D0616949

China's Energy Strategy

China's Energy Strategy
The Impact on Beijing's Maritime Policies

edited by Gabriel B. Collins, Andrew S. Erickson,
Lyle J. Goldstein, and William S. Murray

NAVAL INSTITUTE PRESS
Annapolis, Maryland

Naval Institute Press
291 Wood Road
Annapolis, MD 21402

© 2008 by The United States Naval Institute
All rights reserved. No part of this book may be reproduced or utilized in any form
or by any means, electronic or mechanical, including photocopying and recording,
or by any information storage and retrieval system, without permission in writing
from the publisher.

Library of Congress Cataloging-in-Publication Data
China's energy strategy : the impact on Beijing's maritime policies / edited by
Gabriel B. Collins ... [et al.].
    p. cm.
  Includes bibliographical references and index.
  ISBN 978-1-59114-330-7 (alk. paper)
  1. Sea power—China. 2. Energy policy—Political aspects—China. I. Collins,
Gabriel B.
  VA633.C55 2008
  387.50951—dc22
                        2008009016
Printed in the United States of America on acid-free paper

14 13 12 11 10 09 08   9 8 7 6 5 4 3 2
First printing

To our parents

Brian and Stephanie Collins

Peter and Tay Erickson

Robert and Susan Goldstein

Bingham and Louise Murray

Contents

Gabriel B. Collins, Andrew S. Erickson,
Lyle J. Goldstein, and William S. Murray

Introduction

WITH ALMOST THREE DECADES of double-digit growth, China's continuing rapid development is both breathtaking and unprecedented in world history. Just as remarkable, this process has been peaceful and has avoided—at least thus far—triggering the instability in the international system that many had predicted. Today the prospects for peace remain good. China is increasingly intertwined within a web of interdependent commercial and institutional interactions; the Chinese president has no military experience and appears to be almost entirely focused on issues of domestic stability and development; advocates of Taiwan independence seem for the moment to be in retreat; and Beijing's newly agile diplomacy has delivered major breakthroughs in a variety of important relationships that have previously been problematic, including those with India, Russia, and Vietnam.

Yet, there are still certain disconcerting tendencies. It was once hoped that Hu Jintao might emerge as a liberal reformer, but this has not been the case and there has been little or no progress on the issue of political reform. Moreover, reports of violent rioting by a disgruntled underclass emerge with increasing frequency, which suggests a considerable level of public dissatisfaction with various policies. Chinese nationalism remains a potent and potentially destabilizing factor, as demonstrated in April 2005 when the Japanese consulate in Shanghai was seriously damaged by angry mobs. Chinese military modernization continues apace—even though the People's Republic of China (PRC) seems to face its most benign strategic environment since its founding in 1949. The buildup of the last decade has yielded the world's most advanced conventional ballistic missile force, which has garnered perhaps the most attention from foreign military analysts. But this is a very broad front effort, and Chinese progress in the key military realms of aerospace and maritime development has been on display recently during Beijing's 11 January 2007 antisatellite weapon test, and before that on 26 October 2006 when a Chinese diesel submarine reportedly penetrated the protective screen of the U.S. Navy's *Kitty Hawk* carrier battle group in the vicinity of Okinawa.

The China Maritime Studies Institute (CMSI) was formally established at the Naval War College in October 2006 to study China's evident turn toward the seas. Our aim is to create a center for excellence in the study of Chinese maritime development, especially as it pertains to commercial and military affairs. CMSI draws on the extensive Asia-Pacific expertise that has been assembled on the faculty in Newport over the last decade and uses a variety of unique methodologies, including a strong focus on Chinese-language sources. CMSI has succeeded in producing high-quality research for the U.S. Navy and for the scholarly and policy communities more generally. One final point regarding the new institute is vital: maritime cooperation is a theme that figures prominently in almost all current and planned future CMSI activities, including this volume. Indeed, Chinese–American maritime security cooperation was the theme for CMSI's 2007 annual conference. The CMSI team is wholly committed to a balanced and objective approach to studying China's maritime development.

Most prominent among the institute's activities is the annual conference. The first CMSI conference focused on Chinese undersea warfare, and a resulting book, *China's Future Nuclear Submarine Force,* was published by Naval Institute Press in 2007. The present volume has emerged, following considerable research, from CMSI's second annual conference, "Maritime Implications of China's Energy Strategy." In examining the possible relationship between China's evolving energy strategy, on the one hand, and its naval strategy, on the other, this conference attempted to explore a possible interconnection between China's economic and military strategies. In a broader sense, the conference sought to examine the prospects for a Chinese national security strategy that reaches beyond "offshore defense" and even beyond Taiwan. In a sense this initiative strives to open a debate concerning whether

Beijing aspires to be a powerful regional player or a genuine global power with the attendant robust aerospace forces and blue water fleet.

Participants at the 6–7 December 2006 conference included industry analysts, China specialists, and U.S. military officers. Noteworthy among the participants were several retired ambassadors and flag officers, including former Commander-in-Chief, U.S. Pacific Command and ambassador to China Admiral Joseph W. Prueher, USN (Ret.). Among the U.S. Navy representatives were senior officials from the Office of the Chief of Naval Operations, as well as from Commander, U.S. Third Fleet.

The organizers of this conference purposefully chose to welcome a variety of viewpoints to this important dialogue, including perspectives held by analysts who view China as an emerging economic and military threat and those who believe that China is becoming a vital "stakeholding" partner in global commerce and security. A wide range of perspectives on Chinese energy and naval strategies—and the relationship between these strategies—are evident in the chapters of this book. This reflects CMSI's broader commitment to an open, pluralistic, and scholarly approach to studying Chinese maritime development. In this regard, we believe it is significant that most of this book's chapters draw substantially on original Chinese sources—many not previously referenced in English-language scholarship—to better acquaint the reader with the sophisticated and voluminous Chinese strategic literature on both energy security and naval development.

This conference focused on three concrete questions: (1) What is China's energy strategy? (2) What role might energy dependence play in China's emerging naval modernization? (3) What are the implications of China's energy strategy for maritime strategy? Some consensus findings, along with major points of disagreement, are described below.

With respect to China's overall energy strategy, the economist contingent noted that China's gross national product may continue to grow at its present pace for two decades or more. Despite diversification of energy suppliers and investment in alternative energy sources (e.g., nuclear power) and several pipelines to China being built or in discussion, analysts believed, Beijing's growing fossil fuel dependence and its reliance on seaborne supplies would not be reduced significantly. It was noted that Beijing seeks to vastly increase the energy efficiency of its economy, but participants were deeply skeptical that this could be achieved, even though many believed that Beijing is likely to reestablish an energy ministry in the near future. Finally, it was emphasized in the course of several presentations that China's energy diplomacy in

Central Asia, the Middle East, and especially Africa has been highly effective and may rely on unconventional methods.

Many analysts at the conference addressed the issue of an interconnection between Chinese energy and naval strategies. In particular, it was widely agreed that many Chinese (including, especially, PRC naval analysts) are concerned by the possibility of a U.S. energy embargo against China (possibly aided by Japan, India, or both), for example, in a Taiwan crisis. It was suggested that this issue may already be serving as a rationale for China's accelerated naval development, particularly "beyond Taiwan" (the latter an area of increasing confidence for Beijing), because Chinese naval analysts seem to believe that the People's Liberation Army Navy (PLAN) cannot contest critical energy sea lines of communication (SLOC) now or in the near future. One cogent summary of China's national security viewpoint on the so-called Malacca Dilemma (马六甲困局) with naval implications might be a concerted effort to make the U.S. "not willing to block, not daring to block, and not able to block" ("不愿阻断, 不敢阻断, 无法阻断") China's energy lifeline.[1] This Chinese conception seems to hint at a strategy of cultivating interdependence first while simultaneously hedging against conflict with both robust deterrence and also further development of energy transport and military capabilities to ensure security if deterrence fails. Participants at the conference broadly agreed with the notion that energy issues will likely compel the PLAN to be used increasingly in nonconflict situations in a wider variety of regions. One of those regions is likely to be the Indian Ocean, although in the near and medium term China would appear to face a large ambition–capability gap. In this regard, while PLAN development has been moderate in scope (numbers of platforms) and any change in that trajectory would be obvious to outside observers, there have been enormous and strategically significant qualitative achievements in the last decade.

Conference participants also considered the implications of China's energy strategy for the development of U.S. maritime strategy. Participants widely agreed that emerging Chinese access denial and littoral sea control capabilities require the U.S. Navy to carefully consider SLOC security in East Asia: credible capability must be retained without inadvertently generating perceptions of aggressive intent. In addition, the point was made that the United States may ultimately be more vulnerable than China to oil supply disruption because of higher dependence on imported fossil fuels within its overall energy mix. Finally, many of the participants suggested that the PLAN seems to have reached a crucial strategic turning point. In that light, it was surmised that opportunities for external engagement may be substantial, and that such engagement could help to foster a maritime "stakeholder" mentality within the Chinese Navy.

While there were substantial areas of consensus among conference participants, there were also some interesting areas of disagreement. The assembled specialists differed on the extent to which various Chinese actions were centrally planned and controlled. For instance, the actual degree of state control over Chinese oil companies was a subject of debate. Some participants downplayed the overall importance of the military aspect of China's energy security policy while others maintained that the strategic aspects are salient. A related question concerned whether energy is the true motivation for China in territorial disputes in the East and South China seas. Analysts also had different opinions concerning the likely extent of Chinese capabilities over the next decades, particularly with respect to People's Liberation Army (PLA) power projection beyond China's close-in waters. They differed concerning whether China's increasing clout in Africa (and the developing world more generally) serves U.S. interests. Finally, there was disagreement about whether China might be receptive to a more robust U.S. naval engagement, and the extent to which U.S. naval policy might or might not be able to influence the scope and pace of China's naval modernization. Whether China should be explicitly discussed in the developing U.S. maritime strategy as a unique challenge also formed another sharp point of debate among the participants.

This volume is divided into four parts. The first part, "China's Energy Future and National Security Strategy," establishes a foundation for this study by surveying Beijing's economic and military development and consequent energy needs and policy challenges. The initial chapter, by James Mulvenon, considers the role of energy in the development of the PLA as well as Beijing's strategic options for defending its growing energy access. Mulvenon demonstrates that the PLA is taking the issue of fuel scarcity seriously from an operational perspective. Chas W. Freeman Jr. then assesses the comparative energy vulnerabilities of China and the United States and the prospects for bilateral cooperation in this regard. The third chapter by Daniel H. Rosen and Trevor Houser evaluates the intersection between China's potential future economic growth and energy demand. David Pietz then offers detailed analysis of China's energy sector. Mikkal Herberg provides an overview of the strategic implications of China's growing efforts to acquire and utilize liquefied natural gas as an alternative to more polluting fuels, especially coal. As Chinese energy requirements increase, the security of the relevant SLOC has become a major topic for discussion in Beijing. In the final chapter of part I, Gabriel B. Collins and Andrew S. Erickson consider the motives and the strategic implications of developing a nationally flagged Chinese tanker fleet.

Part II, "China's Global Energy Access," offers in-depth studies of China's efforts to acquire energy around the world. James R. Holmes and Toshi Yoshihara contend that the vital importance of energy imports from the Middle East dictates that China's growing strategic focus, while limited at present, will be directed not into the Western Pacific but rather toward the Indian Ocean. Saad Rahim outlines the substantial recent progress in relations between Beijing and Riyadh, which may result in significant Saudi assistance in China's development of both oil refining capacity and a strategic petroleum reserve (SPR). Although China cannot genuinely compete with the United States in Riyadh, Beijing is subtly gaining influence in Saudi Arabia. Ahmed Hashim analyzes the long-standing ties between Iran and China while uncovering factors that over the long term may limit the development of a true strategic partnership. Sino–Iranian relations are subordinate to Sino–American relations in Beijing's calculus because the trade relationship between the United States and China is so robust. Clifford Shelton examines China's increasing success in parlaying economic assistance and an ethic of noninterference into increasing access to African oil reserves. A case in point involves the Central African Republic, whose entire embassy in Beijing is seemingly funded by China in exchange for rights to mineral exploration. Vitaly Kozyrev situates China's quest for energy and military security in the complex terrain of Eurasia, where China's substantial diplomatic achievements have rendered its borders relatively secure. Kozyrev argues that China intends to be simultaneously a continental and a maritime power. In a chapter devoted to Sino–Japanese competition for sovereignty and resources in the South China Sea, Peter Dutton proposes innovative legal solutions to a complex and volatile dispute over gas fields in the East China Sea. Finally, John Garofano considers the strategic significance of the South China Sea, not only for Beijing's national development but also for Washington's geopolitical interests. Garofano describes China's increasingly effective projection of soft power in the South China Sea region and evaluates future prospects.

Part III, "China's Naval Development and Concerns Regarding Energy Access Denial," considers scenarios of great concern to both the United States and China. Gabriel B. Collins, Andrew S. Erickson, and Lyle J. Goldstein begin by surveying the views of Chinese naval analysts on the maritime threats related to energy confronting Beijing and Beijing's potential responses. They demonstrate that that there is not only acute concern in China about these issues but also openness to the possibility of maritime cooperation in the energy security domain. Bernard D. Cole then surveys the role energy has played in Chinese maritime strategy since 1949. Cole assesses that China's navy today has the most capable conventionally powered submarine force in the world, a large and improving surface combatant force, and significant forces in other maritime mission areas. China's navy is already able to overpower Taiwan's navy, it offers a serious potential match for the Japanese Maritime Self-Defense Force, and it poses a thought-provoking challenge to possible U.S. naval intervention in a Taiwan scenario. While Cole maintains that energy security will remain a PLAN mission, he concludes that this mission is unlikely to become a major planning consideration for China's naval modernization. James Bussert subsequently reflects on the PLAN's development of surface combatants and their potential use in future defense of China's SLOC. Contrary to much conventional wisdom, this naval analyst suggests that global SLOC missions will be within reach of the PLAN in coming decades. Bruce Elleman reviews naval blockades in East Asia and the factors that influence their success or failure, demonstrating that China has ample experience with blockades, of which it has repeatedly been victim. In their concluding chapter to this section, Gabriel Collins and William S. Murray also challenge prevailing wisdom, both within China and abroad, by concluding that inherent interdiction difficulties as well as growing Chinese access denial and retaliatory capabilities would make it difficult to execute in practice, potentially counterproductive, and likely very risky for any foreign power to attempt an energy blockade of China.

The final part, "China's Energy Security and U.S.–China Relations," considers larger strategic and policy implications, especially as they may pertain to the future of the U.S. Navy. Ronald O'Rourke enumerates recent PLAN development and suggests that it is critical for Washington to retain presence, influence, and operational capacity in the Western Pacific by remaining committed to robust naval development and deployment. Dan Blumenthal probes aspects of China's maritime and energy development that may raise concerns in Washington, and warns in particular of unsavory regimes that benefit from China's quest for energy as well as of the instability that could flow from China's building of a genuine blue water fleet. In the end he concludes that the responsibility lies with Beijing to reorient its energy policies in line with market forces to allay suspicions about its larger strategic goals. Jonathan D. Pollack confronts this conflictual paradigm head-on, arguing that the concept of energy security itself is deeply flawed and conducive to dangerous myth-making on both sides of the Pacific. He focuses instead on probing the ways in which China and the United States might work together, potentially as partners in a "thousand ship navy," to mitigate a shared problem.

The opinions expressed in this volume are those of the authors and editors alone and in no way reflect the official policies or assessments of the U.S. Navy or any other entity of the U.S. government. The editors wish to thank each of the respective authors for their outstanding research contributions. In addition, we extend profound thanks to many at the Naval War College who played important roles in executing a successful conference and producing this volume, in particular: Danling Cacioppo, Michael Cardin, Peter Dombrowski, Cristina Hartley, Jim Lewis, Debbie Maddix, Susan Moretti, Jo-Ann Parks, Robert Rubel, Michael Sherlock, and Doug Smith. We wish to give special recognition to Gigi Davis, an exemplary professional who has invested many late nights in this effort. CMSI wishes to thank Raytheon Integrated Defense Systems for its continuing support of Asia-Pacific studies at the Naval War College through a generous gift to the Naval War College Foundation. Finally, we appreciate the diligent and exceptional work of the editorial team at Naval Institute Press on this second volume in the series Studies in Chinese Maritime Development.

Before embarking on the intellectual journey embodied by this fine collection of papers, it is worth recalling that historically China has not been aggressive and expansionist. During the apex of its power, the so-called Middle Kingdom did not generally colonize far-flung domains and its borders have remained more or less stable over a long period of time. Still, basic international relations theory tells us that the rapid rise of great powers is often accompanied by grave instability. The bloody conflicts of the last century are at least partly attributed to this phenomenon.

At the time of our 2006 conference, several participants noted that the event fell on the sixty-fifth anniversary of the tragic Pearl Harbor attack of 7 December 1941. This was entirely coincidental, of course, but we should nevertheless use the opportunity to solemnly reflect on the value of peace in the Asia-Pacific region and, at the same time, on how the strength of our navy can help guarantee that peace. It is widely agreed by historians that the major causes of the deadly war in the Pacific more than six decades ago were Japan's requirement for external resources, its perceived vulnerabilities, and the associated ideologies that then took hold in Tokyo. The durable peace that has prevailed in East Asia for decades is testimony to the power of cooperation over confrontation under conditions of foresight and goodwill.

We live in a world increasingly defined by China's rapid and continuing rise. For the benefit of all countries, we must proceed with a clear understanding of the interconnectedness between energy, international conflict, and maritime security at a variety of levels. The entire world would lose if the history of sixty-five years ago were to repeat itself in this dynamic region.

June 2007

Note

1. 凌云 [Ling Yun], "龙脉" ["The Dragon's Arteries"], 现代舰船 [*Modern Ships*] (October 2006): 19.

PART I

China's Energy Future and
National Security Strategy

James Mulvenon

Dilemmas and Imperatives of Beijing's Strategic Energy Dependence: The PLA Perspective

Introduction

CHINA'S GROWING ENERGY SECURITY DILEMMA, driven by its dramatically increasing demand and concomitant dependence on global oil supplies, has risen to become a prominent topic for strategic discussion both in China and internationally. Most commentators acknowledge the critical equities of the Chinese People's Liberation Army (PLA) in these strategic debates, often speculating about its policy preferences and capabilities, but few have subjected the issue to sustained analysis.[1] This chapter seeks to redress this oversight by answering four core questions:

- How important is the energy factor in China's ongoing military development?
- How does the energy factor impact various tradeoffs in PLA development?

- Can Beijing defend far-flung energy sea lines of communication (SLOC) now and in the future?
- How vulnerable is Beijing to coercion by energy blockade?

From the outset, however, it must be noted that China meets 90 percent of its energy needs from domestic sources, primarily coal.[2] Yet China became a net importer of oil in 1993, and its dependence on foreign petroleum sources is expected to increase in the coming years from its current level of 40 percent to as much as 75–80 percent in 2020. The central focus of this chapter, therefore, is China's growing reliance on the importation of petroleum, and its corresponding implications for military and security issues.

Energy and PLA Development

When examining the role of energy in the PLA's development, it is useful to disaggregate the topic at the strategic, operational, and tactical levels. The strategic level primarily centers on China's national energy strategy and the extent to which the strategy reflects PLA preferences and incorporates and defends the PLA's bureaucratic equities.[3] One can speculate about the PLA's role in the planning and decision making associated with that strategy. On the first point, energy security issues are prominent in the documents of the 11th Five-Year Plan (2006–10), which focuses "sustainable development" through "energy supply security, environmental protection and energy efficiency and savings."[4] Anecdotal interview evidence suggests the PLA provides inputs into this planning process, which is run by Zhang Guobao's energy office under the National Development and Reform Commission, through a variety of indirect means, such as position papers or attendance at key internal meetings.

At the operational level, one can speculate as to whether there is an articulated PLA energy strategy and how that strategy is implemented. Given that the military does not publish a formal energy strategy, we can only deduce its strategy from external behavior and the writings of military analysts. In their writings, PLA authors highlight the need for China to develop independent and reliable access to oil from both domestic and international sources, "identifying China's growing reliance on oil imports as a vulnerability that could be exploited by the United States."[5] In particular, these analysts "worry that the United States could use its influence in oil-rich regions to limit China's access to oil or, in the event of a Sino–American conflict, to disrupt the flow of oil to China."[6] The primary window into the PLA's possible energy policies is the national defense mobilization system, which is responsible for mobilizing the civilian economy, including energy supplies, for the military in times of crisis and war (for more on the connection between energy and defense mobilization, see the final section of this chapter).

Finally, at the tactical level, PLA units are actively engaged in a campaign of energy conservation. Open and internal military sources strongly suggest that the PLA has been focused on conservation of energy for a number of years, even preceding the recent spike in crude oil prices. A February 2004 article in *People's Liberation Army Daily*, for example, summarized the PLA's energy policy guidance as follows: "Over the past few years, the PLA has been oriented toward reducing consumption and increasing efficiency in terms of . . . POL [petroleum, oils, and lubricants] development in order to promote military changes with Chinese characteristics in the context of socialist market economy."[7] Joint logistics departments at the military region level have been told that they should "love oil as though it were blood and value oil as though it were gold."[8] Troopers at lower levels explicitly understand what is driving the need for efficiency, reportedly grumbling at an automobile regiment's POL management symposium, "The oil situation that China faces leaves no room for optimism. We have jumped from number two in the world when it comes to POL consumption and 43 percent of our oil supply comes from imports. Conserving energy and conserving oil should be an imperative duty of the officers and soldiers."[9]

Efforts to conserve fuel are most clearly documented in the People's Liberation Army Air Force, which reportedly has its own "fuel saving work" leading small groups. To reduce fuel consumption, air force units lower taxi time before and after sorties by towing, lengthen sorties to include multiple training subjects and thereby reduce the number of times the engines need to be started, increase the use of simulators, improve analysis of weather to reduce the incidence of dumping excess fuel, and consolidate maintenance schedules to reduce engine starts.[10] Simulation training for Second Artillery units has also been directly linked to a desire to conserve fuel,[11] and the use of computer networks and radio-frequency identification cards prevents waste and fuel thefts (the "escape, emit, drip, and leak" policy).[12] The net result of these efforts across the military, measured in tons of fuel conserved, is not known, but the intensity of the propaganda campaign is a clear indicator of its importance to the leadership.

Energy Security and Trade-Offs in PLA Development

The Chinese energy security dilemma is both a facilitator of and a constraint upon PLA development. The energy security debate facilitates PLA development writ large in two ways. First, defense of the oil-related SLOC provides an additional strategic mission for the PLA and is therefore another justification for higher defense spending, especially on investments related to the deployment of a credible blue water navy. Second, in a related way, energy security creates a new, legitimate arena for PLA participation in security planning and decision making with civilians, particularly given the need for naval expertise in the process.

But China's energy security problems also act as a constraint upon PLA development. First, higher global oil prices, driven in part by Chinese demand, put pressure on high-tempo training and operations. PLA interlocutors in a semiofficial dialogue on defense budget transparency revealed in November 2006 that the PLA had been forced to spend 10 billion renminbi (RMB) (approximately $1.3 billion) more in 2006 for fuel costs than expected.[13] Second, People's Republic of China (PRC) dependence on global energy supplies potentially constrains PLA adventurism vis-à-vis a wide range of scenarios involving Taiwan, Japan, and the United States, especially when faced with the prospect of an economically crippling blockade of foreign oil supplies. (For more on the features of this scenario, see the final section of this chapter.)

Energy Security and Defense of SLOC

Before leaping to a discussion of the PLA's capability to defend energy-related SLOC, especially the Strait of Malacca, one must ask a first-order question: do Beijing and the PLA *want* to defend the SLOC? An affirmative answer is clearly the conventional wisdom, but when examined more closely, this supposed truism may be predicated on shaky assumptions and mirror-imaging. Indeed, the PRC has benefited greatly from the global freedom of navigation provided by the U.S. Navy (USN), particularly during the last twenty-five years of opening to the outside world and economic modernization. It is arguably still in China's interest to "free-ride" on this "public good" for the foreseeable future, given the high political, diplomatic, military, and, most important, fiscal costs of replacing it with an indigenous substitute.

Granted, Beijing's confidence in the neutral nature of USN-provided freedom of the seas has been undermined since the mid-1990s. The 1993

Yinhe incident, in which the USN shadowed a ship suspected of transporting chemical weapons precursors only to discover later that there were no materials on board, was a shock to the PRC system and is regularly cited as evidence of ill intent on the part of the United States. Subsequent international crises reinforced these views. The 1995–96 missile tests near Taiwan, which resulted in the deployment of two carrier strike groups, confirmed in the minds of PLA strategists that they needed to prepare to deter and even defeat U.S. naval forces in a Taiwan scenario. Operation Allied Force and the North Atlantic Treaty Organization bombing of the PRC embassy in Belgrade convinced most of the Chinese security community that U.S. foreign policy operated according to a more expansive and intrusive understanding of sovereignty, further undermining the perception of the U.S. military as a protector of global norms. More recently, China has been reluctant to join the Proliferation Security Initiative, believing that seizures at sea violate both international law and principles of sovereignty, though the commander of China's navy, Wu Shengli, recently expressed interest in joining the "1,000 Ship Navy" effort to maintain international maritime security.[14]

With these events as backdrop, it is no surprise that PLA strategists would view China's dependence on USN protection of critical SLOC as a source of frustration and motivation and would therefore seek to develop an independent means of securing key energy supply routes. But does the PLA have the capability now to assume this mission, or is there any prospect of the capability in the near term? The short answer is no, though PLAN modernization since the late 1990s has been impressive. In the past decade, China's modern shipbuilding complex has produced an astonishing twelve new classes of surface and subsurface combatants armed with advanced weapon systems, including four types of submarines (Song-class SS, Yuan-class SS, Shang-class SSN, Jin-class SSBN[15]), five types of guided missile destroyers (Luzhou, Luyang I, Luyang II/Lanzhou, Luhai, Luhu), and at least three new types of guided missile frigates (Jiangwei II, Jiangkai, and Jiangkai II), as well as at least six new types of amphibious landing craft (Yukan, Yuting I, Yuting II, Yuhai, Yudeng, and the Type 2208 wave-piercing catamaran).[16] Following upon its deployment of two Russian-built Sovremennyy-class guided missile destroyers (DDG) and four Kilo-class submarines, the PLAN has also ordered and received two additional Sovremennyys and eight Kilos.

Despite these significant increases in both the quantity and quality of Chinese naval power, however, the fleet still appears to be undersized and undertrained for global blue water patrolling, not to mention SLOC protection under contested conditions. To be fair, the PLAN's increasingly frequent global port visits do display a growing confidence in blue water operations, but the Chinese navy is still primarily a brown and green water navy. Apart from the sheer number of hulls required for the mission, the key bottlenecks, underscored in a handful of unpublicized problems on the voyages to date, are replenishment and supply.[17] Not only does the PLAN lack a sufficient number of auxiliary oiler replenishment ships, China does not currently have, and—if its long-stated policies continue—will never have, the logistics support of foreign naval bases like the United States. To offset this problem and perhaps to prepare for a future in which the PLAN can implement its own protection of key SLOC, Lieberthal and Herberg point out that "China has greatly increased cooperation, port access agreements, and maritime ties with Pakistan, Bangladesh, and Myanmar in an apparent effort to be better positioned to protect its maritime energy transport routes during a future crisis."[18]

In the meantime, however, the PRC is likely to continue to free ride on the security provision of the USN. If and when Beijing decides that this dependence is intolerable and has the naval capability to provide its own freedom of navigation, then U.S.–China relations will have reached a major strategic tipping point. But that moment seems years if not decades away, despite the current tensions in the relationship.

Beijing and Its Vulnerability to Energy Blockade

The key driver of Chinese energy demand has been the explosive growth of the Chinese economy since the late 1970s. Over the span of twenty years, the Chinese gross domestic product (GDP) has quadrupled while energy consumption has doubled.[19] The PRC is now the second-largest consumer of oil behind the United States and the third-largest importer of oil in the world.[20] Chinese energy demand accounts for one-third of the growth in oil demand over the last decade. More important, China's ratio of oil importation to total consumption is expected to continue to widen, from its current level of 40 percent to more than 70 percent in 2020. Of this imported petroleum, 75 percent is expected to come from the Middle East, with 50 percent passing through the Strait of Malacca.[21]

Painfully aware of the implications of its growing dependence on imported oil, the Chinese government is attempting to mitigate the impact with a wide range of policy initiatives. According to National Defense University professor Bernard Cole, the Chinese government is trying to maintain oil security through expanded domestic production, increasing the efficiency of refineries, signing contracts with foreign suppliers, and gaining "exploration rights and production control over energy fields in foreign nations."[22]

China has also taken significant steps toward building a strategic petroleum reserve, in part to counter a possible energy blockade.[23] In March 2001 it was reported that during the 10th Five-Year Plan (2001–5) China would invest 20 billion RMB to establish a strategic petroleum reserve by 2003.[24] Building the reserves evidently ran into delays because in October 2004 it was reported that China would formally launch its strategic petroleum reserve program in 2005.[25] However, in January 2005, Zhang Xiaoqiang, vice minister of China's National Development and Reform Commission, stated that China would start filling its strategic oil reserves in 2006, although ten million barrels of storage capacity would be ready for use in August 2005 in the city of Ningbo.[26] According to the Asia Pacific Energy Research Centre, China plans to develop its strategic petroleum reserves in three stages with the eventual goal of storing ninety days of imports by 2020, an amount recommended by the International Energy Agency. Though the exact starting date of the first stage may now be inaccurate, the overall plan for developing China's strategic petroleum reserve appears to remain intact.

- By 2005, China's oil reserves are to have a storage capacity equal to thirty-five days of imports, of which fourteen days of reserves would be managed directly by the government and twenty-one days would be managed by state-owned enterprises.

- By 2010, the economy's oil stockpiles should equal fifty days of imports, of which twenty-two days will be managed by the government and twenty-eight days by public companies.

- By 2020, it is anticipated that the strategic oil supply stockpiles will reach the IEA standard of ninety days, with a total capacity of 40 to 50 million tons.[27]

China is building four strategic petroleum reserves on its coast to facilitate the transfer of crude oil from ports. The reserves are located in Zhenhai, Zhejiang province; Daishan, Zhejiang province; Huangdao, Shandong province; and Dalian, Liaoning province.[28] Construction of the Zhenhai facility began on 2 December 2003 and is the first reserve slated to be filled. It is also the largest reserve and will hold 10 million cubic meters when it is completed in 2008.[29] One Chinese author, however, has cautioned that China should also build a petroleum reserve in China's midwest due to the vulnerability of the coast to attack.[30] It should be noted that the petroleum reserve at Ningbo, referenced above, has not been mentioned in the press as one of China's four strategic petroleum reserves. From Chinese press reporting, there is no indication of any partial or complete foreign ownership or control of any of these emerging tank farms, nor is there any real clarity on the distinction between Chinese commercial or state ownership or control of the infrastructure. Indeed, the dominance of state oil companies (China Petrochemical Corporation, China National Petroleum Corporation, China National Offshore Oil Corporation) and the statist nature of the Chinese economy may make such distinctions irrelevant to the discussion, and any comingling of commercially directed assets from strategic assets has been left intentionally ambiguous.

Energy and Defense Mobilization

Energy supplies are a critical sector in China's plans for defense mobilization in crisis or war. One Chinese source states that gasoline constitutes 65 percent of all wartime supplies.[31] One source discloses that the PLA also has two types of strategic petroleum reserves: war preparation reserves (战备油料处被) and another type for normal use (周转油料储备). Wartime oil reserves are divided into strategic oil reserves, campaign oil reserves, and tactical oil reserves. These reserves are administered by the General Staff Department, military regions, services, and tactical forces. Normal use reserves are supplied by support troops at the tactical level. Oil reserves are administered by both local governments and the military. Ordinarily crude, partially refined oil, and military-civil use oil products are administered by local reserves. Petroleum for exclusive military use is administered by the military.[32] The exact size of these reserves is unknown.

Even if China did have enough petroleum stockpiled to support a large-scale military operation, the prospect of a U.S. blockade of China and strikes against its strategic petroleum reserves would likely encourage the Chinese government to ensure against disruptions to its oil supply by increasing oil imports in the months before an invasion. In fact, the Chinese may have already pursued this course of action during past periods of potential disruptions in supplies. In January 2003, in the run-up to the invasion of Iraq, China increased its oil imports, presumably as a hedge against disruptions as a result of the war. If China increased oil imports before the Iraq War, there is reason to believe that it would also increase purchases before a war over Taiwan. This stockpiling effort could be one of the best indicators and warning of PLA preparations for conflict.

But would this stockpiling be sufficient for either the PLA or the country at large in the event of an energy blockade? Part of the answer depends on the nature of the blockade itself. If the USN declares a quarantine area around China to include both Chinese- and foreign-flagged shipping but does not conduct kinetic attacks against land-based reserves, then Beijing's stockpile could provide a limited cushion while the crisis played out. While the operational credibility of this quarantine is itself problematic from a logistics and economic perspective, the blockade could also be "virtual" in implementation and would rely on the full force of U.S. diplomatic and trade relationships. If, however, the United States crosses the escalation threshold of carrying out strikes on the mainland against selected POL targets, the true brunt of China's dependence on foreign oil could be felt quite quickly, exacerbated by the concomitant capital flight and economic pressures. While oil only represents approximately one-fifth of China's national energy mix, China imports more than half of that amount, and there are few if any cost-effective substitutes for air or ground transportation. If predictions hold true about the increase in China's dependence on foreign oil from its current level of 40 percent to 60–80 percent in the next decade or so, then Beijing's vulnerability will only get worse over time, not better.[33]

Conclusion

The Chinese military is clearly concerned about China's growing dependence on foreign sources of oil, both in terms of the constraints it potentially places on operations as well as the strategic vulnerabilities it creates for Chinese diplomatic and security interests. Ironically, this situation is a consequence of China's economic success and rising global power, and it highlights the extent to which the sources of Beijing's growing leverage in international affairs is balanced with a set of potentially painful costs, particularly if it reduces China's options in pursuing its supreme national interest: reunification of Taiwan with the mainland. Beijing's projected oil demands over the coming decades are simply too large to be overcome by any combination of policies and strategic reserves. For PLA planners, this may provide further confirmation of the need for military planning and acquisition focused on a speedy and decisive resolution of the Taiwan issue, thereby preventing foreign powers intent on foiling the effort from playing the "energy card."

At the same time, China's increasingly serious interdependencies in the energy sector may empower those in the system who favor nonmilitary solutions to the Taiwan issue and may in fact reduce the chances of Sino–U.S.

military conflict in the western Pacific. Most troubling, increasing Chinese dependence on foreign sources of energy could cause Chinese to act with desperation and to be willing to accept the dangers of escalation in a Taiwan conflict, much as Japan felt pressured to preemptively attack Pearl Harbor in December 1941.

Notes

1. The most notable exception is Erica Strecker Downs's excellent dissertation, "China's Energy Security," submitted in January 2004 to Princeton University.

2. The major exception to this generalization is transportation, which is disproportionately dependent on petroleum.

3. It is not clear that China actually has an articulated energy strategy, given the complex landscape of bureaucratic and commercial interests involved, but the planning documents described in the text are the closest approximations of Beijing's guiding principles and serve as the interpretative basis for concrete decisions.

4. Erik Nilsson and Selina Lo, "Forum Tackles 'Balancing Act,'" *China Daily,* 7 November 2006.

5. Downs, "China's Energy Security."

6. Downs, "China's Energy Security." For more detail on these debates, see Erica Downs, "The Chinese Energy Security Debate," *The China Quarterly,* no. 177 (March 2004): 21–41.

7. "PLA Boosts Its Capability in Quartermaster Material and POL Support," *Liberation Army Daily,* 12 February 2004.

8. Liu Daoguo, "Making 'War Blood' Even More Accessible—Record of Military Region Units Putting Great Effort Forth to Enhance Standardized Management in POL Supply," *Zhanqi bao* [*Battle Flag News*], 1 November 2005, p. 1.

9. Ibid.

10. These conservation efforts have increased in importance in part because of the PLAAF's (People's Liberation Army Air Force) increased training tempo. In particular, see various articles in the 24 June 2006 issue of the PLAAF's newspaper, *Kongjun bao* [*Air Force News*].

11. Liang Qingwei and Zhang Rong, "Higher Training Quality, Lower Fuel Consumption—A Base Gained Double Benefits from Using Simulation Training Devices," *Huojianbing bao* [*Rocket Force News*], 25 July 2006, p. 1.

12. Wang Kaibin, "Give Prominence to Key Support Areas, Cut Down On 'Escape, Emit, Drip, and Leak'; Second Artillery Adopts Effective Measures to Ensure Ample Supply of Good Quality Fuel for Training," *Huojianbing bao* [*Rocket Force News*], 22 April 2006, p. 1.

13. This figure was confirmed in the December 2006 white paper released by the Chinese government. See *China's National Defense in 2006* (Beijing: State Council

Information Office, December 2006), chapter IX, http://english.people.com.cn/whitepaper/defense2006/defense2006.html.

14. P. Parameswaran, "U.S. Asks China to Help Maintain Global Maritime Security," *Agence France-Presse*, 10 April 2007.

15. For information about the Shang- and Jin-class boats, see Richard D. Fisher Jr., "Trouble Below: China's Submarines Pose Regional, Strategic Challenges," *Armed Forces Journal*, March 2006.

16. For more information, see http://www.sinodefence.com/navy/.

17. For example, the first PLAN flotilla to make a port call on the U.S. mainland, consisting of the Luhu-class guided missile destroyer *Harbin* (DDG 112), *Zhuhai* (DDG 166), and the oiler *Nancang* (AO 953), broke a fuel line en route, forcing PACOM to provide a replacement via helicopter.

18. Kenneth Lieberthal and Mikkal Herberg, *China's Search for Energy Security: Implications for U.S. Policy* (Seattle, Wash.: National Bureau of Asian Research, 2006), 23–24.

19. For studies on the roots and scale of Chinese energy demand growth, see Lieberthal and Herberg, *China's Search for Energy Security*; Philip Andrews-Speed, Xuanli Liao, and Ronald Dannreuther, "The Strategic Implications of China's Energy Needs," Institute for International Strategic Studies, Adelphi Papers no. 346, 2002; Erica Strecker Downs, *China's Quest for Energy Security* (Santa Monica, Calif.: RAND, 2000); Downs, "China's Energy Security"; Joe Barnes, "Slaying the Dragon: The New China Threat School," in *China and Long-Range Asia Energy Security: An Analysis of the Political, Economic and Technological Factors Shaping Asian Energy Markets* (Baker Institute for Public Policy, April 1999); International Energy Agency (IEA), "China's Worldwide Quest for Energy Security" (Paris: IEA, 2000); U.S. China Economic and Security Review Commission, "China's Energy Needs and Strategies," Washington, D.C.: U.S. Government Printing Office, 2003, http://www.uscc.gov/hearings/2003hearings/transcripts/031030tran.pdf; and Ross H. Munro, "Chinese Energy Strategy," in *Energy Strategies and Military Strategies in Asia*, report for the Office of Net Assessment, Department of Defense (McLean, Va.: Hicks & Associates, Inc., 1999).

20. As a caveat, it should be noted that China lags well behind the United States in energy efficiency.

21. Lieberthal and Herberg, *China's Search for Energy Security*, 12.

22. Bernard D. Cole, *"Oil for the Lamps of China": Beijing's 21st Century Search for Energy* (Washington, D.C.: National Defense University, 2003), 52–53.

23. This section draws heavily from Kevin Pollpeter and Keith Crane, *The Economic Indicators of People's War* (Santa Monica, Calif.: RAND, DRR-3621-DIA, March 2005).

24. "China Government to Set Up Petroleum Reserve Base," ChinaOnline, 30 March 2001.

25. "China to Build Four Major Oil Reserve Bases," *People's Daily*, 10 October 2004.

26. "Strategic Oil Reserves to Be Filled Next Year," *China Daily*, 7 January 2005.

27. Asia Pacific Energy Research Centre, *Energy in China: Transportation, Electric Power and Fuel Markets* (Tokyo: Asia Pacific Research Centre, 2004), 50.

28. "China to Build Four Major Oil Reserve Bases," *People's Daily*, 10 October 2004.

29. "China Starts Building New Oil Reserve Bases," *Business Daily Update*, 29 June 2004; and Li Juanqiong, "中国将把战略石油葬在哪里? 圈定四大储备基地" ["Where Will China Establish Its Petroleum Reserve? Deciding on Four Reserves"], Xinhua, 2 December 2003.

30. Li Songlin, "关于建立我国战略石油储 备体系的思考" ["Thinking of Establishing the System of China Strategic Petroleum Storage"] [Translation Provided], 军事经济研究 [*Military Economic Research*] (September 2003): 18.

31. Li Zhiyun, Du Lihong and Zhang Wenjing, 高技术战争后勤保障政治工作 [*High Technology War Logistics Support Political Work*] (Beijing: Military Sciences Press, 2004), 147.27.

32. Lu Linwen, "油料储备" ["Petroleum Reserve"], in 中国战争动员百科全书 [*China War Mobilization Encyclopedia*], Qian Shugen, ed. (Beijing: Military Sciences Press, 2003), 150.

33. China's current oil import dependency stands around 50 percent. Chinese domestic oil production appears likely to climb slightly in coming years and then plateau. Taken in conjunction with oil demand growth that could range from 3 to 6 percent annually (thus adding more than 200,000 billion barrels to demand each year), Chinese oil import dependency is poised to continue rising and could exceed 60 percent by 2010–12. Many variables will influence actual import growth, however, and there is therefore some variation in the estimates cited in other chapters in this volume. For data to support the above estimate, see "China's 2006 Oil Import Dependency at 47 pct, Up 4.1 pct Points from 2005," *Forbes*, 12 February 2007, http://www.forbes.com/business/feeds/afx/2007/02/12/afx3420562.html.

Chas W. Freeman Jr.

Energy as China's Achilles' Heel?

THIS EDITED VOLUME DISCUSSES the security of China's energy supplies. In some dire circumstances, it is perhaps fair to say that the United States might actually be against energy security for China. Presumably, in those same circumstances, the Chinese would be against such security for the United States. Thus, a crucial question arises: who would have the advantage in such a contest?

It would be fairly easy for the U.S. Navy to interdict Chinese seaborne oil imports. These come mainly through the straits of Malacca and Lombok, and Macassar in Indonesia, which we have the capacity to seal off to tankers bound for China. The People's Liberation Army's Navy has not developed any capability to defend these trade routes against lesser navies, still less ours. The U.S. Navy could also quite easily blockade Chinese ports. So there is little question that the United States could cut China off from seaborne energy supplies.

China is worried about these vulnerabilities and is attempting to address them—this issue is discussed later in this chapter—but, for now, let us continue on the theme of possible confrontation over energy trade.

Americans are to a large extent in denial about the fact that the United States now imports about 12 million barrels of oil per day (bpd), or almost 70 percent of our oil consumption. China imports only 3.8 million bpd, or somewhat less than half of its requirements, and brings in proportionately more than we do over land. To put this in perspective, China is only a bit more dependent on imported as opposed to home-produced oil than the United States was at the time of the 1973 Arab oil embargo. It is true that in relative terms, China's current take from the Persian Gulf states is higher than that of the United States, but oil nevertheless plays a much less important role in the Chinese energy economy than it did in ours even back then. Today imported oil accounts for only about one-third as much of the overall Chinese energy diet as it does of ours. The Chinese may now be recapitulating our history by developing an addiction to imported oil and gas, but the fact remains that you have to go back to long-forgotten bygone days to find a period when the United States was as little dependent on imported oil as the Chinese now are for their overall energy supply.

The point here is really quite simple. Mirror-imaging is always a potential problem for analysis; it is a potentially fatal problem for analysis of energy dependence. In the United States, "energy" means oil and gas, mainly imported oil and, increasingly, imported gas. In China, "energy" means fossil fuels, in particular coal, which provides more than 65 percent of the country's primary energy consumption each year. However, from the perspective of "energy security," the discussion focuses on oil consumption, nearly 50 percent of which must be imported, and natural gas, which is now being imported as liquefied natural gas (LNG). An interruption of oil imports would now be catastrophic for the American economy; it would be damaging but still far short of fatal for the Chinese.

So could the Chinese take retaliatory action to disrupt U.S. energy imports if we sought to interfere with theirs? It is not my intention to do their targeting—conventional or unconventional—for them. It will suffice to simply remind the reader that the last time the U.S. Navy did serious convoying of oil tankers was when the United States was the world's largest exporter of petroleum, not its biggest importer. Things are different now than in the glory days chronicled in *Victory at Sea*, and China is not Imperial Japan. U.S. imports now account for almost 27 percent of the world's oil trade. (Japan's imports, on which Japan is totally dependent, are another 10 percent.) China accounts for less than 6 percent. The security stakes are very much higher for the United States than they are for China.

Our Navy can destroy the oil trade of others. Can it protect our own? Is it in our interest to put ourselves in a position where we must attempt to do so? Are the ships that are being built for the U.S. Navy suited to this task? Should Washington risk setting up a situation in which our forces have to undertake this difficult mission? Does it matter that rocket-propelled grenades in zodiacs or dhows, junks, or outrigger canoes can now take down supertankers?

One can make one's own judgment about the vulnerability of tankers transiting Hormuz, Malacca, Lombok-Macassar, the Panama and Suez canals, or the Cape of Good Hope. But it is absolutely clear that Lloyd's of London and the rest of the insurance industry will assess the risk the minute there is a whiff of a real problem. The insurance industry can be counted upon to boost insurance, and thus shipping costs, to extraordinary levels, greatly increasing the cost of oil and gas to everyone, if anyone—no matter how righteous—starts blowing up LNG carriers or sinking oil tankers, wherever they are bound.

Then again, the United States increasingly depends on imports of product, not just crude. Our domestic refining capacity is both limited and highly concentrated. If an unaimed blow from Hurricane Katrina could knock out 10 percent of that capacity, what might a foreign enemy determined to engage in tit for tat through sabotage be able to do in time of war?

Fortunately, the only conceivable casus belli for a major Sino–American conflict is the unresolved issue of Taiwan's relationship to the rest of China, and the danger of a Taiwan conflict is rapidly receding. It is worth noting, however, that with the possible exception of Japan, the United States would have no overt allies were such a conflict to break out. Even the Australians, who have been with us in every war for the past one hundred years, would sit out a war over Taiwan. In such a war, our allies would be neutrals with no inclination or obligation to suspend their trade with China.

It is not irrelevant in this connection that China is developing a wide array of foreign energy supply arrangements. A very few of these are with countries, such as Iran and Sudan, from which the United States has chosen not to import oil and gas, but most are with countries like Angola, Nigeria, Saudi Arabia, and Venezuela—oil exporters on which we ourselves are heavily dependent. It is entirely possible that these countries might take efforts by Washington to disrupt their trade with Beijing amiss—and react by cutting off their sales to the United States. Finally, in arrangements that are likely in time to be replicated with others, China is negotiating with Saudi Arabia to allow the kingdom to own and operate part of China's strategic petroleum reserve as well as refineries and petrochemical plants. An attack on such foreign-owned and -operated facilities would be an act of war against their owners as well as China. Such an attack could impose much more consequential collateral damage on the attacker than on China.

A metaphor of local interest makes the larger point: the China Maritime Studies Institute annual conference took place in Rhode Island, my native state—an international byword for patriotic parades and organized crime, to which I come home when I wish to feel slender and listen to English as it should be spoken. Any Rhode Islander will tell you that people who cannot get along without storing a lot of gasoline in the garage should think twice about taking up arson as a hobby—especially in Mafia neighborhoods—or, for that matter, where there are unfriendly guys from Shanghai.

It appears the Chinese agree. Rather than treating energy security as a primarily military problem, they seem to be approaching it as a complex set of issues in which the military dimension is only one component and perhaps, at that, the least salient.

Chinese concern about energy policy disarray and dissatisfaction with the level of coordination between policies affecting domestic and foreign sources of energy have finally combined to produce a consensus on the need to create a ministry of energy for China. A less solid consensus supports the creation of a national security council to coordinate various aspects of Chinese foreign relations.

Meanwhile, despite occasional lofty talk about energy independence and the undeniable existence of a U.S. Department of Energy, America still has no coherent programs to promote energy company research into synthetic and renewable energy resources, to funnel investment into new energy capacity and infrastructure, or to curb the growth in our dependency on imports of oil and gas. Even without an energy ministry, China has made solid progress at doing all three.

The Chinese emphasis on coal; coal conversion; hydro, solar, wind, biomass, and nuclear power; and natural gas from Central Asia and Siberia is directed in part at holding down seaborne oil and gas imports. Recent Chinese emphasis on oil sand development in Canada, which is second only to Saudi Arabia in reserves of this so-far unexploited energy source, represents yet another significant effort at diversification.[1] China has, and plans to have, a much more diversified energy menu than the United States with, crucially, much heavier reliance both on coal and on renewable sources of energy, enabled by restrictions of oil and other liquid fuels to the transportation sector.

Oil and gas are in some senses indistinguishable for purposes of energy security. Both move to market by ship or pipeline. Natural gas is now increasingly transported by sea in liquefied form. Chinese imports of LNG have just begun, but both the United States and China are rapidly increasing or planning to increase seaborne imports of LNG from producers like Qatar, Australia, Indonesia, and—in the case of China—Iran. China may build an expensive pipeline to Turkmenistan to supplement planned pipelines to gas fields in Russian Siberia, in part as a hedge against sole dependence on maritime trade in gas. China is also increasing its strategic storage capacity. It now has only about thirty days of oil reserves in storage, but given the late 2006 drop in oil prices, it has begun to fill oil storage facilities that it had kept empty when prices were higher.

Even more than the United States, China has the potential to save a lot of energy. Doing so is a key part of its strategy for achieving energy security. Despite China's very low rates of per capita energy consumption (which are only about 14 percent of U.S. per capita consumption), China consumes between 7 and 11.5 times more energy than Japan to produce one dollar of gross domestic product (GDP), and it is about 4.5 times less efficient than is the United States. If China has further to go in energy efficiency, this also makes it much easier for it to conserve and thereby curb growth in demand for imported oil and gas   all the more so because Chinese consumers have not yet become accustomed to the high levels of energy consumption that are taken for granted in the United States.

The current Chinese government seems belatedly to have found both the vision and the will to do serious demand management, something American politics will not permit. China's mainly market-driven efforts to boost the efficiency of its currently energy-wasteful economy offer the opportunity for great increases in energy efficiency. China now aims to cut energy consumption per unit of GDP by about 4 percent annually in coming years, with special attention to oil and gas consumption. Still, even if China's imports of both grow much more slowly than its economy, they will inevitably go up rapidly, given the speed of the country's economic growth.

Therefore, even if the mainstays of Chinese energy policy are diversification, innovation, conservation, and constraints on the role of oil and gas in the Chinese economy, China has to be concerned about the vulnerability of oil and gas imports to disruption, whether by natural or man-made events. So far, China appears to be continuing to rely primarily on political and economic measures rather than focusing on using the Chinese navy to address this issue. China's cultivation of cordial ties with Africa, where it is now the largest foreign investor, is a case in point well illustrated by the recent Sino–African summit in Beijing. China's willingness to subordinate other priorities to the consolidation of energy-purchase relationships with sometimes difficult partners abroad also testifies to this. So too does China's stress on drawing foreign suppliers into the ownership and operation of refineries on its territory in order to consolidate their dependence on the China market and give them an incentive to continue to supply it even in times of adversity.

On the military side, for now, at least, China—like everyone else—seems prepared, if not content, to allow the U.S. Navy and its sister armed services to continue unselfishly to bear the burden of protecting the world's energy supplies and ensuring freedom of navigation for the benefit of energy producers and consumers around the world. One of our most lovable characteristics as Americans has been our apparent willingness to bear any burden and pay any price to preserve our freedom to "gas-guzzle" and to guarantee foreigners the right to join us in this most sacred of all liberties. In the long term, however, it is difficult to believe either that the United States will be willing to continue to provide such a free ride to allies, friends, and competitors alike, or that China will not wish to develop an independent capacity to secure its overseas energy sources and trade routes. Energy security is a subject we should be discussing with the Chinese.

The fact is that China does not trust U.S. maritime policy. Washington's innovations like the Proliferation Security Initiative appear to project a disdain for both sovereignty and traditional principles of international law that the Chinese are not alone in seeing as both ominous and potentially destabilizing. If international law is no protection, countries like China will have to "pack a pistol" when they venture abroad. In the absence of mutual trust, proposed antipiracy patrols in the Straits of Malacca, desirable as they may be, also excite Chinese concerns. China, like the littoral states, wonders whether these patrols are really intended to defend the global commons or to gain de facto control over their energy jugular.

The nearly two-decade-long absence of friendly interaction between the U.S. and Chinese navies, except intermittently at relatively high levels, often in connection with ship visits, has fed mutual suspicion. If this gap in our international relations is not corrected, it will nurture Chinese concern over the implications of continuing to rely on the U.S. Navy for the defense of China's energy trade and the security of its choke points. It will add to Chinese reluctance to contemplate cooperation and burden-sharing with the United States in support of freedom of navigation and the security of the world's energy trade. This in turn will increase the incentives for China to acquire independent naval power projection capabilities with which to defend its supply lines on its own. Thus, despite clear common interests, the lack of present cooperation between the U.S. Navy and its Chinese counterpart undermines the prospects for future cooperation, and the absence of interaction increases the possibility of future contention.

Such contention could be very damaging to both countries but mainly, as argued earlier in this chapter, to the United States. For the foreseeable future, it will be America's market that is most dependent on imports, not China's, though China's dependency will grow. Despite popular perceptions, it is also still the U.S. market, not China's, that more than any other drives energy prices, though China's impact on prices will be ever greater in the future. Meanwhile, price rises or supply disruptions affect us more than China and will continue to do so for the foreseeable future.

As the two largest consumers of energy, the United States and China have many problems in common. We could gain a lot by working together rather than at cross-purposes. A strategy aimed at working with China to boost mutual as well as global energy security would have several elements. It would integrate China as rapidly as possible into the G-7 global economic management system. It would bring China into the International Energy Agency, thereby coordinating the strategic petroleum reserve system and facilitating Chinese contributions to the mitigation of energy emergencies rather than, as at present, allowing China to have a free ride on other nations' oil stockpiles, including that of the United States. It would encourage, not seek to exclude, Chinese access to Central Asian and Russian oil and gas fields for which China is the most proximate (and thus most cost-effective) market, thereby reducing pressure on China to compete with the United States for supplies that are more advantageously located in relation to the American market. Such a cooperative strategy would work with China on ways of increasing the use of domestic energy sources (e.g., using coal in environmentally friendly ways or developing renewable energy resources that could obviate the need for China to import ever more oil and gas). And, most important to the U.S. Navy, it would seek patiently to enlist China along with other energy consumers in support of freedom of navigation, antipiracy patrols, and protection of strategic lines of communication.

Would the Chinese be willing to work with the United States in this way? Would the People's Liberation Army Navy be willing to cooperate directly with the U.S. Navy or at least work out a division of labor in support of the U.S. Navy's mission of safeguarding the global energy commons? I think the answers to these questions are almost certainly "yes," though we will never know unless we ask. Will we ask? China is such a useful cure for our post–Cold War case of enemy deprivation syndrome and as such provides such a convenient rationale for building more nuclear submarines and the like that, no doubt, some in our country will not want to ask. But I think that, in our own interest, we should.

In conclusion, China is worried about its rising dependence on energy imports, but it has a lot less reason to be worried than the United States does. Signaling an intention to threaten Chinese energy security could have a lot of adverse consequences for the United States, and it is hard to find many benefits. We would almost certainly be better off recognizing that, as the world's two largest consumers of energy, the United States and China have common interests that should draw us together rather than pull us apart. And if we can find a way of working with the Chinese in the energy arena, rather than against them, we will almost certainly both be better off.

Note

1. Chinese focus on Canadian oil sands may not be sustained. As this volume went to press, CNPC was cutting back its operations in Canada in order to expand heavy oil operations in Venezuela. See "CNPC Shifts Oil Focus Away from Canada—Reports," Reuters, 13 July 2007, http://uk.reuters.com/article/venezuelaMktRpt/idUKN1337819120070713.

Daniel H. Rosen and Trevor Houser

Scenarios for the Chinese Economy

Introduction

CHINA'S FUTURE ENERGY FOOTPRINT will be determined principally by the larger question of its macroeconomic growth in the years ahead. The policy choices made in light of that macro eventuality are the secondary variable. It is helpful, therefore, to begin a discussion of China's energy strategy with a review of the country's present economic situation, the forces propelling it and constraining it, and scenarios for economic growth in the years ahead. This chapter will provide such a review, albeit in a cursory manner. We will briefly offer our point of view on the energy footprint implications of this macroeconomic growth, including discussion of the key policy choices that enter into the equation.

Present Economic Situation

At the end of 2006 China had an economy of about $2.7 trillion, up 10.7 percent in inflation adjusted terms from $2.3 trillion in 2005.[1] It would have been more than $60 billion *lower* as expressed in U.S. dollar terms were it not for the gradual but noticeable appreciation of the renminbi (RMB) that has occurred since summer 2005.

China's greater than 10 percent growth is exceptional, and doubling in just six years is phenomenal. But consider, too, that the whole economy of China is only 5 percent of world gross domestic product (GDP) of $44.4 trillion. The economy of California is three-quarters as big as that of China. The United States' and European Union's are each about ten times bigger, and Japan's is more than twice as large. Figure 1 depicts these comparators.

Figure 1. GDP Comparators

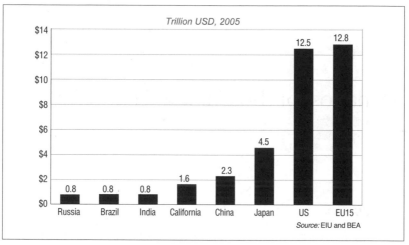

Economists classify economic activity in two different ways helpful to understanding the nature of China's commercial dynamism. The first is by sector: primary sector is agriculture, secondary sector is industry including manufacturing, and tertiary sector is services. Although 340 million of China's total labor force of 758 million in 2005 were involved in some form of agriculture, the value of China's economy today is heavily weighted to industry. In the third quarter of 2006, 49.8 percent of GDP was industrial activity, the majority of that manufacturing. Services activity has also taken off over the past ten years, now representing 39.2 percent of GDP. Importantly, the kind of services being performed in recent years is less unskilled (e.g., pushing bricks in a wheelbarrow) and more skilled. This leaves only 11 percent of GDP in agriculture, which is surely a historic low for this ancient economy. And yet China is still self-sufficient in food, in the aggregate, and in fact is poised to become a major competitive power in higher-value, labor-intensive cropping. Overall, the concentration of Chinese economic activity in manufacturing distinguishes it from other economies at similar income levels. See figure 2 for a depiction of these sectoral shares.

Figure 2. Composition of GDP by Sector

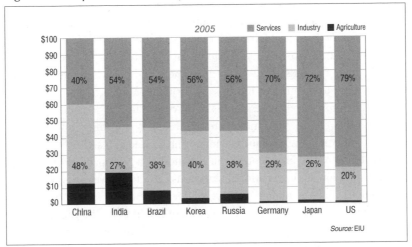

Source: EIU

The second way in which GDP can be classified is by expenditure type: namely, consumption (by households), investment (by businesses), government spending, and the balance of exports minus imports. While all Chinese statistics are problematic, the GDP by expenditure data are especially so; nonetheless, they are important and provide at least a gross picture of the economy. Many people think that China's growth over the past twenty-five years has been export-led, as Japan's or South Korea's was at the corresponding stage of development. That was not generally the case because China did not run systemic trade surpluses for most of the reform period. The past two years have been glaringly exceptional in this regard because China is now running a very large current account surplus amounting to over 8 percent of GDP as of June 2006, and hence growth is partly export-led.

Investment also constitutes an exceptionally large share of China's GDP at present, reaching 42.6 percent in 2005. This is considered by some to be unsustainably high because business investment must subsequently serve to meet consumer demand in order to have been justified, and with such massive investment outlays many simply assume that much of this spending will fail to pay a return, and thus turn into bad debt (because a large portion of it—35 percent or so—is made with borrowed money). Others argue that, while high,

China's large investment share is more or less reasonable given the basic infrastructure being built and structural adjustment taking place nationwide.

Consumption, at 38 percent of GDP in 2005, is thought to be somewhat low. Indeed, it has fallen off from 52.5 percent in 1981.[2] While growing at a robust 13–14 percent per year, consumption still does not satisfy many observers who think that it must, or should, make up a larger share of China's growth both for reasons of fairness (i.e., so that China depends less on foreign demand—exports—to fuel its development) and reasons of good domestic policy (i.e., relying so heavily on investment and exports creates a major, inevitable risk to the growth model). By thriving on foreign demand, China could suffer inordinately when there is a downturn in U.S. demand. Yet some point out that official data understate the weight of consumption in China, and that the expenditure balance is not as imbalanced as it seems.[3]

Government spending enters the equation at a nominal 13.9 percent of GDP. This is low by international standards. The true level of government spending in China is higher because a large share of state bank lending to state companies that shows up as investment might better be thought of as government spending. Regardless of that anomaly, the overall level of government expenditure is almost certain to increase dramatically in the years immediately ahead because public investments in a wide range of critical services cannot be postponed any longer. The urgency of undertaking these investments will in fact precipitate a new era in China's macroeconomic structure, as the shift of government spending to education, healthcare, other transfer payments, and environmental remediation opens up areas previously financed by government (especially infrastructure) to more private investment. Figure 3 depicts the division of China's GDP by expenditure.

The geographic and urban/rural distribution of economic activity in China illustrates the severe unevenness of China's development to date. When reform began in the late 1970s, there was relatively little income inequality in China: everyone was equally poor. Figure 4 offers a view of the divergence in incomes now characteristic of the Chinese economy: GDP per capita in Shanghai is over six thousand dollars, at the level seen by the Organization for Economic Cooperation and Development (OECD) for South Korea only fifteen years ago! In poor interior provinces, meanwhile, incomes are an order of magnitude lower. While it could be said until recently that incomes were rising for each and every decile of Chinese, albeit at different rates, survey data now being discussed suggest that some groups saw real income declines in 2001–3. While there is a good likelihood that the rising sea is once again lifting all boats (especially because farm produce prices

Figure 3. GDP by Expenditure

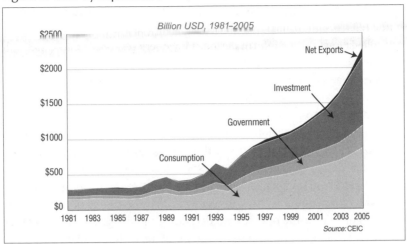

Figure 4: Provincial/Municipal GDP per Capita

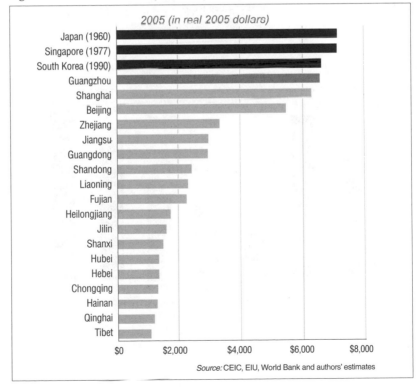

grew significantly after 2003), the geographic inequalities in Chinese income and related tendencies to social instability should not be discounted with blithe reference to the fact that China had achieved a record amount of poverty alleviation over the reform period, a knee-jerk response that—while still true—is insufficient to guarantee stability in the years ahead.

The urban/rural dynamic is also a fundamental and critical characteristic of present economic conditions in China. China is still roughly 40 percent urban and 60 percent rural in population. Urban economies naturally generate greater income flows while also bringing social challenges. China is urbanizing with dizzying rapidity, with 170-plus cities of more than 1 million people now on the map and another 100 or more approaching that level.[4] Yet with 60 percent of the population still rural, there is in fact a massive reserve of migration yet to come; this will constitute the core engine of China's continued growth over the next several decades. This contrasts with both other emerging economies that also have large rural populations but cannot manage the political economy challenges of urbanization (India) and those that have already transitioned to be largely urban (Latin America): figure 5 compares China to some peers in these regards.

Figure 5. Urbanization

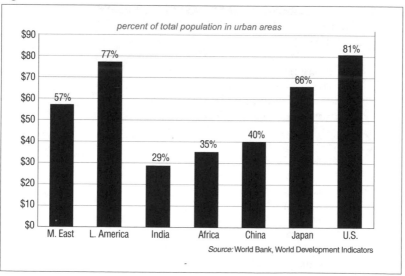

Source: World Bank, World Development Indicators

Background Forces Responsible

So far we have summarized the state of China's economy today in more or less static terms. To achieve our goal of providing reliable scenarios for China's economic footprint in the future—and hence clarifying the energy footprint that derives from it—we must identify key forces underpinning and impelling economic growth to date and, ultimately, ask whether those are the same forces needed to maintain growth in the future, and whether they will be sustained.

Productivity Versus Factor Accumulation. One way to increase the output of an economy is simply to add more inputs into it; this is referred to as factor accumulation, and obviously would produce growth that was illusory in the end, as was the case in the former Soviet Union. A far healthier recipe for prosperity is productivity-driven growth. If output can be increased without changing the amount of inputs (including labor, resources, energy, and capital), then one or more forms of productivity growth are in the mix, and these gains are thought to be more sustainable and desirable. The literature on the role of productivity in explaining China's growth is voluminous and mixed. Certainly during the 1980s gains from redistributing inputs to sectors where they could be better used, and from increased productivity within individual firms, played a leading role. The 1990s were a mixed story in this regard, and given the extraordinary level of investment in recent years (as discussed earlier), caution is warranted before applauding productivity. Nonetheless, recent analysis of the growth in total profit at indigenous Chinese firms—profit growth that has impressed many observers—concludes that productivity growth deserves significant credit.[5] We believe that productivity growth has played an important role in many (though not all) firms and sectors in the past, and that there are significant opportunities to drive growth based on productivity enhancement in the years ahead.

Fixing Incentives. Under socialism "surplus" profit was not necessarily retained by the individual or firm that had managed to generate it. It was largely absorbed (or reabsorbed, since the state was the main provider of working capital in the first place) by the state. Ideology asserted that economic agents could be productive without a personal profit motive, and that a diffuse sense of collective ownership was capable of motivating innovation and striving. In reality things did not play out that way: innovation, growth, and efficiency suffered in comparison to performance in market-oriented economies with commitments to private property and gain. Since 1980 China's economic growth has been driven by restoration of profit incentives.

Early on, the household responsibility system (包产到户) drove productivity because farming households were permitted to retain some of the fruits of their labors and hence pursued efficiency gains. In the early 1990s Beijing decided to let state-owned firms retain much of their "surplus" profit and thus gave them a good reason to increase profitability while the "ownership" of "state-owned enterprises" was left to be fully worked out in the future. This has led to the current debate over whether they should be paying more of a "dividend" to the state as shareholder and, if so, then to which unit of government. Through the 1990s to today a loosening of administrative controls on residency and work choices has restored incentives for individuals and firms to adjust past behavior and choices in order to increase incomes, and this certainly contributes to rapid urbanization.

Despite the significance of restored incentives over twenty-five years, the mother lode of basic private property sanctity law is yet to come. Farmers are most vulnerable to reallocation of their land, and hence their incentive to undertake capital improvements is undermined. State enterprises of various classes still suffer from murkiness in ownership definitions. Restrictions on civil society and related low consciousness about ownership of "the commons" of China—including the environment writ large—contribute to epic failures to internalize the costs of industrialization and make the principle that polluters should pay for the damage they do an enforceable legal construct. These and many other incentive problems remain to be addressed.

Encouraging Competition. A key aspect of China's post-1979 economic reform was embracing the power of competition. Internally, China slowly dismantled many horizontal and vertical monopolies, created new firms to compete with incumbents, worked against interprovincial trade barriers, fought anticompetitive practices, and restored incentives to compete. Externally, barriers to foreign trade and investment were gradually reduced such that new competitors from abroad were introduced to the domestic marketplace in most industries. While in almost all cases much remains to be accomplished and signs of partial backsliding frequently emerge, in general China has shown an enthusiasm for competition rarely encountered among developing economies. We have even described China as achieving competition-led growth in the past and continue to use that term.[6] If China were to shy away from encouraging competition, it would reduce the future economic growth outlook. Some groups in China today, including those sometimes called the "New Left," prescribe such a course. We do not think this view will assume a commanding place in Chinese policy.

Demographics. Fixing incentives and encouraging competition have been the right policy stances to promote growth in China, but the absolute extent of their success is a function of the underlying demographics. The enormous population of 1.3 billion people is the basis of China's tremendous comparative advantage in labor-intensive economic activity, and its existing and potential domestic demand. And yet, absolute gains would be diluted over an increasing population and would not generate such poverty alleviation if not for the success of the "one child" policy in stabilizing the demographic expansion. The very modest growth of China's demographic base is almost unique among low-income developing countries and is a pillar of Chinese exceptionalism. Meanwhile, the shift from a rural past to an urban future is the high-torque driver of economic expansion in China and has many decades still to play out fully. At the same time, however, population policies are already establishing the conditions for rapid aging of China's workforce in years to come.[7]

Policy Consistency and Streamlined Ideological Debate. Finally, we consider the consistency of China's pragmatic policy stance toward reform to be a foundational contributor to economic growth past, present, and future. China has sidestepped the all-consuming ideological debates about growth models that have slowed political economy reforms in so many other developing countries. Instead of first ratifying an official endorsement of a particular growth strategy and implementing it thereafter, China has done the opposite: the ideological rhetoric of socialism has been left in place in official discourse while a wholly different set of policy ideas has been applied in practice. This has created its own set of problems in the management of ostensible orthodoxy and evolution of the regulatory state, but analysts from foreign firms, sovereign ratings agencies, international financial institutions, and other domains are fairly agreed that the risk of policy instability—a major component of emerging market risk in other locales—is low in China. Maybe too agreed: this condition will not last forever, and evidence of more explicit factional politics on policy directions is mounting. However, we continue to see this aspect of China's model supporting growth as we know it for some time to come.

Where to from Here?

Working from our knowledge of present economic performance, and in cognizance of the long-standing driving forces supporting economic growth, it is now time for us to analyze scenarios for China's future economic performance. Ten years ago our scenario outlook was for a decade of 7–8 percent growth, with risks on the upside (meaning that growth might exceed expectations). Through most of the 1990s the majority of China's economic watchers were skeptical about the foundations of Chinese growth and doubted that it could be maintained. We "bulls" were in the minority; far more common were "bears" forecasting the coming collapse of China or that Chinese growth was a "dream." Today our outlook for the next decade is 10–11 percent growth, with risks on the downside. We will elaborate why.

Let us take economic performance over the past year as a baseline and consider what adjustments to it are likely over the coming decade. Consumption growth in the range of 13 percent per year is likely to remain stable or go up. Why? Discretionary savings against unfunded liabilities will come down, driving consumption. There are at least three reasons for this. First, wages and income are rising for most urban Chinese—and it is urban Chinese who constitute the engine of consumption. (The flow of rural dwellers into urban China augments this, as well as raising farm prices relative to manufactured goods prices, which is prorural consumption.) Second, government is moving and will move further to fund safety net systems to reduce the incentive for massive precautionary savings. Third, the younger generation of urban Chinese is less conservative than their elders and simply consumes more of its income and saves less.

Investment has been high as a share of GDP and has been concentrated in real estate and infrastructure. Much of investment is bank-financed, between state banks and state enterprises, and might better be thought of as government spending. The decision by firms to reinvest so much of retained earnings in sometimes dubious expansion reflects a mix of poor corporate governance (which diminishes the amount of profits given to shareholders—including government shareholders—as dividend) and essentially negative rates of return if they save (a result of financial sector immaturity, to state it briefly). The ratio of value added to capital input in enterprise is lowest for wholly state-owned firms, followed by majority state-owned firms, then minority state-owned firms, and higher for private and foreign invested firms: the pattern is as clear as day.

Most of these characteristics are changing or will change in the near future and will thus alter the scenario for the investment component of China's economic path. End-year 2006 investment will come in around $1.4 trillion, over 50 percent of GDP, and growing at a year-on-year pace of 20–30 percent (only recently slowed to below 20 percent). To the extent that such a high level of investment is a problem, we expect Beijing to simply explain some of it away by "conceding" that a portion of what has shown up as investment is in fact consumption, such as the purchase of cars by firms (investment) that are in reality for personal use of managers (consumption). While Beijing is unlikely to refute the argument that a significant amount of "investment" is actually government spending, senior officials are probably not annoyed with this line as long as it helps palliate foreign anxieties about overinvestment. We foresee the stated amount of investment to be reduced from trend soon, just as the amount of service sector activity in GDP was lifted with a simple accounting restatement in December 2005.[8]

Yet that will not change the actual investment taking place. Other measures will: real estate and land conversion regulatory moves are already slowing the growth of almost $300 billion a year in real estate investment. Withheld approvals and emergency reviews are arresting investment in additional capacity in cement, steel, electricity generating, aluminum, and other basic industries. Pressure to withhold bank loans alone will not fully control the investment story, however, because only 21 percent of total fixed asset investments (FAI) as of October 2006 is bank financed, the majority being funded from retained earnings and other internal sources. Other policies, including the payment of dividends by state-owned enterprises to the state and better minority shareholder rights at nonstate firms, are being contemplated to vacuum up that extra liquidity instead; the shareholding structure of listed firms in China has been reformed more generally to help improve corporate governance. On the incentives side, corporate treasurers may find better alternatives to building an infinite number of new factories in the future now that the equity market is moving upward (though so fast that a correction is likely). Nonequity savings vehicles like money market demand deposits may well have to show a higher return as a result or risk seeing interest dry up in light of soaring stocks.

The scenario for investment that we see as most likely is as follows: government shifts from directly and indirectly financing national, provincial, and municipal hard infrastructure projects to financing a trillion dollars' worth of unfunded healthcare and educational, environmental, and other public goods that have simply not been paid-in to date. In this sense we see a case of government spending–led growth in China over the coming two decades. Investment does not dry up, however, but rather is picked up by domestic and foreign institutional investment in infrastructure and other long-term growth, through deepening of the bond market. Currently government is crowding institutional investors, including enterprises with overbrimming corporate coffers, out of making these investments, which professional money managers should be pleased to compete over once given an opportunity. So we see investment restructured and growing at a less frothy pace keyed to longer term debt markets rather than short-term FAI cycles. While the structure of investment changes, it should continue to be a strong positive contributor to growth for ten to twenty years at least.

Having touched on the behavior of government spending within the context of investment, we are left with laying out a point of view on net exports. In 2006, China ran a trade surplus of $177 billion: this approaches 7 percent of GDP, a glaring imbalance. Yet China has not structured its GDP growth around large export surpluses traditionally and already has a headache from managing such a large dollar pile of foreign exchange reserves. We see net exports moving back toward balance over the coming five years (it may take that long) for a wide range of reasons. First, the RMB has moved up somewhat against the U.S. dollar, making dollar-denominated goods cheaper in China and Chinese goods slightly pricier abroad. (The RMB has actually depreciated against the Euro, however, falling along with the dollar.) Second, China intends major politically motivated buying. Third, Chinese export competitiveness in labor-intensive manufacturing is under siege from lower-labor-cost nations (like Vietnam) while its ability to move up the value chain into the space held by more sophisticated economies is limited for the time being. Fourth, China does not possess the process and production methods critical to addressing its own domestic environmental crisis and will necessarily see trade competitiveness shift back toward OECD manufacturing firms as environmental crisis takes hold. Important in these regards are maintenance practices, diagnostic tools for assessing manufacturing problems and inefficiencies, and pollution abatement systems. (We see this as a medium-term phenomenon, not a far-off scenario.)

Downside Risks and Concluding Thoughts

These are the components of our expectation that China will most likely maintain its 10–11 percent GDP growth trajectory, with concommitant growth in appetite for energy, commodities, and other economic inputs. Recent changes in the nature of China's economic growth, which we discussed more fully in a report for the Peterson Institute for International Economics, mean that energy demand is likely to grow as fast as the economy as a whole, a sharp departure from China's historic trends.[9] But, unlike the 1990s during which the likely surprise was growth higher than expected, we think the risks are to the downside for the coming decade or two. The reason is that the microeconomic comparative advantages China has embraced—principally, a shift toward better utilizing its labor endowment—have been well developed by now, and the economic challenges of impelling growth further require governmental skills and leadership that have not been hitherto demonstrated. In fact, we think that China suffers from a host of comparative disadvantages that must be addressed in order to enjoy potential growth of 10 percent or higher.

Table 1 summarizes these comparative disadvantages. Here we will illustrate just a few examples. First, China has established a commanding presence in global labor-intensive, low-end manufacturing. But this manufacturing is commoditized and margins are very low and shrinking further as a result of low barriers to entry and other aspiring locales both within China (the interior) and outside (Vietnam, India, etc.) eager to create jobs at margins that are untenable in even moderately developed settings such as Shanghai, Tianjin, or Shenzhen. Meanwhile, China has systematic troubles expanding activities "downstream"—closer to consumers in overseas locations where distribution and retail margins are more lucrative because its firms are inexperienced operating under normal legal and regulatory regimes where high service-component customer interaction is the basis of value creation.

Table 1. China's Comparative Disadvantages

China's comparative disadvantages	Advantages for Western firms
FACTORS OF PRODUCTION	
Capital market inefficiency	Outperform in capital intensive sectors
The curse of labor	Greater flexibility of technology-intensive firms
Innovation gap	High returns to innovation
Environmental inefficiency	Opportunity for environment/resource-efficient products
LEGAL/POLITICAL SYSTEMS	
Governance technology	Faster standard and policy cycles
Competition policy	Superior responsiveness to consumer demand
Legal system weakness	Legal-intensive industries (e.g. finance)
Political reform risk	Higher certainty in strategic planning
COMMERCIAL ISSUES	
Margin compression in manufacturing	Higher returns to creativity
Slow to internationalize	Superior global brand management
Tax aversion/IT	Higher returns to IT
Undervalue intangibles	Better economies of scope

Moreover, beyond the microeconomic concerns, the economic development model of China has been predicated on not internalizing environmental costs of manufacturing, which can be huge for low-cost operators, and on either command and control or, paradoxically, laissez-faire governance inputs to the marketplace. There is a real crisis already today in Chinese environmental conditions. Internalizing environmental costs is becoming not merely an option but rather as necessary a step as repairing levees before a hurricane: failure to do so will wipe out existing economic activity. For lack of experience and technological know-how in operating beyond a labor-intensive model, the marginal cost of switching to environmentally benign process and production methods will be much greater for Chinese firms than for OECD firms accustomed to tighter operating conditions. The environmental cost burden of not addressing these issues is quickly becoming untenable in terms of clean water availability, diminished crop yields due to atmospheric pollution, and inability to move up the ladder into higher value goods due to contamination and food and product safety concerns.

On the governance side, China is facilitating more rapid growth than, for example, India or Brazil by permitting local authorities to rezone property for industrial or commercial use with no due process or social justice considerations: GDP maximization is the sole imperative. In this regard, the one-party authoritarian political system can employ command and control measures that accelerate growth in the near term. Paradoxically, much of the output growth in China since 1979 has entailed getting government out of the way entirely and simply letting individual greed find a way to increase output. There is nothing wrong with that except that at higher levels of income a key ingredient for higher valued-added economic activity is the role of government as regulator, honest-broker, and enforcer of the common good. China has no experience in providing these governmental inputs. The type of government that got China from $200 per capita to the $1,800 per capita enjoyed today will look little like the government that gets the economy to $10,000 per capita a few years hence. And yet there is no road map for changing the political system, and indeed the need for contestability and accountability in higher income economy government systems seems incompatible with regimes currently in place.

For all these reasons, we think there are downside risks to China as it tries to maintain maximum growth in its next phase.

Notes

1. Absolute numbers are rounded.

2. See Nicholas R. Lardy, "China: Toward a Consumption-Driven Growth Path," in *Policy Briefs in International Economics*, Institute for International Economics, October 2006, [number PB06-6] for a concise discussion of the state of consumption. Available at http://www.iie.com/publications/pb/pb06-6.pdf.

3. See Kroeber et al., "China Retail: A Nation of Shoppers?" *China Insight*, Dragonomics Advisory, 27 November 2006.

4. James Jao, "Healthy Growth of Cities," *China Daily*, 24 April 2006.

5. See Ha Jiming and Xing Ziqiang, "Growing Productivity Drives Up Profit Margins," *CICC Macroeconomics Research*, 22 November 2006.

6. See, for instance, http://www.asiasource.org/news/at_mp_02.cfm?newsid=17651.

7. "China Faces up to Aging Population," Xinhua News Agency, 7 January 2005, www.china.org.cn/english/2005/Jan/117070.htm.

8. "Reduced from trend" means that the stated amount of investment will be less than was originally forecast.

9. Daniel H. Rosen and Trevor Houser, "China Energy: A Guide for the Perplexed," (Washington, D.C.: Peterson Institute for International Economics, 2007), http://www.iic.com/publications/papers/rosen0507.pdf.

David Pietz

The Past, Present, and Future of China's Energy Sector

Introduction

SINCE REFORM BEGAN IN 1978 China has increasingly expanded its global footprint. In virtually every realm of international exchange—scientific, technical, demographic, cultural, and economic—China has developed an important stake. But it is not simply a one-way relationship. Indeed, while smooth and efficient functioning of these networks is vital to China's continued reform agenda, the vitality of these networks has likewise become dependent upon China's active participation and support. Certainly the most obvious expression of this mutual dependence is the global economy. Although the temptation exists to leverage the "China factor" for partisan political purposes, there is no shortage of reasoned analysis that suggests that China has become inextricably intertwined with the global economy. Simply put, what happens in China matters to national economies around the world. One critical issue of this global integration is the maritime implications of China's growing dependence on international markets generally, and on the global oil markets specifically.

By the mid-1990s, China's massive economic growth had propelled it beyond the nodes of international exchange, namely the foreign capital and export market arenas that engaged its attentions to that point. As early as 1993, China's domestic source of energy supplies fell short of demand. To continue fueling rapid economic expansion, China was impelled to enter the global energy markets. The nature of this participation in energy networks was a source of confusion and debate among political and economic elites in China. Discourse about China's acquisition of energy and regulation of energy use was complicated by the fact that China's energy sector, particularly its oil and gas segments, has occupied, and continues to occupy, a space somewhere between the state and the market. It is this rather ambiguous position that has led some foreign observers to suggest that China's recent "going abroad" strategy to secure foreign energy resources has largely been state-directed while others have argued that there is very little state direction to China's international energy investments.

A specific goal of this chapter is to strike an analytical balance that seeks to recognize some of the complex features of China's energy sector. As suggested above, China's principle energy actors negotiate a space that is increasingly influenced by the dynamics of the international energy markets. Conversely, to suggest that a consensus does not exist among political elites, and that energy actors are entirely immune to such consensus, underestimates the still considerable power of the political center. One might also add to this mix an aversion to energy dependence. The political discourse of many national constituencies is seemingly influenced by the dream of energy independence, but the memory of China's recent historical experience—a memory tinted by a sense of aggrievement toward a world often deemed hostile to it—may add an additional element to this sentiment.

The overarching goal of this chapter is to provide a context by which to approach the chapters that follow. The objective is to provide a broad overview of China's energy sector (with special emphasis on oil and gas). This chapter will address the following questions:

- How do oil and gas fit into China's energy structure, and what are the prospects for energy alternatives?
- To what extent, if at all, do China's oil and gas producers serve as arms of state policy? What are the primary drivers of China's oil and gas producers? Who coordinates China's energy policy?
- What would be the impact of a significant maritime conflict involving China on the world oil market? How much would China suffer

relative to other importers? What is the status of China's strategic petroleum reserve (SPR) and how will it eventually be used?

These questions lead to two important conclusions that this chapter highlights, namely (1) over the next thirty years, despite the growing presence of hydroelectricity, nuclear, and other renewables, oil and coal will continue to fuel China's growing energy appetite; and (2) while China's exposure to international energy markets will indeed increase substantially over the next several decades, the continued dominant position of domestically sourced coal in its fuel mix will mitigate its vulnerability to disruptions in international maritime energy transport.

China's Energy Structure

The growth of China's energy sector is a function of rapid growth of gross domestic product since 1978. Although some observers have suggested that the reporting system in China promotes inflated growth rates, China has clearly enjoyed the fastest rate of growth among all major economies of the world.[1] Official annual growth rates between 1980 and 2004 consistently hovered in the 9–10 percent range, as described in table 1. Throughout the reform period, the state has utilized a variety of administrative methods to engineer growth of at least 8 percent per year because this rate has been viewed as necessary to absorb workers laid off by the privatization of state-owned enterprises. Economic growth is projected to moderate to roughly 7 percent to 2015, and to roughly 4.5 percent thereafter to 2030. The important relationship between economic growth rates and energy use is suggested by energy intensity data (energy per unit of GDP), a topic to be addressed further.

Table 1. World GDP Growth (average annual growth rates)

	1980–90	1990–2004	2004–15	2015–30	2004–30
United States	3.1	3.0	2.9	2.0	2.4
Europe	2.5	2.2	2.3	1.8	2.0
Pacific	4.2	2.2	2.3	1.6	1.9
Russia	—	–0.9	4.2	2.9	3.4
China	9.1	10.1	7.3	4.3	5.5
India	6.0	5.7	6.4	4.2	5.1
World	2.9	3.4	4.0	2.9	3.4

Source: World Energy Outlook 2006 (Paris: International Energy Agency, 2006), 59.

China's energy supply has exhibited broad-based growth across the energy spectrum (see table 2). With the exception of oil and gas, sources of primary energy will be supplied domestically. China's rich coal deposits will continue to fulfill all demand requirements. The greatest potential for increases in China's supply spectrum will come from the hydroelectric, nuclear, and gas sectors. Over the next two to three decades, China, virtually alone among major economies of the world, will aggressively develop hydroelectric generation capacity, particularly in the west and southwest where China has considerable untapped water resources available. Although a nascent environmental movement has appeared in China during the past decade, primarily as a consequence of angst over the Three Gorges Dam Project, the state appears committed to develop hydroelectric capacity in these regions.

Table 2. Total Primary Energy Supply (million tons of oil equivalent)

| | 1990 | 2004 | 2015 | 2030 | SHARE (%) | | | ANNUAL GROWTH (%) | |
					2004	2015	2030	2004– 2015	2004– 2030
Coal	534	999	1,604	2,065	61	64	61	4	2.9
Oil	116	319	497	758	20	20	22	4.1	3.4
Gas	16	44	89	157	3	4	5	6.7	5.1
Nuclear	0	13	32	67	1	1	2	8.5	6.4
Hydro	11	30	56	81	2	2	2	5.7	3.8
Biomass and Waste	200	221	222	239	14	9	7	0.1	0.3
Other Renewables	0	0	8	29	0	0	1	*	*

* No data.

Source: World Energy Outlook 2006 (Paris: International Energy Agency, 2006), 59.

Growth in China's nuclear sector has perhaps the greatest potential to increase beyond the projections currently offered by the International Energy Agency and other forecasting organizations. The international climate for nuclear generation has experienced a transformation during the past several years of global energy concerns. This transformation has been marked by renewed calls for the construction of nuclear capacity in a variety of contexts around the globe. This, coupled with increasing environmental concerns stemming from fossil fuel consumption in China, may well increase investment in its nuclear generation sector over the next several decades. Although an increase in capital investment in the nuclear generation sector in China is quite likely over the next thirty years, the total component of nuclear generation will remain relatively small.

China's natural gas sector has been slow to develop despite substantial government rhetoric to the contrary a decade or so ago. One significant accomplishment has been the west-to-east pipeline. The four-thousand-kilometer pipeline completed in late 2004 transports gas from Xinjiang province to China's eastern market centered in Shanghai (with a design capacity of 12 billion cubic meters per year). There has also been discussion of a second west-to-east pipeline as part of China's Eleventh Five-Year Development Plan for National Economic and Social Development (2006–10). Internationally, China has discussed a variety of gas supply scenarios with Kazakhstan, Turkmenistan, and Uzbekistan. The China National Petroleum Corporation (CNPC) has reportedly been engaged in a natural gas pipeline feasibility study with Kazakhstan's KazMunaiGaz. In addition, reports over the past several years suggest that CNPC has been in talks with Russian officials over linking the Siberian natural gas grid to China. Although such pipeline projects remain in the future, investment to effectively exploit the gas resources of the Sichuan Basin and to build an effective internal distribution system continues to plague China's gas sector. Over the next several decades, however, China will continue to promote investment that will ultimately generate 5–7 percent annual growth in natural gas supplies.

Despite the relatively strong per annum increases in hydroelectric, nuclear, and gas supply, China's economy will unquestionably remain carbon-based. If one projects the percentage share of individual fuels across the supply spectrum over the next twenty to thirty years, coal and oil will continue to dominate energy supply. Coal supply will decline slightly on a per share basis but will continue to comprise 60–65 percent of China's total primary energy supply while oil, again with a slight decline, will constitute 20–22 percent.

Overshadowed by the recent discussions about the impact of Chinese demand on world oil markets is the fact that China continues to be one of the top five producers of crude in the world (see table 3). Although their production lags well behind Saudi Arabia, Russia, and the United States, China's oil companies have gradually exploited offshore resources and have consistently and successfully employed secondary and tertiary recovery methods to coax increased production out of mature fields in the East and Northeast (e.g., the Daqing and Shengli oil fields). There is, however, a domestic and foreign consensus that China's oil production will simply have to continue relying on these successes to hold crude production in the range of 3.5–3.8 million barrels per day over the next several decades.

Table 3. Top Twenty Oil Producing Countries (2005, million bpd)

Saudi Arabia	9.48
Russia	9.40
United States	7.61
Iran	3.98
China	3.63
Mexico	3.42
Norway	3.22
Canada	3.14
European Union	3.12
Venezuela	3.08
United Arab Emirates	2.54
Nigeria	2.45
Kuwait	2.42
Iraq	2.13
United Kingdom	2.08
Libya	1.72
Angola	1.60
Brazil	1.59
Algeria	1.37

Source: 2005 CIA World Factbook, available at https://www.cia.gov/cia/publications/factbook/rankorder/2173rank.html.

Although there continues to be hope that China's west will one day become a major oil producing region, distance from markets and complex geology continue to make production in the region economically unattractive. Irrespective of the singular potential of oil fields in the west, an accounting of China's proven oil reserves indeed suggests that it will increasingly rely on oil imports (see figure 1). According to data from late 2005, China's proven reserves total 18 billion barrels (see figure 2).[2] Although this figure may serve to impress (government statistical inflation may also be at play here), this reserve equates to only fourteen years of reserves-to-production ratio.

Figure 1. China's Oil Production (million barrels per day)

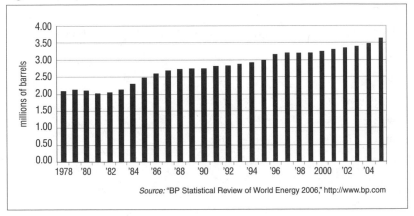

Figure 2. Global Proven Oil Reserves (billion barrels)

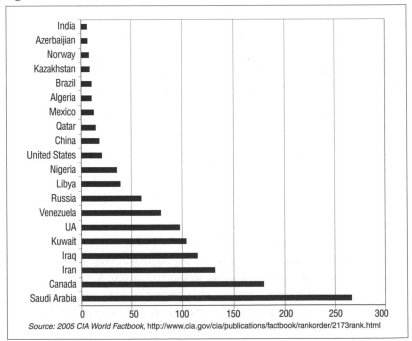

According to projections by the International Energy Agency, China's primary energy demand will increase by 2.6 percent annually to 2030 (see table 4). The demand profile over the next two decades will show healthy percentage increases in gas, nuclear, and hydroelectric consumption. However, average annual increases in coal and oil, while not as large as other fuels in the demand mix, will translate into overwhelming significance. Indeed, although coal demand is projected to grow at a relatively modest 2.3 percent annually, it will continue to dominate China's energy mix as it will constitute over 50 percent of primary energy demand (see figure 3). Similarly, increases in annual oil consumption will not approximate increases in that of gas, nuclear energy, or hydropower but will continue to constitute roughly one-quarter of China's primary energy demand (see figure 4). So, although annual growth rates of China's consumption of nuclear, gas, and hydropower will be impressive, and may indeed significantly surpass present forecasts, over the next thirty years China will not significantly lessen its dependence on coal and oil to fuel its economy.

Table 4. Primary Energy Demand in China (million tons of oil equivalent)

	1971	2002	2010	2030	2002–30
Coal	192	713	904	1,354	2.3%
Oil	43	247	375	636	3.4%
Gas	3	36	375	636	5.4%
Nuclear	0	7	21	73	9.0%
Hydro	3	25	33	63	3.4%
Biomass and Waste	164	216	227	236	0.3%
Other Renewables	0	0	5	20	0%
Total	405	1,244	1,940	3,018	2.60%

Source: World Energy Outlook 2004 (Paris: International Energy Agency, 2005), 264.

Figure 3. Primary Energy Demand by Fuel, 2010 and 2030

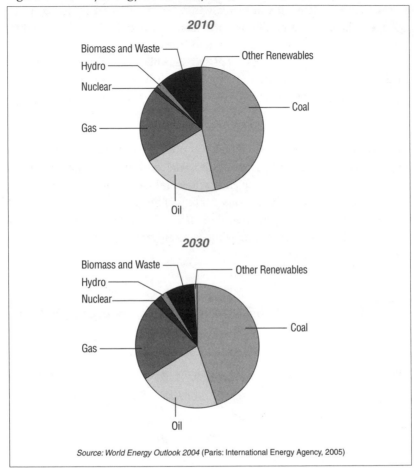

Source: World Energy Outlook 2004 (Paris: International Energy Agency, 2005)

Figure 4. China's Oil Production and Consumption, 1986–2006*

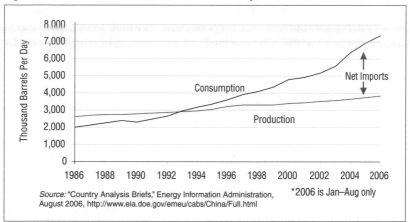

Source: "Country Analysis Briefs," Energy Information Administration,   *2006 is Jan–Aug only
August 2006, http://www.eia.doe.gov/emeu/cabs/China/Full.html

China's energy supply and demand dynamics will mean the country will increasingly impact world energy markets. Because oil and gas production will lag considerably behind projections for demand, China will have no other option than to import these supplies (see figure 5). China became a net importer of oil in 1993, and its dependence on foreign oil has steadily increased. Production was 3.6 million barrels per day (bpd) by 2005 while demand neared 7 million bpd.[3] This ratio between production and demand is projected to continue such that by 2030 China's total oil imports will equal nearly 80 percent of its total oil consumption.[4]

Figure 5. China's Oil Imports as Percentage of Demand

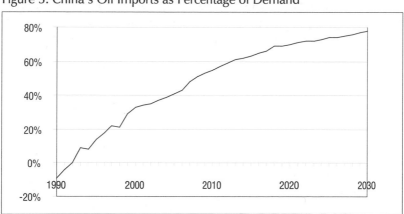

Source: "China's Growing Demand for Oil and Its Impact on U.S. Petroleum Markets," Congressional Budget Office, April 2006, http://www.cbo.gov/ftpdocs/71xx/doc7128/04-07-ChinaOil.pdf, 49.

Although the picture for natural gas in China is not one of such extreme import dependence, gas imports will nonetheless reach roughly 30–40 percent of demand.[5] The fact that India will also continue to influence global gas markets will make Asia an important driver of world gas markets (see figure 6).

Figure 6. Natural Gas Supply in China and India by Source, 2003, 2015, and 2030 (trillion cubic feet)

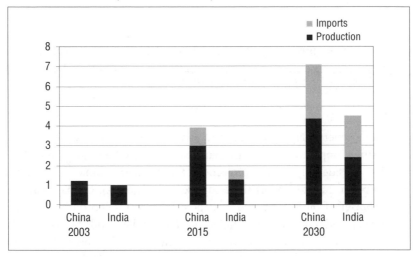

Where will China source these imports of oil and gas? Although China has made assiduous attempts to diversify its sources of international oil and gas resources (see table 5), a simple look at global reserves clearly indicates the major sources of China imports of energy for the next several decades— and these sources of energy are no different from those for every major importing country.

Table 5. 2005 Oil Imports into China

Origin	Thousands of barrels per day	Percent of total
USA	8.4	0.2
Canada	–	0
Mexico	–	0
South and Central America	107.3	3.2
Europe	12.1	0.4
Former Soviet Union	398.1	11.8
Middle East	1,359.7	40.2
North Africa	64.3	1.9
West Africa	574.4	17.0
East and Southern Africa	134.6	4.0
Australasia	24.9	0.7
Japan	69.0	2.0
Other Asia Pacific	625.7	18.5
Unidentified	6.0	0.2

Source: "BP Statistical Review of World Energy 2006," http://www.bp.com/liveassets/bp_inter net/globalbp/globalbp_uk_english/reports_and_publications/statistical_energy_review_2006/ STAGING/local_assets/downloads/spreadsheets/statistical_review_full_report_work book_2006.xls#'Oil - Trade movements'!A1

The Middle East, with by far the largest proven reserves in the world, will continue to be the primary source of China's oil. By 2015 and beyond, 70 percent of China's imported oil will be sourced from the Middle East. Beyond this, West Africa and Russia will be secondary sources of supply. Although the Middle East will also continue to be a major source of gas imports to China, Southeast Asia and Oceania will be important suppliers as well.

An important component of China's energy profile is energy intensity, or how much energy China employs to generate a unit of gross domestic product. On the eve of China's economic reforms beginning in the 1980s, China's economy was already endowed with high energy intensities as a result of the economy's emphasis on heavy industrial production during the Maoist period. Distinctly different from other developing economies that were making the more typical transition from agrarian economies to light industrial economies (with accompanying higher energy intensities), China was transitioning from an inefficient heavy industrial profile to production geared toward light industrial products. As a result, China's energy intensities decreased by 30 percent in the 1980s. From another perspective, China's growth in total energy consumption was 50–60 percent of GDP growth rates from 1980–90. The shift from heavy industry to light industry was also accompanied by efforts to improve productivity and a general upgrading of production technology. In virtually all sectors of China's economy, energy inputs increased more slowly than production output rates. The improvements in energy-use efficiency came from all energy sectors including petroleum. Oil consumption per unit of GDP dropped more than 30 percent in the 1980s.[6]

This trend of decreasing oil intensities during the reform period experienced a reversal in 2002–3 as energy demand exhibited a rather dramatic shift relative to GDP growth. During this period, energy demand grew 30 percent faster that GDP growth rates. The reasons for this transition appear to be related to a change in China's economic structure as more energy intensive industries such as cement and chemical production increase their relative share of economic output. Currently, China consumes two-fifths of the world's cement while also consuming one-quarter of world aluminum and one-fifth of world steel. The recent spike in energy intensities suggests that unrestrained demand may endanger long-term economic growth. China's recent ability to meet its goal of quadrupling GDP by 2020 will hinge on its reducing its energy intensities. And it certainly has room to do this. To generate every $1 of GDP, China uses 3 times as much energy as the global average, 4.7 times more than the U.S., and 11.5 times more than Japan.[7] The investments required to significantly improve China's energy efficiency will be large but necessary to reach the economic growth rates the regime has targeted. However, given the continued importance of heavy industrial production in China's economy, energy intensities in China will likely not reach the low levels likely to be achieved in North America or Europe over the next few decades.

Between the Market and the State

Since 1978 the evolution of the energy sector in China has been marked by the increasing influence of the market on the institutional organization and actions of the state-owned companies responsible for producing and refining crude oil and natural gas, and for transporting and distributing the resulting products to Chinese consumers. Although this process has been marked by episodes of advance and retreat, this evolution has resulted in the three main state oil and gas corporations occupying a space that can best be described as somewhere between the state and market.

Before 1978 a host of ministries had authority over a highly segmented oil and gas industry. In the 1980s, however, authority over upstream and downstream sectors of the business was dominated by several state corporations. First, the China National Offshore Oil Corporation (CNOOC) was created in 1982 and was endowed with control over all offshore oil and gas development. In 1983, the China Petrochemical Corporation (Sinopec) was created and given control over most of China's refining industry. In 1989, the Ministry of Petroleum was abolished and the China National Petroleum Corporation (CNPC) was set up with control over onshore exploration and development. The rationale for establishing state-owned corporations was to promote more professional management over the industry by separating them from highly politicized state ministries. This was in line with the overall current of downgrading the Communist Party's authority over management decisions throughout the economy. Sinopec and CNPC, however, remained firmly within the purview of state planners.

China reorganized its oil industry in 1998. The restructuring created two vertically integrated giants: CNPC and Sinopec. During early 1998 references were often made to creating CNPC and Sinopec in the image of Korea's *chaebol*. Ostensibly, the goal was to increase efficiency through introduction of limited competition between the two companies. In reality, the objective was to concentrate control over the domestic market in the hands of CNPC and Sinopec. The cornerstone of the reforms was an asset swap between CNPC, which had previously dominated production, and Sinopec, which had dominated refining. The two companies divided China's market geographically. CNPC controlled the north and west regions while Sinopec concentrated in east, central, and south China. Control over the new companies lay in a three-tier structure. At the top, the State Development Planning Commission had responsibility for long-term project development and approval while the State Economic and Trade Commission controlled subordinate bureaus, such as the State Administration of Petroleum and Chemical Industries, which formulated overall petroleum policy and coordinated CNPC and Sinopec.

To fund the consolidation of the domestic petroleum markets, as well as to finance future production and refining investments, the central government announced in 1999 that the state oil companies would swap debt for equity by listing shares in Hong Kong and New York. To attract investors, the government announced major restructuring initiatives for each company to reduce production costs and improve labor productivity. As part of this plan CNPC became a holding company and listed its core exploration, refining, and marketing company, PetroChina, on the Hong Kong and New York stock markets. Along with listing of the CNOOC, this development has critically moved Chinese oil companies toward the market because their financial performance is subject to stockholder scrutiny. An additional development that widened China's national oil companies' exposure to the market was China's accession to the World Trade Organization (WTO). The initial proposals included provisions to open China's petroleum distribution and retail markets to international competition within three to five years. These provisions fulfilled the goal of many international oil companies, which made access to domestic retail networks a key condition for additional investments in China's upstream and downstream oil sectors.

An additional set of reforms designed to streamline the formulation of national energy policies and institutions was introduced in 2005. The centerpiece of this reform was the creation of the State Energy Office under the State Resource and Development Commission. This office reports to the Energy Leading Group, led by China's Premier Wen Jiabao. The creation of this newly centralized energy policy apparatus was impelled by the recognition of the critical impact that energy supply and demand has on overall economic performance, particularly the recognition by powerful political elites that China's aggressive targets for economic growth—doubling GDP by 2020—will require a fundamental restructuring of China's energy use. As such, two important goals of China's energy administration will be to promote demand-side policies and greater efficiency of energy use.

Throughout the administrative evolution of China's energy sector, cost-based energy prices have largely remained the norm. As part of the petroleum industry restructuring plan of 1998, the government announced a change in the domestic crude and product price system. The stated goal was to bring prices in line with prevailing international market prices, but the results were something less. Domestic crude prices were brought in line with international prices, but product prices continued to be set by the state to meet the goals of protecting the domestic refining sector.

China appears to have a preference for importing crude rather than product. The domestic refining sector has been crucial to the state and the domestic economy. Although recent data are not widely available, some 40 percent of all state revenue during the late 1990s from state-owned enterprises came from the refining sector.[8] A relatively recent expression of this determination to support the domestic refining sector occurred in the aftermath of the East Asian Economic crisis in the late 1990s and early 2000s. At that time, the Singapore product markets were awash with a surplus of cheap refined products (e.g., diesel and gasoline). Instead of importing large quantities of cheap product, which might normally be expected given the relative inefficiency of the domestic refining sector in China, Beijing imposed administrative controls (under the rubric of "antismuggling" provisions) to restrict the import of cheap products that would undercut the artificially high domestic product prices set by the state pricing authority.

One consequence of emphasizing crude imports and domestic refining is that the state and national oil companies are more exposed to the international crude markets and to the sea lines of communication (SLOC) that connect those markets. Thus, the state and national oil companies have directed a great deal of effort to secure dependable sources of crude abroad.

A great deal of attention has been given to China's "go out" strategy of securing reliable overseas sources of crude oil. Indeed, China's national oil companies have aggressively increased their investment activities around the globe, particularly in the Middle East, Africa, and Central and Southeast Asia (see table 6). As China projects oil and gas import dependencies to grow, the move abroad to secure stable sources of supply should come as no surprise. What is of greatest concern to many analysts is the nature of these investments. China's presumed preference for equity oil interests (and, one might add, long-term supply contracts) is seen by some as an attempt by China's oil companies (operating under strong state control) to take oil production from the international marketplace.

Table 6. Chinese Petroleum Companies' Investments Abroad

Region	Number of Deals	% of Deals	Key Countries
Eurasia	21	15	Russia, Kazakhstan, Uzbekistan
Middle East	25	18	Saudi Arabia, Oman, Iran
Africa	37	27	Sudan, Angola, Algeria, Nigeria
Northeast Asia	3	2	Mongolia
Southeast Asia	31	22	Indonesia, Australia, Papua New Guinea
Latin America	16	11	Venezuela, Brazil, Ecuador, Peru
North America	6	4	Canada
Total	139	100	

Source: Adapted from Kenneth Lieberthal and Mikkal Herberg, "China's Search for Energy Security: Implications for U.S. Policy," *NBR Analysis* April 2006, 17, no. 1: 15.

Although China does indeed appear to favor gaining stakes in overseas oil fields, the reasons for doing so are not unique to Chinese oil companies. International oil companies also favor acquiring upstream stakes because they can often "book" reserves and improve their financial standing, thus pleasing their investors. Although China's main oil producers have thus far only sold minority stakes to private investors, CNPC plans an additional $6 billion share offering in Shanghai that will likely increase pressure on CNPC to perform for shareholders.[9] Sinopec and CNOOC may elect to follow suit after CNPC's offering. Moreover, no matter what the level of privately held shares, all of the Chinese company managements aim to please the real big boss: the Chinese Communist Party, whose cadres often help determine the fate of oil executives once they leave business.

The percentage of international equity oil returning to China has been increasing and will likely continue to do so as China's dependence on imported energy grows during the next several decades. Although data on equity oil imports to China remain elusive, the most recent figures for 2005 suggests that such equity imports constituted roughly 10–15 percent of China's total oil imports.[10] The other source of concern to many, particularly to international security analysts in the United States, is the tendency of China's state oil companies to engage in deals with what the United States considers to be "rogue states."[11]

All three state oil companies have acquired exploration and production interests abroad. CNPC is reported to have production interests in twenty-one countries on four different continents.[12] Certainly one of CNPC's most visible investments is in Sudan, where it has spent nearly $20 billion. Other recent investments include the purchase of PetroKazakhstan (with eleven oil fields and seven exploration blocks), the purchase of Enchana oil and gas assets in Ecuador, and of Petro Canada oil and gas assets in Syria. Sinopec purchased a controlling stake in Udmurtneft (a Russian unit of British Petroleum) in June 2006. Udmurtneft is reported to have one billion barrels of proven reserves.[13] In addition to reported interest in Canadian oil sands assets, Sinopec has been pursuing oil and liquefied natural gas deals in Iran. In 2004 Sinopec inked an agreement with Iran to acquire a controlling interest in the Yadavaran oil field (with a reported production capacity of 300,000 bpd).[14] CNOOC, too, has been aggressively seeking overseas oil and exploration assets. In addition to acquiring assets in Nigeria, Equatorial Guinea, and Kenya, CNOOC purchased Repsol-YPF's Indonesian oil interests in 2005, making CNOOC the largest player in Indonesian offshore oil.[15]

Perhaps the most visible attempt to acquire international assets occurred in 2005 when CNOOC attempted to acquire Unocal for 18.5 billion U.S. dollars. The attempt failed in part because of a firestorm of criticism the impending deal generated in American political circles, but the aftermath of CNOOC's bid suggests the degree to which China's oil companies are indeed as much market actors as they are actors subject to Chinese state control. In an attempt to provide CNOOC greater maneuverability to quietly pursue deals that might otherwise provoke skepticism from capital markets and other public comment (e.g., government), CNOOC management proposed to its shareholders that the parent company be granted freedom to pursue investments abroad. Significantly, shareholders rejected the proposal, which could have significantly insulated the company's investments from shareholder scrutiny and other external concerns because the parent company is fully state held while the CNOOC Ltd. subsidiary that sought to purchase Unocal is 29.36 percent privately held and 70.64 percent state held.[16] The vote strongly suggested that shareholders were comfortable with CNOOC's current reporting requirements that mandate full disclosure of capital investments.

Given the evolution of China's energy institutional structure and investment practices, particularly the oil and gas segments, one might best term the energy sector as being "mercantilist with Chinese characteristics." Over the past ten years, comments by state officials evince clear sentiments about China's sense of energy insecurity. These comments suggest a certain distrust of global energy markets, particularly as they are seen as dominated by the large international oil companies and the geopolitical influence of the United States. In addition, there is a widespread sense that China's national oil companies operate from a position of weakness because they are relative newcomers to the international markets. Clearly, there is a brand of "resource diplomacy" being practiced by the Chinese state—a sort of diplomacy similarly pursued by many, if not most, states around the world. Conversely, China's national oil companies, while clearly operating with an understanding of state goals (to the degree that one can speak of abiding "state goals"), must also operate within a competitive international market and within the strictures of commercial success because many of their assets are subject to shareholder scrutiny.

The simultaneous realities of pressures from the state and the market are expressed in the range of behaviors exhibited by the three main Chinese national oil and gas companies. CNPC is clearly more attuned to state direction, as evidenced by many of the more controversial international oil and gas investments made under its purview. At the other end of the spectrum is CNOOC, whose behavior in international markets is clearly molded by commercial concerns. In between lies Sinopec. Despite the current obsession with labeling China's energy policy (e.g., "mercantilist with Chinese characteristics"), one might more accurately say that the sector "muddles through." In essence, Chinese energy policies are guided by state goals, but these "policies" are implemented by companies with different priorities, resulting in an energy sector that at times appears centrally controlled and at other times looks chaotic (a suggestion of significant market behavior).

The Impact of Disruption of International Oil Flows and China's Strategic Reserves

The impact of a disruption of oil imports into China would undoubtedly be significant. As indicated earlier, China's dependence on imported oil will approximate 70 percent of demand by 2030. Most of this oil will be sourced from the Middle East and Africa. In addition to the Strait of Hormuz, a critical global "chokepoint" is the Strait of Malacca. According to the International Energy Agency, 11 million bpd flowed through the Strait of Malacca in 2003, representing 14 percent of world oil demand. By 2020, the equivalent of 20 percent of world oil demand will flow through this same "chokepoint."[17] The vast majority of this oil is fueling the economies of China, Taiwan, Korea, and Japan. The relative influence that a disruption of supply would have on China versus other countries in the region is worth noting. As mentioned earlier, the strategic choice that China appears to have made regarding a preference for importing crude versus product will amplify this growing dependence on supply from abroad. However, in a time of crisis in the Middle East, for example, China could tap into the Singapore product markets with relative ease and speed (assuming adequate storage facilities).

In either event, the impact of a maritime conflict involving China on the world oil markets would undoubtedly be significant given the growing dependence of China on those markets. One must, however, offer an important caveat on the relative effect of a crude supply disruption between China and other East Asian economies. Although China's demand for imported oil will indeed grow significantly over the next several decades, one must not forget the continued importance of coal to China's economy. Coal will continue to provide over half of China's energy supply by 2030. Thus, to the degree that one can forecast the potential comparative effects of a disrup tion of oil supply on countries in the region, the fact that China is not as dependent on imported energy as other countries should be noted. The critical question facing defense planners is to what degree the Chinese economy could continue to function in the event of an energy supply disruption such as a bottleneck in the Malacca Strait. This question is obviously difficult to gauge with any precision, but given the degree of oil import dependencies, the answer would likely be measured in months, not years.

One way that China is seeking to minimize reliance on SLOC is by aggressively developing overland pipelines to deliver oil and gas from Central Asia and the Russian Far East. A 200,000 bpd pipeline between Kazakhstan and China's northwest was christened in early 2006. Plans call for a doubling of capacity by 2010. Crude oil from both Kazakhstan and Russia is presently being transported. Chinese energy officials are also engaged in aggressive negotiations with Russian officials to access a 2,500-mile pipeline that is currently under construction. Although Russia has not clearly indicated where the final terminus of the pipeline may be, it continues to suggest that both China and Japan may ultimately have access to pipeline oil. There have also been reports that China has been in negotiations with the government of Burma to construct a pipeline connecting the two countries. Because Burma does not produce significant quantities of crude, the presumed intent of the pipeline from Chinese side is to source crude from Africa and the Middle East that would not traverse the Strait of Malacca.[18]

Since the beginning of the second war in Iraq, China has accelerated its plans to construct a strategic oil reserve. China's 10th Five-Year Plan (2000–2005) called for the creation of a reserve. The first facility to be completed was at Zhenhai with a capacity of 33 million barrels (see table 7). Three more facilities slated to be completed in the next five years will hold a total of roughly 100 million barrels, roughly equivalent to twenty days of imports. The ultimate size of China's strategic reserves has not been established. The final SPR size may not yet be fully determined, but current reports indicate that the reserve will initially provide thirty days of import coverage with the ultimate goal of storing ninety days of imports by 2015.[19]

Table 7. First Phase of China's Strategic Petroleum Reserve

Location	Completion Date	Capacity (barrels)
Zhenhai (Zhejiang Province)	October 2006	33.0 million
Aoshan (Zhejiang Province)	End 2008	31.5 million
Huangdao (Qingdao Province)	?	19.0 million
Dalian (Liaoning Province)	?	19.0 million

The eventual decision to develop a strategic petroleum reserve followed years of disagreement among political elites about the benefits of a reserve. Generally speaking, the central issues of debate centered on cost and effectiveness. Many felt that the cost of building an SPR was prohibitive given the necessity of creating a social welfare system in China that could ameliorate the consequences of the privatization of the state-owned sector. Second, those opposing an SPR argued that such reserves have simply lost their effectiveness and are a relic of past oil market realities. They maintained that oil markets in the new millennium were different from the market of the 1970s and 1980s. The new market was one in which all major consuming countries could cooperate to alleviate a global crisis and could withstand a period of high energy prices during a supply disruption. Although the objections by important bureaucratic actors shaped the discussion of a Chinese SPR, the general sensitivity to resource disruption coupled with the increasing degree of oil dependency predicted for China convinced the government to pursue an SPR.

The critical issues surrounding China's strategic reserves now center on how the government will manage the reserves.[20] Because China is not a member of the Organization for Economic Cooperation and Development (OECD), there may be little incentive to manage the reserves in cooperation with the International Energy Agency (IEA). Representatives from OECD countries also worry that China will use the reserves as a mechanism to mitigate price increases in the domestic market. Such use of a reserve for market purposes is contrary to the purpose of strategic reserves as articulated by the IEA. In China there is a general concern with the political implications of committing to international cooperative agreements regarding SPR facilities and SPR drawdown policies. Historically, China has had a predilection for bilateral relations. China has favored these types of arrangements because it feels it has greater room for maneuverability and greater opportunities to secure its interests. Any potential for China to participate in multilateral cooperative agreements regarding SPR management and drawdown policies will be mitigated by the general desire to maintain freedom of diplomatic initiative, particularly in the Middle East—a region in which China may feel that diplomatic initiative would be unduly constrained by active incorporation into the agenda and policies of IEA member countries.

Enduring Issues in China's Energy Sector

Following an examination of China's past and future energy supply demand dynamics and the institutional and policy drivers of the energy sector, this chapter concludes by examining several critical issues that may continue to shape China's energy situation.

The first issue is the problematic relationship between energy and economic growth. As figure 7 suggests, over the past twenty-five years China's GDP and energy consumption growth rates have experienced rather dramatic fluctuations. These fluctuations may be endemic to a rapidly developing economy. In any event, the critical point is that throughout this period, in the absence of an effective monetary system to regulate the economy, China's government has resorted to manipulating energy supply to regulate its economy. Two examples illustrate this point. The government faced serious inflation in 1994 and a deflationary spiral during 1998–99. In both instances, government planners aggressively imposed regulatory measures on the petroleum sector as a means of addressing macroeconomic ills (either inflation or deflation). The net result was to constrain petroleum consumption.

Figure 7. China's GDP and Energy Demand Growth

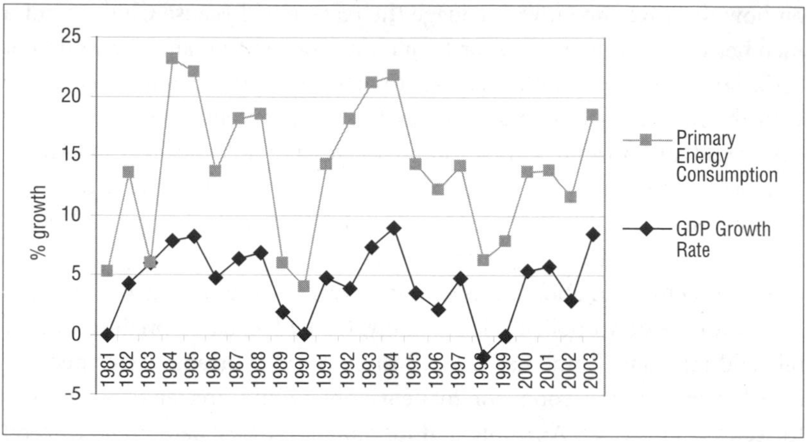

Source: *China Statistical Yearbook 2005*, Chapters 3 and 7, http://www.stats.gov.cn/tjsj/ndsj/2005/indexeh.htm.

Before 1994 the two most critical elements of the oil industry were set for liberalization: import licenses and price controls. The decision to pursue liberalization was prompted by the return of strong economic growth following the downturn that occurred beginning in 1989. Robust economic growth challenged the ability of the state to supply the energy needed to sustain this growth. Thus, deregulation was deemed necessary to meet the demands of a growing economy. The problem, however, was that growth had reached dangerous proportions. Intent on reducing inflationary pressures, thereby short-circuiting potential urban social unrest, the government quickly abandoned further petroleum market liberalization and reasserted regulatory control over the industry. Petroleum imports were restricted and price controls reinstated. The goal was to slow economic growth by rationing energy inputs.

In the face of mounting pressures generated by the East Asian financial crisis in 1997–98, China repeatedly promised that economic growth would meet the official goal of 8 percent. At the end of 1998, official growth was 7.7 percent, close to 8 percent, but clearly feeling the effects of deflationary pressures then endemic in the region. The government attempted to reinflate the economy with a series of measures designed to spur domestic demand and protect domestic industries from cheap imports, particularly imports from countries that had devalued their currencies. The government also implemented policies designed to protect domestic industries from international competition. A diesel import ban was instituted in August 1998 to protect domestic refiners from cheap international products. Although one could argue that cheap energy inputs can benefit a flagging economy, Chinese petroleum policy was guided by other considerations. It chose to retain high price supports for domestically produced products while banning imports. In other words, it rationed supply.

The point of these cautionary tales is to suggest that Beijing may well again regulate supply–demand dynamics for macroeconomic needs. This advance–retreat pattern instructs us to view short-term fluctuations in China's energy data with an understanding of the underlying causations.

The second enduring issue of China's energy sector is its relationship to the continued legitimacy of the Chinese Communist Party. The fundamental legitimacy of the Party lies in its ability to manage two issues: (a) protecting territorial integrity (the Taiwan question), and (b) sustaining economic growth. The imperative of maintaining economic growth will further the interests of the state in maintaining an activist energy policy and maintaining as much influence as it can with the national oil companies. This concern is also informed by the legacy of concern from the 1960s and 1970s over self-sufficiency in energy (and food, one might add). This concern was driven by the imperative of sustaining China in a world that was deemed hostile to it. Continued insecurity about its global position, fueled by a strong sense of historical aggrievement, may well further impel the state to maintain a firm presence in the energy sector. Therefore, despite the undeniable transformative effects that exposure to international markets has had on China's energy sector, it would be premature to conclude that statist influence will be completely removed any time soon.

Notes

1. See Agnus Maddison database, OECD Development Centre.

2. *World Energy Outlook 2006* (Paris: International Energy Agency, 2006), 86.

3. Energy Information Administration, Country Analysis Briefs, http://www.eia.doe.gov/emeu/cabs/China/Full.html.

4. Ibid.

5. Ibid.

6. David Pietz, *Fueling China: Oil and Gas Demand to 2010* (multiclient study for Energy Security Analysis, Inc., 2000).

7. Wenran Jiang, "China's Quest for Energy Security," *China Brief* 4 (14 October 2004): 20.

8. Ibid., 21.

9. "PetroChina Plans US $6B A-share Offer," *China Daily*, 21 June 2007, available at http://www.china.org.cn/english/BAT/214592.htm.

10. The Energy Information Agency states 8.5 percent, while Erica Downs of the Brookings Institution states 15 percent. See http://www.eia.doe.gov/emeu/cabs/China/Full.html; and Erica Downs, *The Brookings Foreign Policy Studies Energy Security Series: China* (Washington, D.C.: Brookings Institution, 2006), www3.brookings.edu/fp/research/energy/2006china.pdf, 43.

11. For a superb analysis of these issues see, Erica S. Downs, "The Chinese Energy Security Debate," *The China Quarterly* (March 2004): 21–41.

12. http://www.eia.doe.gov/emeu/cabs/China/Full.html.

13. Ibid.

14. Ibid.

15. Ibid.

16. For more context, see Kenneth Lieberthal and Mikkal Herberg, "China's Search for Energy Security: Implications for U.S. Policy," *NBR Analysis* 17, no. 1 (2006): 23.

17. *World Energy Outlook 2004* (Paris: International Energy Agency, 2004).

18. http://www.eia.doe.gov/emeu/cabs/China/Full.html.

19. "China's SPR: Massive Buildup, Policy Imperatives," University of Alberta China Institute, Reuters, 2 April 2007, http://www.uofaweb.ualberta.ca/chinainstitute/nav03.cfm?nav03=58765&nav02=57484&nav01=57272.

20. For further information on China's SPR, see Gabriel Collins, "China Fills First SPR Site, Faces Oil, Pipeline Issues," *Oil & Gas Journal* 20 (August 2007): 20–29.

Mikkal Herberg

The Geopolitics of China's LNG Development

Introduction

THE NATIONAL SEARCH FOR ENERGY SECURITY has become a key strategic issue for the major powers of Northeast Asia as energy demand mushrooms while domestic energy supplies remain limited and increasingly under strain. Strategic concerns for securing and safeguarding future energy supplies, retaining reliable energy transportation, and ensuring reasonable energy costs are spread across the entire fuel spectrum, from oil to natural gas to coal to electricity supplies. However, national concerns for different energy sources vary significantly because of the vastly different international market and trade structures along with different geopolitical dynamics affecting the supply and transportation of each fuel. Consequently, the geopolitics of the natural gas and liquefied natural gas (LNG) markets is quite different from the geopolitics of global oil markets.

China's booming energy demand and growing reliance on imported supplies has thrust energy security to the center of the strategic concerns of government leaders. Most of this anxiety has focused on oil now that China imports more than 40 percent of its total oil consumption and is likely to be importing two-thirds of its oil needs within ten years. In response, the Chinese leadership and China's national oil companies (NOCs) have embarked on an aggressive and wide-ranging global search to secure access to future oil supplies. However, natural gas use in China is very low; imports have begun only very recently and, therefore, strategic concerns for future natural gas supplies are far more muted. Nevertheless, China is likely to become a major importer of natural gas in the form of LNG and via long-distance pipelines. Therefore, the salience of secure gas supplies and transportation will inevitably rise rapidly on the leadership's security agenda.

This chapter analyzes the geopolitics of China's growing natural gas and LNG consumption and how this consumption is likely to factor into China's broader energy security and strategic agenda. The analysis suggests that gas and LNG supply security will become an increasingly important issue for the leadership and a factor in Chinese foreign and strategic policy for many of the same reasons that oil is a strategic concern. Nevertheless, because of the peculiarities of China's future energy consumption patterns and the different character of long-term global oil and natural gas markets and supply conditions, the salience of the issue is likely to remain far less intense than is the case with oil and will arise much later as a major factor in Chinese strategic behavior.

The chapter is organized in four parts. The first section reviews the growing role of natural gas in China's energy future and outlines Beijing's early plans to expand LNG and pipeline gas imports and infrastructure. The second section briefly analyzes the industry and international trade dynamics of gas and LNG that differentiate it from oil and that drive a different pattern of geopolitics and a different energy security calculus compared to oil. The third section examines Beijing's current LNG strategy, the somewhat erratic recent evolution of LNG policy, and conflicting and cross-cutting market and political influences on Beijing's LNG plans. The fourth section analyzes a range of geopolitical and regional implications of China's LNG development and provides a range of conclusions on the salience of LNG security concerns, the relationship to oil security concerns, and the way that LNG is likely to influence Beijing's strategic and energy diplomacy behavior.

Natural Gas and LNG Development

The relatively low salience of current government concerns over natural gas and LNG supply security reflects first and foremost the fact that natural gas use in China is very low. Natural gas presently accounts for roughly 2 percent of overall energy consumption compared with coal, which accounts for two-thirds of total energy use. By comparison, gas accounts for an average of 23 percent of total energy consumption globally. Virtually all of China's modest gas needs are met with domestic production, notwithstanding a tiny fraction now met by imports with the first LNG arrivals in mid-2006.

However, China's government has embarked on a series of policies to rapidly increase gas use to help reduce the growing use of coal for electricity generation, to diversify overall energy use, and to provide cleaner-burning fuel for environmental reasons. Current plans call for double-digit annual rates of growth in gas use and for gas to make up 8 percent of energy demand by 2020.[1]

In order to boost gas use, Beijing is accelerating domestic gas exploration and development and expanding the national gas pipeline system to transport more gas from fields in north, central, and western China to the major cities along the east coast. Traditionally, most of eastern China's modest gas use has been for fertilizer production and a rapidly growing petrochemical industry with gas supplies coming mainly from the petroleum heartland of large, old oil and gas fields in northeastern China. But in the wake of recent new gas development in western China, a major west-east 2,500-mile pipeline has been built to move gas from the sparsely populated Xinjiang Uyghur Autonomous Region to Shanghai. Sichuan province traditionally has been a sizable gas-producing region as well, but only recently has the government moved to accelerate gas development in Sichuan and build regional pipelines to link up to east China's dynamic cities. Major new discoveries have also been logged in north central China's Ordos Basin, which is being linked with new regional pipelines into the west-east trunkline to move to eastern coastal China. Finally, gas exploration is encouraged in China's offshore waters (the South China Sea, the Pearl River Basin, the East China Sea, and the Bohai Basin) where gas discoveries historically have outweighed oil discoveries. This also has the advantage of being near the fast-growing coastal cities to meet their gas demands. Aware that regulatory and pricing policies affect demand, the government is also working to develop gas demand and markets by creating more effective regulatory structures, increasing flexibility in gas pricing and transport, and promoting more gas use in electricity generation.

According to current plans, gas demand is likely to begin significantly outrunning domestic production beyond 2010, and a growing share of gas needs will have to be met with imports, both as LNG and by long-distance pipeline. The U.S. Department of Energy and the Lawrence Berkeley National Laboratory forecast that imports will account for 40 percent of

China's total gas needs by 2020.[2] Most of the demand will be along the east coast where economic and industrial growth is so dynamic.

Unlike the case of oil, in which future imported supplies will come largely from outside Asia, significant LNG and pipeline gas imports will be available from within the Asia-Pacific. Southeast Asia is home to a number of major LNG producers including Australia, Indonesia, Malaysia, and, in the future, East Timor. Pipeline gas supplies will also be available from Southeast Asia. China is currently studying the feasibility of building a major gas pipeline through Burma to move offshore Burma gas north to southern China. In Northeast Asia, both pipeline gas and LNG will be available. Russia's 9.6 million metric tons per year (mmt/y) Sakhalin 2 project, led by Shell and now majority owned by Gazprom, is already contracting for sales of LNG to begin very soon to Japan and South Korea. Pipeline gas imports to China are also being proposed from Russia's Sakhalin 1 project run by ExxonMobil and Rosneft, with Gazprom a likely new partner. Russia's president, Vladimir Putin, has promised in recent state visits to Beijing to build two large pipelines: one to bring gas from West and East Siberia to China and one to link up with the west-east trunkline to move gas to China's east coast. Unfortunately, the Kremlin has been very slow to follow through on these promises.[3] For example, a plan to build a major gas pipeline from East Siberia's Irkutsk region to northeastern China and on to Korea has been delayed for several years by Kremlin politics and following the reorganization and recentralization of Russia's oil and gas industry. In Central Asia, China is also discussing future potential long-distance pipeline gas supplies from Turkmenistan and Kazakhstan, both of which are likely to have significant supplies available in the longer term.

While significant amounts of gas will be available from the Asia-Pacific region and Eurasian sources, LNG supplies are also likely to be needed from major Persian Gulf LNG suppliers. In 2004–5 Qatar was one of the final three competitors to supply China's first LNG regasification project in Guangdong, a contract that ultimately went to the Northwest Shelf consortium in Australia. China's Sinopec has signed a preliminary memorandum of understanding (MOU) for a major LNG project with Iran from the massive offshore South Pars gas field that would provide long-term LNG supplies to China. Most recently, China National Offshore Oil Corporation (CNOOC) has signed an MOU for another potentially large LNG project tapping the North Pars gas field.[4] Oman and Yemen are other significant potential Middle East LNG suppliers to China over the long-term.

Given plans for rapidly expanding gas use in China, combined with the growing supply of LNG being developed in Asia and globally, China is expected to be a major force in Asian and global natural gas and LNG markets in the future. As table 1 suggests, recent forecasts indicate China is likely to be importing 40 percent of its gas supplies by 2020.

Table 1. China Natural Gas Production and Imports (billion cubic meters)

Year	Domestic Production	Imports
2004	42	0
2020	120	90

China is likely to be the second largest incremental buyer of LNG in Asia over the next ten to fifteen years, behind South Korea. China's original development plans included 50 mmt/y of LNG capacity annually by 2020 with the balance of gas imports coming by pipeline, which will account for roughly 25 percent of China's total gas consumption and 60 percent of gas imports. But with a recent slowing of LNG developments, the U.S. Department of Energy now forecasts that China's LNG imports will rise from 1 mmt/y in 2006, when imports were inaugurated, to a range of 21–26 mmt/y by 2015.[5] If all the new LNG import terminals currently being proposed are built, capacity could rise to well over 50 mmt/y as early as 2015.[6] So LNG is likely to loom relatively large in China's energy future although there is a substantial range of uncertainty over volumes. A key question is whether Chinese consumers will be able to afford imported gas whose price currently exceeds coal and internal Chinese gas prices. Over the past year Sinopec and other firms have slowed their gas import plans due to sustained high international LNG prices.

The Geostrategic Calculus of LNG Versus Oil

Analysis of China's future LNG plans and geopolitics must be informed by a clear understanding of the market and industry characteristics of the use of gas and LNG as compared to the use of oil. There is an inevitable temptation to assume that the energy security characteristics of natural gas and LNG import dependence largely mirror the very acute security concerns over oil and to draw similar conclusions about the impact of LNG concerns on China's future strategic behavior. However, the differences between the two sectors are considerable, and it is misleading to assume that the two pose precisely comparable energy security concerns.

First, China's oil import dependence dwarfs current gas import dependence and will continue to do so for the long-term. China is already more than 40 percent dependent on imports for its total oil needs and is headed for 75–80 percent oil import dependence by 2020. By contrast, gas imports began in early 2006 and dependence will only begin to be measurable after 2010. Assuming relatively robust gas demand growth, import dependence may rise to 30–40 percent by 2020 and could be lower. Hence, although gas dependence has already been raised in policy discussions in Beijing as an energy security concern, it will likely become a significant energy security concern for the leadership primarily after 2010, and it will remain a secondary concern in comparison to oil security.

Other characteristics of gas use also tend to dampen the salience of energy security drivers. Most importantly, gas has several substitutes as a fuel source for many of its main uses, particularly for electricity, which can be generated using coal, hydropower, nuclear power, and even oil. This is particularly the case in China, where coal is plentiful and cheap as a power generation fuel. Oil's main use is for transportation and industry, for which there are no reasonably economic substitutes. Moreover, until recently LNG supplies were ample and prices were low; this has changed significantly in the past several years, driven by rising oil prices. Also, in terms of global market structure, there is no natural gas cartel to inject arbitrary political supply constraints into the marketplace. Although lately there has been some discussion of such a gas cartel, its formation is fairly unlikely due to the supply structure globally in which regional markets dominate rather than a global market.

Nevertheless, there are characteristics of the gas industry and the global LNG business and markets that do introduce important strategic dimensions to LNG markets and investments. In a sense, the LNG business is much more "vertical" than that of oil (i.e., all the links in the LNG business value chain are tightly linked in large, integrated projects and require strong government support). LNG involves very high transportation costs relative to the value of the gas resource, unlike oil, which increases the risks in large LNG capital investments and creates strong incentives for state involvement and state-to-state deals. Investments in LNG projects are enormous, even by the standards of the very capital-intensive global energy industry, and require complex synchronization of investments, huge multinational financing requirements, multilateral lending agencies, and generally very long-term contracts of up to twenty-five years. LNG also involves very tight links through the value chain from the production phase through tanker transportation to regasification plants to the final gas consumer. This requires strategic government participation on both the producer and consumer-government sides. Most contracts include onerous "take-or-pay" clauses whereby LNG buyers are required to commit to tight limits on how much they can vary their off-take of gas, whether they need the gas or not. Reduced purchases in one period are required to be made up with larger purchases in later periods. Also, the development of the end-user gas markets as well as the upstream project host governments' involvement makes the LNG business very "policy dependent" (i.e., heavily contingent on reliable, consistent, and transparent government policies to build gas demand among end-user markets). All these characteristics together inject strongly political and government dimensions into the LNG industry that make China's growing long-term reliance on LNG more than just a matter of markets.

China's LNG Strategy: Key Policy Considerations

Although Beijing, broadly speaking, is trying to accelerate gas use and LNG development, a number of key energy and security policy considerations have influenced the pace at which China is moving toward growing use of LNG. First, while significant LNG import dependence is a long way off, Beijing's acute energy security concerns over oil import dependence have in part spilled over into a vague but palpable concern over too rapidly developing a too-heavy dependence on imported natural gas and LNG. A similar debate has developed in the United States, where rising LNG imports could eventually make the United States as dependent on gas imports as it already is on oil imports (current U.S. oil import dependence is about 60 percent). Consequently, Beijing continues to promote increased domestic gas production in north-central and western China, Sichuan province, and offshore. In other words, Beijing's basic instincts for energy self-sufficiency militate toward relying mainly on domestic gas supplies, supplemented by imports as needed to fill the gap. Therefore, future gas import dependence will hinge on the pace of domestic gas demand growth, which is highly contingent on effective government energy policies and the pace of success in finding new domestic gas reserves.[7] In turn, the eventual scale of LNG imports will depend on how successful China is in promoting gas demand and how comfortable Beijing becomes with growing gas import dependence.

LNG consumption will also depend on Beijing's strategic trade-off among gas import sources between LNG and pipelines, as well as the very sensible impulse to diversify risk as much as possible among countries supplying imported gas. Furthermore, much will depend on the future price of LNG and pipeline gas in Asia and how competitive imported gas prices are with domestic gas development and delivery costs. Beijing has already shown a strong sensitivity to the recent sharp rise in world LNG prices that has tempered earlier enthusiasm for LNG. LNG import prices will also be weighed against the prices demanded in negotiations on potential pipeline gas imports from Russia (Sakhalin 1, West Siberia, and East Siberia/ Irkutsk), Burma, and Central Asia. Finally, LNG growth is fundamentally driven by demand and consumers' ability to pay. This, in turn, is dependent on NDRC regulatory and pricing decisions. Therefore, LNG growth will be strongly affected by the growing competition among the three major NOCs to develop new LNG import terminals and by expanding domestic gas business opportunities. China's three NOCs see LNG import projects and investment in upstream LNG projects abroad as major new and profitable business opportunities. This has led to an avalanche of new import project proposals. CNOOC has had the early monopoly on LNG development and imports and has controlled China's import facilities currently under development. It now has equity investments in two Asian LNG consortiums in Indonesia and Australia. But the other two major companies, with China National Petroleum Corporation (CNPC) the largest company and dominant upstream player and Sinopec the dominant downstream refining company, have been given government approval to promote development of their own LNG regasification projects along the eastern coast.

These various cross-cutting factors mean that LNG strategy and the eventual scale of LNG imports and energy security calculations in Beijing inevitably reflect a complex blend of energy security, market, and competitive influences. This helps explain what has been and is likely to remain a somewhat muddled LNG strategy that has run the gamut from early enthusiasm to a significant pullback in interest, followed most recently by a cautious return to LNG markets.

The phase of early enthusiasm for LNG exhibited up until 2004 led to the recent completion of China's first LNG regasification plant near Shenzhen in Guangdong province, which is likely to ultimately have a capacity of 6 mmt/y and which received its first shipment in mid-2006. A second import facility under construction in Fujian is scheduled for completion in 2008 and will likely have a 3 mmt/y capacity. Both projects were developed by CNOOC. The bidding by major LNG exporters to supply the first two plants was intense. The government and CNOOC ultimately chose

Australia's Northwest Shelf for the Guangdong plant and Indonesia's Tang-guh project for the Fujian plant. The Guangdong project was reported to have achieved the lowest LNG prices in recent market history at fewer than three dollars per thousand cubic feet.

A key element of CNOOC's LNG strategy has been to demand an equity stake in the upstream LNG production project as part of the price for sup-pliers' opportunity to access China's potentially enormous future LNG and gas market. In effect, CNOOC insists on integrating back upstream into the production process to gain expertise and influence in future LNG mar-kets. The upstream end of LNG projects also tends to be the most profitable part of the LNG chain. The equity stake requirement also mirrors to some extent the emphasis on equity stakes and physical control that has charac-terized China's energy security strategy toward oil supplies. CNOOC gained a significant equity stake in Northwest Shelf's upstream consortium led by Woodside and Shell and also a stake in Indonesia's Tangguh consortium led by BP. Ground has just been broken for a new plant in Shanghai, also spon-sored by CNOOC, to be completed in 2009. This early period of enthusiasm and the competitive instincts of the NOCs generated eight to ten other pro-posals for future LNG re-gasification plants along China's coast over the next ten years, many sponsored by CNPC and Sinopec.

Beginning in 2005, China's enthusiasm for LNG began to wane sharply due to the enormous rise in LNG prices on the back of rising world oil prices and combined with frustrating and ultimately failed negotiations with Aus-tralia's Gorgon LNG consortium. At one point the government stated that it would wait until LNG prices came back down before it would move forward on contracting large new supplies.[8] At the same time, Beijing was stung by widespread international criticism for supposedly driving up world oil prices with its enormous oil import buying binge in 2004. While China's govern-ment has continually tried to deflect that criticism, which in many ways was quite unfair, it became concerned that it might also be blamed for high LNG prices if it continued pressing for new supplies in an increasingly tight world LNG market. Finally, Russia began to promote much more aggres-sively its proposals to build large gas pipelines from Siberia to China, which would provide an alternative and potentially lower-cost gas import option. In response, the government began to slow approvals for new LNG import deals and projects. Presently only two future plants have been approved. They will be located at Ningbo and Qingdao, where relatively affluent indus-trial and residential consumers can afford higher gas prices than can many of their counterparts elsewhere in China.

Nevertheless, in the past year China has begun to consider new LNG deals again, albeit at a somewhat measured pace, as Beijing increasingly accepts that high LNG prices may not be falling any time soon, as Russia seems continually unwilling to move forward on repeated promises to build new gas pipelines to China, and as price negotiations with the Russians stall.[9] In a new major LNG supply deal signed recently, Malaysia will supply the CNOOC Shanghai terminal just beginning construction. As mentioned earlier, in October 2004 Sinopec signed an MOU for a major LNG project with Iran in which Sinopec would have a significant equity stake. CNOOC also signed an MOU in late 2006 for an equity stake in developing the giant North Pars gas structure for an LNG project. And CNPC has signed an MOU for a strategic cooperation with Norway's Statoil, which may include participation in Statoil's planned Phase 6–8 development of LNG in the South Pars field.[10] CNOOC also signed an October 2006 "spot" LNG deal with Shell and Malaysia which signifies Beijing's and CNOOC's new, more sophisticated approach to LNG markets.[11] There is also new movement on the pipeline gas import side. Although Russia has been extraordinarily slow on developing gas pipelines from Siberia, it seems more likely to move forward on Exxon-Mobil's tentative deal with China's CNPC to build a pipeline to send gas to China from the Sakhalin 1 project along the Russian Pacific coast to northeastern China. And a potential gas pipeline from Burma has now moved to the feasibility study phase.

Geopolitical and Regional Implications

The global and regional geopolitics of LNG and natural gas are somewhat different from the geopolitics of oil, but the search for energy security in each case raises a similar set of energy security dilemmas and implications for China and for the United States. First, some significant differences need to be kept in mind. As discussed earlier, the scale of LNG import dependence will almost certainly be much lower, and the availability of domestic gas and substitute fuels will be much greater. Therefore, Beijing's energy security responses are likely to be less assertive when compared to the government's major strategic concern and response over securing future oil supplies. Moreover, Beijing's strategic response to LNG import dependence will occur primarily after 2010, whereas oil import dependence is a compelling and immediate concern. Hence, while there is an underlying strategic discomfort in Beijing over an already excessive reliance on imported LNG that is likely to gradually increase over the next decade, most of the slow pace in moving forward has been a function of market and commercial problems, such as high prices and tight global LNG markets or slow domestic market gas demand development, rather than strategic concerns. The strategic situation for future pipeline gas imports is much the same. China has been seeking new pipeline supplies but has been slowed by the high delivered costs of most pipeline options and by Russia's slow and halting response to China's proposals.

Nevertheless, rising LNG imports will tend to reinforce many of the same geopolitical trends driven by China's global reach for oil supply security and will aggravate the leadership's general angst over secure future energy supplies to fuel China's growing economy. For the United States, this suggests that LNG is likely to reinforce many of the areas of tension between China and the United States over global energy markets and energy diplomacy.

It is worthwhile to discuss the relevant global market issues and geopolitical issues separately. In terms of market issues, China's growing scale of LNG use and growing impact on LNG prices and tight global LNG supplies seems likely to fuel and reinforce the growing sense of geoeconomic competition for energy resources and oil supplies among the United States, China, Japan, India, South Korea, and Europe. Tensions over U.S.–China energy competition seem likely to be impacted particularly strongly since it seems that the other major new entrant to the world LNG market will be the United States, whose future LNG demand could be large enough to literally alter the shape of global LNG demand and prices. These tensions will be aggravated by what appears likely to be very tight world LNG supplies and continuing very high LNG prices for the foreseeable future, mirroring the tense, supply-constrained atmosphere in today's global oil markets.

The propensity for growing competition for supplies of natural gas globally and regionally is also likely to feed energy market rivalries for natural gas pipeline supplies, particularly regarding the future direction of Russia's enormous potential natural gas exports. In particular, an increasingly competitive atmosphere is developing over who will receive the lion's share of Russia's pipeline gas exports, with China and the rest of Asia on one side and Europe on the other. Europe already depends heavily on Russian gas supplies, accounting for roughly one-quarter of Europe's gas supplies, and this dependence is destined to grow in the future. At the same time, Russia is negotiating with China and other Northeast Asian consumers for large potential future gas exports to Asia. For Russia and Gazprom to fulfill the full long-term, post-2010 gas export volumes being contracted with Europe and volumes simultaneously being touted to Asia and China, Gazprom will need to make massive new investments in developing new fields in West Siberia to offset declining long-term production from its older fields. At the same time, Russia has heavy long-term commitments to meet growing gas consumption domestically. There is widespread concern, particularly voiced by the International Energy Agency (IEA), that Gazprom and Russia are not investing currently in sufficient new gas supplies to meet their export promises to both Europe and Asia, as well as meeting domestic demand.[12]

Russia's emerging strategy has been to rely increasingly on Central Asia, particularly Turkmenistan and Kazakhstan, to provide gas to meet domestic and some export gas needs. This will help to free up more West Siberian gas to meet Europe's future needs. Russia has deftly used its geographic position between Central Asia and Europe, the lack of alternative gas pipelines to the West, and its long-term political leverage as the dominant power in the region to squeeze Turkmenistan, Kazakhstan, and Uzbekistan into committing to new gas pipeline deals to move their future gas exports north and west to Russia.[13] This presents Asia and China with two problems for obtaining gas from Eurasia. First, even with augmented Central Asia gas supplies, it is not clear that Russia is investing sufficiently in West and East Siberian gas development to also meet Asia's needs. Moreover, although China and Japan have been negotiating with Turkmenistan and Kazakhstan on possible new gas pipelines to move their future gas east to China and the rest of Asia, Russia's deals to take a large share of Eurasia's gas toward Europe and Russia means that there may be insufficient gas available to justify building very long and expensive gas pipelines from Central Asia to Asia.[14] Combined with Russia's crude use of natural gas as a diplomatic and economic lever to boost its political and economic influence in both Europe and Asia, this is setting off a growing sense of zero-sum competition for future gas supplies between Asia, especially China and Europe.

A second set of market issues relates to the global governance of energy markets and the rising future importance of natural gas as a global fuel. China's rising LNG market impact will reinforce the growing role that China will play in global oil markets as its oil demand mushrooms over the next two decades. Global gas consumption and interregional trade are expected to rise very strongly in the future. Gas and LNG are becoming key issues in such areas as global energy market management, including serious energy security concerns over future supply availability, the reliability of long-distance LNG maritime transportation, and the sanctity of cross-border pipeline gas contracts. With China's growing scale of LNG and pipeline gas imports from long distances, it becomes even more important that China have a seat at the table in global institutions that will address global oil and gas supply security concerns. This reinforces the need to find ways to bring China into cooperative arrangements on emergency oil supplies and market management with the IEA and with key international groups, such as the Group of Eight, that address global energy security issues at the highest level.

In geopolitical terms, China's growing dependence on LNG is likely to impact some important U.S. strategic interests. As suggested earlier, China's anxiety about supply security for LNG will not be of the same order as the immediate concerns over oil supplies. However, at the margin, LNG will reinforce several Chinese concerns over energy security as well as reinforce several developments of strategic concern for the United States. First, growing LNG consumption and imports will reinforce China's focus on the sea lines of communication (SLOC) through which a significant portion of China's LNG will flow. Chinese analysts have already identified the control of the SLOC in Southeast Asia as a key oil import concern, particularly as the large majority of future oil imports will come from west of the Strait of Malacca (i.e., the Persian Gulf and Africa through the Indian Ocean, the Strait of Malacca, and the South and East China Seas).

The case of LNG is slightly different because a large portion of China's LNG needs are likely to be met by seaborne supplies from Southeast Asia, including Australia, Indonesia, and Malaysia, with likely smaller volumes flowing from the Gulf and Africa. Hence, as compared with oil, LNG will exert less influence in China's concerns over the Strait of Malacca as an energy transit route but will still feed Chinese concerns over control of the Southeast Asian sea lanes and control of the South and East China Seas. Thus, in the post-2010 period, LNG imports are likely to contribute to China's incentives to project naval power in Southeast Asia and, to a lesser extent, the Strait of Malacca and the Indian Ocean. This is consistent with the recent efforts of the People's Liberation Army Navy to boost its naval capabilities in the South and East China Seas and port access in the Indian Ocean. To the extent that this is the case, LNG dependence will add fuel to the naval rivalry with India, Japan, Indonesia, and most importantly, the United States as China builds its blue water naval power projection capacity.

This raises the further question of whether LNG supplies could be a serious strategic vulnerability in the case of regional conflict with the United States. Broadly speaking, LNG seems likely to remain a far more marginal source of strategic concern for China in the extreme case of a potential future conflict with the United States and the risk of a U.S. naval embargo on LNG supplies. Based on current forecasts (admittedly subject to a large degree of uncertainty) by 2020 China could be importing roughly 40 percent of its gas needs, with roughly one-half of imports coming from seaborne LNG and one-half via overland pipeline.[15] Of the overland pipeline supplies, the largest share is likely to be from Russia's East Siberia, some possibly from Central Asia, and a relatively small share from the south via Burma. Of the seaborne LNG, more than half is likely to be from Australia, Indonesia, and Malaysia and possibly a small amount from Russia's Sakhalin LNG with the balance from east of the Strait of Malacca from the Persian Gulf (Iran, Qatar, Oman, Yemen) and West Africa.

Consequently, an embargo on seaborne LNG would affect perhaps 20 percent of China's total gas consumption. While this would be problematic for China's economy, a modest reduction in electricity supplies, petrochemical production, and residential and commercial gas supplies would not seem to create severe short-term economic or war-waging challenges. Gas is likely to account for a very small share of electricity supply given the continued dominance of coal and hydroelectric in power generation. The IEA projects that gas will account for only 5 percent of electricity generation in 2020 compared with 75 percent from coal.[16] Overland pipeline gas supplies from Russia and Central Asia could possibly be boosted for a period of time. But given the substitutability of gas by other fuels (coal, hydro, nuclear, and renewables) and its relatively much smaller role in China's total energy needs (at most 8–10 percent), gas shortages would appear reasonably manageable.[17] Commercial and potentially strategic stocks of stored gas supplies could also help mitigate and delay any severe impact. One important caveat to this analysis would be whether overland pipeline gas supplies were also interdicted by destroying gas pipeline infrastructure bringing gas from Russia, Central Asia, and Burma. The impact of gas shortages in this case would be much more significant. The potential damage from an oil supply cutoff would likely exceed that of a gas supply cutoff. This is because oil's primary use in any modern economy is as a transport fuel (for which there are no readily available substitutes), whereas gas is primarily used as a chemical feedstock or for electrical power generation (for which there are available substitutes). It is also worth recalling that by 2020, China is expected to be importing up to 60 percent of its oil needs, mostly by seaborne tanker from west of the Strait of Malacca, with oil overall meeting approximately 25–30 percent of China's total energy needs.

Expanding LNG supply and investment relationships with Southeast Asia will also reinforce growing economic, trade, and diplomatic ties between China and Southeast Asia, and Beijing's influence in the region will grow. In fact, LNG and gas are likely to be more important factors than oil in the energy geopolitics between China and Southeast Asia. However, the extent to which LNG will be a major factor in rising Chinese influence is less clear. Economically, the relationship is being driven by enormous trade and financial flows that will dwarf the scale of energy and gas trade as China moves to cement a full free trade agreement with the Association of Southeast Asian Nations (ASEAN) by 2010.[18] The enormous gravitational force of China's economy is the broader driver for this relationship so it would be an exaggeration to attribute too much of the blossoming Sino–Southeast Asia relationship to LNG and energy relations.

With that caveat, Beijing's influence and ties with Indonesia and Australia, in particular, will be strengthened by the addition of LNG trade to growing economic and trade ties.[19] China's CNOOC already has investment stakes in Australia's Northwest Shelf LNG consortium and in Indonesia's Tangguh LNG project. It has unsuccessfully sought stakes in Australia's Gorgon project and Indonesia's Bontang project on Kalimantan. China's first LNG terminal in Guangdong took its first shipment of LNG in mid-2006 from Australia's Northwest Shelf project, and the second terminal scheduled to open in Fujian in 2008 will source from Indonesia's Tangguh. Both CNOOC and CNPC have significant stakes in Indonesian offshore oil and gas production, and Indonesia sees China as an important potential new source of exploration and development investment at a time when the other international majors are scaling back due to Indonesia's unstable and unattractive investment environment.[20] Beijing has signed some form of strategic energy alliance with both countries.

LNG will undoubtedly be very significant in China–Australian ties, but China's influence will also be driven by other resource trade in coal, iron ore, and recently uranium. Some have already begun to speculate that Australia, traditionally a strong U.S. ally in the region, will move toward a more Beijing-centered regional strategy. Australia's recent statement that suggested some hesitance to be drawn into a potential future confrontation between the United States and China over Taiwan may be a harbinger. If this is the case, LNG and gas will be one of the key drivers but, from this author's perspective, only one driver among many. Much the same can be said about LNG and gas impact on the China–Indonesia relationship. It is also worth keeping in mind that the Asia–Pacific regional LNG market and the global LNG market appear likely to remain very tight with demand for LNG outrunning available supplies for the foreseeable future. That means that Australia and Indonesia have many alternative markets for their LNG; in other words, it is a seller's market, which reduces the extent to which LNG purchases become strategic leverage for China.

Another key dimension in China's Southeast Asian relations will be the extent to which LNG and gas transport issues affect long-running tensions between China and the region over maritime territorial disputes and whether China and the region can work together on SLOC issues and China's "Malacca Strait Dilemma." This is another issue that is probably being influenced much more by the overall strengthening of Sino–ASEAN relations due to economic convergence than by energy and LNG ties.

Conversely, both China's clear desire to maintain future access to potential energy and gas resources in contested areas of the South China Sea and its desire to exert some future influence over the SLOC of Southeast Asia and the Strait of Malacca suggest that Beijing is likely to become more assertive in pursuing its maritime territorial and LNG transit interests in the region. This would suggest that these LNG-related energy drivers will tend to add to tensions between Beijing burgeoning and the region over these issues. However, energy and gas trade and the more important overall mushrooming of Sino–ASEAN economic relations also provide incentives for China to adopt a more cooperative posture that reflects the broadening and diversity of its interests in the region. Thus far, China has seemed to prefer taking a more cooperative posture on the issues related to energy territorial claims and transit issues. For example, China has signed two recent broad agreements with ASEAN on territorial and cooperation issues. The first of these was the November 2002 "Declaration on the Conduct of Parties in the South China Sea" that commits the signatories to "peaceful settlement" of territorial disputes. The second was the October 2003 "Treaty of Amity and Cooperation," which renounced the use of force and called for increased economic and political cooperation. Another hopeful sign was the recent agreement between China, the Philippines, and Vietnam to conduct joint oil and gas exploration in the South China Sea. All these signs suggest that Beijing wants to avoid letting energy and maritime border disputes undermine its broader efforts to engage Southeast Asian states more constructively on trade, financial, and energy ties.[21]

A final issue in China's energy ties with Southeast Asia with strategic implications for the United States involves Burma. Recent decisions by the junta in Burma make it increasingly likely that a gas pipeline will be built to move gas from newly discovered offshore Burmese fields to southern China. India has been competing to have these supplies pipelined west to India, rather than China, but it appears that China's gravitational pull for the junta was much stronger than India's. For Washington, this suggests that gas sales will add to incentives for Beijing to remain the key patron for Burma, hindering U.S. progress in isolating that regime.

China's continuing efforts to forge a major LNG relationship with Iran will contribute to strengthening that evolving strategic relationship, with consequences for U.S. efforts to isolate Iran. As other countries' major oil companies increasingly defer on their investment commitments to Iranian oil and gas projects due to growing geopolitical risks and uncertainty, China's NOC's apparent willingness to move forward on major LNG and oil development projects puts China in a position to be key to Iran's future oil and gas export prospects.[22] China's decision to seek LNG from Iran rather than Qatar is also particularly interesting. Qatar, a proven, rapidly growing major LNG exporter, had offered an extremely competitive bid to supply China's first LNG terminal in Guangdong. China instead awarded the first two contracts to Australia and Indonesia. Iran, on the other hand, has yet to complete its first LNG project despite years of negotiations. This suggests several things. First, China places a strategic premium on nearby Southeast Asian LNG supplies as opposed to Persian Gulf supplies. Second, China also appears to see Qatar as a close U.S. strategic and economic ally while Iran is clearly far more independent of U.S. influence. This makes Iran a more attractive choice despite the fact that it is not yet a proven exporter. Iran also has the world's second largest gas reserves after Russia.

China's imports of both LNG and pipeline gas, over the longer term, are likely to support China–Russia energy as well as diplomatic ties that are being driven by the prospects of growing oil exports from Russia to China and increased Chinese oil company investments in Russian energy supplies. However, this process is unlikely to be smooth due to Russian concerns about providing energy to China, its growing regional rival for power, and by competition outlined earlier between Russia and China over access to Central Asia's future gas exports. Relations between the two over potential gas imports from East Siberia and Pacific Russia have been somewhat tortured due to capricious Russian policies toward energy exports to Asia generally and China in particular, as well as by the decision-making paralysis caused by the Kremlin's ongoing efforts to gain complete control over the main gas projects being developed in East Siberia before moving forward with major export decisions. These projects include both Sakhalin 1 and 2 as well as the Kovykta gas pipeline project proposed in the Irkutsk region. China has shown some interest in LNG imports from Shell's Sakhalin 2 project and recently has negotiated a proposal for pipeline gas to come from ExxonMobil's Sakhalin 1 project. Having forced their way into a majority share of Shell's Sakhalin

2 project, Russian energy and environmental authorities are now increasing pressure on ExxonMobil and its Japanese partners to cede an ownership and control share in the Sakhalin 1 oil and gas project. As Gazprom eventually exerts control over both Sakhalin 1 and 2, these two projects are increasingly likely to be combined into a single LNG export stream, which could free up some of that supply for export to China.[23] A gas pipeline to China from Kovykta also will become more probable when Gazprom and British Petroleum/Russian Oil Company eventually work out an arrangement to give Russia control of that project.[24] In sum, as the control issues regarding gas supplies and exports from East Siberia and Sakhalin are sorted out in favor of Gazprom and the Kremlin over the next few years, it will open the door more widely to both Sakhalin LNG and Kovykta pipeline gas to eventually flow on a significant scale to China. Added to the ties driven by growing oil exports to China, expanding LNG and gas-pipeline gas should strengthen the energy dimensions of stronger Sino–Russian ties generally.

A corollary effect of this will likely be to further aggravate already tense China–Japan energy relations. Japan is in the process of seeing its strong position in controlling the disposition of Sakhalin gas supplies eroded with the Kremlin's effective takeover of these projects and the potential redirection of some of these future supplies to China rather than Japan. Japan has been a major equity partner in both the Sakhalin 1 and 2 projects. But it has seen its 45 percent share of the Sakhalin 2 LNG project cut to 10 percent with the recent encroachment of Gazprom into that project, which could ultimately reduce the amount of that LNG which flows to Japan. And Japan faces the prospect of sharply reducing its stake in Sakhalin 1 when Gazprom is likewise brought into that project with the possibility that a significant portion of the gas likely to be exported from that project will find its way to China instead of Japan. This is also likely to further strain Russo–Japanese relations, which are already burdened by a range of serious tensions and growing Japanese frustration with Russia over delays in oil and gas export projects to Japan.

Conclusion

In a broad sense, China's future growth in natural gas imports will reinforce many of the same energy security concerns that come with rising oil import dependency. LNG will be one part of a larger gas import supply security concern for Beijing's leaders. LNG is likely to reinforce the speed and scale of China's naval expansion in the Southeast Asia region and the Indian Ocean and, hence, add to U.S. concerns over China's long-term intentions regarding its naval buildup. LNG will also reinforce China's involvement in Iran, which will exacerbate U.S. concerns that China will be supporting the diplomatic interests of Iran. Therefore, it is important that the United States begin to engage China more actively to find ways to ensure safe energy transport through the sea lanes of Southeast Asia. The United States also needs to begin planning for growing influence by China in key gas exporting regions, such as the Gulf, Russia, and Central Asia, and to find common ground with China on shaping developments in these regions, which are crucial to U.S. energy and strategic interests.

Notes

1. For an excellent discussion of China's gas industry and plans, see David Fridley, "Natural Gas in China" in *Natural Gas in Asia: The Challenges of Growth in China, India, Japan and Korea*, ed. Ian Wybrew-Bond and Jonathan Stern (Oxford: Oxford University Press, 2002), 5–64; see also, Jonathan Sinton et al., *Evaluation of China's Energy Strategy Options* (Berkeley, CA: Lawrence Berkeley National Laboratory, China Energy Group, May 2005).

2. For this data and discussion of China's LNG demand and terminal plans, see *International Energy Outlook 2006*, Energy Information Administration (Washington, D.C.: U.S. Department of Energy, GPO, 2006), 44–47.

3. On recent difficulties, see "Russia, China Plot Thickens," *World Gas Intelligence*, Energy Intelligence Group, 4 April 2007, p. 1.

4. "Iran, China Agree on North Pars Gas Field Development," *Xinhua Economic News*, 22 May 2007.

5. See the "Natural Gas," in *International Energy Outlook 2006* (Washington, D.C.: U.S. Department of Energy, Energy Information Agency, 2006), 46, available at http://www.eia.doe.gov/oiaf/ieo/pdf/nat_gas.pdf.

6. Ibid.

7. For example, see "China's Sinopec Shelves LNG, Shifts to Local Output, Pipelines," *International Oil Daily*, 14 December 2006.

8. "Low Domestic Gas Prices May Dampen China's LNG Imports: CNOOC," *Asia Pulse*, 2 December 2005; "Beijing Moves to Control Construction Pace of New LNG Terminals," *International Oil Daily*, Energy Intelligence Group, 19 September 2005.

9. For a discussion of recent cross-currents affecting LNG's growth in China, see "Natural Gas: Putting the Cart before the Horse," *Petroleum Economist*, 1 December 2006, p. 12.

10. Song Yen Ling, "CNPC, Statoil Ink Upstream, LNG Deal," *International Oil Daily*, 5 March 2007.

11. For an indication of the growing acceptance of higher LNG prices, see Richard McGregor, "China LNG Deal Hints at Easing of Price Limits," *Financial Times*, 9 May 2007; and "China's CNOOC to Import 25m Tonnes of Natural Gas by 2010," *BBC Monitoring Asia Pacific*, 10 November 2006.

12. For the IEA's views, see Claude Mandil, "Russia Must Act to Avert Gas Supply Crisis," *Financial Times*, 21 March 2006.

13. See "Russia's Central Asian Score," *Petroleum Intelligence Weekly*, 16 May 2007, p. 1; and Sergei Blagov, "Russia Celebrates Its Central Asian Energy Coup," *Eurasianet*, Eurasianet.org, 16 May 2007.

14. Stephen Blank, "Turkmenbashi in Beijing: A Pipeline Dream," *Eurasianet*, Eurasianet.org, 10 April 2006.

15. *World Energy Outlook 2004* (Paris: International Energy Agency, 2004), 143.

16. *World Energy Outlook 2004*, IEA, 268.

17. *World Energy Outlook 2004*, IEA, 264.

18. "Interview: China-ASEAN FTA to Help Bring about Asia's Economic Integration," *People's Daily Online*, 31 October 2004, available at http://english.people.com.cn/200410/31/eng20041031_162255.html.

19. For a fuller discussion of these issues, see Mikkal Herberg, "China's Search for Energy Security and Implications for Southeast Asia," in *China, the United States, and Southeast Asia: Contending Perspectives on Economics, Politics, and Security*, Chapter 5, Routledge Press (forthcoming).

20. *Petroleum Report Indonesia, 2005–2006*, U.S. Embassy, Jakarta, 12–14.

21. See Herberg, "China's Search," 76–79.

22. For example, see "China Holds Key to Iran's Stalled Development," *Petroleum Intelligence Weekly*, Energy Intelligence Group, 21 May 2007, p. 1.

23. "Gazprom's Arrival Changes Outlook for Sakhalin Gas," *Petroleum Intelligence Weekly*, Energy Intelligence Group, 23 April 2007, p. 1.

24. "Let the Kovykta Battle Begin," *World Gas Intelligence,* Energy Intelligence Group, 31 January 2007, p. 4; see also Anne-Sylvaine Chassany, "Russia Oil Minister: Undecided on How to Develop Kovykta Gas Field," *Dow Jones Newswire*, 31 May 2007.

Gabriel B. Collins and Andrew S. Erickson

Chinese Efforts to Create a National Tanker Fleet

CHINESE SHIPPING FIRMS are aggressively expanding their oil tanker fleets. Although China's state energy firms support national energy security goals in their rhetoric, and China's state shipbuilders are striving to lead global production, commercial forces will almost certainly determine how these ships are employed. China's internal energy politics are complex. National, provincial, and commercial actors often pursue their interests in ways that support their own objectives, sometimes at the expense of Beijing's. And, given China's unwieldy bureaucracy and lack of an energy ministry, it is unclear to what extent larger objectives are conclusively defined and coherently enforced. Energy security considerations may have some influence in determining China's naval force structure, however. The Chinese navy's ability to protect energy transport routes is currently embryonic, at best. China's present naval buildup seems focused on Taiwan and other claimed territorial areas, and its tanker fleet buildup is best explained as pursuit of commercial gain. Yet the majority of new tankers being built for Chinese shipping firms will fly China's flag, which arguably helps to set a legal basis for militarily protecting these vessels. As Chinese naval power and oil import dependency rise, security-minded factions in China's leadership may use the country's resource needs to justify further pursuit of blue water naval capabilities. At this critical crossroads in its naval development, China's leaders would do well to understand that the security of their nation's maritime oil transport lies in the inherent difficulties facing any force trying to disrupt it, rather than on any other single factor.

China's Evolving Energy Situation

The global oil shipping system transports oil from some of the world's most unstable areas. It has functioned through wars, hurricanes, embargoes, and canal closures. While commercial tanker operators engage in apolitical pursuit of profit, however, the U.S. Navy's maintenance of the freedom of navigation that makes their operations possible is subject to complex geopolitical conditions. The People's Republic of China (PRC)'s rise as a commercial and military power over the past three decades is drawing renewed attention to a system that governments and private consumers around the world have long taken for granted.

Maritime oil transport will be increasingly important to China in coming decades. China became a net oil importer in 1993 and a decade later was the second-largest-consuming and third-largest-importing nation.[1] In 2006 China imported 40 percent of its oil, or 2.9 million barrels per day (bpd). China currently imports roughly 45 percent of its oil supply. China's rising motor vehicle ownership, its plans to double the size of its road network, and its domestic firms' huge fixed investments in steel, petrochemicals, and other energy-intensive basic industries could drive oil imports to as much as 60 percent of total oil demand by 2016. China is on track to become the world's second largest net oil importer by 2015. The International Energy Agency estimates that by 2020 China could import around 7 million bpd of crude oil, or double today's imports.[2] Over the next fifteen years China's share of world oil consumption will more than double, with imports possibly rising to 80 percent by 2025.[3] Despite new domestic fields, a highly touted pipeline from Kazakhstan, and planned lines from Russia, Chinese oil demand growth will likely overwhelm increases in nonmaritime oil supplies. Much of the new demand, therefore, will be met by seaborne oil shipments.

Inspired by growing concerns about oil insecurity, interested Chinese parties advocate the construction of a state-flagged and, to a large extent, domestically constructed fleet of oil tankers capable of hauling up to three-quarters of Chinese oil imports by 2020.[4] Although PRC-owned tankers can currently transport less than 20 percent of China's oil imports, Chinese shipyards and shipping companies, driven by a combination of commercial and political concerns, are assembling a fleet of state-flagged very large crude carriers (VLCCs) that could carry upwards of 50 percent of Chinese oil imports by 2016.[5] In practical terms, this means that more than fifty Chinese-flagged VLCCs could be plying the seas a decade from now.

Official Concern

China's explosive post-1993 oil import growth surprised analysts and officials. Indeed, Beijing disbanded its Energy Ministry in 1993 because the leadership expected China to remain energy self-sufficient.[6] By 2003 the combination of the Iraq War, exploding domestic oil demand, and a leadership increasingly wary of reliance on the U.S.-led international economic system made oil security a central concern in China's energy debate.

Under President Hu Jintao China is taking multiple steps to secure its oil supply. It is continuing to support the "go out" policy in which Chinese national oil companies aggressively seek overseas oil fields. Beijing is encouraging state oil companies to build joint venture refineries in China that will be fed with earmarked oil supplies from Saudi Arabia and Kuwait, thus providing guaranteed crude streams because oil exporters would not likely cut off oil to their own refineries. China is simultaneously enhancing downstream security by building a strategic petroleum reserve, expanding its internal and external pipeline networks, and boosting its refining capacity and ability to handle a wider range of crude oil grades.

Chinese shipping companies and shipyards are constructing a tanker fleet capable of hauling a substantial portion of Chinese oil imports. While efforts to ensure upstream security by defending overseas oil fields are precluded by China's inability to project power overseas, a larger tanker fleet will help to develop what China—like many nations—regards as a critical, strategic industry and may help enhance the security of seaborne oil imports.

A large, state-flagged tanker fleet may help to ensure the security of China's oil imports because it could deter a future adversary from interdicting China-bound tankers to pressure China's leadership. This would be particularly true in crisis situations short of a shooting war. State flagging of tankers can be a legal prerequisite for military protection and raises the stakes for a potential blockader, who might otherwise see a distant blockade as a way to pressure China in such a crisis situation. The possibility also exists, however, that Chinese tanker operators may, in effect, be manipulating Beijing's oil insecurity for commercial gain. The key variable is the relationship between

China's government and its national oil companies, which, if left to their own devices, typically put profits before politics.

Some observers characterize China's tanker buildup as a centrally driven plan. This remains a point of contention. The authors' interviews with Chinese scholars familiar with the central government's current energy policies suggest that Beijing has no coherent plan at present for the creation of a national tanker fleet. However, articles from state-controlled Xinhua News Agency and *China Daily* feature analyst Luo Ping from the National Development and Reform Commission (NDRC)–affiliated Institute of Comprehensive Transportation calling for at least 60 percent of oil imports to be carried by Chinese shipping companies, which are now rapidly expanding their tanker fleets.[7] According to *China Daily*, Peng Cuihong, a senior official at the Ministry of Communications' Water Transport Department, has stated that China will build additional oil tankers to reduce reliance on foreign tankers.[8]

Perhaps most significantly, a *China Daily* editorial (which would not appear without at least some form of tacit official sanction) echoes Luo's call:

> As the world's second largest oil importer, our overseas supplies are vulnerable. Inadequate ocean shipping capacity is a weakness that could prove fatal. We have cause for worry with around 85 percent of our entire oil imports transported by foreign-flag vessels. This is acceptable when business is just business. But we are not in a perfect world. The best way to minimize our vulnerability is to increase our preparedness for less than normal times. It is well within our reach to have more than 60 percent of our oil imports carried by Chinese-flag tankers, if that is what we need for oil security. The government should not economize on this strategic national interest. It has the financial resources to make it happen. The subsequent shipbuilding orders will in turn be a major boost to home shipyards. The authorities' idea to encourage more domestic shipping companies to enter the ocean-faring business is a good one. . . . We can also handle the technology. Several domestic shipyards have been building large crude oil carriers for years. We applaud the Ministry of Communications' determination to upgrade our self-reliance in ocean shipping. It is an insightful decision that will help guarantee a more comfortable position in the kind of special times we hope will never come.[9]

Despite its increasing economic influence and growing presence in energy-rich areas around the world, China's lack of an energy ministry, and hence a lack of a clear centralized policy process, makes it difficult for outsiders to understand the formation and content of its energy policies. This is particularly true when dealing with maritime energy transport security, which includes both economic and military concerns. Some Chinese scholars state that Beijing's energy policy is largely determined and articulated by NDRC, a branch of China's State Council. Premier Wen Jiabao reportedly devotes substantial time to energy issues as head of the State Council's Energy Leading Group, which solicits NDRC's inputs.[10] NDRC documents tend to focus on general aspects of national energy consumption and conservation, however, not maritime or military issues. A variety of institutions in China's People's Liberation Army Navy (PLAN)[11] focuses on the security aspects of Chinese energy and likely influences PLAN energy strategy but is not easily accessible to foreign scholars.[12]

Analyzing China's energy transport industry will elucidate the larger, sometimes competing considerations that inform Beijing's quest for reliable energy supplies. China's oil tanker buildup appears to be driven primarily by commercial factors at present. The geopolitical implications of China's growing maritime trade and oil demand, however, necessitate careful examination of the impetus behind China's desire to increase its presence in the world tanker market.[13] According to one PLAN researcher, China's maritime trade could equal $1 trillion by 2020, nearly four times the 2006 figure of $270 million (10 percent of China's gross domestic product).[14] Because much of China's growing oil demand must be met with seaborne imports, Beijing's evolving oil transport practices may have significant maritime commercial and security repercussions in East Asia and beyond.

Beyond Taiwan

China's future tanker fleet could have significant geopolitical effects if China makes protecting oil and other resource shipments a major priority. China needs secure seaborne oil imports to sustain economic development. At the same time, at least some Chinese officials fear that the United States might seek to interrupt Chinese oil imports in a future conflict.[15] In a speech to PLAN officers attending a Communist Party meeting on 27 December 2006, President Hu Jintao bluntly stated that China needs a "powerful . . . blue water" navy prepared to uphold national interests "at any time."[16] This may entail creating a long-distance sea line of communication (SLOC) protection capacity.

Not surprisingly, China's 2006 defense white paper reiterates President Hu's assertions. This official appraisal of China's strategic environment and the proper responses thereto states that, "the impact of economic globalization is spreading into the political, security, and social fields. . . . Security issues related to energy, resources, finance, information, and international shipping routes are mounting."[17] Many Chinese naval analysts' writings echo the need to protect Chinese commerce far from Chinese shores.[18] Yet to date, China's naval modernization efforts appear to have been oriented almost exclusively to defense of China's maritime periphery, and to solving the "Taiwan problem." Protecting maritime resource supply lines may be a key driver of PLAN development for contingencies "beyond Taiwan."

Some Chinese analysts advocate strengthening the PLAN so that it can intervene in trouble spots such as the Strait of Malacca.[19] Wu Lei, a prominent Chinese energy scholar from Shanghai International Studies University, explains that "fear that the U.S might cut [energy shipments] off as a result of the deterioration of Sino–U.S. relations over the Taiwan issue drives much of Beijing's modernization of its navy and air forces."[20] Identifying and analyzing the strategic rationale behind China's tanker-fleet expansion may help to illuminate China's maritime development strategy.

Why an Expanded Tanker Fleet?

Despite likely future increases in oil imported overland, China will have to continue to rely on maritime transport for the majority of its increasing oil imports. This is partly for reasons of geography: 76 percent of Chinese oil imports in 2006 came from the Middle East and Africa.[21] A new pipeline from Kazakhstan will likely carry up to 200,000 bpd within the next year and up to 400,000 bpd by 2011. A similar pipeline to supply China with 200,000 bpd of Russian oil will come fully online some time in 2009–10, adding as much as 500,000 bpd of total new overland supply.[22] A major new oil field discovered in the Bohai Gulf by PetroChina could deliver up to 200,000 bpd within three years, for a total of ~700,000 bpd of additional nonmaritime oil supply by 2010.[23] Yet even assuming a conservative 8 percent growth in annual demand (as compared to 14.5 percent in 2006), Chinese oil demand would increase by more than 1 million bpd during that same three year period. Moreover, as table 1 indicates, seaborne oil imports are Beijing's most cost-effective option. Thus, for the foreseeable future, China's seaborne oil imports will continue to increase and to represent the dominant share of overall oil imports. In 2006, over 85 percent of oil entering China came by sea.

Table 1. Sample Oil Transport Costs to China

Transport Mode	Route	Distance	Total Cost ($/barrel)	Cost/barrel/ 1,000 km
Tanker*	Ras Tanura-Ningbo	7,000 km	$1.14	$0.163
Pipeline**	Angarsk-Skovorodino	2,700 km	$2.14	$0.793
Train***	Angarsk-Manzhouli	1,000 km	$7.19	$7.19

  * VLCC at $65K/day, 2 million barrels cargo
 ** based on Russian Transneft tariff of 58¢/ton/100 km
*** based on weighted average of Russian Railway's oil tariffs to Zabaikalsk and Naushki

Perhaps driven by fear that major naval powers could sever China's maritime oil supply lines, a growing contingent of Chinese analysts and policymakers advocates major tanker fleet development. In August 2003, China's government reportedly established a "Tanker Working Group,"[24] though this assertion that has been disputed by at least one prominent Chinese scholar.[25] By 2010, one source reports, Beijing intends to transport 40–50 percent of its oil imports in PRC-flagged tankers. By 2020, it hopes to carry 60–70 percent.[26] Chinese analysts predict that their country will need more than forty VLCCs by 2010, each of which will be able to carry upwards of 1.5 million barrels of oil in order to meet these goals.[27] For an explanation of various tanker designations, which are based on hauling capacity, see table 2.

Table 2. Tanker Size Guide

Panamax	50,000–80,000 dwt of capacity (1 ton = 7.33 barrels of oil)
Aframax	80,000–120,000 dwt
Suezmax	120,000–180,000 dwt
Very Large Crude Carrier (VLCC)	200,000–300,000 dwt
Ultra-large Crude Carrier (ULCC)	300,000–550,000 dwt

Beijing considers shipbuilding to be a strategic sector.[28] Although security concerns are, to some extent, driving China's tanker fleet buildup, its biggest short-term effects will probably be commercial. Japan and South Korea, in particular, face major competition from Chinese tanker builders. According to China State Shipbuilding Corporation's plan, by 2015 China will overtake Japan and South Korea to become the world's largest shipbuilder.[29] Figure 1 shows those tanker builders with total orders exceeding 2 million deadweight tons' (dwt) worth of shipping. It also depicts these firms' home countries' total share of new construction for long-haul tankers. With nearly 30 percent of global tanker orders, China has already displaced Japan as the world's second largest builder of long-haul tankers.

Figure 1. Main Global Long-Haul Tanker Builders

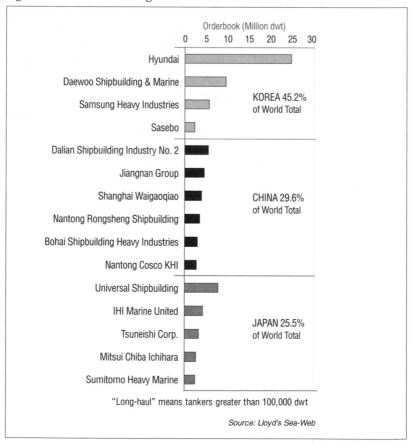

The Malacca Dilemma

More than 85 percent of Chinese oil and oil-product imports pass through the Strait of Malacca.[30] Some Chinese analysts fear that Malacca and other bottlenecks such as the Strait of Hormuz could easily be closed by terrorism, piracy, or the navies of the United States or regional powers in the event of a conflict over Taiwan or some other serious Sino–American crisis. They write that whoever controls Malacca also controls China's oil security, and that China's inability to secure Malacca would be "disastrous" for national security.[31]

To some Chinese analysts, the U.S. Navy is not the only threat to China's maritime energy supply lines. They worry that the rapidly modernizing Indian navy could use its superiority vis-à-vis China's PLAN in the Indian Ocean to gain strategic leverage.[32] Beijing also distrusts Tokyo and worries about the capabilities of the Japanese Maritime Self-Defense Force due to historical enmity; because Japan competes with China for energy resources in Russia and the East China Sea; and because Japan is a major ally of the United States and cooperates closely on many strategic issues with India.

China will continue to rely on maritime oil shipments because there are simply no economically viable alternative means of shipping oil from most remote sources to China's refineries. For sources overseas, tankers are the only option. These maritime shipments, moreover, will likely pass through the Strait of Malacca for the foreseeable future. Despite its geographical funneling and the limited risks posed by terrorists and pirates, Malacca will remain a primary oil shipping route simply because of the cost (in additional time, fuel, and ships) of using alternative maritime routes such as the Lombok Strait, or even circumnavigating Australia.[33] Beijing will have to find a way to work within these realities.

Commercial Factors

Beijing's relationship with tanker operators is best characterized as "the government builds the stage and the companies play." The government sets certain ground rules, but the companies enjoy substantial freedom to pursue their own commercial objectives within understood limits. This relationship and understanding probably extends to building national oil transport capability as well.

Managers of shipping companies appear generally content to let the central government promote the shipbuilding/shipping industry at the broad policy level. In fact a Chinese energy expert has told one of the authors the idea of a Chinese national oil tanker fleet, while widely discussed in various forums, is a "rhetorical device for China's shipbuilding industry to justify more central government interest."[34] Yet, like state oil companies, Chinese shipping companies may resist government interference in their daily operations. If chartering tankers to national and private operators worldwide on an individual basis is more profitable than serving Chinese national oil companies in accordance with central policy directives, shippers will favor the more profitable approach. Similarly, if national energy companies find it more cost-effective to have foreign tanker operators haul their oil, they may oppose a forced marriage with Chinese oil shipping firms. Observers will be able to learn more about these relationships once Chinese state-owned shipping firms such as China Ocean Shipping Corporation start taking large-scale VLCC deliveries, perhaps as early as late 2007 and early 2008. To better understand how Chinese shipping companies and national oil companies will interact, analysts will need access to significant chartering data spanning at least a year.

At present an estimated 90 percent of China's oil shipping capacity serves foreign clients.[35] Reassigning these vessels to domestic firms would not help China's long-distance oil transport situation. According to *Lloyd's Sea Web*, only eighteen of these ships are VLCCs suitable for economically transporting crude oil from the Middle East, Africa, and other distant suppliers. The bulk of China's current fleet consists of smaller Aframax, Panamax, and Handysize vessels designed for short-haul oil trading. China will need more than forty VLCCs to meet its goal of carrying 50 percent of imports on Chinese tankers by 2010.

Attempting to control maritime oil transport will likely cost more than outsourcing oil transport to private shippers. When the major Western oil companies ("Seven Sisters") dominated the global oil market in the 1960s, they ran large maritime divisions with tankers dedicated to hauling their production, which for most roughly equaled their refinery throughputs. Oil companies trimmed their tanker fleets after the Organization of Petroleum Exporting Countries renationalized the majors' Middle East production. Hiring private tankers to carry oil imports may be more cost effective than acquiring and maintaining a large tanker fleet. Although tanker rates have been strong over the past several years, the oil shipping business is highly cyclical, and when shipping rates fall, companies that paid high prices when rates were elevated will lose money. Like other modern oil companies, China's national oil companies rely primarily on independent tanker operators to haul their oil. In 2006, Sinopec chartered two-thirds as many VLCC spot voyages as did ExxonMobil (103 to 149). In 2007, it may out-charter ExxonMobil.[30]

If Beijing hopes to foster long-term strategic cooperation between domestic oil shippers and the national oil companies (some of which are among the world's leading VLCC charterers), it may have to offer tax breaks and other financial incentives. Otherwise, the shipping firms will likely utilize their ships based almost exclusively on "nationality-blind" commercial criteria.

Financing

As table 3 indicates, several Chinese shipping firms that specialize in energy shipping, or have substantial positions in the business, have held initial public offerings of stock since 2005.[37] This is another indicator of the fundamentally commercial character of Chinese firms' energy shipping operations. Because Chinese firms (particularly state-owned enterprises) are major employers and generate large tax revenues, it is unlikely that Beijing will permit them to sell controlling shares. Foreign and domestic investors are nevertheless likely to pursue these limited options because of restricted access to other investment opportunities within China's energy sector and Beijing's skillful linking of investment, technology transfer, and market access. A senior Chinese energy official has told one of the authors that China is constructing oil tankers not as part of a security-focused central government policy, but rather to gain economic benefits, particularly by reducing tanker financing rates.[38]

Table 3. Chinese Energy Shipping IPOs

Company	Amount	% of Total Capitalization	Purpose	Date	Exchange
China Merchants Energy Shipping	$727 million	35	Raise capital for fleet expansion	Nov. 2006	Shanghai
COSCO Holdings	$1.22 billion	29	Boost international profile, raise capital	June 2005	Hong Kong

Sources: Lloyd's List, International Herald Tribune, Nelson's Public Company profiles

Shipping Sector Parallels with Oil Company–Central Government Relations

The relationships between China's national energy companies and central government may foreshadow how those between tanker operators and the central government will unfold. China's main oil producing and importing companies are China National Petroleum Corporation (CNPC), China National Offshore Oil Corporation (CNOOC), Sinopec, and Sinochem. Between 2000 and 2002, CNPC, Sinopec, and CNOOC all sold minority stakes to outside investors. CNPC and CNOOC made the publicly held portions of their firms into subsidiaries, PetroChina and CNOOC Limited. These share sales (typically around 20 percent) allowed the companies to raise operating cash and boost their international profile while retaining clear state control. Figure 2 illustrates Chinese oil companies' links to the central government.

Figure 2. China's Oil Pyramid

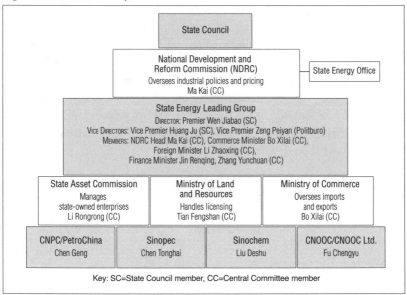

Key: SC=State Council member, CC=Central Committee member

Although Chinese energy companies are state-controlled, their corporate interests frequently influence high-level energy policy decisions.[39] It is widely believed, for instance, that much of the initial impetus behind China's "go out" oil field acquisition push actually came from CNPC.[40]

Over the past decade, Chinese national oil companies have adhered to a business model unlike that of Western firms. They are often criticized for subverting the market by offering "package deals" backed by state banks' soft loans and other enticements. Chinese state-owned companies are willing to "overpay" for deals and often accept lower rates of return than private oil companies. These tendencies stem from a combination of relative inexperience in international energy deal-making, access to subsidized financing from Chinese state banks, low accountability to shareholders, and nonbusiness incentives created by top executives' dual company and Party roles.

That said, Chinese oil companies appear to be placing increased emphasis on profitability. For example, PetroChina oil marketers have stated that transporting back to China oil produced in distant fields is too expensive.[41] In accordance with sound business principles, they favor selling local production locally and acquiring crude oil for Chinese use closer to home.

Had CNOOC successfully acquired American producer Union Oil Company of California (UNOCAL) in summer 2005, it would probably have continued to sell UNOCAL's Gulf of Mexico production on the U.S. market because it made greater economic sense to do so. Likewise, CNPC often sells a substantial portion of its Sudanese production on the world market rather than shipping it back to China.[42] This suggests that despite the "go out" policy's political overtones, Chinese producers' crude oil shipping decisions tend to be driven by economic rather than strategic concerns.

The shipping industry's incentives for expansion appear similar to those of most Chinese oil and gas producers. The "national oil, nationally carried" oil transport concept parallels the "go out" oil acquisition policy. Both approaches involve commercial interests pursuing profits under the banner of enhancing national energy security.

Aggressively seeking deals overseas allows Chinese oil companies to expand production while casting themselves as "servants of the Chinese nation" by generating tax revenue and increasing the import share of Chinese-produced oil. State energy companies generate more than 20 percent of all tax revenue produced by state-owned enterprises.[43] Such contributions please the Communist Party, which can influence oil executives' future prospects. Many top executives have occupied, and in some cases continue to occupy, high-level political positions in conjunction with their business roles. For example, CNPC president Jiang Jiemin has served as governor of Qinghai province, and Sinochem vice president Zhang Zhiyin is a delegate to the 10th National People's Congress. In addition, there exists an informal "revolving door" by which good performance at the helm of an oil company can greatly advance an official's career. Wei Liucheng successfully managed CNOOC Limited's initial public offering in 2001 and was rewarded with governorship of Hainan upon leaving CNOOC in 2003.[44]

Some shipping industry executives also have political careers. Dr. Qin Xiao, chairman of China Merchants Group, is a member of the 10th Chinese People's Political Consultative Conference and served as a deputy to the 9th National People's Congress.[45] Generally, however, successful shipping executives do not yet seem to enjoy as many plum positions as do their oil industry counterparts. Nonetheless, China's shipping industry is acquiring the aggregate financial clout to justify an important political role. As it continues to grow, its location along China's populous, politically influential east coast, growing ranks of workers, and contribution to national and local coffers may give it more political influence. Thus, if China's shipping industry generates sufficient profits and tax revenue, political rewards for shipping managers will likely resemble those currently enjoyed by successful oil executives.

On the whole, China's state shipyards and shipping companies appear to be broadly following the model of the state oil and gas companies. In peacetime, state-controlled oil carriers will attempt to influence government policies in ways beneficial to their business but, when the government wants something in return, will ultimately put profit before politics. In a crisis scenario, by contrast, state-owned vessels would stand ready to be pressed into service, Chinese analysts write.[46] Having a state tanker fleet is not an oil security panacea, however. Potential flaws in China's emerging approach will be discussed shortly.

China's Shipbuilding Industry

Beijing has powerful economic incentives to bolster its shipbuilding sector. Shipbuilding strengthens the entire industrial chain, including the steel industry, the metallurgical and machine-tool sectors, and others. VLCCs recently built in Chinese yards have required approximately 884,000 man-hours to complete.[47] Chinese sources calculate that, in general, every 10,000 dwt built can create 100,000–200,000 man-hours of employment for Chinese workers.[48] Thus, direct shipyard labor accounts for only about 15–20 percent of the entire amount of employment generated by building a ship. At present, China's shipbuilding industry directly employs more than 275,000 workers.[49] Thus, on the basis of job creation alone, China's government has good reason to support its shipbuilders.

As mentioned earlier, Chinese ship owners and operators presently control eighteen VLCCs. Roughly half of the vessels (by hulls, not tonnage) in China's fleet are small, old tankers better suited for the coastal and short haul trades than for international oil transport. Meng Qinglin, a senior manager of Dalian Ocean Shipping Company, estimates that Chinese tankers are 30 percent older than the international norm.[50] The ships' average carrying capacity is also better suited to medium-distance oil carriage, rather than the long trip from Africa or the Persian Gulf, as Chinese crude oil tankers average 116,000 dwt (as opposed to the Japanese fleet's average of nearly 200,000 dwt per vessel). Figure 3 compares China's current VLCC fleet with those of other major oil importers.

Figure 3. Oil Import Dependency vs. Tanker Fleet Size

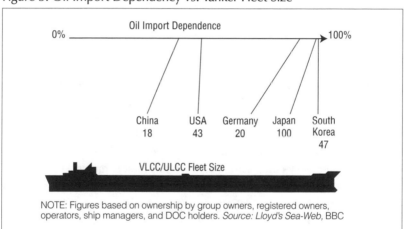

NOTE: Figures based on ownership by group owners, registered owners, operators, ship managers, and DOC holders. *Source: Lloyd's Sea-Web*, BBC

While China's VLCC fleet is smaller than those of more oil-reliant nations, this is changing rapidly as a combination of government policies, domestic commercial interests, and sizeable commercial advantages in building tankers drive increasing tanker construction in Chinese yards. Tankers form a major portion of Chinese yards' output and will continue to do so, as shown in figure 4. It should be noted that the majority of Chinese yards' long-haul tanker orders are actually being built for foreign buyers.

Figure 4. PRC Shipbuilding Production by Deadweight 1989–2009

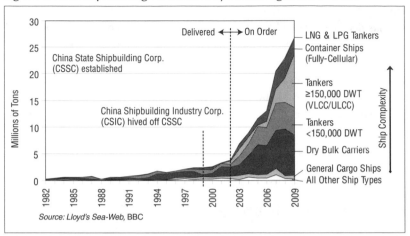

Source: Lloyd's Sea-Web, BBC

Figure 4 demonstrates the success of Chinese firms in winning orders for new tankers. According to *Lloyd's Sea Web*, of the 21 million dwt of Suezmaxes and VLCCs currently on order or under construction in Chinese yards, roughly 13 million dwt are being built for foreign operators. Although China lags Japan and Korea in technology and yard management practices, the large number of foreign tanker orders seems to endorse the Chinese shipbuilding industry's increasing quality at unbeatable prices. Western ship owners interviewed by the authors indicate that Chinese yards' low prices as well as a desire to establish relationships with rapidly growing Chinese shipbuilders drive their current orders.[51] Chinese ship quality, which recently was suspect, is rapidly improving, even if it has not yet reached the high level of South Korean– and Japanese-built vessels. Recognizing this increase in quality, foreign buyers are considering ordering chemical tankers and other more complex ships, in addition to the tankers and bulk carriers that have thus far dominated their orders.[52]

While two of China's large state-run shipyards (Shanghai Waigaoqiao and Dalian No. 2) are considered to be among the world's top ten, other yards still experience regular delays and quality control problems. China's entire ship subcomponents industry remains weak, creating a situation in which Chinese yards are excellent at hull fabrication but must import many key internal parts. Indeed, South Korean builders have even begun to construct hull blocks in China and barge them back to South Korea for final assembly. To boost the subcomponents industry, Chinese yards often force ship buyers to source engines and other subcomponents in China when they order vessels. Otherwise, ship buyers interviewed by the authors indicate, both they and the ship operators would favor Korean- and Japanese-made engines and other internal parts.[53] In sum, China's low labor costs and large land areas for yard expansion give it a distinct edge in building bulk carriers, tankers, and other less complex "commodity" ships. Chinese yards' current order books indicate a continued focus on building tankers and bulk carriers over the next two to three years. Table 4 summarizes Chinese shipbuilders' strengths and weaknesses relative to those of their primary competitors.

Table 4. Chinese Shipbuilding Industry vs. Main Competitors

PRC	Japan/South Korea
Bulk of ships built are of low complexity.	More proficient at high-value ship contruction.
Lower prices.	Higher prices.
Gaining technological proficiency, but still behind state-of-the-art.	Main yards are technologically state-of-the-art.
Relatively weak domestic innovation capacity.	High domestic innovation capacity.
Willing to customize ships.	Emphasize series production, little customization.
Lower labor costs.	High labor costs, but partially offset by higher technical proficiency.
Has significant land area for physical expansion.	Must build yards overseas and outsource, since space for expansion is scarce.
Extensive co-siting of commercial and military shipbuilding.	Commercial and military shipbuilding separated. Much less military shipbuilding activity at present.
Quality control problems.	Excellent quality control.
Problems with on-time delivery.	Timely delivery.
Weak marine equipment industry (only 40% of ship equipment is domestic).	Japan has strong marine equipment industry (95% of ship equipment is domestic); 85% of South Korea ship equipment is domestic.
Lower degree of integration between shipbuilding and supporting industries such as steel and marine equipment.	Higher integration due to old industrial groupings (*keiretsu* and *chaebols*).

Shipbuilding seen as a "pillar industry" in all three countries. The idea is that the industry can promote wider industrial development.

Broader Effect on the Tanker Market?

Some Chinese observers worry that China's aggressive tanker-building program, which is occurring amid record high tanker chartering rates and profits, could outstrip demand and depress tanker rates.[54] Some advocate acquiring secondhand tankers as an antidote. Building tankers without close regard for what the ship market can absorb might depress freight rates, however, and could create a situation in which Chinese shipyards profit while shipping companies suffer losses. Many tankers under construction today will enter the market in 2008–9. Continuing strong oil demand growth in the developing world (particularly Asia) will have to be met primarily with long-haul crude imports from the Middle East and could help underpin the VLCC market. Russia's delays in bringing East Siberian crude onto the Asian market may also uphold demand for VLCCs to carry Middle East and African crude. Long-haul product exports from the Middle East will also create incremental VLCC demand in coming years.

Changes to the market for new ships may also increase China's shipbuilding market share without causing undue depression of shipping rates. For example, shipping industry personnel interviewed by the authors indicate that Japanese heavy industrial firms are considering making a gradual exit from shipbuilding. This would open market share for Chinese shipyards, possibly allowing them to accelerate construction efforts without overbuilding.

Benefits for Oil Import Infrastructure

In 2005 only three ports—Qingdao, Zhoushan, and Shuidong—could directly berth tankers displacing 200,000 dwt or more, such as the VLCCs that deliver crude from Africa and the Middle East. Consequently, China is rapidly preparing specialized facilities at Ningbo, Quanzhou, and Maoming on China's southeast coast to handle 200,000–250,000 dwt oil tankers.[55]

Connecting oil ports with users throughout the country has become a major priority. Chinese analysts recommend rapidly upgrading China's oil transport system (e.g., pipelines, harbors, ships, shipyards, and oil transport lines), along with governing laws and regulations.[56] In particular, improving China's domestic oil pipeline network would enhance energy security. Robust capacity to shift oil supplies rapidly between major demand and import areas would introduce a degree of redundancy in case an incident closed one or more major VLCC-capable ports. An improved pipeline network would also bolster the effectiveness of China's growing strategic petroleum reserve by allowing rapid infusion of supplies into an integrated market in the event of a crisis. By 2010, Chinese companies plan to expand the country's pipeline network for oil, gas, and other products from 40,000 to 65,000 km.[57]

Can a Larger Tanker Fleet Ensure Oil Security?

Chinese analysts fear that the U.S. Navy, and even allied navies, might blockade energy shipments to China in a showdown over Taiwan or some other crisis.[58] Chinese "hawks" such as Zhang Wenmu believe that China's Navy must modernize because its ability to secure SLOC and ensure the safety of China-bound shipments seriously lags behind China's growing import demand.[59] In their view, a national tanker fleet would bolster the security of the nation's oil supply only if PLAN units had the capability to escort Chinese tankers in a crisis.

China may also be concerned that an outside power could exert financial and diplomatic pressure on the home countries of major tanker operators (e.g., Greece or the Bahamas) to force them to cease carrying oil to China. Chinese analysts emphasize that the United States in particular has demonstrated a robust capability to bring comprehensive financial, military, and diplomatic pressure to bear on adversaries. Having the capacity to haul a majority of Chinese oil imports on vessels owned by Chinese state and private shipping companies would ensure that an opponent could not use such a tactic to pressure China in a situation short of war.

Some Chinese analysts claim that using Chinese-flagged and -operated tankers would help secure oil shipments from unstable areas such as Africa and the Middle East.[60] To be sure, a national tanker fleet cannot protect oil importers from the internal security problems endemic to many oil-exporting countries. Civil war, terrorism, and many other factors could prevent supplies from ever reaching Chinese tankers. Yet while the internal instability of supplier countries may be unavoidable, an importer with its own tanker fleet and a blue water navy enjoys greater ability to ensure energy security once the oil leaves the exporting country. Protecting tankers and downstream infrastructure (e.g., refineries and distribution networks) is usually simpler than trying to protect oil fields in distant countries jealous of their sovereignty. Protecting an "upstream" oil or gas field thousands of miles away would entail a large, rapid joint military deployment that is beyond the capability of nearly all oil importers other than the United States. And even if an importer boasted substantial force projection ability, its response would likely come too late to prevent a supply cutoff. It is unclear to what extent some of China's more hawkish and mercantilist analysts have considered these realities.

Tanker Protection Options

Tankers can be protected with escorts and by convoying. Shippers resist convoy operations because it hinders their flexibility and adds costs. Naval officers likewise tend to dislike escort missions, which cede the initiative almost entirely to the enemy. Convoying is also highly asset-intensive, particularly when facing aerial, surface, and subsurface threats. Assuming that two VLCCs per day would be needed to meet Chinese oil demand, the logistics of implementing such a convoy system would overwhelm today's PLAN. A weekly group of fourteen VLCCs would require roundtrip steaming time of thirty-three days from the Persian Gulf to China, plus a two-day turnaround period to take on supplies and cargo. This thirty-five-day cycle, repeated weekly, would likely correspond to a need for more than twenty-five escorting surface warships and support vessels. Logistics ships would be necessary to refuel the escorts on both the inbound and outbound legs of the voyage (since PLAN-escorted VLCCs would be vulnerable to attack when transiting the Indian Ocean after offloading in China). Additional ships would likely be required to perform maintenance and repair on the escorts.[61]

This rough calculation gives a basic idea of the tremendous number of surface warships required to escort convoys. Even if China's navy acquired sufficient surface combatants in the coming years to perform sustained convoy operations, China's leadership would still be forced to choose between escorting tankers and keeping sufficient forces in the main theater of conflict to win the fight that triggered the blockade. Recognizing this reality, a number of Chinese analysts write that it will be some time before China can realistically defend distant energy SLOC.[62]

The second strategy for protecting shipping entails taking the fight to the enemy, attacking his bases, and driving him from the area. A Chinese doctrinal textbook notes that in order to avoid continually fighting at a time and place of the enemy's choosing, protective forces would have to work aggressively and "attack the enemy force immediately after locating it." The authors also emphasize that "covering forces should attack the enemy first in an effort to destroy the attacking enemy before it unfolds or uses weapons."[63] To accomplish these objectives, however, Chinese forces would need to achieve sea and air control at a specific time and place (i.e., where the ships being escorted are at any particular moment), a capability that China has yet to demonstrate far from its shores.

Implications of Further Chinese Naval Development

The pattern of Chinese naval acquisitions in recent years suggests that Beijing is not seeking to directly escort tankers, at least for now. To be sure, China has a growing modern submarine force (including roughly fifty-eight attack submarines, albeit at varying levels of readiness), new land-attack cruise missiles, long-range strike aircraft, and a formidable ballistic-missile force with which it could attack the bases of any country that imposed a blockade or lent its support to the blockading power. China's navy also has approximately seventy-two major surface combatants, fifty medium and heavy amphibious lift vessels, and forty-one coastal missile patrol craft.[64] At present, China is simultaneously building two classes of attack submarine (Yuan and Type 093) and purchasing one (the Kilo) from Russia. These submarines could eventually launch land-attack cruise missiles such as Russia's 300 km range Klub or China's Dong Hai-10, the latter reportedly having been test-fired and designed to strike targets 1,500 km away.[65] These missiles might have a maritime strike mission.[66] Finally, the PLA's 2nd Artillery commands a force of more than nine hundred short- and medium-range ballistic missiles.[67]

Most of the naval platforms that China is currently developing, however, with the exception of its Type 094 SSBNs and Type 071 landing platform docks, seem to have been acquired with a clear focus on a Taiwan contingency, rather than on escorting oil tankers over long ranges. Some of China's more modern ships and aircraft do have the necessary endurance and weapons to project combat power slightly farther, into the South China Sea, and to a limited extent, into parts of the Western Pacific. The PLAN's limited number of oilers, tenders, and other replenishment vessels severely constrains China's long-distance operational capability, however. China's burgeoning shipbuilding industry has the wherewithal to produce large numbers of these, but shipbuilders have so far focused on commercial vessels.

Nevertheless, China's rapidly increasing defense budget (officially $45 billion in 2007[68] and estimated by the U.S. Defense Intelligence Agency to be as high as $85 billion to $125 billion for that same year[69]) may allow for an ambitious building program. In fifteen to twenty years, China could acquire the capability to execute long-distance SLOC protection missions. Already, for instance, China's new J-10, SU 27, J-11, and SU-30 aircraft, and the weapons they can carry, represent a major improvement over their predecessors.

Of course, Chinese forces still must master aerial refueling in order to make these aircraft relevant in a distant SLOC defense campaign. In their studies of Operation El Dorado Canyon (the U.S. attack on Libya in 1986) and other U.S. aerial campaigns, Chinese analysts note that aerial refueling can give tactical aircraft (such as the SU-30 or J-10) strategic strike range.[70]

China is also developing significant missile capabilities that would be useful in a SLOC protection campaign. China's formidable SS-N-22 Sunburn supersonic antiship cruise missile (ASCM) can be fired from its four Russian-made Sovremennyy-class cruisers. Every surface warship launched by China in the past decade (with the possible exception of the new landing platform dock) carries sophisticated, long-range YJ-series ASCMs, which compare well with foreign systems. It is important to recall that a single Chinese-made C-802, which is likely less capable than China's newer ASCMs, nearly sank an Israeli Haanit-class frigate during the summer 2006 war between Israel and Hezbollah.[71] China is also thought to be in the process of developing antiship homing warheads for its ballistic missiles, which would be extraordinarily difficult to defend against.[72]

Surface vessels operating far from their home ports would also require strong organic air defense capabilities. Rapid improvements in air defense and surface warfare are already evident in the PLAN's three most recent classes of surface combatants, all of which mount sophisticated air search and missile guidance radars, and long-ranged vertically launched surface to air missiles (SAMs). China's Luyang II destroyers (hulls 170 and 171) carry the HHQ-9 SAMs, its two Luzhou-class destroyers have a marinized SA-20, and its four or five Jiangkai II frigates under construction in early 2007 have vertical launch cells and phased array and guidance radars that suggest a similar capability.

These measures will gradually enhance China's power projection options. "The long-range SAM systems [that the Luzhou and Luyang II destroyers] possess will provide Chinese surface combatants with an area air defense capability as they operate farther from shore and outside of the protection of land-based air defense assets," states Scott Bray, deputy senior intelligence officer for China in the U.S. Navy's Office of Naval Intelligence. "Under the protection afforded by these advanced area air defense destroyers, which are also equipped with long-range ASCMs, the Chinese Navy can operate combatants such as two recently acquired Sovremennyy II [destroyers]. These long-range engagement and air defense capabilities now being fielded by the PLA(N) give China a significantly improved capacity for operations beyond the littoral in support of SLOC protection."[73]

Improved destroyers and air defenses will not alone afford China SLOC defense capabilities, however. China's navy presently lacks a robust antisubmarine warfare (ASW) capability. As such, PLAN ships engaged in distant SLOC protection would be highly vulnerable to an adversary's attack submarines and mines.[74] Although the PLAN's newer large surface combatants can carry ASW helicopters, most appear to lack modern hull-mounted or towed sonars.[75] There is also little evidence that China is in the process of acquiring truly long-range maritime patrol aircraft, which are essential for ASW missions.

China's growing retaliatory capacity would help to insulate it from coercive pressure short of war. In the event of hostilities, China might be able to deny outside forces access to its maritime periphery, or launch retaliatory attacks against enemy forces in portions of SLOC nearest to China. But while China has made substantial qualitative improvements in its navy over the past decade, thereby avoiding the block obsolescence of several platforms, it does not yet possess the overall force structure to support multiple missions to defend contested SLOC. "At present," the U.S. Department of Defense judged in 2007, "China can neither protect its foreign energy supplies nor the routes on which they travel, including the Straits of Malacca."[76]

Should China develop significant SLOC defense capabilities in coming years, several indicators will be apparent to foreign analysts. First, China would have to purchase or produce a substantial contingent of long-range oilers, tenders, and other replenishment vessels. Such prioritization of naval construction might require the establishment of shipyards dedicated to military ship production. Second, China would have to acquire reliable overseas bases (e.g., in the Indian Ocean). As James Mulvenon has emphasized in his chapter, this would seem to represent a significant departure from Chinese foreign policy post-1949, a central tenet of which has been commitment to forego the permanent basing of military forces in other nations.[77] Third, in order to achieve viable, lethal ASW capabilities, a substantial force of PLAN nuclear attack submarines would need to go on frequent extended deployments. Such a force has proved enormously difficult and expensive for the U.S.S.R., and even the United States, to acquire. In order to increase its power projection capabilities, China might also develop some form of deck aviation (e.g., one or more aircraft or helicopter carriers), or even hospital ships. Finally, to achieve high levels of presence and readiness, China's navy would have to deploy a substantial portion of its forces at all times. To support this increased operational tempo the PLAN would need to develop the ability to conduct sophisticated repairs to ships remotely—either through tenders or overseas repair facilities. This would also require the maturation of advanced levels of doctrine, training, and human capacity, none of which are currently obviously present in China's navy, but all of which are well within the capability of China to develop.[78]

Calling an Opponent's Bluff

Unless China's navy can attain outright naval and air superiority in a given sea zone, carrying oil in Chinese-flagged tankers during wartime might render Beijing *more* vulnerable to interdiction of its energy supply because—at least in theory—foreign navies could easily determine which tankers were bound for China. It might seem, then, that absent a substantial blue water naval capability—which may be decades away—China is making itself a target by constructing a state-controlled, Chinese-flagged tanker fleet.

If so, Beijing's best option might be to rely on private third-party tanker operators, whose deliveries could be effectively stopped only by a close blockade of Chinese ports—in turn exposing the blockading state's naval forces to a wide range of military threats and almost certainly sparking a larger conflict whose repercussions would presumably exceed any likely political gains for that state. Alternatively, reflagging Chinese-owned tankers to Liberia, Panama, or another flag-of-convenience state would force an interdicting navy to go to much greater lengths to identify a tanker's ownership and ultimate destination.

Nonetheless, because of international legal norms, having a Chinese-flagged tanker fleet import oil for the government might indeed help to ensure China's energy security during crises short of war. It is likely not lost on China that embargoes and other forms of economic coercion are a key nonkinetic instrument that major powers may use to pressure a foe. Under international law, a PRC-flagged tanker in government service would enjoy the substantial protection of China's flag. If an outside power interdicted such a vessel, China would have grounds to claim that its sovereignty had been breached sufficiently to threaten its national well-being, thereby justifying a serious armed response. The escalatory barrier created by putting state-flagged vessels into government service would thus deter adversaries from interdicting PRC oil shipments unless hostilities were either imminent or already underway. While legal norms are sometimes disputed, sidestepped, or even ignored in wartime, it is difficult to imagine a scenario short of major war in which an adversary would risk triggering escalatory behavior by Beijing.

PRC-flagged tankers hauling oil for any of the state-controlled Chinese producers may be deemed by some states to meet the criteria for sovereign immune status. During a crisis, moreover, oil carried on Chinese-flagged tankers not already being shipped on behalf of PRC state-owned oil companies could rapidly be resold at sea to any number of PRC government entities, thus creating the necessary legal conditions to assert sovereign immune status for the tanker.[79] Based on *Lloyd's Sea Web* data, thirty-one of the forty-two VLCCs currently on order in Chinese yards for Chinese shipping companies are slated to fly the PRC flag (of the other eleven, five will be Panamanian-flagged and six will fly the Hong Kong S.A.R.'s flag). Figure 5 depicts China's increasing propensity to place its VLCCs, which would be the primary vessels hauling oil through the Indian Ocean and other potentially vulnerable SLOC, under Chinese flag.

Figure 5. PRC Tanker Flagging

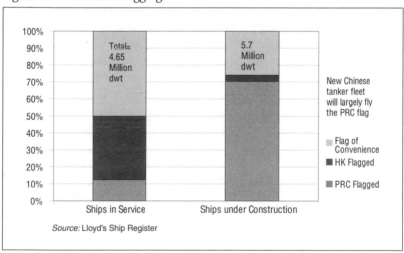

Even without state flagging, normal commercial factors would make a distant oil blockade of China extremely difficult to implement, even during full-scale hostilities. Several factors make interdicting private tankers at sea difficult in practice. The oil shipping sector is highly globalized (e.g., with tankers perhaps owned by a Norwegian company registered in the Bahamas, commanded by a Dutch captain, flagged in Panama, crewed by Pakistanis and Filipinos, carrying oil originating in Saudi Arabia to Japanese buyers).

This national diversity makes it extremely difficult to determine a tanker's ultimate destination.

At any given time, a tanker's bill of lading might not accurately reflect the true end destination of its oil cargo. The oil market is also highly liquid, allowing oil cargoes to be bought and sold at sea. In normal commerce, cargoes may be bought and sold dozens of times while still on the high seas; some may change hands thirty times between time of loading in the Persian Gulf or West Africa and arrival at the final destination in East Asia or Europe. Additionally, supertankers often carry "parceled out" cargoes (i.e., 500,000 barrels may be bound for Singapore, 500,000 barrels for South Korea, and 1,000,000 barrels for Japan or China). Bills of lading can also easily be falsified, a technique regularly used by smugglers, to pass through a distant blockade set up in the Malacca Strait or another chokepoint far from the Chinese coast.[80] Finally, unless the blockading power were willing to risk environmental disaster by disabling or sinking uncooperative tankers, it would likely lack sufficient military assets to board and take control of such ships, as fifty-two oil tankers per day pass through the Malacca Strait alone.[81] Compounding matters, due to China's crucial role in the global economy, blockaders would face major diplomatic pressure to curtail their operation and allow normal trade to resume.

Seeking lower insurance rates is another possible rationale for a state tanker fleet. Under normal operating conditions, hull insurance for a tanker is between 2.5 and 3.75 percent of ship value on an annualized basis. Thus, the operator of a $130 million VLCC can expect to pay $8,900–13,300 per day in insurance costs. However, if insurance firms declare an area a War Risk Exclusion Zone (e.g., in the Persian Gulf), rates can climb to 7.5 to 10 percent of ship value on a *daily* basis, meaning that the same VLCC operator would now have to pay between $8.9 and $13.3 million per day to insure his or her ship while it was in the danger zone. Assuming three days in the Gulf each time the vessel loaded oil, the operator would have to pay from $26.7 to $39.9 million per trip. Even in the best of markets, VLCCs rarely command more than $100,000 per day. Yet to pay off the projected war risk insurance costs, a VLCC making the thirty-three-day trip from the Gulf to East Asia would have to earn more than $1 million per day—an unrealistic sum.

Commercial ship owners would only operate under such conditions if an outside power either paid them such rates or offered insurance and a guaranteed profit payment as part of an oil transport deal. State-owned ships could conceivably self-insure and forego paying insurance premiums in order to maintain continued oil delivery service to the home country. For all these reasons, a domestically flagged tanker fleet makes some strategic sense, at least from Beijing's security-focused perspective.

Security Implications

Not all contingencies threatening Chinese energy security involve an armed conflict. A terrorist attack on a Saudi export terminal that suddenly tightened world oil markets, for example, might be sufficient to trigger a government "call" on state-run tankers.[82] It might prove difficult for Beijing to press PRC-flagged tankers into state service during a crisis, however. Assuming that PRC tanker operators followed normal peacetime operating principles, their VLCCs could be chartered out to shippers in places as far afield as Nigeria, Venezuela, or northwest Europe. Given the distances involved, it might take thirty days or more for these vessels to reach Chinese ports, even if they immediately broke contracts and headed for China.

If it had advance warning, China's central government might notify tanker operators ahead of time, pay contract termination penalties, and preposition state-owned tankers for crisis oil deliveries. However, numerous commercial observers carefully track tanker movements, meaning that even covert Chinese preparations would be noticed quickly. Other major powers would rapidly realize that China was marshalling assets and might interpret such actions as a sign that Beijing anticipated hostilities. Rather than helping to ensure national security, therefore, a decision to call on PRC flagged tankers during times of major tension could well cause other actors to assume the worst—thereby precipitating a more serious crisis.

The security of China's maritime oil transport lies in the inherent difficulties facing any force trying to disrupt it. It would be very difficult to interdict private tankers bound for Chinese ports. The global oil market is highly fungible; ship destinations are unclear because cargoes are often resold at sea; and oil can be transshipped to China through third ports in the region. In addition, the number of tankers transiting key chokepoints would likely far exceed any potential blockading navy's physical ability to take control of uncooperative ships, unless it were willing to accept the diplomatic, environmental, and military consequences of using disabling fire.[83] These factors, in addition to the legal considerations mentioned earlier, explain both Chinese preoccupation with acquiring state-flagged tankers and why during peacetime Beijing can allow Chinese shipping companies to operate them under normal commercial principles.

Conclusion

Anxiety over the security of maritime oil supply is one factor shaping decision making as interested actors promote the development of a large Chinese tanker fleet and Beijing contemplates the construction of a blue water navy. For the foreseeable future, particularly during peacetime, Chinese tanker operators will work almost exclusively within the framework of the existing global tanker market. Circumventing this system by forcing Chinese shippers to serve Chinese oil producers at any cost would be economically unsound. Energy subsidies are a parallel case in point. China already pays its state oil companies billions of dollars in subsidies annually to compensate them for losses they incur by purchasing oil at market prices and selling products made from that oil at government-capped rates within China. Already pressures are mounting for Beijing to reduce these and other energy subsidies, which have recently resulted in supply shortages.[84]

Tanker operations driven by economic opportunity are likely to be more profitable than those driven by state directives. Moreover, commercial deals with foreign tanker operators will tend to further integrate Chinese shipping and shipbuilding firms into the global oil shipping sector. The precedent set by China's national energy companies in emphasizing profit over politics whenever possible (e.g., in equity oil sales to the international market rather than to China) also favors the adoption of a largely commercial approach to tanker fleet operation. Although China has spent billions of dollars on overseas equity oil acquisitions, the flagship state firm CNPC sells a sizeable portion of its equity oil on the international market.[85]

Given the Chinese leadership's current bias toward state-led oil security policies, Beijing likely hopes that Chinese shippers will come to haul a large percentage of China's oil imports. However, the final outcome will likely depend much more heavily on shipping economics than it does on politics. In essence, if a Chinese VLCC working for a Chinese oil company is making $50,000 per day, but could generate $60,000 per day on a different route serving an international oil company, absent substantial incentives or compulsion from China's government, it will choose the more profitable route. China's central government faces an uphill fight in coordinating energy policy in general, let alone oil transportation policy. Indeed, in recent discussions, a well-placed Chinese energy policy expert indicated that the process of establishing an Energy Ministry has been arduous and that the plan could fail.[86]

Chinese state and private companies seek to profit from shipbuilding and tanker operation during peacetime while the government likely believes that it is hedging its bets against future threats to oil shipments by supporting a large tanker buildup. Security concerns are probably shaping Beijing's desire and efforts to have Chinese tankers haul Chinese crude imports. To date, China has been "free riding" on the U.S. Navy's global SLOC security guarantee. Yet China's rising maritime energy interests and naval power could lead it to seek a much more active SLOC security role. A steady and secure supply of oil and other imported resources fuels the economic growth that helps the Chinese Communist Party maintain its hold on power. Thus, anything that disrupts this flow would represent a grave threat to regime survival and Beijing could be expected to react strongly. Over the longer term, as China develops greater international interests, increasing comprehensive national power and confidence vis-à-vis Taiwan's status may finally allow China's navy to cast its strategic sights on blue waters and develop power projection capabilities sufficient to protect Chinese tankers progressively farther afield.

As such, in coming years, China's growing oil and gas import needs, together with the actions Beijing is taking to secure those supplies, have the potential to become a serious international maritime security issue. As the PLAN continues to modernize, outside observers should bear in mind that nations' intentions and desires often grow in parallel with expanding capabilities. Energy and resource supply security may thus become a powerful "beyond Taiwan" driver of Chinese blue water naval development.

As the next Five Year Plan takes shape, China's leaders will make crucial decisions concerning the extent to which China's navy should expand its power projection ability, a factor closely related to China's energy strategy. These decisions, in turn, will shape strategic perceptions, doctrine, and force structures for the next ten to twenty years. Identifying and analyzing the strategic rationale behind China's apparent intent to create a state-led tanker fleet expansion can help inform U.S. strategy and policies concerning China, particularly as Washington clarifies and implements its own maritime strategy.

Washington should use this window of opportunity to make the case to Beijing that, for the time being, the world oil market is a far better guarantor of energy security than a state tanker fleet protected by a blue water navy. While these are clearly sensitive topics in which both sides have great strategic stakes, judicious use of U.S.–China navy-to-navy exchanges and bilateral consultations may help the world's two largest energy consumers achieve sustainable, if competitive, coexistence.

Notes

An earlier version of this essay appeared as Andrew Erickson and Gabriel Collins, "Beijing's Energy Security Strategy: The Significance of a Chinese State-Owned Tanker Fleet," *Orbis* 51, no. 4 (2007): 665–84.

1. The data in this paragraph are derived primarily from the U.S. Department of Energy's Energy Information Administration, http://www.eia.doe.gov/emeu/cabs/ China/Background.html; and Sinopec's 2006 Annual Chinese Oil Import and Export Situation Analysis.

2. The U.S. currently imports between 10–12 million bpd of oil and products.

3. Office of the Secretary of Defense, *Military Power of the People's Republic of China 2007*, Annual Report to Congress, 8.

4. 乔恩言 [Qiao Enyan], "石油企业在国家石油安全战略中的作用" ["Petroleum Enterprises and Their Use in National Oil Security Strategy"], 现代化工 [*Modern Chemical Industry*] (2005): S1, 9–12.

5. By comparison, Japanese tankers can haul over 90 percent of the energy consumed by that nation.

6. Erica Downs, *Brookings Foreign Policy Studies Energy Security Series: China* (Washington, D.C.: Brookings Institution, 2006), 6.

7. "China Must Carry 60% of Seaborne Oil Imports on Local Shippers," *Xinhua Financial Network News*, 14 June 2007; "More Oil Tankers Taking to the Sea," *China Daily*, 14 June 2007, http://www.chinadaily.com.cn.

8. "More Oil Tankers Taking to the Sea."

9. "Oil Security at Sea," *China Daily*, Opinion/Commentary, 14 June 2007, p. 10, available at www.chinadaily.com.cn/opinion/2007-06/14/content_894050.htm.

10. Interviews in Beijing, December 2006; NDRC website, www.eri.org.cn.

11. These include the Naval Research Institute in Beijing, the Command and Staff College in Nanjing, and the Naval Submarine Academy in Qingdao.

12. Authors' interviews with Chinese scholars, 2007.

13. Japan and Vietnam also appear highly interested in creating state flagged tanker fleets to protect oil shipments.

14. 徐起 [Xu Qi], "21世纪初海上地缘战略与中国海军的发展" ["Maritime Geostrategy and the Development of the Chinese Navy in the Early 21st Century"], 中国军事科学 [*China Military Science*] 17, no. 4 (2004): 75‑81. Translation by Andrew Erickson and Lyle Goldstein published in *Naval War College Review* 59, no. 4 (Autumn 2006): 46–67.

15. Authors' discussion with Chinese energy expert, April 2007.

16. "World Briefing/Asia: China: Hu Calls For Strong Navy," *New York Times*, 29 December 2006; David Lague, "China Airs Ambitions to Beef Up Naval Power," *International Herald Tribune*, 28 December 2006, http://www.iht.com/bin/print. php?id=4038159.

17. *China's National Defense in 2006*, Information Office of the State Council, People's Republic of China, 29 December 2006, http://www.fas.org/nuke/guide/china/doctrine/wp2006.html.

18. Zhang Wenmu, "Sea Power and China's Strategic Choices," *China Security* (Summer 2006): 17–31; Xu Qi, "Maritime Geostrategy."

19. 李杰 [Li Jie], "石油，中国需求与海道安全" ["China's Oil Demand and Sea Lane Security"], 舰船知识 [*Naval & Merchant Ships*] (September 2004): 10–13.

20. Wu Lei and Shen Qinyu, "Will China Go to War over Oil?" *Far Eastern Economic Review* 169, no. 3 (April 2006): 38.

21. Data derived from LexisNexis.org.

22. Li Fangchao, "Russia-China Oil Link Nears Completion," *China Daily*, 15 June 2007, http://www.chinadaily.com.cn/china/2007-06/15/content_894794.htm.

23. "China's Newly Found Oilfield Boasts Reserve of 7.35 bln Barrels," Xinhua, 3 May 2007, www.chinaview.cn.

24. 杨明杰 [Yang Mingjie, ed.], 海上通道安全与国际合作 [*Sea Lane Security and International Cooperation*] (北京：时事出版社) [Beijing: Current Affairs Publishing House, 2005], 123.

25. Interview, Beijing, June 2007.

26. 罗萍 [Luo Ping], "国油国运: 中国能源的安全保障线" ["National Oil, Nationally Hauled: China's Energy Security Lifeline"], 中国远洋航务公告 [*Maritime China*] (February 2005): 38–40.

27. Ibid.

28. "Shanghai Shipbuilding Reaches for New Heights," *China Daily*, 6 September 2003.

29. "China's Shipbuilding Industry Booms," Xinhua Economic News Service, 13 June 2006.

30. Telephone interview with Department of Defense official, March 2007.

31. 李小军 [Li Shaojun], "论海权对中国石油安全的影响" ["Mahan's *Sea Power* and Its Influence on China's Oil Security Strategy"], 国际论坛 [*International Forum*] 6, no. 4 (July 2004): 16–20.

32. 陈安刚, 武明 [Chen Angang and Wu Ming], "马六甲海峡: 美国凯觎的战略前哨" ["Malacca: America's Coveted Strategic Outpost"], 现代舰船 [*Modern Ships*] (December 2004): 11–14.

33. 杨明杰 [Yang Mingjie, ed.], 海上通道安全 [*Sea Lane Security*], 106.

34. Interview, Beijing, June 2007.

35. "China Urged to Beef Up Ocean Oil Shipping," *Asia Pulse*, 15 March 2006, available at http://www.lexisnexis.com.

36. Katherine Espina, "Sinopec Trawls for More Supertankers," *International Herald Tribune*, 30 April 2007.

37. Much of the global shipping IPO activity of the past two years has occurred in the dry-bulk sector, but strong tanker markets have driven a number of energy shipping offerings outside Asia as well.

38. Interview, Beijing, June 2007.

39. Downs, "The Chinese Energy Security Debate," *China Quarterly* 177 (March 2004): 21–41.

40. Downs, *Brookings Foreign Policy Studies*, 38–39.

41. Ren Xiaoyu, "Analysis and Opinions on How PetroChina Markets Its Equity Oil," *China Oil and Gas*, no. 4 (2002): 50–52.

42. Downs, *Brookings Foreign Policy Studies*, 44.

43. Steven Lewis, Baker Institute for Public Policy, Rice University, "Reform in Chinese Energy Policy: The NOCs at Home and Abroad" (presentation at U.S. Naval War College, 12 February 2007.)

44. Joseph Kahn, "Profit or Politics? Chief of CNOOC Faces a Delicate Balancing Act," *New York Times*, 7 July 2005.

45. China Merchants Group website, http://www.cmhk.com/en/management/default. htm.

46. 杨明杰 [Yang Mingjie, ed.], 海上通道安全 [*Sea Lane Security*], 123.

47. 郑长兴 [Zheng Changxing], "2005年中国船舶工业发展特点" ["2005 China Shipbuilding Industry Development Characteristics"], 机电设备 [*Mechanical & Electrical Equipment*] 2 (2006): 33–34.

48. Qin Xiao, "Energy Transportation Issues in China's Energy Security Strategy," 中国能源 [*China Energy*] 26, no. 7 (July 2004): 4–7.

49. 张凯 [Zhang Kai], "江苏船舶工业的盛会" ["A Life and Death Test for Jiangsu's Shipbuilding Industry"], 机电设备 [*Mechanical & Electrical Equipment*] 3 (2006): 16; and "Current Capacity, Future Outlook for Japanese, Chinese Shipbuilding Industries," *Sekai no Kansen*, 9 March 2006, OSC# FEA2006030902654.

50. "Major Chinese Operator Calls for Maritime Oil Transport Development," BBC, 10 March 2006, http://www.lexisnexis.com.

51. Authors' interview with representatives of Western shipowners currently building tankers in Chinese yards, March 2007.

52. Ibid.

53. Ibid. The ship buyers prefer Korean or Japanese parts if they are more reliable. Chinese shipyards want to sell their own parts regardless of their quality.

54. The tanker industry has suffered from dramatic swings in profitability, with times of high profits (and little or no overcapacity) leading to massive shipbuilding splurges which quickly lead to subsequent overcapacity and industry consolidation and bankruptcies.

55. 杨明杰 [Yang Mingjie, ed.], 海上通道安全 [*Sea Lane Security*], 124.

56. Ibid., 123.

57. "By Year End 2010, the Length of China's Oil Pipeline Network Will Grow by 25,000 KM," *Oil & Capital*, 26 February 2007, www.oilcapital.ru/print/news/2007/02/261024_105757.shtml.

58. See, for example, 查道炯 [Zha Daojiong], "三问中国未来石油安全" ["Three Questions about China's Future Oil Security"], 中国石油企业 [*China Petroleum Enterprise*] 6 (2006): 116–19,

59. Zhang Wenmu, "中国的能源安全与可行战略" ["China's Energy Security and Policy Choices"], 税务研究 [*Taxation Research Journal*] 10 (2005): 11–16.

60. Qin Xiao, "Energy Transportation Issues in China's Energy Security Strategy," 中国能源 [*China Energy*] 26, no. 7 (2004): 5.

61. For further explanation, see the chapter by Collins and Murray, part III this volume.

62. 杨明杰 [Yang Mingjie, ed.], 海上通道安全 [*Sea Lane Security*], 119.

63. Wang Houqing and Zhang Xingye, eds., *The Science of Campaigns* (Beijing: National Defense University Press, 2000), 304.

64. Office of the Secretary of Defense, *Military Power*, 3.

65. Robert Hewson, "Chinese Air-Launched Cruise Missile Emerges from Shadows," *Jane's Defence Weekly*, 31 January 2007, http://www8.janes.com; Wendell Minnick, "China Tests New Land-Attack Cruise Missile," *Jane's Missiles & Rockets*, 21 September 2004, http://www.janes.com/defence/news/jmr/jmr040921_1_n.shtml.

66. See, for example, 王伟 [Wang Wei], "战术弹道导弹对中国海洋战略体系的影响" ["The Effect of Tactical Ballistic Missiles on the Maritime Strategy System of China"], 舰载武器 [*Shipborne Weapons*], no. 84 (August 2006) 12–15.

67. This section draws heavily on Erickson's testimony on the "PLA Modernization in Traditional Warfare Capabilities" panel, "China's Military Modernization and its Impact on the United States and the Asia-Pacific" hearing, U.S.–China Economic and Security Review Commission, Washington, D.C., 29 March 2007, http://www.uscc.gov/hearings/2007hearings/transcripts/mar_29_30/mar_29_30_07_trans.pdf, 72–78. William Murray contributed extensively to the preparation of this testimony.

68. "A Fair Exposition of China's Defense Budget (Opinion)," *People's Daily*, 6 March 2007, http://english.people.com.cn/200703/06/eng20070306_354817.html.

69. Office of the Secretary of Defense, *Military Power*, 25.

70. 凌朝 [Ling Chao], "伊尔-78飞向中国" ["The IL-78 Comes to China"], 兵工科技 [*Ordnance Industry Science & Technology*], no. 10 (2005) 19–23.

71. See Matt Hilburn, "Hezbollah's Missile Surprise," *Seapower* 49, no. 9 (September 2006): 10–12.

72. Eric A. McVadon, "China's Maturing Navy," *Naval War College Review* 59, no. 2 (Spring 2006): 90–107, http://www.nwc.navy.mil/press/review/documents/NWCRSP06.pdf. See also 王慧 [Wang Hui], "攻击航母的武器装备" ["Anti-carrier Weapons Systems"], 当代海军 [*Modern Navy*] (October 2004): 35.

73. Scott Bray, "Seapower Questions on the Chinese Submarine Force," U.S. Navy, Office of Naval Intelligence, 20 December 2006, http://www.fas.org/nuke/guide/china/ONI2006.pdf.

74. Andrew Erickson, Lyle Goldstein, and William Murray, "China's 'Undersea Sentries': Sea Mines Constitute Lead Element of PLA Navy's ASW," *Undersea Warfare* 9 (Winter 2007): 10–15.

75. China's Jiangkai II frigates have bell mouths on their sterns from which towed arrays might be deployed.

76. Office of the Secretary of Defense, *Military Power*, 8.

77. See, for example, Sun Shangwu, "PLA 'Not Involved in Arms Race'," *China Daily*, 2 February 2007, http://www.chinadaily.cn/china/2007-02/02/content_799222.htm; "'PLA Making Great Efforts to be More Open'," interview of Lieutenant-General Zhang Qinsheng, deputy chief of the General Staff of the People's Liberation Army (PLA) by Sun Shangwu, *China Daily*, 2 February 2007, p. 12, http://www.chinadaily.cn/cndy/2007-02/02/content_799207.htm.

78. The authors thank William Murray for his assistance with this paragraph.

79. See High Seas Convention (1958), Article 8; United Nations Convention on the Law of the Sea (1982), Articles 32, 58(2), 95 and 236; A. Ralph Thomas and James C. Duncan, "Annotated Supplement to the *Commander's Handbook on the Law of Naval Operations*," *U.S. Naval War College International Law Studies* 73 (1999): 110, 221, 259, 390; Chairman of the Joint Chief of Staff Instruction 3121.01B (January 2005); Joel Doolin, "The Proliferation Security Initiative: Cornerstone of a New International Norm," *Naval War College Review* 59, no. 2 (Spring 2006), 29–57. The authors thank Professor Peter Dutton for his extensive guidance concerning maritime legal issues.

80. For further information, see this volume's chapter by Murray and Collins.

81. 岳来群 [Yue Laiqun], "突破马六甲困局" ["Finding a Way Out of the Malacca Dilemma"], 中国石油企业 [*China Petroleum Enterprise*], (April 2006): 6.

82. If global oil supplies suddenly tightened due to a major crisis in the Middle East and a bidding contest for remaining oil supplies ensued, it is highly conceivable that China would want its oil cargoes carried on PRC-flagged tankers.

83. For further explanation, see the chapter by Murray and Collins.

84. Shai Oster and Patrick Barta, "China Raises Price of Fuel Amid Shortage," *Asian Wall Street Journal,* 1 November 2007, pp. 1, 32.

85. Gary Dirks, "Energy Security: China and the World," (speech at "International Symposium on Energy Security: China and the World," Beijing, China, 24 May 2006).

86. Interview, April 2007.

PART II

China's Global Energy Access

James R. Holmes and Toshi Yoshihara

China's Naval Ambitions in the Indian Ocean

THE CHAPTER ARGUES THAT AN INCREASINGLY sea power–minded China will neither shelter passively in coastal waters nor throw itself into competition with the United States in the Pacific Ocean. Rather, Beijing will direct its energies toward South and Southeast Asia, where supplies of oil, natural gas, and other commodities critical to China's economic development must pass. There China will encounter an equally sea power–minded India that enjoys marked geostrategic advantages. Beijing will likely content itself with "soft power" diplomacy in these regions until it can settle the dispute with Taiwan, thereby freeing up resources for maritime endeavors farther from China's coasts.

What Kind of Sea Power?

That China has turned its attention and energies to the seas has become a staple of Western commentary on East Asian international relations. Indeed, China is pursuing sea power—measured by the Mahanian indices of commerce, bases, and ships—and it is building up a powerful navy with dispatch. What kind of sea power will China become? Will Beijing pursue a purely defensive naval strategy, sheltering within its coastal waters, as many prognoses maintain? Or will its massive naval buildup lead to competition for supremacy in the broad Pacific, as other equally capable analysts predict? The answer offered here: neither. Once it secures the East, Yellow, and South China seas to its satisfaction, Beijing will direct its nautical energies not eastward but toward the south and southwest, where its interests in energy security and economic development lie. Chinese officials have already made concerted efforts at soft power diplomacy in regions adjoining vital sea lines of communication (SLOC). They have reached out to countries throughout Southeast and South Asia, and their efforts have yielded a fair measure of success.

While its interests may prompt China to attempt to amass hard naval power in these regions, it is worth pointing out that (a) capabilities will not match Chinese intentions anytime soon; (b) Chinese naval ambitions in the Indian Ocean region will run afoul of those of India, another rising great power operating far closer to home; and (c) whatever its leanings in the abstract, Beijing must tend to matters in East Asia before it can apply its energies to building up naval forces able to vie for supremacy in the Indian Ocean region.

China's Strategic Interests in the Indian Ocean

The paramount concern animating Chinese interests in the Indian Ocean is energy security, an imperative that has been widely debated in media and academic studies. The nation's energy use has more than doubled over the past two decades, exacerbating its dependency on energy imports.[1] In 2003, China surpassed Japan as a consumer of petroleum, moving into second place behind the United States.[2] That same year, foreign supplies accounted for more than 30 percent of total Chinese oil consumption, prompting fears in Beijing that any disruption to energy shipments would check the nation's economic development.[3] News reports documenting nationwide power outages and projecting severe oil shortages in the coming decades have given rise to fears that China will fail to manage its economic transition.[4]

Longer-term projections suggest that this energy crunch will persist. U.S. government analysts forecast that Chinese oil demand will at least double over the next two decades.[5] While estimates from nongovernmental analysts vary significantly, most agree that Chinese oil demand will double the 2000 figure by 2020.[6] In 2003, moreover, the U.S. Energy Information Administration predicted that foreign supplies would account for 75 percent of Chinese demand by 2020.[7] The U.S. National Intelligence Council projected that Chinese oil consumption would have to increase by 150 percent by 2020 to sustain a healthy rate of economic expansion. If so, Chinese demand for oil will nearly equal the U.S. demand forecast for that year.[8]

This seemingly insatiable appetite for energy resources has brought tremendous domestic political pressure on Beijing to ensure an uninterrupted flow of energy. Chinese officials have sought out supplies of oil and gas as far away as the Persian Gulf and the Horn of Africa. Energy, then, has compelled Beijing to cast anxious eyes on the SLOC. The security of the waterways stretching from China's coastlines to the Indian Ocean has taken on special policy importance for Beijing.

Raw geopolitics is also at work. While Sino–Indian relations have seen steady improvement since the late 1990s, geopolitical calculations have long furnished a backdrop to bilateral ties. India is the dominant power in the Indian Ocean region, and, given its great-power potential, it could very well rise to become a peer competitor of China over the long term.[9] Given these dynamics, any Chinese attempt to control events in India's geographic vicinity would doubtless meet with Indian countermeasures. The Chinese recognize that India's energy needs, which resemble China's own, could prod New Delhi into zero-sum competition at sea.[10]

Chinese thinkers, moreover, voice special concerns about India's geopolitical ambitions beyond the Indian Ocean. According to the Chinese scholar Hou Songlin, India's "Look East Policy" toward the Association of Southeast Asian Nations (ASEAN) carries maritime implications. While New Delhi is focusing on economic cooperation for now, declares Hou, the second stage of its eastern-oriented strategy will expand into the political and security realms. Indeed, he prophesies that Indo–ASEAN cooperation on counterterrorism, maritime security, and transnational crime fighting represents part of an Indian "grand strategy to control the Indian Ocean, particularly the Malacca Strait."[11]

Another Chinese observer, Zhu Fenggang, postulates that Indian maritime strategy envisions aggressively extending naval missions from coastal regions to blue water expanses. For Zhu, New Delhi's objectives include, in ascending order: (1) homeland defense, coastal defense, and control over maritime economic zones; (2) control of the waters adjacent to neighboring littoral states; (3) unfettered control of the seas stretching from the Hormuz Strait to the Malacca Strait in peacetime, and the capacity to blockade these chokepoints effectively in wartime; and (4) the construction of a balanced oceangoing fleet able to project power into the Atlantic Ocean by way of the

Cape of Good Hope and into the Pacific by way of the South China Sea.[12] If so, the latter stages of Indian naval development will plainly encroach upon China's traditional sphere of influence in general and its energy security interests in particular.

The Chinese have also devoted substantial attention to the security dilemma posed by the U.S. Navy's dominance of the high seas stretching from the Persian Gulf to the Indian Ocean to the South China Sea. They worry, understandably, that American naval prowess will hold China's sea-dependent economy hostage in times of crisis. In particular, the Malacca Strait, the maritime portal for virtually all of China's Persian Gulf oil, preoccupies Chinese thinking.[13] In the view of Shi Hongtao: "From the perspective of international strategy, the Straits of Malacca is without question a crucial sea route that will enable the United States to seize geopolitical superiority, restrict the rise of major powers, and control the flow of the world's energy. . . . It is no exaggeration to say that whoever controls the Strait of Malacca will also have a stranglehold on the energy route of China. Excessive reliance on this strait has brought an important potential threat to China's energy security."[14]

Sounding a similar note, Zhang Yuncheng argues that "excessive reliance of China's oil on the Malacca Strait means that China's energy security is facing a 'Malacca predicament,' that is, if some accident occurs or if the strait is blockaded by foreign powers, China will be facing [a] tremendous energy security problem."[15] Zhang no doubt has the United States in mind as the foreign power most likely to interdict shipping in or along the approaches to the Malacca Strait. Zhu Fenggang warns explicitly that the United States and Japan might jointly seal off the Strait as a coercive strategy against China.[16]

The Indian Ocean is plainly one maritime expanse in which America might hypothetically interrupt Chinese oil supplies. An editorial in *Ming Pao* portrays recent U.S. overtures toward India as part of a diplomatic strategy animated by the calculation that "whichever country controls the Indian Ocean controls East Asia."[17] As the editors observe, "Oil is shipped from the Gulf via the Indian Ocean and the Straits of Malacca to China, Korea, and Japan. If another [power] holds the lifeline, the three oil-importing countries will suffer severe blows. Because [the U.S.] strategy is to hold sway over the 'oil route,' the U.S. has in recent years showered attentions on India, Vietnam, and Singapore, all of which lie on that route."[18]

Some Chinese strategists consider the Indian Ocean an arena in which the United States will strive to contain Beijing's broader aspirations. They appraise Washington's military realignment in the Asia-Pacific region in stark geopolitical terms. Applying the "defense perimeter of the Pacific" logic elaborated by Secretary of State Dean Acheson in the early Cold War, they see their nation enclosed by concentric, layered island chains. The United States and its allies can "encircle China," "squeez[e] China's strategic space," or "blockade the Asian mainland (China in particular)" from island strongholds where powerful naval expeditionary forces are based.[19]

Analysts who take such a view conceive of the island chains in various ways. Strikingly, some of them include Diego Garcia, a key U.S. military base in the Indian Ocean, as an element in these geostrategic belts enveloping China's coasts. Writing in *Guofang Bao*, Jiang Hong and Wei Yuejiang depict the first island chain—normally thought of as originating in Japan to the north and terminating in the Philippines or Southeast Asia to the south—as extending all the way through the Indonesian archipelago to Diego Garcia in a single, sweeping arc.[20] In their conception, the second island chain runs through Guam—another forward redoubt for U.S. forces—ending at Australia. Another observer, He Yijian, explicitly links strategic bombers based on Guam to potential contingencies in the western Pacific—particularly contingencies related to Taiwan.[21] Yet another commentator, Li Xuanliang, sees Guam and Diego Garcia as an interactive basing dyad that enables the Pentagon to shift forces nimbly from Northeast Asia to theaters as remote as Africa and back.[22]

Clearly, then, China faces a daunting array of potential challenges in the Indian Ocean. Yet it is important to emphasize that, for now, these dilemmas remain largely in the realm of abstract speculation. First, the Chinese recognize that a steady flow of energy resources is an international public good and that everyone would suffer should this public good be interrupted. Only in extreme circumstances such as a shooting war over Taiwan would the United States resort to a naval blockade—even assuming it could make good on a blockade.[23] Second, China is superior to India across most indices of national power, allowing Beijing to exert pressure to counter New Delhi's nautical ambitions. The recent Sino–Indian rapprochement, furthermore, promises to temper competitive forces between the two resurgent powers. Third, although Chinese commentators routinely condemn U.S. observers for promoting a "China threat theory," they are prone to hype Washington's strategic intentions toward Beijing. In effect they promote an "America threat theory" of their own. How real this threat is remains to be seen.

Soft-Power Response to the Indian Ocean Imperative

China's actual and rhetorical responses to its energy vulnerabilities and to its great-power relations with India and the United States in the Indian Ocean suggest that Beijing is crafting a sophisticated, long-term strategy aimed in part at securing its maritime position.

First, Beijing has carefully choreographed its diplomacy in the region to support the leadership's objectives. Intriguingly, Chinese diplomacy in and around the Indian Ocean region has tapped an obscure figure (at least in the West) from Chinese maritime history. Zheng He, the Ming Dynasty's "eunuch admiral," commanded seven voyages of trade and discovery in Southeast and South Asian waters (1405–33). Beijing has woven Zheng and the expeditions of his "treasure fleet"—named after the silks, porcelains, and other valuables it carried to trade with foreign peoples—into an intricate, sophisticated diplomacy depicting the rise of Chinese maritime power as a new phase in a benign regional dominance that had its origins six centuries ago. Beijing has directed much of this charm offensive at maritime nations throughout Southeast and South Asia, where resource-laden Chinese vessels ply the same waterways once traversed by the Ming treasure fleet.

Zheng He helps Beijing apply its soft power at sea, in large part by letting Chinese diplomats mold expectations about how the nation will conduct its naval affairs. This eases worries aroused by its ambitious naval buildup and in the process reduces fellow Asian sea powers' propensity to band together against Chinese naval pretensions. Several themes pervade China's maritime diplomacy. First, Chinese officials and commentators invoke the treasure fleet's voyages to make a geopolitical point, reminding their countrymen and foreign governments that China boasts a proud tradition as a seafaring power despite its traditional landward orientation. Under the Dragon Throne's tributary system, foreign sovereigns throughout Southeast Asia and the Indian Ocean littoral once acknowledged Chinese suzerainty. Beijing plays up the beneficent characteristics of the tributary system, declaring that China will inevitably follow the Ming path to dominant yet self-denying sea power.

And China's ancient mariner allows Beijing to upstage the West, advancing its aim of regional preeminence. On a recent trip to Europe, Premier Wen Jiabao reminded audiences that the Chinese seaman had "sailed abroad earlier than Christopher Columbus," in vessels larger than and technologically superior to the backward fleets put to sea in fifteenth century Europe.[24] In 2003, during President Hu Jintao's historic state visit to Australia—a visit that won media plaudits, in contrast to the tepid reception afforded President

George W. Bush shortly before—the Chinese leader cast Zheng He's expeditions as a historical basis for the Sino–Australian relationship. In a speech to parliament, he declared, "The Chinese people have all along cherished amicable feelings about the Australian people. Back in the 1420s, the expeditionary fleets of China's Ming Dynasty reached Australian shores. For centuries, the Chinese sailed across vast seas and settled down in what they called Southern Land, or today's Australia. They brought Chinese culture to this land and lived harmoniously with the local people, contributing their proud share to Australia's economy, society and its thriving pluralistic culture."[25]

Hu's claims that Chinese mariners reached Australia and settled there during the Ming Dynasty were dubious, but his overall message was indisputable: China's power and presence in maritime Asia far predate those of Europeans. His statement also indirectly justified seagoing endeavors far beyond China's shores, thereby helping satisfy the Chinese populace's penchant for nationalism—a critical goal for Beijing as the appeal of communism dissipates, leaving little to bind the Chinese people together as a nation.

Second, to support Beijing's claim that it is pursuing a "peaceful rise" to great-power status, Chinese spokesmen accentuate the predominantly peaceful nature of Zheng He's endeavors.[26] This helps assuage fears in Asian capitals of China's naval buildup, which in short order has produced a leap in combat power. "The essence of Zheng's voyages does not lie in how strong the Chinese navy once was," declared Xu Zuyuan, China's vice minister for communications, "but in that China adhere[d] to peaceful diplomacy when it was a big power. . . . Zheng He's seven voyages to the West [explain] why a peaceful emergence is the *inevitable outcome* of the development of Chinese history"[27] (emphasis added). Chinese officials intimate that, had the Ming Dynasty not outlawed maritime pursuits after Zheng He's final voyage, Asian history would have taken a different—and presumably more humane—course under Chinese dominance.[28]

Third, and closely related, Chinese officials contrast Zheng He's expeditions of commerce and discovery with "Western geostrategic theory," which is purportedly "rooted in aggressive and expansionist goals" and manifests itself in imperial conquest and exploitation.[29] Chinese power, they suggest, benefits all peoples in the region. Declared Premier Wen while visiting the United States, Zheng "brought silk, tea and the Chinese culture" to foreign peoples, "but not one inch of land was occupied."[30] Guo Chongli, China's ambassador to Kenya, proclaimed, "Zheng He's fleet [was] large. . . . But his voyages were not for looting resources"—code for imperialism—"but for friendship. In trade with foreign countries, he gave much more than he took," fostering "understanding, friendship and trade relation[s] between China's Ming Dynasty and foreign countries in southeast Asia, west Asia and east Africa."[31]

The overt message to countries uneasy at Chinese ambitions: despite China's ascendancy in Asia, it can be counted on to refrain from territorial conquest or military domination. The implied message: Chinese mastery of the seas is preferable to that of the United States, the self-appointed guarantor of the Asian sea lanes.

In short, Beijing has used Zheng He to fashion a maritime diplomacy that bestows legitimacy on China's naval aspirations in Southeast and South Asia, mollifying littoral nations skeptical of Chinese pretensions; undercuts America's claim to rule the waves in the region; and appeases Chinese nationalism, thereby helping the communist regime maintain its rule. This represents an impressive use of soft power.

What kind of tangible dividends and payoffs this type of diplomacy would yield should China enter the arena more assertively nonetheless remains unclear. A preliminary appraisal of the strategic effects of Chinese diplomacy nevertheless provides a helpful analytical guide for the future. To date, most of the literature has focused primarily on Chinese efforts at developing soft power through bilateral and multilateral diplomacy and economic inducements.[32] In other words, analysts have riveted their attention on the supply side of Chinese soft power, paying less attention to the reactions this form of outreach has elicited from target audiences. Only a few studies have sought to gauge tangible regional reactions to China's charm offensive. Early indications conveyed in these studies suggest that China's civilizational and historical appeal in Southeast and South Asia is indeed enjoying a renaissance.[33]

Yet there is ample reason to remain somewhat skeptical about these findings. First, linking the effects of soft power to concrete policy outcomes is an inherently hazardous methodological task. The ability of soft power to shape behavior is based largely on influencing perceptions and impressions, which can be vague or fleeting. Attraction to a nation or susceptibility to its charm is particularly difficult to measure. As such, existing studies rely on ephemeral and indirect benchmarks, such as opinion polls, the popularity of the Chinese language with foreigners, and the spread of Chinese educational institutions, as evidence that Chinese actions and identity have broad appeal.[34]

Second, even if such indicators validate Chinese popularity, they may not accurately convey the strategic calculus of the weaker states in Southeast and South Asia. In fact, current scholarship suggests that China's neighbors have adopted sophisticated diplomatic and military strategies that defy notions of a linear progression toward geopolitical alignment with major players in the region, especially China, the United States, and India. The ASEAN states, for example, have adroitly pursued strategic hedges designed to preclude the need to choose sides and to diminish the zero-sum nature of great-power competition in their region.[35]

In this broader geostrategic context, it is unclear what lasting effects Beijing's Zheng He narrative will engender, either in Southeast Asia or beyond. At the very least, further research will be required to accurately determine the relationship between Chinese diplomacy and regional governments' policy responses to Beijing's overtures.

China Seeks Indian Ocean Footholds

Rather than await empirical proof that its soft-power strategy is working, Beijing is pressing ahead. Securing beachheads in the Indian Ocean basin represents a precursor to a more vigorous future strategy in the region. China has cultivated close relationships with littoral states that are likely to look favorably on—or, at any rate, refrain from objecting to—a Chinese naval presence in their vicinity. Chinese efforts to negotiate basing rights have earned the moniker "string of pearls" in the United States.[36] In general, this term refers to bases and seaports scattered along the sea routes linking the Middle East with coastal China, augmented by diplomatic ties with important states in these regions. Interestingly, the notion of a string of pearls swiftly took on an aura of legitimacy. Analysts and officials incorporated it into everyday discourse, both in the United States and abroad.[37] It has become common parlance, for instance, among Indian sea-power analysts.[38] But the term is based more on inferences U.S. observers have drawn from Chinese activities in the region than on a coherent national strategy codified in Chinese doctrine, strategic commentary, or official statements.

In any event, the string-of-pearls concept does help to explain China's pattern of behavior in the Indian Ocean region. Beijing could leverage its informal strategic alliances with Myanmar and Pakistan, two countries that have granted basing rights, to counterbalance U.S. power, check India's rise, and monitor maritime activities carried on by these maritime competitors.[39] Some of these states also provide alternative routes that bypass the chokepoint at Malacca. Chinese strategists have urged Beijing to build oil pipelines through Myanmar and Pakistan. The more ambitious among them advocate digging a canal across Thailand's Kra Isthmus. While the political merits, technical feasibility, and cost-effectiveness of these various proposals remain dubious, the level of interest paid to them suggests an acute sensitivity on Beijing's part to the nation's energy security dilemma. China, in short, is gradually laying the foundations of a strategic maritime infrastructure that would enhance both its economic prospects and its military access to the Indian Ocean.

To gauge the near-term effectiveness of these efforts, it is worth examining one of Beijing's best-known "pearls." China has invested heavily in the construction of the port facility in Gwadar, in western Pakistan. Pakistani officials involved in the project trumpet its geostrategic significance.[40] Premier Wen Jiabao signaled the importance Beijing attaches to the facility by personally attending the ceremony marking the successful conclusion of the project's first phase. Strategically located near the Strait of Hormuz, the new seaport represents both a new economic gateway and a military opportunity for Beijing:

- In terms of energy security, Gwadar could act as a strategic hedge, giving Beijing a work-around should the United States blockade the Strait of Malacca during a Taiwan contingency or some other Sino–U.S. clash. Persian Gulf oil could be offloaded at the port and transported (or pumped, should plans for a pipeline bear fruit) overland to China.[41] Beijing might find the high price of such an alternative worth paying for assured energy supplies in the face of a U.S.-imposed embargo.

- From a military standpoint, Gwadar already offers a useful installation for monitoring commercial and military traffic through the critical chokepoint at Hormuz. Over the longer term, should China develop a navy robust enough to project credible power into the Indian Ocean, then the port promises to allow Beijing—for the first time—to directly shape events in the Persian Gulf.

All of that said, Gwadar by no means represents a trump card for China, either in energy security or military terms. Consider the seaport's strategic attributes, delineated by Alfred Thayer Mahan as position, strength (or defensibility), and resources.[42] Gwadar's geographic position near the Strait of Hormuz evidently excited Beijing's attention, but geography is not everything:

- First, Beijing's effort to outflank U.S. naval operations using an overland route might itself be outflanked in wartime. Should Washington direct the U.S. Navy to interdict Chinese petroleum shipments, it would probably do so within the confines of the Persian Gulf, where tracking and intercepting shipments bound for Hormuz is a fairly simple matter for U.S. warships and aircraft. Cargoes bound for Gwadar, and thence for transshipment to China, might never reach the Pakistani seaport in the first place. This would severely degrade its strategic value to Beijing.

- Second, the port is not readily defensible. The terminals occupy a small peninsula connected to the mainland by a narrow spit of land, around half a mile across at its narrowest point. Slowing or halting the flow of oil and other cargo out of the port facility should present few problems for a superior naval power—a vulnerability that surely is not lost on U.S. and Indian naval strategists. Until and unless the People's Liberation Army Navy (PLAN) can defend Gwadar against cruise missiles or naval air strikes emanating from the sea, the port's strategic worth will be less than it might appear for Beijing.

- And third, politics might work against Chinese use of the base in times of crisis. Although Beijing has sought to wring guaranteed access to Gwadar from Islamabad, it is hard to envision Pakistani officials exposing brand-new port facilities—facilities they see as a major part of their nation's economic future—to American counterstrikes during a shooting war. Nor is it obvious that Islamabad would jeopardize relations with Washington for the sake of energy cooperation with Beijing. In short, Pakistan might well balk at taking part in Sino–U.S. hostilities.

However useful an asset Gwadar is in peacetime, then, wartime conditions threaten to vitiate its strategic value—unless the People's Liberation Army (PLA) manages to amass enough military power in its vicinity to defend it against nearby U.S. forces.

Recognizing how tenuous Beijing's position in the Indian Ocean basin remains, some Chinese analysts espouse a stronger, outward-looking navy able to deter or defeat attempts by other powers to stop the flow of energy resources through regional SLOC. Drawing upon history, Zhang Wenmu, a prominent proponent of Chinese sea power, maintains that trade has always been inseparable from naval dominance; together these two factors furnish the basis for great-power ascendancy. Zhang acknowledges China's failure to develop military means adequate to protect its energy security, exhorting the Chinese leadership to emulate the rise of Western sea power.[43] Zhang warns ominously, "We must be prepared as early as possible. Otherwise, China may lose everything it has gathered in normal international economic activities, including its energy interest, in a military defeat."[44]

Similarly, two Chinese academics conclude that the nexus between economic vitality and military power compels Beijing to pursue a capable navy: "Ocean power has a permanent meaning to the trade of coastal countries, and the backup of a country's ocean power is its navy. Therefore, the long term approach toward ensuring open sea lane and potential ocean resources is to [develop] a modern ocean-going navy."[45]

Perhaps the most thoughtful spokesman for Chinese naval power is Professor Ni Lexiong of the Research Institute of War and Culture, Eastern China Science and Engineering University. As Ni asserts, "it is China's necessary choice to build up a strong sea power" to guard against "threats posed to our 'outward-leaning economy' by some strong nations."[46] He clearly has China's vulnerability to sea-lane disruptions by the United States in mind. Intriguingly, he links the cross-strait stalemate to China's inability to safeguard its economic interests on the high seas. Ni argues that if China were "checked by the U.S. on the Taiwan matter, if our lifeline at sea once again falls into the hands of the U.S., we will give the U.S. another bargaining chip over the issue of Taiwan."[47]

As for the question of how China might defend its seaborne energy transport in Southeast Asia, one study denigrates the string-of-pearls strategy, contending that powerful PLAN forces must be built and deployed to the region to uphold it:

> The Kra Isthmus canal, the Sino-Burmese and Sino-Pakistani oil pipelines, would not be able to fundamentally avoid the impact of the navies of major powers. If the fleets of such powers directly intercept our tankers in the Persian Gulf, the Arabian Sea, or the Suez Canal . . . the above-mentioned three schemes would all become meaningless. Thus, before the Chinese navy's ocean-going squadrons can achieve some kind of force parity with the navies of major powers in the Indian Ocean, the security problem of China's oil transport routes and straits cannot be resolved.[48]

The assumption implicit in the statement above—that is, that China is determined to or has already embarked on a naval modernization program that will allow the PLAN to rival the navies of the major powers—says much about attitudes emerging among Chinese strategists. More startling still, the two authors call on Beijing to develop a comprehensive maritime strategy that seeks to open an outlet into the Indian Ocean "so as to break out of the encirclement for the rise of the Chinese nation and its maritime rejuvenation, and open up a brand new ocean waterway leading to victory."[49]

Such rhetorical flourishes aside, these analysts have clearly set their sights on extending Chinese naval power far beyond East Asian littoral seas.

If one assumes that these steps are being (or could be) coordinated as a part of a coherent national strategy, then incremental gains in Chinese leverage and presence in the Indian Ocean region are the foreseeable result. Indeed, this tripartite strategy can be seen as a series of well-coordinated, sequential maneuvers: (1) diplomatic work combined with (2) efforts to negotiate forward naval basing rights may lend legitimacy to (3) a more robust Chinese naval presence in the Indian Ocean basin. Even if that is the case, however, this strategy is largely a work in progress, and it bespeaks long-term Chinese aspirations. Beijing will lack the capacity for overt naval competition in the region for some time to come, and the pace and scope of its activities in the Indian Ocean will be limited by priorities far closer to home.

But China Will Encounter a Sea Power–Minded India

As it expands its interests in the Indian Ocean, waging a vigorous soft-power diplomacy and backing maritime aims with material power, China will encounter another rising power—India—that entertains nautical ambitions of its own. Like China, India discerns real, compelling interests in the Indian Ocean, and it enjoys venerable seafaring traditions that offer a major reserve of soft power. Strategists in New Delhi phrase their arguments in intensively geopolitical terms—jarringly so for Westerners accustomed to the notion that economic globalization has rendered armed conflict passé. And the Indian economy has grown at a rapid clip—albeit not as rapidly as that of China—allowing an increasingly confident Indian government to yoke hard power, measured in ships, aircraft, and weapons systems, to a foreign policy aimed at primacy in the Indian Ocean region.[50] Indeed, Indian thinkers as well as outside observers often speak of an Indian equivalent to the Monroe Doctrine that seeks to place the region off-limits to external politico-military intervention.[51] If intervention is necessary, imply Indian leaders, India should take the lead rather than give outsiders a pretext for doing so.

Such a doctrine will inevitably have a strong seafaring component to it. In 2004 New Delhi issued its first public appraisal of the nation's oceanic surroundings and how to contend with those surroundings. Straightforwardly titled Indian Maritime Doctrine, the document (much like Beijing's most recent defense white papers) describes India's maritime strategy largely as a function of economic development and prosperity: "India's primary maritime interest is to assure national security. This is not restricted to just guarding the coastline and island territories, but also extends to safeguarding our interests in the [exclusive economic zone] as well as protecting our trade. This creates an environment that is conducive to rapid economic growth of the country. Since trade is the lifeblood of India, keeping our SLOC open in times of peace, tension or hostilities is a primary national maritime interest."[52]

Among the "strategic realities" that the framers of the Indian Maritime Doctrine discern, the trade conveyed by the sea lanes traversing the Indian Ocean ranks first. Roughly forty merchantmen pass through India's "waters of interest" every day. An estimated $200 billion worth of oil transits the Strait of Hormuz annually, while some $60 billion transits the Strait of Malacca en route to China, Japan, and other East Asian countries reliant on energy imports.[53]

India's geographic location and conformation rank next in New Delhi's hierarchy of strategic realities. Notes the Indian Maritime Doctrine, "India sits astride . . . major commercial routes and energy lifelines" crisscrossing the Indian Ocean region. Outlying Indian possessions such as the Andaman and Nicobar islands sit athwart the approaches to the Strait of Malacca, while the Persian Gulf is near India's western coastline, conferring a measure of influence over vital sea communications to and from what amounts to a bay in the Indian Ocean. While geography may not be destiny, the document states bluntly that "by virtue of our geography, we are . . . in a position to greatly influence the movement/security of shipping along the SLOC in the [Indian Ocean region] provided we have the maritime power to do so. Control of the choke points could be useful as a bargaining chip in the international power game, where the currency of military power remains a stark reality."[54]

The Indian Maritime Doctrine prophesies a depletion of world energy resources that will render the prospect of outside military involvement in India's geographic environs even more acute than it already seems. Modern economies' dependence on the Gulf region and Central Asia "has already invited the presence of extra-regional powers and the accompanying Command, Control, Surveillance and Intelligence network. The security implications for us are all too obvious." Sizable deposits of other resources— uranium, tin, gold, diamonds—around the Indian Ocean littoral only accentuate the factors beckoning the attention of outside maritime powers to India's environs.[55]

Indian leaders, then, take a somber view of the international security environment. In the "policycentric world order" that New Delhi sees taking shape, economics is "the major determinant of a nation's power." While "India holds great promise" owing to its size, location, and economic acumen, its "emergence as an economic power will undoubtedly be resisted by the existing economic powers, leading to conflicts based on economic factors." The likelihood that competitors will "deny access to technology and other industrial inputs," combined with "the shift in global maritime focus from the Atlantic-Pacific combine to the Pacific-Indian Ocean region," will only heighten the attention major powers pay to the seas.[56] A buildup of Indian maritime power represents the only prudent response to strategic conditions that are at once promising and worrisome in economic terms.

Clearly, then, New Delhi will not allow a buildup of Chinese naval power in the Indian Ocean to go uncontested. Do Indian officials have in mind a "Monroe Doctrine" as all-encompassing as the one the Grover Cleveland administration proclaimed in the 1890s when Secretary of State Richard Olney informed Lord Salisbury—head of government for the predominant naval power of the day—that the United States was "practically sovereign" in the Americas and that its "fiat is law upon the subjects to which it confines its interposition," owing primarily to "its infinite resources" and "its isolated position," which "render it master of the situation and practically invulnerable as against any or all other powers"?[57] This is doubtful. Indeed, the United States itself only briefly hewed to Olney's extravagant version of the Monroe Doctrine, recognizing that it had neither the material power nor the need to police an entire hemisphere. American control of the Caribbean basin, traversed by SLOC critical to U.S. economic and security interests, was enough.[58]

By invoking the doctrine, New Delhi has nonetheless signaled its reluctance to allow any outside power to gain territories in the Indian Ocean basin or to police the region—perhaps in search of an excuse for territorial aggrandizement. And India clearly wants the wherewithal to make good on its claim to preeminence in the region, with naval officials openly declaring that the nation needs a blue water navy to fulfill the missions set forth in the Indian Maritime Doctrine.[59]

Strategic Determinants of China's Naval Ambitions in the Indian Ocean

An expansive Chinese maritime strategy in the Indian Ocean basin—especially a strategy backed by hard power, manifest in PLAN forces—will thus meet with countervailing soft and hard power deployed by a resurgent India. At least three determinants stand out among the myriad factors bearing on China's naval ambitions in the region:

- **Determinant 1: Taiwan and the China Seas.** China's efforts to radiate influence into the Indian Ocean region will hinge on its ability to secure waters nearer home. For Beijing, regaining control of Taiwan, the midpoint of the first island chain and a potential base for "foreign forces" to interfere with Chinese shipping, tops the strategic agenda. Asserting a measure of control over SLOC transiting the Indian Ocean must await settlement of this matter of surpassing importance. To borrow from Barry Posen, Beijing must first put to sea (and aloft) forces able to mount a "contested zone" against United States and perhaps allied forces attempting to intervene in a cross-strait contingency. As Posen observes, "The closer U.S. military forces get to enemy-held territory, the more competitive the enemy will be. This arises from a combination of political, physical, and technological facts. These facts combine to create a contested zone—arenas of conventional combat where weak adversaries have a good chance of doing real damage to U.S. forces.[60]

In short, a country operating in its geographic environs enjoys certain advantages even over a vastly superior foe. Proximity to the prospective theater of conflict, nearby land bases for aircraft and missiles, and a formidable force of submarines based near the prospective conflict area are only a few elements of China's nascent contested zone. But until Beijing acquires or builds sufficient capabilities to defend this zone against intruding American forces, Chinese leaders will relegate less immediate priorities such as threats to Chinese shipping in the Indian Ocean to secondary status. Amassing a local superiority of force over the largest force the U.S. military and its Asian allies would likely throw against the PLA is task enough for now.

- **Determinant 2: Rival Claimants to Soft Power in the Indian Ocean.** Even China's impressive soft-power diplomacy in the Indian Ocean region, as exemplified by its use of Zheng He's voyages, will find itself rivaled by Indian soft power. Indian maritime history presents with New Delhi its own counterpart to the Ming treasure voyages, as K. M. Panikkar, the father of Indian maritime history, noted some sixty years ago. True, India turned inward during the long era of Mughal supremacy, occupying itself with continental affairs, but only after Hindu mariners had plied Indian Ocean waters for centuries. Hindu shipwrights, like those who built Zheng He's treasure fleet, constructed "compartmented" vessels that resisted sinking after heavy weather or battle.[61] Seafarers propagated Indian cultural and political influence throughout the Indian Ocean basin, not to mention eastward into the South China Sea, until the downfall of Hindu maritime supremacy in the thirteenth century. The nation's "usable past," to borrow Henry Steele Commager's phrase, thus furnishes ample basis for Indian maritime soft power.[62] Deft Indian diplomacy could check Chinese advances in this realm.

While Beijing may well ease concerns about its growing naval might, then, it will find it difficult to convince coastal nations in the Indian Ocean littoral that the PLAN should be the principal guardian of maritime security in the region. This will be especially true should China mishandle the Taiwan question, squandering the soft power it has painstakingly accumulated in recent years. Consider: what if Beijing attempted to settle the cross-strait dispute by force, as it has repeatedly threatened to do, but the Taiwanese populace defied assumptions and held out against this onslaught? And what if an insurgent movement arose to battle the Chinese occupation, even after government forces went down to defeat?

As the United States has found in Iraq, a prolonged, bloody conflict undertaken without the UN imprimatur can sap a great power's capacity to rally other nations behind its foreign-policy ventures. Indeed, a protracted and valiant struggle against Chinese coercion, even if ultimately unsuccessful, would likely undermine Beijing's sovereign claims over the island, win over international sympathy in favor of the Taiwanese, and further delegitimize China's use of force. Beijing might see its stock plummet in maritime Asia, even after a victorious war in the Strait. In all likelihood, India would be left ascendant in the Indian Ocean region, given its emphasis on naval diplomacy, humanitarian relief, and other peacetime missions.

The United States (to the chagrin of soft-power proponents such as Joseph Nye) is not a serious claimant to oceanic soft power in South Asia. Whether it can augment its influence through close ties with India is unclear. While Washington may find in New Delhi a natural partner or friend in the region, as analysts who play up ideological affinities between the two English-speaking democracies contend, it is unlikely that the two nations will be natural *allies*.[63] Some Indian observers point out that even the Anglo-American "special relationship" only emerged from trying circumstances— circumstances that are unlikely to be duplicated in the Indian Ocean, given the constraints on Chinese power in the region.[64] Absent such a threat, Washington may find it difficult to enlist Indian soft power until and unless China begins mounting a sizable challenge to Indian interests in the region.

- **Determinant 3: Rival Contested Zones.** China is not the only beneficiary of Posen's concept of the contested zone. Should China attempt
  to amass hard power—embodied in PLAN expeditionary forces stationed along the string of pearls—in the Indian Ocean region, it will
  inevitably encounter an India accustomed to predominance in its
  neighborhood and determined to uphold that predominance against
  all comers. If Beijing can hope to mount a contested zone against the
  U.S. Navy, New Delhi can hope to mount a contested zone against the
  PLAN—which remains far inferior in absolute terms to the U.S. Navy
  and faces permanent, pressing concerns in the China seas—for the
  foreseeable future. While tremendous difficulties beset New Delhi—
  the guns-and-butter dilemma, a hodgepodge of foreign-supplied military hardware and the interoperability problems this brings—the
  Indian navy will in all likelihood continue to enjoy local superiority
  over its prospective Chinese competitor for some time to come.

Operational and Force-Structure Determinants

With all this in mind, how do the PLA's capabilities measure up to Beijing's goals in the Indian Ocean region? Is Beijing effectively matching ends
with means? Consider a best-case scenario from China's standpoint. What
would happen the "day after" the mainland regained control of Taiwan,
either peacefully or after a military operation in which the PLA suffered neg-
ligible human and material losses? Would this enable China to make itself
the leading power in the South China Sea and the Indian Ocean, measured
in hard-power terms?

Not for some time to come. In order to assert control over the SLOC
traversing South and Southeast Asia, the PLAN needs to add certain platforms to its order of battle, beyond those needed to mount a contested zone
in the East Asian littoral. To complicate matters for Beijing, certain capabilities useful in a Taiwan contingency hold little relevance for SLOC defense.
As currently configured, advanced military assets such as shore-based tactical fighters, land-based short-range ballistic missiles, and ground-based
surface-to-air missiles would be of limited use in missions beyond littoral defense. Discounting capabilities designed specifically for a cross-strait
confrontation reveals a naval force that remains inadequately equipped to
project credible power into the Indian Ocean. Indeed, at present, the PLAN
possesses only enough surface combatants and conventional submarines to

serve as the nucleus for a modest cruise-missile navy consisting of at most three to four combined strike groups.

What, then, will the PLA need for the SLOC-defense mission, assuming China decides to build up hard power in a day-after-Taiwan scenario? It will not need a force symmetrical with that of the U.S. Navy, centered on big-deck aircraft carriers. More modest, less expensive platforms can perform the SLOC-defense function adequately. Some capabilities needed in the PLAN inventory include:

- **More—and More Modern—Destroyers and Frigates.** Quantity has a quality all its own, as Soviet Admiral Sergei Gorshkov liked to remark. Bernard Cole points out that, despite its impressive progress, the PLAN still has fewer than twenty modern surface combatants, the most useful assets for patrolling the sea lanes.[65] Warships with organic surveillance capacity will be at a premium. It will take some time for Beijing to construct additional warships for South China Sea and Indian Ocean patrol duty, even assuming the navy has perfected the Aegis-like combat system installed in its latest guided-missile destroyers. If the PLAN starts building larger ship classes, as opposed to the three- or four-ship classes it has put to sea up to now, this will signal that it is satisfied with its technological progress and can now focus on accumulating mass. Until Beijing breaks out of its rather sporadic procurement pattern of the past decade, which bespeaks a deliberate effort at fleet experimentation, it will be unable to field a naval force with sufficient depth to cope with attrition and the strains of blue water operations. In other words, serial production of cruisers and destroyers would signal confidence in PLAN hardware, emboldening Chinese leaders to deploy navy units farther offshore.

- **More Organic Naval Air Power.** China's navy suffers from three interrelated weaknesses that could be best reversed by robust naval aviation. First, "maritime domain awareness," the U.S. Navy's term of art for oceanic surveillance, is the key to effective SLOC defense. Over-the-horizon surveillance and targeting remains a weak spot for the PLAN, even in home waters where it enjoys the luxury of nearby land-based sensors and aircraft. Second, despite the navy's recent advances in anti-air and antisubmarine warfare, PLAN surface combatants remain highly vulnerable to attacks from modern submarines and aircraft. Third, the most glaring gap in the inventory is the absence of sustainable, long-range combat power. A concerted effort to develop or acquire plentiful long-range aircraft and ship-based helicopters for maritime surveillance, patrol, and antisubmarine-warfare missions will be necessary before China can hope to assert control over SLOC beyond the waters adjacent to the Chinese mainland.

While China's aircraft-carrier ambitions remain an enigma to Western observers, the operational benefits these floating airfields promise across a wide range of offensive and defensive missions are beyond question. Accordingly, carriers designed for SLOC defense could be an attractive option—though not an absolute necessity—for Beijing. As one study notes, China need not build prohibitively expensive large-deck carriers resembling those in the U.S. Navy. As a stopgap measure, pending the construction of larger platforms in the future, a mid-sized helicopter carrier may be sufficient to fulfill the navy's short- and medium-term needs.[66]

- **More Combat-Logistics Platforms.** At-sea sustainment—the ability to refuel, rearm, and take on stores under way—is a perennial shortcoming of the PLAN. A fleet of forward-deployed oilers, ammunition ships, and refrigeration ships will be critical if China wants to emplace itself as a leading power in the Indian Ocean basin. Doubts about the navy's skill at underway replenishment are undoubtedly overstated. Indeed, PLAN units have already demonstrated this capacity on a small scale during a variety of port visits around the globe. Becoming proficient at delicate alongside operations nevertheless promises to take time. And even if logistics vessels are stationed at all of the string-of-pearls seaports, Chinese commanders will confront the tyranny of distance in this vast region. Gwadar would help, but it would be no panacea.

For some time to come, then, China's naval ambitions in the Indian Ocean will take second place to security interests closer to home. Mounting a contested zone adjacent to China's coasts—with regaining Taiwan as the key intermediate step—is and will remain uppermost in the minds of sea-power thinkers in Beijing. Nevertheless, the three broad operational requirements identified here give policymakers tangible benchmarks by which to measure China's progress at aligning strategy and military means with longer-term political objectives.

If and when China resolves these urgent concerns satisfactorily, the nation's leadership can reorient its gaze along the SLOC connecting the Horn of Africa and the Middle East with Chinese seaports. But formidable obstacles will loom, even then, and it remains far from clear that China will manage to match its expansive Indian Ocean diplomacy with equally expansive naval means. Beijing understands its limits. For now, soft power offers China an inexpensive way to project influence into new geographic domains without backing up its diplomacy with large military forces. Available PLAN forces already allow Beijing to undertake a modest slate of missions in South and Southeast Asia. China will not, for instance, repeat its mystifying blunder of 2004, when it remained conspicuously aloof from the tsunami relief effort—allowing India, Japan, and the United States, its chief rivals at sea, to harvest goodwill from their naval diplomacy.

It is precisely China's prolonged material weakness along the sea lanes that could allow Washington and New Delhi to forge a near-term maritime partnership with Beijing. Cooperation in areas such as disaster relief, maritime domain awareness, and counterterrorism could lay the groundwork for a more durable partnership in maritime Asia, alleviating the concerns about sea-lane security that could prod China in a more ominous direction. Considering the stakes, it would be worth the effort U.S. and Indian leaders would expend in negotiating such a partnership.

Notes

James Holmes and Toshi Yoshihara are professors in the Strategy and Policy Department at the U.S. Naval War College. The views voiced here are theirs alone. An earlier version of this chapter appeared as James Holmes and Toshi Yoshihara, "China's Naval Ambitions in the Indian Ocean," *Journal of Strategic Studies*, 2008.

1. Asia Pacific Research Centre, *Energy in China: Transportation, Electric Power and Fuel Markets* (Tokyo: Asian Pacific Research Centre, 2004), 5.

2. See U.S. Energy Information Administration, "China," EIA Country Analysis Briefs, July 2004, http://www.eia.doe.gov/emeu/cabs/china.html.

3. A RAND study of China's economic vulnerabilities posited a scenario in which a 25 percent contraction in global oil supplies resulted in a sustained tripling of prices over a ten-year period (2005–15). The study concluded that China would suffer an annual reduction of 1.2–1.4 percent to its economic growth rate. The expected consequences of an energy crisis were among the most severe economic setbacks the study considered. See Charles Wolf Jr. et al., *Fault Lines in China's Economic Terrain* (Santa Monica, Calif.: RAND, 2003), 105–16.

4. See, for instance, "Mainland May Face a Crippling Oil Shortage by 2020," *South China Morning Post*, 26 July 2004.

5. U.S. Energy Information Administration, "China."

6. Philip Andrews-Speed et al., *The Strategic Implications of China's Energy Needs* (London: International Institute of Strategic Studies, July 2002), 25.

7. Guy Caruso, EIA Administrator, Testimony to U.S.-China Economic and Security Review Commission, 108th Congress, 30 October 2003, 8.

8. U.S. National Intelligence Council, *Report of the National Intelligence Council's 2020 Project: Mapping the Global Future* (Washington, D.C.: Government Printing Office, December 2004), 50, 62.

9. David Walgreen, "China in the Indian Ocean Region: Lessons in PRC Grand Strategy," *Comparative Strategy* 25 (2006): 59. For a Chinese perspective on India's rise, see Deng Ruixiang, "Assessing the Question of India's Rise," *Guoji Wenti Yianjiu* 1 (2006): 37–42.

10. See for example Zhang Lijun, "Analyzing India's Energy Strategy," *Guoju Wenti Yianjiu* 5 (2006): 65 66.

11. Hou Songlin, "India's 'Look East Policy' and the Development of Indian-ASEAN Ties," *Dangdai Yatai* 5 (2006): 42.

12. Zhu Fenggang, "The Impact of the Maritime Strategies of Asia-Pacific Nations," *Dangdai Yatai* 5 (2006): 34.

13. Some 80 percent of China's oil imports, accounting for 40 percent of total Chinese oil consumption, passes through the strait, giving rise to what Chinese president Hu Jintao has called China's "Malacca Dilemma." U.S. Office of the Secretary of Defense, *Annual Report on the Military Power of the People's Republic of China, 2005* (Washington, D.C.: Government Printing Office, 2005), 33. On China's demand for petroleum, see David Hale, "China's Growing Appetites," *National Interest* 76 (Summer 2004): 137–47.

14. Shi Hongtao, "China's 'Malacca Straits,'" *Qingnian Bao*, 15 June 2004, Foreign Broadcast Information Service (hereafter FBIS), FBIS-CPP20040615000042.

15. Zhang Yuncheng, "The Malacca Strait and World Oil Security," *Huanqiu Shibao*, 5 December 2003, FBIS-CPP20031217000202.

16. Zhu, "Impact of the Maritime Strategies," 36.

17. Editorial, "U.S.-Indian Alliance against China," *Ming Pao*, 17 August 2005, FBIS-CPP20050817000043.

18. Ibid.

19. Qing Tong, "2002: Focus on Guam," *Kuang Chiao Ching*, 16 October 2002, FBIS-CPP2002101800075; Wang Jisi, Ni Feng, and Zhang Liping, "Impact of US Global Strategic Adjustment on China," *Zhongguo Shehui Kexueyuan Yuanbao*, 7 January 2004, FBIS-CPP20040121000126; Dan Jie and Ju Lang, "Russian Strategic Bomber to Fly to China," *Jiandai Wuqi*, 1 March 2005, FBIS-CPP20050328000206.

20. Jiang Hong and Wei Yuejiang, "100,000 US Troops in the Asia-Pacific Look for 'New Homes,'" *Guofang Bao*, 10 June 2003, 1, FBIS-CPP20030611000068.

21. He Yijian, "The United States Is Busy Deploying Troops in Asia," *Liaowang*, 13 May 2002, 54–55, FBIS-CPP20020521000054.

22. Li Xuanliang, "U.S. Military's 'New Guam Strategy,'" *Liaowang Dongfang Zhoukan*, 18 June 2006, 18–19, FBIS-CPP20060619718001.

23. The participants at a recent conference on "Maritime Implications of China's Energy Strategy," held at the Naval War College, Newport, Rhode Island, on 6–7 December 2006, generally questioned the U.S. Navy's ability to sustain an effective blockade of Chinese energy supplies.

24. "Premier Wen's Several Talks During Europe Visit," Xinhua, 16 May 2004, FBIS-CPP20040516000069. Wen sounded similar themes during a spring 2005 trip to South Asia. See Xiao Qiang, "Premier Wen's South Asian Tour Produces Abundant Results," Renmin Ribao, 13 April 2005, FBIS-CHN-200504131477. Reporting on the efforts of Yao Mingde, the official in charge of organizing activities to commemorate the treasure voyages, the official news service Xinhua observed that "Zheng He's fleet surpassed all other marine navigators of his time in scale, sophistication, technology and organizational skills in his seven sea trips, which were a great event in the world's navigation history." "China Launches Activities to Commemorate Sea Navigation Pioneer Zheng He," Xinhua, 29 September 2003, FBIS-CPP20030928000052.

25. Hu Jintao, "'Constantly Increasing Common Ground': Hu's Speech to Australian Parliament," 24 October 2003, http://www.australianpolitics.com/news/2003/10/03-10-24b.shtml.

26. Zheng Bijian, "China's 'Peaceful Rise' to Great Power Status," Foreign Affairs 84, no. 5 (September/October 2005): 18–24. Zheng is a close advisor to President Hu.

27. See, for instance, "China Celebrates Ancient Mariner to Demonstrate Peaceful Rise," Xinhua, 7 July 2004, FBIS-CPP20040707000169.

28. Xu Qi, "Maritime Geostrategy and the Development of the Chinese Navy in the Early Twenty-first Century," trans. Andrew S. Erickson and Lyle J. Goldstein, Naval War College Review 59, no. 4 (Autumn 2006): 53–54. Xu's article originally appeared in China Military Science, China's foremost journal of military affairs.

29. Xu, "Maritime Geostrategy," 52.

30. Chen Jian and Zhao Haiyan, "Wen Jiabao on Sino-US Relations: Cherish Harmony; Be Harmonious but Different," Zhongguo Xinwen She, 8 December 2003, FBIS-CPP20031208000052.

31. "Kenyan Girl Offered Chance to Go to College in China," Xinhua, 20 March 2005, FBIS-CHN-200503201477.

32. Matthew Wheeler, "China Expands Its Southern Sphere of Influence," Jane's Intelligence Review, 1 June 2005, http://www.janes.com/security/international_security/news/jir/jir050523_1_n.shtml.

33. Bates Gill and Yanzhong Huang, "Sources and Limits of Chinese 'Soft Power,'" Survival 48, no. 2 (Summer 2006): 24–25; Andrew Erickson and Lyle Goldstein, "Hoping for the Best, Preparing for the Worst: China's Response to US Hegemony," Journal of Strategic Studies 29, no. 6 (December 2006): 965–66.

34. Sheng Ding and Robert A. Saunders, "Talking Up China: An Analysis of China's Rising Cultural Power and Global Promotion of the Chinese Language," East Asia 23, no. 2 (Summer 2006): 3–33.

35. Shannon Tow, "Southeast Asia in the Sino-U.S. Strategic Balance," *Contemporary Southeast Asia* 26, no. 3 (2004): 434–59; Denny Roy, "Southeast Asia and China: Balancing or Bandwagoning?" *Contemporary Southeast Asia* 27, no. 2 (2005): 305–22; and Evelyn Goh, "Great Powers and Southeast Asian Regional Security Strategies," *Military Technology* (January 2006): 321–23.

36. The term first appeared in a *Washington Times* article after originating in a Booz-Allen study commissioned by the Pentagon's Office of Net Assessment. See Bill Gertz, "China Builds Up Strategic Sea Lanes," *Washington Times*, 18 January 2005, http://www.washtimes.com/national/20050117-115550-1929r.htm.

37. See, for example, Christopher J. Pehrson, *String of Pearls: Meeting the Challenge of China's Rising Power Across the Asian Littoral* (Carlisle, PA: Strategic Studies Institute, U.S. Army War College, July 2006); Lawrence Spinetta, "Cutting China's 'String of Pearls'," U.S. Naval Institute *Proceedings* 132, no. 10 (October 2006): 40–42; Sudha Ramachandra, "China's Pearl in Pakistan's Waters," *Asia Times*, 4 March 2005, http://www.atimes.com/atimes/South_Asia/GC04Df06.html; Hideaki Kaneda, "The Rise of Chinese 'Sea Power,'" *Philippine Daily Inquirer*, 22 September 2005, 11.

38. Author discussions with Indian analysts, Institute for Defence Studies & Analyses, New Delhi, 6–16 November 2006.

39. Lee Jae-Hyung, "China's Expanding Maritime Ambitions in the Western Pacific and the Indian Ocean," *Contemporary Southeast Asia* 24, no. 3 (December 2002): 553–54.

40. With twelve berths in place or in planning, and with the capacity to receive deep-draft merchant ships, the port facility could easily play host to Chinese warships. See Government of Pakistan, Ministry of Ports and Shipping, presentation on Gwadar Port Project, http://siteresources.worldbank.org/PAKISTANEXTN/Resources/293051-1114424648263/Session-VII-Fazal-Ur-Rehman.pdf; Government of Pakistan, Board of Investment, "Gwadar," http://www.pakboi.pk/News_Event/Gwadar.html; "About Gwadar," Gwadar Port website, http://www.gawadarport.com/main/Content.aspx?ID=1; Tarique Niazi, "Gwadar: China's Naval Outpost on the Indian Ocean," *China Brief* 5, no. 4 (25 February 2005), http://www.jamestown.org/news_details.php?news_id=93.

41. Islamabad and Beijing are jointly studying a pipeline project connecting Gwadar with the western Chinese province of Xinjiang. See "Gwadar-China Oil Pipeline Study Underway," *Pakistan Observer*, 4 September 2006, http://pakobserver.net/200609/04/news/topstories12.asp?txt=Gwadar-China%20oil%20pipeline%20study%20underway.

42. Alfred Thayer Mahan, "The Strategic Features of the Gulf of Mexico and the Caribbean Sea," in *The Interest of America in Sea Power, Present and Future*, ed. Alfred Thayer Mahan (Boston: Little, Brown, and Company, 1897; reprint, Freeport, NY: Books for Libraries Press, 1970), 283–92.

43. For a similar argument, see Yan Xuetong, "The Rise of China and Its Power Status," *Chinese Journal of International Politics* 1, no. 1 (2006): 5–33.

44. Zhang Wenmu, "China's Energy Security and Policy Choices," *Shijie Jinji yu Zhengzhi (Global Economics and Politics)* 5 (14 May 2003): 11–16, FBIS-CPP 20030528000169.

45. Liu Xinhua and Qi Yi, "China's Oil Security and Its Strategic Options," *Xiandai Guoji Guanxi (Contemporary International Relations)* 12 (20 December 2002): 35–46, FBIS-CPP20030425000288.

46. Ni Lexiong, "Sea Power and China's Development," *Liberation Daily*, 17 April 2005, 4, U.S.-China Economic and Security Review Commission website, http://www.uscc.gov/researchpapers/translated_articles/2005/05_07_18_Sea_Power_and_Chi nas _Development.pdf.

47. Ibid., 7.

48. Liu Jiangping and Feng Xianhui, "Going Global: Dialogue Spanning 600 Years," *Liaowang* 5 (1 July 2005): 14–19, FBIS-CPP20050719000107.

49. Ibid.

50. For a good recent overview, see Donald L. Berlin, "India in the Indian Ocean," *Naval War College Review* 59, no. 2 (spring 2006), 58–89, http://www.nwc.navy.mil/press/review/documents/NWCRSP06.pdf.

51. See for example Devin T. Hagerty, "India's Regional Security Doctrine," *Asian Survey* 31, no. 4 (April 1991): 351–63; John W. Garver, *Protracted Contest: Sino-Indian Rivalry in the Twentieth Century* (Seattle. University of Washington Press, 2001), 31; C. Raja Mohan, "Border Crossings," *South Asia Monitor,* May 2006, http://www.southasiamonitor.org/2006/may/news/17view2.shtml.

52. Government of India, INBR-8, *Indian Maritime Doctrine* (New Delhi: Integrated Headquarters, Ministry of Defence [Navy], 25 April 2004), 63.

53. Ibid., 63–64.

54. Ibid., 64.

55. Ibid., 64–65.

56. Ibid., 65–67.

57. Richard Olney to Thomas F. Bayard, 20 July 1895, in *The Record of American Diplomacy: Documents and Readings in the History of American Foreign Relations*, 4th ed., ed. Ruhl J. Bartlett (New York: Knopf, 1964), 341–45. The classic account of the Monroe Doctrine is Dexter Perkins, *A History of the Monroe Doctrine* (Boston: Little, Brown and Company, 1963), 228–75.

58. James R. Holmes, "Roosevelt's Pursuit of a Temperate Caribbean Policy," *Naval History* 20, no. 4 (August 2006): 48–53.

59. See for instance Rajat Pandit, "India's Chief of Naval Staff—Blue-water Navy Is the Aim," *Times of India,* 1 November 2006, http://timesofindia.indiatimes.com/Bluewater_Navy_is_the_aim/articleshow/262611.cms; Ranjit B. Rai, "India's Aircraft Carriers Programme: A Steady Sail Towards Blue Water Capability," *India Strategic*, October 2006, 42–44; "Extending the Navy's Reach: Navy Chief Speaks to *India Strategic*," *India Strategic*, October 2006, 23–33.

60. Barry R. Posen, "Command of the Commons: The Military Foundation of U.S. Hegemony," *International Security* 28, no. 1 (Summer 2003): 22.

61. Panikkar extolled Hindu mariners' accomplishments while also paying tribute to Zheng He's voyages. K. M. Panikkar, *India and the Indian Ocean: An Essay on the Influence of Sea Power on Indian History* (New York: Macmillan, 1945), 28–36; K. M. Panikkar, *Asia and Western Dominance: A Survey of the Vasco Da Gama Epoch of Asian History, 1498–1945* (New York: John Day, n.d. [1954?]), 35–36, 49, 68, 71.

62. Henry Steele Commager, *The Search for a Usable Past and Other Essays in Historiography* (New York: Knopf, 1967), 3–27. Commager explored founding Americans' quest for common history, traditions, and legends to bind the new nation together.

63. For a sampling of commentary on the Indo–U.S. relationship, see Stephen J. Blank, *Natural Allies? Regional Security in Asia and Prospects for Indo-American Strategic Cooperation* (Carlisle, PA: Strategic Studies Institute, U.S. Army War College, September 2005); C. Raja Mohan, "India and the Balance of Power," *Foreign Affairs* 85, no. 4 (July–August 2006): 17–32; Ashton B. Carter, "America's New Strategic Partner?" *Foreign Affairs* 85, no. 4 (July–August 2006): 33–44.

64. Author discussions with Indian scholars, Salve Regina University, Newport, Rhode Island, 19 September 2006.

65. Bernard D. Cole, "The Energy Factor in Chinese Maritime Strategy" (paper presented at conference on "Maritime Implications of China's Energy Strategy," Naval War College, Newport, Rhode Island, 6 December 2006).

66. Andrew Erickson and Andrew Wilson, "China's Aircraft Carrier Dilemma," *Naval War College Review* 59, no. 4 (Autumn 2006): 30–37.

Saad Rahim

China's Energy Strategy toward the Middle East: Saudi Arabia

CHINA BECAME A NET IMPORTER OF OIL IN 1993, an event which had a dramatic impact on the country's autarkic model. Forced to look outside its borders for its most strategic commodity, China naturally turned its attention to the largest holders of hydrocarbon reserves in the world, namely the Middle East Gulf states. In doing so, it quickly ran up against the fact that the United States has long maintained a strategic interest in the region and, in the aftermath of the Gulf War, positioned significant armed forces there. Beyond the U.S. presence, Chinese planners were also concerned with the fact that the region as a whole has always been one of the most volatile areas in the world, especially over the last century. Given these factors, the Chinese looked elsewhere initially for their oil, starting with Sudan and Southeast Asia. Over time, however, the scale of China's import requirements have forced it back to the Middle East, and projected future oil demand will bring ever-increasing Chinese (and, indeed, global) reliance on the Gulf producers. While Chinese deals in Iran have dominated headlines, the more critical relationship over the long term will be the one emerging between Saudi Arabia and China. Intersecting strategic interests between the two countries have markedly changed their level of energy interdependence and will continue to do so for the foreseeable future. Recent actions include extensive Chinese investment in Saudi energy infrastructure; substantial Saudi investment in Chinese refineries, possibly including partial Saudi ownership of China's Strategic Petroleum Reserve; guaranteed Saudi oil exports to China of 1 million barrels per day by 2010 (double 2006 levels); and Chinese participation in a limited opening of the Saudi gas sector.

This new partnership is unfolding as part of a new energy architecture that is beginning to take form. The post–World War II energy architecture was implemented in a manner that relied on the United States as the key market and as the guarantor of sea lane security. These benefits were extended to Europe and Japan as well, allowing them to participate in the architecture in a way that allowed them to fuel their economic growth. Now, however, a new pattern is emerging wherein both the centers of supply and demand are shifting eastwards. Over the coming decade and beyond, the Middle East will be called upon to produce a substantially larger percentage of the world's oil than it currently does, as mature hydrocarbon basins in the Organization for Economic Cooperation and Development countries begin to decline rapidly, and new discoveries in West Africa and elsewhere peak and begin their inevitable decline. Concurrently, China and India will become two of the three most prominent drivers of increased energy demand (the United States being the other), continuing the trend first seen in 2004 when China alone was accountable for 40 percent of the growth in world oil demand that year. As a result of these trends, and increasingly as a result of coordinated planning, political relationships, and market mechanisms, the key producers and consumers of the future are creating physical (infrastructure), political (diplomatic alliances), and commercial (long-term contracts and cross-investment) ties. China and Saudi Arabia remain the key drivers on their respective sides, and thus the tenor and temperature of that relationship is critical to the success or failure of this new energy architecture. The manner in which this relationship evolves and how it is received by other parties, especially the United States, will determine whether the emerging architecture enhances or threatens global energy security. As of now, however, while China and Saudi Arabia have embarked on the initial stages of a deepening commercial relationship, these efforts fall far short of a strategic partnership or a putative threat to U.S. interests.

Chronology

Although the fit between the world's fastest-growing energy market and the world's largest resource holder seems to be a natural one, the relationship has been a long time coming and is still evolving. Certain trends and patterns are already becoming clear, however. After many years of alternating between ignoring the Middle East and supporting various "revolutionary-minded" groups in the region, China has finally come to terms with the fact that there is the possibility of mutual benefits from a strategic partnership. China has become very active in the region in recent years on a number of fronts, making its value proposition on two lines: access to burgeoning Chinese market demand and the possibility of some type of strategic partnership. The second possibility became much more important and appealing to certain producers, namely Iran and Saudi Arabia, in the wake of September 11, as they sought a strategic counterweight to the United States. The defining characteristic of China's involvement in the Middle East energy sector has been the willingness to overlook ideological constraints that have limited the activities of the United States and other Western nations.

Somewhat surprisingly, given the amount of coverage now dedicated to the Sino–Saudi relationship, the two countries have only very recently established anything resembling a dialogue. While limited military sales between the two took place in the 1980s (see the following for details), formal diplomatic relations were not established until 1990 and initially remained driven primarily by discussions around potential further arms deals. Following the first Gulf war, the relationship was put on hold because China was loath to continue selling arms in a region of overwhelming strategic significance to the United States, especially a region where the United States maintained a large military footprint. In fact, the next high-level contact did not take place until almost a decade later, when then–Crown Prince (now King) Abdullah visited China in 1998. This visit coincided with the Asian Financial Crisis, which had severely affected both parties, albeit for different reasons. While China had other matters on its mind at the time, for Saudi Arabia it became clear that deepening its relationship with, and understanding of, a critical demand area and emerging consumer should be a key component of its energy management strategy.

Abdullah's outreach was reciprocated by then–President Jiang Zemin's visit to Riyadh the next year, during which the two sides laid the foundation blocks for a "strategic oil partnership." What that means in practice is still unclear, even to both parties. However, some insight may be gleaned from the details of the agreement signed, which stipulated that Saudi Arabia would open its domestic oil and gas market to China except for upstream oil exploration and production.[1] In return, China agreed to open its downstream sector to Saudi Aramco.[2]

Shortly thereafter, by 2002, Saudi Arabia had become China's leading for-eign supplier of crude oil. As figure 1 and figure 2 demonstrate, although the kingdom's relative position has fluctuated on a monthly basis, it remains one of the top suppliers to China.[3] This is a significant move by energy industry standards given that China had long built up supply relations with a variety of other countries, including Oman and the United Arab Emirates (UAE). The next step came as part of a broader regional effort when in 2005 the China-Arab Cooperation Forum and China-GCC Framework Agreement were established. The two initiatives are meant to delineate the parameters for future economic cooperation.

Figure 1. Top Suppliers of Chinese Crude Oil Imports, 2002–2005

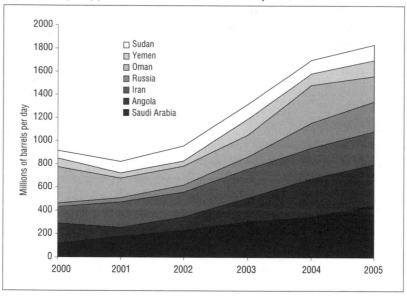

Figure 2. Changes in Key Chinese Suppliers, 2000 versus 2005

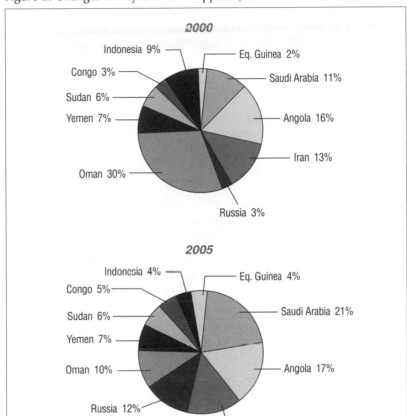

Until this year, then, relations had been initiated but were relatively low-key. Starting in early 2006, however, the relationship appears to have taken a qualitative step forward. In January, King Abdullah visited China on his first trip outside the Middle East since becoming monarch of the kingdom in August 2005, thus becoming the first sitting Saudi monarch to visit China since the two countries established relations in 1990. The two sides signed another broad pact covering "cooperation in oil, natural gas and minerals" but, as before, have yet to reveal the details. Additional negotiations were reported on a plan for building a crude pipeline from Saudi Arabia to China via Pakistan, but this remains a highly speculative prospect.

A few months later, in April 2006, President Hu Jintao made a return visit to Riyadh. His visit resulted in the signing of a Memorandum of Understanding that yielded the first concrete measures in the relationship, namely statements that Saudi Aramco is committed to supplying Sinopec and its affiliates with a minimum of 1 million barrels per day of Arabian crude by 2010 (a 39 percent increase from current levels).[4] Volume agreements of this type with a specific country are a relatively rare, although not unheard of, occurrence on the part of Saudi Aramco, which generally prefers to deal with term and spot contracts, therefore on a more market-driven basis.

One other card that the Chinese have played, albeit intermittently, is that of the Muslim connection. Approximately 20 million Chinese adhere to the Islamic faith, and thousands of them make the journey to Saudi Arabia each year to perform Hajj, the obligatory religious pilgrimage all Muslims are required to perform at least once in their lifetime. Although China generally does not treat religious minorities favorably, it recognized the link to the Middle East that Chinese Muslims gave the government. This process began following the Iranian Revolution, when China realized that "it was necessary to treat its own Muslims in a way that would not harm its relations with Iran."[5] The use of Hajj pilgrims as unofficial emissaries became more and more common, and "such contacts created, for the first time, a favorable opinion of China among both religious and political leaders in Saudi Arabia."[6]

China has realized that merely trading with a country is not enough to secure goodwill in the long run, and that a deeper, multifaceted and nuanced strategy needs to be employed to be moved to the front of the line for favored projects. In fact, by now almost all of the Gulf countries have entered into similar, multitiered bilateral agreements with China.

Military/Security History

While the Gulf has remained an American-managed region since the middle of the twentieth century, and therefore is generally closed to any moves that might be construed as "strategic" or threatening to U.S. interests, China's first real forays into the Gulf, particularly with Saudi Arabia, were primarily military sales. China has supplied weaponry to various states in the region, including sophisticated missiles and guidance systems to both Iran and Saudi Arabia.

Stymied by Washington's "special relationship" with Riyadh, China chose instead to go the route of providing what the United States could not or would not, namely missile technology. China reportedly sold fifty-six

CSS-2 intermediate-range (3,100 km) missiles to Saudi Arabia in the mid-1980s. However, a deterioration in Saudi–American relations following the events of 11 September 2001 led the Saudis to seriously reexamine the costs, benefits, and ultimate future of the relationship. Had matters not improved, as they seem to have done over the course of 2005, Saudi Arabia may have looked to China to provide an expanded security and strategic role in the region. Whether China, for its part, would have been willing or able to play such a role is perhaps doubtful, but any such move would represent a significant departure from previous policies.

While China will not be able to replace the United States or its role in the Gulf in any meaningful way in the foreseeable future, any further strain in the Saudi–U.S. relationship may prompt a reestablishment of military sales, especially in the face of regional trends surrounding Iran and Iraq.

How the region deals with the dual issue of a collapsing Iraq and a resurgent Iran remains very much uncertain. China has strategic and commercial interests in both countries, and therefore how it chooses to play its role will have broader repercussions, particularly in its relationship with Saudi Arabia, not to mention the United States.

Following Saddam's invasion of Kuwait in 1990, China abstained from the UN Security Council resolution authorizing use of force against Iraq. China also began calling for an end to sanctions as early as 1994 and, together with France, held up the reparations claims made by Kuwait, saying that more proof and time were needed to establish the correct amount due. These moves were entirely motivated by self-interest and were recognized by the beneficiary as such. Iraq awarded China National Petroleum Corporation (CNPC) the rights to develop the al-Ahdab field for $1.3 billion, in the event that the UN sanctions were lifted. China and Iraq also signed a preliminary agreement for the Halfayah field but were unable to finalize terms. With the second largest proven reserves in the world, Iraq was an opportune place for China to begin its first large-scale overseas investments aimed at securing future sources of energy.

These agreements with Iraq were likely a major factor in China's adamant opposition to the U.S. invasion of Iraq in 2003. In fact, China threatened to veto any resolution brought to the Security Council authorizing the use of force, which was one of the reasons the United States was forced to go in without a UN mandate. Given that there is unlikely to be a resolution of either the security or hydrocarbon regulatory issues in the foreseeable future, China will likely have to look elsewhere for the time being. An important issue in Iraq's reconstruction will be the awarding of contracts to develop the country's one major resource and product. The new Iraqi government will be closely watched to see if it will honor old contracts and if it will award new contracts to companies from other nations.

If the security situation continues to deteriorate, and a collapsing Iraq pulls neighboring countries into its vortex, either through floods of refugees, an extension of conflict across border areas, or armed intervention by regional powers on behalf of their proxy interest groups inside Iraq, China may be looked upon by the region to help manage the situation. China's options for doing so are limited, however. China was reluctant to commit troops to the 2003 invasion and certainly would not do so now, and it is limited in its other response capabilities. Short of total collapse, Chinese companies have a higher tolerance for security risk than most international oil companies, and thus might be willing to begin oil operations even in an uncertain environment, should their contracts be revived. This would allow some funds to begin flowing, although whether at that point it would be to the central government or the regional authorities is an open question. Helping Iraq produce more oil to bring to the market would have been viewed somewhat negatively by Saudi Arabia a few years ago because that would have forced the latter to cut back some of the market share it had gained in the wake of the Gulf War, but given the tightness in the market today, the Organization of Petroleum Exporting Countries (OPEC) could likely absorb Iraqi increases with minimal pain, and thus the Sino–Saudi relationship would remain unaffected.

Iran, however, may be a different story. Other than a brief period in the 1990s, Saudi Arabia has always been concerned with Iran as a strategic competitor in the region. It was Saudi Arabia who led the funding of Iraq during the Iran-Iraq War, pouring billions into that country to help it face off against Iran. Iran's apparent push to acquire a nuclear weapon has greatly alarmed Saudi decision makers because this would definitively tip the balance of power in the region. At the very least, this would likely force the Saudis to repair and reinforce their relationship with the United States, a potentially risky decision from a domestic politics viewpoint. Domestic opposition to increased dealings with the United States runs high among both religious and more secular sectors of Saudi society. Saudi Arabia would thus prefer to deal with Iran through other means, which is where China comes into the equation. One of the reasons Iran has pursued this current course is that it feels "protected" by China and Russia; Iran believes neither country will allow the Security Council to move forward in authorizing military force against it. To date, this has certainly proven true and, although Saudi Arabia has no wish to see another military conflict so close to home, has rankled Saudi Arabia. China is also facilitating Iran's activities in another way: by investing in its energy sector. Chinese national oil companies (NOCs) and Iran have signed a series of deals encompassing oil and gas exploration and production (E&P) and liquefied natural gas (LNG) deliveries. Iran is thus subject to far less financial pressure than it might otherwise be feeling.

Although Saudi Arabia certainly does not view the Chinese–Iranian relationship with any favor, it has not yet risen to the level of an issue that might significantly impact Sino–Saudi relations. Should matters take a downward turn from here, however, that possibility remains open.

Oil Deals

Although a very recent entrant on the international oil scene, at least from a corporate perspective, China has made substantial strides in securing fields and production rights and is beginning to undertake larger and more complex projects. In less than ten years, Chinese companies have managed to secure fields in Sudan, Iran, Saudi Arabia, Kuwait, Iraq, and Kazakhstan, to name but a few areas. The crucial point to note here is that China has been able to secure these deals despite its lack of world-class technical expertise primarily by leveraging two approaches (often in concert): offering extremely favorable contract terms and utilizing "soft power" and arms sales linkages.

China, as noted earlier, has been working since 2000 to secure a long-term, tangible relationship with Saudi Arabia. In fact, as soon as China became a net importer and began to realize both the importance of Saudi oil and the U.S. near-monopoly in terms of strategic concerns, it began looking for ways to get its foot in the door. With the Saudis' gradual shift of power away from the United States beginning in 1995, China has seen a golden opportunity to offer itself as the alternative, and the effort has begun to pay dividends.

Saudi Arabia has also realized the benefits of having unfettered access to one of the world's largest consumers of oil. China's need for imported oil, specifically imported Middle Eastern oil, is set to grow at an extraordinary rate in the coming years. However, a problem arose in the early stages of the burgeoning relationship: Chinese demand is mostly for light, sweet crude oil, and not the heavy, sour crude that Saudi Arabia generally produces. Saudi Arabia thus came to realize that to make its oil attractive to the Chinese market, it would have to provide some assistance. The result of the two conflating trends was that China and Saudi Arabia entered into the 1999 agreement mentioned earlier, under which China will allow Saudi companies to make downstream refinery investments in China, and in return Chinese companies will be active in upstream oil activities in Saudi Arabia.

In terms of the first part of the agreement, work began with the construction of a major refinery and petrochemical project in Quanzhou city in the province of Fujian. The complex is being built to handle up to 240,000 barrels per day (bpd) of high-sulfur Saudi crude oil. Construction began in July 2005 and is scheduled to be completed by the first half of 2008. Petrochemical products are to include ethylene, polyethylene, and polypropylene, among others. The Saudis are contributing $750 million out of the total $3 billion required. The companies participating in the project were Sinopec (50 percent stake), Saudi Aramco (25 percent), and ExxonMobil (25 percent). However, the project stalled for some time over a dispute brought by ExxonMobil regarding marketing of the products. Although the dispute has recently been resolved, it is important to note that subsequent projects undertaken by the Saudis and Chinese do not include any international oil companies (IOCs).

For example, the next project between the partners is to be an ethylene project, agreed upon in 2006. The agreement covered a joint venture between Saudi Aramco and Sinopec, establishing the Fujian Ethylene JV (joint venture), with an ethylene steam cracker with a capacity of 800,000 tons per year (tpy); a 1 million tpy aromatics unit; and a 650,000 tpy polyethylene unit.[7] A 300,000 tons crude berth and associated utilities will also be built. Production from this facility is slated to begin in early 2009.

It is important to note, however, that there are occasional bumps in the road of the Sino–Saudi partnership; specifically, regarding the marketing side of the Quanzhou/Fujian deal, Sinopec only agreed to establish a retail joint venture involving six hundred service stations and proved unwilling to cooperate with the other partners in the wholesale sector for the entire province. Saudi Aramco holds a 22.5 percent stake in the Fujian marketing joint venture, with Sinopec (55 percent), and ExxonMobil (22.5 percent) holding the rest. Furthermore, cooperation in the trading company has been complicated because Beijing has tightly regulated retail prices and reportedly does not want to share the financial risk with the Saudi side.

Nonetheless, Saudi Aramco has followed up the Quanzhou deal with another one recently, signing an MOU to acquire a 25 percent stake in the greenfield (i.e., new development) Qingdao refinery in Shandong province. Sinopec, Shandong International Trust Investment Corp., and Qingdao International Investment Trust hold the remaining shares. The estimated total investment for the project is 9.7 billion yuan (approximately $1.2 billion).

Saudi Aramco and Sinopec reached a follow-on agreement to supply Saudi crude to the 200,800 bpd (10 million tpy) refinery which would be expanded to 400,000 bpd, due to be completed by end 2007. The first phase of the investment is 1.2 billion yuan ($150 million), and both sides have definitively indicated that final approval of the deal is forthcoming shortly.

The Qingdao refinery is strategically a very important project for Sinopec, as it would allow the Chinese company to challenge PetroChina (owned by CNPC, Sinopec's domestic NOC rival) on its home turf in northeastern China. Saudi Arabia has shown an interest in marketing the oil products in Shandong province, but Sinopec appears reluctant to give even more influence to Saudi Aramco. Sinopec will likely ship in Saudi crude for the Huangdao storage (18.4 million barrels) near the refinery and use that as the primary feedstock.

The Saudis are showing via these projects that they are truly committed to cementing their role in the Chinese market and are providing even more financing and technical assistance to complete projects. The Quanzhou development is an important test case for the two sides (Saudi Arabia and China) because its likely success will prove the logic of such tie-ups in the future. Specifically, the project will prove that it makes sense for the Saudis to build "captive capacity" in its target market; by building refineries that are calibrated for the specifications of Saudi crude, this makes it more difficult and more expensive for the refinery to process crude from other suppliers. Chinese refining capacity is not well suited to heavier Saudi crudes, but the Saudis are said to have shifted some of their lighter crudes to the Chinese market from other customers with more developed refining infrastructure. An additional motivation may be the "Asian premium" of roughly $1 per barrel for Saudi crude.[8]

On the other hand, Sinopec–Aramco deals allow Aramco a stable receiver for its crude production *and* entrance into the Chinese wholesale and retail product market. However, it has been suggested that Aramco is probably selling its crude oil to these refineries at below-market prices to compensate for the low capped prices of refined products in the Chinese market. But the deals are also beneficial for Sinopec because it needs the foreign investment to fund its ambitious project slate. Also, the deals ensure a stable supply of crude for its refinery and more stable oil prices. Aramco's rationale for taking a loss, if indeed it is doing so, is that China's wholesale market is likely to open up to foreign investment in late 2007 and 2008, and Aramco's moves are thus designed to pre-position in anticipation of such an opening, given the company's interest in expanding its presence in this market. Also, because this is direct investment by Saudi Arabia in China's downstream sector, the crude oil supplied to China's refineries is not limited by OPEC export quotas, which provides additional incentive.

Chinese Investment in Saudi Arabia's Energy Infrastructure

By entering the Saudi upstream sector, Chinese companies have succeeded where many other oil companies have not. In what is widely seen as one of the most portentous shifts in Saudi oil (and by extension foreign) policy, the awards in the recent Saudi gas bidding round all went to non-U.S. companies. This is especially significant for China because it was able to secure one of the most promising blocks—designated areas in which a company has exploration rights—and thereby establish a true foothold in the Saudi upstream sector.[9] Sinopec was awarded an 80 percent stake in the exploration and development project of Block B of the Rub-al Khali (Empty Quarter) gas fields (38,800 square km).

Sinopec landed the deal by agreeing to take minimal amounts of royalty-free condensate (30 million barrels, compared to the second place bid of 150 million barrels) and to conduct extensive (and expensive) seismic work.[10] Sinopec has said it will invest $300 million in the first phase of exploration alone, drilling wells and conducting seismic surveys. The exploration period is divided into three phases totaling up to ten years, with the second and third phases optional. It has a twenty-five-year production term, with the maximum term of the whole contract set at forty years. The deal itself is unlikely to yield much in the way of commercial returns for Sinopec, and indeed one of the reasons the IOCs did not win any blocks was because they were unwilling to accept a rate of return as low as Sinopec's. For Sinopec, however, securing the rights to this project fulfilled a number of aims. First, it helped Chinese companies establish a presence in the most critical hydrocarbon producer in the world, a presence that to that date had been lacking. Second, it allowed Sinopec to expand its experience in upstream gas E&P activity, a key driver for the company as it seeks to become more corporatized and commercially well-rounded. While Sinopec has some experience with domestic gas, this type of project will allow it to make a significant improvement in this area of its E&P portfolio.

Block B is estimated to hold reserves of 800 billion cubic meters (bcm) of natural gas, of which 300 bcm are recoverable and about 15 bcm could be produced per annum. From the Saudi perspective, giving the concession to the Chinese NOCs does not bring some of the commercial benefits, such as technology transfer, that the projects might have brought in under Western IOCs. The fact that this deal has gone ahead despite a clear-cut commercial driver can thus be seen as a sign that Saudi Arabia wants to develop a more robust strategic relationship with China as a hedging strategy against the United States, partly by allowing long-term strategic concerns to outweigh short-term commercial goals.

This move has substantial implications for future development in Saudi Arabia, and it provides China with the funds, experience, and impetus to go after future projects in the same manner. For Saudi Arabia, although the focus has historically always been on oil, gas development is becoming increasingly important. Given the demographic boom the country is experiencing, the electrical power needs are going to be enormous. Gas and power will be especially critical for desalination activities, without which Saudi Arabia will be short of potable water. Gas is also a crucial component of the expansion of the petrochemical sector, an area that is being looked at to provide substantial job growth. Once again, China was able to capture a critical project by following a shrewd policy of sacrificing short-term gains for a more fruitful long-term strategic vision.

The trend of cross-investment between the two countries thus remains strong, especially in the downstream sector. Saudi Arabia has an aggressive strategy in the petrochemical industry because it wants to have a 15 percent share of the global plastics market by 2020 and to boost ethylene output to 14 million tons by 2010 (it is 7 million tons at present). The chairman of the Saudi Arabian General Investment Authority, Amr Al-Dabbagh, has suggested that "instead of the Chinese watching their market share globally shrinking, they would be better off being part of the action." Rather, he maintains it makes economic sense for Chinese firms to process petrochemicals in Saudi Arabia instead of shipping energy and raw materials home to do it there, given the abundance of cheap energy and feedstock in the kingdom and a lack of the same in China.

Saudi Investments in China's Energy Infrastructure

As part of this process, Sinopec, together with the Netherlands' AK, recently won a construction contract bid for Saudi Arabian Basic Industries Corporation's (SABIC, the major state-owned petrochemical producer) 400,000 tpy polyethylene project and 400,000 tpy polypropylene project, involving $760 million of investment. Sinopec holds 50 percent of both projects. Overall, Saudi Arabia needs to invest $50 billion over the next fifteen to twenty years to become one of the top three producers in the sector. SABIC is currently the world's seventh largest petrochemical producer, but it intends to move into one of the top positions as soon as is feasible.

To this end, SABIC is negotiating with the Dalian Shide Group regarding the formation of a joint venture to expand the former's ethylene presence in China. The project itself would be a 50–50 joint venture and would involve the construction of a 400,000 tpy ethylene plant in Huludao, Liaoning province. The investment required is estimated to be approximately $5.2 billion, but the project overall needs to be approved by the National Development and Reform Commission.

SABIC, meanwhile, is also considering cooperation with Sinopec in its refining and petrochemical project in Tianjin (Northeast China). This project, in turn, involves expanding Sinopec subsidiary Tianjin Petrochemical's 110,000 bpd refinery to 250,000 bpd; building a cracker with a capacity of 1 million tpy; and constructing units for petrochemical derivatives. The project is estimated to cost $3.1 billion, with start-up slated for late 2008 or 2009. No other foreign investor has yet established a foothold of similar value in northeastern China. Western majors BP, Shell, and ExxonMobil have been limited to building petrochemical plants in eastern and southern China. The Chinese government is encouraging companies to integrate petrochemical units with refineries. But the issue for foreign investors is how to market refined oil products, unless they sell through their Chinese distribution network.

SABIC has also shown interest in another 400,000 tpy polyvinyl chloride plant in Liaoning, in cooperation with the Jinzhou-based Jinhua Chemical Group. The Shide Group, in turn, is also considering building a chemical plant in Saudi Arabia.

Other future energy plans include ongoing negotiations by Sinopec to build a refinery in Saudi Arabia with Saudi Aramco. The Saudis, for their part, have been promoting the idea of a strategic oil reserve facility in Hainan, but agreements since then have been stalled because the Saudis wanted to run and own it and the Chinese, to date, have turned down the suggestion.[11] The Aramco Overseas Company has opened an office in Shanghai, China, to tap local manufacturing competence and material supply services.

Reports have suggested that Saudi Arabia may use its price flexibility to try to secure a long-term energy relationship in China by undercutting competitors. The contracting process for Saudi crude is opaque enough to do so, and Riyadh has the lowest extraction costs of all producers. This would be similar in nature and application to the 2001 "July shift" vis-à-vis Japan in which Saudi Arabia supposedly offered Japan oil at a rate that undercut the UAE's price, and Saudi's exports grew by 20.7 percent while the UAE's exports dropped by 19.7 percent.

Trade

While the natural synergies on the energy front are obvious and are beginning to be jointly exploited, general trade is also on the rise. Traditionally, the relationship had been markedly one-way, with China providing Saudi Arabia with manufactured goods, and Saudi in return shipping minimal amounts of crude. Beginning in 2000, however, this relationship reversed itself in dramatic fashion. While Chinese exports to Saudi Arabia continued to increase steadily, Saudi exports to China increased greatly in 2000. The increase is partially a nominal effect due to the run-up in prices, but an increase in oil volumes has been the real driver. Saudi Arabia currently provides about 17 percent of China's oil imports and is its second largest supplier. China contracted to buy 500,000 bpd of Saudi crude in 2006, a number that is forecast to double by the beginning of the next decade.

Chinese efforts in Saudi Arabia have included the building of a "trade city" within Jeddah, where everything from textiles to chemicals and commodities will be sold. China has in fact already become the seventh biggest trading partner of Saudi Arabia, despite establishing formal relations only a few years ago, with trade between the two countries totaling over 1 billion dollars worth of goods every year. China and Saudi Arabia are also studying a plan on the establishment of a fund to encourage investment between the two countries. The Saudis are trying to encourage Chinese investment in sectors outside of energy, including transport, health care, and life science.

The kingdom is looking for partnerships with Chinese companies to mine for phosphate in northern Saudi Arabia and build rail lines to transport the raw material to Jubail and Dammam on the Gulf coast. There it would be used for making fertilizers that would be shipped to Chinese and Asian markets. A Chinese company is said to have agreed to invest in a $4 billion bauxite refinery to produce alumina or aluminum oxide, a resource the mainland needs to make aluminum but has been lacking.

Role of Chinese NOCs and Service Companies

Chinese NOCs, with their improving technical capacity and government mandate to secure access to energy resources abroad, have been key in the emerging Sino–Saudi relationship. Sinopec's contract to conduct geological work in the Saudi Empty Quarter is a critical example of this type of cooperation.

There is no question that, given projected Chinese oil import requirements, the Chinese will have to look at the Middle East as the most critical supplier of its crude in the future. However, in terms of targeting the region for access, little has been done directly in the Middle East as of yet. This is not because the Chinese government does not realize the long-term centrality of Middle East crude supplies, but rather because it feels that it cannot overtly target the region without alarming other global powers. The Chinese government's instructions to China's NOCs rank the Middle East as one of the most important regions in terms of priority in their quest for overseas energy assets, but efforts to date have focused on less politically sensitive areas such as Southeast Asia and Africa. The Chinese are faced with a dilemma: in terms of volumes, both the Middle East and Central Asia make the most sense, but both regions are overshadowed by outside powers—Russia, in the case of Central Asia, and the United States, in the case of the Gulf. About 60 percent of China's oil imports already come from the region that holds greater petroleum reserves and production than anywhere else in the world. But Beijing fears that Washington has already established hegemonic power over the Middle East and might easily interdict supplies bound from there to China. The NOCs (CNPC, Sinopec, and China National Offshore Oil Corporation) represent an excellent mechanism for China to establish a presence of strategic value in the Middle East in a nonthreatening manner, and thus will be the preferred tool for Chinese activities in the region.

Another part of the emerging Chinese strategy for securing projects in the Middle East has been China's focus on providing oil services as a supplement to E&P operations. China Petroleum Engineering and Construction Corporation (CPECC), the construction arm of CNPC, began in 1983 to undertake projects in Kuwait, Iraq, and Pakistan. Its strategy has rested on competing for subcontracts and small turnkey contracts. The real boost to this approach began occurring in the mid-1990s when CPECC won an oil-storage reconstruction project in Kuwait valued at $400 million. By leveraging this experience, CPECC was able to secure projects elsewhere in the region, contributing to a $10 billion final value of all Chinese overseas oil-service contracts by the end of 1997. In fact, over the period 1992–97, oil material and equipment exports grew 710 times, from $0.43 million in 1992 to $322 million in 1997. Another company that did very well during this time was the Great Wall Drilling Company (GWDC), set up in 1993. GWDC was able to capture growing drilling opportunities in Sudan, Egypt, Qatar,

Tunisia, Nigeria, Oman, and other parts of the Arab world. Saudi Arabia in particular has taken to hiring Chinese service companies and drilling crews in the face of global shortages in the sector.

Conclusion

It is critical to realize that China has been successful in pursuing its partnership in Saudi Arabia because it has brought a number of factors to the table, including political support, the prospect of building on military technology transfers initiated in the 1980s, soft-power ties, and a "no-questions-asked" policy on the Saudi domestic politics front.

China's current initiatives are strictly civil and commercial. The Chinese argue, and the Saudis acknowledge, that the bulk of Saudi oil exports will move to Asia in the future for purely economic reasons (rising demand and low transport costs). Riyadh wants to begin expanding its position in this market, if only as a way of reducing its traditional commercial over-reliance upon the United States.

The warming of relations between Riyadh and Beijing has been possible in part because they do share certain interests. China has long been more supportive of the Palestinians than has the United States, and Beijing shares Riyadh's conviction that America's program for regime change in the Middle East is destabilizing and that it has used the "war against terror" to cloak the expansion of its global influence. At the same time, the ideological rapport of China with the antimodern monarchies of the Gulf is even weaker than its allegiance to Tehran, and one of the dirtiest secrets of the international arms trade is that China's imports of military electronics and software from Tel-Aviv make it one of Israel's main trade partners.

Thus, neither the Chinese nor the Saudis view their agreements as an erosion of the kingdom's long-standing military and political dependence upon the United States. No other country can deliver the quantity or quality of troops for the defense of the Arabian Peninsula that the United States can. The Saudis and all of the other Arab Gulf states will have to continue relying upon American protection, and they will continue to pay for it by awarding most of their arms contracts to U.S. firms and informally guaranteeing that they will continue to keep the U.S. market well supplied with oil.

But improved relations between Beijing and Riyadh will give the latter a little more autonomy, a bit more breathing space. And they will form a small step in the former's quest for energy security, a step that will become more significant over time. Some experts think that 50 percent of China's oil imports will come from the kingdom by 2010. Others think that the Saudi capacity to expand production to meet Chinese demand has been over-estimated. Either way, the Middle East alone does not hold the solution. But while Chinese–Saudi relations are unlikely for the foreseeable future to become a "strategic relationship" rivaling that of the United States and Saudi Arabia, a deepening commercial partnership is emerging, to the benefit of both players and indeed the world at large.

Notes

1. Upstream activities focus solely on the discovery and production of hydrocarbons, prior to transportation or refining.

2. Downstream oil refers to activities pertaining to the refining and processing of crude oil into usable products ranging from heating oil to diesel to gasoline, as well as the retail and marketing aspects of these products; it can sometimes extend into petrochemicals as well. Downstream gas refers to the distribution and marketing of gas; when used in terms of liquefied natural gas (LNG), the definition extends to the point of regasification as well.

3. "Oil Imports from All Sources on the Increase," Ministry of Commerce of the People's Republic of China website, 6 March 2007, http://english.mofcom.gov.cn/arti cle/newsrelease/significantnews/200703/20070304425961.html.

4. "Arabian crude" is the term for the slate of crudes produced by Saudi Arabia; the slate then encompasses heavy, medium, and light grades.

5. Mohammed bin Huwaidin, *China's Relations with Arabia and the Gulf: 1949-1999* (London: RoutledgeCurzon, 2002).

6. Ibid.

7. "Cracking" is a petroleum refining process in which gas, oil, and other "heavy" petroleum feedstocks are broken down under heat and pressure in the presence of a catalyst in order to increase the yield of gasoline, diesel, jet fuel, and other high value "light" petroleum products. A "cracker" is a tower-shaped device that accomplishes this process.

8. The "Asian premium" is a quasi-official surcharge that results in Middle Eastern oil shipped to Asia, on average, costing $1/barrel (freight on board) more than Middle Eastern oil being shipped to Europe or America. Reasons given by the Middle Eastern producers for this premium vary, but one clear contender is the desire, especially on the part of the Saudis, to capture and maintain market share in the key Western markets. The Middle Eastern producers have viewed this subsidy as a way to maintain a strategic link to the Western powers.

9. Readers should note that Saudi Arabia still has not opened its upstream oil exploration and production to foreigners.

10. Royalty-free condensate is hydrocarbon liquids found in natural gas, on which the company will not have to pay royalties. Thus, lower royalty-free condensates means that the company has agreed to take fewer such barrels and will pay royalties much earlier in the production cycle.

11. The Saudi interest in commercial storage facilities and refineries in China stems from the fact that sour Saudi crude is often not an appropriate feedstock for most of China's existing refineries. By investing in downstream infrastructure in China, the Saudis are helping to ensure Chinese demand for Saudi crude oil.

Ahmed Hashim

China's Evolving Relationship with Iran

SEVERAL CENTURIES AGO THE CHINESE EXPLORER Zhang Qian (126 BC) established the first known contact between China and the territories that incorporated modern Iran, known in his time as Parthia. Naturally as an explorer he wrote a report on life in Parthia, which he referred to as "Anxi," a Chinese transliteration of Arsacid, the name of the ruling Parthian dynasty at the time. As Zhang reported:

> Anxi is situated several thousand li west of the region of the Great Yuezhi (in Transoxonia). The people are settled on the land, cultivating the fields and growing rice and wheat. They also make wine out of grapes. They have walled cities like the people of Dayuan (Ferghana Valley), the region contains several hundred cities of various sizes. The coins of the country are made of silver and bear the face of the king. When the king dies, the currency is immediately changed and new coins issued with the face of his successor. The people keep records by writing on horizontal strips of leather. To the west lies Tiaozi (Mesopotamia) and to the north Yancai and Lixuan (Hyrcania).[1]

Not surprisingly, both the Iranians and the Chinese make a great deal of the long-standing contacts between their mutual ancient civilizations. When the president of the People's Republic of China (PRC) Jiang Zemin made his historical official visit to Iran in 2002, the first by a Chinese leader since the emergence of the Islamic Republic of Iran (IRI), he and Iranian president Mohammad Khatami spared no effort to highlight the civilizational aspect of the ties even as they promised to further promote bilateral relations. Jiang was quoted by the English-language *Tehran Times* as saying: "Our forefathers began friendly exchanges through the world-famous Silk Road more than 2,000 years ago."[2] The theme was continued by Beijing's ambassador to Iran, Sun Bigan, who said that China and Iran were seeking to "revive their golden Silk Road ties."[3] In his new and authoritative study of Sino–Iranian relations John Garver highlights this aspect of the bilateral relationship. But he also points out that it is primarily based on more tangible factors, which he then examines skillfully in considerable detail.[4]

Indeed, neither the Iranians nor the Chinese were interested in merely waxing lyrical over their ancient ties during the course of the Chinese leader's historic visit to the Islamic Republic. Both instead were determined to develop their bilateral ties on a concrete basis. In the past decade and a half relations have grown dramatically because of the PRC's insatiable energy needs and Iran's hunger for technology, consumer goods, and its desire to create a tight web of interdependence with the growing economies of the non-Western world. Nonetheless, the relationship still has a long way to go; contrary to alarmist analyses and journalistic observations, the bilateral relationship between the IRI and the PRC is not strategic in the way that long-standing Sino–Pakistani relations have been. This is the underlying theme of this short study of the relationship. The PRC cannot afford to put all its eggs in the Iranian basket; it is developing energy relations with many countries apart from the IRI.[5] Moreover, the latter's poor and inexorably declining relations with the West, particularly the United States, over the Iranian nuclear controversy and its activities in turmoil-ridden Iraq have acted to limit the expansion of Sino–Iranian relations.[6] The PRC is not going to damage its important ties with the United States over the Iranian nuclear controversy. The Iranians, for their part, have recognized that there are limits to how far China and other major powers— such as Russia—will go to insulate Iran from sanctions as a result of its nuclear proliferation activities that the international community suspects is taking place. In this context, the PRC supported the limited sanctions imposed on the IRI by the United Nations Security Council in late December 2006 in Resolution 1737, which restricted sales of some technology, curbed the right to travel of Iranian officials involved in the nuclear program, and reiterated its call for Iran to suspend all enrichment-related and reprocessing activities. With these considerations in mind, this chapter will explore the origins of the contemporary bilateral relationship between the two countries and the nature of the economic and energy relationship, and will conclude with a closer examination of the obstacles that limit the further evolution of their bilateral ties.

Historical Background to Contemporary Sino-Iranian Relations

Imperial Iran and the People's Republic of China established commercial and trade relations in 1950, one year after the emergence of the PRC. But it was not until 1971 that they established formal diplomatic relations. The ruler of Iran, Mohammad Reza Shah, was fervently anti-Marxist and viewed the machinations of radical powers with considerable loathing. This sentiment was based, no doubt, on Iran's historical experiences with its huge and interfering neighbor to the north, first Tsarist Russia and then the Soviet Union. The Shah never forgot Soviet mischief-making in northern Iran, specifically in Azerbaijan and Kurdistan after World War II. The PRC did not figure in this, of course. But the Sino–Soviet split in the early 1960s did not mean much in Iranian strategic considerations until much later. Indeed, the Sino–Soviet break did not make the former any more savory, as far as the Iranian monarch was concerned. In a conversation with Dr. Henry Kissinger and U.S. official Harold Saunders in 1969 the Iranian monarch indicated that he was worried by Chinese adventurism along the Soviet–PRC border.[7] The Shah expressed his fears shortly after the fierce border clashes between the two Communist giants in March on Damanski Island on the Ussuri River. Moreover, the PRC supported the Marxist-inspired rebellion in the province of Dhofar in the Sultanate of Oman, which was strategically located on the southern shores of the Strait of Hormuz. As the self-appointed guardian of Persian Gulf security following the British decision to withdraw from "east of Suez," the Iranian ruler intervened in this conflict to support the forces of conservatism and stability.[8]

Bilateral relations improved significantly from the mid-1970s; particularly when Deng Xiaoping took over power in the PRC in 1976 and set the country on the road to the Four Modernizations (advancements in agriculture, industry, science and technology, and national defense) and a rapid improvement in relations with the West as part of an overall policy of "reform and opening up." In this context Iran, which was then an ally of the West and a major client of the United States, saw much merit in stronger strategic ties with the PRC, a major anti-Soviet power. Moreover, at the regional level, the Shah was very much concerned with the weakening of neighboring Pakistan following its devastating defeat in the Indo–Pakistan War of 1971, and like

China's leadership he viewed pro-Soviet India with considerable suspicion. One could argue that there were elements of a strategic Sino–Iranian consensus concerning the baleful impact of the close Indo–Soviet relationship on the subcontinent. But in no way did this constitute a strategic alliance between Imperial Iran and the PRC. Last but not least, the Shah did not see the PRC as a model for economic development and modernization; for him the Asian power that Imperial Iran needed to emulate was Japan.

The Shah fell from power as a result of the 1979 Revolution and was replaced by a radical Islamic Republic under Ayatollah Khomeini. Relations between the PRC and the new revolutionary republic were not warm. Iran's new rulers remembered that Mao's anointed but short-lived successor Hua Guofeng had visited the Shah in 1978. Furthermore, while the PRC was improving its relations with the West, Iran under its new rulers was seemingly bent on alienating the West as much as possible. This was reflected not only in Khomeini's ideology of "Neither East nor West," which highlighted his rejection of the Marxist socialist and the Western capitalist paths to progress, and substitution of an Islamist one, but also in the Iranian takeover of the U.S. Embassy in Tehran and the incarceration of American hostages for 444 days. This breach of diplomatic norms, which continues to poison U.S.–Iranian relations, was viewed with considerable opprobrium by the rest of the world, including by the PRC. The Iranians retorted that the Chinese themselves had done something similar in 1948 to the U.S. consulate in Shenyang (Mukden). Nonetheless, the PRC opposed the imposition of sanctions on the IRI for its breach of diplomatic norms.

During the first few years of the 1980s the IRI was under its most radical phase, generally referred to as the First Republic, during which its energies were focused on fending off internal and external enemies and consolidating the revolution along Islamic lines. Ironically, at that time there were many within the hierarchy of the IRI who saw Maoist China as a role model in everything from economic self-sufficiency, revolutionary fervor, and war-making capabilities along the lines of people's war. Among the most fervent exponents of this line of thinking was Iranian defense minister Mustafa Chamran, who died in the early stages of the Iran-Iraq War; it was due to him that much of Iran's initial resistance to the Iraqi invasion of Iran was organized as a popular war by armed citizen militias and revolutionary forces.

By the mid-1980s the exigencies of the Iran-Iraq War and the IRI's desperate need for arms supplies to replenish its deteriorating U.S.-equipped military provided the impetus for Tehran to reach out to Beijing. The PRC first began exporting missiles to the IRI in 1985. Iran acquired jet fighters, tanks, and large stores of ammunition from the PRC. The regular Iranian military—accustomed to high-tech Western weaponry—was not particularly keen on lower-grade military technology from the PRC; instead, most of the Chinese weaponry was used either for training purposes or went to equip the Islamic Revolutionary Guards Corps. Iran's most notable acquisitions were missiles. The PRC sold the IRI large quantities of antiship missiles and provided it with technical help for its surface-to-surface missile program. However, at the same time the PRC was also supplying Iran's co-belligerent, Iraq.[9] Given this context, it is difficult to argue that there was a strategic foundation behind the relationship at that stage. Iran was desperate to counter Iraqi air power's reach into Iran, and China was driven by commercial considerations to sell ballistic missiles. But throughout the 1990s China continued to provide Iran with ballistic missiles and also with the requisite technology, equipment, training, and testing that allowed Iran to proceed with the indigenous production of ballistic missiles based on Chinese and North Korean designs.[10] Following U.S.–China summits in 1997 and 1998, Beijing decided to halt the sales of ballistic missiles and associated technologies.[11] But doubts continue to exist concerning whether Beijing has acted to effectively curtail the activities of Chinese companies in promoting the development of Iran's missile programs. The United States and its intelligence services are skeptical.[12] China was suspected of helping Iran modify its antiship missiles in 1999–2000. Nonetheless, over the course of the past decade North Korea moved into position as the key country in aiding Iran's ballistic missile programs.

Emergence of Close Sino–Iranian Relations in the 1990s

The onset of the 1990s witnessed the development of closer bilateral relations between the two countries due to profound strategic changes in the regional and international arenas.

The Strategic and Economic Context

The end of the Iran-Iraq War in 1988 found Iran devastated and in dire need of economic reconstruction. In 1989 the parliamentary speaker Hashemi Rafsanjani won the presidential elections and sought to promote political liberalization, economic development and reconstruction, and a greater opening to the outside world. Rafsanjani inaugurated the "Second Republic," a Thermidorian reaction against the radicalism and rhetoric of the 1980s. The Iranians began to pay greater attention to the Chinese experiment in development and modernization. With over 70 million people, Iran, along with Turkey and Egypt, is one of the Middle East's largest consumer markets. It has a large, educated population, a significant industrial base in need of modernization, and a dire need for technology and capital goods. While the energy aspect of the bilateral relationship is important (as will be discussed below), it is erroneous to think that economic relations are limited to energy. On the contrary, as has been extensively detailed by Garver, they range the gamut from construction of the Tehran metro to airports, paper mills, and refineries.[13] Initially, Sino–Iranian economic relations and trade were not substantial. They reached $713 million in 1993. While witnessing a sharp reversal in 1994, it registered a 20.2 percent increase in the first quarter of the following year.[14] They continued to rise thereafter and in 2002, totaled $3.742 billion, with Chinese exports to Iran accounting for $1.396 billion while Iranian imports to China totaled $2.346 billion. China's exports to Iran grew 34.8 percent more than China's total exports. From 1999 to 2002, bilateral trade value between China and Iran grew nearly twofold, and China's exports to Iran doubled. During the same period, Iranian imports to China increased by 242 percent. From January to August 2003, the bilateral trade value neared $3.8 billion, exceeding the entire value of 2002. Both countries were interested in expanding the economic relationship further. On 23–24 October 2003 the Chinese and Iranians held an extensive trade seminar in Beijing. It was the first seminar held in China specifically on trade exchanges with the Iranian market. During the seminar representatives from both Chinese and Iranian enterprises discussed the future prospects for Sino–Iranian economic and trade relations, Iran's investment environment, and problems that the Chinese could expect to encounter with trade and investment in Iran. By 2006, 250 Chinese firms were engaged in industrial and construction projects in Iran. In a measure of the importance that personalities have played in the deepening of the bilateral ties between these two Asian powers, the architect of the explosion in Iranian trade and commercial relations with China was Iranian ambassador Fereydoun Vardinejad whose tenure in Beijing ended in 2006.[15]

In 1989 China underwent the upheavals of Tiananmen Square rebellion, which were occasioned by the belief of students, intellectuals, and urban workers that the Communist Party had become too repressive and unresponsive to people's needs. This rebellion, which was ruthlessly crushed, was watched carefully by the Iranian government, which was mindful of growing postwar popular discontent within its own borders. The suppression of the rebellion soured PRC relations with the West and, much to Iran's delight, the close anti-Soviet strategic bond between Beijing and Washington began to unravel.

The UN-sanctioned coalition war to eject Iraq from Kuwait in early 1990 came as a massive shock to the Iranian government. Clearly, Iran was pleased by Iraq's utter defeat; indeed, for the first but not the last time, the United States did Iran a favor against a regional nemesis as many Iranian officials pointed out then and again in 2002 when the United States destroyed the Taliban regime in Afghanistan and removed Saddam Hussein from power in April 2003. What shocked the Iranians was the ease with which Iraq's military was dispatched by the high-tech U.S. armed forces. This conventional revolution in military affairs affected the perceptions and plans of all major powers including the Chinese military, the People's Liberation Army.

The Post–Cold War Era

By late 1991 the ailing Soviet Union and its system in Eastern Europe finally collapsed, to be replaced by a much diminished Russia surrounded by fully independent states in Eastern Europe as well as new states in Central Asia that sought to cut their remaining links with the metropole and were beset with massive internal problems. The end of the Cold War was heralded as a victory by the West; Iranian and Chinese glee at the collapse of the Soviet Union was tempered by the realization that this event also heralded the rise of U.S. "unipolar preeminence."[16] One should not underestimate the opposition of both the IRI and the PRC to America's rise to primacy and the unease with which they have witnessed its use of that power, particularly during the administration of George W. Bush. From the onset of the post–Cold War era, both Tehran and Beijing have expressed their distaste for a unipolar world and their commitment to forging the emergence of a multipolar one.

It was also in the 1990s that the international community began to pay closer attention to yet another ominous aspect of the bilateral relationship: Chinese aid to the Iranian nuclear program. Sino–Iranian cooperation in the nuclear arena began in the mid-1980s when the IRI decided to revitalize its once-vibrant nuclear energy program that the Shah had started in the 1970s. In 1991, China announced an agreement to supply Iran with a 20 megawatt (MW) research reactor. This was followed in September 1992 by an agreement under which China announced its intent to supply two 300 MW pressurized water reactors to Iran, whose construction would be completed over ten years. This intended agreement caused the international community to pay attention—and not for the last time—to the emerging Iranian nuclear program. Many international observers and countries did not accept the IRI's claim that it was seeking nuclear energy to generate electricity. In short, the IRI was suspected from the early 1990s of seeking to develop a nuclear weapons capability.

From the very beginning, the PRC argued that its nuclear cooperation with the IRI was legitimate and in full compliance with International Atomic Energy Agency (IAEA) safeguards provisions. The controversy over Iran's intentions in the nuclear arena generated considerable headaches for China because of U.S. displeasure and alarm. Although during the administration of President George H. W. Bush the United States admitted that there was no evidence of deliberate Chinese support for an Iranian nuclear weapons capability, Washington was nonetheless wary of any support given to Tehran's nuclear infrastructure.[17] The United States exerted pressure on China to explain and cease its activities in the nuclear arena with Iran. In October 1992 China canceled the deal to supply Iran with the 20 MW research reactor. But during much of the 1990s China and Iran, it seems, continued to discuss the proposed sale of two 300 MW reactors. China also assisted Iran in the building of uranium enrichment and conversion facilities.[18]

Suddenly, in May 1995, Chinese foreign minister Qian Qichen assured U.S. secretary of state Warren Christopher that China had canceled the 300 MW reactor sale.[19] The cancellation may have been due to two separate factors. First, the U.S. may have exerted sufficient pressure on China to cancel the proposed construction of the reactors. The export of U.S. nuclear technology and equipment to the PRC may have been contingent upon the cancellation of the deal with the IRI. Second, the Chinese may have decided to cancel it because they had begun to experience significant differences with the Iranians over technical and financial issues. This is not far-fetched. Both Russia and China have found the Iranians to be difficult economic partners—their historical fear of economic and political domination by outside powers makes them tough negotiators. In October 1997, China reportedly promised the United States that it would provide no further nuclear assistance to Iran. Despite this assurance, it is still not clear that China has fully suspended all nuclear activity.[20]

The burgeoning bilateral relationship in the 1990s was cemented by the initiation of high-level mutual visits by senior officials. When former Iranian leader Mohammad Khatami visited the PRC in 2000, officials of both countries stressed the necessity of building a Tehran–Beijing axis to confront the rise of the United States. During the course of the visit Iranian observers began to take note of China's economic importance and of its growing weight in international affairs: "The Iranian president's visit to China should open wide vistas of cooperation. . . . China is a world apart. It is a country with its own culture and identity on the international political scenes. Blessed with huge manpower and natural resources, it has carved up for itself a unique and independent status despite the plots of the U.S. and the merciless propaganda of the Western mass media."[21] But Khatami's visit to the PRC was more than a "love-fest." Both Khatami and Jiang Zemin stressed that bilateral relations between the countries in the political, economic, social, and cultural fields had developed along sound and dynamic paths and that they needed to be enhanced further in the twenty-first century on the basis of mutual respect for sovereignty, territorial integrity, and peaceful coexistence. In this context, the two leaders agreed

- to strengthen cooperation in energy, transportation, telecommunication, science and technology, industry, banking, tourism, agriculture, mining, and promotion of cooperation between the petrochemical companies of both countries in the oil and natural gas arenas.

- to promote world multipolarization. They stressed the need to establish an equitable, just, fair, and reasonable new international political and economic order that is free of hegemonism and power politics and is based on equality.

- to remain committed to a world free from nuclear, biological, or chemical weapons. They stressed that the international regime for eliminating and prohibiting the proliferation of weapons of mass destruction should be permanently and indiscriminately applicable to all regions and countries with no exception. And at the same time, both sides took note of the legitimate rights of any country for peaceful uses of nuclear energy, chemical, and biological technology in a transparent manner under the supervision of the relevant international organizations.

- to work together for the realization of a comprehensive, just, and lasting peace in the Middle East with the belief that a sustainable peace in the region cannot be attained without recognition of the rights of the Palestinian people, including the right of the Palestinian refugees to return to their homeland.

- to promote the view that the security and stability of the Persian Gulf should be safeguarded by the countries in the region free from outside interference.

- to combat the manufacture, distribution, and trafficking of illicit drugs.[22]

Two years later in April 2002 President Jiang Zemin visited Iran and held extensive discussions on regional strategic and bilateral economic and trade issues with President Khatami who reiterated the constant theme that Iran and China are ancient civilizations with long-standing contact and relations. He added that both countries are "developing nations and have identical or similar views on a wide range of major international and regional issues."[23]

It is not surprising that the two countries would stress strategic common-alities. The official visit came in the wake of the devastating 11 September 2001 attack on the United States by al-Qaeda. Both China and Iran expressed opposition to international terrorism; however, the leaders of the two coun-tries also warned about hegemonism in international politics and looked forward to the emergence of a multipolar world. More specifically, both were worried by the deteriorating situation in the Middle East, China because of its growing economic interest in the region and Iran because it was clearly caught in the middle of the deepening instability. The global war on terror was raging in Afghanistan, which had been a sanctuary for al-Qaeda. Both China and Iran expressed their desire to see Afghanistan restored to security, stability, and sovereignty. In this context, the two leaders also expressed con-siderable concern over the growing U.S.–Iraqi confrontation. China and Iran have expressed their determination to see Iraq implement all relevant resolu-tions of the United Nations Security Council, but they also maintained that Iraq's territorial integrity and sovereignty should be respected and that no armed intervention by any country should be initiated against Iraq.[24]

The two leaders also extensively discussed their growing bilateral rela-tionship. Jiang Zemin specifically stressed this aspect of the relationship: "In recent years, Sino-Iranian economic relations and trade have achieved signif-icant development; the volume of trade between the two countries has been increasing by the year; and their economic and technological cooperation has been expanding steadily. The Chinese government attaches great impor-tance to China's economic relations and trade with Iran and supports Chinese enterprises in conducting diverse forms of trade and economic cooperation with the Iranian side on the basis of equality and mutual benefit." Indeed, at the time Sino–Iranian bilateral economic relations were becoming the focus of attention, particularly in the energy field.

The Energy Context

In the wake of Khatami's historic visit to China in 2000, Sino–Iranian economic and commercial relations picked up considerably. Much of it was focused on expanding Iranian exports of oil to China. In October 2000 a five-member delegation of the Zhuhai Zhenrong Corporation visited Iran for a week and engaged in long negotiations with the National Iranian Oil Company for a contract to supply China with 12 million tons of crude oil for the year 2001. Indeed, petroleum was slated to become a critical element in the burgeoning Sino–Iranian relations. In January 2007 imports from Iran almost tripled from December 2006's level of 738,000 tons to 2.214 million tons. This made Iran the largest exporter of oil to China for January 2007.[25]

The Middle East is clearly important in China's oil needs. The region holds roughly two-thirds of the world's oil. When China became an oil importer in 1993, it realized that Asian producers would not be able to make up the shortfall. Therefore, when it began to look farther afield, it was logical that its view of the global energy map focused on the Middle East. In 1990 China imported 1.15 million tons of oil from the Middle East; in 2004 it imported a total of 45 million tons. This represents a fortyfold increase over the course of fourteen years.[26] But when China entered the Middle East in the mid-1990s, it did so with little understanding of the complex and complicated intertwining of energy and politics. It directed its attention toward Iraq, a country with vast reserves of proven oil. The only problem was that Iraq under Saddam Hussein was a pariah state under the most stringent United Nations sanctions regime in history. China sought to develop some of Iraq's more promising reserves and therefore advocated lifting the United Nations sanctions that prevented investment in Iraq's oil industry and limited sales of its production. China was practically salivating at the chance to extract oil from some of Iraq's major central and southern oil fields. In particular, it wanted to begin working on the al-Ahdab field in central Iraq under a $1.3 billion contract signed in 1997 by its largest state-owned firm, China National Petroleum Corp. The field's production potential was estimated at ninety thousand barrels a day.

China also pursued rights to a far bigger prize—the Halfayah field, which could produce three hundred thousand barrels a day. Together, those two fields might have delivered quantities equivalent to 13 percent of China's domestic production in 2002.[27] When the United States went to war against Iraq in March 2003 and toppled Saddam in early April 2003, China's stake in Iraq was wiped out. This forced China to see that oil is heavily intertwined with politics and strategic competition, and it intensified its push to seek multiple sources of oil and not to focus on one region or country. According to Pan Rui, a professor of international relations at Fudan University in Shanghai: "Iraq changed the government's thinking. The Middle East is

China's largest source of oil. America is now pursuing a grand strategy, the pursuit of American hegemony in the Middle East. Saudi Arabia is the number one oil producer, and Iraq is number two [in terms of reserves]. Now, the United States has direct influence in both countries."[28]

After 2003 China's National Oil Companies and the government realized that they could not rely on one or two oil production areas. The PRC enhanced its energy relations with Iraq's neighbor, the Islamic Republic of Iran. Iran is one of the biggest oil producers in the world, and as of January 2006 Iran was credited with having 132.5 billion barrels of proven oil reserves. This figure included discoveries made in 2004 and 2005 in Kuskh and Husseinia in Khuzestan province. These recent discoveries put Iran in second place globally after Saudi Arabia in the size of proven oil reserves.[29] In November 2004 China and Iran signed a massive energy deal that was estimated to be worth between $70–100 billion. The deal stipulated that China will purchase Iranian oil and gas in addition to helping develop Iran's Yadavaran oil field near the Iraq border. That same month China and Iran decided to set up a joint venture to build huge tankers to deliver Iranian liquefied gas to the PRC. In another deal also concluded in 2005 China also agreed to purchase $20 billion in liquefied natural gas from Iran over the next quarter century. Bilateral commercial relations hit a record of $9.5 billion in 2005, compared with $7.5 billion in 2004.[30]

In December 2006 CNOOC Group and the Iranians signed a memorandum of agreement whereby the former would invest $11 billion in the construction of liquefied natural gas facilities. By late 2006, all three of China's top national oil companies had signed massive oil and gas deals with Iran. The main thrust of Sino–Iranian bilateral economic relations is focused on the construction sector in Iran where Chinese companies now play a key role and in the energy sector.[31] It is the growing ties in the energy sector that has focused the attention of strategic analysts on the nature of Sino–Iranian ties and what they mean in the economic and geopolitical arenas, particularly for the United States.

From Economics to Strategic Partnership?

In analyzing growing economic and energy cooperation between China and Iran, is it possible to talk of an emerging political and strategic axis? One strategic analyst stated in testimony before the U.S.–China Economic and Security Review Commission: "there is no evidence that the Chinese leadership is seeking to forge a strategic alliance with Tehran."[32] It is not clear that it is accurate to interpret Sino–Chinese relations as being directed against the United States or solely in terms of implications for U.S. regional and global strategic and economic interests. Both countries are clearly uncomfortable with the American domination of the post–Cold War international system. But this has not crystallized into shared strategic principles.

Moreover, there are some obstacles standing in the way of deepening Sino–Iranian bilateral relations. The IRI is problematic in many ways. It drives a hard bargain in business deals; it has complicated and Byzantine regulations that were designed to protect the country from foreign exploitation, a fear that was hardwired into the Iranian political cultural mind-set after many years of "nefarious" activities by Britain and the United States. Many of the deals signed between China and Iran have not been consummated. There have been a number of irritants in the specifics. The Chinese have expressed considerable dissatisfaction with the high price of the energy deals with Iran. The Chinese are also mystified by some of the seemingly unnecessary obstacles or delays in the way of potentially lucrative deals. On the other hand, it also looks as if the Iranians—increasingly mindful of their penchant for needless bureaucratic obstacles and inspired by a desire to maintain goodwill with China in a time of tension with the West—have begun to speed up deals and to "rationalize" their cumbersome and time-consuming procedures.[33] Added to this was Iran's determination to master the nuclear fuel cycle—a determination that put it at loggerheads with the West and has put China in an uncomfortable position. It would not be too far-fetched to argue that China is not sure whether it wishes to invest further in Iran so long as the political climate between that country and the wider international community is fraught with tension. The Chinese have paid attention to discussions in the West over the feasibility of a U.S. attack on the Iranian nuclear infrastructure. Not surprisingly, while China moved to enhance its relations with Iran, it also began to develop extensive relations with other oil producers around the world.[34]

There is also something missing in the Sino–Iranian bilateral relationship that is never mentioned in the numerous statements referring to their past connections. Notwithstanding the common sense of victimization and domination at the hands of the West, the PRC does not yet elicit passions—positive or negative—in the way Britain and Russia/Soviet Union used to do and the United States does today. This may be due to the fact that both the IRI and PRC still do not know much about each other. The closest that the PRC has come to stirring strong passions among Iranians had nothing to do directly with Sino–Iranian relations but more to do with the lessons of the

famed and so-called Chinese model of economic development that was originally set in motion by the Four Modernizations.

As Sino Iranian relations in the commercial and economic sectors pro-
gressed in the 1990s, the Iranians began to pay greater attention to the Chinese experiment in development and modernization, particularly because
the IRI seemed to be failing in these areas while the PRC was making great
progress. As a result of its failure to meet popular aspirations, it was clear to
many within the senior hierarchy of the Iranian elite that their system was
facing a serious crisis of legitimacy. Indeed, in 2000 no less a person than
the secretary of the Supreme National Security Council, Dr. Hasan Rowhani,
first broached the subject of legitimacy in a major speech:

> My topic of discussion is perhaps the most important challenge which the
> Islamic Republic of Iran is currently facing in the domestic scene and per-
> haps in the international arena.
>
> Our Islamic system is presently confronted with a wide variety of domes-
> tic and international challenges, both ideological and practical in different
> arenas such as cultural, economic, legal and other social fronts. *But the most
> crucial challenge faced by our system is the question of legitimacy* . . . legiti
> macy is the principal basis of every system of government and without this
> real foundation, the continued existence of any regime would only become
> possible through violence and repression. Legitimization is the policies and
> programs of a system for sustaining, supporting and stabilization of itself.[35]

Stimulated by the legitimacy deficit of the IRI, a debate arose in Iran over
the merits of the so-called Chinese model. This has been described as a strategy of implementing economic development and modernization that satisfies pent-up popular aspirations in parallel with the maintenance of political
authoritarianism. More specifically, it is viewed as a way of opening the oil-
producing nation's economy to the world and building ties with the West
while maintaining restrictions on political, social, and cultural freedoms.
Many within the Islamic conservative camp viewed the model as being applicable to the IRI.[36] If the IRI were to succeed in implementing its own version
of the Chinese model, the legitimacy of the regime would be considerably
enhanced by successful economic development and growth, and there would
be no need to alter or sacrifice the political, social, and cultural pillars of the
Islamic system.

But many Iranians have viewed the notion of the Chinese model in
Iran with derision; some Iranian officials such as former Iranian ambassador Fereydoun Vardinejad, an Iranian expert on China who had lived in that

country for several years, doubt its applicability to Iran because of different political and cultural mores and vastly different geopolitical circumstances.[37] Vardinejad expresses his belief that "the Chinese model is a suitable model for China," and added that "as a nation, we [Iran] have our own views and theories." He goes on to add:

> We hardly adapt to other models. . . . Besides, our geographical, economic and political situations are very different from those of China. China is a country with a single political party and a highly centralized system of decision-making. The Chinese model calls for economic development based on political authority and security. This model docs not go well with our geographic, strategic, social, and political conditions. It is not clear that we would be able to implement this model. The Chinese model has been influenced by their geography, their Oriental characteristics, the ideas of Confucius, and post 1978–1979 political conditions in China. . . . The Chinese model is the product of China's own history.[38]

Other Iranian political analysts and reformers followed Vardinejad in criticizing the applicability of the Chinese model to Iran, but many went further and have denounced it because it does not offer political liberalization. One of Iran's leading political analysts, Mahmoud Sariolghalam, professor of international relations at Shahid Beheshti National University, argued that China was able to implement its economic model of development because of its strategic weight in the international system, as presumably reflected in its seat in the United Nations Security Council and its large population. Moreover, and of considerable importance, China's rapprochement with the West began in the early 1970s, when Beijing was seen by the United States as a useful counterweight to the Soviet Union and before human rights and democracy became universal concerns for the international community.[39] In short, it is quite evident that the Chinese model with "Iranian characteristics" would only be applicable if there were an Iranian rapprochement with the West. But Irano–Western rapprochement looks to be unlikely because of serious differences between the two sides. Sariolghalam also argues that the "Chinese model could not work because Iranians will not be satisfied solely with economic development. In Chinese popular culture, people tend to conform. Iranian history is exactly the reverse. The Shi'ites have a long tradition of rebellion against authority." Sariolghalam's reading of Chinese history is not accurate. Like Iran, that country's history has been punctuated by a series of often bloody revolts, rebellions, and insurrections. But Sariolghalam is right in arguing that Iran would have to change its anti-American foreign policy to achieve major economic progress.

Moreover, even many of Iran's conservative commentators are not too keen on the Chinese model. For example, Amir Mohebian, the editor of the conservative newspaper *Resalat*, rejected the concept of the Chinese model for Iran, arguing that "we accept democracy. We know at present that we can survive and save our Islamic Revolution only by ruling in a democratic manner. Democracy is not against our system, but there are versions of democracy."[40] In a recent and detailed analysis of the Iranian political scene a U.S. researcher has enumerated three considerable obstacles that the IRI is bound to face in trying to seriously follow the Chinese model:

- Macroeconomic challenges that the regime has proven incapable of resolving and is unlikely to resolve.

- Concentration of economic power in the hydrocarbon industry and the rampant corruption and patronage within it.

- Lack of political will to revamp the economy and adopt market economics. This is aggravated by the reluctance of the outside to invest in Iran's economy due to political risk and structural economic problems.[41]

The final authority on the so-called Chinese model was certainly its architect in China, namely Deng Xiaoping who reportedly told the visiting president of Ghana, Jerry Rawlings, in September 1985, "Please don't copy our model. If there is any experience on our part, it is to formulate policies in light of one's own national conditions."[42]

The issue of a Sino–Iranian strategic consensus or axis is also inevitably linked to the growing crisis between the IRI and the global community over Tehran's determination to master the nuclear fuel cycle, much to the chagrin of the West, particularly the EU-3, namely France, Germany, and the United Kingdom. The Iranian nuclear standoff dramatically escalated on 10 January 2006 when Iranian officials broke the IAEA seals on equipment at the Natanz facility to restart small-scale uranium enrichment activities, ending a two-year suspension of its enrichment program. The international response was swift and unequivocal. The EU-3, which had over the last two years been engaged in protracted negotiations with Tehran to look for a solution to the Iranian nuclear issue, immediately suspended planned talks and, together with the United States, called for an emergency session of the IAEA Board of Governors. China's reaction was to counsel restraint by both sides. While expressing concerns over the Iranian nuclear crisis, Beijing has called on the EU-3 and Iran to resume negotiations. Kong Quan, foreign ministry spokesman, stated at a press conference on 12 January 2006 that China hoped that Iran would do more to enhance mutual trust for resuming the talks. In a meeting with Ali Larijani, secretary of the Iranian Supreme National Security Council and Tehran's top nuclear negotiator, Chinese state councilor Tang Jiaxuan expressed his concerns over the worsening nuclear tension, stressing that "all parties concerned should step up diplomatic efforts to create favorable conditions for the resumption of talks on the Iranian nuclear issue."[43]

Meanwhile, Beijing had indicated its opposition to the use of sanctions against Iran and emphasized that the dispute should be resolved within the IAEA framework through negotiation. China also suggests that member states to the Nuclear Nonproliferation Treaty are entitled to peaceful use of nuclear technology so long as they comply with the nonproliferation provisions. "We oppose the habitual use of sanctions, or threats of sanctions, to solve problems. This only complicates problems," reiterated Foreign Ministry spokesman Kong Quan at a 26 January 2006 press conference. He added that the Iranian nuclear issue should be resolved within the framework of IAEA: "In the current context, the most feasible approach is still the negotiation between the three EU countries and Iran. For this reason, we are much supportive of carrying on the negotiation. Iran and the EU expect further positive role of China. We have taken note of this wish, and stayed in close contact with all parties concerned, so as to translate our joint effort into real outcome, that is to say, to re-launch the negotiation between the EU and Iran and strive for progress."[44] But the PRC had no qualms about joining the United States, the EU-3, and Russia in agreeing to refer Iran to the United Nations Security Council when it failed to halt its enrichment program.[45]

In early January 2007 the UN Security Council implemented limited sanctions on Iran. But these sanctions have had little impact on curtailing that country's activities in the nuclear arena, the growing discord within the country over President Mahmoud Ahmedinejhad's confrontational strategy notwithstanding. China continues to face a dilemma concerning how it will proceed on the Iranian nuclear issue, if the crisis continues without resolution. Beijing wants to be seen as a responsible rising power supporting the principles of nuclear nonproliferation while trying to maintain an amiable relationship with Iran to protect its important energy interests in the oil-rich country. Yet China also does not want to strain its ties with the United States and other major Western powers. Many experts believe that Iran's strong economic ties with both the PRC and Russia are bound to make it more difficult for the United States to put pressure on Tehran's aspirations in the nuclear arena and to prevent its emergence as the regional superpower in the Middle East. While the PRC did play a role in the construction of the IRI's nuclear infrastructure from the mid-1980s to the mid-1990s, it does not seek the emergence of a nuclear Iran. However, the PRC is certainly not in favor of either sanctions or a military attack on the IRI. It has resisted Western efforts to "punish" Iran for seeking to master the nuclear fuel cycle.

The Iranians have watched this with considerable interest. They know that neither Russia nor the PRC are in favor of their nuclearization, but they have used Russian and Chinese obstructionism to proceed further in their endeavors in this arena. As Hasan Rowhani, former head of Iran's Supreme National Security Council, intimated a couple of years back, the IRI cannot count on active support from the PRC for his country's nuclear stance.[46] Many Iranian analysts and observers have rightly pointed out that the PRC is not going to sabotage its extensive bilateral relations with the United States for those with Iran. Sino–American trade was valued at $170 billion in 2005; in 2010 it is expected to reach $300 billion. In short, China is more important to Iran than Iran is to China. But in contrast to the strong influence that the PRC has over the Democratic People's Republic of Korea, there is little that China can do by itself to sanction Iran, something Iranians are well aware of. However, there is a clear Iranian perception that their strategy must not put China in a difficult position—that is to say, a position where it will have to make a choice—because the Iranians know that this would not be to their advantage. Hence, this is the reason why the Iranians are being extremely careful in the nuclear arena that they do not push too far ahead of what Russia and China would be willing to bear.

It has also been argued that the Shanghai Cooperation Organization (SCO), in which the IRI has observer status but not membership, is a possible vehicle for Tehran to transform its relations with the PRC and Russia into a more genuinely strategic one. The SCO is a seemingly powerful intergovernmental international organization founded on 15 June 2001 by China, Russia, Kazakhstan, Kyrgyzstan, Tajikistan, and Uzbekistan. These six member states cover an area of over 30 million square kilometers, or about three-fifths of Eurasia. They have a total population of 1.455 billion, or about a quarter of the world's total. The IRI would like to join the organization to benefit from greater economic cooperation as well as to further its own plans for creating energy interdependence, fighting drugs and (Sunni) Islamist extremism, and transforming itself into a land bridge between the SCO countries and the Persian Gulf. But it is not clear whether it is a budding strategic alliance of these six countries and any other potential additions. Moreover, it is not clear that it can be the vehicle for the deepening of Sino–Iranian relations. The SCO suffers from major problems of coordination between its member countries. There are also major structural obstacles standing in the way of further strengthening the SCO into a genuine group of like-minded regional states that see eye to eye on a wide variety of issues.[47]

Conclusion

Despite media assertions to the contrary, the Sino–Iranian relationship is currently not a true strategic partnership (unlike the U.S.–Saudi relationship). China is nonetheless highly interested in increasing its position in the Iranian energy sector and as such is reluctant to cooperate in international efforts to impose sanctions on Tehran. While China currently purchases more than 400,000 bpd of oil from Iran, this is not "equity oil" produced from fields in which Chinese firms have investment stakes. Rather, Chinese buyers are purchasing crude just as Japanese, Indian, or European buyers do and then having it shipped to China. Thus, China's current maritime energy security concerns with respect to Iran mainly revolve around a fear that any U.S. military operation against Tehran's nuclear facilities could interrupt Iranian oil supplies, which comprise between 15 and 20 percent of Chinese imports.

Iranian liquefied natural gas (LNG) projects are currently moving very slowly due to investors' fears of political instability in the region, the Iranian government's refusal thus far to provide appealing upstream investment terms, and continuing pricing disputes between Sinopec and its Iranian partners.[48] Once the Iranian LNG export facility construction begins in earnest, it could be at least three to four years before significant Iranian supplies are shipped to China. Assuming that the LNG contracts signed by state oil trader Zhuhai Zhenrong and Sinopec come to fruition, China could be importing more than 10 million tons of LNG per year from Iran.

In coming years, Iranian LNG development may have a more direct bearing on China's maritime energy security stance than does oil. Because the LNG market is less liquid than the crude oil market, China might not be able to obtain supplies elsewhere rapidly if Iranian LNG supplies were interrupted by internal problems or naval interdiction by a hostile power. As such, at some point after 2010, China may come to take a deeper interest in Persian Gulf maritime energy security than it does now, as growing LNG (and oil) supplies are sourced from Iran.

At present however, China is forced to walk a delicate diplomatic balance as it tries to protect diplomatically a key energy supplier while simultaneously striving to avoid provoking Washington. A 2005 analysis on great power influences on Sino–Iranian relations states "If we move forward too quickly, we will arouse the ire of the West, which of course does not mesh with our goal of 'rising peacefully.' If on the other hand we move too slowly, we may lose opportunities to develop the relationship, which would also harm our national interests."[49]

Increased Chinese oil and LNG imports from Iran will make China a stakeholder in the country, but for at least the next five years, we are unlikely to see China push for a serious hands-on role in protecting energy shipments from Iran.

Notes

1. Sima Qian, *Records of the Grand Historian: Han Dynasty I & II*, trans. Burton Watson, rev. ed. (Hong Kong and New York: The Research Centre for Translation, The Chinese University of Hong Kong, and Columbia University Press, 1993), 123.

2. "China and Iran Move Closer," BBC News, 20 April 2002, http://news.bbc.co.uk/1/hi/world/middle_east/1941030.stm

3. Ibid.

4. John Garver, *China and Iran: Ancient Partners in a Post-Imperial World* (Seattle: University of Washington Press, 2006).

5. See Richard Spencer, "Tension Rises as China Scours the Globe for Energy," *Daily Telegraph*, 19 November 2004, http://www.telegraph.co.uk/news/main.jhtml?xml=/news/2004/11/19/wchina19.xml&sSheet=/news/2004/11/19/ixworld.html; Peter Goodman, "Big Shift in China's Oil Policy with Iraq Deal Dissolved by War, Beijing Looks Elsewhere," *Washington Post*, 13 July 2005, p. D1; Su-Ching Jean Chen, "China's Oil Safari," *Forbes*, 9 October 2006 http://www.forbes.com/energy/2006/10/06/energy-african-oil-biz-energy_cx_jc_1009beijing_energy06.html; William Mellor and Le-Min Lim, "China Drills Where Others Dare Not Seek Oil," *International Herald Tribune*, 2 October 2006, http://www.iht.com/articles/2006/10/01/bloomberg/bxchioil.php.

6. Shen Dingli, "Iran's Nuclear Ambitions Test China's Wisdom," *Washington Quarterly* 20, no. 2 (2006): 55–66.

7. Memorandum of Conversation, "The Shah of Iran, Henry Kissinger, Hushang Ansary, Iranian Ambassador to U.S., and Harold Saunders," 11 April 1969, Department of State, declassified 7 May 2002.

8. Eckehart Ehrenberg, *Rustung und Wirtschaft am Golf: Iran und seine Nachbarn, 1965–1978* [*Arms Buildup and Economics in the Gulf: Iran and Its Neighbors, 1965–1978*], no. 11 (Hamburg: Deutsche Orient Institut, 1978).

9. In the 1980s the lion's share of Chinese arms exports to the Middle East went to cobelligerents Iran and Iraq. There was also a one-time large sale of intermediate-range ballistic missiles to Saudi Arabia.

10. Bates Gill, "Chinese Arms Exports to Iran," *Middle East Review of International Affairs* 2, no. 2 (May 1998), http://meria.idc.ac.il/journal/1998/issue2/jv2n2a7.html; see also "Iran Missile Milestones—1985–2004, The Risk Report," 10, no. 3 (2004), http://www.wisconsinproject.org/countries/iran/missile-miles04.html; "Chinese Missile Exports and Assistance to Iran," Nuclear Threat Initiative, Monterrey Institute Center for Nonproliferation Studies, 2007, http://www.nti.org/db/china/miranpos.htm.

11. This did not last long because in 2001 the PRC, or rather Chinese firms, were suspected of resuming ballistic missile cooperation with Tehran. In particular, American officials have expressed concerns that Chinese firms have aided in the development and the technical enhancement of Iran's major ballistic missile, the 2,000-kilometer-range Shahab-3; the most detailed and up-to-date analysis of Iranian ballistic missile programs is Uzi Rubin, *The Global Reach of Iran's Ballistic Missiles*, Research Memo. 86, Institute for National Security Studies, Tel Aviv University, November 2006.

12. "Chinese Missile Exports and Assistance to Iran," Nuclear Threat Initiative, Monterrey Institute Center for Nonproliferation Studies, 2007, http://www.nti.org/db/china/miranpos.htm.

13. Garver, *China and Iran*.

14. Gao Bianhua, "Sino-Iranian Trade Rebounds," *China Daily,* 23 May 1995, p. 5 in FTS19950523000066, "Trade Increases with Iran After 1994 Decline," Open Source Center at https://www.opensource.gov/portal/server.pt/gateway/PTARGS_0_0_200_975_51_43/http.

15. Kamel Nazer Yasin, "China and Iran: Unlikely Partners," *Eurasia Net, Business & Economics,* 4 April 2006, http://www.eurasianet.org/departments/business/articles/eav040406.shtml; "Ambassador Says 'Chinese Model' Cannot Be Implemented in Iran," *Sharq,* 22 December 2004, p. 6, OSC# IAP20041223000037.

16. Garver, *China and Iran*, 95–138.

17. "Chinese Sales to Iran Raise Nuclear Concerns," *Arms Control Today* (December 1991): 24–26.

18. For more details of the nature of Sino–Iranian nuclear cooperation and the obstacles it faced see Alexander Montgomery, "Social Action, Rogue Reaction: U.S. Post-Cold War Nuclear Counterproliferation Strategies," PhD dissertation, Stanford University, September 2005, 153–200, especially 178–80.

19. Ibid.

20. There is now a voluminous literature on the Iranian nuclear program and on the international community's reactions to it. The analysis in this paper comes largely from The Nuclear Threat Initiative, http://www.nti.org/db/China/niranpos.htm.

21. S. Nawabzadeh, "New Phase in Iran-China Ties," *Kayhan International*, 26 June 2000, p. 2.

22. "Iran and China Call for Multi Polar World Versus Unipolar," Iran Press Service, 22 June 2000, http://www.iran-press-service.com/articles_2000/june_2000/khatami_china_22600.html.

23. Yang Guoqiang, Jiang Xiaofeng, and Jiang Xianming, "Jiang Zemin Attends Welcome Ceremony Hosted by President Khatami and Holds Talks with Khatami," Xinhua Domestic Service, Beijing, GMT 20 April 2002 in CPP20020420000057, Open Source Center, https://www.opensource.gov/portal/server.pt/gateway/PTARGS_0_0_200_975_51_43/http.

24. Ibid.

25. The data for the preceding paragraph were derived from the following sources: "Iran Biggest Crude Supplier to China," *The Standard*, http://hkstandard.hk/news_detail.asp?we_cat=10&art_id=39240&sid=12465708&con_type=1&d_str=20070302; "China," Country Analysis Briefs, Energy Information Administration, www.eia.doe.gov.

26. Raquel Shaoul, "Japan and China's Energy Supply Security Policy Vis-à-vis Iran: An Analysis of a Triangular Relationship," *Iran-Pulse*, no. 6 (6 December 2006).

27. Peter Goodman, "Big Shift in China's Oil Policy," *The Washington Post*, 13 July 2005, p. D1.

28. Ibid.

29. "Iran," *Country Analysis Briefs*, Energy Information Administration, www.eia.doe.gov.

30. "Report on PRC-Iran Cooperation in Developing Yadavaran Oilfield," *Shiji Jingji Baodao*, 22 February 2006, OSC document #CPP20060223050003; "China Bids to Revive Mega Iran Energy Deal," *Agence France-Presse*, 17 December 2005; Rowan Callick, "China in $128bn Iran Oil, Gas Deal," *The Australian*, 29 November 2006; "Iran's Oil Exports to China Soared 80% in '05," *Sinocast China Business Daily News*, 12 July 2006, http://www.uofaweb.ualberta.ca/CMS/printpage.cfm?ID=47962.

31. "Iran's Exports to China Soared 80% in '05," *SinoCast China Business Daily News*, 12 July 2006, http://www.uofaweb.ualberta.ca/CMS/printpage.cfm?ID=47962.

32. Prepared Statement of Dr. John Calabrese, Scholar-In-Residence, Middle East Institute and Assistant Professor, American University, Washington, D.C., "The Impact of the Sino-Iranian Strategic Partnership, Testimony Before the U.S.-China Economic and Security Review Commission," 14 September 2006.

33. "China's Energy Investment Plans in Iran," Reuters, 21 December 2006, https://www.uofaweb.ualberta.ca/CMS/printpage.cfm?ID=54769.

34. For more details see Shai Oster, "China's Oil Hunt Heats Up Abroad"; and "Quest for Oil and Gas Intensifies," *Lloyd's List*, 23 February 2007, http://www.uofaweb.ulberta.ca/CMS/printpage.cfm?ID=57200.

35. *Iran*, 18 November and 13 December 2000, www.iran-newspaper.com.

36. Another model for economic development and modernization that was viewed as more pertinent was the success of Malaya, a fellow Muslim state. Yet another group of reformers within the Iranian political system, the so-called Iranian neoconservatives are not interested in the Chinese model; they are apparently mesmerized by the Japanese model of development.

37. Sahar Namazikhah, "Iran's Ambassador to China in Interview with Sharq: Chinese Model Cannot Be Implemented in Iran," *Sharq*, 22 December 2004, in IAP 20041223000037, Open Source Center, https://www.opensource.gov/portal/server.pt/gateway/PTARGS_0_0_200_975_51_43/http.

38. Ibid.

39. Nancy Bernkopf Tucker, "China and America: 1941–1991," *Foreign Affairs* (Winter 1991–92), http://www.foreignaffairs.org/19911201faessay6114/nancy-bernkopf-tucker/china-and-america-1941-1991.html; Chi Su, "U.S.-China Relations: Soviet Views and Policies," *Asian Survey* 23, no. 5 (May 1983): 555–79.

40. "The Backlash Against Democracy Assistance," Report by the National Endowment for Democracy, Prepared for Senator Richard Lugar, Chairman, Committee on Foreign Relations, U.S. Senate, 8 June 2006, http://www.ned.org/publications/reports/backlash06.pdf.

41. Elliot Hen-Tov, "Understanding Iran's New Authoritarianism," *Washington Quarterly* 30, no. 1 (2006–7): 163–79.

42. Wei-Wei Zhang, "The Allure of the Chinese Model," *International Herald Tribune*, 1 November 2006, http://www.iht.com/articles/2006/11/01/opinion/edafrica.php.

43. Jing-dong Yuan, "China and the Iranian Nuclear Crisis," *China Brief* 6, no. 3 (1 February 2006), http://jamestown.org/publications_details.php?volume_id=415&issue_id=3605&article_id=2370730.

44. Kevin Dumouchelle, "Iran Nuclear Crisis," *Washington Post*, 18 January 2006, http://www.washingtonpost.com/wp-dyn/content/article/2006/01/18/AR2006011801131.html.

45. "Russia, China Agree to Refer Iran to Security Council," *Bloomberg*, 31 January 2006, http://www.uofaweb.ualberta.ca/CMS/printpage.cfm?ID=44132.

46. See Chen Kane, "Nuclear Decision-Making in Iran: A Rare Glimpse," *Middle East Brief*, no. 5 (May 2006), www.brandeis.edu/centers/crown/publications/Mid%20East%20Brief/Brief%205%20May%202006.pdf.

47. Zhao Huasheng, "Security Building in Central Asia and the Shanghai Cooperation Council," http://src-h.slav.hokudai.ac.jp/coe21/publish/no2_ses/4-2_Zhao.pdf.

48. As noted earlier, Iranians' extreme fear of being dominated or taken advantage of by foreigners can make then extremely tough business negotiators. At present, foreign firms wishing to invest in the Iranian oil industry must deal with "buy back" contracts in which they develop a field, and then once it begins producing, the foreign firm hands the field back over to National Iranian Oil Company. The firms then gets its costs reimbursed and gets a share of oil and gas profits, assuming that the field produces as agreed upon and that international oil and gas prices remain

strong. Foreign investors complain that buy back contracts force them to bear all of the risk because they may not be fully recompensed if a field doesn't meet production expectations.

49. Xiong Xiaoqing, Yang Xingli, Liu Jinzhao, Ai Shaowei, and Zhang Chaoyang, "Influence of Big Powers to the Relationship Between China and Iran." *World Regional Studies* (September 2005): 64–70.

Clifford Shelton

The Energy Component of China's Africa Strategy

BEIJING'S AMBITIOUS GOALS for economic growth have created a sharp increase in demand for oil, which has caused China to go overseas in search of this vital strategic commodity. China's global outreach for oil resources, commonly termed "oil diplomacy," increasingly involves Africa.[1]

Beijing has targeted Africa as a significant part of its global energy security strategy.[2] China's relations with Africa, although politically motivated in the past, have recently become both more diversified and economically focused. This shift toward economically motivated engagement has created both a surge in trade between Africa and China and a higher priority for African affairs in Beijing's energy security.[3]

China is obtaining access to African oil in large part by providing investment without political conditions. This offers opportunities for Africa to secure new investment partners, develop infrastructure, and increase trade, but this also simultaneously undermines efforts to further good governance and sustainable economic development. Although China is successfully extracting African resources, its increasing presence and heightened economic interests will likely exert pressures that will draw Beijing into African civil conflicts. China already maintains a military presence in Sudan and is strengthening military cooperation with other African countries, including Angola and Zimbabwe.[4]

While China could seek the purchase of oil resources directly from the global market, Beijing instead has embarked on a longer-term strategy to develop the oil infrastructure of African countries and explore for other depositories.[5] This strategy is likely to have both positive and negative long-term effects for U.S. interests. While it could increase global oil production to a significant degree, this would almost certainly come at the price of much greater Chinese influence on the continent.

The energy component of China's Africa strategy has implications for American strategic interests in Africa and for the continent's overall economic and political development. Other interested parties such as the European Union also stand to lose political leverage across the continent in response to Chinese activities.

The United States, which Africans view as having long neglected their continent, has been forced to review its strategy in response to China's rapid advancements. Washington is suffering setbacks in the battle of public diplomacy on the continent and stands to lose even more political leverage among many African nations by insisting on tying aid to political changes, good governance, or sustainable economic development. To many African leaders, such conditions can be avoided by instead securing Chinese investment.

Despite its moral ambivalence, China's Africa strategy could present new opportunities for economic development as well as greater integration for African nations into the international system. To obtain these opportunities Africa's leaders need to actively bargain with Chinese leadership to ensure their economic benefit.

This study aims to further understand the role that Africa plays in China's overall energy strategy as well as the positive and negative externalities that could arise from this new relationship.

China's Global Energy Strategy

China's continued economic growth and development hinges on access to imported energy. Oil, in particular, is required both to fuel China's industrial growth and to power its expanding transportation networks. China's military is critically dependent on oil as well.

In 2005, China consumed approximately 6.5 million barrels a day.[6] This represents 7 percent of global oil consumption, making China the second-largest global consumer of oil, ahead of Japan and second only to the United

States, which accounts for 25 percent of oil consumed.[7] These figures are projected to increase substantially, with China's oil appetite rising fourfold between 2006 and 2030.[8]

Coal represents the majority of China's energy consumption, comprising 55 percent of the energy consumed in China. Oil makes up a relatively modest 11.1 percent.[9] As Beijing's economy expands and more oil-hungry cars, trucks, and planes take to the roads and skies, the current reliance on coal resources will shift increasingly toward oil. The legitimacy of the Chinese Communist Party and China's leaders is thought to be critically dependent on the continued growth of China's economy, which is figuratively lubricated with imported oil. This has made energy security a top priority for the Chinese Communist Party and is consequently a tremendous issue for global security as a whole.

China's leaders and scholarly community have detected many shortcomings in their current energy situation and have sought a variety of means to ensure national energy security in the future.[10] To this end, China's leaders plan to increase their access to foreign oil sources, stabilize alternative transportation systems for the shipment of that oil, restructure the way in which Beijing stores its oil reserves, and diversify China's global trading partners.[11]

It must be noted that Chinese scholars are very concerned about the U.S. reaction to their energy security strategy and appear to base their decisions upon a series of predictions that they feel the United States would likely make.[12] One source suggests that China's energy security strategy has five components. An aspect of this supposed strategy is to increase its use of oil resources and reduce the use of other energy sources, like coal. Second, China hopes to develop technology to reduce its dependency on oil imports. This would directly complement China's technology collaborations with companies such as South Africa's SASOL in nuclear energy cooperation.[13] Third, Beijing plans to develop more infrastructure to utilize reusable energies like hydro or solar power. Fourth, Beijing hopes to moderate consumption of oil resources through technology and government policy. Finally, China hopes to exert greater influence on the global oil marketplace to reduce the risk of price fluctuations.[14]

The majority of Chinese oil imports (approximately 56 percent) come from the Middle East. The Asian continent provides approximately 14 percent of China's oil imports while Africa supplies approximately 23 percent.[15] Oil imports from the Middle East and Africa are transported to China by sea, through the Indian Ocean to the Strait of Malacca and finally through the South China Sea. Chinese analysts worry that their nation's dependence on the Strait of Malacca subjects its sea-based oil imports to great risk from American military might. Beijing is thus in the process of increasing over-land shipments of oil resources, primarily from Russia and Kazakhstan.[16] It is unlikely that there will be sufficient overland supplies to meet China's grow-ing thirst for imported oil, however. Therefore, the absolute amount of Chi-nese seaborne oil imports is forecast to grow.

An apparent Chinese strategic objective is to expand and diversify its oil suppliers. This component of China's energy strategy places a premium on robust engagement with Africa.[17]

Africa's Place in China's Energy Strategy

The African continent, particularly areas of West and Central Africa, has become an especially important source of non-OPEC oil production growth, accounting for approximately 16 percent of global oil production. Nigeria, with 35.2 billion barrels of oil in reserves, is Africa's largest oil producer at 2.4 million bpd. Angola, the continent's second-largest oil producer, generates 1 million bpd with a reserve of 5.4 billion barrels. Sudan produces 300,000 bpd with a reserve of 563 million. Equatorial Guinea produces 300,000 bpd, with 12 million in reserves, and Chad produces 200,000 bpd, with a 900-million-barrel reserve. Other African countries with substantial oil pro duction and reserves in the millions include the Republic of Congo, Cam-eroon, Côte d'Ivoire, the Democratic Republic of Congo, South Africa, and Ghana. Oil from the Gulf of Guinea is predicted within five years to com-prise around 21 percent of the world's developed oil reserves.[18] China wants as much access to this oil as possible.[19]

African countries export approximately 3.8 million barrels of oil per day, of which only 2 percent (90,000 barrels) is consumed on the continent. Thirty-eight percent of the remainder, roughly 1.5 million barrels, is exported to North America, and 35 percent, or about 1.3 million barrels, is exported to Asia. The remainder of these resources is exported to Europe and South America.[20] Twenty-three percent of China's imported oil originates from Africa, over 730 thousand barrels a day, which represents a large portion of African oil exports to the Asia.

In 1997 African oil represented approximately 14 percent of global oil exports at 5.8 million barrels of oil a day. Ten years later that production increased 35.5 percent to 7.8 million barrels a day. It is predicted that by the year 2020 exports will increase by another 40 percent to 11 million barrels a day of oil. Africa is thus of great strategic importance to Chinese oil security.[21]

China has moved aggressively into oil-producing nations of North Africa, particularly Sudan. Using a long-term strategy, Chinese firms have invested heavily in the country and have developed much of its energy and oil infrastructure. China's investment in Africa became more apparent to the rest of the world after the Darfur crisis arose in Sudan in February 2003. Yet China's National Petroleum Company had already begun investing within the country in the 1990s in cooperation with the Sudanese government in what was called the Greater Nile Petroleum Operation Corporation. China currently controls 40 percent of the Sudanese oil market.[22]

Many Gulf of Guinea offshore oil discoveries, while rich, are located in deep water. Developing these sources poses technological challenges that exceed Chinese oil company capabilities. Only large multinational oil companies and a select few state companies (namely Brazil's Petrobras) have the relevant expertise and technology to exploit these resources. This capability gap impels China to continue to develop other oil sources farther inland as it works to broaden its oil supplier base.[23] China is also collaborating with other nations to develop better technology for alternative energy resources and economization of petroleum resources. China has been working with South Africa specifically in areas of nuclear energy technology cooperation.[24]

The Ease of Connection

Beijing has been able to make such strong headway into African oil resources partially because of its relatively long and substantive presence on the continent. China became involved with Africa after its own successful communist revolution while much of Africa struggled for independence. The political climate of the time in which Africa was isolated from the Western world made the cultivation of African allies particularly attractive to China.[25] The superpower rivalry also enabled China to gain influence as a legitimate nation. During this time the Chinese supported different African independence movements while providing aid and infrastructure development.[26]

Under Deng Xiaoping China was able to successfully maintain positive relations with African nations while opening up to the Western world and beginning to structure itself into a market-based economy.[27] Almost twenty years later China's relationship with Africa has changed markedly. Whereas China historically aligned strategically with Africa for political reasons, the imperatives of energy security have caused Beijing's Africa strategy to shift toward economics.

In 2000 China established the China–Africa Cooperation Forum, a multilateral organization focused upon increasing trade and investment between African nations and China. Since then trade between China and Africa has almost doubled, increasing from $11 billion in 2000 to $18 billion in 2003. Trade also surged 50 percent between 2002 and 2003 and was projected to exceed $30 billion by the end of 2006.[28]

In contrast to some aid offered by Western nations, China has neither as high a demand for return on investment nor as high a level of consumer visibility. These features give Beijing a slight advantage when engaging Africa, especially within the many nations that possess political and business cultures grounded in the development of long-term personal relationships.

The aforementioned factors have all contributed to the warm reception that many African leaders give to China's engagement efforts. This positive impression of Chinese steps resonates with many African diplomats who see Beijing's efforts as a new opportunity to secure needed development and investment. In a series of interviews conducted within the African business and diplomatic community in Beijing, the ambassador from Lesotho, Uganda's coffee trade representative to China, the First Premiere of the Nigerian embassy, and the standing ambassador of Ethiopia all voiced strong enthusiasm for the new Sino–African economic ties.[29]

The Carrot of Investment

On average, oil revenues account for 75 percent of the GDP of Africa's oil exporters. Oil makes up 60, 77, 86, and an astounding 95 percent of the GDPs of Algeria, Libya, Nigeria, and Angola, respectively.[30] These African governments typically raise revenue through taxation, levies, royalties, signature bonuses, production-sharing agreements, and joint ventures. These governments also decide which oil companies they will allow to operate within their borders.[31]

Many African states lack the means necessary to produce, extract, or distribute exploitable resources. They also, unfortunately, cannot by themselves develop the infrastructure required to provide basic services for their citizens. China has been able to exploit these shortcomings by providing Africa with the capital that can mitigate this shortcoming. Beijing's oil companies also arrive with extraction technology and infrastructure in exchange for energy resources.[32]

China's Africa policy states its ambition to promote "mutual benefit, reciprocity, and common prosperity" while "respecting African countries' independent choice of the road of development."[33] China maintains close government-to-government relations with African states, imposing neither conditions for reform nor development in exchange for loans. This differs markedly from Western countries or other donor organizations like the World Bank, which commonly impose conditions (e.g., eradication of corruption) in return for investment.

More than seven hundred Chinese construction and technology companies are established throughout Africa. Additionally, large Chinese state-owned construction and engineering companies such as the China Geological Engineering Group and the China Civil Engineering Corporation have branches in a number of African countries. These private and state-owned companies frequently build Chinese-funded infrastructure. These projects allow Chinese companies to maintain close relations with African governments and to secure state contracts.[34] Significantly, in 2007 the African Development Bank held its annual meeting in China—a first. Although China is one of the bank's twenty-four non-African stake owners, this meeting's location clearly expresses the growing economic relationship between China and Africa. Similarly the 2006 China–Africa Cooperation Forum brought together in Beijing an enormous contingent of leaders and businessmen from both sides. This forum, which is the largest multilateral convention dedicated to Sino–African relations, is held every three years.

China incurs some surprising costs in exchange for a guarantee on energy supply. For instance, the People's Republic of China (PRC) pays the salaries of staff and the up-front costs for the Central African Republic (CAR)'s Beijing embassy in exchange for further rights to engage in oil exploration within the CAR's interior.[35] The CAR, which underwent a military coup in 2003 and is still plagued with guerrilla activity, has difficulty securing Western investment. Not so with China, which offers an easy alternative with immediate tangible benefits.

Opportunities and Pitfalls of China's Strategy

The PRC's investment strategy certainly offers opportunities for Chinese and African interests. In the short term, African nations enjoy an alternative source of capital free from the constraints and conditions levied by traditional sources such as the International Monetary Fund or the World Bank. China, being less risk-averse in its engagement strategy than are many Western nations, is also willing to invest in countries such as Sudan or the CAR that have a higher level of political insecurity. Chinese investment, despite these factors, could offer the possibility of creating the stability necessary to allow these nations to begin to develop and prosper.

From an African perspective, greater Chinese engagement has the potential to create a herd effect, driving other nations to invest in Africa, particularly as competition for global oil resources heightens. Countries along the Gulf of Guinea have used such competition to negotiate more beneficial terms.

The short-term benefits for the Chinese in making such loans and investments are obvious. Investment in Africa helps China secure specific quantities of oil and other resources in contract form, gain access to African markets for Chinese goods, and diversify its trading partners. Maintaining close relations with African governments also bolsters the PRC's position as an international power. China has been able to position itself as a power broker within the region by providing representation for African nations in the United Nations, thereby gaining international support for its One China policy. Such "South–South" partnerships also further China's long-standing ambition to become a leader of the developing world.

China's African investment strategy also presents many pitfalls for Africa and global security, however. Free of demands for economic and political reform, Chinese investment prolongs the failures of oil-rich African nations' governments. Although immediately benefiting the elite, it does little for their nations' poor. Beijing readily engages in trade and business practices known to stunt the development of domestic industry and exacerbate environmental problems. Consequent increases in unemployment and income inequality will further jeopardize African nations' political security unless countered by sustainable economic development, something China has shown scant interest in facilitating. The internal conflicts that roil oil-rich Angola, Nigeria, and Sudan will therefore likely continue as economic inequality increases and disdain for existing governments swells.

China is also establishing a legacy of supporting disreputable governments in such African nations as Zimbabwe and Sudan. This creates both an international and a mass African backlash against China as Africa's political climate worsens. Opposition to Beijing's actions is developing in African populations, perhaps stemming from China's unconditional support of Robert Mugabe and the crippling of the textile industries in South Africa, Nigeria, and Lesotho. Most notably, China has generated considerable African enmity for its unwillingness to intervene in Sudan's Darfur crisis. This antagonism will likely grow in the event of Beijing's continued close oil ties with Khartoum or additional Chinese vetoes of UN resolutions to stop the ongoing genocide.

The Taiwan Question in China's Africa Strategy

Another Chinese–African objective is to reduce Taiwanese influence. The China–Taiwan rivalry for African diplomatic relations dates back to the establishment of the PRC and Beijing's subsequent quest for international legitimacy and recognition. As this book went to press, only six African countries (Burkina Faso, Gambia, Malawi, Senegal, São Tomé and Príncipe, and Swaziland) maintained formal diplomatic relations with Taiwan. Of these, none is a significant producer of oil. The remaining forty-seven African states all recognize Beijing as the sole legitimate government of China.

The motivation for African nations to choose between recognizing Taiwan or China is largely a question of aid. In many cases, the amount that Taiwan provides for African nations exceeds general standards. For example, when Taiwan established diplomatic relations with Chad in 1997, it agreed to provide $125 million in aid—more than half the country's total.[36]

Most African countries do not object to China's One China policy or its antisecession law, and thus effectively support China's efforts to block Taiwan's independence movement. While it can be argued that many African nations that share similar experiences with separatist movements may be inclined to support China's policy in any case, the economic incentives to support Beijing are also readily identifiable. China makes it very clear that those African nations that do not recognize Beijing's authority over Taiwan will not receive China's development projects and will also be denied access to facilitation organizations such as the China–Africa Cooperation Forum.[37]

In a recent interview, a minister of the Nigerian embassy in China explained that the Chinese government continually pressures the Nigerian government about Taiwanese presence in the country. Hence, a Taiwanese trade center established in 1992 in the capital, Abuja, was forced by President Olusegun Obasanjo to relocate to Lagos. China continues to pressure Nigeria to have the trade center removed altogether from the country.[38] Similar incidents are said to have taken place in countries like Lesotho and South Africa, both of which have historically had a large Taiwanese presence.[39]

African Conflicts and China's Military Involvement in the Continent

The PRC's increasing dependence on African resources will inexorably lead Beijing to become further enmeshed in African political affairs, especially those of oil producing nations. It will be in China's great interest to prevent not only activities that would risk imperiling the export of African energy but also those that would threaten the favored governmental bodies that legitimize China's resource extraction.

Sudan and Zimbabwe both serve as good bellwethers of the inevitability of Chinese involvement in African conflicts. In Sudan, UN efforts to pressure the government in Khartoum to end the Darfur crisis were stymied by China's veto. In Zimbabwe, China can be regarded as the main factor responsible for President Robert Mugabe's continued grip on power. China's energy interests in the country are primarily related to coal as opposed to oil, but it must be noted that coal supplies over 69 percent of China's energy. Mugabe has established a "Look East" policy that aims to court the political and economic support of Asian allies, primarily China.

Zimbabwe has experienced high levels of economic decay and political oppression following the European Union's introduction of economic sanctions in response to electoral fraud and political violence. Despite these challenges, Beijing has helped Mugabe retain power by maintaining substantial bilateral trade between the two countries. China's interest in Zimbabwean resources and markets, and the absence of a Western presence, propelled Beijing's close relationship with a leader shunned by the majority of the international community. The PRC has also built new presidential palaces and buildings for Mugabe to, in effect, "grease" the relationship.

Despite this, the past year has shown evidence of a slight shift in Beijing's policy toward countries with questionable governments. After receiving negative feedback from the international community, China has moved to try to distance itself from Mugabe. President Hu Jintao pointedly failed to visit Harare in early 2007 on his extensive trip to Africa, although he did travel to most of Zimbabwe's neighbors. With the approaching 2008 Olympics, Beijing also finds itself underneath the international community's judgmental microscope. Beijing has also moved to quell growing negative international reaction by supporting the deployment of UN peacekeeping troops in Sudan.

These hints of shifts in policy toward Africa may not be motivated solely by ambitions of better relations with the West. Beijing is becoming increasingly aware of the possibility that an anti-Chinese backlash from Africans could hinder Chinese economic benefits on the continent. Reports of poor working conditions within Chinese companies and the undercutting of domestic industries have created small but growing pockets of anti-Chinese sentiment on the continent.

Beijing is starting to pay some other costs associated with investing in unstable regions. In 2007 an Ethiopian rebel attack on the Chinese oil field in

Ogaden resulted in seventy-four Chinese and Ethiopian workers killed and seven Chinese workers kidnapped. If China were to be ostracized as a negative entity across Africa, its vulnerability to similar acts of violence could greatly increase. Chinese companies, which had heretofore enjoyed a degree of agreed immunity among Nigerian rebels, lost this benefit in early 2007 when Chinese workers were kidnapped and held for ransom.[40] Furthermore, the 2006 elections in Zambia were split between pro- and anti-Chinese candidates. This split was likely in response to exploitative working conditions of Chinese companies, not to mention these companies' threats to halt relations if the candidate Michael Sata, heavily critical of China, was elected.[41]

Chinese military involvement in Africa, though currently marginal, could increase in the future. China maintains a military presence in nations of very high-risk and high-energy importance. A study published in *The National Interest* notes Chinese military presence in Sudan to protect the nation's interest in the oil fields directly south of Darfur.[42]

Chinese military attachés are present in member states of the Southern African Development Community. These nations include Angola, Botswana, the Democratic Republic of Congo, Lesotho, Malawi, Mauritius, Mozambique, Namibia, the Seychelles, South Africa, Swaziland, Tanzania, and Zimbabwe. Chinese military detachments make visits and provide training for the local military in Zimbabwe, Angola, and the Democratic Republic of Congo,[43] all of which possess significant oil reserves and recognize Beijing as the sole legitimate government of China.[44]

Arms Sales in Africa

China's African arms trade dates to the beginning of the Cold War. Originally motivated by ideology, such dealings are now driven primarily by profit. Although this shift in motivation has precipitated a decline in sales since the 1990s, recent and future sales are likely to influence African politics.[45] China's arms trade with Africa constituted 10 percent of all conventional arms transfers to the continent between 1996 and 2003.[46] Significant known arms transfers include those that fueled Eritrea's civil war in the late 1990s from which China may have received more than $1 billion.[47] In a possible indication of future high technology business, in late 2004 China arranged to sell Zimbabwe twelve FC-1 fighter jets and one hundred military vehicles for approximately $200 million.[48] Human rights groups have alleged that China has supplied weapons to Sudan in violation of a UN arms embargo.[49]

Implications for U.S. Security

The United States is ill served by its failure to respond adequately to China's African energy pursuits. In comparison, Chinese–African interaction is at a very high level, thereby creating a strong foundation for future Chinese public diplomacy and political influence efforts. This is exemplified by the China–Africa summit held in Beijing in November 2006.[50] For a variety of reasons, the United States does not have as large a public diplomatic presence in Africa. This could prove to be a major hindrance to U.S. interests in times of African political strife or heightened energy security pursuits.

Additionally, countries with high levels of poverty and despair are also likely incubators for anti-Americanism. As an active and engaged African partner, China is well positioned to manipulate that tendency should it suit Beijing's interest to do so. Further, if China's economic engagement helps lift African nations out of poverty, then Beijing, and not Washington, will get the credit and the resulting influence and support.

In contrast to the optimistic scenario of the preceding paragraph, if China's investments do not improve Africa's plight and instead aggravate it, then international efforts to stabilize the continent will be thwarted, resulting in increased violence, mass migration, and other forms of chaos. A viable investment option led by Washington that promotes African security and stability will hedge against either unbridled Chinese gain (at measurable Western expense) or abject failure.

Policymakers should also note that promising new oil reserves are being found in deep waters in the Gulf of Guinea region. China's lack of deepwater extraction technology provides the United States with a unique advantage in the region. China does, however, have a strong political influence in those countries that could slow or prevent U.S. extraction efforts. In the meantime, there can be little doubt that Chinese oil companies will develop, buy, or steal the technology necessary to pursue such deposits. Simultaneously, Chinese firms are exploring the remaining reaches of the African continent in search of untapped reserves.[51] Taken together, these factors suggest that a window of opportunity for the United States to further its interests in Africa may be closing. One thing is certain: where the United States does not engage, China will.

The United States can and should play an important role in preventing nightmare scenarios that could arise in Africa. One strategy would be to continue to engage China and to use increasing influence in Beijing to encourage the PRC to be a more responsible stakeholder in Africa's future. Another would be to urge U.S. businesses to operate in Africa, through tax incentives and other mechanisms, and thereby help to create the conditions necessary for sustained development. These goals could also be pursued through other economic means such as debt relief, low-cost loans, and reductions in agricultural protectionism. Accomplishing this without abandoning the U.S. core values of regard for human rights and promotion of democracy, however, will challenge America's brightest policymakers. Nevertheless, an increase in U.S. attention to and effort on the African continent is necessary to better understand, complement, or compete against the effects that unhindered Chinese investment has created.

The recent establishment of the United States Africa Command (AFRICOM) has the potential to be a positive move in the direction of fostering a more effective U.S. presence on the continent. According to a U.S. State Department press release, "By creating AFRICOM, the Defense Department will be able to coordinate better its own activities in Africa as well as help coordinate the work of other U.S. government agencies, particularly the State Department and the U.S. Agency for International Development."[52] The launch of AFRICOM sends a positive message to Africa that Washington views the African continent as being of great strategic interest and should facilitate further American aid, security assistance, and business involvement in Africa. The 2007 announcement of the launch of AFRICOM coincided with President Hu Jintao's visit to Africa, however, and perhaps sent an unintended message of competition to Beijing.

Notes

1. See "China's National Energy Strategy and Reform," China Development Forum 2003, Development Research Center of the State Council, Diaoyutai State Guesthouse, Beijing, China, 15–17 November 2003; Kang Sheng, "The American Factor of China's Africa Oil Security and Diplomacy," World Economy and Politics 4 (2006): 79–81. U.S. leaders must recognize that China's efforts to increase its political and economic clout across Africa constitute rational pursuit of its national interests. Chinese methods, which include turning a blind eye to poor governance, often offend Western sensibilities about human rights and political freedom. But Chinese investment and development activities on the continent can advance both African and American interests. China's aggressive approach to engagement in Africa is likely to become more balanced and sophisticated in the future in response to the increasingly heavy burden of international scrutiny and criticism. China is relatively inexperienced at playing international politics at the level of international responsibility commensurate with its emerging role as a rising regional/global power and faces a learning curve with respect to its Africa policy. Washington must

use Beijing's lack of experience to its advantage in furthering U.S. diplomatic goals. Chinese efforts in Africa can lead to a more prosperous and stable Africa but only if they are tempered with a strong and sustained U.S. counter presence. The alternative would be an Africa depleted of resources, wracked by conflict, and condemned to perpetual chaos. Surely that is not in any nation's interest.

2. Shu Xianlin and Chen Songlin, "African Oil and China's Energy Security," *Journal of the University of Petroleum, China (Edition of Social Sciences)* 20, no. 5 (October 2004): 5–9.

3. Esther Pan, "China, Africa, and Oil," Council on Foreign Relations, Backgrounder, 26 January 2007, http://www.cfr.org/publication/9557/.

4. "China Replaces Peacekeepers in Sudan," *PLA Daily* (Xinhua), 26 January 2007. There are also reports that China has stationed four thousand paramilitary personnel (possibly People's Armed Police) in Sudan to protect Chinese workers and infrastructure. Peter Brookes, "The Ties That Bind Beijing," *National Review Online*, 20 April 2006, http://www.nationalreview.com/comment/brookes200604200753.asp; "Zimbabwe Reveals China Arms Deal," *BBC Online*, 14 June 2004, http://news.bbc. co.uk/2/hi/africa/3804629.stm.

5. Zhong Yanqiu, Sun Guoqing, and Ma Fengcheng, "African Petroleum Resource Has Exploration Potential," *Petroleum Geology & Oilfield Development in Daqing* 21, no. 1 (February 2002): 79–80.

6. CIA World Factbook, https://cia.gov/cia//publications/factbook/geos/ch.html#Econ.

7. Ma Fengliang, "Study on Petroleum Security of China" (in Chinese), *Journal of Petroleum Chemical Industry Technology and Economy*, no. 20 (2004): 1.

8. International Energy Outlook 2006, "World Oil Markets," Energy Information Administration, http://www.eia.doe.gov/oiaf/ieo/oil.html.

9. Zheng Zhong and Chen Yizheng, "Strategy Study of China Energy Security in Its Resource Exploration and Utilization" (in Chinese), *Resource Development & Market* 22, no. 2 (2006): 137.

10. Zhang Bo, Chen Chen, Liu Ming, and Chen Zao. "The Status Quo of China Energy Security and Sustainable Development," *Geological Techno-Economic Management* 26 (February 2004): 56–67.

11. Gao Hongtao and Ding Hao Li Liang, "Current Situation of Petroleum Consumption in China and Its Strategic Thinking" (in Chinese), *China Safety Science Journal* 14, no. 8 (2004): 29.

12. Wang Wei, "African Oil Development and the Western World's Scramble for Possession" (in Chinese), *West Asia Africa* 4 (2003): 74–76; Xin Hua, "Europe and America's Scramble for African Oil Strategy" (in Chinese), *Global Watch* 7 (2004): 57.

13. "Five Major Countermeasures for China's Energy Security," excerpt from *Yunnan Energy Conservation News*, 15 January 2006, 36.

14. "Five Major Countermeasures," 36.

15. Liu Shihua, Zhang Huiyao, and Hu Guosong, "A Tentative Analysis on Oil Import Security of China" (in Chinese), *Journal of Petroleum Chemical Industry Technology and Economy* 3, no. 21 (2005): 14.

16. Wei Jinsheng and Yang Weiliang, "China's Oil Import Strategy Analysis" (in Chinese), *Statistics and Strategic Policy* 14 (July 2005): 44.

17. "Major Points of China's Oil Import Strategy" (in Chinese), *Foreign Investment in China* 5 (2005): 16–19.

18. Yao Guimei, "Strategic Consideration on Exploitation and Utilization of African Mineral Resources" (in Chinese), *West Asia and West Africa Journal, Chinese Academy of Social Sciences* 2 (2003): 53–57.

19. Wang Li Min, "Investment in Africa to Be Aspired—2nd Africa Petroleum, Energy & Mining Investment Forum," *International Oil Economics* 4 (2006): 46–50.

20. Nick Kotch, "African Oil: Whose Bonanza?" *National Geographic Online*, September 2005, http://www7.nationalgeographic.com/ngm/0509/feature3/index.html.

21. Shu and Chen, "African Oil and China's Energy Security," 5–9.

22. "Sudan Oil and Human Rights," *Human Rights Watch* (2003): 63, http://www.hrw.org/reports/2003/sudan1103/.

23. Cui Hong Wei, "Fulfilling China's Energy Security Strategy," *Journal of World Economic Research* 6 (2005): 23–27.

24. "Five Major Countermeasures," 36. See also, "Nuclear Power in China," World Nuclear Association, http://www.world-nuclear.org/info/inf63.html.

25. Phillip Snow, *The Star Raft: China's Encounter with Africa* (New York: Weidenfeld & Nicolson, 1988), 144–85.

26. Peter Andrews Poole, "Communist China's Aid Diplomacy," *Asian Survey* 6, no. 11 (November 1966): 622–29.

27. Ian Taylor, "China's Foreign Policy towards Africa in the 1990s," *The Journal of Modern African Studies* 36, no. 3 (September 1998): 443.

28. "Council Promotes Sino-African Ties," *Financial Times Information*, 18 November 2004.

29. Lefa Mokotjo, Solomon Rutega, Jibril Dama Audi, and Eyassu Dalle, interviews by author, Beijing, June–July 2005.

30. Liu Xin-hua, "Analysis of America's Oil Diplomacy in Africa in Recent Years" (in Chinese), *International Forum* 5, no. 5 (2003): 36–41.

31. Ian Gary, "Bottom of the Barrel: Africa's Oil Boom and the Poor," *Catholic Relief Services*, June 2003, http://www.earthinstitute.columbia.edu/cgsd/STP/documents/Bottom_of_the_Barrel_English_PDF.pdf.

32. Zong He, "Sino-African Friendship, Cooperation and Common Development," *West Asia Africa* 2 (2005): 55–59.

33. "China's African Policy," People's Republic of China Foreign Ministry, http://www.fmprc.gov.cn/eng/zxxx/t230615.htm.

34. Shang Chun Xiang, "The Prologue to Energy Diplomacy," *Economic Outlook*.

35. Eric Lembe, Central African Republic diplomat, interview by author, Beijing, 20 June 2005.

36. Philip Liu, "Cross-Strait Scramble for Africa: A Hidden Agenda in China-Africa Cooperation Forum," *Harvard Asia Quarterly* 5, no. 2 (2001), http://www.asiaquarterly.com/content/view/103/40/.

37. Liu, "Cross-Strait Scramble for Africa."

38. Jibril Dama Audi, Nigerian First Premiere to China, interview by author, Beijing, 22 June 2005.

39. Lefa Mokotjo, Kingdom of Lesotho Ambassador to China, interview by author, Beijing, 23 June 2005.

40. Understood level of immunity in relation to Chinese companies in Nigeria taken from personal interview with Jibril Audi.

41. "China Intervenes in Zambian Election," *Financial Times,* 5 September 2006.

42. David Hale, "China's Growing Appetites," *The National Interest* 76 (2004): 141.

43. "China, Zimbabwe to Strengthen Military Ties," Xinhua News Agency, 31 July 2006.

44. "Angolan, Chinese Military Delegation to Discuss Cooperation," BBC News, 9 August 2004.

45. Daniel Byman and Roger Cliff, "China's Arm Sales: Motivations and Implications," RAND Corporation, 1999, http://www.rand.org/pubs/monograph_reports/MR1119/.

46. Esther Pan, "China, Africa, Oil," 12 January 2006, http://www.cfr.org/publication/9557/.

47. Ibid.

48. Ibid.

49. "Arms Transfers to Sudan Fuel Serious Human Rights Violations," *Amnesty International,* 5 May 2007, http://web.amnesty.org/pages/sdn-080507-news-eng.

50. Chen Aizhu and Lindsay Beck, "Chinese African Summit Yields $1.9 billion in Deals," *Washington Post,* 6 November 2006, p. A17, http://www.washingtonpost.com/wp-dyn/content/article/2006/11/05/AR2006110500742.html.

51. Lembe interview.

52. Vince Crawley, "U.S. Creating New Africa Command to Coordinate Military Efforts," U.S. Department of State, 6 February 2007, http://usinfo.state.gov/xarchives/display.html?p=washfile-english&y=2007&m=February&x=20070206170933MVyelwarCo.2182581.

Vitaly Kozyrev

China's Continental Energy Strategy: Russia and Central Asia

CHINA'S APPEARANCE AS A KEY GLOBAL PLAYER of the "great energy game" has prompted constant international speculation about the far-reaching geopolitical implications of China's thirst for fossil energy resources. Since China became a net petroleum importer in 1993, its ambitious "going out" strategy[1] and growing oil import dependency have raised the risks and vulnerabilities of crude oil supply and transportation from economically and politically volatile oil-producing markets and regions. Until recently, the geographical model of China's energy sourcing has been one-dimensional: in 2003, Saudi Arabia, Iran, Angola, Oman, Yemen, and Sudan provided China with almost two-thirds of Beijing's imported oil.[2] Despite expanded energy cooperation with oil and natural gas suppliers in Latin America, Australia, and Central and Southeast Asia, China's interests in the Persian Gulf and Africa remain intact, and roughly 80 percent of its oil imports continue flowing through the Strait of Malacca.[3]

The U.S.-led global war on terror has shifted the regional geopolitical setting in the "Greater Middle East," forcing China to confront increased oil price instability and political uncertainty in oil-producing regions. China's dependency on the U.S. naval protection of the critical maritime oil transport routes has increased substantially. Operation Iraqi Freedom and China's unprecedented growth of oil demand in 2003 brought the issue of strategic resource imports to Beijing's national security agenda.[4]

Beijing's sense of energy insecurity, coupled with the Taiwan predicament, drives its maritime ambitions. Zbigniew Brzezinski once noted that China's economy (like the other Asian economies) is "almost exclusively dependent on cargo carried by ships—including oil imports," which is "absolutely essential."[5] China considers its maritime-power status to be an important component of its grand strategic aspirations. While previously limited, growing Chinese strategic sea power may ultimately challenge American military preeminence in the western Pacific.[6]

These developments have raised the problem of coherence between Beijing's maritime interests and the continental strategy of China as a major land power in Eurasia. The continental strategy has long been integrated into China's conception of "peaceful development," which requires a favorable international environment. But it is the issue of energy security that prompts Beijing to reassess the importance of China's "strategic rear." To ensure stability of supply from the oil-rich neighboring states, China has strengthened its military capabilities by reorganizing the army into combined arms battle groups, and the heavy armored corps in Xinjiang are designed to safeguard relevant oil fields in Central Asia.[7] In the diplomatic field, China's policy of regional integration has been a success: Beijing has deepened its energy partnership with Kazakhstan, Uzbekistan, and Turkmenistan, and the economic and energy agenda of the Shanghai Cooperation Organization (SCO) has expanded. In recent years, Sino–Russian partnership in the energy sphere has developed from uncertainty to a full-fledged cooperation.

It is therefore important to explore the parameters of China's continental energy strategy. This chapter argues that to secure its energy supply, Beijing strives to maintain a balance between the continental and maritime options, and its concrete behavior in Eurasia is determined to a large extent by a combination of the basic Chinese geopolitical perceptions and energy security concerns in the changing international environment. China seriously considers the northern and northwestern vectors of its energy diplomacy as a real opportunity to diversify its petroleum supply away from the "Malacca dilemma."

It is noteworthy that China's efforts to set up its footholds in the resource-rich Eurasian landmass takes place in the context of increasing Russian isolation from the West, creating a potentially positive overlap of Russian and Chinese interests in the region. Moscow intends to consolidate and develop its ability to supply Asia's rising demands, and China seeks to secure access to stable, adequate supplies of oil and gas for its industrial and public needs. The politically and economically motivated convergence of interests of China, Russia, and their Central Asian partners might enable Beijing to realize an optimistic scenario in which up to 40–50 percent of crude oil and 100 percent of natural gas import demands could be covered by continental supplies.

This scenario, however, is unlikely to happen, due to a number of economic and political obstacles. There is a fundamental tension between the interests of Russia (a supplier seeking secure demand at acceptable prices) and China (a consumer looking to ensure future access to supplies at an affordable price) that prevents the strategic cooperation from running very deep. Compounding this fundamental tension between producer and consumer is a competitive dynamic for relative influence in an area that both major powers view as strategically significant: Central Asia. Russia is looking to maintain or restore some degree of Moscow-centric orientation or even dependence, while China is seeking to ensure that the power dynamics in its strategic rear do not once again pose a threat to its territorial integrity. Finally, the Central Asian states, while opting to cooperate with their neighboring great powers in the energy sphere, also strive to keep their foreign policy options open.

This chapter explores these geopolitical dynamics and the role of overland oil supplies in the context of China's continental energy security. In the first section Chinese perceptions of continental energy security and its strategic interests in Eurasia are analyzed in their relationship with Beijing's understanding of the global dynamics mixed with its traditional geopolitical conceptions of continental sufficiency. The next section is devoted to such factors as Russian strategic perceptions in the energy sphere and to a new geopolitical arrangement in Eurasia that helps China and Russia mitigate frictions and bolster closer energy cooperation based on the shared geopolitical concerns and the principles of the new international order. A special focus is devoted to the dynamics of the Sino–Russian and the broader Sino–Russo–Central Asian energy dialogues within the framework of the SCO in particular. Finally, the chapter explores the sustainability of continental energy supply to China by evaluating its financial and technological components as well as its political and economic risks.

Fundamentals of China's Energy Security and the Role of Central Asia and Russia

China's leaders view the world as anarchic, with Beijing on its own when it comes to providing for its energy needs. This prompts China to seek diversification away from the Persian Gulf, which is vulnerable to seaborne disruption. In its survey of alternative sources, Russia and Central Asia provide an attractive alternative source. To justify prospective partnerships with Russia and Central Asia, Chinese policymakers apply traditional geopolitical perceptions of China as a "strategic link" between the sea powers and the continental Eurasian hinterland. Engaging the Central Asian energy producers will help China drive regional economic development and secure its geopolitical position.

In Beijing's view, the post–Cold War global crisis and the clash of civilizations led to imbalances of power. Chinese theorists compare post-1991 global order with the anarchy of the Warring States era.[8] From this perspective, the Trans-Caspian region is pivotal for China's regional strategy. This idea, in fact, resembles Halford MacKinder's theory of a "heartland" encompassing the continental center of Russia and the contiguous regions of Central Asia and the Middle East. Although China in its geopolitical calculus in Central Asia does not appear to explicitly seek Pax Sinica,[9] the Central Asian region falls into the sphere of China's vital interests, with a special emphasis on eastern Kazakhstan (the "Seven Rivers" region) as a strategic zone for defending China beyond its mainland territory.[10] Therefore, the status of Central Asia in Chinese eyes is similar to Russia's perception of the "near abroad." The overlapping interests of Russia and China in Central Asia influence Sino–Russian interaction. Both China and Russia are concerned about regional political stability, which might be undermined by separatism, ethnic and religious conflicts, or political insurgency.

In the era of the global war on terror, China acknowledges America's role in Eurasia but formulates its geopolitical goals to prevent U.S. transformation into a military threat to China, and to check the probable rise of a new secondary regional power capable of shifting the strategic balance of power. Yet, more importantly, it also seeks to establish a regional order that will help China safeguard its economic interests and exclude the United States from regional territorial or energy disputes.[11]

It is also noteworthy that, according to Chinese theories, the country's role in Eurasia stems from its central position in East Asia—at the junction of the land and the sea. Being "a land-and-sea power" (陆海兼备的大国),

China tends to extend both toward the Eurasian heartland and into the Western Pacific. Li Xiaohua stresses that because China lies between the major land powers (Russia and India) and in close proximity to maritime activities of the major sea powers (the United States and Japan), it seeks to play a bridging role in order to avoid a "geopolitical dilemma."[12] To play this role, China should be strong economically and maintain mutually beneficial friendly relations with the neighboring countries, Russia in particular.[13]

For China and its neighbors, geopolitics has thus far fostered cooperation rather than conflict. This formula conforms well to China's new "security conception" introduced by Jiang Zemin in 1998. It calls for security through codevelopment and cooperation between the neighboring countries. Proactive security strategy in Eurasia implies economic support of the smaller nations, to secure their "self-reliance" and to avoid one-sided dependency on any great power, including even China itself. Thus geoeconomic engagement secures geopolitical influence.[14] Chinese strategists presume that a stable partnership with Russia is possible based on mutual economic interests: Russia's thirst for foreign investments and China's quest for Russian oil. In striving for codevelopment and coprosperity, China and Central Asia also share common interests. In the realization of the program of "grand western development," the Chinese northwest and Central Asia can eventually be transformed into the "strategic extension of China's western periphery" (西部周边的战略延伸).[15]

To secure its advancement beyond the western periphery, Beijing's policymakers have formulated the major premises of China's energy strategy. The first basic premise is that the anarchic character of the global energy system, rather than the "peak oil" problem, contributes dramatically to today's world energy insecurity.[16] In the view of most Chinese leaders, according to one Chinese source, the geopolitics of energy dramatically affects the international order. In the spirit of a "harmonious world" theory, they optimistically believe, however, that the international community is moving toward a more structured and stable energy system. In the period of transition, a fierce competition between both oil-consuming and oil-supplying groups of states persists. Many Chinese are skeptical about stated U.S. policy to ensure a liquid world spot market for oil, and acknowledge that in the new system of global control over energy resources, the new emerging market economies (including China's) will continue to compete with the major Western oil consumers. This might aggravate U.S.–China relations and, perhaps, lead to conflict over control in the Middle East. By 2020 the number of global oil suppliers will be reduced to such countries as the OPEC Persian Gulf states

(Saudi Arabia, Iran, Iraq, Kuwait, the United Arab Emirates, and Qatar), Russia, Western Africa, Venezuela, North Africa, Mexico, and Canada. At the same time, Chinese observers hope that OPEC's relative position in China's oil-supply balance will fall and be displaced by a number of the non-OPEC countries, including Russia and Central Asia.[17]

The second basic premise is that growing East Asian energy consumption will boost global oil demand in coming decades. Chinese experts predict that by 2010 East Asian demands for crude oil will rise to 30 million bpd, whereas local (Asian) oil output will remain near 8 million bpd. China is likely to be the major contributor to Asia's "energy dilemma."[18] Chinese and Western estimates show that the "petro-dragon's" import volume will rise to 4.1 million bpd in 2010, and 5.1–6.1 million bpd in 2020 (whereas total demands will reach 7.6 million bpd and 10.2 million bpd, respectively).[19] Experts believe that prospective crude supplies to Asia will continue to come from the Persian Gulf. The IEA predicts that by 2015 70 percent of China's oil imports will come from the Middle East.[20] To avoid risky dependency on specific supplies, Chinese leaders proclaim that Beijing should import no more than 30 percent of its needs from a single region. The rising African share in China's imports and the decline of its reliance on the Middle East supply from 48 percent in 2005 to 45 percent in 2006 has demonstrated Beijing's efforts to reduce risks of single-supplier dependence in its oil import strategy.

The third basic premise of Chinese strategy is its focus on international energy cooperation. The looming uncertainty regarding access to Persian Gulf oil resources may, therefore, raise the problem of resource conflicts within the Asian region. To prevent conflicts, Beijing's regional energy strategy seeks to create a solid foundation for robust energy cooperation, which seems to be the key solution to future imbalances of supply and demand in Asia. While competing with India and Japan for oil, Beijing is inclined to engage the oil-producing and oil-consuming countries within a multilateral framework that may be based on the APEC or ASEAN+3 structures, or even on a new ad hoc mechanism to regulate diverse interests. To enhance international energy cooperation, China has been working through the World Trade Organization (WTO), engaging in dialogues with the OPEC countries, and engaging other major international economic and financial institutions. China (as well as Russia and India) signed a memorandum of cooperation with the International Energy Agency (IEA), and numerous forums within the framework of the China–IEA partnership showed their effectiveness. By internationalizing its energy security approach, China gains opportunities to interact with major oil and gas suppliers, to obtain new oil-development and oil-refining technologies, and to gain experience in energy conservation and stockpiling practices.[21]

China seeks active participation in all types of international resource trade and cooperation. In addition to its initial strategy of direct contract purchasing, China seeks to "broaden oil supply channels" by participating in transnational projects of oil and gas exploration and development by establishing long-term "operational" sites of Chinese-controlled oil production. Chinese scholar Tong Xiaoguan comments that China has actively increased its equity acquisitions and that it participates in international tenders to obtain the right to develop oil and gas fields. Moreover, China is also working to attract big international oil producers to construct refineries and petrochemical plants on Chinese territory.[22]

The fourth strategic premise is China's traditional call for resource self-sufficiency. It is noteworthy that in addressing this issue of energy security China chooses domestic options first. Zhou Dadi, a prominent Chinese expert from the China Energy Research Institute, does not even mention the "going out" strategy as China's primary option.[23] This course of "standing firmly domestically, carving out internationally" has been formulated by top Chinese leaders and will be embodied in the anticipated new Energy Law, which will cover rationalization and energy conservation, rebalancing China's current energy mix, reshuffling China's energy distribution system, exploiting nontraditional and renewable energy sources, and promoting domestic oil and gas development and exploration. Much emphasis is placed on the key role of the market mechanism in the sphere of energy resource supply. At the China–EU summit in Helsinki on 12 September 2006, Premier Wen Jiabao stressed that in its energy strategy China prioritizes self-reliance, economizing, and technological advancement. He also pointed to the substantial potential of renewable energy resources for China.[24]

The establishment of a national strategic petroleum reserve (SPR) is a high priority for China's state energy authorities. National strategic reserve sites located in Zhoushan (Zhejiang province), Qingdao (Shandong province), and Dalian (Liaoning province) are currently under construction. One of the largest sites at Zhenhai (Ningbo, Zhejiang province) began operation in summer 2006. China's initial goal is to secure reserves (including "commercial" ones) equivalent to thirty days of oil consumption. Experts believe that China's ultimate objective is to store at least 700 million barrels of crude, which, in the view of some Chinese analysts, may be comparable to the strategic petroleum reserves of the United States and at current consumption rates would be equal to roughly ninety days of oil supply.[25]

Russia and Central Asia are indispensable to China's energy security at the international, regional, and national levels. Aggregate proven petroleum reserves of Russia, and three former Soviet Republics—Kazakhstan, Uzbekistan, and Turkmenistan—account for approximately 10 percent of the total world proven reserves. More than one-third of global natural gas deposits are located in Russia and the Central Asian region. With less than 3 percent of the world's population, Russia possesses 26.6 percent (47.82 trillion cubic meters) of world's proven natural gas reserves and 6.2 percent of global proven (74.4 billion barrels) crude oil reserves.[26] From the outset of Vladimir Putin's presidency, Russia has gradually risen as a global energy superpower. Its daily oil production has increased from the average 7.25 million bpd in 2002 to 9.23 million bpd in 2006 and accounts for 10 percent of global oil output.[27]

Central Asia's proven petroleum reserves account for about 50 billion barrels, and its discovered natural gas deposits contain over 8 trillion cubic meters.[28] In the Central Asian region, Kazakhstan is the biggest oil producer: while its own annual oil demand does not exceed 80 million barrels, Kazakhstan produces about 1.36 million bpd and exports more than 1 million bpd of crude. The Kazakh government seeks increase of oil production up to 2 million bpd in 2010 and 3 million bpd by 2015.[29] Having relatively small proven reserves of oil (totally about 1 billion barrels), Uzbekistan and Turkmenistan are unable to compete as petroleum suppliers with Kazakhstan but have significant potential as natural gas suppliers.[30]

It is quite logical that the Chinese authorities take proper account of the substantial reserves in the neighboring regions. The energy potential of China's northern "backyard" provides it with additional options to advance its energy security interests. The role of Russia and the Caspian Basin will grow in Beijing's energy mix as it works to diversify its oil import sources. In most official reports, Russia and Kazakhstan are rated as the second (behind the Middle East) or the third (behind the Middle East and Africa) regional source of crude oil supply to China.[31]

Apparently China's long-term security calculations prioritize continental options given the strategic significance of China's northwestern rear. As Aaron Friedberg noted in 2005, China "is and has historically been a land power. Its 'natural sphere of influence' will include Central Asia and continental Southeast Asia."[32] This creates favorable geopolitical conditions for the Sino–Russo–Central Asian energy nexus. Recently, the broader international situation in the region has helped Beijing to convert its geopolitical schemes into practical policies. The success of China's continental endeavors ultimately depends on a number of intertwined economic and political factors as well as on the changing strategic situation in the region.

Mikkal Herberg has noted that "in the settlement of the 'energy dilemma' each nation chooses the balance between cooperative and competitive strategies."[33] China's global quest for oil indeed combines assertive policies and cooperative approaches. In addition, China's government realizes that its energy cooperation with Russia and Central Asia should be based on principles that transcend pure market calculations. In Beijing's view, an unfavorable international geopolitical environment dramatically affects the parameters of energy partnership. China seeks to avoid problems by engaging Russia and the Central Asian states on the basis of shared political perceptions and values. This idea may be a key driver of China's interest in the SCO. China elaborates on its old and new geopolitical modeling and seeks an energy alliance with overland energy suppliers.

Energy Nexus in the Eurasian Heartland

A Sino–Russo–Central Asian energy nexus has emerged as a strategic game with a number of domestic and international variables. As often happens in a strategic interplay between the game participants, political decisions and assessments are based on each party's perceptions of the others' preferences and policies. Chinese strategy in continental Eurasia has been in constant flux as Beijing learned more about Russian strategic perspectives and the roots of uncertainty in the proclaimed energy cooperation. Despite steps toward energy partnership, it was not until U.S.–Russia relations soured (in part due to U.S. policy in the post-Soviet space and the "color revolutions") that real Sino–Russian strategic cooperation in the oil and gas sphere began.

It was symbolic that in July 2006 the first barrels of crude oil that flowed into the newly opened Chinese SPR site at Zhenhai came from Russia. This remarkable episode demonstrates that the energy dialogue between the great Eurasian powers has reached new heights. For the last two years, the two states have improved their relationship, and one may conclude that a Sino–Russian energy alliance is not far from becoming a reality.

The shift in the energy cooperation between the two countries has been unprecedented. Though very promising in early 2003, the Sino–Russian energy agenda was damaged by Russia's unexpected turn in its oil export policies from China to Japan, disavowing its previous commitment to supply Siberian crude by pipeline solely to China. The pipeline from eastern Siberia to Chinese Daqing, so much anticipated in Beijing, was outbid by the competing route to Perevoznaya Bay, near Nakhodka on Russia's Pacific coast.[34]

The Yukos affair, and Moscow's subsequent turn to the project favorable to Japan, humiliated Beijing, and Moscow's "betrayal" was perceived in China as Russia's pro-Western intent to change the balance of power in the region in favor of the United States and Japan. Beijing's initial reaction was a result of its realist interpretation of Russian policy as part of the U.S.-designed plan of "getting support from Japan" (借助日本), "engaging Russia" (拉拢俄国), and "constraining China" (防范中国). In the view of many Chinese observers, Moscow prioritized the Pacific Ocean export route due to pressure from Japan, and, by extension, its U.S. ally. Along with skyrocketing oil prices in 2003–5, Moscow's pro-Japanese inclination affected Beijing's behavior in its relationships with Russia. China tried to use the "carrot and stick" approach, and at the top level Beijing continuously demonstrated its strong demand in an attempt secure exclusive access to prospective fossil fuel supplies from Russia to the Asia-Pacific markets.[35]

But the *realpolitik* assumption that Russia was choosing between "pro-Western" Japan and "anti-Western" China in the spirit of a balance of power game was misleading. It is true that in the first years of Putin's presidency Moscow regarded its oil and natural gas supply to the United States (and to the West in general) as one of the few pillars of the anticipated Russo–American partnership, particularly in the new post-9/11 international environment. Andrei Tsygankov characterizes Putin's policy as an attempt to "reengage the West in order to acquire its recognition for Russia as a great power."[36] But the Kremlin leaders realized that Western-bound Russian crude export infrastructure had reached its capacity limit and required huge investments in further expansion, while the traditional reserve base of oil production was declining. Thus, new policies should have been implemented to help redirect part of Russia's exports to satisfy the demand of quickly growing Asia-Pacific consumers. The situation in the natural gas markets was also changing as liberalization of the European gas market raised risks for Russian exports, further natural gas exploration and production required substantial investments, and Asia-Pacific gas demand rose rapidly.[37]

These economic changes prompted Russia's reassessment of its strategic priorities, and the new approaches were reflected in the "The Energy Strategy of the Russian Federation until 2020," officially published in 2003. The Russian leadership was concerned about the prospect of development of new oil and gas fields. Moscow's energy authorities confirmed that, if production continued to focus only on the proven reserves in the traditional oil development areas, 30–40 percent of the national resource base would be exhausted by 2015–20. The exploration and development of oil and gas in the new territories required, according to official estimates, $40–50 billion of additional investments.[38] To consolidate resources, the Russian government in March 2005 implemented a new "Subsoil Resources Law," aimed at the restoration of the central control over existing and prospective oil/gas fields by means of setting up a new licensing regime.[39]

Furthermore, Moscow officials recognized that without intensive development of the resources in eastern Siberia and Sakha (Yakutia), Russia's ambitious goal to maintain the current level of oil production (about 10 million bpd) in 2010 and even raise it in 2020 would be unfeasible due to the slow growth or even stagnation in the main oil fields of western Siberia. Some leading Russian experts believe that by 2020 eastern Siberian (including Sakhalin) oil production in Russia should reach at least 1.6 million bpd. This might help Russia to raise its Asian oil exports from today's 3–4 percent to 9 percent in 2010 and up to 30 percent in 2020. Experts predict that Russia will increase total annual gas production to 710–730 billion cubic meters (bcm), 15 percent of which will be provided by the new natural gas fields in eastern Siberia. The structure of Russian natural gas exports will also change in favor of Asia-Pacific countries, and their share will amount to more than 25 percent of the aggregated export.[40]

In 2002–5, therefore, Russia faced a strategic energy policy dilemma: would its energy exports primarily be directed to the West, through the Black Sea ports and the terminals in the Baltic Sea and the Kola Peninsula; or should Moscow channel its oil and gas flow to the East, thereby solidifying its position among the Asia-Pacific oil consumers and stimulating the development of the vast and underdeveloped Russian Far East? Putin's team appears to advocate a balanced approach between East and West.

Chinese analysts misinterpreted the setback in China's energy cooperation with Russia as Moscow's "strategic deviation" from partnership with Beijing. For Chinese observers, it was unclear whether Moscow would prioritize its relationship with the West to the detriment of its relationship with the East. It took some time to evaluate the outcomes of dramatic struggle among the Russian elite groups over resource control and distribution.

In fact, however, in dealing with Beijing, Moscow's actions have never been motivated by such ideological extremes as a one-sided pro-Western stance or by the "China threat" theory. Vicissitudes in Russia's eastward export strategy since 2003 have never led to a drastic disruption of the energy agenda with China. Even at the peak of uncertainty between Russia and

China, it was inaccurate to forecast the death of the two nations' energy cooperation.[41] China has never been excluded from Russia's list of potential oil and gas customers. Despite Chinese concern that Moscow has made a dramatic pro-Japanese shift on the pipeline issue, the Russian authorities since 2003 have reiterated their intent to carefully consider Chinese interests.[42]

In December 2004 the Russian government expressed its principal position that East Siberian pipeline construction should extend both to the Pacific Ocean and Chinese Daqing. In April 2005 a governmental decree was issued stipulating that a line be built from Taishet (Irkutsk region) to Perevoznaya Bay in the Russian Far East, with a branch to China to be constructed from Skovorodino town (Amur region), 70 km from the Chinese border. It was announced that the pipeline's capacity should be 1.6 million bpd and its cost would be $11.5 billion. The realization of the project was delayed due to environmental concerns (due to its proximity to Lake Baikal, the world's largest freshwater repository). Eventually, at the Russo–German summit in Tomsk (April 2006), President Putin approved the project and demanded that Transneft shift the pipeline route 40 km to the north of Lake Baikal. The first stage of the main pipeline construction   from Taishet to Skovorodino—will be completed by the end of 2008.[43]

Initially the Chinese leaders seemed to hardly understand the "integrative" logic of Moscow's attitude to China in the energy sphere. In trying to settle the energy export dilemma and raise its role as a major global supplier of energy resources, Moscow was inclined to consider China as part of the broader Asia-Pacific market, which Moscow perceived as a single entity, embracing China, Japan, South and North Korea, Southeast Asia, and the Pacific shore of the United States. Russia has been interested in the stability of the Asia-Pacific market as a whole to bolster its economic benefits. Russia's "integrative" approach toward East Asian regional energy cooperation was demonstrated by Moscow's quest for a stable regional hydrocarbon market backed by Northeast Asian strategic petroleum reserves. While apparently supportive of multilateral cooperation in investment, which is seen as enhancing market predictability and transparency, Russia seeks to retain control of energy reserves and infrastructure.[44]

A number of key projects in the energy sphere, initiated by Russia in 2001–3, in fact, bore a very strong regional integrative component. The production-sharing agreements (PSA) of the oil and gas projects "Sakhalin 1" (which began operation in 2001) and "Sakhalin 2" (operative since 2002) became the most illustrative examples of practical realization of such an "international" approach of Russia toward its export policy.[45] In addition to the multinational character of the projects' stockholders (including Russia, the United States, Japan, India, and China), oil and gas export from Sakhalin was supposed to be diversified among several consuming countries in the Asia-Pacific region. The Sakhalin Energy Company (Sakhalin 2) concluded a contract in 2004 on LNG supply to the United States and Mexico for the period of twenty years. Russian officials also confirmed in summer 2003 that Moscow was indeed interested in China's participation in exploring the island's offshore energy resources.[46] Another example was the agreement on natural gas supply to East Asia from the Kovykta gas field. In November 2003 an agreement between Rosneft, Sinopec, and the Korean Gas Corporation was inked in Moscow. The parties agreed to set up a 4,887-km gas pipeline to China and, further, to South Korea, with the transportation capacity of 34 billion cubic meters annually over thirty years, starting in 2008 and reaching its peak in 2017. According to the original agreement, China expected to receive a total volume of 600 billion cubic meters of natural gas over that period.[47]

One may assume that Russia's logic of a unitary Asia-Pacific market is irrational. Perhaps Russia would benefit from having China and Japan bidding against each other and rising the price of the hydrocarbon assets. By being persistent in inviting Japan to make investments in the energy infrastructure, Russia's leaders seem willing to capitalize on simultaneous participation of Beijing and Tokyo in developing Russian oil fields in Siberia.[48] But Moscow appeared to be unable to pursue a coordinated marketing policy due to the existing contradictory sales strategies performed by the major oil producing companies, the pipeline monopolist Transneft, and the central government with its competing entrepreneurial ministries and agencies. Therefore, Moscow has long preferred to remain ambiguous concerning the question of pipeline construction from Siberia, and it was only China's ongoing pressure that made Russia confirm its intent to have the "Chinese vector" of Russian energy export policy unchanged.

While playing a waiting game, in 2004 Beijing strategists came to understand the domestic and international reasons behind Russia's strategic uncertainty. The Chinese leaders accepted the Russian perception of the prospective Asian market as the integrated and organized one. Beijing acknowledged that Russia desires the ability to sell oil to a wide variety of customers, rather than remaining tied to a single buyer who can use the sunk cost of a China-bound pipeline and supporting infrastructure as leverage for seeking further price concessions. Once the supplier commits more than $1.5 billion into developing dedicated fields and infrastructure to send oil to China, the Chinese are in a more powerful price negotiating position, assuming they have other ways to obtain oil (e.g., by sea). China positively assessed the process of renationalization of the energy industry in Russia: it gave the Chinese negotiators more opportunities to make a deal with two Kremlin-controlled vertically integrated corporations, Gazprom and Rosneft, rather than with a number of private operators.[49] The growing role of the state bureaucracy in the energy sphere helped China to negotiate the "package" of issues with Russia, in which oil and gas could be integrated with the broader context of the Sino–Russian strategic partnership.

In 2004 Gazprom was empowered as the government's agency for the realization of the United Program of Gasification of the Russian Far East. The infrastructure of eastern Siberian gas supply, distribution, and sales have since depended on this state monopoly. Exploiting its connections to President Putin, Gazprom raised its role in Russian energy policy, domestically and internationally. In 2005 China's negotiations with Gazprom and the fact that Rosneft purchased Yuganskneftegaz (Yukos's largest asset) helped Beijing to further secure its strategic interests in Russia.[50]

In October 2004 China and Russia started institutionalizing their energy cooperation. The mechanism of the prospective partnership was based on the governmental dialogue and on the "strategic partnership" between the state-controlled oil and gas corporations. Gazprom and Rosneft were assigned to be the companies performing the agent role in the cooperation with China. An official in the Russian Ministry of Industry and Energy explained in an interview with the *Vedomosti* newspaper that Gazprom and Rosneft implemented two lines in relations with foreign companies: "Gazprom exchanges assets for foreign assets under Russian control, while Rosneft swaps foreign money for Russian assets also under Russian control."[51]

Under the tight control of Putin's aides, namely, Igor Sechin, deputy chief of Russia's presidential staff (chairman of the board of directors, Rosneft), and first deputy prime minister Dmitry Medvedev (chairman of the board of directors, Gazprom), the companies embarked on maintaining a strategic dialogue with China. A set of normative documents shaped energy cooperation between Beijing and Moscow. On 14 October 2004 China National Petroleum Corporation (CNPC) and Gazprom sealed an "Agreement of Strategic Cooperation" laying the foundation for future gas exports to China and gas storage construction. To implement the agreement in practice, the parties set up a Joint Coordinating Committee and a certain number of working groups for different businesses under the coordination of a permanent Gazprom-CNPC Joint Working Group.[52]

China successfully built on Russia's "cooperative" approach toward the "integration" of Asian markets. At multilateral and bilateral meetings, Chinese diplomats have consistently promoted the idea of regional economic integration (including energy) as the key article of the Shanghai Cooperation Organization's agenda. In the concrete policy of regional cooperation, Beijing used the "Kazakhstan card" to obtain Moscow's accord on guaranteed oil supply to China.

China's involvement in energy projects in Kazakhstan preceded Russian plans to build a pipeline to China. In 1997, the Kazakh government reached an agreement with China on the pipeline construction linking western Kazakhstan oil fields (Aktobe) with a few refineries close to Urumchi, in China's Xinjiang province. The 3,200 km pipeline was supposed to transport at the minimum 400,000 bpd of crude oil and can carry up to 1 million bpd if additional Russian oil supplies (e.g., from Omsk) materialize. Construction of the domestic part of this pipeline in Kazakhstan (Kenkiyak-Atyrau) and of the pipeline arm to Druzhba-Alashankou (China) was completed in 2005.

It has been very important for Beijing to avoid a Russo–Kazakh clash over petroleum supply and transit to China. Beijing thus strove to integrate the potentials of Russia and Kazakhstan as the largest prospective oil suppliers to China, and this project was performed on the basis of "regional integration and partnership" fully supported by Russia. When negotiating with Kazakh president Nursultan Nazarbayev in 2003, Hu Jintao raised the issue of Russia's participation in joint oil supply to China to fill the entire 400,000 bpd capacity of the pipeline to the border city of Alashankou, China (Kazakhstan is able to supply up to 200,000 bpd). Subsequently, Nazarbayev conveyed this idea to the Russians. By this arrangement with Astana, Beijing demonstrated its awareness of a "special" type of relationship between the Kazakh and Russian elites, and shortly thereafter the Kazakhs and some Russian petroleum companies (TNK-BP and Samaraneftegas) came to an agreement on their participation in oil supply through Kazakhstan to China.[53]

Despite the setback in relations, Beijing in 2003–5 never gave up its effort to achieve a foothold in the Russian and Central Asian energy market. Chinese leaders were driven in their actions by the need to safeguard prospective fossil fuels supply to China as the situation in the Middle East deteriorated. But the real breakthrough in Sino–Russo–Central Asian energy cooperation occurred after the "color revolutions" in the post-Soviet space dramatically changed the character of Russo–Western partnership and created a new environment for the strategic energy game unfolding in Central Asia.

New Dynamics of Sino–Russo–Central Asian Energy Cooperation in the Aftermath of the "Color Revolutions"

America's support of the "color revolutions" in Georgia, Ukraine, and Kyrgyzstan and its "democratic offensive" in Eurasia in 2003–5 were followed by a major setback in the U.S.–Russian relations and the weakening of energy cooperation as a pillar of sustainable Russo–Western partnership. These changes have substantially increased the pace of development for China's "continental strategy," which now opens the new perspectives for China's strategic setting. However, Washington's "transformational diplomacy" and the ambiguous role of the West in the "Eurasian heartland" make the energy strategic game in the region more complicated.

After supporting the "colored revolutions" in the post-Soviet space, the United States sided with the European leaders in criticizing Russia for "politicizing energy issues" after the Russo–Ukrainian "gas wars" of 2005–6. This spat showed how differently Moscow and its European customers perceive the idea of "energy security." Moscow has been reluctant to accept the principle of "non-discriminatory conditions for trade in energy materials, products and energy-related equipment based on WTO rules," promulgated by the European Energy Charter Treaty (1994), which was signed by the Russian government but never ratified by the State Duma.[51] It is clear that, since the respective statements on multilateral energy cooperation were made at the Group of 8 summit (July 2006), neither the EU nor the United States has been willing to substantially increase oil/gas imports from Russia. Furthermore, many of the long-term contracts regulating Russia's gas supply to Europe will soon expire, and the new terms of future energy agreements with European customers remain uncertain.

Under such circumstances, the Kremlin's "eastern vector" rhetoric in 2005–6 has acquired a very important strategic meaning. Mikhail Delyagin, director of the Russian Institute of the Problems of Globalization, emphasized in November 2006 that Western policy "pushes Russia away" from the West and accelerates its redirection to "China and China-related Southeast Asian countries." Apparently, the "Chinese alternative" thesis is instrumental for bargaining with the EU partners.[55]

The program of eastward expansion of Russia's gas transportation network to Asia (with the hope of increasing the Asian share of natural gas exports to one-third of the total outbound gas supply by 2011) is thus economically realistic, and it conforms to Moscow's "broader Asia" market strategy while providing leverage in Russia's trade interaction with the European

Union. However, despite its economic importance, the "diversification issues" in Russo–Euro–Central Asian energy interaction are not likely to undermine dramatically the whole system of fossil resources supply and distribution in Eurasia. Eventually Europe will have to secure its coherent engagement with Russia, and, as the recent International Crisis Group report concludes, "steps to improve energy security with Russia are more of a priority than a Caspian shortcut."[56]

But what might be more significant for the analysis of Russia/Central Asia behavior and China's energy strategy is that Western "democratic offensive" and energy "counter-diplomacy" in the region complicate the strategic energy game between the great powers in Eurasia. Dramatic shifts in the U.S.–Eurasian strategy and the political consequences of "color revolutions" strengthen realist arguments in Russia's policymaking and strategic thinking. Since 2005 Russia has considered prioritizing energy supply to China to balance against the United States and to help Beijing prevent possible petroleum supply disruptions to China from the Middle East. There are many in Russia's leadership who regard the "China choice" as part of the global strategy to counter "American hegemony."[57] This assumption fuels the ideas of "a new Russian mission" to promote the creation of an alternative scheme of hydrocarbon flows in Eurasia beyond Western control and with Russia, Central Asia, and Iran at the center of the "energy club." This was proposed by President Putin at the SCO summit in Astana in July 2005.

Beijing appeared to be responsive to Russia's new approach and promptly capitalized on Moscow's fear of a possible setback in its energy cooperation with Europe—a fear that drove the Kremlin to solve its "energy dilemma" in favor of Asia. China has also worked to establish a "friendly and trustful" relationship with Russia through a series of formal and informal contacts at the central and local levels. Local officials in China received a directive from Beijing to activate the relationship with Russia, and the 2006 "Year of Russia in China" activities contributed to the advancement of Sino–Russian cooperation.[58]

Chinese diplomats ably incorporate the Russia-desired principle of the "integrated Asian market" into the new Sino–Russian energy partnership and seek to promote Russia's strategic and commercial interests in the Asia-Pacific region. A special emphasis now is placed on the coordination of the partners' strategies, based on the consideration of strategic, political, and market factors as well.[59] Although oil and gas sales to China remain an issue of "high politics" in the Kremlin (as in Beijing), on the practical level the partners emphasize the complementary, nonbinding, mutually beneficial, and market-oriented character of energy cooperation. Informally, the energy game is fraught with bargaining, brokerage, and bluffing. Officially, it is "a gentleman's game." In the "Joint Declaration of the People's Republic of China and the Russian Federation," signed by the Chinese and Russian presidents during Putin's March 2006 visit to China, energy cooperation is labeled as an important part of the Sino–Russian strategic cooperative partnership. But the two parties acknowledge their respective rights to diversify markets and sources of energy supply, stating that in energy cooperation "both Russia and China have adopted a *pluralistic* [emphasis added] strategy."[60] The Chinese counterparts admit that this partnership, based on the "win–win" principle, is developing in accordance with the "practices of observing disciplines and law, respecting the host country's local culture, belief and customs," and that it sets "much value on local employment and social public utilities, as well as environmental protection."[61]

The "new stage" of the Sino–Russian energy partnership appears to be a manifestation of Beijing's shift in its approach to its continental energy strategy toward a more complex web of transnational relations and businesses. To accelerate cooperation, Chinese experts advocate varied forms of partnership, including joint exploration and development of oil and gas, joint pipeline construction, and the establishment of a special fund for development of the oil sector in Russia and China. The success of these endeavors is determined by effective "work with the railroad ministry, the companies, and local authorities."[62]

Within the new framework of strategic interaction, substantial progress in the Sino–Russo–Central Asian energy cooperation has been achieved:

- New developments have been made in solidifying the financial and legal foundations of Russia's oil exports to China. Following Rosneft's controversial $9.3 billion purchase of Yuganskneftegaz in December 2004 (partially credited by the Chinese banks), the two governments in May 2005 secured agreements between banking institutions and insurance companies to provide the guarantees of China's loans to the Russian banks and partners in the energy sphere.

- China was invited to participate in the prospective oil and gas projects in eastern Siberia and the Russian Far East. In July 2005 Rosneft and Sinopec Shanghai Petrochemical Company signed a protocol to create a joint venture that would explore for hydrocarbons off Sakhalin Island.[63] Rosneft concluded a special "Agreement on Long-Term Cooperation" with CNPC, which shaped the contours of a joint oil exploration program, which includes drilling exploratory wells in eastern Siberia. The scope of the anticipated Sino–Russian cooperation was expanded in March 2006 by concluding intergovernmental "Framework Agreement on Deepening Petroleum Cooperation by Establishment of Joint-Ventures in China and Russia," "Protocol on Investment Evaluation of Crude Oil Branch Line to China between CNPC and Transneft," and "Protocol on Gas Supply from Russia to China," signed by CNPC and Gazprom.[64] When CNPC vice president Zhou Jiping addressed the Energy Forum on 23 March 2006, he dubbed this progress "a new stage of development" in the Sino–Russian partnership.[65]

- East Siberian pipeline construction has been in progress, and China has become more confident about the possibility of pipeline construction from Siberia. By April 2007 Transneft had built 860 km of the first 2,757 km stage from Taishet to Skovorodino, and the first leg of the pipeline is likely to be accomplished in late 2008. Transneft will build the 70 km spur from Skovorodino to the Sino–Russian border, and CNPC intends to invest more than $400 million to link the East Siberian pipeline with its new 600,000 bpd, 965 km pipeline from the Russian border to Daqing, which is to be constructed by December 2008.[66]

- Kremlin-supported Rosneft has become a key promoter of Moscow's East Asian energy strategy and the major oil supplier to China.[67] Without Igor Sechin's support, China could hardly coordinate the interests of the prospective Russian oil producers and major competing transportation companies (Transneft and Russian Railways). Rosneft and CNPC have demonstrated their desire for integrated cooperation, which opened the doors for equity acquisition in both countries; oil exploration and development in Russia; and the refining, processing, and marketing of petroleum production in China. Strategic relations with CNPC help the Russian and the Chinese companies to cooperate in joint bidding for oil exploration and development. The first Rosneft–CNPC joint enterprise, "Vostok Energy Ltd.," was established on 16 October 2006 with the Russian company as a 51 percent stakeholder. Another joint venture, "Chinese-Russian Eastern Petrochemical Company," will operate a 200,000 bpd oil refinery in China and will also manage up to three hundred gas stations in China.[68] Rosneft may also help CNPC set up another joint enterprise on Russian territory.[69] The purchase by CNPC International of $500 million of shares in Rosneft's IPO on 19 July 2006 can be labeled as the culmination of the mutual investment cooperation between the two giants.[70] Rosneft has also started its cooperation with another Chinese leading corporation, Sinopec. In July 2006 Sinopec acquired the first significant Chinese equity stake in the Russian oil sector by bidding $3.5 billion for a former TNK-BP subsidiary, Udmurtneft (located in the Volga-region Republic of Udmurtia).[71] Some observers in Russia have called this deal "political." The development of Rosneft-Sinopec cooperation led to the general "Agreement on Strategic Cooperation" between the two companies, signed during Russian Premier Fradkov's visit to China in November 2006.

- Chinese participation in the Sakhalin projects has also become feasible. Rosneft supports granting Chinese companies expanded access to Sakhalin's oil and gas deposits. Since 2003 Rosneft has been competing with Gazprom to obtain state licenses for development and production on Sakhalin. Natural gas exports depend on Gazprom policy, except for the "Sakhalin 1" production site operating under PSA. However, Rosneft possesses a number of stakes in oil-rich sections in the Sakhalin shore zones.[72] As a stakeholder in the "Sakhalin 1" project (20 percent), the company supported main operator Exxon-Mobil's plan to sell all natural gas to China. In October 2006 ExxonMobil and CNPC signed an agreement whereby at least 8 bcm of Sakhalin 1 gas would be piped to China's northeast.[73] Rosneft is also ready to supply China with up to 2 million tpy of crude oil. Rosneft holds a 49.8 percent stake in the "Sakhalin 3" project, together with Sinopec (25.1 percent) and Sakhalin Petroleum Company (25.1 percent). Recently, Sinopec has been competing with Russian companies and a South Korean firm to secure a larger stake in "Sakhalin 3," after the 25.1 percent equity share of Sakhalin Petroleum Company was reportedly transferred to other companies.[74]

- Beijing has strengthened its relationship with Gazprom based on the agreement on strategic partnership and the "Protocol on Natural Gas Supply from Russia to the PRC," signed in March 2006 with CNPC. The protocol fixed the major accords on the gas-supply timing, amount, routes, and gas-pricing formula principles. After the documents were signed, Putin enthusiastically announced that Russia would consider building two pipelines to deliver a total of 60–80 bcm of natural gas annually to China. Alexander Medvedev, deputy chairman of Gazprom, has stated that beginning in 2011, Gazprom will supply 68 bcm per year of gas to China through the eastern (Kovykta-Blagoveshensk) and western (Altay-Xinjiang) lines.[75] Russia also urges joint LNG production with China aimed at supplying East Asian markets.[76]

- Sino–Kazakh initiatives to secure joint supply of Kazakh and Russian oil to China have paved the way for extended cooperation in the region. Following the "integrative" logic, the Russian oil companies have become more determined to use the Kazakhstan routes for oil exports to China. Russia no longer regards Kazakhstan as a competitor and now prefers to cooperate with this pivotal Central Asian state. In November 2006 Rosneft expressed its desire to supply oil through the Kazakh pipeline from Samara to Atyrau. Rosneft chairman Bogdanchikov's official statement indicated that Rosneft would like to supply China with 1.5 million tpy of oil through the Kazakhstan pipeline with the possibility of future increases. Transneft confirmed that Russian oil shipments via the Kazakhstan pipeline would reach 7 million tpy (51.3 million barrels) in 2007.[77] Joint Russo–Central Asian supply to China, should it be realized, will turn a new page in the geopolitical setting in the "Eurasian heartland." Motivated by political (Western pressure in the post-Soviet space) and economic factors (risk aversion in dealing with competing suppliers in the Chinese market), Moscow has strengthened its partnership and cooperation with Astana through a series of governmental agreements signed by Putin and Nazarbayev in Uralsk, Kazakhstan, in October 2006.

- A new "energy club" has been proposed. At a Shanghai summit of the SCO in June 2006 Putin called for the establishment of an Asian energy club to further develop economic cooperation among Russia, China, and the four Central Asian nations. Russia views the SCO energy club as a mechanism to unite oil, gas, and electricity producers, consumers, and transit countries. At the SCO summit, Putin called it a "very timely proposal to create the energy club of the Shanghai Cooperation Organization and to expand cooperation in the transport and communication sectors."[78] The SCO member states and observer countries broadly supported the idea of placing energy cooperation issues on the Organization's agenda.[79] Kazakh prime minister Daniel Akhmetov stressed that the SCO states should focus on energy security as "the pivotal challenge for our countries' economic development."

Iranian president Mahmoud Ahmadinejad also welcomed Putin's proposal, saying that "the increasing role of energy and the presence of oil consumers and producers among member states have provided conducive grounds for cooperation." He also suggested that Russia and Iran could cooperate on jointly setting natural gas prices "in the interests of global stability." A special working group was established in the aftermath of the summit and submitted proposals for prompt establishment of such a structure.[80]

- New favorable conditions for Beijing's advancement in the area of China's "geoeconomic extension" since 2003 helped the Chinese oil and gas companies to strengthen their footholds in Central Asia. Kazakhstan has become the key partner in China's Central Asian strategy.[81] Kazakhstan started to pump crude oil to China in May 2006 through the 988-km-long Sino–Kazakh oil pipeline (Atasu-Alashankou), which had been completed in December 2005. Pipeline oil deliveries, which would reach 200,000 bpd in 2006, will increase to 400,000 bpd by 2011 and supply oil to Chinese refineries in Sichuan province. The existing Kazakhstan–China oil pipeline is likely to be extended in length to 3,000 km.[82] Railroad deliveries of oil from Kazakhstan to China from Shimkent through the Druzhba station at the border will also increase.[83] In 2005 CNPC AktobeMunaiGas Corporation (in which China's stake is 66.7 percent) produced 43.8 million barrels of oil and 2.7 billion cubic meters of natural gas but swapped most of the oil to refineries in Russia.[84] China's CNOOC successfully acquired PetroKazakhstan for $4.18 billion in October 2005, taking over assets including full or part ownership of eleven oil fields and licenses for seven exploration blocks in Kazakhstan's South Turgai Basin with production capacity of up to 143,000 bpd of crude oil.[85] Finally, CITIC Group's recent $1.9 billion acquisition of Karazhanbas oil field (in western Kazakhstan) from the Canadian company Nations Energy will secure 50,000 bpd oil output from a deposit with proven reserves of 340 million barrels of oil. Kazakhstan's state-owned KazMunaiGaz is reported to be building a refinery aimed at exporting petroleum products to China or other markets.[86]

- Uzbekistan's appeal to China for political support in the aftermath of the Andijon events resulted in the Sino–Uzbek partnership agreement signed in May 2005. A dramatic shift in Tashkent's political orientation, followed by the United States' November 2005 withdrawal from the Karshi–Khanabad air base, enabled China to expand its businesses in Uzbekistan's energy sector. CNPC established a joint venture with Uzbekneftegaz, offering $600 million of investment in oil and gas exploration and development. CNPC also acquired a license to explore and produce oil and gas in twenty-three oil and gas blocks in Uzbekistan's Bukhara-Khiva region and in Ustyurt field.[87] Remarkably, China is trying to involve Kazakhstan, Uzbekistan, and Turkmenistan (although the last is not a member of the SCO) in the establishment of a pipeline network for prospective oil and gas supply from these countries. There are three projected trans–Central Asian gas pipeline routes: (1) from Turkmenistan and Uzbekistan via Almaty to China; (2) from western Kazakhstan through Tymerkent in southern Kazakhstan to Almaty; and (3) from Russia's city Omsk to Almaty via Astana. Sino–Kazakh joint projects include a $2 billion reconstruction of the "Uzbekistan-Kazakhstan" gas line and building the "Almaty-Ürümqi" gas pipeline.[88]

- In 2005 China received an opportunity to strengthen its positions in Turkmenistan. Former President Niyazov's consent to cooperate with China in the development of gas fields in Turkmenistan was a strategic breakthrough for Beijing. Having obtained an additional argument in its natural gas bargaining with Russia, China also hedged against probable growth of Western influence in Turkmenistan's energy sphere (and new President Gurbanguly Berdymuhammedov does not rule out future partnership with the West in the Caspian region considering participation in the future Trans-Caspian gas pipeline). Despite the recent developments of the joint Russo–Turkmen–Kazakh landmark agreement on building a pipeline along the Caspian coast to export Turkmen gas via Russia, Beijing hopes to build a gas pipeline from Turkmenistan with annual capacity of 30 billion cubic meters to be supplied for thirty years starting in 2009.[89] The pipeline will presumably run from Turkmenistan through Uzbekistan and Kazakhstan. China also intends to sign a production-sharing agreement for the development of a new gas area on the right bank of the Amu Dar'ya river.[90]

Chinese energy policy's regional context is becoming a decisive factor in Sino–Russian cooperation. It drives the leaders of China and Russia to adjust their energy strategies and to seriously consider Central Asia's economic and political dynamics. Beijing's breakthroughs in its energy relationships with Russia and Central Asia have been determined by the character of its continental energy strategy. But these developments have also been affected by exogenous factors and political contingency. Russia's foreign energy relationships have rapidly become "politicized." Dramatic structural changes in the region and setbacks in Russo–U.S. and Russo–EU relations narrowed Russia's options and drove it to more aggressively seek oil and gas export possibilities in Asia. This "politicization of the energy sphere" not only buttressed Russia's advancement into the Chinese market but also broadened the common agenda of Russia and Central Asian states. Their leaders have to combine integrative and competitive strategies to secure their role in the Asian markets under the growing political and economic pressure from the West.

Sustainability of China's Continental Energy Options

In the changing international context, China's energy strategy in Eurasia fosters growing regional cooperation in the sphere of oil and gas supply to the energy hungry "dragon." The recent developments in Sino–Russo–Central Asian energy partnership based on bilateral and multilateral arrangements have been very promising, and preliminary estimates of prospective fossil fuels imports from the "Eurasian heartland" provide some data to support an optimistic scenario of the future share of China's oil and gas demands which might be covered by continental supplies. However, a number of economic and political factors in the strategic energy game in Eurasia raises the question about the sustainability of continental supply. Among these factors are Western policies in Central Asia, prospective tensions of Russia's and China's interests in Central Asia, and the "balancing" behavior of the Central Asian states, which remain dependent on natural resource exports and are thus economically and politically vulnerable.

How sustainable would China's continental energy options be? Can China secure a continuous supply of imported fossil resources in the foreseeable future? To answer these questions, one should evaluate a number of key factors and risks which might affect China's advancement in the "Eurasian heartland."

Among the many political factors, major risks for sustainable continental energy supply stem from the *highly competitive strategic interaction* between the Eurasian suppliers of energy resources (Russia in particular), and the Western actors. This noncooperative game has boosted Sino–Russo–Central Asian cooperation with the emphasis on security and economic issues. Motivated by both economic and political reasons, Russia sees the East Asian energy markets as a way to hedge its future risks in dealing with the West and pursues a seesaw policy of counterbalancing between Europe and Asia.

Russian leaders understand that the turn toward vibrant Asian markets may lead to competition with other energy suppliers. Considering competition to be unavoidable, Moscow is working to bargain with and engage potential competitors both in European and Asian markets. Russia lacks an effective mechanism to prevent completely the rerouting of energy resource transit routes to bypass Russian territory. Moscow had to swallow a bitter pill in summer 2006 when Astana agreed to pump its offshore Caspian oil through the Baku-Tbilisi-Ceyhan pipeline system. As a result, Russia may lose nearly one-third of the current volume of Caspian oil transit through the facilities of the Caspian Pipeline Consortium. In addition, a new Trans-Caspian oil pipeline may be constructed from Kazakhstan to Baku, paralleled by another gas pipeline linking Turkmenistan, Kazakhstan, Azerbaijan, Georgia, and Turkey with potential extension to Europe.

Still, in this competition, Sino-Kazakh-Russian cooperation is important. Both China and Kazakhstan exploit Russia's political complexities in the "near abroad" and the weaknesses in its energy cooperation with the West. Beijing hopes to maximize gains from its policy of geoeconomic expansion in the region. By cooperating with Astana, Chinese strategists place indirect pressure on Russia to be more forthcoming with respect to China's role in Russia's energy strategy. But Chinese and Kazakh interests are not identical. Astana tries to limit Chinese control of the local equities at a level much lower than the Western stakes in the Kazakh economy. Kazakhstan purposefully allows Chinese companies to invest in its oil and gas sectors. It also plays an indispensable role in Sino–Russian relations by permitting Russia to sell West Siberian oil to China through the Kazakh pipeline network. Astana thus demonstrates its good-neighborliness toward China, securing increased oil supply to China's northwest while committing to remain a serious partner vis-à-vis its prospective American and European investors.

Astana has its own perception of the energy alliance in Eurasia. Kazakhstan's strategy mirrors its growing ambitions as a great power in Eurasia. Kazakh leaders support modernization, which helps ensure regime stability. Astana receives support from the West, China, and Russia—all of which consider Kazakhstan pivotal in Central Asian geopolitics. Astana supports these integrative ideas and hopes to raise its role as a transit country for the other Central Asian republics—particularly Turkmenistan and Uzbekistan—in their energy cooperation with China. But, most importantly, Kazakhstan offers a long-term Eurasian oil collaboration program to mitigate emerging competition with Russia in Asian energy markets and to justify the establishment of a Kazakh–Russian oil cartel to coordinate petroleum exports into Asian (and, likely, European) markets. This proposal, made by the Kazakh presidential administration's premier think tank, conforms to the ideas of energy cooperation within the SCO and opens new perspectives in Kazakh–Russian relations for seeking a coordinated policy vis-à-vis China.[91]

Moscow accepts the rules of the game as proposed by Nazarbayev. The Kremlin understands that Astana's main objective is to pursue a multivector foreign policy strategy and, with Kazakhstan's growing commitments to Western partners in mind, consents to supplementing Kazakh deliveries to China with Siberian oil. Moscow tacitly accepts its loss of transit profits in the Caspian Pipeline Consortium and agrees to redirect the oil export flows to China using the Kazakh transit facilities. Russia is willing to bear the cost of maintaining Kazakhstan's balancing position between China and the West in order to help Astana avoid excessive dependency on either side. By developing such a "pragmatic partnership," Moscow helps Astana to keep a distance from the major players, thus securing its own role in the regional cooperation, including in the SCO structures. Russia's interest in multilateral cooperation in the region lies in diversification of export routes and reduction of price and political risks in the energy market. By promoting the SCO energy club, Russia is working to hedge against unexpected political turnarounds by the Central Asian countries. Making some concessions to Astana—on matters such as oil transit, the pricing of Gazprom's natural gas purchases in Kazakhstan, and Russo–Kazakh swapping schemes for oil supply to refineries—Moscow seeks a unified mechanism of supply to the developing Asian markets.[92]

China seems to be interested in creating a Russian–Kazakh oil cartel to satisfy China's oil demands. Beijing is likely to appreciate Astana's effort to fill the pipeline to Xinjiang with both domestic and Russian oil, which would be significant for implementation of China's strategy to safeguard half of its oil imports from the strategic "northern rear."[93] But China seeks a dominant role in the evolving integrative mechanism in the Eurasian heartland. Beijing in fact opposes a Russian monopoly on energy resource supply and transport infrastructure. Trying to work out the common SCO agenda in the energy sphere, Beijing focuses on its bilateral strategic relations with the Central Asian states. Despite alarmist Western media reaction to Putin's SCO energy club initiative, the SCO today is able to manage only a few marginal projects in smaller states (e.g., the Sangtudinskaya and Rogunskaya hydropower stations in Tajikistan and two blocks of the Kambaratinskaya hydropower station in Kyrgyzstan).[94] China may be interested in energy alliances in central

Eurasia, but only if its interests as a consumer are secured. The formation of a system of natural gas price coordination under Russian or Russo–Iranian–Kazakh control would lessen China's own bargaining position in negotiating energy deals with Russia and the Central Asian suppliers.

Therefore, having accepted the idea of the energy club, Beijing remains cautious in its support of Gazprom's desire to form "a global network of natural gas distribution" and weighs seriously the pros and cons of a Russian-led "Gas OPEC" establishment.[95] In response to speculation concerning the nature and role of the energy alliance, President Putin had to downplay suggestions of a formal gas cartel. Putin stressed that "our companies are holding talks about pooling efforts in the oil and gas sphere. . . . There is no gas version of OPEC . . . but simply a joint enterprise." Vladimir Milov, a former Russian deputy energy minister, said that the prospect of such a cartel is unrealistic.[96] In short, Russia's integrative initiatives, within the SCO or beyond, should be regarded as a way to prevent growing Russo–Central Asian and Russo–Chinese competition in the energy sphere. Besides, as Igor Tomberg aptly observes, this energy initiative can play the counterbalancing role against China's assertive economic expansion in the Central Asian region.[97]

The character of Russian and Central Asian policymaking process will also affect the sustainability of China's continental strategy. Having opted for the "eastward energy strategy," Russian political elites still face the problem of an "East-West dilemma" and reformulation of the energy security concept in a changing strategic environment. Russia, as it is shown in this chapter, actively promotes a cooperative approach toward neighboring states in the energy sphere. Yet securing a long-term national domestic consensus in the country's energy strategy remains critical for China's capability to safeguard its interests in dealing with Russia.[98]

Apart from Russia's concerns about the "resource character" of its exports to China, the clash of interests between two major partner companies of China—Rosneft and Gazprom—has become one of the key factors affecting the Sino–Russian energy partnership's sustainability.[99]

Both companies intensively promote their businesses in China, but their strategies reflect diverse interests of different powerful groups both in the center and at the local level. The companies failed to merge in 2005–6 due to divergence of interests and the differences in their respective strategies.[100] Interestingly, as the significance of Russo–Chinese energy ties grew, Gazprom and Rosneft began competing with each other and that eventually impacted their relationships with the Chinese counterparts in different business projects. Gazprom seeks full control of all natural gas deals with China.

With Putin's personal support, the gas monopolist in July 2006 received the legitimate right to be the "single export window" for Russian gas, including (yet to be) produced LNG in Sakhalin or Shtockman gas fields. Even Rosneft was not allowed to export its natural gas from the "Sakhalin 3" project, jointly owned with the Chinese. Although the export right procedure is not applicable to the PSAs, ExxonMobil's agreement with CNPC on the "Sakhalin 1" gas supply to China was not coming into effect due to Putin's personal request to refrain from making gas export decisions without Gazprom's approval.[101]

Gazprom seeks full control over natural gas export to China from Kovykta gas field in Irkutsk Region. However, TNK-BP is the license holder in Kovykta, and, despite agreements between Gazprom and TNK-BP on the terms of exploration of this giant gas deposit, the Kovykta option might long remain a paper project for China. In the Far East, Gazprom is actively purchasing existing gas pipelines in the Russian Far East, including the 375-km-long Komsomolsk-na-Amur-Khabarovsk branch (completed in December 2006) and the Sakhalin-Komsomolsk-na-Amur pipeline, and the construction of a Khabarovsk-Vladivostok gas pipeline is planned. According to Gazprom documents, Sakhalin gas fields (including those belonging to Rosneft) would become the Russian Far East's resource base for gasification.[102]

The competition between the major Russian companies was contained in November 2006 when, under Putin's pressure, Gazprom and Rosneft signed a strategic cooperation agreement, which demands a coordinated policy in oil and gas exploration, production, and in exports of hydrocarbon fuels to Asia as well. Thus Gazprom receives access to Rosneft's gas fields on the Yamal Peninsula and in Sakhalin Island, and Rosneft obtains a stable market for its natural gas.[103]

Examination of Rosneft and Gazprom's China policies makes it clear that Moscow and Beijing differ in their perceptions of primary goals and the terms of bilateral energy cooperation. At present, for Russia it is more important to secure long-term agreements with potential buyers of Russian natural gas in Asia. Gas export routes are usually predetermined geographically, and, unlike crude oil, the cost of transportation does not permit flexible sales in different markets. Gazprom intends to secure long-term contracts with China on natural gas deliveries in order to justify the expensive western and eastern gas pipelines. For China, today's gas purchase from Russia is not a matter of survival. Chinese companies may consider buying Russian natural gas for the big cities in China's northeast and the Beijing area at a reasonable price to supplement costly natural gas deliveries from the Gansu and Ningxia region. Recent agreements between CNPC and ExxonMobil ("Sakhalin Energy") on pipeline deliveries of natural gas to Manchuria, or Shandong, demonstrate China's readiness to start its "gas program" now. This may also help China preserve its developed gas fields in the north as a strategic deposit. China is even more interested in transit supply of Russian (Central Asian) natural gas to South Korea and Japan, which will be a factor in China's importance in the region in the future. But, in general, China can defer extensive purchase of Russian gas until 2015, and this may affect Russia's position in its talks with the CIS and EU counterparts.[104] The forecast of Russia's East Asian natural gas supply in table 1 shows sustainable growth of China's share in the total exports.

Table 1: Russia's Natural Gas Export to Asia-Pacific (bcm)

Region/Year	2010	2015	2020	2025	2030
West Siberia	0	15	30	40	60
East Siberia and Sakha Republic	0	30	60	82	82
Sakhalin Island	13.4	13.4	18	20	23
TOTAL	13.4	58.4	108	142	165
Including to China	5	40	78	102	125

Source: Institute of Oil and Gas Geology and Geophysics, Russian Academy of Sciences, Siberian Branch, 2006; A. Korzhubaev, "The Prognosis of Development in Russia's Oil and Gas Industries, and New Perspectives of Hydrocarbon Exports," *Problemy Dalnego Vostoka*, Moscow 5 (2006), 54.

China demands that Gazprom supply gas at a lower coal-related price rather than Gazprom-suggested "average basket of oil production price." China has been asking for the gas deliveries at a cost of $30–35 per thousand cubic meters at the Russo–Chinese border. Vladimir Milov calculates that the Kovykta project would be profitable only if the sale price of 1,000 cubic meters of natural gas exceeds $75. Russian suppliers may well have proposed the same price that Kazakhstan accepts in its sales to Russia—$140 per thousand cubic meters. Numerous negotiations and Gazprom-CNPC Joint Working Group effort made no progress in the Sino–Russian bargain on a natural gas sale price.[105] China is also unlikely to accept Gazprom's plan to acquire natural gas distribution companies on Chinese territory. Presumably, should the gas supplies be started, Russia would be satisfied with joint possession of local assets together with the Chinese partner companies, which might be preferable for Beijing. There is also the problem of developing sufficient natural gas resources to supply to China, as well as the asymmetric natural gas demands in China's northern and southern provinces, but these problems do not seem to be prohibitive for Sino–Russian natural gas cooperation.

While Russia attempts to secure gas deals with China, China seeks additional oil from Russia. Beijing considers pipelines to be a way of safeguarding energy security vis-à-vis vulnerable seaborne supplies, at least to a limited extent.[106] Chinese economists inexorably claim that Beijing must make Moscow depend on China as a buyer. The pipeline supply from Russia would help China engage Russia, and there are many reasons for doing this. Obviously, China is much concerned about the growing influence of other great powers in the oil-rich Siberian region. Furthermore, Beijing leaders seem to understand that "strategic" pipelines may strengthen geoeconomic and geopolitical interdependence between supplier and consumer, and the cost of aggression against the country-consumer from the third party rises. In general, to attain strategic goals in Siberia and the Russian Far East, China improves its political and market intelligence capabilities in Russia.[107]

Notwithstanding the progress in the East Siberia pipeline construction, China remains concerned about the project realization. The closer the final date of the Taishet-Skovorodino pipeline extension, the more Chinese experts express concerns about Russia's inability to tap sufficient volumes needed for the commercial feasibility of pipeline transportation. It is a matter of China's vital interests to secure at least 1 million bpd of oil supply to Skovorodino, because 400,000 bpd are supposed to be further delivered by railway to Nakhodka terminal Kozmino, and the balance of 600,000 bpd would go to China.

Western analysts doubt that East Siberian reserves can fill the pipeline.[108] Chinese experts seem to be more optimistic, focusing on the general fact that the East Siberian pipeline to China will connect prospective oil fields in Krasnoyarsk state, Irkutsk region, the Sakha Republic, and the Evenky Autonomous District, which totally contain 22.4 billion barrels of probable and 4.2 billion barrels of proven reserves of crude oil.[109] Specialists from the Siberian Branch of the Russian Academy of Sciences argue that at the beginning, western Siberian low-sulfur oil will become the main resource to be piped to China. Future oil supply to China will partially be secured from eastern Siberian reserves: in 2010 East Siberian and Sakha oil production will rise to 250,000 bpd, and by 2020 crude output in these areas will reach 1.8–2.1 million bpd of oil, including Sakhalin Island production.[110] Projected

Siberian oil production is shown in table 2:

Table 2: Russia's Oil Output Forecast (w/condensate*)

Region / Year	2010	2015	2020	2025	2030
	millions of barrels/day				
West Siberia	7.05	7.07	7.17	7.19	7.28
European Part of Russia	2.45	2.35	2.25	2.18	2.05
East Siberia/Sakha-Yakutia	0.25	0.86	1.23	1.43	2.25
Far East (Sakhalin)	0.47	0.51	0.60	0.67	0.72
Russia Total	10.22	10.79	11.25	11.47	12.3

* Condensate is a liquid hydrocarbon product that occurs in gas reservoirs and is also obtained when raw natural gas production is processed for sale. It may also be called natural gas liquids (NGL) and is chemically and physically very similar to gasoline. Natural gas liquids can be classified according to their vapor pressures as low (condensate), intermediate (natural gasoline), and high (liquefied petroleum gas) vapor pressure. Condensate can help improve gas project economics because of its high sale value.

Source: A. Korzhubaev, *The Prognosis of Development in Russia's Oil and Gas Industries, and New Perspectives of Hydrocarbon Exports* (Institute of Oil and Gas Geology and Geophysics, Russian Academy of Sciences, Siberian Branch, 2006), 51.

The table data demonstrate that, should East Siberian/Far Eastern oil output reach 1.8 million bpd in 2020, it may be sufficient to secure the planned 1.6 million bpd of oil to be supplied through the East Siberian pipeline to Asian consumers, including China and Japan. Rosneft optimistically estimates that eastern Siberia will provide in 2015 more than 1 million bpd of oil, which may secure Russia's supply to China.[111] The problem is that even the discovered reserves may not be developed quickly. Although the Chinese branch from Skovorodino is likely to be completed in late 2008, according to Rosneft reports, China will get only half (i.e., 300,000 bpd) of the needed crude from a new pipeline.[112] Rosneft actively supports pipeline construction, confirming that oil production from Vankorskoye oil fields 150 km southwest of Igarka town in Krasnoyarsk state would help start filling the pipeline with oil.[113]

In other words, the major challenge that the Chinese petroleum companies face comes not from the deficit of Russian energy resources but instead from an unpredictable outcome of inherent struggle between contending Russian companies over resource access, ownership, export, and transportation. The problem of fierce competition for resource deliveries between powerful groups of Kremlin-affiliated oligarchs may postpone pipeline building or affect fossil fuels supply from specific producers, from western Siberia in particular. The powerful railway minister Vladimir Yakounin, a member of Putin's inner circle, successfully promotes his "Oil for China" program. This plan involves making huge investments in the "southern arm" of the Trans-Siberian route, especially the Karymskaya-Zabaikalskaya branch. To complete the reconstruction, the "Russian Railways" corporation will invest more than $500 million. Railroad deliveries might be increased to 600,000 bpd in the future, and recent developments show that, in the battle for oil transportation to China, the railway lobby is likely to trump the advocates of pipeline deliveries.[114]

In this game between oil producers (primarily Rosneft), pipeline constructors (Transneft), and the Russian Railways ad hoc solutions are substituting for key strategic decisions about the final buyer of petroleum. For producers, it is crucial to get access to a cheaper transportation means. Transportation companies seek quick capital return, no matter in which direction the oil flows.[115] To maintain the balance of interests, the authorities have to allow the major beneficiaries get an access to exports, relevant for their political and financial weight. Therefore, more than 60 percent of the expected 600,000 bpd of oil in Skovorodino is likely to be delivered further to Nakhodka by railroad transport, which would receive higher profits as compared with even direct railroad oil supply via Manchuria to China.

Here lies the root of Russia's uncertainties about prospective volumes of eastward export supply. Backed by the powerful railway lobby, governmental officials often refer to the slow development of oil fields in eastern Siberia.[116] Lack of confidence concerning Moscow's strategic preferences stirs up anxieties in the headquarters of Chinese energy companies. Russia regularly gives China reason to doubt that the China pipeline project will actually materialize. Ecological reasons have been replaced by Russia's demands that China provide oil purchase guarantees to Russia. Oil transportation tariffs have become a constant focus of bilateral negotiations on energy issues. After the geography of the first Taishet-Skovorodino leg was changed in 2006, the cost of its construction ($11 billion) has been close to the anticipated cost of the whole pipeline to the Pacific Ocean in the original version. Therefore, the previous estimated cost of $2.06 billion in the case of Taishet-Daqing delivery must now double, and the announced $5.21 billion Transneft cost of future pipeline delivery to Kozmino looks unrealistic. In the previous scheme, delivering eastern Siberian oil directly to China was reasonable and the Chinese market (compared with the Nakhodka route) was the most logical from the commercial perspective.[117]

The above-mentioned political and economic obstacles should be considered in the forecasts of China's continental imports of fossil fuels. Broadly-publicized numbers of the planned supplies to China from Russia and Central Asia could be used to depict an optimistic scenario for China. But thorough consideration of the possible hurdles facing this scenario and a more conservative approach are essential to shape a realistic projection of the future achievements of China's continental energy policy. In table 3 two different scenarios, optimistic and moderate, are offered.

According to the optimistic scenario, China might be able to safeguard its "northern" continental supply at the level of 2.4 million bpd of petroleum and 110–130 billion cubic meters of natural gas by 2020, accounting for 40–50 percent of Chinese oil imports and about 100 percent of natural gas imports in 2020.[118] However, the accomplishment of this scenario will depend heavily on the ongoing strategic game between the major powers, and on the dynamics of regional development. Therefore, in the moderate scenario, China might obtain up to 1.35 million bpd of crude oil from its Eurasian partners, and, should western Siberian gas deposits be linked to Xinjiang via Russian Altay, China's overall demand for imported natural gas might be totally satisfied. Under the realistic scenario China's dependence on its "Eurasian rear" will grow but would not exceed 30 percent of the total crude oil imports.

China's efforts in the energy sphere in central Eurasia and Russia are likely to secure more stable continental fuels supply in the future. China's growing dependency on its Eurasian rear will not exceed one third of the total global oil and gas supply. But even these "moderate" needs should be protected, given the lack of sufficient resources and high costs of oil and gas fields' exploration and development, inherent political instability of the post-Soviet regimes, domestic competition, and the lack of strategies in the producing countries. External influence on the proceeding of the great energy game in Eurasia is also essential for China's successful energy hunt. China hopes to cooperate with the great powers, seeking for sustainable oil and gas supply from the vulnerable international markets.

Conclusion

China's continental energy strategy is based on Beijing's growing perception of the reliability of the central Eurasian region. Energy security is

Table 3: Major Sources and Volumes of China's Continental Oil and Gas Supply

Source	Operator	Projected Supply Volumes (2020)	Realistic Volumes (2015)
OIL			
Railroad deliveries from Siberia	Rosneft (including Vostok-Energy), Gazpromneft, Udmurtneft, Lukoil, TNK-BP, Surgutneftegaz, Urals Energy, and others	500,000–600,000 bbl/d (300,000–360,000 bbl/d is expected to be delivered in 2007).	270,000–300,000 Bbl/d
East Siberian pipeline (Skovorodino-Daqing branch)	Rosneft and the pool of companies	600,000 bbl/d	300,000 bbl/d
Sakhalin Island exports	Rosneft and Gazpromneft, Exxon-Mobil	400,000 bbl/d	50,000 bbl/d
Transit of Russian oil through Sino-Kazakhstan Oil Pipeline	Rosneft, LukOil, Surgutneftegaz, Gazpromneft, and others	400,000 bbl/d	200,000–300,000 Bbl/d
Sino-Kazakhstan Oil Pipeline Caspian deliveries	Kazmunaigas, OJSC Karazhanbas munai, and others	400,000 bbl/d	400,000 bbl/d
Railroad oil supply from Uzbekistan via Almaty	Uzbekneftegas	20,000 bbl/d	n/a
GAS			
West Siberia ("Altay"), East Siberian pipeline, and Sakhalin gas supplies	Gazprom, Rosneft	80–100 billion cu m/year	60–100 billion cu m/y
Turkmenistan-Uzbekistan-Kazakhstan gas supplies	Central Asian operators	30 billion cu m/year	30 billion cu m/year

Sources: Minpromenergo, Transneft, Rosneft, Russian Academy of Sciences, China Office of the National Energy Leading Group.

perceived by China's leaders primarily in terms of safety and sustainability of supply. This approach integrates geopolitical calculations and such important issues as domestic economic development and social stability, resource supply, and the growth of fuel consumption. China's Eurasian energy diplomacy is based to a great extent on the basic traditional geopolitical perceptions. In the present international environment, China postulates that its role as a key Eurasian player and as a balancer between the land and the sea powers will grow in the future.

Beijing's continental strategy combines the cooperative approach with elements of realpolitik implanted into the regional context. In the energy game unfolding in the Eurasian heartland, the interaction between the major players—ambitious Russia seeking great power status; modernizing Kazakhstan with its present political stability, pragmatic diplomacy, and aspirations of becoming a pivotal energy power; and fuel-hungry China with overwhelming economic power, anxious about third countries' incursion in its "northern rear"—generates contradictory tendencies with multiple variables. This requires virtuous diplomacy, substantial investment capabilities, and a credible power projection capability to secure Beijing's energy interests in continental Eurasia.

At the same time, a new tendency toward consolidation drives Sino–Russo–Central Asian relations and energy cooperation. Integrative regional partnership may secure cooperative, mutually beneficial relations between the suppliers—Russia and Central Asian states—and the main consumer—China. The latter will not necessarily seek realist-minded control of continental oil and gas supplies to China. Beijing will promote regional integration and Russia will remain a key partner of China within the SCO, although China will keep its hands free for independent action. For Russia, the "Energy Club" proposal is an attempt to coordinate the interests of the main players. China will participate in any kind of cooperation, but, because of fundamentally conflicting interests of the players, the probability of a universal, robust energy alliance is low.

The sustainability of Sino–Russo–Central Asian energy partnership is less affected by economic or technical factors, or the lack of resources. There will not be many economic or technological threats to Russian and Central Asian oil supply to China unless the political climate changes. For a number of Kremlin oligarchs and interest groups in the center and at the local level, a new turn to the Chinese (or Asian) option increases their confidence and assertiveness when bargaining with the United States and European Union over issues of energy security. China will capitalize on the negative developments of the relationship between Russia and the West.

A change in Western attitudes may weaken the pro-Chinese orientation of the Russo–Central Asian energy strategy. Other political factors affecting China's continental policies include Russian and Central Asian domestic political instability (factionalism and continuous political struggle in Russia) and the fact that Russia's foreign policy remains highly contingent upon Western actions. Finally, Russia's ad hoc energy strategy, notwithstanding officially declared goals, may suddenly change under the impact of bureaucratic policies or growing concerns about a "China threat."

Notes

This chapter is part of the author's research on China's grand strategy and foreign policy and is supported by Karl Loewenstein Fellowship in Political Science and Jurisprudence at Amherst College. This study is conducted in collaboration with the China Maritime Studies Institute at the United States Naval War College, on the initiative of Professor Lyle Goldstein and the organizers of the Conference "Maritime Implications of China's Energy Strategy," 6–7 December 2006 in Newport. The author is grateful to the editors and reviewers of this volume—Gabe Collins, Andrew Erickson, Lyle Goldstein, Bill Murray—and the two anonymous reviewers for their invaluable constructive comments on the earlier draft of this chapter. I wish to thank Samuel Grausz, William J. Norris, Anoop Menon, Sergey Sevastyanov, and Charles Ziegler, whose careful readings helped greatly to improve the chapter. The author also thanks Andy Anderson for his assistance in preparing the key geographical and statistical data.

1. The "go out" strategy of ambitious expansion into the international market and the parallel exploration of domestic and foreign resources were formulated by the Chinese leaders in the mid-1990s. In 1997, Chinese premier Li Peng's call for the "going out" strategy marked a new era in Beijing's "energy diplomacy" and has brought Chinese companies to the global energy markets. The strategy received the approval of the 15th Plenum of the Chinese Communist Party in October 2000 as part of the Proposals to the 10th Five-Year Plan. Jiang Zemin at the 16th Party Congress in November 2002 labeled it "a realization of the new stage of China's open policy." As a result, by 2005 China's overall foreign investments exceeded $50 billion, and thousands of Chinese enterprises were involved in the global business activity for approximately $135 billion. "十五期间中国 '走出去' 战略有力推动对外经济合作" ["'Go Out' Strategy Significantly Promoted International Economic Cooperation in the Years of the Tenth Five-Year Plan"], www.gov.cn/gzdt/2006-02/13/content_187120.htm.

2. Pak K. Lee, "China's Quest for Oil Security: Oil (Wars) in the Pipeline?" *The Pacific Review* 18, no. 2 (2005): 270.

3. For example, according to the official statistical data of the National Development and Reform Commission (NRDC), in 2005 China imported 38.34 million tons of crude oil from Africa, which accounted for 30 percent of its oil imports (in total China imported 126.82 million tons of crude oil in 2005), http://english.china.com/zh_cn/business/energy/11025895/20061019/13685339.html. Chinese experts hold that continuous growth of oil supply from Africa is currently a matter of high priority, though it cannot substitute for petroleum exports to China from the Middle East. See, for example, 郝瑞彬, 王伟毅 [Hao Ruibin and Wang Weiyi], "21世纪中国石油安全与中俄石油合作" ["China Petroleum Security and Sino-Russian Petroleum Cooperation in the Twenty-first Century"], 中国矿业 [*China Mining Industry*] 15, no. 3 (March 2006): 7.

4. In May 2003 China became the world's second-largest consumer of oil, consuming 5.46 million bpd, 35.6 percent of which had to be imported. In his speech at the governmental economic conference on 29 November 2003, President Hu Jintao for the first time explicitly defined energy and finance as the major components of China's national security policy. The text of Hu Jintao's speech was published at http://finance.beelink.com.cn/20040615/1605588.shtml. On China's growing oil demands see: 陈勉 [Chen Mian], "专家建议: 中国应重视石油战略安全" ["Proposals of an Expert: China Must Consider Security of Oil Strategy"], 开放潮 [*Open Tide*], no. 3 (2003): 22; 刁秀华 [Diao Xiuhua], "新世纪中俄能源合作" ["Sino-Russian Energy Cooperation in the New Century"], 西伯利亚研究 [*Siberian Studies*] 32, no. 1 (February 2005): 18, 20; Amy Myers Jaffe and Kenneth B. Medlock, "China and Northeast Asia," in *Energy and Security: Toward a New Foreign Policy Strategy*, ed. Jan H. Kalicki and David L. Goldwyn (Washington, D.C.: Woodrow Wilson Center Press; Baltimore: The Johns Hopkins University Press, 2005), 267.

5. Zbigniew Brzezinski, *The Choice: Global Domination or Global Leadership* (New York: Basic Books, 2004), 108–9.

6. See, for example, *The People's Liberation Army and China in Transition,* ed. Stephen J. Flanagan and Michael E. Marti (Washington D.C.: National Defense University Press, 2003); 叶自成. [Ye Zicheng], 中国大战略 [*The Grand Strategy of China*] (Beijing: Zhongguo shehui kexue chubanshe, 2003), 324–36.

7. On the People's Liberation Army (PLA) reorganization, see Martin Andrew, "PLA Doctrine on Securing Energy Resources in Central Asia," The Jamestown Foundation, *China Brief*, 9 July 2006, http://www.asianresearch.org/articles/2900.html; on Xinjiang deployment see Martin Andrew, "PLA Doctrine on Securing Energy Sources in Central Asia," *China Brief* 6, no. 11 (2006): 6.

8. О.В. Зотов. «Евразийские Балканы» в геополитике Китая: значение для России» Восток. Афро-Азиатские общества: история и современность, М., январь 2001, no. 4. [O. V. Zotov, "'Eurasian Balkans' in China's Geopolitics: Implications for Russia," *Oriens-Vostok: Afro-Asiatskie Obshestva: Istoria I Sovremennost*, no. 4 (January 2001): 105]

9. В.Л. Андрианов. Формирование «Большого Китая»: геополитическое измерение. В кн. Китай в мировой и региональной политике: история и

современность. М., 2000 [V. L. Andrianov, "The Establishment of Greater China and Its Geopolitical Dimension," in *China in World and Regional Politics: History and the Present* (Moscow, 2000)].

10. В.П. Ощепков. Россия и Китай в зеркале региональной геополитики. М., 1998 [Oshepkov, *Russia and China in Regional Geopolitics*, 52]

11. "邱 斌, [Qiu Bin], 美国的亚洲地缘政治战略与中国的选择" ["The United States' Geostrategy in Asia and China's Choice"], 江西教育学院学报 [*Journal of Jiangxi Institute of Education*] 24, no. 1 (2003): 13–14.

12. See 李小华 [Li Xiaohua], "欧亚大陆地缘政治新格局与中国的选择" ["The New Geopolitical Setting in Eurasia and China's Choice"], 现代国际关系 [*Journal of Contemporary International Relations*], no. 4 (1999): 14–15. Chinese geopolitical thinkers intensively elaborate on China's status as a "sea-and-land power" from a theoretical perspective. An interesting example is Liu Jiangyong's conception of China's pacifying role in the relationship between the land and the sea powers, see Liu Jiangyong, "地缘战略需要海陆和合论" ["Geostrategy Requires the Theory of the Land and Sea Powers' Pacification"], 学习时报 [*The Study Times*], 25 April 2006, http://theory.people.com.cn/GB/41038/4330005.html.

13. Qiu Bin, "The U.S. Geostrategy," 14; Li Xiaohua, "New Geopolitical Setting"; 叶自成, [Ye Zicheng], 地缘政治与中国外交, 北京, 北京出版社 [*Geopolitics and Chinese Foreign Policy*] (Beijing: Beijing chubanshe, 1998).

14. Zotov, "'Eurasian Balkans' in China's Geopolitics," 115–16.

15. 唐绍 [Tang Yun], 大搏杀: 世纪石油之争 [*The Great Clash: A Fight for Oil in This Century*] (Beijing: 世界知识出版社 [Current Affairs Press], 2004), 162–63, 214.

16. Official reports of the National Energy Leading Group suggest that China should be ready to adapt to the challenge of "peak oil" by 2040. "我国利用国外石油资源战略分析" ["Analysis of China's Strategy of Reliance on External Oil Resources"], Report, 中国电力企业联合会 [China Association of Electric Power Producers], 2 November 2006, http://www.chinaenergy.gov.cn/news.php?id=12319.

17. Tang Yun, *The Great Clash*, 162–63, 214.

18. In 2006 China's oil product demand reached 7.05 million bpd and will rise to 7.44 million bpd in 2007. "China 2006 Oil Product Demand Forecast Unchanged at 7.05 mln bpd–IEA," 12 September 2006, http://www.forbes.com/home/feeds/afx/2006/09/12/afx3009137.html.

19. "2020年我国石油对外依存度将超60%" ["China's External Dependency on Oil Imports Will Grow to 60 Percent in 2020"], 证券时报 [*Zhengjuan shibao*], 22 November 2006. Russian economists estimate that petroleum consumption in China would reach the level of 9.2 million bpd much earlier than 2020. See H. Байков, Г. Безмельницына. Мировое потребление и производство первичных энергоресурсов. Мировая экономика и международные отношения), 2003, no. 5, [N. Baikov and G. Bezmelnitzina, "Global Consumption and Production of Hydrocarbon Resources," *World Economy and International Relations*, Moscow, no. 5 (2003): 50].

20. "China's External Dependency on Oil Imports Will Grow to 60 Percent in 2020," 116; Adla Massoud, "Oil May Fuel Sino-US Conflict," *al Jazeera*, 29 June 2006, http://www.globalpolicy.org/security/natres/oil/2006/0629massoud.htm.

21. These conventions usually involve a spectrum of organizations and corporations as well as the key officials of other international institutions (Asian Development Bank, United Nations Industrial Development Organization, Asia Pacific Economic Cooperation, European Union, World Bank, etc.). See, for example, the Agenda of China Economic Forum to be held in Tianjin in January 2007.

22. "Analysis of China's Strategy."

23. Zhou Dadi formulated the following "strategic" preferences: (a) to pursue the policy of energy saving; (b) to optimize energy consumption: raise effective use of coal, shift oil, and gas share in the energy mix; (c) to develop projects of alternative energy production; (d) to modify the oil transportation system; (e) to lay out a comprehensive policy of national energy security, including an early warning system in case of operational disruptions; (f) to consider environmental problems; and (g) to improve the system of state regulation of the energy sector. "权威专家解读新能源战略 优化能源结构非常重要" ["Authoritative Experts Introduce the New Energy Strategy, Considering the Importance of the Energy Structure Optimization"], December 2005, http://finance.beelink.com.cn/20040713/1628080.shtml.

24. "温家宝谈中国能源战略基本方针" ["Wen Jiabao Speaks on the Fundamentals of China's Energy Strategy"], Xinhuanet, 13 September 2006, http://www.chinaenergy.gov.cn/news.php?id=9869; China heavily invests into its own energy production. Deputy Director of Energy Bureau Xu Yongsheng, in his recent report "The Development of the Chinese Industries in 2007," stated that within two years China will become the largest energy-producing country globally, http://www.chinaenergy.com.cn/news.php?id=12497.

25. "国家战略石油储备计划明年在镇海率先启动" ["The National Strategic Oil Reserve Is Scheduled to Start Its Operation in Zhenhai Next Year"], 12 October 2004, http://auto.sohu.com/20041012/n222439012.shtml. Japanese commentators believe that in 2005 China was able to secure more than twenty days of reserve supply; see Jamie Miyazaki, "Beware the Petrodragon's Roar," *Asia Times Online*, http://www.atimes.com/atimes/China/FF10Ad05.html. Indian experts estimate that Chinese SPRs at the initial cost of $725 million are designed to hold seventy-five days' reserves, not thirty days', as it is announced officially. Sudha Mahalingam, "Energy Vulnerability," *The Hindu*, http://www.hindu.com/2004/03/02/stories/2004030200961000.htm.

26. The statistical data are based on BP Statistical Review of World Energy 2006 (www.bp.com). In absolute figures, BP's estimates of Russia's proven reserves (74.4 billion barrels) of oil does not differ much from the Chinese statistics, which show that Russia's current proven petroleum reserves account for 61.3 billion barrels (8.2 billion tpy). See Hao Ruibin and Wang Weiyi, "China Petroleum Security and Sino-Russian Petroleum Cooperation in the Twenty-first Century," 5. According to some conservative estimates, proven oil deposits in Russia reach 48.6 billion barrels (6.7 billion tons). *Russia Business Consulting (RBC) Report* (Moscow, 2005), 11. Experts

of Russian Academy of Sciences claim that Russia's probable reserves contain up to 44 billion tons (329.1 billion barrels) of crude oil (12–13 percent of the world) and 127 trillion cubic meters of natural gas. The statistics were obtained from the text of "The Energy Strategy of the Russian Federation until 2020" (Moscow, 2003), 57.

27. «Нефтяной рывок» ["Oil Leap Forward"], *Vzglyad Online*, 18 August 2006, http://www.vz.ru.

28. BP Statistical Review of World Energy 2006; "中亚将成为世界主要以应急能源供应地" ["Central Asia Will Become Global Critical Energy Supplier at Emergency"], 国家发改委能源局 [*NRDC Energy Bureau Report*], 20 November 2006, http://www.chinaenergy.gov.cn/news.php?id=13022.

29. Trade Environmental Database case studies, Kazakhstan and Oil, American University, http://www.american.edu/projects/mandala/TED/kazakh.htm.

30. In 2005 natural gas output in Kazakhstan, Turkmenistan, and Uzbekistan reached 23.5 billion, 58.8 billion, and 55.7 billion cubic meters respectively. See BP Statistical Review of World Energy 2006. The estimates of Uzbek gas production made by China Office of the National Energy Leading Group are slightly higher (60 billion cubic meters), see "Central Asia Will Become Global Critical Energy Supplier at Emergency," NRDC Energy Bureau Report, 20 November 2006.

31. See "Analysis of China's Strategy"; Tang Yun, *The Great Clash,* 204.

32. Aaron Friedberg, "The Future of U.S. China Relations. Is Conflict Inevitable?" *International Security* 39, no. 2 (Fall 2005): 29.

33. Mikkal E. Herberg, "Asia's Energy Insecurity: Cooperation or Conflict?" in *Strategic Asia 2004–05: Confronting Terrorism in the Pursuit of Power,* Mikkal E. Herberg, ed. (Seattle & Washington, D.C.: National Bureau of Asian Research, 2004), 347.

34. The Russian oil giant Yukos, which owned several prospective oil fields in eastern Siberia, was the first to declare its intent to ship oil to China. Both production and transportation were to be conducted by private companies and railway export deliveries of crude oil reached 82,000 bpd in 2004. In May 2003, during Hu Jintao's first visit to Russia as the top Chinese leader, a general agreement was signed between Yukos and Sinopec regarding the construction of a 2,300 km oil pipeline from Angarsk (the Irkutsk region) to Daqing (Heilongjiang province) to secure transportation of up to 600,000 bpd of crude oil (almost 30 percent of the Chinese import at that time) for twenty-five years to come. However, in January 2003 Russia and Japan agreed that the latter would make $5 billion of investments to the Nakhodka pipeline project on the condition that Russia guaranteed up to 1 million bpd of crude oil export to Japan. In autumn 2003 Moscow clearly showed that it was tilting toward the Nakhodka project due to "environmental risks" of the pipeline construction to Daqing. The projected Japanese investments rose to $7 billion at that moment, to boost further exploration of Siberian oil fields. The conflict with Yukos escalated since then making the China pipeline probability appear low. The change of Moscow's preferences in the pipeline issue, as well as a scandalous Sinopec dislodging from the Russian state-controlled "Slavneft" privatizing auction (December 2002) stirred up bitter resentment in China against the "strategic partner."

35. China used such levers as Russia's WTO membership, weaponry trade, nuclear power cooperation, trade, and security issues to exert pressure on the Kremlin. It is noteworthy that, despite being offended by Russia's inconsistency, Beijing never directly criticized the Russian authorities on the official level. It described the Yukos case as a purely domestic affair and insistently claimed that the oil pipeline project to Daqing was officially inserted into the Russian energy strategy in August 2003.

36. Tsygankov holds that in supporting the U.S.-led GWOT, Moscow promptly proposed some new areas, namely, counterterrorism and energy cooperation, in which Russia could have developed its relationship with the West, and that these proposals were initially welcomed with enthusiasm in the West. As early as in October 2001, at the U.S.–Russian "energy summit" in Houston, the two presidents embarked on the practical realization of these proposals. These new developments in U.S.–Russia relations were labeled by the author as the "great power pragmatism." Andrei P. Tsygankov, *Russia's Foreign Policy: Change and Continuity in National Identity* (Lanham, Md.: Rowman & Littlefield, 2006), 137–38.

37. Alexey A. Makarov, "Russia's Resources in Asia," paper presented at the Taipei-Moscow Forum Round-Table, National Political University, Taiwan, 28 November 2004.

38. "The Energy Strategy of the Russian Federation," 58–60. Igor Ivanov, Secretary of the Russian Security Council, has recently stated that unless new oil fields are intensively exploited, the old oil deposits will be more than 70 percent exhausted by 2030, and the oil production in Russia will drop from the current 9.8 million bpd to 2.5 million bpd. *Interfax*, June 8, 2007.

39. Правительство РФ одобрило законопроект «О недрах» ["The Government Adopted the 'Subsoil Resource Law'"], http://top.rbc.ru/index.shtml?/news/day themes/2005/03/17/17122649_bod.shtml.

40. "The Energy Strategy of the Russian Federation," 45, 63, 69–70. Andrei Dementiev, deputy minister of Industry and Energy, stated in September 2006, "Eastern direction" within the energy strategy and policy is an adequate answer to the global challenges and risks that Russia faces, this is in fact implementation of the policy of markets diversification and supply directions while minimizing risks of transit territories." See "Russia's Energy Strategy as Current Development Program for the Fuel and Energy Complex," the report of Deputy Minister of Industry and Energy Andrei Dementiev at the Valdai International Discussion Club, September 7, 2006, http://www.minprom.gov.ru.

41. Lyle Goldstein and Vitaly Kozyrev, "China, Japan and the Scramble for Siberia," *Survival* 48, no. 1 (2006): 172–73.

42. Top officials from the presidential administration and the government, as well as the management of the operating and transportation companies (Rosneft, Gazpromneft, Transneft), remained confident about the possibility of satisfying both Japanese and Chinese interests in the pipeline construction. Besides, the Russian government promised to increase railway supplies to China up to 300,000 bpd in 2010. Anna Skornyakova, "The Pipeline Will Be Replaced by Rails," Трубу заменят

на рельсы, «Независимая газета» [*Nezavisimaya Gazeta*], 26 August 2004, http://www.ng.ru/economics/2004-08-26/3_truba.html.

43. Alexey Shoglov, "To the North of the Lake Baikal," 8 August 2006, http://www.strana.ru. Eventually the route of this pipeline was moved several hundred kilometers northward closer to the major oilfields of eastern Siberia. Major pro-Kremlin petroleum companies (Rosneft and Surgutneftegaz, in particular) saved substantial financial resources by avoiding constructing additional pipelines to link their oil producing areas to the East Siberian pipeline.

44. These conceptions of a solid market for Russia in Asia were reflected in the governmental blueprint of its Energy Strategy. In the section addressed to Russia's diplomatic institutions, the program specified the sequence of high-priority consumers of Russia's oil export: the CIS, Eurasia, Northeast Asia, the EU, and, finally, the United States. "The Energy Strategy of the Russian Federation," 41–42.

45. The Sakhalin 1 project is led by ExxonMobil Corporation with a 30 percent stake. Rosneft holds 20 percent, India's ONGC (Oil & Natural Gas Corp.) holds another 20 percent, and the remaining 30 percent is in hands of the consortium of Japanese companies.

46. Заключено соглашение о поставках сахалинского газа в Мексику ["The Agreement on Sakhalin Natural Gas Supply to the U.S. and Mexico is Signed"], 15 October 2004, http://www.regnum.ru/news/342516.html; "Russian Ambassador on the Issues of Bilateral Energy Cooperation," Xinhua News, 11 June 2004, http://russian1.people.com.cn/31521/2564471.html.

47. http://www.cheyou.com.cn/shnews/2003-11/18/content_73041.htm .

48. The Russian side reiterated its position regarding Japanese investments in the "East Siberia-Pacific Ocean" pipeline construction during Russian prime minister Mikhail Fradkov's visit to Japan in February 2007. In addition, Rosneft proposed to the Japanese business circles to build a joint refinery (with the capacity 400,000 bpd) in the Russian Far East, with an estimated investment of $5–7 billion. Tokyo anticipates fast accomplishment of the Pacific arm of the pipeline to start buying eastern Siberian oil in the Russian port terminal. See "Japan Is Invited to Participate in the 'East Siberia-Pacific Ocean Project,'" http://vstoneft.ru/news.php?number=293.

49. Vertically integrated corporations handle a product throughout the entire value chain: production, transportation (in the case of gas companies), refining, and distribution.

50. Beijing consistently pursued a more assertive policy of energy cooperation with Russia, and despite the risks, in January 2005 the Chinese government approved a $6 billion credit to help Moscow conclude the controversial Yuganskneftegaz acquisition. In exchange, CNPC signed a contract with Rosneft that obliged Russia to supply 48.4 million tons per year of crude oil by rail up to 2011 for the amount of $15 billion. "郑东生, [Zheng Dongsheng], 俄罗斯的能源外交与中俄能源合作" ["Russian Energy Diplomacy and Sino-Russian Energy Cooperation"], 当代世界 [*Dangdai Shijie*], no. 9 (2005): 40.

51. "Rosneft Finds Chinese Sponsor for 51% in Udmurtneft–Paper," *RIA Novosti Agency*, 21 June 2006, http://en.rian.ru/russia/20060621/49818321.html.

52. "On the 5th Meeting of Joint Coordinating Committee between Gazprom and CNPC," 13–15 December 2006, http://www.gazprom.com/eng/news/2006/12/22045.shtml.

53. See Leila Muzaparova, Лейла Музапарова, «Пути углубления энергетического сотрудничества между Казахстаном и Россией» на конференции «Стратегическое партнерство Казахстана и России: современное состояние и перспективы развития» (Алматы, 1 ноября 2006 г.) ["The Patterns of Energy Cooperation between Kazakhstan and Russia," paper presented at the conference "Strategic Partnership between Kazakhstan and Russia: Current Situation and Prospects for Development," Almaty, 1 November 2006], http://www.apn.kz/news/article6849.htm.

54. "The Energy Charter Secretariat, Status of Membership" (May 8, 2007) in the Energy Charter Treaty, Brussels, http://www.encharter.org/fileadmin/user_upload/document/Public_ratification_Treaty.pdf. The Russian leaders, concerned about the future of the "sovereign democracy," consider it dangerous to allow an equal free access of European consumers to the Russian fossil fuels and energy infrastructure. Western partners of Russia are also moving to lessen their dependence on Russian energy supplies.

55. See Mikhail Delyagin's speech: "Energy Security: Imagined and Real Problems," Conference "Strategic Framework of EU Eastern Policy," Bratislava, 9–12 November 2006, http://forum/msk/ru/material/economic/16140.html. In June 2006, Gazprom head Alexey Miller requested that European partners provide Gazprom with detailed information on anticipated volumes of prospective EU consumption "to build up the company's own export strategy, in the Chinese direction, in particular." A few days later, Gazprom's top officials had to explain to the European customers that Gazprom's reserves were substantial enough to fulfill all export contracts and satisfy growing demand in Asia. Газпром готовит плацдарм на Востоке ["Gazprom Establishes Its Eastern Base"], *Izvestia*, 23 June 2006, 10. On the concrete Sino–Russian energy agenda see "Going East," The Eighth Meeting of the Russian-Chinese Sub-commission on Cooperation in Energy, 17 October 2006, http://www.minprom.gov.ru/eng/press/news/155.

56. "Central Asia's Energy Risks," *International Crisis Group Asia Report,* no. 133, 24 May 2007, Brussels, 36–37, http://www.crisisgroup.org/home/index.cfm?id=4866&l=1.

57. See, for example, the anti-Western rhetoric of Russian top managers Miller of Gazprom and Vainshtok of Transneft in spring 2006: С.Вайншток объединился с А.Миллером в борьбе за независимость от Запада ["S. Vainshtok Allied with A. Miller in the Fight for Independence from the West"], 25 April 2006, http://www.neftegaz.ru/lenta/show/63194/. On the anti-American context of Russo–Chinese cooperation, see Sergey Livishin, С.В.Ливишин. 2006 год–Год России в Китае. Новое качество партнерства. *Проблемы Дальнего Востока*, 2006, no. 1 ["2006 Is the Year of Russia in China: A New Quality of Partnership," *Far Eastern Affairs*, Moscow, no. 1 (2006): 21].

58. Alexander Lukin, director of the SCO Analytic Center in Moscow Foreign Relations University, in a personal interview with the author, noticed that in the aftermath of Putin's March 2006 visit to China, many of the local party and governmental leaders demonstrated unexampled amicability to the Russians after they received a directive from above.

59. At the opening ceremony of the "Moscow Energy Dialogue" in late October 2006, Russian industry and energy minister Victor Khristenko stated that cooperation "should be established on the basis of comparison and coordination of national energy strategies in order to minimize risks on the energy carrier market." See «Создание нового языка глобальной энергобезопасности». Вступительное слово Виктора Христенко на главной сессии Международной энергетической недели "Московский энергетический диалог" ["Creating a New Language of Global Energy Security," Minister Victor Khristenko's welcoming speech at the opening ceremony of "Moscow Energy Dialogue," 31 October 2006], http://www.minprom.gov.ru/appearance/showAppearanceIssue?url=activity/energy/appearance/24

60. Совместная декларация Российской Федерации и Китайской Народной Республики ["Joint Declaration of the Russian Federation and the People's Republic of China"], Beijing, 21 March 2006, http://www.kremlin.ru/interdocs/2006/03/21/1851_type72067_103421.shtml?type=7206.

61. "Win-Win for Sino-Russian Oil-Gas Cooperation," CNPC president Chen Geng's speech at the Sino-Russian Business Summit Forum, Beijing, 23 March 2006, http://www.cnpc.com.cn/english/xwygg/speeches/200603280004.htm.

62. Zhou Jinkui, "中俄石油产业合作的基础, 契积及模式" ["The Foundation, Opportunities, and Models of Chinese-Russian Cooperation in Petroleum Production"], 世界经济研究 [Global Economic Studies] 88, no. 2 (2005): 87–88.

63. In July 2005 an agreement between Rosneft and Sinopec was concluded on the joint development of the Venin block in the Sakhalin 3 project (crude reserves are estimated as 400 million bpd and natural gas reserves as 578 billion cubic meters). "Rosneft Opens Sakhalin to the Chinese," Kommersant, 4 July 2005, http://www.kommersant.com/p588631/r_1/Rosneft_Opens_Sakhalin_to_the_Chinese/.

64. See the list of documents signed at the Russo–Chinese summit, 21 March 2006, available at the official website of the president of the Russian Federation, http://www.kremlin.ru/events/articles/2006/03/103278/103438.shtml.

65. "Sincere Collaboration and Win-Win Strategy Mark a New Stage for Sino-Russian Oil-Gas Cooperation," CNPC vice president Zhou Jiping's speech at the Sino–Russian Business Summit Forum, Beijing, 23 March 2006, http://www.cnpc.com.cn/english/xwygg/speeches/200603280003.htm.

66. OAO Transneft and the CNPC have agreed to build the "Chinese border leg" based on the "Protocol on studying the design and construction of the oil pipeline from Skovorodino to PRC border." The companies negotiated the cost of this pipeline which exceeded the initially planned amount. See "Transneft Warns of China Route Cost Rise," Petroleum Argus Monthly (Argus Nefte Transport—Far East), April 2007, 5.

67. Being the leading producer of crude oil, the company currently accounts for 25 percent of Russian crude to China, and by 2010 it intends to increase oil deliveries to China up to 400,000 bpd. Former Rosneft vice president Yuri Matveev proposed in 2005 that by 2015 the company's oil production will reach 2.5 million bpd, and 2.8 million bpd in 2020. Yuri Matveev, Особенности развития нефтегазового комплекса на Востоке России ["The Character of Oil and Gas Complex Development in Russia's Far East"], presentation at the First International Far Eastern Economic Congress, 27–28 September 2005, Khabarovsk, www.dvcongress.ru/Doklad/Matveev.pdf.

68. Vostok Energy will conduct exploration and development along the prospective East Siberian pipeline route and aims to produce within three to five years 200,000 bpd of oil. It is unclear, however, whether oil from the new fields will be supplied to China through the East Siberian pipeline. "Rosneft Turned to the East," *Vzglyad Online*, 17 October 2006, http://www.vz.ru/economy/2006/10/17/53187.html.

69. It was reported that CNPC will establish a joint venture with Russia's South Ural Petroleum Company to undertake oil and gas exploration projects involving a CNPC investment of $7 million to $7.5 million. Although the sums involved are small by industry standards, CNPC will obtain a new foothold in the strategically important Orenburg region and, perhaps, be able to use local production and transportation infrastructure linking this area to Kazakhstan. "CNPC to Ink US$7-Million Russian Deal," *China Daily Online*, 1 December 2006, http://www.chinadaily.com.cn/bizchina/2006-12/01/content_747838.htm.

70. Although China reportedly sought a $3 billion stake (it ultimately got only half of the BP acquisition of $1 billion), CNPC later stressed that China's subscription proposal was submitted after "thorough evaluation of the [initial public offering] process was conducted by CNPC experts," to demonstrate the "pragmatic character" of officially sanctioned Sino–Russian business cooperation in the energy sphere. "CNPC Subscribed Rosneft Shares," 19 July 2006, seen at: http://www.cnpc.com.cn/.

71. The purchase was made in cooperation with Rosneft, and, according to the option agreement signed by Sinopec and Rosneft, the new holding managing company is owned by Rosneft (51 percent) and Sinopec (49 percent). Sinopec's investment gives it access to Udmurtneft's proven reserves of 551 million barrels of oil and probable deposits of up to 922 million barrels. Its production stands at 120,000 bpd of crude oil, and it will probably become a substantial resource of petroleum exports from Russia to China via Kazakhstan. Sergei Sanokoyev, head of the Russo-Chinese Center for Trade and Economic Cooperation, commented on this acquisition: "If two years ago the Chinese did not discuss the question of acquiring less than a blocking stake, now they are willing to take it stage by stage and not aim for a big step immediately in the development of relations." From Catherine Belton, "Chinese Buy Udmurtneft for Rosneft," *The Moscow Times*, no. 3436 (21 June 2006): 1. See also *Russian Profile Online*, http://www.russianprofile.org/resources/business/russian companies/rosneft.wbp.

72. Rosneft owns 20 percent of the "Sakhalin 1" project and holds licenses in "Sakhalin 3" (Veninsky sector), "Sakhalin 4" (Zapadno-Shmidtovsky sector), and "Sakhalin

5" (Vostochno-Shmidtovsky and Kayagansko-Vasyukansky sector). The company successfully won the governmental auction in July 2006 to obtain a twenty-five-year exploration and production license for the western part of the Kaurunanis-kaya zone near Sakhalin Island, with 1.5 million tpy of probable reserves of oil and 2.5 billion cubic meters of natural gas; http://www.russianprofile.org/resources/busi ness/russiancompanies/rosneft.wbp.

73. "Sergei Bogdanchikov Interview to Xinhua Agency," 22 March 2006, http://xinhua net.com.cn.

74. Xinhua News, 13 December 2006.

75. "Gazprom Establishes Its Eastern Base," 10. The western route would link west Siberian gas fields with China's Xinjiang province and pass through Russia's Altay state directly to the 54-km-long part of the Russo–Chinese border. The Altay gas pipeline will cost $5–10 billion depending on the route. "Gas Pipeline Will Not Be Constructed across a Special Natural Preserved Zone," 6 April 2006, http://www. altaiinter.org/news/?id=10259; *Kommersant-Novosibirsk*, 5 April 2006. The second pipeline, proposed earlier, would follow the Severobaikalsk-Skovorodino-Blagoveshensk-China routes, carrying 30–40 bcm per annum of natural gas from the Kovykta gas field. Unlike the western route, the project of a gas pipeline from East Siberia has received the support of the local authorities. "Gas Pipeline to China Will Go through Blagoveshensk," 18 February 2005, http://www.amur.info/ news/2005/02/18/10.html.

76. "Khristenko Does Not Rule Out the Possibility of Russia's and China's Joint LNG Production," *The People's Daily Online*, 22 March 2006, http://russian.people.com. cn/31518/4229368.html.

77. "Rosneft Established Its Representative Office in China. It Will Coordinate the Company Activities in the Asian Region," 9 November 2006, http://www.rosneft. ru/; *RIA Novosti Agency*, 31 October 2006, http://www.rian.ru.

78. Valeria Korchagina, "Putin Calls for Energy Club in Asia," *The Moscow Times*, no. 3433 (16 June 2006): 5.

79. In Joint Communiqué of 2006 SCO Summit, energy cooperation was called a priority. *The People's Daily Online*, 15 June 2006, http://english.people.com.cn.

80. Igor Tomberg, "Energy Outcome of SCO Meeting in Dushanbe," RIA Novosti Agency, 20 September 2006, http://en.rian.ru/analysis/20060920/54104304.html. At the fifth meeting of the Heads of Government Council of the SCO in Dushanbe, Tajikistan, on 15 September 2006, the Russian delegation, headed by Premier Frad-kov, elaborated on the idea of the Asian energy club. Discussing the club's feasibility, Russia focused on ensuring the SCO countries' mutual access to power grids, improving existing gas shipment networks, and providing nuclear fuel cycle services for member states. The energy club's rationale was clear to the participants as Russia proposed implementing several bilateral and multilateral energy projects, such as oil and gas exploration, production, and shipment, and development of power grids to supply excess electricity to neighboring countries. See "Russian Prime Minister M. Fradkov's Speech at the Heads of Governments Council of the SCO in Dushanbe," 15 September 2006, circulated copy, p. 4.

81. Andrew Erickson and Lyle Goldstein pointed to a pivotal role of Kazakhstan in Chinese strategies in their recent article. Andrew Erickson and Lyle Goldstein, "Hoping for the Best, Preparing for the Worst: China's Response to U.S. Hegemony," *Journal of Strategic Studies* 29, no. 6 (2006): 963.

82. Т.Таубалдиев. АО «Казтрансойл»: сотрудничество с Китаем в области транспортировки нети. В кн. Казахстан и Китай: стратегическое партнерство в целях развития. Материалы международной конференции. Алматы: ИМЭП, 2006 [T. Taubaldiev, "AO KazTransOil and Its Cooperation with China in the Sphere of Oil Delivery," in *Kazakhstan and China: Strategic Partnership for the Purposes of Development* (Almaty: Institute of World Economy and Politics, 2006), 33–34.]

83. Л.Музапарова. Казахстанско-китайское энергетическое сотрудничество: оценка потенциала и направления развития. В кн. Казахстан и Китай: стратегическое партнерство в целях развития. Материалы международной конференции. Алматы: ИМЭП, 2006 [L. Muzaparova, "Kazakh-Chinese Energy Cooperation: Potential Evaluation and Patterns of Development," in *Kazakhstan and China: Strategic Partnership for the Purposes of Development*, 21–22.]

84. CNPC Central Asia Projects Data, http://www.cnpc.com.cn/.

85. CNPC Central Asia Projects Data.

86. Information data bank, 26 October 2006, http://www.sinorusoil.com/ru/news/?id=52.

87. "China, Uzbekistan Sign $600 M Oil Agreement," *China Daily Online*, 26 May 2005, http://www.chinadaily.com.cn/english/doc/2005-05/26/content_445707.htm; "China, Uzbekistan to Strengthen Cooperation in Oil and Gas Sectors," Xinhua News Agency, 28 August 2006.

88. "石化行业 检测报" ["Report on Petrochemical Industry"], *Bimonthly Journal*, 22 October 2004, available at http://www.lib.buct.edu.cn/.

89. "Energy Summit Gives Putin New Trump Card. Trans-Caspian Gas Pipeline Project in Question," *Spero Forum*, 17 May 2007, http://www.speroforum.com/site/print.asp?idarticle=9487.

90. Россия внимательно наблюдает за расширением туркмено-китайского экономического сотрудничества ["Russia Attentively Observes the Development of Turkmen-Chinese Economic Cooperation"], 1 September 2006, http://www.iamik.ru/; Казахстан открыл путь туркменскому газу в Китай ["Kazakhstan Opens a Path to China for Turkmen Gas"], *Nezavisimaya Gazeta*, 26 December 2006, www.ng.ru.

91. L. Muzaparova, "Kazakh-Chinese Energy Cooperation: Potential Evaluation and Patterns of Development," 21–22.

92. Yury Solozobov, Комитет энергетической безопасности ["The Committee of Energy Security"], http://apn.kz/publications/article4771.htm; Olga Steblova, Нефтяной картель и логистические олигополии ["Oil Cartel and Logistics Oligopolies"], 17 November 2006, http://www.gazeta.kz/art.asp?aid=83470.

93. Muzaparova, "Kazakh-Chinese Energy Cooperation," 27.

94. "Russian Prime Minister M. Fradkov's speech at the Heads of Governments Council of the SCO in Dushanbe," 15 September 2006. A circulated copy, p. 4.

95. Chinese analysts interpreted the possibility of the "Gas OPEC" formation between Russia, Algeria, Libya, Kazakhstan, Uzbekistan, and Iran in the spirit of Western assessments. See, for example, "俄罗斯欲建天然气欧佩克?" ["Russia Urges to Create Gas OPEC?"], 新华网 [Xinhuanet Online], 11 July 2006.

96. Stephen Boykewich, "A New OPEC in the Making?" The Moscow Times, no. 3437 (22 June 2006): 1.

97. Tomberg, "Energy Outcome of SCO Meeting in Dushanbe,"

98. Gabriel Collins points to an "X factor" on Russia's way to energy great power status: Byzantine internal politics that "stifle investment and reflect the sharp divide between the interests of major energy exporters and major consumers"; Gabriel Collins, "Global Energy Heavyweights," Oilandgasinvestor.com, December 2006, 64.

99. Far Eastern Affairs, no. 3 (30 June 2006): 71.

100. Gazprom's oil fields and electricity power grid acquisitions fomented much discontent among the Russian elites. After acquiring one of the biggest oil-producing companies in western Siberia, Sibneft, in 2005, Gazprom oil management announced that the corporation would raise its petroleum production up to 1 million bpd in 2008–10. This volume may rise if the Russian gas monster acquires TNK-BP's share in "Slavneft" (output 500,000 bpd). Moreover, if it gets the entire Russian share in TNK-BP itself, its annual oil production capability will rise to about 1.8–2.0 million bpd. The two companies' aggressive policy of equity acquisition boosts competition for resource development and exports. Gazprom recently acquired halves of the foreign investors' stakes in the "Sakhalin 2" project (Royal Dutch Shell, Mitsui, and Mitsubishi). This restoration of the governmental control over the main "Sakhalin 2" reserves will enable Gazprom to make decisions on Sakhalin 2 oil and gas exports, including to China. See Vladimir Milov, "Petrostate: State Control Restoration Will Lead to Economic Stagnation," interview with Novaya Gazeta, no. 96 (22 December 2005); see also Expert Online, 28 October 2006; FT, 22 December 2006, 1.

101. Stephen Boykewich, "Gazprom's Export Monopoly Cemented," The Moscow Times, no. 3447 (6 July 2006): 1; Miriam Elder, "TNK-BP Executive Targeted in Probe," The Moscow Times, no. 3537 (10 November 2006): 1. Gazprom has also considered increased gas supplies to China from Sakhalin, and its recent acquisition of part of Royal Dutch Shell's stake in "Sakhalin 2" makes the probability of natural gas exports from Sakhalin to China very high. Gazprom and Chinese firms may also conduct joint natural gas exploration. According to official estimates, Russia has only explored 8 percent of gas resources in Siberia, 11.5 percent in Russia's Far East, and 6 percent of offshore gas resources. See "Khristenko Does Not Rule Out the Possibility of Russia's and China's Joint LNG Production," The People's Daily Online, 22 March 2006, http://russian.people.com.cn/31518/4229368.html.

102. Vassily Sukhanov, "Oil and Gas Industry Is Ceded to the State," 19 December 2006, http://www.km.ru, 14 June 2006.

103. Газпром пустил Роснефть к трубе ["Gazprom Provided Rosneft with Access to the Pipelines"], Vzglyad Online, 28 November 2006, http://www.vz.ru/economy/2006/11/28/59004.html; "Gazprom, Rosneft Join in Venture," The Moscow Times, no. 2550 (29 November 2006): 6.

104. It was reported that China is unlikely to need Russian gas before 2015, British-based energy consultant Wood Mackenzie proposed in 16 October 2006, http://www.uofaweb.ualberta.ca/chinainstitute/.

105. "Gazprom, CNPC Differ on Price of Russian Gas," 16 November 2006, http://www.fcinfo.ru/.

106. Tang Yun, The Great Clash, 207.

107. 郝瑞彬, 王伟毅。[Hao Ruibin and Wang Weiyi], "21世纪中国石油安全与中俄石油合作" ["China Petroleum Security and Sino-Russian Petroleum Cooperation in the Twenty-first Century"], 中国矿业 [Zhongguo kuangye] 15, no. 3 (2006): 7–8.

108. Gabriel Collins, "Fueling the Dragon: China-Bound Pipelines Are Russia's Most Realistic Asian Energy Option," Geopolitics of Energy 28, no. 9 (2006): 12–19; on the feasibility of East Siberian pipeline see, e.g., Leslie Dienes, "Observations on the Problematic Potential of Russian Oil and the Complexities of Siberia," Eurasian Geography and Economics 45, no. 5 (2004): 319–45; Leszek Buszynski, "Oil and Territory in Putin's Relations with China and Japan," The Pacific Review 19, no. 3 (2006): 287–303.

109. 李福川, [Li Fuchuan], "影响中俄石油管道项目的两个最重要因素" ["Two Important Factors of Influence on Sino-Russian Oil Pipeline Construction"], 俄罗斯中亚东欧研究 [Russia, Central Asia and Eastern Europe Studies], no. 1 (2005): 84.

110. http://www.transneft.ru/press/Default.asp?LANG=RU&ATYPE=8&ID=12108.

111. Geographically, the oil pumping will be made in four zones of eastern Siberia, mapped around the famous oil fields, namely, Vankorskoye, Yurubcheno-Takhomskoye, Chayandinskoye, and Verhnechonskoye. Rosneft experts are confident that current potential of East Siberian Oil Production may secure output 1.05 million bpd of oil by 2015. See: Yuri Matveev, "The Character of Oil and Gas Complex Development in Russia's Far East," 5–6.

112. http://www.uofaweb.ualberta.ca/chinainstitute/.

113. Alexander Sapronov, Rosneft vice president, informed that Vankorski oil field deposits contain about 3 billion barrels of crude oil, and the company will pump about 380,000 bpd; Роснефть ждет ВСТО ["Rosneft Waits for ESPO Pipeline"], 25 April 2006, http://www.neftegaz.ru/lenta/show/63209.

114. "China to Get Only Half of Oil from New Pipe," Reuters News, 23 November 2006, http://www.uofaweb.ualberta.ca/chinainstitute/nav03cfm?nav03=43664&nav02=43096.

115. Vladimir Milov concludes that both the East Siberian oil pipeline and the Altay gas pipeline would be unprofitable projects, and it is the pipeline building company that would benefit the most. See, for example, Коммерсант [Kommersant] 197, no. 3528 (2006 October 20).

116. Sergey Fedorov, head of the government policy department at the Natural Resources Ministry, said that the further construction of the East Siberian pipeline could be postponed by years because of lack of proven reserves and production in eastern Siberia. See "Siberian Oil Might

Flow to China, Not Primorye," *Vladivostok Times*, 15 April 2007, http://vladivostoktimes.com/show.phP?id=9231&r=8&p=10.

117. Gabriel Collins argues that the revenues from piping oil to the Pacific coast would be lower than if oil were piped directly to China and that Russian oil producers would provide their oil only if the supplies are politically motivated. See Collins, "Fueling the Dragon," 13.

118. This generalization may not be applicable to China's southern provinces, where dependence on LNG imports would grow. According to the Chinese estimates, China's energy consumers are expected to give preference to natural gas consumption, which will get 9–10 percent in the fuel balance by 2010. By 2020 the figures of natural gas annual consumption will rise from current 30 billion up to 200 billion cubic meters, 120 billion of which will be imported. See http://www.chinaview.cn, 6 January 2005.

Peter Dutton

Carving Up the East China Sea

As the primitive society pushed ahead and the population of clan groups increased, the balance between the material requirements of the clan groups and the total quantity of the natural materials for living in their localities was upset . . . resulting in the earliest form of war of human society.

The Science of Military Strategy, 2005

The dispute over the continental shelf in the East China Sea . . . is a battle of energy and a battle of geography. It is a fight for the benefit of the ocean, and it is a contest for development of a country and the destiny of its people.

Naval and Merchant Ships, 2006

IT IS A TIMELESS AND FUNDAMENTAL QUESTION: Must competition for scarce resources inevitably lead to conflict? Today, that age-old question is often asked in reference to the many sites in the world's oceans in which neighboring coastal states are contending with each other for the authority to claim the potentially vast sources of hydrocarbons embedded in the continental shelf and the fishing rights to the waters above it.

With more than a billion people to feed and a surging economy that demands ever more energy, the People's Republic of China (PRC) has become one of the world's fiercest competitors for the ocean's resources.[1] China's oil consumption, already the second largest in the world after the United States, is forecast by some to grow to 590 million metric tons in 2020 (up from 220 million tons in 2000), nearly three-quarters of which will be imported by that time.[2] By some estimates, gas and oil deposits in the central area of the East China Sea could go a long way toward alleviating the energy deficit the country faces.

The Chunxiao Natural Gas Development Project, an area of hydrocarbon exploitation by the Chinese, is publicly estimated to contain a reserve of 65.2 billion cubic meters (bcm) of natural gas and 12.7 million tons of oil.[3] This development project, which involves American and European oil companies as minority stakeholders, lies in the heart of the disputed zone in the East China Sea.[4] China has accommodated and cooperated to develop disputed areas with several other of its maritime neighbors and even to resolve some of those disputes amicably—most notably those with Vietnam, the Philippines, and Malaysia, with whom it shares overlapping claims in the South China Sea;[5] nonetheless, the competition between China and Japan over the resources in the East China Sea remains confrontational, causing some concern that the competition for regional predominance between these two powerful nations could trigger armed conflict if not carefully managed.[6]

In the recent statements of Chinese leaders—such as the conciliatory meeting in early August 2006 with the Chinese ambassador to Japan, Wang Yi—and in the recent decrease in Chinese research in the disputed zone, there are glimmers of hope that China will pursue policies of cooperation with Japan.[7] Additionally, China reopened talks with Japan in July 2006 to attempt to resolve competing claims to the gas reserves in the East China Sea.[8] In the South China Sea, by contrast, China completed cooperative development agreements with Vietnam and the Philippines in March 2005;[9] it did so again recently with Malaysia in a manner that implicitly accepts Malaysian, rather than Chinese, sovereignty over the disputed portion of the South China Sea.[10] These latter decisions reflect Beijing's active wooing of support from Association of Southeast Asian Nations members as part of its "peaceful rise" strategy.[11] However, the strategic situation between China and Japan is significantly different. Even with China's accelerated economic development, Japan still possesses the second-largest economy in the world and consumes a proportional share of global petroleum resources—resources China may also need to continue its economic rise and the rejuvenated international status it desires.[12] More important, however, is the fact that Beijing sees Tokyo as a potential rival for predominance in Southeast Asia, a perception that despite a recent thaw in relations makes the possibility of long-term cooperation and compromise in the East China Sea less likely.[13]

The focus of the dispute between China and Japan in the East China Sea is an expanse of nearly seventy thousand square nautical miles of water space that constitutes the overlap between China's claim—which reaches from the mainland eastward to the Okinawa Trough just west of the Ryukyu Islands chain—and Japan's claim along a line equidistant from the shores of each state (see map 1). China asserts its claim to the full continental shelf—and the waters above it—on the basis of the continental shelf provisions in the 1982 United Nations Convention on the Law of the Sea (UNCLOS), and Japan correspondingly points to the provisions related to the exclusive economic zone as the legitimate starting point to determine a maritime boundary.

In part the dispute arises from the fact that UNCLOS essentially imported existing international law related to the continental shelf without also incorporating the pre-UNCLOS maritime delimitation standard based on equidistance.[14] Alongside it, UNCLOS set new law governing the creation of exclusive economic zones—that is, the waters above the continental shelf extending to two hundred nautical miles from the shoreline—stating only that "an equitable solution" should be achieved in delimiting maritime boundaries for both the continental shelf and the exclusive economic zone.[15] UNCLOS provides no guidance as to just what factors constitute an equitable means of dividing between two claimants the seabed with its resources and the water column with its resources. Many international courts and tribunals have reverted to the equidistance standard with corrections for factors such as offshore islands, disparate lengths of opposing coastlines, and economic considerations.[16] Still, because signatories to UNCLOS are bound only to its provisions and not to the decisions of international tribunals, no unified standard exists to bring stability and predictability to this volatile area of international law.

Map 1. China and Japan's Claims in the East China Sea

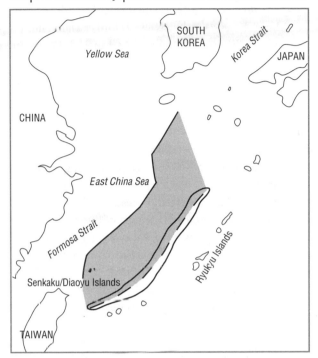

The shaded area marks the disputed zone in the central East China Sea. Japan claims delimitation should be based on the median line; China views the Okinawa Trough as the appropriate boundary. The Senkaku/Diaoyu Islands lie between Taiwan and Okinawa. They have been disputed between China and Japan since the mid-1980s. Today the dispute's stakes are high because possession of the Senkakus can have major ramifications for seabed demarcation under UNCLOS. Whoever possesses the islands could theoretically claim a 200 nm EEZ around them if they are treated as true islands, as opposed to "rocks." See Robert Marquand, "Japan-China Tensions Rise Over Tiny Islands," *Christian Science Monitor*, 11 February 2005, http://www.csmonitor.com/2005/0211/p01s03-woap.html.

The Chinese Position on the East China Sea

Since the period of negotiations that led to the United Nations Convention on the Law of the Sea, China has advocated that the "middle line" principle should be considered merely one delimitation method out of several, rather than the mandated means to achieve a fair and reasonable result, especially in cases that involve both continental shelf boundaries and exclusive economic zone boundaries.[17] China has consistently adhered to this position, and today, with virtually a unanimous voice, Chinese scholars and political actors alike argue that the "principle of fairness" and the "principle of natural extension"—referring to the coastal state's automatic authority over the continental shelf as the natural extension of its continental territory—are the most equitable means of resolving their maritime delimitation disputes in the East China Sea.[18]

Out of this legal perspective arises a theme that recurs with remarkable consistency in the statements of Chinese scholars (and government authorities): the sense that the continental shelf off the coast of China is actually historical Chinese territory, not simply an area to be claimed under the international regime of oceans law. One discussion of the topic by Chinese maritime scholars refers to the regression of water during the Ice Age, extending the Yellow and Yangtze and other rivers out onto the continental shelf, where they deposited silt from the Chinese mainland. On this basis, the scholars claim that "the East Sea continental shelf is a natural extension of Chinese territory."[19] This emphasis helps to put in context the strength of feeling by many Chinese, who seem to view competing claims on the continental shelf as actual encroachments on their rightful repossession of the continental shelf and its resources. Accordingly, the Chinese position on delimitation is that the entire continental shelf under the East China Sea—from the mainland coast to the Okinawa Trough just west of the Ryukyu Islands chain—should be Chinese and that delimitation of the maritime boundary should therefore occur in that area (see map 1).[20]

These same scholars view compromise on the economic resources in the water column above the continental shelf through a different lens. Their position that China should also rightfully claim the majority of the waters in the East China Sea is based on concern for the Chinese fishermen who "would lose their traditional fishing grounds . . . [causing] unacceptable losses to the Chinese fishing industry."[21]

Just as nationalism is reflected in the Chinese view of the continental shelf, there is also a nationalist aspect to China's view of its exclusive economic zone claim over the East China Sea. The language of UNCLOS recognizes coastal state sovereignty over the territorial sea and implicitly conveys the full jurisdictional authority of the state in that area. However, it affords coastal states only specified sovereign rights in the exclusive economic zone and no more jurisdiction than is necessary to enforce those rights.[22] UNCLOS specifically provides all states the right to high seas freedoms in the exclusive economic zone of a coastal state, subject only to the "due regard" standard that is also applied on the high seas."[3] Chinese commentators, however, treat the concepts of sovereignty and sovereign rights as if the distinction were insignificant and argue that coastal states have, for instance, "sovereignty . . . over the natural resources," as opposed to the sovereign right to harvest them.[24]

Using this approach, the Chinese assert that "it is perfectly justifiable, reasonable and legal for the coastal State to exercise exclusive jurisdiction within [the exclusive economic zone, and] although other states enjoy freedoms of navigation, overflight, and the laying of undersea cables and pipelines within this zone, such freedoms are conditional and restricted."[25] The view that a coastal nation has authority in the exclusive economic zone that approaches full sovereignty—at least over the resources—may be contrary to the purposes of the drafters of UNCLOS and a novel approach to maritime law, but it is a view that is widely held among influential Chinese and one that informs their positions on boundary disputes. They view maritime boundary negotiations as essentially "winner takes all" endeavors, which actually result in enhanced or depleted sovereignty for the coastal state.[26]

The Japanese Position on the East China Sea

Japan too, as a major importer of energy resources and one of the world's strongest economies, has interests in the resources of the continental shelf.[27] Nonetheless, Japan bases its claim to water space and the continental shelf resources under it on provisions in UNCLOS related to the exclusive economic zone, which have significant differences from the continental shelf provisions and allow Japan to make a legitimate claim on more of the East China Sea than do the provisions on which China relies. Specifically, while China relies on the "principle of natural prolongation" (found in Article 76) on the continental shelf and refers to the Okinawa Trough just off the Ryukyu Islands as a natural, geomorphological dividing point, Japan relies on the "equidistance principle," as articulated in many of the maritime delimitation decisions of international courts.[28] Japan is critical of China's claim, with some support from the International Court of Justice, which has ruled out geomorphology as a relevant basis under international law for most maritime delimitations.[29] Thus, Japan asserts that neither in law nor in fact should the Okinawa Trough form the basis for a maritime delimitation, since geomorphologically it is just an "incidental impression in an otherwise continuous continental shelf" and therefore not a true boundary.[30] Accordingly, Japan concludes, an equitable division of the East China Sea should be devised through an equal division of the waters created by drawing a line equidistant to the baselines of the Chinese coast and the baselines of the Ryukyu Islands chain (see map 1).[31] The legal basis for the dispute between the two states is therefore one of interpretation of the text of UNCLOS and of the relevant factors, as developed through the application of international maritime law by other states and international bodies, that should sway in favor of one interpretation or the other in the particular case of the East China Sea.

Three Options for Peaceful Delimitation

Despite the legal difficulties, there are reasons to hope that the political will for a peaceful and lasting compromise may be developing. For instance, both sides have agreed to cooperation;[32] both sides have agreed to seek an equitable solution through negotiation;[33] both sides agree that shared fishing rights are mutually beneficial and have agreed to a joint fishing regime;[34] both sides express an interest in joint development of the hydrocarbon resources of the East China Sea;[35] and perhaps most importantly, both sides recognize the potential for undesirable conflict and agree to exercise self-restraint and apply international law as expressed in and through UNCLOS in formulating a solution.[36] These areas of agreement provide a substantial basis upon which to forge cooperation and compromise, reached in accordance with international law of the sea, which will serve to decrease tensions in the region and increase the efficient use of the East China Sea's resources.

A Single Integrated Boundary

Perhaps the single best guide to the international law that governs resolution of maritime boundary disputes like the one in which the Chinese and Japanese find themselves engaged in the East China Sea is the 1984 *Case Concerning the Delimitation of the Maritime Boundary in the Gulf of Maine Area* (the Gulf of Maine Case), decided by the International Court of Justice.[37] In that case, as do the Chinese and the Japanese today, Canada and the United States found themselves in a dispute involving overlapping continental shelf claims, overlapping exclusive economic zones, and the proper means of drawing a maritime boundary in resource-rich waters with historical use by the people of both countries.[38] The international law of boundary delimitation was at the time (and remains, as we have seen) fraught with ambiguity that encouraged parties to stake out and stand by irreconcilable approaches to drawing a common and accepted maritime border. Canada and the United States were unable to resolve their differences through negotiation because there was no commonly accepted set of principles from which to start realistic negotiations. However, the factors considered and the approach taken by the International Court in the Gulf of Maine Case can shed light on a fruitful path forward in the East China Sea.

Canada and the United States disputed the appropriate basis on which to demark the international maritime boundary in the Gulf of Maine (see map 2). Canada's position was based on a straightforward rendering of the principles of the equidistance line (for laterally adjacent coasts) or the median line (for opposite coasts), which hold that unless there are special circumstances, an equal division of the areas of overlap is the most equitable result.[39]

Map 2. Gulf of Maine: Fishery Zone and Continental Shelf Claims

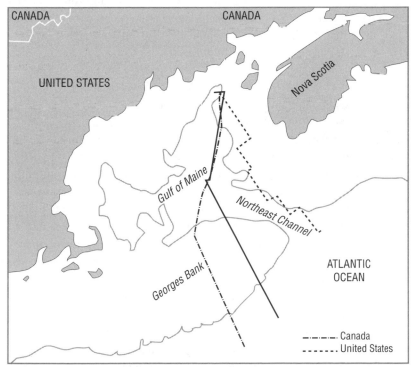

International Court of Justice Year 1984, 12 October 1984, *Case Concerning Delimitation of the Maritime Boundary in the Gulf of Maine Area (Canada/United States of America)*. The solid line represents the boundary set by the Court to delimit both the exclusive economic zone and the continental shelf.

The American position was that holding strictly to the equidistance principle would lead to an inequitable division of the waters; accordingly, the United States urged the Court to apply a more nuanced balancing of relevant factors to achieve an equitable result.[40] Specifically, the American side argued that the Court should blend considerations of continental shelf delimitation and economic zone delimitation. In such blended situations, the United States argued, international law requires the Court to apply equitable principles, such as consideration of the geographic features of the relevant coastlines; ecological features, including the nature and location of commercial fish stocks; and special circumstances, such as the historical dominance over the area by American fishermen and government authorities for more than two hundred years.[41]

The Court began its analysis of relevant international law and the parties' positions with an important observation—that it was not determining a true boundary between sovereign states but merely delimiting zones of jurisdiction or sovereign rights outside each state's sovereign waters.[42] The Court recognized that the international community had relevant rights in these areas that would not be affected by whatever the Court decided because, presumably, the international rights in these waters were predominant and would therefore remain unchanged regardless of which coastal state ultimately possessed the rights to the resources in the disputed area.[43]

The key to the Court's ultimate decision was an essential acceptance of the U.S. position that geographic circumstances are relevant to maritime delimitation decisions. In an unexpected move, however, the Court decided to define what the parties had not: it took an expansive view of what constitutes the Gulf of Maine, to include the protrusions caused by Cape Cod Bay and Massachusetts Bay on the American side and the Bay of Fundy on the Canadian side (see map 2), a position that neither party had apparently anticipated.[44]

Fundamentally, the Court rejected delimiting a maritime boundary based solely on either the basis of the continental shelf or the exclusive economic zone. In doing so, it determined that international law requires that delimitation in such complex, overlapping zones be based on equitable criteria in relation to the geographical features of the region.[45] Having rejected either geomorphological or resource-related attributes as a basis for delimitation, the Court drew a boundary based on the geography of the adjacent and opposing coastlines, adjusting it for relevant special circumstances in order to achieve an equitable result. The first special circumstance of which the Court took note was the presence of the adjacent Bay of Fundy, which it used to increase the overall allocation of space to Canada. The Court also took note of a few very small Canadian islands in the Gulf of Maine and adjusted the line slightly to give them only half effect, in order to avoid cutting into the U.S. allocation of space by an amount disproportionate to the islands' diminutive size. Finally, the Court chose to divide the Georges Bank between the parties because "a decision which would have assigned the whole of Georges Bank to one of the Parties might possibly have entailed serious economic repercussions for the other," given the historical dependence of the inhabitants of both countries on the fishing resources in that area.[46]

Applying to the East China Sea the same rules that the International Court of Justice applied to the Gulf of Maine, China and Japan can negotiate agreement of a single maritime boundary. An equitable division of the space can be achieved using geographical features as a starting point and taking into account the special circumstances. One special circumstance is the dispute over the Senkaku/Diaoyu Islands; another is historical patterns of use by each country. In order to achieve an equitable result that does not harm the long-term interests of either party, accommodation of these issues must be considered.

One omission in the Chinese literature—and a fairly curious one, in light of the Gulf of Maine Case—is any assertion that the Yellow Sea should be taken into account as a special circumstance in addressing an appropriate ratio to guide allocation of water space between the two countries. The International Court having held that the adjacent presence of the Bay of Fundy as a dependent body of water of the Gulf of Maine should weigh in Canada's favor when delimiting the maritime boundary, one would think that the Chinese might make the same claim for the effect of the Yellow Sea on China's rightful allotment of the waters of the East China Sea. But recently the description by a pair of Chinese oceans scholars of the northern border of the East China Sea as "the Yangtze River's entrance at Qidong to the southwest corner of the Korean peninsula" specifically excluded the Yellow Sea, thus excluding that sea as a consideration in this context.[47]

Delimiting a single boundary to mark both the exclusive economic zone and the continental shelf between China and Japan has the benefits of clarity and certainty, and it therefore minimizes the potential for future conflict over resource rights and sovereign jurisdiction. However, given the suspicion that hangs over the relationship between the two countries because of the history of Japanese use of force against China to pursue territory and resources, the likelihood that this kind of comprehensive solution to the boundary dispute can be successfully negotiated is remote. The positions of these states are too divergent; agreement on relevant factors and the weight to be given them is unlikely;

and, because of the confused state of the law, each side has at least some legal support for its position as to the proper location of a unified boundary. Therefore, other approaches to boundary delimitation should be considered.

Multiple Functional Boundaries

Chinese scholars have been considering another potential model for peaceful and equitable resolution of the boundary dispute: delimitation of nonidentical boundaries for the continental shelf and for the economic zones in the waters above it.[48] An example of this type of dispute resolution can be found in the Australia–Papua New Guinea Border Treaty, which set a precedent for creativity in international dispute resolution and founded the practice of cooperative jurisdiction between interdependent states.[49] The two states, which share only a maritime boundary, agreed to four distinct types of boundaries between them: sovereign boundaries between territorial waters in the narrow Torres Strait, in which overlapping territorial water claims existed; a seabed boundary; a fisheries boundary in the water column; and a special reservation area for aboriginal peoples living on the islands in the Torres Strait. This agreement broke new ground, so to speak, in that the two states agreed to exclusive jurisdiction in separate forms over the same space. Additionally, the two states recognized the special status of islands with cultural and historical significance and accommodated those values by carving out a special zone for them.

The preamble to the treaty addresses the fundamental values that the two states applied in coming to the creative solution and that they sought to protect and preserve by accepting multiple boundaries. It especially emphasizes freedom of navigation and overflight, conservation and sharing of fishing resources, regulation of seabed mineral resources, the importance of preserving the marine environment, and the desire to protect the historical way of life of Torres Strait Islanders and indigenous coastal peoples.

The multiple boundary approach helps resolve the tension left within UNCLOS between delimitation of exclusive economic zones and delimitation of the continental shelf. Although the Australia–Papua New Guinea Treaty was negotiated before the convention, it presaged at least one answer to the thorny dilemma presented by the two approaches to maritime delimitation. As one Chinese scholar has noted,

> Although the UN Convention on the Law of the Sea adopted a compromise position between the "natural extension principle" [of continental shelf

delimitation] and the "centerline principle" [of exclusive economic zone delimitation] . . . it only provided guidance in the most general terms saying that states should proceed in accordance with international law . . . in order to attain an equitable solution. Although this stipulation sets down the principle of peaceful and equitable dispute resolution . . . it is nonetheless overly general and simplistic and lacking in rigorous standards, and as a result the two sides engaged in a border negotiation often wind up offering widely divergent or even contradictory interpretations of this principle in actual practice. . . . And with regard to whether the exclusive economic zone and the continental shelf should share the same boundary or have two different boundaries, the Convention on the Law of the Sea was completely silent.[50]

Although this scholar probably overstates the "silence" of UNCLOS concerning boundary delimitation methods where both exclusive economic zone and continental shelf boundaries are under consideration, if the Chinese and Japanese governments were to apply this multiple boundary method to the dispute in the East China Sea, each principle could be applied to its own zone.[51] The delimitation of the seabed boundary may be based on the continental shelf approach of "natural extension," taking into account primarily geomorphological factors of the seabed to delimit this boundary and adjusting for "special circumstances" such as the presence of the Senkaku/Diaoyu Islands, which will be discussed below. With regard to the exclusive economic zone, a separate boundary could be established using the median line principle, achieving an equitable result by again adjusting for such special circumstances as the ratio of the length of each state's coastline, the presence of the Yellow Sea adjacent to and arguably a part of the East China Sea, and the historical use of the waters by each state's coastal population for fishing and harvesting of other resources.[52] Boundaries thus established would have the benefit of resolving a long-standing source of friction between China and Japan, and they would allow for the exploitation of hydrocarbon resources in the wide expanse in the middle of the East China Sea that each side has agreed not to develop.[53]

In the negotiated compromise reached by the Australians and the Papua New Guineans, each side was confident of future stable relations between them, but future stability across the East China Sea is less assured. The most significant aspect of the treaty between Australia and Papua New Guinea is clearly the implementation of a delimitation system of overlapping jurisdictions, which will require substantial and perpetual cooperation between the two states to implement effectively. In other words, Australia's ability to exploit its seabed rights will be forever dependent on Papua New Guinea's acquiescence to Australia's presence in the waters over which Papua New Guinea has economic jurisdiction, and vice versa.

In the Gulf of Maine, another location in which international stability between the negotiating states was reasonably ensured, the parties chose to implement a single boundary to guarantee future peaceful relations concerning the maritime space and the resources contained within it. Jurisdictional authority in the Torres Strait region was also successfully separated, but between Australia and Papua New Guinea the possibility for friction continues unless each state habitually accommodates the other. Habitual accommodation has worked reasonably well between Australia and Papua New Guinea, which have no long history of antagonism and neither of which is presently vying for regional predominance. It might have worked well between the United States and Canada, but each side wisely chose to avoid even the possibility of friction. However, in the case of China and Japan, hope for such accommodation over time is rather far-fetched, given the long history and recent geopolitics. Chinese scholar Li Yi of the College of Political Science and International Relations at Beijing University, in commenting on this multiboundary approach, has suggested a compromise that may help to reduce tension in the East China Sea—that the area of overlap formed by the two different boundaries (continental shelf and exclusive economic zone) be designated a joint development zone.[54] Although such an agreement would move relations a step closer to the harmony each side professes to desire, it still relies on political compromise to diffuse tension, and history suggests that such compromise, if ever achieved, would be fleeting because the fundamental bases for mistrust have not been addressed. That said, a third approach to maritime delimitation—creation of a zone of shared jurisdiction—is worth examining to determine whether any agreement in existence could offer a stability-building compromise.

Joint Jurisdictional Zones

The idea of creating a zone of mutual jurisdiction was to some degree taken up in the Australia–Papua New Guinea Treaty, in relation to "reservation zones" set aside for free use by the indigenous population. In that case, neither state party to the treaty is authorized to exercise jurisdiction—except its seabed or fishery rights—without the concurrence of the other state party.[55] This is an approach to boundary and resource disputes well known to the Chinese. In May 1979, for instance, Deng Xiaoping, then vice premier, proposed to Japan that the dispute over the sovereignty of the Senkaku/

Diaoyu Islands be resolved "through bilateral negotiations and joint development, without touching upon the issue of territorial sovereignty."[56]

Joint Use and Development

On Christmas Day in 2000, Vietnam and China signed a comprehensive—and creative—maritime delimitation agreement for the waters of the Tonkin Gulf (Beibu Gulf, to the Chinese).[57] The Tonkin Gulf is a stretch of water bounded by Vietnam on the west, mainland China on the north, and China's Hainan Island on the east. The agreement created the first finalized maritime border between China and a neighboring coastal state. It divided the waters roughly equally, delineating territorial waters and exclusive economic zones and allocating continental shelf rights.[58] In this case, the exclusive economic zone and the continental shelf boundary are conterminous. The creative aspect of the agreement is the establishment of a joint fisheries zone in waters with historical significance to both countries in the middle of the gulf (see map 3).[59] Fishing vessels of both states have the right to fish for a period of twelve years—with three years of automatic extensions—after which the waters will revert to full sovereign control on either side of the agreed-upon line. Since the agreement came into effect on 30 June 2004, China and Vietnam have begun joint maritime research and joint patrols in the fisheries zone.[60]

Map 3. Tonkin/Beibu Gulf Co-fishing Area

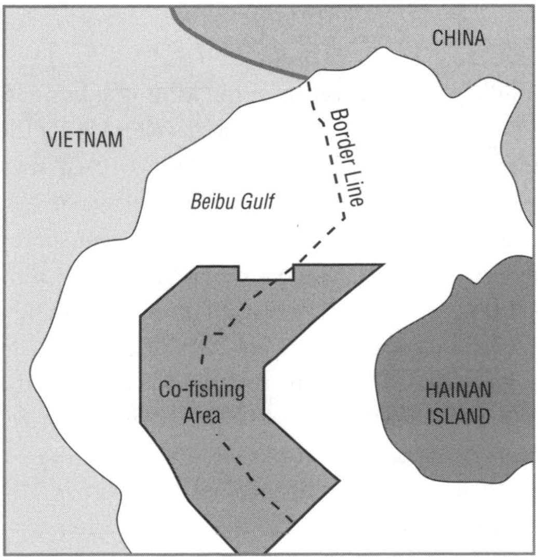

CHINA

VIETNAM

Beibu Gulf

Border Line

Co-fishing Area

HAINAN ISLAND

Creation of the fishing area constituted a key aspect of maritime boundary negotiations between China and Vietnam.

This agreement demonstrates that the two states, which have engaged in open conflict over border and resource disputes in recent decades, can move beyond the past to peaceful resolution of their differences to mutual benefit. As one Chinese commentator noted,

> The delimitation and fishing agreements between the two countries are mutually beneficial. It shows that the two sides are fully capable of resolving historical problems through friendly consultation. It will also boost the development of bilateral ties and promote lasting stability, neighborliness, amity and overall cooperation between the two countries. At the same time, it will further strengthen mutual political trust and their cooperation in other fields, which are favorable to the peace and stability of the [Tonkin] Gulf area.[61]

Indeed, China and Japan had a similar burst of bilateral sentiment in 1997 when they signed an agreement for cooperative fisheries management in the East China Sea. However, unlike the growing cooperation between China and Vietnam in the Tonkin Gulf, the intervening years since the China–Japan East Sea Fisheries Agreement have been unproductive in reaching a larger settlement and are better characterized by reported tense, and occasionally armed, standoffs between the two powers.[62] Even if the political circumstances do not currently permit the 1997 agreement to serve as the starting point for cooperative compromise across the East China Sea, the possibility of a broader, long-term solution could be improved if China and Japan took smaller confidence-building steps toward that goal.

Joint Business Development

One such confidence-building step was taken in the form of a business arrangement by China, the Philippines, and Vietnam to develop jointly the hydrocarbon resources under the South China Sea. Although each state maintained its rival claim of sovereignty over all or portions of the Spratly Islands, the three countries agreed in March 2005 to perform a joint survey of potential hydrocarbon deposits in the disputed areas of the South China Sea.[63] Each country claims sovereignty over some or all of the Spratly Islands, which pepper the South China Sea, and accordingly each claims rights to the continental shelf and exclusive economic zone that would pertain to the islands under the UNCLOS framework. The tripartite agreement authorizes the state-owned oil companies of each country (China National Offshore Oil Corporation, the Philippine National Oil Company, and the Vietnam Oil and Gas Corporation) to engage in joint seismic exploration, sharing costs equally, as a commercial transaction specified to last three years and to have no effect on political claims.[64]

Cooperation among state-owned oil companies is certainly not new, but an agreement among rival claimants—whose rivalries led to armed skirmishes in the 1970s, '80s, and '90s—to cooperate in the development of maritime resources while postponing final agreement over sovereignty is a potential model for cooperation between China and Japan in the East China Sea. One of the stumbling blocks to a final agreement between China and Japan is a lack of shared information about the nature of likely resources under the East China Sea's continental shelf. Suspicion by each of the exploratory activities of the other is in part responsible for the heightened tensions and increased potential for military conflict.[65] Joint exploration in the East China Sea using the Spratlys cooperative business plan as a model could lead to joint development with mutual benefits and will at least afford a more complete picture of the resources available for negotiation. Even though it may be a small step in a much longer process, an agreement on joint exploration would form the basis for increased trust and confidence and demonstrate a real desire by each side to move forward cooperatively. Additionally, China and Japan have each stressed the importance of the resources in and under the East China Sea to their respective economies, and joint exploitation may result in more efficient use of the oil and natural gas resources available to lessen each country's dependence on external energy supplies.

Establishing a joint development zone in the East China Sea, either through a business-based agreement or a mechanism that allows for joint resource exploitation for a period of time, has the benefit of building upon the factors upon which China and Japan both already agree. It helps alleviate each country's need for resources without touching the "third rail" of sovereignty, the issue on which neither side seems ready to compromise. Perhaps most importantly, joint development could serve as the foundation of trust and confidence necessary to move forward on a comprehensive delimitation agreement. That said, the potential for conflict remains as settlement of the key issue of sovereignty is once again put off for another day. Perhaps that is the most that can be hoped for, given the complicated political factors that make negotiations in the East China Sea so difficult.

Taiwan and the Senkaku/Diaoyu Islands Dispute as Complicating Factors

Significantly complicating factors in the delimitation of the maritime boundary in the East China Sea are the dispute over the sovereignty of the Senkaku Islands (known as Diaoyu Islands in both mainland China and Taiwan) and the unique status of Taiwan.[66] The Senkaku/Diaoyu Islands are a group of five small uninhabited rocky islets, the largest of which is 3.6 square kilometers in area.[67] Historically, they were known to the Chinese and mentioned in official documents as early as the Ming dynasty (1368–1644), but there is no evidence they were ever taken under effective administration or control by the Chinese, the necessary element under international law for a state to assert legitimate sovereignty over territory.[68] They have been administered and controlled by Japan since 1895—with the exception of the post–World War II occupation by the United States between 1945 and 1972—based on Japanese claims of discovery in about 1894. China's view is that they were stolen from Chinese control as a result of the 1895 Sino–Japanese War and should have been returned to China after World War II.[69] Military posturing between Chinese and Japanese naval forces in the waters around these islands has been intense in recent years, including aggressive Japanese tracking of a Han-class Chinese nuclear submarine in the area in November 2004 and joint U.S.–Japanese naval exercises to practice defending the islands in November 2006.[70]

Resolution of the issue of sovereignty and the naval tensions that attend it, however, are only the first complicating factors concerning these islets. An equally strident argument is ongoing over the extent of water and continental shelf space to which this small but crucial group of outcroppings is entitled—regardless of which side receives final sovereignty over them. The crux of the problem is, again, ambiguity in the language of UNCLOS, which states that if these outcroppings can be considered islands—that is, if they can support human habitation or commercial activity—they should normally receive a full two-hundred-nautical-mile exclusive economic zone. However, if they are merely rocks—that is, if they cannot sustain human habitation or commercial activity—they receive no exclusive economic zone or continental shelf.[71] Although the islands have never been inhabited and have not sustained commercial activity of any kind in approximately eighty years (they were used briefly around the turn of the last century to harvest guano and perhaps at various times as a refuge for fishermen) the dispute remains whether they could support human habitation or commercial activity, and thus whether the exclusive economic zone and continental shelf boundaries in the East China Sea should be adjusted for them.[72] The difference is not insignificant: perhaps as much as eight thousand square miles of ocean space—and the rich resources in and below the water that go with it—are at stake.

Taiwan's status is another complicating factor to boundary delimitation, given the visceral way in which Beijing reacts to any suggestion that Taiwan has a legitimate status apart from the rest of China.[73] Nonetheless, Taiwan maintains an independent claim over the Senkaku Islands, and Taiwanese fishing boats have historically plied the waters around the islets and continue to do so regularly with nationalistic support from portions of the Taiwanese population and their representatives in government.[74] Japan's geostrategic support for Taiwan will remain an obvious irritant to the prospects of a lasting peaceful compromise in the East China Sea, but on a practical level, Taiwan's nonacceptance of any agreement between Tokyo and Beijing could prevent meaningful application of confidence-building measures that would form the necessary first step of any lasting agreement.

The Chinese reaction to these two concerns—the Senkakus and Taiwan—demonstrates that unresolved territorial claims remaining from the period of Japanese aggression during World War II still evoke strong Chinese memories of suffering as a nation at the hands of outside colonial powers. This in turn may limit the freedom of the Chinese government to compromise with the Japanese and at the same time maintain legitimacy in the eyes of its populace.

China May Not Want to Resolve the Dispute

It is entirely possible that regardless of the overtures of friendliness recently extended to the Japanese by Chinese leaders, the Chinese may not actually see it as in their best interest to settle these disputes. The tension between China and Japan over resources, boundaries, and sovereignty in the East China Sea—and especially the confrontation over Japanese administration of, and claim of sovereignty to, the Senkaku/Diaoyu Islands—provides the PRC government with a lever of nationalism with which to divert the attention of the Chinese people from domestic difficulties and shore up support for the central government during times of domestic political competition.[75] In this context Chinese leaders have historically used economic advantage and territorial nationalism as two sources of legitimacy—emphasizing economic progress during periods of prosperity and blaming outside powers during times of instability.[76]

One reason why China has successfully negotiated a path forward in its disputes with Vietnam, Malaysia, and the Philippines in the South China Sea but has refused to do so with similar disputes with Japan in the East China Sea is that China has never been dominated by the former states: accommodation with them allows China to portray itself as internationalist and cooperative with its neighbors. Put simply, Japanese aggression within the living memory of many Chinese makes Japan a ready source of nationalist fervor. Whenever Chinese leaders desire to enhance Chinese nationalist sentiment, they need only remind their people of the territorial disputes in the East China Sea to call to mind Japan's occupation of large portions of Chinese territory only decades ago. This, combined with an unbending stand against Japanese encroachment on China's maritime claims, demonstrates to the Chinese people that the PRC government will never again allow outside powers to humiliate them. Thus, by negotiating cooperatively with its other neighbors but remaining in controlled conflict with Japan, China balances its domestic and regional political messages in a way that contributes both to domestic stability and regional rise.

It is likely that there exists a spectrum of contending causal forces that move international relations between China and Japan along a sliding scale between cooperation and competition.[77] Domestic political concerns, international power dynamics, resource requirements, economic fluctuations, and even major events like the 2008 Summer Olympics can move their relationship from a static competitive dynamic toward cooperation. Perhaps Hu Jintao's recent signals of rapprochement with Japan after the election of Prime Minister Shinzo Abe reflect confidence by Beijing in China's economic future and a desire for international goodwill before the Olympics and that the time may indeed be right to move forward on the East China Sea dispute. But China's long-term strategic interests are still captive to its geographic position, bounded as the mainland is by the island chain that runs along China's coastline from the Kuriles to the archipelagoes of the South China Sea. As James R. Holmes and Toshi Yoshihara have observed,

> China's naval and air modernization efforts point to a build-up toward a strategy of sea denial against U.S. forces seeking to intervene in Asian waters. . . . [In time of conflict], the closer U.S. military forces get to [Chinese] territory, the more competitive the [Chinese] will be. This arises from a combination of political, physical, and technological facts. These facts combine to create a contested zone—arenas of conventional combat where weak adversaries have a good chance of doing real damage to U.S. forces.[78]

In other words, because it provides the Chinese with a larger operational space within which to contest legitimately the presence of non-Chinese warships, it may be to China's military advantage to maintain its claim over the full breadth of the waters of the East China Sea, from the mainland to the Okinawa Trough and the doorstep of American bases on Japanese territory, rather than to reach a compromise with the Japanese that might restrict China's legitimate freedom of action during any future conflict.[79] Still, China has no short-term interest in allowing the dispute over maritime boundaries in the East China Sea to get out of hand and spill over into actual conflict. Only if its assertion of sovereignty over Taiwan were severely threatened would China be likely to take military control over the full extent of its East China Sea claim.

Charting the Course

Before agreement can be reached, China must conclude that it is genuinely in its interest to compromise with Japan. This is no small hurdle. Beijing may perceive managed conflict as an essential tool in maintaining political legitimacy as China develops the "harmonious society" that Hu Jintao intends to build.[80] Accordingly, until China's domestic growing pains are eased and Taiwan's status is settled, there may never be a policy toward Japan that is fully cooperative. Still, effective interim steps can be taken that will ensure that the current competition does not unintentionally escalate into open conflict.

First, agreement should be reached that the Senkaku/Diaoyu Islands dispute is to be removed from the equation through agreement that no matter how the sovereignty question is ultimately settled, the islets will receive no territorial effect beyond the twelve-nautical-mile territorial sea. The waters around the islands could be designated a joint fisheries zone on behalf of China, Taiwan, and Japan, with a cooperative approach to policing—perhaps on a rotating basis. Stakeholders with hydrocarbon exploration and exploitation concessions in the area could be given financial compensation for affected rights.[81] Deng was right: the way forward requires both sides to "shelve the dispute over sovereignty and proceed with mutual development."[82]

Additionally, first steps toward building trust and confidence for mutual development could be undertaken by an agreement to abide scrupulously by the provisions of the 1997 Fishing Agreement and to build a joint enforcement team composed of both Chinese and Japanese officials to police the East China Sea fisheries zone. This should be followed by a new agreement, similar to the existing agreement between China, Vietnam, and the Philippines, to develop jointly the hydrocarbon resources in the disputed area of the East China Sea. Furthermore, both sides should agree that during the period of joint development, final boundary delimitation will be negotiated in good faith.[83] Negotiators should consider the advantages and disadvantages of delimitation of a single boundary as opposed to multiple boundaries, paying special attention to solutions that promote permanent avoidance of friction.

If a negotiated settlement cannot be reached during that period, both sides could demonstrate their commitment to the rule of international law, as Canada and the United States did in the Gulf of Maine, by agreeing to submit specified questions to an international tribunal as called for in UNCLOS. The stated commitment of both states to resort to the rule of law rather than to confrontation and intimidation would offer hope that the region can move beyond the geopolitical rhetoric that has informed public discourse to date and would serve as a model of accommodation and cooperation between former competitors.

So far, China and Japan seem to be talking past each other rather than to each other in their public discourse surrounding their dispute over the East China Sea. However, the stakes are high, given the possibility that supposedly "managed" conflict can always result in unintended war.[84] Substantial economic and political benefits could be derived from a cross-sea détente, but this would require both sides to choose to set aside old grudges and move forward cooperatively rather than competitively. The examples provided by the agreements between the United States and Canada and between Australia and Papua New Guinea demonstrate that international law charts several productive paths for this way forward. Tokyo and Beijing should begin this journey by developing a trusting and cooperative spirit through step-by-step implementation of precursor agreements similar to the tripartite agreement for hydrocarbon exploration in the Spratlys and to the joint fisheries agreement between China and Vietnam. Only then will East Asia be able to demonstrate that competition for scarce resources need not inevitably lead to conflict.

Notes

An earlier version of this article appeared as "Carving Up the East China Sea," *Naval War College Review* 60, no. 2 (Spring 2007): 49–72.

Epigraph: Epigraphs from Peng Guangqian and Yao Youzhi, eds., *The Science of Military Strategy* (Beijing: Military Science Publishing House, Academy of Military Science of the Chinese People's Liberation Army, 2005), 2; and Yang Lei, "Behind the Disputes in the East China Sea between China and Japan," *Naval and Merchant Ships* 27, no. 6 (2006) 22.

1. Kosuku Takahashi, "Gas and Oil Rivalry in the East China Sea," *Asia Times*, 27 July 2004, www.atimes.com.

2. Ibid.

3. "Development Project Awarded," *Tenaris Pipeline Services News*, November 2003, p. 6, www.tenaris.com/archivos/documents/2003/704.pdf.

4. Ibid.

5. Greg Austin, *China's Ocean Frontier: International Law, Military Force and National Development* (Canberra: Allen and Unwin, 1998), 152–61.

6. Norimitsu Onishi and Howard W. French, "Ill Will Rising between China and Japan," *New York Times*, August 2005. Despite thawing relations between China and Japan, development of oil and gas fields in the East China Sea continues to be a source of friction. As recently as November 2006 Japan's request that China halt new production in the disputed waters was met with obfuscation by a spokesperson of Republic of China's foreign ministry. Takahashi Hirokawa and Shigeru Sato, "Japan Asks China to Halt Gas Output in Disputed Field," *Bloomberg*, 1 February 2007, www.bloomberg.com/apps/.

7. "PRC Naval Vessel Activities in East China Sea 'Drop Sharply' in 2006," *Sankei Shimbun*, 4 November 2006. For Wang Yi's meeting, Jiang Wenren, "China and Japan: Reconciliation or Confrontation," *China Brief*, 16 August 2006, p. 5. The focus of the meeting was reportedly one of the most promising things the two countries could do to advance reconciliation.

8. "China, Japan Hold Talks on East China Sea Gas Reserves," *Taipei Times*, 9 July 2006, p. 5.

9. "Crossfire War: South China Sea," *Times of Oman*, 15 March 2005.

10. Michael Richardson, "Sovereignty Tussle Key to China-ASEAN Ties," *Straits Times* (Singapore), 9 November 2006.

11. Charles Hutzler, "China Promotes 'Peaceful Rise' to Quell U.S. Fears," *Wall Street Journal*, 13 September 2005, p. 13.

12. Peng and Yao, eds., *The Science of Military Strategy*, 443.

13. Richard Halloran, "The Rising East," *Honolulu Advertiser*, 10 September 2006; Doug Struck and Rajiv Chandrasekaran, "Nations across Asia Keep Watch on China," *Washington Post*, 19 October 2001, p. 23.

14. John Donaldson and Alison Williams, "Understanding Maritime Jurisdictional Disputes: The East China Sea and Beyond," *Journal on International Affairs* 59, no. 1 (2005): 141.

15. Satya N. Nandan and Shabtai Rosenne, eds., *United Nations Convention on the Law of the Sea 1982: A Commentary*, vol. 2 (Dordrecht, Neth.: Martinus Nijhoff, 1993), 827–29. The basic provisions of the 1958 Convention on the Continental Shelf were retained; however, UNCLOS does provide additional regulation of the outer limits of legitimate coastal state claims to the continental shelf.

16. Donaldson and Williams, "Understanding Maritime Jurisdictional Disputes," 141–42.

17. Zhang Dongzhiang and Wu Weili, "A Discussion of the Sino-Japanese Delimitation Issue in the East China Sea and Its Settlement," *Shijie Yu Zhengzhi,* 14 April 2006, translated FBIS CPP20060427329001, pp. 35–42.

18. U.S. Defense Dept., *Department of Defense Maritime Claims Reference Manual,* DoD 2005.1-M (Washington, D.C.: December 2003), 106; Zhang and Wu, "A Discussion of the Sino-Japanese Delimitation Issue in the East China Sea and Its Settlement," 35; 张耀光, 刘锴 [Zhang Yaoguang and Liu Kai], "东海油气资源及中国, 日本在东海大陆架划界问题的研究" ["A Study of East Sea Oil and the China-Japan East Sea Continental Shelf Demarcation Dispute"], 资源科学 *[Resources Science]* 27, no. 6 (November 2005): 11 para. 3.1.

19. Zhang and Liu, "A Study of East Sea Oil," 11, para. 3.3. See also Zou Keyuan, "Historic Rights in International Law and in China's Practice," *Ocean Development and International Law* 32, no. 2 (April 2001): 163, where the author states, "In China's view, a claim derived from historic rights may seem more forceful and valid in law than claims simply based upon the EEZ concept."

20. 杨雷 [Yang Lei], "中日东海争端的背后" ["Behind the Sino-Japanese Dispute in the East Sea"], 舰船知识 *[Naval & Merchant Ships]* (June 2006).

21. Zhang and Liu, "A Study of East Sea Oil," 11.

22. Compare UNCLOS Article 2, "The *sovereignty* of a coastal state extends . . . to an adjacent belt of sea, described as the territorial sea," with Article 56, "In the exclusive economic zone, the coastal state has *sovereign rights* for the purpose of exploring and exploiting, conserving and managing the natural resources" and "*jurisdiction* as provided for in the relevant provisions of this Convention" [italics added].

23. UNCLOS Article 58 specifically states that "in the exclusive economic zone, all States . . . enjoy . . . the freedoms referred to in Article 87," concerning freedom of the high seas.

24. See, for example, 李广义 [Li Guangyi], "论专属经济区军事利用的法律问题" ["On Legal Issues Associated with the Military Usage of Exclusive Economic Zones"], 西安政治学院学报 *[Journal of Xi'an Politics Institute]* 18, no. 2 (2005): 56.

25. Ibid., 54–55.

26. See, generally, ibid., 54.

27. Japan imports 80 percent of its oil, 88 percent of which comes from the politically unstable Middle East. For a good discussion of the varying interests between China and Japan in development of hydrocarbon resources under the East China Sea, see Zhang and Liu, "A Study of East Sea Oil."

28. Moritaka Hayashi, "Japan: New Law of the Sea Legislation," *International Journal of Marine and Coastal Law* (November 1997): 570, 573–74. UNCLOS Article 74 states that delimitation shall be based on international law and in order to achieve an "equitable solution."

29. Since UNCLOS allows states to claim continental shelf rights out to two hundred nautical miles regardless of the features of the seabed, the International Court of

Justice concluded that where opposing coasts are less than two hundred nautical miles apart, the geological and geomorphological characteristics of the seabed are entirely irrelevant to delimitation. *Case Concerning the Continental Shelf (Libya and Malta)*, International Court of Justice, Judgment of 3 June 1985, paras. 39–41.

30. Mark J. Valencia, "East China Sea Dispute: Ways Forward," Pacific Forum CSIS PacNet 47, 15 September 2006, www.csis.org/.

31. Hayashi, "Japan," 570, 573–74.

32. Mayumi Negishi, "Teikoku Oil Seeks Rights to Test-Drill in Disputed Seas," *Japan Times*, 29 April 2005; James Brazier, "China and Japan: Friendlier Still," *AsiaInt Political and Strategic Review* (December 2006). See also Ji Guoxing, "Maritime Jurisdiction in the Three China Seas: Options for Equitable Settlement," Institute on Global Conflict and Cooperation, October 1995, www.ciaonet.org.

33. Permanent Mission of the People's Republic of China to the United Nations Press Conference, "Foreign Ministry Spokesman Qin Gang's Comments on China's Relevant Oil and Gas Exploration in the East China Sea," www.china-un.org/eng/fyrth/t269599.htm; *White Paper on China's National Defense*, Xinhua, 2002, p. 16. It is also worth noting that both countries have accepted the requirement of UNCLOS Article 74(1) to settle disputes in order to "achieve an equitable solution . . . through negotiation."

34. Mark J. Valencia and Yoshihisa Amae, "Regime Building in the East China Sea," *Ocean Development and International Law* 34 (2003): 189, 193–96.

35. "Japan, China to Discuss Disputed Gas Field in July," Reuters, 30 June 2006; Valencia, "East China Sea Dispute"; Brazier, "China and Japan."

36. UNCLOS, Article 74(1). For self-restraint, Mayumi Negishi, "Teikoku Oil Seeks Rights"; Valencia and Amae, "Regime Building in the East China Sea," 189, 191; James C. Hsiung, "Sea Power, Law of the Sea, and China-Japan East China Sea 'Resource War,'" conference paper, Forum on China, Institute of Sustainable Development, Macao, 9–11 October 2005, www.nyu.edu.

37. *Case Concerning the Delimitation of the Maritime Boundary in the Gulf of Maine Area* [hereafter Gulf of Maine Case], *1984 Yearbook of the International Court of Justice*, 246.

38. To be precise, the parties requested the court to assist in the delimitation of a "200-mile exclusive fishery zone," but in the intervening years, with the growing acceptance of the term "exclusive economic zone" established in the United Nations Convention on the Law of the Sea, both parties have accepted the newer concept and changed their terminology accordingly.

39. Gulf of Maine Case, 300.

40. Ibid., 258–60.

41. Ibid., 284.

42. Ibid., 265.

43. Ibid. Whether the Court was correct in its assessment is debatable. For instance, different states have different treaty obligations vis-à-vis third states for such rights

as fishing and hydrocarbon exploitation that could well be affected by the Court's choice of boundary. Additionally, coastal states differ with regard to their understanding of passage rights available to the international community in the waters and airspace over them. China in particular maintains that it has the right to regulate many activities in the airspace above its exclusive economic zone despite the fact that UNCLOS specifies that they are international in character. Thus, as maritime boundaries change, so do the zones of interpretation and obligation change.

44. Ibid., 270.

45. Ibid., 278.

46. Ibid., 343.

47. Zhang and Liu, "A Study of East Sea Oil"; Yang, "Behind the Sino-Japanese Dispute," 22–24.

48. 李毅 [Li Yi], "论澳巴海洋边界划分方法之特色及其对中日东海海域划界之借鉴意义" ["A Discussion of the Distinguishing Features of the Division Methods for the Maritime Boundary between Australia and Papua New Guinea and the Lessons of and Significance for the Delimitation of the Maritime Boundary between China and Japan in the East China Sea"], 东北亚论坛 [Northeast Asia Forum] 14, no. 3 (2005): 30–34.

49. The treaty, which consists of thirty-two articles and nine appendixes, was concluded in 1978 and came into effect in February 1985. It is available online from the Australian Government Publishing Service at www.austlii.edu.au.

50. Li, "A Discussion of the Distinguishing Features."

51. The equidistance line method is mentioned in neither UNCLOS Article 74 nor Article 83, which relate to delimitation of exclusive economic zone and continental shelf boundaries. Both articles require, however, that delimitation be "effected by agreement on the basis of international law" and "in order to achieve an equitable solution." This is a significant departure from Article 6 of the 1958 Geneva Convention on the Continental Shelf, which required the equidistance line method unless historical title or special circumstances existed. Donaldson and Williams, "Understanding Maritime Jurisdiction Disputes," 135–56.

52. For a thorough treatment of this approach, see, generally, Li, "A Discussion of the Distinguishing Features."

53. "Japan Foreign Minister Defends PRC Marine Survey in EEZ," Tokyo Sankei Shimbun, 21 June 2001, BIS JPP20010621000023.

54. Li, "A Discussion of the Distinguishing Features."

55. Treaty between Australia and the Independent State of Papua New Guinea, Part 2, Article 4.

56. Li, "A Discussion of the Distinguishing Features."

57. "China, Vietnam Ink Deals Ending Tonkin Gulf Border Row," Kyodo News International, 1 January 2001.

58. "VN-China Gulf Pact to Enhance Relations," *Vietnam News*, 2 July 2004, www.vietnamnews.vnanet.vn/. Under the agreement, Vietnam is entitled to 53.23 percent of the Gulf's total area and China is entitled to 46.77 percent.

59. Xiao Jianguo, "Drawing the Line," *Beijing Review*, www.bjreview.com.cn/.

60. "Chinese President and Party Leader to Visit Vietnam," *Vietnam Net*, 11 November 2006, www.vnn.vn.

61. Xiao, "Drawing the Line."

62. Christian Caryl, with Akiko Kashiwagi, "A Risky Game of Chicken," *Newsweek* (International Edition), 18 September 2006; Kosuke Takahashi, "Gas and Oil Rivalry in the East China Sea," *Asia Times*, 27 July 2004, www.atimes.com; Tim Johnson, "Rift between Two Asian Powers Grows Wider," *Philadelphia Inquirer*, 8 May 2006; Valencia, "East China Sea Dispute."

63. "Crossfire War: South China Sea," *Times of Oman: International News*, online edition, 15 March 2005.

64. "Beijing, Manila, Hanoi Strike Deal over Spratleys' *[sic]* Oil," *AsiaNews*, online edition, 15 March 2005.

65. Andrea R. Mihailescu, "UPI Energy Watch: More Security Challenges," eurasia21.com, 16 March 2005; "Chunxiao Oil/Gas Field to Be Completed This October," *People's Daily Online*, 21 April 2005.

66. China's Law of the People's Republic of China on the Territorial Sea and the Contiguous Zone, effective 25 February 1992, specifically states that the land territory of the People's Republic of China includes the Diaoyu Islands. *Department of Defense Maritime Claims Reference Manual*, 108.

67. Austin, *China's Ocean Frontier*, 162.

68. Ibid., 163–64.

69. Zhang and Wu, "Discussion of the Sino-Japanese Delimitation Issue," 35; Austin, *China's Ocean Frontier*, 163.

70. "Japan's Navy Denies Practice Invasion," Associated Press, 31 December 2006, www.newsmax.com. For a thorough discussion of the Han incident, see Peter Dutton, "International Law Implications of the November 2004 'Han Incident,'" *Asian Security* 2, no. 2 (2006): 87–101.

71. UNCLOS, Article 121.

72. Austin, *China's Ocean Frontier*, 168.

73. Yang Lei, "Behind the Dispute."

74. "New Party Blasts Government on Tiaoyutais," *Taipei Times*, 23 April 2005.

75. Erica Strecker Downs and Philip C. Saunders, "Legitimacy and the Limits of Nationalism: China and the Diaoyu Islands," *International Security*, no. 23 (Winter 1998/99): 114, 116; Norimitsu Onishi and Howard W. French, "Ill Will Rising between China and Japan," *New York Times*, 2 August 2005.

76. For a view to the contrary, see M. Taylor Fravel, "Regime Insecurity and International Cooperation," *International Security* 30, no. 2 (2005): 46–83. Fravel argues

that PRC regime insecurity actually increases the likelihood of compromise. His examples of past compromise, however, all involve land borders in the western portion of China where territorial compromise was seen as the best means of gaining and maintaining control over groups of non-Han Chinese citizens. He acknowledges that where historical Han territorial interests have been at stake, such as in Hong Kong or Macau (and, I argue, the maritime claims in the East China Sea), China has been much less willing to compromise and indeed sees recovery of these territories as central to the legitimacy of the Communist Party regime.

77. For a good discussion of power dynamics in the relations between the United States and China, see Aaron L. Friedberg, "The Future of U.S.-China Relations," *International Security* 30, no. 2 (2005): 7–45.

78. James R. Holmes and Toshi Yoshihara, "China and the Commons: Angell or Mahan?" *World Affairs* 168, no. 4 (2006): 172–91.

79. As one Chinese commentator put it, "If China can control the East China Sea, it can establish a protective screen as a strategy at sea and to enhance its strategic defense from the east"; Yang, "Behind the Sino-Japanese Dispute." See also Ho Szu-shen, "China Interested in Japan's Waters," *Taipei Times,* 9 September 2004, quoting Liu Huaqing, former first vice chairman of China's Central Military Commission, as saying that China's blue water naval strategy is to allow it to move its defense from the coastline to the first chain of outlying islands—Japan, Taiwan, the Philippines, and Indonesia—and perhaps beyond.

80. See, for example, Will Lam, "Hu Jintao's 'Theory of the Three Harmonies,'" *China Brief* 6, no. 1 (2006): 1.

81. This is also discussed by Valencia, in "East China Sea Dispute."

82. Yang Lei, "Behind the Sino-Japanese Dispute."

83. Indeed, UNCLOS Articles 74 and 83 require states to "make every effort to enter provisional agreements of a practical nature and, during this transitional period, not to jeopardize or hamper the reaching of the final agreement."

84. For a description of one such dangerous game of chicken—in October 2004, between the Chinese marine surveillance ship *Haijian* and the Norwegian research vessel *Ramforn Victory,* contracted by the Japanese government to gather data on oil and gas reserves in the disputed area—see Yoichi Funabashi, "Can Dialog Resolve China-Japan Oil Clash in East China Sea?" *International Herald Tribune/Asahi Shimbun,* 13 October 2004. In that incident, Chinese and Japanese crews exchanged warnings, and "the Chinese vessel venture[d] within a hairsbreadth" of Japanese research equipment. In September 2005, a Chinese naval vessel operating in the disputed area reportedly trained its guns on a Japanese P-3 maritime patrol aircraft that was surveilling the area. ("Japanese MSDF Spots Five Chinese Naval Ships near East China Sea Gas Field," Kyodo World Service, 9 September 2005.) Another "brief row" occurred in April 2006, when Chinese authorities banned ship traffic near the Penghu gas fields in the disputed area of the central East China Sea; Johnson, "Rift between Two Asian Powers Grows Wider."

John Garofano

China, the South China Sea, and U.S. Strategy

What we aim is for a sea of conflict to become a sea of cooperation in the near future.

Philippines Foreign Affairs Secretary Alberto Romulo,
7 September 2004

However, due to the intricate situation in the disputed South China Sea areas, oil and gas exploration will undoubtedly become a sensitive issue which might not only bring about conflict, but also problems related to investment and cooperation.

Wu Shicun, president, and Hong Nong, assistant researcher,
National Institute for South China Sea Studies, March 2005

THE SOUTH CHINA SEA (SCS) is the sixth largest body of water on earth, covering an area of some 3.5 million square kilometers. Three-quarters of the world's oil and natural gas trade transits the sea annually, providing a critical economic lifeline between Northeast and Southeast Asia and South Asia, the Middle East, Europe, and North America. It is one of the world's largest sources of fish production, providing the majority of the protein in the diets of many in the Asia-Pacific. Oil and natural gas exploration and production have increased dramatically over the last two decades. Estimates of total reserves continue to vary wildly, ranging from the hope that it is "the next Persian Gulf" to much lower guesses based on the limited amounts that have actually been extracted thus far. One half of the world's merchant fleet sails through the sea lines of communication (SLOC) of the South China Sea and waters around Indonesia. The flow of oil through the SCS is three times that through the Suez Canal and fifteen times that which flows through Panama, and is expected to double by 2020 due to increased energy demand in the region. An interruption would cause major economic harm.[1]

The SCS is also the subject of competing territorial claims that have proliferated since the 1970s and the passage of the United Nations Convention on the Law of the Sea. China, Taiwan, Vietnam, Malaysia, Brunei, and the Philippines are the parties of direct concern, with China having both demanding energy needs and a strong, though perhaps recent, view of ownership of nearly the entire Sea. In addition, other states have strong interests in the Sea. Indonesia has major offshore facilities. Japan receives 75 percent of its oil via the SCS, Taiwan 70 percent. The United States requires freedom of navigation and has a formal treaty with the Philippines as well as growing relationships with other interested parties.[2]

From continued right of free passage for commercial and military vessels and unrestricted access to free market opportunities for oil and natural gas exploration and exploitation, the United States has important national interests at stake in the Greater South China Sea Area (GSCSA). These interests will be increasingly challenged by several current or potential developments, including the inevitable growth of China's power projection capabilities in the region, the spread of nationalism and increasingly strident territorial claims on the part of many of the claimant states, and the discovery of new hydrocarbon reserves or technology allowing the exploitation of existing known reserves. As the primary enforcer or monitor of several of those interests, the U.S. Navy must pay close attention to political and military developments in the region.

This chapter addresses some of the political and military dynamics at play in the SCS and asks the following questions: What is the nature of competing territorial claims? What motivates the People's Republic of China (PRC), and what does this tell us about its likely future claims and behavior? What are its views of oil and gas deposits and how important are these in Beijing's calculations? Do China's neighbors have a strategy for addressing Beijing's claims and interests? What are the prospects for conflict?

This chapter's primary argument is that Chinese presence and influence in the area is likely to grow absent major changes in Association of Southeast Asian Nations (ASEAN) or U.S. policy. The long-term implications include not only less U.S. political and economic influence but also potential erosion of the Navy's freedom of action. Oil and gas deposits are one motivation behind Beijing's policies but are likely viewed as a small if significant "bonus" while the real goal is consolidation of what it considers its sovereign territory. Regional actors, including the United States, must follow a sophisticated set of policies if they are to offset these current trends.

Conflicting Territorial Claims

The potential for conflict lies in the conflicting territorial claims made by China, Taiwan, Vietnam, the Philippines, Malaysia, and Brunei (with a number of other actors holding an interest in the ultimate resolution of the claims), combined with the growing importance of energy to the continued growth of the respective economies. The entire SCS contains about two hundred small islands, rocks, and reefs, most in the Spratly or Paracel island chains.

China and Taiwan both claim the entire SCS based on historical occupation and effective jurisdiction. China, Vietnam, and Taiwan claim all of the Spratly islands, reefs, and rocks that stand or emerge above sea level. The Philippines claims a smaller number of islets within the area it calls Kalayaan ("Freedomland"), basing its claims on non-occupation and "discovery." These states also make conflicting claims about partially submerged rocks in the area. Malaysia claims seven islets that fall within its continental shelf boundary while Brunei claims a narrow, two-hundred-mile-long exclusive economic zone that includes Rifleman Bank in the Spratlys and a small area of the Philippine claim.[3]

No state vigorously espoused or defended territorial claims in the sea until the discovery of potentially meaningful hydrocarbon deposits in the 1970s. At the same time, via negotiations on the United Nations Convention on the Law of the Sea, the international community began to consider how to manage offshore and undersea resources. China soon emerged as the most vociferous and muscular claimant, deploying maps dating from the early twentieth century showing a "dashed, U-Shaped Line" suggesting that the entire sea and its resources were Chinese territory. Beijing cites as further evidence of claim validity voyages across the sea two thousand years ago and continuing to the present. The U-shaped line may first have been delineated in 1914 and was used occasionally through 1947 when Republic of China officials employed it. In any case, it is true that China received few if any challenges to its claims between 1946 and 1971, when the Philippines occupied three islands.[4]

PRC Aggression and ASEAN Diplomacy

China continued to press its claims, seizing and occupying the Paracels from a weakened and distracted Vietnam in 1974, firing on Vietnamese boats in the Spratlys in 1988, and occupying Fiery Cross Reef, within the Philippines exclusive economic zone, in 1988. Most importantly, Beijing then codified its presumed sovereignty over the sea in domestic law on 25 February 1992. Article 2 of the Law of the Territorial Sea and Contiguous Zone asserts that the SCS is Chinese internal waters and that foreign naval vessels therefore must obtain permission before transiting, submarines must surface and fly their flags, and aircraft must obtain permission for overflight rights. Article 8 allows Beijing to take all necessary measures to stop harmful passage while Article 14 authorizes hot pursuit of foreign naval vessels to the high seas.

Malaysian, Philippine, and Indonesian authorities reacted strongly, citing their intention to defend their respective claims, which they viewed as critical national assets. Indonesian foreign minister Ali Alatas declared that the situation was potentially explosive and would worsen if significant oil reserves were discovered. The ASEAN signed its own declaration on the SCS in July 1992, seeking to promote the twin norms of nonoccupation and nonprovocation. ASEAN accelerated its efforts after China occupied Mischief Reef in February 1995, although it continued to adhere to its standard fare of official meetings, norm-building, consensus decision making, and Track II efforts.

ASEAN sought to gain Chinese acceptance of its principles of peaceful coexistence in a format applied specifically to the SCS while maintaining internal ASEAN unity. This was a challenge because nonclaimant ASEAN states were more interested in maintaining good relations with China while the Philippines and Malaysia had overlapping claims themselves. Some further fracturing occurred when Malaysia colluded with China by agreeing to deal on a bilateral basis, to exclude the United States from any negotiations, and even to occupy two more reefs itself, much to the consternation of the Philippines. The Philippines, on the other hand, sought unsuccessfully to raise the issue at the Asian Regional Forum Senior Officials Meeting, at which the United States and Japan were present, which China rejected. This contributed to Manila's moving closer to Washington.

The 1995–96 Taiwan crisis may in fact have changed the balance of internal forces such that by 1997 Beijing's claims shifted to an emphasis on resources. The missile firings following Lee Teng-hui's visit to the United States brought the United States into the picture as a major deterrent to cross-strait conflict. The missile diplomacy supported by People's Liberation Army (PLA) hardliners was not viewed as successful by Jiang Zemin. Jiang lessened the influence of hardliners by expanding the number of deputy chairmen on the Central Military Commission. Admiral Liu Huaqing was retired from the commission in September 1997, and since then the "lost territory" theme has been subordinated to the resources theme.

In 1998 Manila signed a Visiting Forces Agreement allowing U.S. forces to use Philippine facilities and to train its forces. Notably, the agreement was signed in the midst of a dispute with Beijing over an unoccupied atoll in the Spratlys and one week after a letter from then Ambassador Thomas Hubbard to Manila stated that the 1951 Mutual Defense Treaty had both "territorial and situational applications." This letter was interpreted to mean that Washington was moving away from its neutral stance on SCS disputes.[5]

Internal fracturing and the increasing involvement of a superpower led to a renewed ASEAN agreement, which resulted in the November 2002 Declaration on a Code of Conduct in the SCS. The idea of a code of conduct surfaced formally at the 29th Advanced Ministerial Meeting in July 1996 but stalled over Vietnam's desire to include the Paracels and the Philippines' desire to ban any new structures on existing occupied lands. ASEAN made two major concessions rather quickly, which may internally have signaled success for the new security concept. The first was that a code would recognize that disputes should only be resolved bilaterally, as Beijing sought. The second was that the result of these negotiations would be only a declaration on desirable forms of behavior, not an actual code of conduct. China moved more closely to some agreement as ASEAN's concessions were made clear in 1991 and 1992. Then the Philippines backed down on its stipulation of a ban on new structures, which was replaced in Article 5 with an agreement simply not to inhabit uninhabited islands, reefs, and shoals.[6]

Valencia refers to China's policy up to this time as one of "three no's"—no specification of claims, no multilateral negotiations, and no internationalization. Some therefore viewed China's acquiescence to the 2002 Declaration on a Code of Conduct in the SCS as a turning point. Chung is probably more accurate in terming it "a triumph of diplomacy over substance" as it

- does not identify the area to which it applies: the entire SCS, or the Paracel and Spratly Islands, or only the Spratly Islands

- excludes Taiwan, other interested states such as Indonesia, Singapore, Thailand, Japan, the United States, and international organizations such as the United Nations

- does not prohibit erecting or improving/expanding structures on territory already occupied

- states that progress towards an actual Code must be "on the basis of consensus"

- did not invite other countries to associate themselves with the declaration.

As Chung states, however, this did allow the parties to concentrate on the economic portion of their relationship, announcing the next day a Framework Agreement on Comprehensive Economic Co-operation between the Association of South East Asian Nations and the People's Republic of China, with goal of a free trade area by 2010 for China, Brunei, Indonesia, Malaysia, the Philippines, and Singapore, and by 2015 for Cambodia, Laos, Myanmar, and Vietnam. In June 2003 China also signed the Treaty of Amity and Cooperation, ASEAN's foundational document requiring signatories to forgo activities threatening political and economic stability, sovereignty, or territorial integrity. In December 2004 China and ASEAN signed a Five-Year Plan of Action focusing on confidence- and trust-building in defense relations, dialogues and consultation on security issues, cooperation on training military personnel, joint military exercises, and peacekeeping operations.[7]

China's Motivations

It is worth attempting to discern the various possible motivations in Chinese policy toward the SCS in order to hypothesize concerning the extent to which compromise or new solutions are possible. One line of thought might fall roughly into the category of "defensive realism." One analyst emphasizes the role of walls in Chinese history and culture and sees the U-shaped line as southern parallel to Great Wall in north, with James Shoal as the perceived southernmost territory of China. In this view the late addition of this wall to China's strategic thinking is a reflection of the lack of threats from the south until Western industrialization and imperialism. Thus China's official delineation of its territory as including the SCS could be a "pre-emptive act, entered into to guard against future uncertainties, and, furthermore, entered into before any other national entity . . . had sought to decisively deal with issues of sovereignty in the SCS."[8]

While one might view these motivations as allowing for compromise down the line, there is a direct link to the more categorical "lost territories" theme. Citing *New Scramble for Soft Frontiers,* by Lt. Colonel Cui Yuchen of the research office of Chengdu military region, Buszynski notes that China has used the term "living space" extensively and has described the SCS as an area critical for fuel for industry and food for its people into the twenty-first century. This view was supported by Liu Huaqing, who had significant influence on naval doctrine in the 1970s and 1980s as commander of China's navy (1982–88) and vice chairman of China's Central Military Commission (1989–97). As commander of China's navy, Liu emphasized claims to the sea based on the "lost territories" theme. China's patrols and survey crews in 1987, a clash with Vietnamese vessels at Johnson Reef in 1988 and subsequent occupation of several reefs, and the formation of a naval headquarters for the South China Sea in 1989 can all be seen as an outgrowth of his influence and this way of thinking.[9]

There are other indications of a more offensively minded approach to the area. Holmes and Yoshihara describe a trend that could be away from defensive realism.[10] They note that Chinese planners look to Mahan, who instructs them that their contiguous waters are their domain and that dominant sea power is essential. This is in keeping with tradition as well because China has long considered the SCS a national preserve. Mahan's formula of "commerce, bases and shipping" means, among other things, that China needs bases such as Itu Iba, one of the largest in the Spratlys, as well as adjacent cays. Together, the authors note, these would constitute a presence superior to that of Mischief Reef. Beijing will also need, they argue, seagoing communications along the coast and northern edge of the SCS, where opponents could potentially foil operations against Taiwan. The drive for energy security only reinforces these needs.

Furthermore, Beijing is acquiring an ever-increasing ability to shape the security environment of Southeast Asia as well as the perceptions and policies of individual states. China's defense budget continues to experience a fifteen-year trend of double-digit increases, with current spending at between $35 billion and $105 billion and the 2007 budget slated to receive a nearly 18 percent increase in this second year of the current five-year spending plan. Spending is focused on a revolution in military affairs to include "informationization" and communication on force projection and on precision strikes to defeat enemy command, control, communications, and computers (C4) in short order. The military modernization programs were prompted and reinforced by a sequence of international developments, including the rapid U.S. victory in the first Gulf War, the 1996 Taiwan Strait crisis during which the PRC realized it could not then compete with the United States in an operational sense, and the errant U.S. bombing of the Chinese embassy in Belgrade in 1999.[11] The impact on procurement has been dramatic. To highlight only some of the naval and related purchases, Beijing has invested in second-generation nuclear and conventional submarines, frigates, destroyers with deadly antiship missiles, various platforms for amphibious force projection, army attack helicopters, and even aircraft carriers. By 2010 the numbers of destroyers will total up to forty-three; frigates, fifty-five; and submarines, sixty-two. Fourth- and fifth-generation strike fighters, fighter bombers, airborne warning and control system–like, close air support, and critical support aircraft are being developed, purchased, and upgraded.[12]

The transformation of the PLAN is aimed at exerting greater control over contiguous waters while deterring larger foes in conflict scenarios. Operationally, China's 2006 defense white paper claims the navy's strategy is to attain "gradual extension of strategic depth for offshore defensive operations and enhancing its capabilities in integrated maritime operations and nuclear counterattacks." According to Timothy Hu, central to this is "the establishment of a sea denial capability to prevent the U.S. Navy from being able to deploy into waters that cover what Chinese naval strategists call the Second Island Chain," stretching from the Japanese islands to Guam and the Marshall Islands. The PLAN's ambitious program of acquiring new classes of submarines will go far toward accomplishing these goals.[13]

While conflict scenarios over Taiwan and North Korea must be foremost in the minds of those responsible for the modernization program, much of the new weaponry provides capabilities and presence that will be relevant to a "post-Korea" and "post-Taiwan" world. The planned development and purchase of tanker aircraft, for example, will afford a new People's Liberation Army Air Force presence over the SCS. Put another way, if the central goal of the buildup has been to defeat Taiwan and deter the United States in a Taiwan conflict scenario, the effect is that by the end of this decade the PRC will have the ability, in the words of the U.S. Department of Defense, to defeat "a moderate-size adversary." These contradict such theses as David Shambaugh's earlier one that "there is scant evidence of the PLA developing capabilities to project power beyond China's immediate periphery."[14]

Indeed, once those conflicts are settled, it is likely Beijing will turn to securing its southern flank where, as with Taiwan, it has what it considers to be unsettled borders. Most potential adversaries there would rank smaller than medium-sized. Coterminous with this shift would be the development, as set forth in a China 2006 white paper on national defense, of the second long-term phase of defense development strategy, covering 2011 to 2020, of a military that might be comparable to that of any second-tier military power, including Japan, Russia, and some Western European countries. Both near- and medium-term plans and acquisitions will provide China with a preponderant naval and air presence in the SCS area.

Energy security and its role in economic development provide a further offensive-oriented set of motivations. Economic modernization has been the overriding goal of Chinese policy since 1978 and is a cornerstone of social harmony and political stability. Central to economic development, of course, is an available, secure, and affordable supply of resources and energy. Regarding energy, China has been a net importer of oil since 1993, with near double-digit economic growth and nearly a quarter of the world's population in a country with about 2.3 percent of proven oil reserves. Oil consumption is expected to reach 10.5 billion bpd by 2020. China will need to import approximately 7.0 million bpd, or up to 60 percent of its total, by 2020. Also, Chinese oil policy thus far conforms well to either a mercantilist or a Maoist doctrine of self-reliance.

Equally important in Beijing's calculations must be the growing demand in neighboring countries. Oil consumption alone in developing countries in Asia will rise by 3.0 percent annually through 2025, thus doubling by volume from about 15 million bpd currently to nearly 34 million. While China will be responsible for fully one-third of this increased demand, growth in other countries is equally important to domestic political and social needs, thus contributing to a "scramble" for whatever incremental oil and gas can be found locally.[15]

The SCS covers an area believed to possess significant amounts of hydrocarbon deposits, and Beijing publicly espouses a highly optimistic view of the oil and gas potential. In 1982 the president of China's geological society made extravagant predictions about the oil resources in the Spratly Island area. China conducted several oceanographic research excursions to the area in 1987, concluding publicly that the southernmost area of the archipelago probably contained substantial deposits. It is significant that the modern phase of armed conflict over conflicting territorial claims dates from this period, as Vietnam soon challenged China's attempts to build naval outposts, culminating in a shooting match and the sinking of a Vietnamese vessel in March 1988, followed the next month by China's occupation of six reefs.

Chinese analysts commonly argue that the SCS, including the Spratlys, could contain 105 billion barrels of oil and 25 billion cubic meters of gas.[16] Proven reserves are a mere 7 billion barrels of oil. A 1994 estimate by the U.S. Geological Survey estimated total reserves in the offshore basins of the entire Sea at 28 billion barrels. Current production is around 2.5 million bpd, with China, Malaysia, and Vietnam most recently increasing their production to contribute to that figure.[17] A common industry rule of thumb suggests that in frontier areas like the SCS, roughly 10–15 percent of projected reserves may be recoverable.

Natural gas usage among developing Asian countries will rise even faster than that of oil, at around 4.5 percent annually through 2025, meaning that demand will triple to more than 21 trillion cubic feet (Tcf) per year. Again, China projects optimistic figures, for example as high as 900 Tcf of recoverable natural gas for the Spratly area and 2,000 Tcf for the entire sea. Few outsiders agree with these estimates. The USGS has estimated all SCS natural gas at 266 Tcf.[18]

Two issues are noteworthy here. First, even a small but secure contribution could have a major positive impact on China's economic growth. Second, Beijing knowingly makes exaggerated claims about the resources believed to be exploitable in the area. Why? Most likely these lend some recognizable justifications to China's territorial claims and therefore some sense of legitimacy that it has a stake in the future of the region. Energy and economic concerns are recognized as legitimate by most states and suggest that there can be some non-zero-sum resolution based on sharing, cooperation or coordination.

If hydrocarbon deposits are depleted or found not to be economically viable, Beijing's claims to having a national interest in the SCS are weakened, and revert to simply historical or legalistic arguments. This would go far to explaining why China is considering drilling a field off the Philippine coast recently judged to be unprofitable, as discussed later.

The SCS is, finally, vital as a SLOC. Virtually all of China's overseas-sourced oil (close to 90 percent)—like much of its trading goods—transits the SCS. Beijing explained its perception of the Spratlys and Paracels as early as 1975 thus: "As it lies between the Indian Ocean and the Pacific, the South China Sea is a vital strategic area. It acts as a gateway to the outside world for the mainland and offshore islands of China. The archipelagoes occupy a position central to the shipping lanes connecting Guangzhou, Hong Kong, Manila and Singapore."[19]

Southeast Asia's Response

China's presence in the SCS continues to grow and with it, its ability to project power there. These new capabilities may give Beijing strong motivations to take a proactive or even aggressive posture regarding activities in the region and its right to control them. It is also clear that Southeast Asian states, at least if left to their own devices, do not appear interested or able to alter this trend line.

Southeast Asian states are certainly not balancing against a perceived China threat—that is, they are not strengthening themselves militarily to a significant extent nor are they forming strong alliances in order to confront a perceived near-term threat.[20] They are rather pursuing a mix of strategies.

Indonesian military leaders privately label China their country's greatest military threat with a major challenge being Chinese claims to the Natuna Islands and the islands' possible energy reserves. Yet Indonesia realizes that China is a major buyer of its bulk commodities and may be a more dependable supplier of weapons than the United States. It thus balances against China less than do Singapore, Thailand, and perhaps the Philippines.

The Singapore–Washington relationship is something between an alliance and a strong friendship. Singapore hosts the U.S. Navy's western logistics base and has built a pier at Changi Naval Base for U.S. carriers. For its part, Thailand remains a "major non-NATO ally" and yet engages with China on economic growth, criticizes Taiwan and Falun Gong, and has offered lukewarm support to the United States concerning Iraq. The Philippines, having clashed with China over Mischief Reef in 1995, the Campones Islands in 1996, and Scarborough Shoal in 1997, clearly perceives an external threat and has realized since the Mischief Reef incident that it is too weak to defend its claims. The Visiting Forces Agreement signed in 1998 and the 2003 Mutual Logistics Support Agreement led to the Philippines being labeled, along with Singapore and Thailand, a "major non-NATO ally" in 2003. Major joint exercises and a U.S. role in fighting the militant group Abu Sayyaf solidify the balancing nature of the Philippines' approach.

Vietnam and the United States have gone further down the road of full diplomatic normalization. The Bilateral Trade Agreement has increased trade dramatically, the states are cooperating on AIDS prevention, and high-level political visits have occurred. Vietnam continues to promote its claims in the SCS by pursuing deals on exploration and prospecting, and violence continues to flare, as in 2005 when Vietnamese fishermen strayed into Chinese waters. Vietnam supports a U.S. military presence and cooperates on counterterrorism, drugs, demining, search and rescue, and disaster relief. Vietnamese observers attend Cobra Gold, U.S. naval vessels now visit Vietnam, and the 2005 visit of the Vietnamese prime minister to Washington promised further cooperation.[21]

Malaysia and the United States have increasingly cooperated since 2001 with defense ties increasing, including a rapidly growing number of U.S. ship visits (e.g., that of the carrier USS *Stennis* in 2004), and providing jungle training for U.S. troops. The former Malaysian prime minister has said publicly that he does not consider the PRC a threat and that China should remain a constructive player. Serious disagreements remain between Malaysia and Brunei, as they do between Thailand and Cambodia.

The one unifying theme to ASEAN state responses is the attempt to use economic cooperation and engagement to manage security relations with China. This is not a new strategic innovation. It derives from a set of ideas about how states may use trade and other economic flows to structure anarchy in ways that create common interests among states, dampen security competition, and support an ordered international system in which the "expectation of war disappears" as states resolve conflicts through "judicial processes, not coercive bargaining."[22] In fact, these ideas have been a constant guiding principle of U.S. policy since the end of the World War II. "It was America," writes Thomas Friedman in *The Lexus and the Olive Tree*, "that drove the creation of the International Monetary Fund, the General Agreement on Tariffs and Trade (GATT) and a host of other institutions for opening markets and fostering trade around the world. And it was the American fleet that kept the sea lanes open for these markets to easily connect."[23]

There is also a prevalent notion that China's transition from a command- to market-oriented economy has generated a significant Chinese interest in integrating peacefully into the present international system.[24]

There are at least two potential problems with this notion in general and its relation to the situation in the SCS. First, the very logic that links liberalism's economic and political constraints against force to international peace may prove unsound. One should not assume that growing economic linkages between China and the ASEAN countries will automatically resolve SCS disputes. In addition, it is possible that small, less complex economies will feel more constrained than will China as economic integration proceeds. This would be particularly true if China continues to work on a bilateral basis to resolve disputes in the SCS, because on the single country level, China plays a bigger role in the economies of Vietnam, Malaysia, Indonesia, and the Philippines than each of them alone does in the Chinese economy.

Ripe for Renewed Confrontation

There are hopeful signs of decreased tension. When China published a map in the 1990s with unclear boundaries, which suggested that the highly productive Natuna gas fields—estimated to contain 5 Tcf of recoverable gas—could fall within Chinese territory, Indonesia held large military exercises and accelerated gas production, with no response from Beijing. The Philippines linked the Malampaya and Camago fields, which lie in waters claimed by China and contain an estimated 2.6 Tcf of natural gas, to three power plants, with no protest by China. China has not objected specifically to Malaysia's exploration of gas fields off Sarawak, also within Chinese claimed waters. Vietnam and China have of course resolved their disputes in the Tonkin Gulf.

Superficially, China's behavior toward SCS conflicts seems to be a "calculative" strategy of seeking resolution on minor issues but postponing essential disputes.[25] The earlier strident claims and military occupations and reinforcements may have given way to a new interest in joint development.[26] The March 2005 Agreement on Tripartite Marine Seismic Work with Manila and Hanoi is a case in point. The Chinese ship *Nanhai* (Hull 502) gathers data which are sent to Vietnam for processing and finally analyzed by experts in the Philippines. Beijing may also have shifted its view of ASEAN and multilateral institutions from that of puppets of the United States to potential allies and assets that must be won over. Concomitant with this has been a nascent shift in self-perception from one of victim to one of burgeoning world power.[27] Some ministries may have concluded that there is a small window of opportunity for maintaining rapid growth, overall strength, and competitiveness.[28]

On the other hand, this chapter has highlighted several issues suggesting that the SCS may be an area ripe for renewed confrontation. First, there is an asymmetry of motivations with respect to the claims made by the PRC and its neighbors and the United States, with China's motivations stronger and likely of longer, if not permanent (or until the territorial issue is settled), duration. A trio of motivations—in particular, nationalism and territoriality, energy security, and influence over vital SLOC—will naturally drive Beijing to exert greater presence and control.

Furthermore, most arguments about dramatically altered perceptions in Beijing are based on very recent short-term trends with limited data or insight into motivations. Beijing needs to be taken at its word (and at the word of its national legislation) that it considers all of the SCS to be sovereign territory. While it may not now be able to enforce right-of-transit approval, the PLAN is developing means that in the future may allow it to do so. And when China is confronted with problems that have no win–win solution and are matters of important national interests—as in dam-building along the Mekong River system—Beijing has shown that it chooses brutal self-interest over cooperation with smaller states.[29]

Recent signs of improved relations do not necessarily bode well for the longer term in the absence of resolution of territorial and resource disputes. First, as this book goes to press, China is considering drilling the Malampaya reserve fields off the Philippine coast, which had been abandoned as unprofitable by Royal Dutch Shell and Chevron, with a possible target date in early 2009. Holding enough reserves to supply China for only four days and costing up to $1 billion to drill, the Malampaya fields might be used by China to gain Philippine concessions for exploring disputed waters near the Spratly Islands that may contain larger reserves.[30] It is unlikely that such benevolence will endure in the event that Beijing spends less money in these areas.

Second, economic integration is unlikely to serve as a realistic strategy for constraining China on matters of vital or important national interests. Beijing views a China-owned or -dominated SCS as an important national interest. Smaller, less diversified economies in the region are likely to feel both more constrained and less motivated to contest a growing Chinese presence in the region. They are not balancing against Chinese power in any substantive way now; even the United States' closest friends are barely "hedging," but rather are merely walking a fine line aimed at avoiding controversy and bad feelings.

Third, there are no clear indications of serious movement away from territorial claims and toward any kind of internationally or multilaterally administered solution. Limited multinational exploration is far from a multinational settlement on the territorial and resource issues. As noted earlier, the 2002 ASEAN Declaration does not address the underlying claims or commit any side to actions that will ameliorate the basic conflicts.

It must also be remembered that most of the recent "good feelings" have come during a time of continued, hopeful exploration. Should the hydrocarbon boon prove disappointing, other issues could move to the fore, including old animosities, the freedom-of-the-seas implications of national prestige (e.g., China's demanding the right to approve transit), and the role of the SCS in a Taiwan contingency, among others. And the current limited cooperation will legitimize China's presence in contested areas: when the China–Vietnam–Philippines joint exploration arrangement moves into the exploitation phase next year, China's presence will be legitimized to a greater extent than ever in a 54,000-square-mile area.

This leaves a creeping importance of the SCS in China's political consciousness coupled with that nation's growing presence and military power, including an expanding power projection capability for the SCS and continued reliance upon economic integration by a number of smaller neighbors with no significant coercive capacity. For the United States, whose national interests in freedom of navigation and SLOC security depend heavily on the political disposition of these states, it should be cause to rethink the largely legalistic position held on the territorial and resource disputes in the SCS, namely, that the United States does not take a position on territorial disputes there. As far as energy security is concerned, China relies to a small extent on gas fields in the South and East China Seas to fuel its economic growth. Yet these maritime regions' real energy security importance comes from their role as vital oil and gas transport corridors through which supplies flow not just to the PRC, but also to Taiwan, South Korea, and Japan. Should the optimistic and hopeful scenarios not pan out, and should there be a movement back toward territorial claims, the PLAN will be in a much better position than previously to enforce them.[31] U.S. policy and naval presence will then also be more important.

Notes

1. See Energy Information Administration, Country Analysis Briefs, South China Sea, March 2006, http://www.eia.doe.gov/emeu/cabs/South_China_Sea/Background. html, and Energy Information Administration, "World Oil Transit Chokepoints: Malacca," http://www.eia.doe.gov/emeu/cabs/World_Oil_Transit_Chokepoints/ Malacca.html.

2. Standard works include Greg Austin, *China's Ocean Frontier* (St. Leonards, NSW: Allen and Unwin, 1998); Mark J. Valencia, Jon M. Van Dyke, and Noel A. Ludwig, *Sharing the Resources of the South China Sea* (Honolulu: University of Hawaii Press, 1997); Lee Lai To, *China and the South China Sea Dialogues* (Westport, Conn.: Praeger, 1999); Liselotte Odgaard, *Maritime Security Between China and Southeast Asia* (Burlington, Vt.: Ashgate, 2002); and Christopher Chung, *The Spratly Islands Dispute: Decision Units and Domestic Politics* (PhD thesis, University of New South Wales, 2004).

3. Valencia, Van Dyke, and Ludwig, *Sharing the Resources*, 8–9.

4. Austin, *China's Ocean Frontier*, chs. 1, 4; see also Ulises Granados, "As China Meets the Southern Sea Frontier: Ocean Identity in the Making, 1902–1937," *Pacific Affairs* 78, no. 3 (2005): 443–52. Vietnam did challenge China's claims in a session of the San Francisco Peace Conference in 1951.

5. Carlyle Thayer, "China's 'New Security Concept' and Southeast Asia," in *Asia-Pacific Security: Policy Challenges*, David W. Lovell, ed. (Singapore: ISEAS, 2003), 101; Leszek Buszynski, "ASEAN, the Declaration on Conduct, and the South China Sea," *Contemporary Southeast Asia* 25, no. 3 (2003): 343–58.

6. Buszynski, "ASEAN, the Declaration on Conduct, and the South China Sea," 343–58.

7. Chris Chung, "The South China Sea Dispute," unpublished manuscript, November 2006. For relevant agreements see *ASEAN Document Series 2005*, 198–216, and *ASEAN Document Series 2004*, 291–312, at http://www.aseansec.org/16805.htm.

8. Peter Kien-Hong Yu, "Setting Up International (Adversary) Regimes in the South China Sea: Analyzing the Obstacles from a Chinese Perspective," *Ocean Development and International Law* 38 (2007): 147–56.

9. Buszynski, "ASEAN, the Declaration on Conduct, and the South China Sea."

10. This entire paragraph draws on James Holmes and Toshi Yoshihara, "China's 'Caribbean' in the South China Sea," *SAIS Review* 26, no. 1 (2006): 79–92.

11. *Jane's Defence Weekly*, 25 April 2007; Jane's Sentinel Security Assessment—China and Northeast Asia, 22 March 2007. PRC defense expenditures remain at approximately 1.5 percent of GDP.

12. Ibid.; Federation of American Scientists, "PLA Navy Facilities," www.fas.org/man/dod-101/sys/ship/row/plan/index.html.

13. Timothy Hu, "China—Marching Forward," *Jane's Defence Weekly*, 18 April 2007. http://www8.janes.com.

14. David Shambaugh, "China Engages Asia: Reshaping the Regional Order," *International Security* 29, no. 3 (Winter 2004/05): 64–99, at 86.

15. "South China Sea Country Analysis Brief, Background," Energy Information Administration, http://www.eia.doe.gov/emeu/cabs/South_China_Sea/Background.html.

16. 张玉坤, 张慧 [Zhang Yukun and Zhang Hui], 戍海固边: 海上安全环境与海洋权益维护 [*Defend the Sea with a Solid Boundary: The Maritime Security Environment and the Defense of Maritime Rights and Interests*] (Beijing: Sea Tide Press, 2003), 39.

17. Energy Information Administration, "South China Sea," http://www.eia.doe.gov/emeu/cabs/South_China_Sea/Background.html.

18. Energy Information Country Analysis Briefs, South "China Sea," United States Department of Energy, Energy Information Adminstration, March 2006, http://www.eia.doe.gov/emeu/cabs/South_China_Sea/Background.html.

19. John Wesley Jackson, "China in the South China Sea: Genuine Multilateralism or a Wolf in Sheep's Clothing?" M.A. thesis, Naval Postgraduate School, 2005, 25.

20. Stephen Brooks and William Wohlforth, "Hard Times for Soft Balancing," *International Security* 30, no. 1 (2005): 72–108.

21. Ian James Storey, "Creeping Assertiveness: China, the Philippines and the South China Sea Dispute," *Contemporary Southeast Asia* 21, no. 1 (1999): 95–118.

22. Michael Doyle, *Ways of War and Peace* (New York: Norton, 1997), 210, 293.

23. Thomas Friedman, *The Lexus and the Olive Tree* (New York: Anchor, 2000), 253.

24. See Bijian Zheng, "China's Peaceful Rise to Great Power Status," *Foreign Affairs* 84 (2005): 18–24.

25. Michael Swaine and Ashley Tellis, *Interpreting China's Grand Strategy: Past, Present and Future* (Washington, D.C.: RAND, 2000).

26. Zou Keyuan, "Joint Development in the South China Sea: A New Approach," *International Journal of Marine and Coastal Law* 21, no. 1 (2006): 83–109.

27. Evan Medeiros and M. Taylor Fravel, "China's New Diplomacy," *Foreign Affairs* 82, no. 6 (2003), http://www.foreignaffairs.org/20031101faessay82604/evan-s-medeiros-m-taylor-fravel/china-s-new-diplomacy.html.

28. Frank Frost, "Directions in China's Foreign Relations: Implications for East Asia and Australia," Research Brief no. 9, 2005, Parliamentary Library, Parliament of Australia, http://www.aph.gov.au/Library/pubs/rb/2005-06/06rb09.htm; David Shambaugh, "China Engages Asia: Reshaping the Regional Order," *International Security* 29, no. 3 (2004–5): 64–99; Kuik Cheng-Chwee, "Multilateralism in China's ASEAN Policy: Its Evolution, Characteristics, and Aspiration," *Contemporary Southeast Asia* 27, no. 1 (2005): 102–23.

29. Alex Liebman, "Trickle-down Hegemony? China's 'Peaceful Rise' and Dam-building on the Mekong," *Contemporary Southeast Asia* 27, no. 2 (2005): 281–305.

30. "China May Drill Philippine Oil that Shell, Chevron Rejected," 29 November 2005, http://www.bloomberg.com/apps/news?pid=10000087&sid=anrzFgfRSYtY&refer=top_world_news.

31. See Bernard Cole, "Oil for the Lamps of China: Beijing's 21st Century Search for Energy," McNair Paper 67, Institute for National Strategic Studies, National Defense University, 2003, 20, http://www.ndu.edu/inss/mcnair/mcnair67/198_428.McNair.pdf.

PART III

China's Naval Development and Concerns Regarding Energy Access Denial

Gabriel B. Collins, Andrew S. Erickson,
and Lyle J. Goldstein

Chinese Naval Analysts Consider the Energy Question

AS CHINA RISES ON THE WORLD STAGE, one of countless interesting uncertainties concerns a possible intersection between China's developing energy strategy, on the one hand, and emergent Chinese naval strategy on the other. Beijing's extremely brisk economic development has vaulted China into the upper ranks of the world's oil importers.[1] China's seaborne oil imports continue to comprise more than 80 percent of total oil imports. While China obtains nearly one-third of its oil imports from Africa and has reduced its Middle Eastern oil import share by roughly 20 percent in recent years, it still faces serious maritime energy security concerns. In 2006, 76 percent of Chinese oil imports came from the Middle East and Africa. Whether this oil comes from Saudi Arabia, Angola, or Sudan, it must cross the long Indian Ocean sea lanes and pass through the Strait of Malacca.

Against this strategic backdrop, it is not surprising that some Chinese naval analysts believe that China needs the military capacity to protect its long and increasingly vital maritime energy supply lines.[2] In recent years, particularly since the mid-1990s, the pace of Chinese naval modernization has accelerated. Interestingly, this growth is not limited to diesel submarines, as one might expect of a Taiwan-centric Chinese military strategy, but also includes impressive surface combatants. These simultaneous trends have prompted some to suggest that there may be a strong linkage between China's energy and maritime strategies. Indeed, the U.S. Department of Defense's 2007 annual report to Congress, *Military Power of the People's Republic of China*, states that "China has . . . offered economic assistance and military cooperation with countries located astride key maritime transit routes. Concern over these routes has also prompted China to pursue maritime capabilities that would help it ensure the safe passage of resources through international waterways."[3]

On 27 December 2006 in a speech to People's Liberation Army Navy (PLAN) officers attending a Communist Party meeting, Chinese president Hu Jintao declared, "we should strive to build a powerful navy that adapts to the needs of our military's historical mission in this new century and at this new stage" and is prepared "at any time" for military struggle.[4] "In the process of protecting the nation's authority and security and maintaining our maritime rights," Hu emphasized, "the navy's role is very important."[5] Hu added that China's "navy force should be strengthened and modernized"[6] and should continue moving toward blue water capabilities.[7] China's 2006 defense white paper offers further detail in support of Hu's assertions, stating that China's "Navy aims at gradual extension of the strategic depth for offshore defensive operations and enhancing its capabilities in integrated maritime operations and nuclear counterattacks."[8] There is a disparity between China's defense white paper, which hardly mentions energy, and the U.S. Department of Defense's report, which discusses energy as a major factor in China's military development. It is therefore necessary to further examine the extent to which China possesses, and will seek to develop, military capabilities to secure its substantial, rapidly growing seaborne energy imports.

The maritime dimensions of China's emerging energy strategy have received considerable attention from scholars and analysts, both inside and outside the People's Republic of China (PRC). Wu Lei, a leading China energy security expert at Yunnan University, explains: "The fact that China's future energy supply is overly dependent on the sea lanes and the fear that the U.S. might cut them off . . . drives much of Beijing's modernization of its navy."[9] In a comprehensive survey of China's energy security by the National Bureau of Asian Research, Kenneth Lieberthal and Mikkal Herberg also point out that "China's increasing dependency on [sea-borne] oil flows . . . is potentially accelerating China's development of the naval capabilities necessary to protect those lanes."[10]

Yet despite significant discussion of why China might not be willing to simply continue free riding on U.S. naval protection of its oil imports, few researchers have attempted to comprehensively analyze energy related writings in Chinese naval and maritime publications. In fact, Chinese maritime writings have become extremely prolific in recent years. There are at least five serious PRC professional publications concerned with naval warfare.[11] In addition, a variety of new books have appeared that discuss the direction of Chinese naval development; in fact, entire publishing houses appear to have been formed around this emerging theme.[12] This chapter will survey the maritime energy security discussions conducted by Chinese naval and energy analysts.

In Chinese naval and energy security source materials, maritime energy security discussions are not pervasive. There are two key reasons for this. First, with the exception of three short periods, the PRC has lacked a central energy ministry with real authority over other energy sector players.[13] Second, analysts are apparently forbidden to publish on certain sensitive topics. For example, a well-informed Chinese scholar recently told one of the authors that "although China is not pursuing a 'String of Pearls' strategy [in the Indian Ocean], we are nonetheless forbidden to publish on that topic."[14] The dearth of specific Chinese sources on maritime energy security makes it vital to consult a wide range of Chinese naval and energy security writings in order to glean insights into the maritime dimension of China's energy strategy.

A simple survey of China's official naval journal, 当代海军 (*Modern Navy*), from 2003–6 reveals only a small number of articles devoted to maritime energy issues. Nevertheless, these articles express major concern with respect to China's energy vulnerability. Moreover, China's naval weakness is highlighted as a major contributing factor to this vulnerability. The tenor of these concerns suggests a strong disinclination by Chinese naval strategists to accept U.S. or Western control over Beijing's "oil lifeline" ("石油生命线").[15] There is no question that this unease helps to fuel China's naval buildup. However, one interesting finding of this study is that Chinese naval analysts are attuned to the complicated reality of China's energy challenge, and express a clear readiness to engage in cooperation with other oil-consuming great powers, including the United States, to secure oil and gas supply stability. In the end, it seems that Beijing is opting for an energy "hedging" strategy that includes diplomatic, commercial, and military aspects, among which the naval component features relatively prominently.

This analysis of energy discussions among Chinese naval analysts will proceed in six steps. First, a context for the naval strategy discussion will be established by briefly examining the broader trends in both energy and naval strategy. Second, the chapter will investigate the distinct maritime ideology that has emerged in China over the last decade and its focus on developing and protecting off-shore resources for China's national development. The third section of the chapter will describe the geostrategic challenges China faces in protecting a supply chain that stretches deep into the Middle East and Africa. The fourth will assess the calculations of China's naval analysts concerning possible threats to this critical energy sea line of communication (SLOC). Bearing these threat assessments in mind, the fifth section will evaluate the recommendations of these analysts regarding the future trajectory of China's fleet development. A final section describes the (somewhat surprisingly) ample cooperative aspects of these naval writings on Chinese energy strategy.

The Context for Naval and Energy Strategy Development

Naval and energy policy vectors are developing within the context of China's peaceful development strategy, and more broadly in a global strategic environment at least partly conditioned by China's "new diplomacy."[16] Beijing's newly agile foreign policy fully develops soft power principles in featuring highly skilled diplomats, a plethora of commercial initiatives, a flexible approach to a variety of previously intractable problems, and dramatic new willingness to shoulder responsibilities for upholding international order (e.g., peacekeeping). There is no question that China's primary focus is on its internal development—it is reassuring, for example, that Beijing's upgrading of road and rail infrastructure seems to have higher priority than the development of many weapons systems. This priority is fully consistent with the emergence of China's fourth generation leadership, which is noteworthy for its lack of experience in military affairs.

Nevertheless, China's military has made dramatic improvements in the last decade, no doubt largely due to the vastly improved economic situation. A major achievement of Chinese foreign policy during this period is that Beijing's continental flanks are now almost entirely secure. This has enabled Chinese military development to focus on improving aerospace and maritime capabilities. The Taiwan contingency has served as a precursor for the creation of the world's most capable conventional, tactical ballistic missile force. China has imported several hundred advanced fighter aircraft from Russia and has now begun serial production of its own indigenous fourth generation fighter aircraft in parallel. Improvements are also evident in the crucial arena of intelligence, surveillance, and reconnaissance capabilities. China's naval development has clearly accelerated. A priority on undersea warfare is evident: China has been building four classes of submarines simultaneously. The "Song incident" near Okinawa on 26 October 2006, when a Chinese diesel submarine reportedly penetrated the protective screen of the U.S. Navy's *Kitty Hawk* carrier battle group in the vicinity of Okinawa, might suggest a new era of skill and confidence among China's submarine skippers.[17] Clear improvements in antiship missiles, high-speed attack vessels, amphibious warfare, and—above all—air defense, when coupled with the improvements described earlier in the aerospace realm, explain why Beijing apparently has increasing confidence that it "controls" the Taiwan issue.[18] Whereas strategic debates have focused on Taiwan contingencies over the last decade, the new strategic questions concern China's wider regional, and potentially global, ambitions.

To answer such questions, it will be critical to understand the state of China's current debate over energy strategy. Chinese energy security writings have become prolific in recent years, reflecting a vigorous national debate among civilian experts and scholars. "Economic liberals" like Zha Daojiong of People's University in Beijing argue that China's path to energy security lies in greater integration with the existing global energy market.[19] Doing so is cheaper and aligns Beijing more closely with the oil-consuming powers that share many of its core interests in this sphere. The liberal approach enables China to benefit from a "mutual fund" effect, in which China's energy risks are lowered because its interests become tightly interwoven with those of other major "investors" in a world oil system that benefits all major consumers and that none wish to disturb.

By contrast, "neomercantilists" such as Zhang Wenmu of Beijing University of Aeronautics & Astronautics take a darker view based on the zero-sum premise that oil supplies are running out and that each consumer must fight for an exclusive piece of the pie.[20] A neomercantilist approach to energy security is driven by distrust of the global oil market and entails paying whatever it takes to secure access to reserves, emphasizing bilateral state-to-state deals, and building up a military force that can secure one's energy supply lines. World Security Institute researchers emphasize Chinese concerns that the United States has shown a "proclivity to embrace oil sanctions and blockades in exercising coercive diplomacy" and that "denial and coercion have been the hallmarks of U.S. oil strategy toward adversaries."[21]

China's petroleum security strategy is evolving as the National Development and Reform Commission and other Chinese energy policy-making bodies realize that equity oil (i.e., direct ownership of oil reserves) does not guarantee oil security. Instead of the previous exclusive focus on securing overseas oil production, the new aim may be to control the transport of oil back to China.[22] For further details concerning China's apparent development of a national tanker fleet for this purpose, see the chapter by Gabriel Collins and Andrew Erickson in this volume.

China's increased emphasis on the mid- and downstream segments of its oil and gas supply chain has direct military implications. Protecting upstream assets (oil fields) is very difficult and requires that substantial ground forces enter a sovereign country and secure the area. Defending midstream assets (e.g., tankers at sea) is more feasible but requires robust naval and aviation capabilities.[23] At present, it seems plausible that China's rapid naval and aerospace force modernization might be driven in part by the perception that China requires the capability to protect its resource supply lines in a crisis.

The Role of Energy in China's New Maritime Ideology

China's new maritime ideology is composed of a number of elements. There is a historical fascination with the exceptional Zheng He episode of the Ming Dynasty. There is an evident determination to grasp an ever-larger share of the world shipbuilding industry, as well as container transport and port operations. But there is also a natural resource/energy component to this emerging ideology that is somewhat Malthusian in character. The logic is that extensive foreign resources are required to sustain China's current growth trajectory and, moreover, that some of the most critical of these required (energy) resources are located along China's maritime periphery. Finally, U.S. military activism in the greater Middle East over the last five years has conditioned the views of Chinese security analysts toward energy questions.

Despite its largely insular and continental history, China appears to be decisively turning to the sea as its trade relationships blossom and resource demand grows. In 2006 maritime industries accounted for $270 billion in economic output (nearly 10 percent of GDP).[24] While the Ming dynasty admiral-navigator Zheng He has become an iconic figure for contemporary China, it is also recognized that he is an exceptional figure in modern Chinese history. As early as the 1980s Chinese intellectuals criticized "the mentality of a servile, static, and defensive people who always meekly hug to mother earth to eke out a miserable living, rather than boldly venturing forth on the dangerous deep blue sea in search of a freer, more exalted existence."[25] This movement, which was quite consistent with the "reform and opening up" (改革开放) ethic of the Deng Xiaoping era, asked "How can the 'yellow' culture of the earth be transformed into the 'blue' culture of the ocean?"[26]

China's new maritime ideology should not be underestimated and does appear to serve as a fundamental basis for developing Chinese naval strategy. What is interesting for the purposes of this study, however, is that energy resources appear to have a distinctly important role within this ideology.

A series of naval strategy books published in the PRC during 2003 under the overarching theme of "The Chinese Nation and the Ocean" establishes a relatively firm link between naval strategy and resource concerns in China. The introduction to one of these books, 蓝色方略 (*The Blue Strategy*), explains that "in today's world, the population is growing as land-based resources are depleted. Conflict and competition over maritime rights and interests are intensifying with each passing day."[27] Another book in the series, 卫海强军 (*A Mighty Force to Protect the Sea*), suggests that "whether or not the serious resource question is resolved will strongly impact how China's development strategy is realized, and whether China can accomplish its rise and rejuvenation." China's ability to resolve "the serious resource question" in a manner that supports its development strategy will require new "resource space" (资源空间) that can only be found in maritime domains.[28] A third book in the series, 戍海固边 (*Defend the Sea with a Solid Boundary*), observes that "turning to ocean resources and also to foreign resources has become a crucial strategic step for sustaining national economic development." In anxious tones, the authors relate, "The world has begun to enter a new era of competition and carving up of the ocean."[29]

Demonstrating that a link between naval and economic power is now well accepted in China, Alfred Thayer Mahan's dictum that commerce is vital to maritime power, and that the best way to threaten and defend it is by engaging the naval forces in decisive battle is pervasive and cited in particular in a recent book by two Chinese naval officers, 海上力量与中华民族的伟大复兴 (*Sea Power and the Chinese Nation's Mighty Resurgence*).[30] Published by the PLA National Defense University in Beijing, it emphasizes the critical role of controlling sea lanes for the purposes of developing sea power, as well as developing the nation's economy. Its authors contend that sea powers have generally enjoyed great geostrategic advantages over land powers—an argument with major implications for China's future development. Once again stressing the link between economic and naval power, the two naval officers note, "from an economic power standpoint, maritime civilizations . . . are far superior to continental civilizations."[31]

Particularly relevant to this discussion of energy security, the authors observe that continental powers have frequently been surrounded and blockaded with considerable strategic effect. Taking a broad look at China's strategic environment, they suggest that "the continental threat to China has dramatically decreased, while maritime threats are increasing on a daily basis."[32] One of the critical reasons for the deterioration of the security situation on China's maritime flank is said to be that its "natural resources are being plundered . . . [for example] in the South China Sea."[33]

Recent American actions have greatly influenced the views of Chinese analysts with respect to energy security. According to a 2004 article on energy security in China's foremost naval journal, 当代海军 (Modern Navy), "The 9.11 events gave the United States an opportunity to assert greater control over the oil-rich Middle East. The wars in Afghanistan and Iraq ensured that Middle Eastern oil and gas was 'in the bag' for the United States."[34] Looking beyond the Middle East to the U.S.–Russian pipeline diplomacy in the Caucasus of the 1990s, this PLAN analyst takes an important lesson: "The competition was not market- or economic-type competition, but rather was a competition to control oil." There is little doubt that the situation in the contemporary Middle East has made an impression. The author of this analysis relates: "The great powers compete for oil [because whichever state] controls the oil can also control the lifeblood of other countries' economic development, [but whichever state] controls the Middle East can control that of the [entire] world economy." Such perceptions are important. If Chinese policymakers see the oil market as U.S. controlled and unreliable and come to doubt Washington's willingness to impartially keep critical oil SLOC open, they might push hard to create a blue water navy. Such actions could mark a strategic tipping point in the Sino–American relationship and could set off a cascade effect of more assertive SLOC security policies by Japan and other major oil importers.

China's New "Grand Canal"

Over a millennium ago the Grand Canal connecting Hangzhou in central China with Beijing in the north became a critical artery for the dynamic growth of Chinese civilization. Over the last decade, the SLOC connecting China to the Middle East and Africa has assumed a similarly vital role as a major "center of gravity" for China's future economic development. A recent article by a PLAN senior captain in the renowned journal 中国军事科学 (China Military Science) illustrates China's growing global maritime interests, stating that today "[China's] open ocean transport routes pass through every continent and every ocean [and] through each important international strait [to] over six hundred ports in over 150 nations and [administrative] regions" and projects that "by 2020, China's maritime commerce will exceed U.S. $1 trillion. It may be[come] necessary to import three-quarters of [China's] oil from overseas."[35] Chinese defense intellectuals have clearly seized on energy SLOC security as a major issue, as evidenced by an edited volume published by the China Institute of Contemporary International Relations (CICIR), which states, "because oil is the most essential commodity of international trade, [SLOC] are also oil channels on the sea."[36] In addition, the PLA's first English-language volume on strategy, *The Science of Military Strategy*, emphasizes that to "ensure the security of [the] channel[s] of [our] strategic energy supply is . . . of great significance to our development in the long run."[37]

China's modern strategists envision their nation as having four strategic sea lanes: east, south, west, and north. The "Western SLOC" (西行航线), running from the Indian Ocean, through the Malacca Strait, to the South China Sea, and finally to the Chinese mainland has particular strategic value for China. Carrying 80 percent of Chinese oil imports, it is "China's 'lifeline' of economic development."[38] Chinese analysts believe that "without SLOC security, one cannot have energy security" and are concerned that more than 75 percent of China's seaborne oil imports flow through a few key maritime arteries.[39] This seemingly disproportionate concentration stems from the fact that even in the modern era, geography, prevailing winds, ocean currents, and weather patterns determine the safest and most efficient maritime shipping routes.[40] Shippers would likely only consider alternate routes if customers were willing to bear the additional transport costs, an unlikely prospect in an era of razor-thin profit margins for a large proportion of consumer goods.

Many Chinese analysts have worked to identify ways to bypass these established routes, but thus far few of their plans appear likely to substantially alter established global oil shipping lanes. According to a map that appeared in the October 2006 issue of 现代舰船 (*Modern Ships*) (see map 1), such alternative routes could in the future include an oil pipeline from Siberia, a pipeline from Pakistan, one running into China from the Burmese port of Sittwe, and finally the just-completed Kazakhstan pipeline that carries oil into western China. The accompanying analysis, however, is skeptical that these pipelines could solve China's "Malacca Problem." Regarding Russia, for example, it is suggested that Moscow's evident distrust of China means that the Kremlin "will not accept putting its lifeline under the control of another great power." Conversely, CICIR scholar Zhang Xuegang maintains that a proposed canal across Thailand's Kra Isthmus "could . . . provide a strategic seaway to the Chinese navy" through which "fleets could . . . more easily protect the nearby sea-lanes and gain access to the Indian Ocean."[41]

Map 1. Conceptual Map of Key Current and Potential Future Chinese Oil Transport Routes

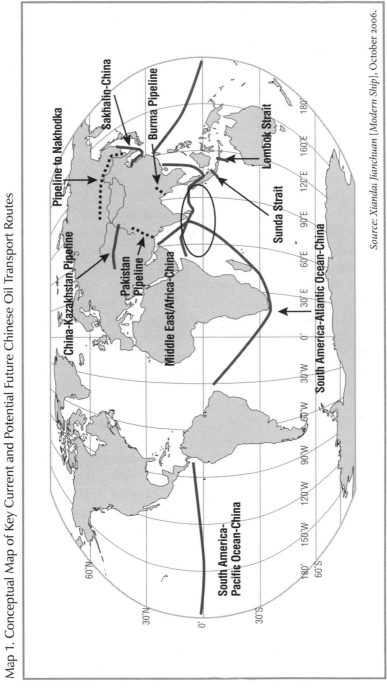

Source: *Xiandai Jianchuan* [*Modern Ship*], October 2006.

In general, it is held that land-based oil pipelines will help diversify China's oil import channels to some extent but that they cannot replace maritime oil transport. Available overland supplies from Russia and Kazakhstan and other areas are insufficient to offset China's rapidly growing seaborne oil imports. Also, offloading seaborne crude in Burma or Pakistan to avoid Malacca makes little economic sense because relatively small volumes of crude will have to be pumped at very high cost to interior parts of China, far from the booming East Coast demand centers, and then redistributed once again from the pipeline termini to main consuming areas.

Moreover, regarding the various pipeline projects, it is suggested that "land-based oil pipelines are China's necessary choice for oil import diversification, and will no doubt advance China's oil security, but land-based pipelines cannot replace the role of sea-borne oil transport, [so] it is not possible to cast off the maritime transport [problem]."[42] Moreover, regarding the various pipeline projects, it is suggested that "actually, the greatest threat to Chinese oil transport through the Malacca Strait is neither piracy, nor terrorism, but rather the massive sea power of the United States. The China-Pakistan and China-Burma pipelines will not diminish the hidden threat to China's oil transport from the United States, Japan and India."[43] Another article in 舰船知识 (*Naval & Merchant Ships*) states more succinctly, "SLOC security is much more important than pipeline transport lines."[44]

It is therefore reasonable to assume that China will continue to rely on the Indian Ocean sea lanes, the Malacca and Hormuz Straits, and the South and East China Seas as its primary oil import channels.

Chinese writers have dubbed the Strait of Hormuz the "Oil Strait" (石油海峡) because China obtains approximately 40 percent to 45 percent of its oil imports from the Middle East, the vast majority of which must flow through Hormuz.[45] Chinese analysts recognize the Middle East's instability, noting that since 1951, ten of sixteen major global oil supply disruptions have originated in the region.[46] Nevertheless, they realize that despite a concerted campaign to diversify away from the Middle East, China will remain heavily reliant on the region for much of its oil supplies. Indeed, a recent PRC analysis notes that over the next ten to fifteen years, oil imports to East Asia through the straits of Hormuz and Malacca will increase, and by 2020 China could be importing nearly 4 million barrels per day of oil from the Middle East (over twice the current average level of 1.5 million barrels per day).[47] Chinese analysts pointedly note that "all [the] oil that China imports from the Middle East and Africa has to go through the Straits of Hormuz and Malacca, but [they] are beyond the reach of the PLAN's power."[48]

Chinese analysts worry about the Hormuz Strait's vulnerability but are even more concerned about Malacca, which they call East Asia's "maritime lifeline" (海上生命线).[49] Eighty percent of Chinese oil imports flow through Malacca, including virtually all of China's imports from the Middle East and Africa (the latter of which represents 26 percent of China's total).[50] For this reason, states one Chinese source, "the Malacca Strait is China's maritime oil lifeline, for China's economic security it is akin to breathing itself."[51]

Chinese naval analysts fear that Malacca, which "has become the strategic throat of China's energy and economic security,"[52] "is extremely narrow, easy to blockade" (十分狭窄，易于封锁).[53] "Whoever controls the Strait of Malacca," therefore, "effectively grips China's strategic energy passage, and can threaten China's energy security at any time. Moreover, China must enter the world; the PLAN must enter the ocean, and has to pass through the Strait of Malacca."[54] These factors produce substantial Chinese concern: "Currently, 95% of China's oil imports are transported by sea; of these, 80% transit the Malacca Strait. This strait is easy to blockade . . . but [this mission] is beyond the power of China's Navy, so that if this occurs, then China's resource security will be gravely compromised."[55]

Chinese naval writings mention piracy and terrorism as threats to the oil flow through Malacca, noting that "in 2001 alone, there were over 600 piracy incidents."[56] The foremost concern, however, is clearly the strong U.S. presence in the region, which has increased with the ongoing global war on terror. China is uneasy with growing U.S.–Singapore security cooperation and the notion that the United States appears to be cementing its regional strategic position under the guise of "combating terrorism." Chinese analysts reserve special scrutiny for what they regard as an American chokepoint control strategy. As quoted in an article in 现代舰船 (Modern Ships), "former National Security Advisor Brzezinski stated revealingly: the Malacca Strait is a key sea area, the control of which [could] check the rise of a great power in the Asia-Pacific Region."[57] Another analyst adds, "Everyone knows that the Malacca Strait is tightly linked to the South China Sea—a so-called second Persian Gulf—and grips the throat of both the Pacific and the Indian Oceans."[58]

The South China Sea is one of China's critical oil transport zones because China-bound oil flowing through Malacca must also transit on its way to southern and eastern China. As one book states, "it is China's portal to the Indian Ocean, a major maritime communications thoroughfare to the West. It also the critical economic portal of many nations to the Middle East, Europe, and Africa, especially with the rapid development of oil extraction and commerce in the Middle East and Southeast Asian regions. The strategic position of shipping in the South China Sea is also extremely important."[59]

Moreover, the South China Sea is a vital transport corridor for liquefied natural gas (LNG), carrying two-thirds of the world's current LNG trade.[60] At present, Japan and South Korea are the region's primary LNG users, but the LNG transport security question is of increasing interest to China, which by 2020 may be importing more than 30 million tons per year.[61] For additional information concerning the maritime implications of Chinese LNG development, see the chapter by Mikkal Herberg in this volume.

China is also keenly interested in producing oil and gas from the South China Sea, which has been called a "second Persian Gulf" (第二波斯湾) by many Chinese observers.[62] As two analysts state, "oil and gas reserves could reach 3.5 billion tons [or more than 25 billion barrels of oil equivalent]. . . . It is one of China's huge resource treasure houses, [and is] extremely important for China's economic development."[63] A PLA publication also claims that the South China Sea possesses "rich oil reserves equivalent to that of Middle East."[64]

While Chinese analysts' reserve estimates are perhaps excessively optimistic, their statements are worth considering insofar as they reveal that Beijing may attach a high value to the region's oil and gas production potential. This could become particularly important if China increases exploration and production activities in the South China Sea as a way to reduce oil and gas import dependency, and thereby reduce vulnerability to SLOC disruption. Some naval analysts have advocated this as one component of a strategy to reduce China's vulnerability to a U.S. energy blockade.[65] In collaboration with China National Offshore Oil Corporation (CNOOC), Hong Kong–based Husky Resources recently made a world-class gas find 250 km south of Hong Kong.[66] If China discovers more fields of this magnitude, it could further increase Beijing's interest in the area.

Chinese observers recognize that major outside powers, particularly Japan and the United States, are determined to maintain freedom of navigation through the South China Sea.[67] As one PRC naval analyst notes, "the U.S. clearly indicates that it has important interests in the South China Sea region. Through the 'American Overseas Interests Act' the U.S. Congress has stated that freedom of navigation in the South China Sea is 'vital' to U.S. national security."[68]

Like the South China Sea, the East China Sea has attracted the interest of Chinese analysts because of its energy resources, the value of which they likewise seem to exaggerate. "The East China Sea's continental shelf could be one of the world's richest oil fields," declares one book on Chinese naval strategy. "The waters near the [disputed] Diaoyu [Senkaku] Islands could become the 'Second Middle East.'"[69] However, the East China Sea is typically mentioned in the context of energy and territorial disputes with Japan, as opposed to SLOC security per se. Nevertheless, this region contains some of China's most important ports, and, unlike the Malacca Strait and Indian Ocean energy lanes, lies near Chinese air and naval bases.

Pervasive in the Chinese naval analyses cited above is the notion that China is currently hemmed in by the natural features of its surroundings, which generally concentrate its maritime energy supply chains in areas where powerful potential adversaries might easily interdict them. One analyst states,

> Looking from the standpoint of strategic geography, the outer fringe of China's sea areas is completely surrounded by island chains. . . . Power to control the SLOC approaching [China's] offshore sea areas is basically in the hands of the U.S. and Japan. These two countries will always attempt to blockade China within offshore waters, [by] installing surveillance networks undersea, on the surface, and in the air [so that] China's naval vessels coming in and out of the island chains will receive tight scrutiny. In wartime, it is possible that PLAN vessels might suffer enclosure, pursuit, blocking, and interception by the enemy.[70]

The next section will explore which threats Chinese naval analysts fear most, and under which scenarios they might arise.

The Perceived Threats to China's Major Energy SLOC

It is often said that U.S. naval supremacy is an excellent guarantor of the global commons and that Beijing actually benefits substantially from the stabilizing role that American naval hegemony plays, perhaps especially with respect to energy markets and the related question of sea lane security.[71] Unfortunately, the writings surveyed here do not suggest that such views are common among Chinese naval and security analysts. Instead, they generally perceive a very substantial naval threat to China's long energy supply line. One analyst notes that oil and gas supply routes often become important military targets in wartime. Taking the Pacific war as an example, he points out that "Japanese tankers became Allied targets and in 1944, Japanese oil imports were halved. By early 1945, Japanese oil imports had basically been stopped."[72]

In analyzing the threats to China's major energy SLOC, Chinese naval analysts contend that this threat does not emanate solely from Washington.

Despite the breakthrough bilateral naval exercises with India in 2005 and Hu Jintao's successful November 2006 visit to India, Chinese analysts are acutely aware and anxious that India commands a dominant position astride China's most important energy SLOC. Chinese naval publications keenly follow Indian naval development.[73] Chinese analysts are impressed by India's naval development, perhaps especially in the realm of naval aviation, and fear that such capabilities could allow New Delhi to "effectively prevent any outside great power's Navy from entering the Indian Ocean."[74] Moreover, Chinese observers also note India's enhanced capability to project power to the East. Indeed, a 2004 article in 现代舰船 (*Modern Ships*) reviews New Delhi's establishment over the past decade of a Far Eastern Fleet (远东舰队), increased operational presence in both the Andaman Sea and in the vicinity of the Malacca Strait, and increased joint exercises with the U.S. Navy.[75] Perceiving an ensuing threat to vital SLOC, one Chinese analyst observes, "the Indian Navy's attention extends from the Arabian Sea to the South China Sea. Tankers carrying China's oil imports pass through Indian Navy controlled seas every day."[76]

According to another Chinese analyst, it is the U.S. Navy presence in the Arabian Sea and the Persian Gulf, together with "the cruising of Indian naval task forces in the Indian Ocean and the Malacca Strait's western entrance, [in addition to] Japan's sending troops overseas and great deployment of Japan Maritime Self-Defense [Force] destroyers [that] invariably constitute overwhelming pressure on China's oil supply."[77] Indeed, other naval analysts have been critical of Japan's deployment to Iraq, arguing that this initiative has more to do with the politics of energy than with any humanitarian motives.[78] In appraising Japan's newly evolving defense posture, Chinese analysts are concerned that "Japan's defense scope has extended to the Taiwan Strait and could include the Malacca Strait. [Also,] Japan has used Singapore's air bases."[79] There was additional concern with respect to an emphasis on the Malacca Strait in the 2005 Japanese defense white paper.[80] Perhaps not surprisingly, PRC naval analysts also closely monitor the military activities of other regional powers near this critical SLOC (e.g., Indonesia).[81]

Nevertheless, as a recent maritime oil security analysis in 现代舰船 (*Modern Ships*) states, "For the forseeable future, the U.S., Japan, and India are the three countries that have the capability to cut China's oil supply lines. However, cutting China's oil supply lines essentially means starting a war with China. . . . Only the U.S. has the power and the nerve to blockade China's oil transport routes."[82] The same Chinese naval analysis suggests two possible scenarios wherein the United States might seek to embargo China's energy supplies. The first would be a Taiwan contingency "if the mainland's military power proved insufficient to deter the United States from intervening."[83] The second is somewhat more vague: "If China's rise is not of a peaceful character, or if the speed of the rise is too rapid, and thus poses an extremely large, extremely rapid and fundamental challenge to American hegemony and the international system, the U.S. could blockade China's maritime oil transport lines, thereby cutting short China's rise."[84]

It is argued that, in addition to the Malacca Strait, American forces could block China's energy sea lanes at multiple points. This is interpreted as a source of considerable leverage for the U.S. Navy vis-à-vis China.[85] Another analysis arrives at similarly stark conclusions: in 1993, there was

> an incident in which the U.S. Navy intercepted the merchant ship 'Yinhe' in the Indian Ocean; ten years later there has been no fundamental improvement in the situation. The U.S. can carry out a 'Yin He'-like interception at any time, and can speed toward and intercept China's tankers in the Indian Ocean. Under these particular circumstances, [China] cannot eliminate the possibility of a similar situation happening again. For example, if war erupts in the Taiwan Strait, once the U.S. intervenes, it could absolutely consider this same strategy, and using its preponderance of sea power in this place far removed from mainland China, cut off China's oil supply.[86]

A similarly pessimistic naval strategy assessment concludes: "At a critical moment of America's choosing, the U.S. military could completely control sea-borne oil transport routes from the Persian Gulf oil-producing countries through the Indian Ocean to our South China Sea by stopping and inspecting transiting ships. In a Taiwan crisis, an American embargo of seaborne oil transport and SLOC cannot be ruled out."[87]

Chinese naval analysts are particularly sensitive to the growth of U.S. influence in and around the Strait of Malacca. One PRC analysis concludes that "whoever controls the Malacca Strait can at any moment threaten China's energy security."[88] Its authors ask whether the Malacca Strait will become yet another American forward military position in the Asia-Pacific (see map 2).[89] Another analysis asserts that there is a "grave, hidden threat" to China's energy security: "Which state can control the Malacca Strait? The United States, of course."[90] PRC naval analysts have noted that during the 1990s the Seventh Fleet logistics command was moved from Subic Bay in the Philippines to Singapore's Changi Naval Base.[91] Referring to the problem of sea lane

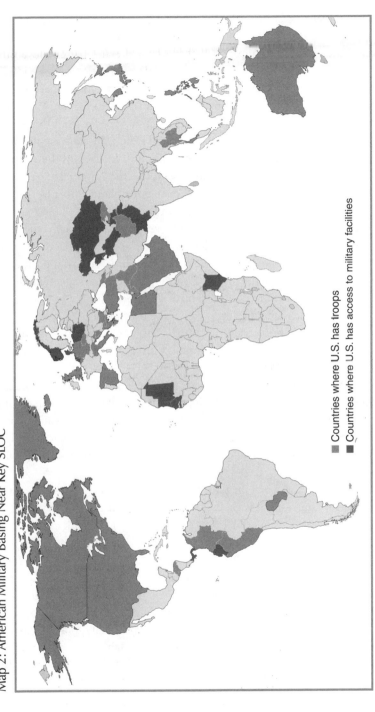

Map 2: American Military Basing Near Key SLOC

Countries where U.S. has troops

Countries where U.S. has access to military facilities

security, it is suggested that "the U.S. establishment of a military base in Singapore indicates that the area can be placed under the control of U.S. military power."[92] Moreover, "it is apparent that the United States has employed the war on terror in order to take control of the Malacca Strait."[93]

One of the most interesting naval strategy discussions regarding the threat to China's energy SLOC concerns a possible link to Taiwan. Most PRC analyses of the Taiwan question tend not to stray very far from the official line that Taiwan is a sovereignty issue pure and simple. By contrast, the book 戍海固边 (*Defend the Sea with a Solid Boundary*) focuses on the strategic value of the island for China. Its authors assert that the Taiwan issue is a matter of survival for China because it will enable mainland China to "project upon the Pacific Ocean's critical strategic sea lanes."[94]

The authors suggest that unfavorable geography, especially the enemy's position on Taiwan, has enabled the adversary to blockade China in the recent past. According to this analysis, Taiwan is critically positioned along the "oil route" from the Middle East to East Asia. It is suggested, moreover, that "if Taiwan fell under the control of a power hostile to China, not only would this mean that this great gate was closed but also that the Taiwan Strait Channel could be blocked. The north coast of China's most convenient channel, the Gonggu Strait, which is just 145 km across, could be blockaded relatively easily by a modern navy."[95]

Chinese naval analysts are well aware that the U.S., Indian, and especially Japanese economies are also highly dependent on seaborne trade in oil and gas. It has even been suggested that, at least in the near term, China's only viable naval response to the embargo scenarios mentioned above would be a strategy of retaliation—an effort to answer an embargo against China with "an eye for an eye."[96]

On this note, and given the paucity of available PLA analyses relevant to SLOC security missions, it is useful to examine here one of the very few that directly addresses the subject. 战役学 (*The Science of Campaigns*), an operationally and tactically focused doctrinal textbook that seems to focus on a Taiwan contingency, was published by China's National Defense University in 2000. While its level of authority is unclear, it represents views of preeminent military thinkers in Beijing. Chapter 12, "Naval Campaigns," contains detailed discussions of how the PLA might counter blockades to which it might be subject, all of which have obvious applicability to a Taiwan scenario.[97] The authors seem to subscribe to generic "Mahanian" theories of sea power. "It is decisively significant to find and assault the enemy first,"[98] the authors state, "We should try to make the first attack a success."[99]

The chapter repeatedly stresses the primacy of offensive initiative to secure command of the sea. The importance of offense is recognized even in situations of Chinese weakness.

"SLOC attack campaigns are not always conducted in situations in which we have superiority. When our naval strength is in an inferior position, and we want to conduct systematic sabotage against enemy SLOCs, the campaign will probably last longer. . . ." The need for China's navy to attack a variety of enemy targets is also emphasized:

> The SLOC attack campaign not only needs inshore SLOC attack, but also needs SLOC attack in the deep sea in order to achieve good campaign effect. Under normal situations, we should attack enemy transportation ships. Nevertheless, in order to accomplish this goal smoothly, we often need to attack enemy escort warships first, even the enemy campaign covering escort. Sometimes, we even need to attack the enemy loading and unloading ports, docks, and airports.[100]

The authors definitely appreciate the value of offensive, not just defensive, mining.[101] For instance, in a section entitled "Attacking and Blocking Enemy Loading and Unloading Ports," the authors state, "we will concentrate the main force on attacking enemy ports, loading and unloading equipment, and transportation ships. When attacking enemy ports, a portion of air force bombers as well as submarines are used to deploy sea mine barriers in the water channels outside of enemy ports to blockade them."[102]

"Active defense" concepts allow for offensive actions even in a Chinese "SLOC Protection Campaign." Thus, "active . . . local offensive operations are an effective measure to reduce and limit enemy capabilities for transportation sabotage combat in a transportation defense campaign."[103] Specifically, "In order to weaken and limit enemy capabilities for SLOC attack, we sometimes need to attack and blockade enemy bases and airports."[104] The authors argue that China's level of offensive measures in a SLOC defense campaign should vary with both relative capabilities and with the operational situation: "When one has a stronger operational force, launch an active offensive to attack the enemy's SLOC attack force. . . . When one does not have the ability to conduct an active attack and the enemy does not attack us, we start to launch transport activities under concealment. . . . When the enemy has started blockade and attack activities, we start the campaign with various anti-blockade and counterattack combat activities."[105]

Despite emphasizing offensive fleet action throughout the chapter, however, the authors acknowledge that the dispersed nature of combat and fleet operations today makes obtaining a single decisive battle difficult.[106] The authors' preference for offensive strategy appears difficult to reconcile with a strategy for the protection of friendly shipping—a difficult, asset intensive, defensive mission. The authors acknowledge that protection of shipping is a defensive mission and that a scarcity of assets will likely limit a navy's ability to protect all shipping,[107] but when it comes to presenting a solution for this dilemma, they fall back on the primacy of offense. This is highlighted by the authors' caveat that "generally speaking, the SLOC protection campaign is a defensive campaign. Nevertheless, active . . . local offensive operations are an effective measure to reduce and limit enemy capabilities."[108] The rest of the paragraph advocates seizing opportunities to attack first whenever they present themselves, even when performing a "defensive" mission.

The authors repeatedly discuss the need for air superiority, and provide recommended guidance for the employment of fighter aircraft in each section. This would be relevant for a Taiwan scenario; but, since the PLAN currently lacks carrier-based aircraft, not for others beyond the range of land-based air. The authors are either discussing Taiwan or implicitly lobbying for PLAN aircraft carrier capability (or both). The section on "Organization and Covering Transport Ships to Load and Unload and Leave Port" seems to discuss a naval expeditionary task force assembling to sail to one common objective as opposed to an ordinary convoy of merchant/cargo ships sailing along the coast.[109] While these statements need to be compared with those in other PLAN doctrinal writings as they become available outside China, it seems reasonable to conclude that Beijing was already carefully evaluating the consequences of a maritime energy blockade seven years ago and was engaged in developing serious countermeasures.

The next section of this chapter addresses the implications of the above threat analyses for the future development of the PLAN—as discussed by Chinese naval strategists.

Naval Implications

Outside observers tend to focus on Chinese development of sea denial capabilities that could be used to repel U.S. intervention in a cross-Strait conflict. Yet China might also be pursuing the ability to project naval power farther than would be necessary in a Taiwan contingency. Moreover, many naval capabilities are highly fungible and could thus be applied both to a Taiwan context and to missions farther afield.

One explanation for China's possible movement toward a blue water navy that might transcend the Taiwan issue could be found in its growing dependency on imported oil and other key economic inputs. In addition to naval discussions of these issues, which have been described in detail earlier, there is a lively debate among Chinese policy intellectuals. Figure 1 shows the key representatives of China's "economic liberal" and "neomercantilist" schools of thought.

Figure 1. China's Energy Security Spectrum

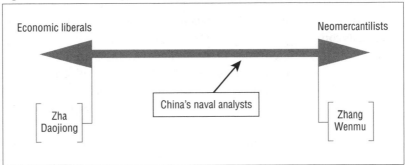

Many PRC energy security analysts from the neomercantilist school perceive the global oil system to be controlled by the United States. They therefore advocate acquiring the naval wherewithal to defend China's growing dependence on secure seaborne oil imports. Beijing University of Aeronautics & Astronautics scholar Zhang Wenmu explains this school of thought: "China is facing fierce competition overseas in obtaining its share of crude oil. . . . [It is therefore necessary to] build up our navy as quickly as possible."[110] Indeed, "China should not only strengthen its naval power and defense to protect imported oil, but also expand its navy to achieve its influence over the offshore resources in the Asia Pacific region."[111] A second source states that "protecting China's sea lines of communication has become an important aspect of maritime security. This is an important new mission for the PLAN."[112] Another analyst adds: "In order to . . . effectively capture sea control in a specific area, [the PLAN] must possess the ability to control passage in and out of important strategic passages in times of crisis."[113] As noted earlier, Chinese security analysts specifically emphasize the importance of the PLAN being able to freely transit the Malacca Strait.[114]

The PLAN's present inability to secure China's long-distance oil transport SLOC or to militarily deter a U.S. blockade greatly concerns Chinese naval analysts.[115] They are painfully aware of the U.S. Navy's superiority over the PLAN.[116] There is a clear sense of urgency: "[China] must . . . strengthen the PLAN and PLAAF so that they possess the capability to defend China's maritime resource and energy supplies, and smash [any] maritime blockades of China's economy or energy supply and defend [China's] own tanker transport passages. . . . Regarding the problems . . . of sea embargo or oil lanes being cut off . . . China must . . . 'repair the house before it rains.'"[117]

To rectify the current weakness of the PLAN relative to such potential naval competitors as the United States, Japan, and India, Beijing is energetically modernizing naval platforms as well as training and operational doctrine. While "China already has a relatively strong navy," it is striving to increase its comprehensive sea power (结合海洋力量).[118]

In 1997, a PLAN flotilla made a historic global circumnavigation. The strategic significance of this event expresses "China's hope to establish its position on the world's oceans, particularly to guarantee its maritime energy channels. Yet because the PLAN's power, technology, and scope lag those of other nations," contends one analyst, "China's future maritime development will emanate from commerce, not military bases."[119] Indeed, a high profile new government-inspired study titled 大国崛起 ("The Rise of Great Powers") suggests that while national power can be furthered by a strong navy, it actually stems primarily from economic development, fueled by foreign trade.[120]

Despite these efforts to both channel China's maritime development in a peaceful direction and to portray it as such to the rest of the world, history suggests that any major military modernization program is likely to unnerve other powers. A move by Beijing from a "near sea" to a blue water naval strategy, even if conducted under the auspices of "commercial protection," may be no different. A recent article in 中国军事科学 (*China Military Science*) states that: "[China's] navy must . . . unceasingly move toward [the posture of] a 'blue-water navy' [and] expand the scope of maritime strategic defense."[121] Chinese analysts have clearly stated the need to acquire power projection instruments to support such increasing naval ambitions. These include long-range area air defense destroyers, helicopter carriers, diesel submarines with air-independent propulsion and cruise missiles, nuclear submarines capable of attacking enemy harbors and land targets, and advanced naval aircraft such as the SU-30 Flanker.[122]

Another PRC naval analysis of maritime rights and resource security explains that China's navy is not sufficiently strong to undertake the energy SLOC security mission because of Beijing's longtime policy of "emphasizing land power at the cost of sea power" (重陆轻海).[123] Hinting at a possible redirection of PLAN strategy, as well as rivalry among PLAN warfare communities, this analysis continues:

> [in order] to build a Navy with a relatively strong, distant ocean-going fighting capacity . . . the [Chinese] Navy cannot only emphasize submarines, [because] a formidable submarine force is only an aspect of [the] "active defense" [积极防御] [strategy]. A modern navy must be comprehensive in nature, thus putting joint warfare at the center of sea power, and [thereby] make aircraft carriers the centerpiece of a multi-functional and multi-use, distant-ocean type of sea power. In order to protect sea lane security and guarantee [China's] maritime interests, we must maintain a certain naval presence, especially in the South [China] Sea, and such vital military and economic regions in strategic locations.[124]

One Chinese analyst recognizes the strategic value of the South China Sea's bathymetry and its pivotal position as both a critical SLOC in its own right and as the entrance to the Strait of Malacca: "If a nuclear submarine were concealed in deep water near the Spratlys, it could counteract the greater portion of the strength of a U.S. 7th Fleet deployment in the Philippines. . . . [Because] this region's water depths can easily be used to hide a submarine . . . it is impossible to use counterattack operations."[125]

As was demonstrated earlier, the need to control the Strait of Malacca, or at least prevent other powers from denying China access to it, is foremost in the minds of Chinese strategists. It is therefore hardly surprising that the PLA appears already to be deploying assets in a pattern that would further this goal.

According to a recent analysis by *Jane's*, China's South Sea Fleet is receiving increasing numbers of military assets. Already, it boasts slightly more destroyers and frigates than either the East Sea Fleet or the North Sea Fleet. Reportedly, a new PLAN or PLAAF air base may be under construction on Hainan Island.[126] Submarines, however, are shifting most dramatically toward Hainan. China might base both Type 093 SSNs and Type 094 SSBNs at a new submarine base proximate to Hainan's Yulin Naval Base (near Sanya City).[127] Already, Internet photos indicate that Song- and Kilo-class diesel submarines, as well as at least one Type 091 Han-class SSN, have been based at least temporarily in Hainan. It may be relevant that China's marine corps is thought to have based all of its units with the South Sea Fleet.[128]

A sustained movement of assets to the South China Sea could imply a PLAN mission beyond Taiwan in pursuit of genuine, if limited, SLOC protection capability. Indeed, a student at Beijing's powerful Central Party School suggests that Beijing's policy intellectuals are supporting a naval buildup:

> Because of the maritime power of the U.S., Japan, etc., we have been overly cautious, and restricted our activities to . . . the inshore and territorial waters . . . [thereby] forfeiting the strategic initiative. . . . We ought instead to be accelerating transformation from an offshore defense navy to an open ocean navy, in the not too distant future possessing absolute sea control within 500 NM, and with deterrence power on the SLOCs through the Malacca Strait to the southern part of the Indian Ocean, not only able to ensure SLOC security, but also able to break the First Island Chain blockade,[129] and in the vicinity of the Second Island Chain (approaching beyond 1,000 NM) intercepting or attacking enemy targets, thereby safeguarding the security of the southeast littoral region.[130]

In this vision, the PLAN might indeed have an offensive mission, even if justified ideologically in the context of "active defense": "In the event of maritime conflict, an important aspect of the two sides being at war would be carrying out SLOC blockades and counterblockades. The PLAN will be charged with the heavy responsibility of ensuring that SLOC are unimpeded, and at the same time breaking the enemy's transport lines and weakening its war potential."[131] This proactive approach to SLOC security is portrayed not as an option but as an imperative: "The strategic passages in the sea areas of China's East (Sea Fleet) and South (Sea Fleet)—e.g., the Korean Strait, the channels of the Ryukyu archipelago, the Bashi Strait, the Malacca Strait, the Lombok Strait, [and] the Sunda Strait—are either places where the PLAN must penetrate the island chains to carry out strategic defense missions, or strategic points where the U.S. and Japan will carry out offensive operations to make surprise attacks on targets on the Chinese mainland and coast."[132]

Increased PLAN presence in SLOC and surrounding areas also has a valuable "shaping" function, as it can "strengthen [China's] power of influence in key sea areas and straits" in peacetime and thereby decrease the chance of its interests being threatened in war.[133]

One of the most ambitious discussions of PLAN development in relation to energy SLOC security is found in a 2006 article from 舰载武器 (*Shipborne Weapons*). This article proposes that in the twenty-first century, as China broadens its naval presence on the world's oceans, Beijing's North Sea, East Sea, and South Sea fleets should transform into a Northern Fleet, a Pacific Fleet, and an Indian Ocean Fleet (印度样舰队). The potential scope and mission of such Northern and Pacific fleets are perhaps beyond the parameters of the present study, but the idea of a Chinese Indian Ocean Fleet could represent a radical shift in the PLAN's response to the SLOC security issue. According to this Chinese analysis, the core mission of the proposed Indian Ocean Fleet would be "to protect [Beijing's] interests in the South China Sea, while at the same time guarding the Indian Ocean navigation route and escorting Chinese oil tankers transiting the Malacca Strait, thus preserving a matter of life and death for China: security of the 'the energy lifeline' and the 'oil straits.'"[134]

The analysis emphasizes the crucial role that aircraft carriers would play in such a PLAN Indian Ocean fleet, in particular if they could coordinate effectively with China's new air defense destroyers. "In order to escort merchant vessels along the entire Indian Ocean route and resolve related crises," the author explains, "China's future Indian Ocean Fleet must have a powerful, open-ocean, escort, combat capability." Additionally, a major mission of Beijing's Indian Ocean Fleet would be "guarding against the Singapore-based U.S. Navy."[135]

China is already making moves that could bolster its strategic position along Indian Ocean oil transport lanes. Writing in China's most prestigious military journal, *China Military Science*, a PLAN senior captain relates: "During the 1990s, China constructed harbor wharves in the eastern Indian Ocean in Burma [and] cleared the Mekong waterways, in order to gain access to the sea in [China's] southwest. . . . China invested $U.S. 1 billion to construct a deep water port [at Gwadar], in order to establish a trade and transport hub for Central Asian nations, and simultaneously expand China's geo-strategic influence."[136]

India and other naval powers will likely react unfavorably to an overt Chinese naval presence in the Indian Ocean region. India already has a formidable naval force, including the aircraft carrier *Viraat* and TU-142 long-range maritime patrol aircraft, which have been used to track Russian made warships transiting the Indian Ocean on their way to China.[137] To sustain a serious naval presence in the Indian Ocean, the PLAN would need to substantially expand its at-sea replenishment capacity and also secure basing rights in Pakistan, Burma, and perhaps Sri Lanka or Bangladesh. India and the United States might put major pressure on these countries not to accept Chinese forces. Indeed, it is noteworthy that the U.S. Marine Corps and Sri Lankan navy held major exercises in October 2006 near the Sri Lankan port of Hambantota, where China is looking to build oil storage and bunkering (ship refueling) facilities.[138] Finally, even if China did somehow overcome the aforementioned obstacles and obtain basing rights, it would be violating a key precept of its foreign policy to date, which emphasizes that China will not base military forces abroad.

A Responsible Stakeholder?

It is perhaps not surprising that Chinese naval analysts are looking to so-called blue water missions, beyond the strict confines of Taiwan contingencies. It is certainly in their bureaucratic interest to do so. Indeed, such bureaucratic interests have fueled naval rivalries in the past. A more surprising finding is the considerable group of Chinese naval analysts that recognize the imperative for China to cooperate with the other oil-consuming powers, particularly the United States.

A major study of China's SLOC security problem, for instance, calls for emphasizing cooperation in international organizations and conventions, laws, and regulations concerning oil transport.[139] A 2004 survey in 舰船知识 (*Naval & Merchant Ships*) reveals many nationalist themes on energy but also concludes that China is "more and more dependent on stability in the Middle East."[140] Of course, this kind of phrasing sounds utterly familiar to Western ears. An analysis from 现代舰船 (*Modern Ships*) concludes, "The energy crisis and maritime SLOC security are not problems that are just confronting China alone . . . but [rather] impact on international sea lane security and stability."[141] A more recent and very detailed analysis from the same journal observes that Persian Gulf instability could significantly harm China's interests and emphasizes that China must cooperate closely with India, Korea, and even Japan in the energy sphere—or else they might join with the United States against China in any conflict.[142] But the overarching requirement is actually to maintain good relations with the United States. There is really no choice in the matter, according to this source, because "the United States could blockade energy shipments to China at any time."[143] This analysis characterizes the 2005 failure of CNOOC to acquire the American UNOCAL Corporation as a serious foreign energy policy setback and elaborates on the causes of this embarrassment for China. It is suggested, moreover, that present U.S.–China relations have, despite the UNOCAL incident and other irritants, stabilized to a large degree. It is also recognized that Washington is unlikely to act against the status quo. Indeed, "If stability can be maintained in U.S.–China relations, then China's maritime oil transport will be basically secure."[144]

A rather remarkable article on the energy issue in China's foremost naval journal, 当代海军 (*Modern Navy*), actually links China's naval buildup with the SLOC mission to the principle of "peaceful development." The analysis asserts that China's "fleets patrolling the vast oceans, protecting commerce from terrorist elements and pirate attacks, will receive praise from the world." All oil trading nations benefit from a stable supply chain, it is said, and "a big and powerful [Chinese] fleet will support a stable supply chain. Thus, in the era of globalization, a formidable navy is not only in our own country's security interest, but is actually a requirement of global security as well."[145] Cooperation with other world navies, and especially those of the developed world, in activities such as counterterrorism, it is said, will effectively dispel the "China threat theory." This analysis concludes that "There is no contradiction between our building of a large fleet and China's peaceful rise."[146] As long as China's navy continuously engages with the outside world, developing opportunities to partner with other countries, then the world will come to accept, and even welcome, a strong Chinese Navy.[147]

Conclusion

This study has found that the energy content within the voluminous output of naval literature in contemporary China is not overly large. Certainly, it could not be described as pervasive—in the manner that discussions of undersea warfare (e.g., air independent propulsion technology) are. Nevertheless, it should be said that there does exist a pointed interest in energy issues among PLAN strategists, and indeed there is a rather distinct general viewpoint. The most critical theme that underlies this perspective is China's perceived current vulnerability to an energy embargo. As one might expect, Chinese naval analysts are extremely reluctant to place their country's oil security in the hands of other great powers, especially the United States. If it does not already serve this role (which it very well might), then the energy issue will likely offer a potent rationale for continuing or even further accelerating China's naval modernization, especially as Beijing's military planners begin to grapple seriously with scenarios beyond Taiwan. Somewhat more unexpected in this study are the findings that Chinese naval strategists candidly admit that their capabilities for protecting China's long energy SLOC are minimal at present. Also, it is somewhat surprising that these analysts, while sounding many nationalist themes, seem guardedly open to multilateral cooperation on energy issues, and appear to understand the importance of trying to preserve good relations with Washington.

Among the many Chinese naval analyses surveyed for this study, perhaps the most sophisticated was the lengthy treatment of the energy question in the October 2006 issue of 现代舰船 (*Modern Ships*). At the conclusion of this analysis, the author articulates a three point strategy, which may incisively summarize the approach taken by the Chinese naval community to the energy question: "[China] must view things from the perspective of keeping the U.S. from cutting its oil supply lines. Concretely speaking, this entails making the U.S. not willing to cut China's oil supply lines, not daring to do so, and not able to do so."[148] Without exaggerating the importance of this particular source, it might be noted that the internal coherence of this statement may actually suggest that it is drawn from official internal policy. It is further suggested that a web of self-interest would keep the United States from wanting to embargo China, and that oil pipelines and agile diplomacy could hinder any attempt by Washington to use this leverage. Most surprising, perhaps, is that this formulation's prescription also calls not just for strengthening naval forces, but nuclear strategic forces as well.[149] This last point may truly illustrate the depth of Beijing's insecurity with respect to the energy issue.

Notes

1. Chinese officials periodically call for oil conservation and reduction of the economy's overall energy intensity, and encourage Chinese state oil and gas producers to diversify away from the unstable Middle East and increase the share of oil imports that come overland by pipeline. However, Chinese oil demand continues to grow strongly (at a rate of 14.5 percent from 2005–6). See Wang Qiyi, "Energy Conservation as Security," *China Security*, no. 3 (Summer 2006): 90, http://www.worldsecurityinstitute.org/showarticle.cfm?id163; "China's Crude Oil Imports Up 14.5% in 2006," *People's Daily*, 12 January 2007, www.english.people.com.cn/.

2. Because of the difficulty in conclusively identifying the authors of many Chinese writings on naval issues, this chapter will use a very broad definition of "naval analyst," namely, one who engages in research and publication concerning naval affairs.

3. Office of the Secretary of Defense, *Military Power of the People's Republic of China 2007*, Annual Report to Congress, 9. The Defense Department's 2006 report echoes these concerns, noting that "securing adequate supplies of resources and materials has become a major driver of Chinese foreign policy. . . . Evidence suggests that China is investing in maritime surface and sub-surface weapons systems that could serve as the basis for a force capable of power projection to secure vital sea lines of communication and/or key geostrategic terrain." Ibid, 1.

4. "World Briefing/Asia: China: Hu Calls For Strong Navy," *New York Times*, 29 December 2006, http://query.nytimes.com/gst/fullpage.html?res=9C0CE3D71F31F93AA15751C1A9609C8B63.

5. David Lague, "China Airs Ambitions to Beef Up Naval Power," *International Herald Tribune*, 28 December 2006, http://www.iht.com/articles/2006/12/28/news/china.php.

6. "Chinese President Calls for Strengthened, Modernized Navy," *People's Daily*, 27 December 2006.

7. "Chinese President Calls for Strong Navy," *VOA News*, 28 December 2006, http://voanews.com/english/2006-12-28-voa41.cfm.

8. China's 2006 defense white paper further states that China's

> Navy is working to build itself into a modern maritime force of operation consisting of combined arms with both nuclear and conventional means of operations. Taking informationization as the goal and strategic focus in its modernization drive, the Navy gives high priority to the development of maritime information systems, and new-generation weaponry and equipment. Efforts are being made to improve maritime battlefield capabilities, with emphasis on the construction of relevant facilities for new equipment and the development of combat support capabilities. The Navy is endeavoring to build mobile maritime troops capable of conducting operations under conditions of informationization, and strengthen its overall capabilities of operations in coastal waters, joint operations and integrated maritime support. Efforts are being made to improve and reform training programs and methods to intensify training in joint integrated maritime operations. The Navy is enhancing research into the theory of naval operations and exploring the strategy and tactics of maritime people's war under modern conditions.

See "China's National Defense in 2006," Information Office of the State Council, People's Republic of China, 29 December 2006, http://www.fas.org/nuke/guide/china/doctrine/wp2006.html.

9. Wu Lei and Shen Qinyu, "Will China Go to War Over Oil?" *Far Eastern Economic Review* 169, no. 3 (April 2006): 38.

10. Kenneth Lieberthal and Mikkal Herberg, "China's Search for Energy Security: Implications for U.S. Policy," *NBR Analysis* 17, no. 1 (April 2006): 23.

11. These would include, at a minimum, 当代海军 [*Modern Navy*], 人民海军 [*People's Navy*], 舰船知识 [*Naval & Merchant Ships*], 舰载武器 [*Shipborne Weapons*], and 现代舰船 [*Modern Ships*]. 当代海军 [*Modern Navy*] is a monthly magazine published by the official PLAN newspaper 人民海军 [*People's Navy*], which is the daily newspaper published by the Political Department of China's Navy. 舰船知识 [*Naval & Merchant Ships*] is a semitechnical monthly publication of the Chinese Society of Naval Architecture and Marine Engineering. 舰载武器 [*Shipborne Weapons*] and 现代舰船 [*Modern Ships*] are both monthly journals published by the state-owned China Shipbuilding Industry Corporation (CSIC), China's largest designer, manufacturer, and trader of military and civilian vessels and related engineering and equipment. In addition to these naval-oriented publications, Beijing's most prestigious military journal, 中国军事科学 [*China Military Science*], is published by the PLA's Academy of Military Sciences.

12. Sea Tide Press [海潮出版社], located in Beijing, publishes such authoritative volumes as 中国海军百科全书 [*China Navy Encyclopedia*], vol. 1 (Beijing: Sea Tide Press, 1998).

13. Kong Bo, "Institutional Insecurity," *China Security* 3 (Summer 2006): 67. Instead, energy policies are developed by a constellation of actors under what Kong Bo of Johns Hopkins University dubs "a high degree of organizational confusion." Bo, "Institutional Insecurity," 65. These include the National Development and Reform Commission (NDRC, a branch of the State Council, whose reports are available at www.eri.org.cn), the state oil and gas producers, and special high-level working groups such as the Energy Leading Group chaired by Premier Wen Jiabao. There is also a nascent State Energy Office, attached to NDRC's Energy Bureau, but it is understaffed, lacks formal authority over energy stakeholders, and is likely so overwhelmed with work that it can only react to events, rather than actually shape policy. See Erica Downs, "Brookings Foreign Policy Studies Energy Security Series: China," Brookings Institution, December 2006, 21, http://www3.brookings.edu/fp/research/energy/2006china.pdf.

Moreover, anecdotal evidence suggests that many Energy Office employees come directly from the state energy companies, particularly CNPC/PetroChina. See Downs, 22. These agencies are primarily concerned with supply, demand, pricing, conservation, and other typically market oriented matters. There appear to be few dedicated civilian experts who focus on both energy and maritime security issues, and the few that do tend to narrowly focus on specific subjects (for example, Southeast Asia experts who study the Malacca Strait). The PLA and PLAN almost certainly pay close attention to energy security, but their views are difficult to track because both organizations are basically closed to foreign scholars. Author's interviews with Chinese scholars in Beijing, December 2006.

14. Author's interview with Chinese scholar, Shanghai, May 2007.

15. 陈安刚, 武明 [Chen Angang and Wu Ming], "马六甲: 美国觊觎的战略前哨" ["Malacca Strait: The United States Covets a Strategic Outpost"], 现代舰船 [*Modern Ships*] (December 2004): 13.

16. Evan S. Medeiros and M. Taylor Fravel, "China's New Diplomacy," *Foreign Affairs*, November/December 2003, http://www.foreignaffairs.org/20031101faessay82604/evan-s-medeiros-m-taylor-fravel/china-s-new-diplomacy.html.

17. See, for example, "U.S. Confirms Aircraft Carrier Had Close Brush with Chinese Submarine," *Japan Today*, 14 November 2006, http://www.japantoday.com.

18. Author's interviews, Beijing, June 2006.

19. See, for example, 查道炯 [Zha Daojiong], "相互依赖与中国的石油供应安全" ["Interdependence and China's Oil Supply Security"], 世界经济与政治 [*World Economics & Politics*], no. 6 (2005): 15–22.

20. See, for example, Zhang Wenmu, "China's Energy Security and Policy Choices," *Shijie Jingji Yu Zhengzhi* [*World Economics & International Politics*], no. 5 (2003): 11–16, FBIS# CPP20030528000169; Liu Xinhua and Zhang Wenmu, "China's Oil Security and Its Strategic Options," *Xiandai Guoji Guanxi* [*Contemporary International Relations*], no. 12 (December 2002): 35–37, 46, FBIS# CPP20030425000288.

21. Bruce Blair, Eric Hagt, Chen Yali, "The Oil Weapon: Myth of China's Vulnerability," *China Security* 3 (Summer 2006): 39.

22. Gabriel Collins, "China's Seeks Oil Security with New Tanker Fleet," *Oil & Gas Journal* 104, no. 38 (2006): 20–26.

23. Enhancing downstream security entails improving domestic energy infrastructure by increasing refining capacity, diversifying refining capacity to accept a broader range of crude oil feed stocks, and establishing a strategic petroleum reserve (SPR). This is, not surprisingly, the easiest of the three areas (upstream, midstream, and downstream) in which to increase energy security. China has made the most progress in this area, perhaps in part because of the overwhelming economic rationale for doing so.

24. "10% of GDP Now Comes From Sea, Says Report," *China Daily*, 10 April 2007, www.chinadaily.com.cn.

25. Chen Fong-Ching and Jin Guantao, *From Youthful Manuscripts to River Elegy: The Chinese Popular Cultural Movement and Political Transformation 1979–1989* (Hong Kong: Chinese University Press, 1997), 221–22.

26. Ibid, 222.

27. 周德华, 陈炎, 陈良武 [Zhou Dehua, Chen Yan, and Chen Liangwu], 蓝色方略：二十一世纪初的海洋和海军 [*The Blue Strategy: Ocean and Navy at the Beginning of the 21st Century*] (Beijing: Sea Tide Press, 2003), 3.

28. 曲令泉, 郭放 [Qu Lingquan and Guo Fang], 卫海强军：新军事革命与中国海军 [*A Mighty Force to Protect the Sea: The New Revolution in Military Affairs and China's Navy*] (Beijing: Sea Tide Press, 2003), 46.

29. 张玉坤, 张慧 [Zhang Yukun and Zhang Hui], 戍海固边: 海上安全环境与海洋权益维护 [*Defend the Sea with a Solid Boundary: The Maritime Security Environment and the Defense of Maritime Rights and Interests*] (Beijing: Sea Tide Press, 2003), 39.

30. 郝廷兵 [Hao Tingbing] (PLA Navy) and 杨志荣 [Yang Zhirong] (PLA Navy), 海上力量与中华民族的伟大复兴 [*Sea Power and the Chinese Nation's Mighty Resurgence*] (Beijing: National Defense University, 2005).

31. Ibid., 32.

32. Ibid., 6.

33. Ibid., 6.

34. This entire paragraph is drawn from 顾祖华 [Gu Zuhua], "维护海上石油安全须有强大海上编队" ["In Order to Safeguard Energy Security, a Massive Naval Fleet Is Necessary"], 当代海军 [*Modern Navy*] (August 2004): 40.

35. 徐起 [Xu Qi], "21世纪初海上地缘战略与中国海军的发展" ["Maritime Geostrategy and the Development of the Chinese Navy in the Early Twenty-first Century"], 中国军事科学 [*China Military Science*] 17, no. 4 (2004): 75–81, trans. Andrew Erickson and Lyle Goldstein, *Naval War College Review* 59, no. 4 (2006): 46–67.

36. 张运成 [Zhang Yuncheng], "能源安全与海上通道" ["Energy Security and Sea Lanes"], in 海上通道安全与国际合作 [*Sea Lane Security and International*

Cooperation], 杨明杰 [ed. Yang Mingjie] (Beijing: 时事出版社 [Current Affairs Publishing House], 2005), 103.

37. Peng Guangqian and Yao Youzhi, eds., *The Science of Military Strategy* (Beijing: Military Science Publishing House, 2005), 446.

38. 达巍 [Da Wei], "中国的海洋安全战略" ["China's Maritime Security Strategy"], in 海上通道安全与国际合作 [*Sea Lane Security and International Cooperation*], 杨明杰 [ed. Yang Mingjie] (Beijing: 时事出版社 [Current Affairs Publishing House], 2005), 361–62.

39. Zhang, "Energy Security and Sea Lanes," 101.

40. Donna J. Ninic, "Sea Lane Security and U.S. Maritime Trade: Chokepoints as Scarce Resources," in *Globalization and Maritime Power,* ed. Sam J. Tangredi (Washington, D.C.: National Defense University Press, 2003), 143–69.

41. Zhang Xuegang, "Southeast Asia: Gateway to Stability," *China Security* 3, no. 2 (2007): 26.

42. 凌云 [Ling Yun], "龙脉" ["The Dragon's Arteries"], 现代舰船 [*Modern Ships*] (October 2006): 12.

43. Ibid.

44. 李杰 [Li Jie], "石油, 中国需求与海道安全" ["Oil, China's Requirements and Sea Lane Security"], 舰船知识 [*Naval & Merchant Ships*] (September 2004): 12. See also 江风 [Jiang Feng], "21世纪中国海军三大舰队构想" ["Prospects for the PLAN's Three Fleets in the 21st Century"], 舰载武器 [*Shipborne Weapons*] (June 2006): 21.

45. Zhang, "Energy Security and Sea Lanes," 107, 108, 118.

46. "Bypassing Hormuz," 世界经济与政治 [*World Economics & Politics*], no. 1 (2006): 49.

47. Ibid., 48.

48. Zhang, "Energy Security and Sea Lanes," 118.

49. Ibid., 107.

50. Ibid., 118.

51. Chen and Wu, "Malacca Strait," 13.

52. 李兵 [Li Bing], "国际战略通道研究" ["International SLOC Research"], PhD dissertation, 中共中央党校 [Chinese Communist Party Central Party School], 1 May 2005, 355.

53. Zhang, "Energy Security and Sea Lanes," 118.

54. Chen and Wu, "Malacca Strait," 13.

55. Jiang, "Prospects for the PLAN's Three Fleets in the 21st Century," 21.

56. 章明 [Zhang Ming], "马六甲困局与中国海军的战略抉择" ["The Malacca Strait Problem and the Future Strategic Choice of the Chinese Navy"], 现代舰船 [*Modern Ships*] (October 2006): 21.

57. Ibid., 21.

58. Chen and Wu, "Malacca Strait," 11–14.

59. Zhang and Zhang, *Defend the Sea with a Solid Boundary*, 50.

60. Zhang, "Energy Security and Sea Lanes," 107.

61. Scott C. Roberts, "China's LNG Program Turns a Corner," Cambridge Energy Research Associates, http://www.cera.com/aspx/cda/client/report/reportpreview.aspx?CID=7328&KID=.

62. Chen and Wu, "Malacca Strait," 12.

63. Zhang and Zhang, *Defend the Sea with a Solid Boundary*, 47.

64. Peng Guangqian and Yao Youzhi, eds., *The Science of Military Strategy* (Beijing: Military Science Publishing House, 2005), 441.

65. Ling, "The Dragon's Arteries," 8–19.

66. "Husky Energy Announces Significant Gas Discovery in South China Sea," *Husky Energy Inc. News*, 14 June 2006.

67. Chen and Wu, "Malacca Strait," 11–13.

68. Ibid., 12.

69. Zhang and Zhang, *Defend the Sea with a Solid Boundary*, 45.

70. Li, "International SLOC Research," 355.

71. See, for example, Robert Looney, "Market Effects of Naval Presence in a Globalized World: A Research Summary," in *Globalization and Maritime Power*, ed. Sam J. Tangredi (Washington, D.C.: National Defense University Press, 2003), 103–32.

72. "Global Energy Structure," China Institute of Contemporary International Relations, Economic Security Study Center, Beijing, 2005, 91.

73. See, for example, the series of very detailed reports in a long series that was initiated in the November 2005 issue of *Modern Navy*.

74. Zhang, "Energy Security and Sea Lanes," 116–17.

75. Chen and Wu, "Malacca Strait," 14.

76. Zhang, "Energy Security and Sea Lanes," 120.

77. Ibid., 119.

78. Gu, "In Order to Safeguard Energy Security," 40.

79. Zhang, "Energy Security and Sea Lanes," 120.

80. Zhang, "The Malacca Strait Problem," 23.

81. See, for example, Li, "Oil, China's Requirements and Sea Lane Security," 13; Chen and Wu, "Malacca Strait," 14.

82. Ling, "The Dragon's Arteries," 15.

83. Ibid.

84. Ibid.

85. Ibid.

86. Zhang, "Energy Security and Sea Lanes," 119.

87. Ling, "The Dragon's Arteries," 12.

88. Chen and Wu, "Malacca Strait," 13.

89. Ibid., 11.

90. Ling, "The Dragon's Arteries," 15.

91. Zhang, "Energy Security and Sea Lanes," 111.

92. Ibid., 118.

93. Chen and Wu, "Malacca Strait," 14.

94. Zhang and Zhang, *Defend the Sea with a Solid Boundary*, 22–24.

95. Ibid. The Gonggu Strait is located in the Ryukyu Island chain nearly due east of Taipei. See Chen Xue'en, *Analysis of the Circulation on the East-China Shelf and the Adjacent Pacific Ocean*, PhD dissertation, University of Hamburg, 2004, 85.

96. This was the position of one Chinese strategist; interview in China, December 2005.

97. The authors thank Lt. Michael Grubb, USN, for the substantial insights that he contributed to this section.

98. 主编 王厚卿, 张兴业 [Wang Houqing and Zhang Xingye, eds.], 战役学 [*The Science of Campaigns*] (Beijing: 国防大学出版社 [National Defense University Press], 2000), 320.

99. Ibid., 330.

100. Ibid, 324–25.

101. For detailed paragraphs on defensive sea mine barrier and using sea mines to "Resist Enemy Blockade of [PLAN] Bases," see ibid., 341, 344.

102. Ibid., 327.

103. Ibid., 336.

104. Ibid., 334.

105. Ibid., 336–37.

106. Ibid., 318–19. This significant consideration is not developed further, however.

107. Ibid., 334–35.

108. Ibid., 336.

109. Ibid., 337.

110. Zhang Wenmu, "China's Energy Security and Policy Choices," *Shijie Jingji Yu Zhengzhi* [*World Economics & International Politics*], no. 5 (May 2003): 11–16, FBIS CPP20030528000169.

111. Liu and Zhang, "China's Oil Security and Its Strategic Options," 35–37, 46.

112. 沈游 [Shen You], "新世纪潜艇创新发展前瞻" ["Looking Ahead at the New Century's Nuclear Submarine Development and Innovation"], 现代舰船 [*Modern Ships*], no. 5 (2005): 15–16.

113. Li, "International SLOC Research," 355.

114. Chen and Wu, "Malacca Strait," 13.

115. Ting, "The Dragon's Arteries," 16.

116. Ibid., 15.

117. Zhang, "Energy Security and Sea Lanes," 122.

118. Da, "China's Maritime Security Strategy," 365. China's 2006 defense white paper clearly prioritizes naval modernization, stating: "The Navy is working to build itself into a modern maritime force of operation consisting of combined arms with both nuclear and conventional means of operations. . . . [It] gives high priority to the development of maritime information systems, and new generation weaponry and equipment. Efforts are being made to improve maritime battlefield capabilities, with emphasis on the construction of relevant facilities for new equipment and the development of combat support capabilities." "China's National Defense in 2006," Information Office of the State Council, People's Republic of China, 29 December 2006, http://www.fas.org/nuke/guide/china/doctrine/wp2006.html.

119. Zhang, "Energy Security and Sea Lanes," 119.

120. As a twelve-part program on China Central Television and an eight-volume book series, "The Rise of Great Powers" has enjoyed considerable popular exposure in China. Reportedly conceived on 24 November 2003 at the CPC Central Committee Political Bureau group session "Study of Historical Development of Major Countries in the World since the 15th Century," and completed in 2006, it attempts to determine the reasons why nine nations (Portugal, Spain, the Netherlands, the United Kingdom, France, Germany, Japan, Russia, and the United States) became great powers.

121. Xu, "Maritime Geostrategy," 75–81.

122. Zhang, "The Malacca Strait Problem," 25.

123. 高月 [Gao Yue], "海权, 能源 与安全" ["Maritime Rights, Resources, and Security"], 现代舰船 [Modern Ships] (December 2004): 7.

124. Ibid., 7.

125. Zhang, "Energy Security and Sea Lanes," 111.

126. Unless otherwise indicated, data in this paragraph are derived from "China's New Sub Base to Make Waves," Foreign Report, Jane's, 2 March 2006, www.janes.com/defence/naval_forces/news/fr/fr060224_1_n.shtml.

127. Presumably, the strategic importance of the Type 094 SSBNs would necessitate the deployment of other naval and air assets to protect them, particularly if they will need to venture beyond the South China Sea to achieve nuclear deterrence against the continental United States with their JL-2 SLBMs. These "bastion" forces could have an additional benefit of improving the PLAN's SLOC security options.

128. "Marine Corps," China Defense Today, http://www.sinodefence.com/navy/orbat/marinecorps.asp.

129. Notably articulated by Adm. Liu Huaqing, commander of China's navy (1982–88) and vice chairman of China's Central Military Commission (1989–97), the First Island Chain is formed by Japan and its northern and southern archipelagoes, South Korea, Taiwan, the Philippines, and the Greater Sunda Islands. The Second Island Chain runs from the Japanese archipelago south to the Bonin and Marianas islands (including Guam) and finally to the Palau group. See 刘华清 [Liu Huaqing], 刘华清回忆录 [*The Memoirs of Liu Huaqing*] (Beijing: People's Liberation Army, 2004), 437. Chinese analysts view the "island chains" alternatively as benchmarks of China's progress in maritime force projection and as fortified barriers that China must continue to penetrate to achieve freedom of maneuver in the maritime realm. See, for example, Alexander Huang, "The Chinese Navy's Offshore Active Defense Strategy: Conceptualization and Implications," *Naval War College Review* 47, no. 3 (1994): 18. Because neither the PLAN nor any other organization of the PRC government has publicly made the island chains an integral part of official policy or defined their precise scope, however, Chinese references to "island chains" must be interpreted with caution.

130. Quotations in this paragraph, unless otherwise indicated, are from Li, "International SLOC Research," 354, 355.

131. Li, "International SLOC Research," 354.

132. Zhang, "Energy Security and Sea Lanes," 124.

133. Ibid.

134. This entire paragraph is drawn from 江风 [Jiang Feng], "21世纪中国海军三大舰队构想" ["Prospects for the PLAN's Three Fleets in the 21st Century"], 舰载武器 [*Shipborne Weapons*] (June 2006): 19–22.

135. Ibid.

136. Xu, "Maritime Geostrategy," 75–81.

137. "China: Facing a Multinational Maritime Morass," *Stratfor*, 15 February 2006, http://www.stratfor.com.

138. "Sri Lanka: Exercises with U.S. Send a Message to China," *Stratfor*, 19 October 2006, http://www.stratfor.com/products/premium/read_article.php?id=278539.

139. Zhang, "Energy Security and Sea Lanes," 124.

140. Li, "Oil, China's Requirements and Sea Lane Security," 11.

141. Gao, "Maritime Rights, Resources, and Security," 7.

142. Unless otherwise specified all data in this paragraph are derived from Ling, "The Dragon's Arteries," 10, 11, 14, 17.

143. Ibid, 14.

144. Ibid, 17.

145. 顾祖华 [Gu Zuhua], "维护海上石油安全须有强大海上编队," ["In Order to Safeguard Energy Security, A Massive Naval Fleet is Necessary"], 当代海军 [*Modern Navy*] (August 2004): 40.

146. Ibid.

147. Ibid.

148. This entire paragraph is drawn from Ling, "The Dragon's Arteries," 19.

149. Ibid. This last sentence clearly suggests the need to examine possible links between China's energy strategy and its nuclear weapons strategy.

Bernard D. Cole

The Energy Factor in Chinese Maritime Strategy

THIS CHAPTER EXAMINES THE ROLE OF ENERGY SECURITY in the formulation and execution of China's maritime strategy. Discussion focuses on two primary factors: first, the growth and modernization of the People's Liberation Army Navy (PLAN), and second, Beijing's views of energy security. The latter question involves increasing demand and the need for increasing supplies, much of which lies overseas, and the need for a naval capability to safeguard the sea lanes of communication (SLOC) over which imported energy resources must flow.

Consideration of these issues will focus on five questions:

- How has Chinese naval development changed over the last decade?

- Is there an acceleration in China's naval modernization program?

- How large a factor is energy in China's naval modernization?

- Could a future PLAN protect China's energy SLOC?

- Would China desire a naval presence in the Indian Ocean or Middle East?

The PLAN has been undergoing a very significant modernization program for the past decade and a half, conducted with a strategic focus on maritime conflict scenarios involving a recalcitrant Taiwan, almost certainly aided by U.S. naval intervention. However, "beyond Taiwan" the future of China's navy will depend on several factors.

First is the trajectory of the nation's economy. Continued impressive growth in gross domestic product and most other significant economic indicators is almost universally assumed but not guaranteed. The stagnation that struck Japan's economy in the 1990s following several decades of dramatic growth is only the most recent evidence of the fragility of national economic prognostication. If the economy does keep expanding, then the People's Liberation Army (PLA) will continue receiving increasing annual budget allocations from the central government. What is not as certain is whether other sources of military financial support, provided by provincial and local governments, will continue to grow or will continue at all in the face of increasing allocations from the central government.

Of course the navy's budget could increase dramatically, exceeding the current proportion of the overall budget. Such an increase presumably would reflect Beijing's decision that at least some of the nation's vital maritime interests were in enough jeopardy to require increased attention by the PLAN. And maritime interests are the most likely area of increased security concern for China's rulers. Taiwan currently heads this list, of course, and any employment of military force to pressure the island will almost certainly feature the PLAN.

Chinese distrust of Japanese foreign policies and potential militarism is a more general concern. The current argument over energy deposits in the East China Sea is the best-known energy-related issue, and a Sino–Japanese problem that demonstrates historic enmity as well as a maritime energy dispute. Beijing's energy concerns are an even more important factor in the third major maritime area of concern: the defense of SLOC.

These strategic maritime concerns must be addressed by Beijing in an environment potentially dominated by the U.S. Navy and heavily influenced by other powerful navies, especially those of South Korea, Japan, and India. Furthermore, despite its long coastline of over 14,000 kilometers, thousands of insular possessions, and an increasing awareness of maritime issues, China's view of national security threats has almost always focused on continental, not maritime, dangers.[1]

Indeed, the PLA remains dominated by the army, with the navy probably able to exert influence in intraservice debates only as effectively as specific maritime-associated national interests justify. China's leaders seem well aware of maritime interests as vital elements in their nation's economic health and their own political legitimacy, and the importance of a capable PLAN. But China's priority for SLOC defense, especially concern for the security of its overseas energy supplies, does not play a major role in its national security policy process. Current PLAN modernization is fueled more by increased national revenues than by a general reordering of military budgeting priorities.

How Has Chinese Naval Development Changed over the Last Decade?

China is now deploying the fruits of a dedicated effort to build a new navy, one capable of confronting modern maritime opponents, especially Taiwan, Japan, and the United States. The objective is not the ability to seize command of the sea in the face of opposition by any of these naval forces but to secure vital national maritime interests, despite the presence or active intervention of these foreign navies.

China's navy has been modernizing since its inception in 1949, of course, but the process intensified during the 1980s and received particular motivation from the 1995–96 Taiwan Strait crisis. Although its naval aviation capability remains the PLAN's least capable warfare community, this is not a significant weakness in view of Taiwan's proximity to the Chinese air force's (PLAAF) many mainland bases, and the increasing integration of naval and air force aviation.

Naval aviation is particularly deficient in antisubmarine warfare and long-range search aircraft; its airborne electronic warfare capability is also weak. PLAN fixed-wing aircraft are all shore-based, with limited numbers of helicopters operating from shipboard. The former category is made up for the most part of fighter and bomber aircraft although it includes a force of longer-range aircraft capable of launching antiship cruise missiles.

The PLAN's helicopter force is small but growing in capability and numbers. Recent at-sea exercises demonstrating the navy's emphasis on operations between ships and aircraft, both fixed- and rotary-wing, have evidenced growing integration between the navy's surface and aviation forces. PLAN combatants also have finally achieved the capability of data-linking with embarked helos.[2]

The Chinese navy's surface combatant force includes fewer than twenty warships capable of operating in an early twenty-first-century naval environment. And these ships—four Sovremennyy-class, one Luhai-class, two Luhu class guided-missile destroyers (DDGs), and approximately twelve Jiangwei-class guided-missile frigates—are armed with limited antiair warfare (AAW) weapons systems. Another forty or so Chinese warships are armed with antisurface ship cruise missiles and in a non–air threat environment could perform SLOC defense duties in Chinese littoral waters.

This force remains significantly limited in the crucial areas of antisubmarine warfare, however, and it is only since the 2005 commissioning of three new classes of destroyers that the PLAN has deployed ships capable of "area AAW." This important capability enables a single ship to provide antiaircraft defense not just for itself, but for a formation of ships. Area AAW is crucial to fleet operations at sea, whether against a U.S. naval task force or for escorting an amphibious task force against Taiwan.

The PLAN's ability to deploy at extended ranges is further limited by the presence of only five replenishment-at-sea (RAS) ships. Indeed, until 2005, each of China's three fleets—the North Sea, East Sea, and South Sea fleets—was assigned just one RAS ship, and two of these are relatively small, displacing just 14,000 tons. Two larger RAS ships—displacing 28,000 tons—entered service in 2005, but it is not clear whether they will replace or augment the two smaller ships.

Beijing has also made a significant investment in amphibious shipping during the past five years. The new ships are relatively small, however, and have not significantly increased the PLAN's ability to conduct multidivision-size amphibious warfare.

Mine warfare should be an important PLAN capability, but one of uncertain competence. The mine clearance force is old, and exercises with late twentieth-century mine clearance technology have only recently been reported.[3] Despite its obvious utility against Taiwan, mine warfare apparently is no more attractive to the PLAN than it is to the Taiwan or U.S. navies. The PLAN's minelaying capability is more formidable and could serve as an effective tool in a maritime campaign against Taiwan.

Some sentiment for acquiring aircraft carriers no doubt is present among naval officers, but there appears little support for this very expensive acquisition elsewhere among China's military and civilian decision makers. Beijing has acquired four decommissioned aircraft carriers during the past quarter-century but none has been viewed as an operating unit. The most recent acquisition was the ex-Soviet Kuznetsov-class carrier Varyag. This hulk has been dry-docked in Dalian, almost certainly to conduct the hull maintenance necessary to keep the ship afloat. The repairs necessary to allow the carrier to operate as such—especially the installation of a functioning engineering plant—have apparently not been completed.[4] Nonetheless, recent reports of the purchase of carrier-compatible Su-33 aircraft from Russia indicate that the PLAN sentiment for acquiring large aircraft-capable ships remains.[5]

The navy's most potent strength lies in its numerous, modernized submarines. It currently deploys an impressive and improving force of conventionally powered submarines. The twelve Kilo-class and twelve to fifteen Song-class conventionally powered attack boats are not well suited for long-range deployments (to the Indian Ocean, for example) but are formidable weapons systems within approximately one thousand nautical miles (nm) of China's coast. As Beijing continues to build Songs or buy Kilos from Russia and as these boats become operational, the thirty or forty older Ming- and Romeo-class boats will probably be decommissioned.

The next likely step in the development of China's submarine force will be the incorporation of an air-independent propulsion (AIP) system into some of its boats. An AIP system enables a conventionally powered submarine to remain submerged for up to forty days (at slow speed) instead of the usual four days before snorkeling is required.[6] The PLAN launched a new indigenously produced submarine in 2004 named the "*Yuan*" by Western observers. This boat was at first thought to be a candidate for AIP installation, but its hull size indicates that it more likely represents a Chinese attempt to replicate the Kilo-class.[7]

The PLAN's five nuclear-powered Han-class attack submarines are old and noisy, and difficult to maintain. The nuclear-powered submarine force will soon improve, however, as the new Shang-class becomes operational. China's past failure to deploy an effective fleet ballistic missile (FBM) submarine will soon change with the deployment of the Jin-class FBM boat currently under construction, with Russian assistance. At least one of these has been launched, and as many as five are thought to be under construction.[8]

China is also following the U.S. example by employing its navy as a diplomatic instrument. Since 1983, the PLAN has periodically deployed two- or three-ship task forces on diplomatic missions to Southeast, South, and Southwest Asia and to the western hemisphere. In 2002, a Luhu-class DDG and an oiler completed a circumnavigation of the globe, a significant accomplishment.[9] Another task force visited the United States in September 2006.

Is There an Acceleration in China's Naval Modernization Program?

PLAN modernization received increased priority and funding after the early to mid-1990s, almost certainly receiving additional impetus following the March 1996 Taiwan Strait crisis. Beijing began acquiring Kilo-class submarines from Russia and began indigenous production of the Song-class submarines in the mid-1990s. The new nuclear submarine program also began during this period. It is unlikely that the modernization of China's submarine force began by coincidence with the PLA's realization of its shortcomings following U.S. naval intervention in the Taiwan imbroglio in 1996.

The events of the mid-1990s no doubt spurred PLAN modernization of its surface combatant fleet as well. In particular, the PLAN realized its weaknesses in specific naval warfare areas, especially AAW. Hence, the new Luyang I–, Luyang II–, and Luzhou-class destroyers and the Jiangkai II frigates appear to be equipped with significantly improved AAW defense systems. An area AAW capability, crucial for fleet operations in opposed scenarios, is apparently included.

PLAN modernization also includes other naval warfare area improvements. Amphibious force growth since the mid-1990s has included significant shipbuilding programs, including almost twenty tank landing ships displacing approximately 3,500 tons and possibly a landing platform dock that may displace more than 10,000 tons.[10] Even more important, however, has been additional amphibious training, even mission specialization, assigned to at least two PLA divisions in the Nanjing and Guangzhou military regions. The marine corps remains at two brigade strength, but its officer accession process has been regularized under PLAN aegis.

PLA aviation capabilities have also benefited. As is the case with amphibious warfare, more significant even than important equipment acquisitions— Su-27s, Su-30s, air-to-air refueling, and AWACs-type aircraft—has been increased air force and naval aviation integration, and advances in operational capabilities, including overwater flights.[11]

The two most important areas of PLAN modernization during the past decade have relatively little to do with hardware. The first is the overhaul of the personnel education and training system that has occurred as the Chinese military strives to enlist and retain personnel capable of mastering the technological complexities of current-day warships. This extends to the second area, the PLAN's revised and seemingly improved training paradigm. The old ship and unit training system, slaved to the calendar year, seems now far more flexible, which enhances the integration of maintenance and shore-based training requirements. The PLAN is also continuing to increase its participation in joint training and exercise activities.

How Large a Factor Is Energy in China's Naval Modernization?

Energy security is defined as "assuring adequate, reliable supplies of energy at reasonable prices and in ways that do not jeopardize major national values and objectives."[12] This includes three primary elements: availability, affordability, and military assurance. First, energy must be available at a confirmed location with access to the energy reserves—especially fossil fuels including petroleum, natural gas, and coal—to satisfy the economic demands of an early twenty-first-century nation. Affordability is the second element in energy security: fuel must be available at an acceptable cost.[13] The third element in energy security is military assurance: China must be able to safely and confidently obtain and import required energy supplies. These three elements are not completely discrete, of course, but are linked by common geographic, economic, political, and military threads.

China's emergence as a global economic power has been accompanied by dramatically increasing energy demand. At the same time, Beijing is modernizing its military to carry out specific national security missions. These two major developments—economic and military—will to a large extent determine the degree of security China will demand for nondomestic energy supplies.

Energy demands and interests are to a significant degree maritime in nature and form a PLAN mission. The 2004 defense white paper notes the "priority [of] the building of the Navy." Beijing is very much aware of the American role in any future maritime energy calculus, including a PLAN strategic view of the American presence in Japan, Taiwan, and the Philippines as a potential "blockade" across China's legitimate maritime security interests.[14]

In the near term, China's efforts to build a navy able to satisfy these maritime security concerns focus on Taiwan; in the midterm, they include the disputes with Japan over natural gas deposits in the East China seabed and with the claimants to South China Sea territories.

China is seeking to emulate the United States by establishing a strategic reserve of petroleum supplies (with ninety days' worth of import coverage planned by 2015–20, in Beijing's case) to counter fluctuations in the international oil market.[15] This plan is under way with the first of at least four petroleum reserve bases under construction near Shanghai and others to be built along China's coast. Two bases will be located in Zhejiang and Shandong provinces while the fourth will be built in China's northeastern Liaoning province.

Guangdong province officials are also campaigning for a strategic reserve to "ensure the economic security of the [Pearl River] delta."[16] The nonmilitary character of these strategic reserves is evidenced in their planned construction as above-ground tank farms near China's coastline, leading to the conclusion that Beijing's interest in securing energy supplies springs from an economic rather than military rationale.

Could a Future PLA Navy Protect China's Energy SLOC?

Asia's vast continental and maritime sweep is commonly divided into Northeast, Southeast, East, South, and Southwest regions, but the increasing globalization of energy producers and consumers, linked by transportation and the world marketplace, dictates that consideration of energy security cuts across and includes all of these regions.

Although China has been primarily a continental power throughout its history, it is a maritime nation as well. First, China relies on its extensive river network for communication, commerce, and energy transportation. Riverine issues are in the main domestic, although international complications arise from rivers on international borders or whose management affects other nations. The Amur, bordered by China and Russia, is an example of the first; the Mekong (called the Lancang in Chinese), with its headwaters in China but its primary impact on the nations of Southeast Asia, marks the second case. This river's headwaters are in southwestern China, but its course through Southeast Asia gives the nations of the Indo-Chinese peninsula—Vietnam, Laos, Thailand, Cambodia—a direct and intense interest in Beijing's attempts to harness the upper reaches of the Mekong for generating hydroelectric power. These efforts are already reducing the river's flow downstream, where it is a vital resource.[17]

Coastal waters, defined here as those lying within 100 nautical miles of China's shore, are in part sovereign, in part international, and marked by the thousands of islands belonging to or claimed by China.[18] Of particular note are the islands disputed with Japan, Taiwan, and Vietnam. Coastal waters are trafficked by ocean-going vessels making or leaving port, of course, but also serve hundreds of thousands of fishing boats, ferries, and coastal commercial craft, including energy carriers.

This maritime area is also sensitive from a naval viewpoint because its control is absolutely necessary for Beijing to maintain national sovereignty, economic autonomy, and security for both regime and people. Second, coastal waters provide China with critical maritime highways, as do the regional waters of East Asia, the third category of maritime dependence.

China's regional maritime arena includes the Yellow, East, and South China seas, which delineate the region from Japan and the Korean Peninsula in the north to the Strait of Malacca in the south. China's interests in these waters by definition pose international issues. China shares maritime boundaries and disputes with North Korea, South Korea, Japan, and Vietnam, as well as maritime disputes with the Philippines, Brunei, Indonesia, and Malaysia.

These seas are crucial to China as sources of food, minerals, transportation, and defense. They are of course international bodies of water, linking China to friends and opponents, both current and potential. Hence, any evaluation of East Asian military balances must include these linkages between China and Russia, Korea, Japan, and the nations of Southeast Asia, all of whom are Association of Southeast Asian Nations (ASEAN) member states. And the United States, by virtue of its omnipresent naval and air forces throughout the Pacific Ocean and adjacent seas, is linked directly to maritime China.

Finally, the oceans of the world are increasingly vital to China's continued economic growth and national well-being, especially under the aegis of "comprehensive national power" frequently noted by Beijing.[19] All these maritime areas are connected, of course, but they are characterized by different conditions and pose different problems for China's civilian and military leaders.

The oceans increasingly concern Beijing because they are necessary for China's continued economic growth, consolidation of its status as a world power, and hence continuation of the Chinese Communist Party (CCP) regime in power. Beijing already deploys the world's second-largest merchant marine, trailing only Panama's "flag of convenience" fleet.[20] China's shipbuilding industry is also among the world's most robust, with the largest shipyard in history under construction in the Shanghai estuary. This city is also the principal container port for Northeast Asia, the third largest in the world. Its maritime importance to China is matched by Hong Kong, which is the portal to southern China and the world's busiest container port.

The PLAN presently is capable only of defending coastal SLOC. Even that capability must be qualified, however, given the proven difficulty of defending surface ships against submarine attack.[21] Defense of China's economic offshore infrastructure is an important PLAN concern; the South China Sea would become an area of primary operations should significant energy resources be discovered in that sea. PLAN forces have regularly deployed to the Paracel Islands since the early 1970s and to the Spratly Islands since the early 1980s. A Chinese military presence has been established on more than a half-dozen of the islands.

Would China Desire a Naval Presence in the Indian Ocean or Middle East?

The Indian Ocean is of particular importance to the issue of SLOC security, given China's increasing dependence on the energy resources of Southwest Asia and the Middle East (to include East Africa). These very long SLOC stretch for thousands of miles—over 5,500 nm from Shanghai to the Persian Gulf, for instance.

There have been a few PLAN cruises to the Middle East during the past ten years, and even one to Western Europe, but these have been unusual deployments by no more than two or three ships.[22] For China to establish a constant or even frequent naval presence in these far waters would require a very significant, dedicated effort by the PLA. That said, PLAN planners may advocate the Soviet policy of the 1970s and 1980s, which stationed a repair ship and a two-four ship task group at distant locations, such as Socotra, in the mouth of the Gulf of Aden.

First, the PLAN would have to acquire ocean-going repair ships and a significant number of RAS ships, enough to deploy one with every task group deploying. An alternative would be to rely on refueling and reprovisioning ports en route, but this would constrain at-sea operational options, tying the ships to shore bases, and placing PLAN operational options at the mercy of the countries in which the ports were located. It would also not address the question of rearming combatants at sea, should that be required. PLAN port facilities would no doubt currently be made available by Burma and Pakistan, and possibly Bangladesh, but the first two of these are among the world's least stable polities, and the third lies effectively in India's bight.

This raises another difficulty with maintaining a PLAN presence in Southwest Asian/Middle Eastern waters: the formidable Indian navy and air force. New Delhi would have to acquiesce to such a presence, and little in the history of Sino–Indian relations or differing national interests would offer reassurance to a Chinese naval strategist evaluating this situation.

Finally, why would Beijing want to establish such a far-flung naval presence? What would be the threat to be confronted? The current and probable threats from terrorism, piracy, or other international criminals are highly unlikely to require or be efficiently countered by naval presence, and Beijing would be wiser to join already in-place international efforts dedicated to improving at-sea security.

Should Beijing decide that the United States, perhaps during Chinese military action against Japan or Taiwan, would try to intercept its SLOC, then PLAN engagement might be envisioned, but to do so on anything more than a sacrificial basis would have to come at the end of a massive, multiyear effort at naval expansion. Such a program would surprise no one and would simply engender corresponding increases in naval and air presence by the United States and probably by India.

Furthermore, PLAN presence in Southwest Asian waters would be based on the defense of SLOC and energy reserves in that region, but China is already moving to establish alternate paths to ensuring their security. These include developing alternate fuel sources within China and establishing shortened or nonmaritime lines of transportation for energy imports. The former effort is already bearing considerable fruit in the areas of hydropower, solar power, and wind power; the latter may be seen in the very considerable and rapid domestic pipeline construction that has occurred in China during the past decade.

These pipelines are built both to improve the weak internal energy distribution system and also to link up to pipelines of foreign origin. The most significant among these are the proposed line from Siberia, designed to take advantage of the huge reserves in Asiatic Russia, and to China's west the line already under construction from the rich fields in Kazakhstan. Additional projects are under consideration or in planning that would enable China to draw on Caspian Basin reserves, either directly, or through a pipeline through Iran to the Pakistani port of Gwadar, expansion of which is being funded and supervised by Beijing.

This would at least shorten the at-sea time for tankers en route to China, as would the pipeline recently approved from Yunnan province through Burma to the coast of the Andaman Sea.[23] Other southern options include a pipeline proposed by Bangkok to run from the Gulf of Thailand to Yunnan; the Thais are also urging construction of a canal across the Kra Isthmus, and the Malaysians for a pipeline across the Malaysian peninsula near the Thai border. The first of these expensive propositions would shorten transit time, and both would eliminate the need for tankers to transit the narrow

Malacca Strait, which is both navigationally constrained and a tempting target for terrorists and pirates. All of these factors mitigate against a decision by Beijing to establish a Chinese naval presence in Southwest Asian or Middle Eastern waters.

China's 2004 white paper on defense directly addressed the importance of national security interests in the coastal and regional maritime areas.[24] The authors described defense of national sovereignty, territorial integrity, and "maritime rights and interest" as "national security goals."

Southwest Asia is the source of roughly 45 percent of China's imported oil while most of its imported natural gas comes from Southeast Asia.[25] Hence, these imports must undergo a long seaborne transit. The PLA is perhaps most directly involved in China's search for energy security through the maritime role of securing SLOC and ocean-bed energy fields, and the United States is viewed as the likely force that will have to be countered.

It would be difficult for even the U.S. military to interrupt China's SLOC over which international energy flows, but these appear vulnerable to PLAN eyes. Should the United States attempt physically to interrupt either SLOC or overland pipelines, it would almost certainly mean directly attacking China, directly attacking other nations (hosting pipelines and their pumping stations), interfering with the peacetime passage of third-country tankers at sea, or all of the above.

The SLOC are most vulnerable not on the high seas but at transit points through narrow straits, including Hormuz, the Nine-Degree Channel, Malacca, Luzon, and Taiwan. The most likely tactic for the United States to employ would be a blockade of Chinese oil port terminals or of these choke points. Such actions would be acts of war against China and other nations, and also would likely not succeed in significantly reducing China's overall energy supply.

Conclusion

China's maritime strategy is one of offshore defense, meaning that the PLAN will strive to "maintain control over the maritime traffic in the coastal waters of the mainland" and the resources in those waters.[26] Delineating the capability necessary to accomplish these goals is not easy, even when focused on the waters extending from the Chinese coast to approximately 100 nm east of Taiwan along a line from the Philippines to Japan, and all of the Yellow Sea.

Continued constructive relations with the nations of Southeast Asia should ease Beijing's concern about commanding the seas bordering the narrow Malacca Strait. Defense of more distant SLOC, from Malacca, between the South China Sea and the Indian Ocean, to the Hormuz Strait at the mouth of the Persian Gulf, would require a quantum leap in PLAN capabilities. Conceivably, however, China could choose to deploy PLAN units as part of a multinational force. Beijing might also follow the Soviet model of stationing small naval task groups in the area, but these would be of limited utility in a threat scenario.

Beijing's decision-making process for using the PLAN to ensure energy security will include answering four primary questions. First, how secure does the CCP leadership feel about its place in power in Beijing? Second, how willing is the Chinese leadership to rely on the world energy market to ensure the affordability, availability, and safe passage of imported supplies? Third, how confident is the leadership about U.S. peaceful intentions, possibly in the face of contentious Chinese actions, such as increasing military pressure against Taiwan? Finally, how much confidence does the leadership have in PLAN capabilities?

The U.S. Navy will protect these SLOC for the foreseeable future, but a Sino–American crisis (over Taiwan, for instance) might drive Beijing to decide that the PLAN has to defend them. China would have to make a major change in national budgeting priorities to build a navy and air force capable of protecting the extended SLOCs that carry much of its imported oil and natural gas. This degree of PLA growth is inhibited by several factors.

First, developing China's economy and ensuring the welfare of its people remains top priority for the government and the CCP. Second, while Taiwan remains the most sensitive issue between Beijing and Washington, the present economic and political situation on the island, U.S. and Chinese interest in keeping the issue within peaceful bounds, and common interest in the campaign against terrorism all mitigate against the reunification issue deteriorating to the point of hostilities. Hence, Sino–American relations should remain peaceful, if frequently contentious.

Third, there is little indication that the Chinese military's strategic paradigm is going to change significantly in the near future. The PLA remains dominated by the army, with the navy only as strong as specific maritime-associated national interests justify. Current PLAN modernization seems fueled by increased national revenues rather than by a reordering of budgeting priorities within the PLA.

In summary, China's navy today has the most capable conventionally powered submarine force in the world, a large and capable surface combatant force, and capable forces in other maritime mission areas. It is already capable of overpowering Taiwan's navy, offers a serious challenge to the Japanese Maritime Self-Defense Force, and poses a thought-provoking challenge to possible U.S. naval intervention in a Taiwan scenario. Energy security will remain a PLAN mission, but is unlikely to become a driver in China's naval modernization.

Notes

1. See, for instance, Ye Zicheng, "China's Sea Power Must Be Subordinate to Its Land Power," *International Herald Leader* [*Guoji Xianqu Daobao*], 2 March 2007, OSC# CPP20070302455003.

2. Author's discussion with Jiangwei III–class frigate commanding officer in May 2006.

3. See, for instance, Guo Weimin and Ma Aimin, "PRC S&T: Visualized Simulation of Image Sonar on ROV," *Fire Control and Command Control* [*Huoli Yu Zhihui Kongzhi*] (February 2006): 66–68, OSC# CPP20060803476001.

4. See pictures at http://www.sinodefenceforum.com/showthread.php?t=529. Also, discussion at MOSNEWS, "China Converts Russian Ship to Build Its First Aircraft Carrier," at http://mosnews.com/news/2005/08/25/chinacarrier.shtml.

5. For instance, see "Senior Military Officer: China to Develop Its Own Aircraft Carrier Fleet," *Wen Wei Po* (Hong Kong), 10 March 2006, OSC# CPP20060310508004, http://www.wenweipo.com/news_print.phtlm?news_id=CH060300007; and see "China Plans to Procure 50 SU-33 Carrier-Borne Fighters from Russia," *Sankei Shimbun,* 6 November 2006, U.S. Pacific Command Virtual Intelligence Center (VIC) website, 7 November 2006, www.vic-info.org.

6. A good explanation of AIP is provided in Richard Scott, "Boosting the Staying Power of the Non-Nuclear Submarine," *Jane's International Defense Review* 32 (November 1999): 41–50.

7. See Andrew Erickson and Lyle Goldstein, "China's Future Nuclear Submarine Force," paper prepared for the U.S. Naval War College, October 2005; and Lyle Goldstein and William S. Murray, "Undersea Dragons: China's Maturing Submarine Force," *International Security* 28, no. 4 (2004): 161–96.

8. This reflects traditional U.S. thinking, however, and Beijing may decide not to follow the paradigm of one SSBN on patrol, a second undergoing maintenance, and a third training for patrol.

9. The flotilla's voyage is summarized in "PLAN World Cruise 2002: Special Report," Asia-Pacific Daily News Summary, PACOM Virtual Information Center Site (VIC) 23 September 2002, http://www1.apan-info.net/. See also Bernard D. Cole, "*Oil for the Lamps of China*": *Beijing's 21st Century Search for Energy* (Washington, D.C.:

National Defense University, 2003), 74. The PLAN's execution of the traditional naval mission of "presence" is detailed in Kenneth W. Allen and Eric A. McVadon, *China's Foreign Military Relations* (Washington, D.C.: The Henry L. Stimson Center, 1999).

10. See Eric Wertheim, *The Naval Institute Guide to Combat Fleets of the World: 2005–2006* (Annapolis, Md.: Naval Institute Press, 2005), 118–19. The landing platform dock is discussed at "PLAN Amphibious Transport Dock 071 LPD," 14 November 2006, http://www.china-defense.com/forum/index.php?showforum=4.

11. For instance, see "Nanjing Military Region Air Force Conducts Night Attack Operation Exercise at Sea," *PLA Daily [Jiefengjun Bao]*, 1 June 2004, www.pladaily.com.cn; also, author's discussion with PLAAF 9th Air Division DCOS, May 2002.

12. Daniel Yergin, "Energy Security in the 1990s," *Foreign Affairs* 67, no. 1 (1988): 11.

13. Discussion of various aspects of these elements is ably presented in *The PRC's Global Pursuit of Natural Resources* (Seattle: The National Bureau of Asian Research, 2006), especially the essays by Philip Andrews-Speed et al. ("Natural Resources Strategy and Resource Diplomacy") and Aaron L. Friedberg ("'Going Out': China's Pursuit of Natural Resources and Its Implications for Grand Strategy"). Also see Erica S. Downs, "The Chinese Energy Security Debate," *The China Quarterly*, no. 177 (March 2004): 21–41.

14. PLA General Wen Zongren, of the Academy of Military Science, cited in the U.S. Department of Defense (DoD), *Report on the Military Power of the People's Republic of China, Report to Congress 2005*.

15. Zhang Guobao, cited as "China's energy tsar," in "China Is Building Strategic Petroleum Reserve," *Dow Jones* (23 May 2004) in *Alexander's* 9, no. 12 (2004), http:www.gasandoil.com/GOC/news/nts42425.htm. One Chinese analyst, Yang Zing, of the Energy Research Bureau, has estimated that ninety days of petroleum reserves would be accumulated until 2015 ("China Builds Four Oil Reserve Bases," *Agence France-Presse [AFP]*, 29 June 2004). Liu Keyu of CNPC's Petroleum Economics and Information Center projected stockpile goals of twenty days' supply in 2005, fifty days' in 2010, and ninety days' in 2020 ("Asia Pacific Daily Summary," *VIC Site*, 16 September 2002), but these amounts have not been realized.

16. "Guangdong to House Oil Reserve Bases," *People's Daily*, 28 February 2006, http://english.people.com.cn/200602/28/eng20060228_246572.html.

17. See information provided in "Mekong River, the Lifeblood of Southeast Asia," http://www.irn.org/programs/mekong; also see Chen Liang, "For China, Xiaowang Dam a Reservoir for Progress," http://www.ipsnews.net/mekong/stories/xiaowan.html.

18. A nautical mile equals approximately 1.2 statute miles. Maritime sovereignty is defined by the 1982 United Nations Convention on the Law of the Sea (UNCLOS), which has been accepted—if not formally signed and ratified—by almost all the world's nations with coastlines. Briefly, it delineates four primary areas of national maritime control: (a) the Territorial Sea extends from a nation's coastline 12 nm seaward and gives sovereign rights over the sea, airspace above it, seabed, and subsoil; (b) the contiguous zone extends from a nation's coastline 24 nm seaward and

gives the control to prevent and punish infringement of its customs, fiscal, immigration or sanitary laws and regulations within its territory or territorial sea; (c) the exclusive economic zone (EEZ) extends to a maximum of 200 nm from a nation's coastline and gives sovereign rights with respect to natural resources and certain economic activities, and to exercise jurisdiction over marine science research and environmental protection; and (d) the continental shelf (the national area of the seabed) may be claimed out to a maximum distance of 350 nm from a nation's coastline and gives sovereign rights for exploring and exploiting the seabed.

19. See, for instance, Hu Angang and Men Honghua, "The Rising of Modern China: Comprehensive National Power and Grand Strategy," paper presented at the KEIP Conference on "China and East Asian Economy," Seoul, 19–20 March 2004, http://www.kiep.go.kr/.

20. *CIA World Factbook*, at https://www.cia.gov/library/publications/the-world-factbook/index.html.

21. The difficulties of combating submarines in World Wars I and II remain largely unsolved; antisubmarine warfare is extremely difficult, time consuming, and resource intensive.

22. See, for instance, "PLA Navy Fleet Makes First Portcall to Hong Kong," *People's Daily*, 11 November 2001, http://english.peopledaily.com.cn/200111/10/eng20011110_84297.shtml; "India, China to Conduct Joint Naval Drills," *Indo Asian News Service*, 25 November 2005, hindustantimes.com; and "PLA Navy Ships Visit Hawaii," *PLA Daily [Jiefengjun Bao]*, 6 September 2006, www.pladaily.com.cn/.

23. "China Wants Pipeline to Myanmar to Secure Oil Supplies," *Straits-Times*, 31 July 2004, in *Alexander's Gas & Oil Connections* 9, no. 16 (18 August 2004), http://www.gasandoil.com/goc/news/nts43358.htm; "China Approves US$998 Million Sino-Myanmar Oil Pipeline," *Asia Pulse News*, 17 April 2006, http://goliath.ecnext.com/coms2/gi_0199-5430136/CHINA-APPROVES-US-998-MLN.html.

24. This and other Chinese defense white papers may be found at http://www.china.org.cn/e-white/index.htm.

25. Philip Bowring, "Oil-Thirsty Asia Looks to Calm Gulf Waters," *International Herald Tribune*, 9 February 2006, http://www.iht.com/.

26. PLAN Commander, Admiral Shi Yunsheng, quoted in "Jiang Made the Final Decision on Adopting Offshore Defense Strategy," *Oriental Daily News [Tung Fang Jih Pao]*, 24 August 2001, OSC# CPP20010824000062.

James Bussert

China's Surface Combatants and the New SLOC Defense Imperative

THE TERM SEA LINE OF COMMUNICATION (SLOC) refers to the oceanic transport routes over which nations engage with one another. The term may also remind readers of the epic battles between submarines and the convoy-escorting warships that struggled to protect merchant ships transporting critical war material across the Atlantic and Pacific oceans.

China, a land power that has been weak and ineffectual in the naval realm, at least in the modern era, rarely comes to mind in this context. The missions of the People's Liberation Army Navy (PLAN) have long focused on coastal defense—a similarity that this institution shares with its prime mentor, the Soviet navy. Other chapters in this volume describe how China's energy needs have created a worldwide network of oil and gas resources that spans waters ranging from hundreds to thousands of miles to reach Chinese ports.

Although the Taiwan issue is the scenario upon which the PLAN appears to be focused at present, the PLAN's (in)adequacy to meet prospective maritime SLOC protection mission is the subject of this chapter. Surely, the inherent difficulty of defending these long sea lanes represents a potential critical vulnerability for today's China. During a war, merchant ships in general and tankers in particular would require naval protection to transit safely. Can current PLAN warships perform the SLOC protection missions; if not, what ship designs and combat systems would be needed to meet PLAN requirements for the evolving SLOC mission?

New Mission—Tough Choices

Peacetime commerce protection has a minimal warship requirement because terrorist attack prevention as well as stop and search roles are missions that are indeed vital in today's maritime security environment but which fall below the threshold of major hostilities between nation-states. This chapter will not examine these activities but will instead focus squarely on wartime "control" SLOC missions, dividing these into green and blue water endeavors.

This chapter will refer to blue waters as the high seas beyond China's continental shelf. Green waters will refer to those sea areas adjacent to China and generally comprising China's two-hundred-nautical-mile exclusive economic zone. The blue and green water SLOC warship and combat systems requirements would be somewhat different. Here it is essential to note that blue water SLOC defense is not simply a future PLAN mission because Chinese warships have routinely supported forces occupying South China Sea bases seized from Vietnam, as well as other contested islets and reefs of the Spratly Islands. Map 1 shows People's Republic of China (PRC) energy transit SLOC that the PLAN might be ordered to protect.

Map 1. People's Republic of China Energy Transit SLOC

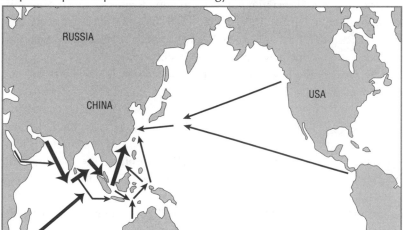

It is evident that some sea lanes would almost certainly be too challenging for the PRC even to attempt to protect, such as the China to Canada or Latin American routes. Other blue water SLOC may not convey enough energy volume to justify the expenditure of limited PLAN assets. The Middle East to China sea lane across the Indian Ocean and the South China Sea, however, is a route that would seem to justify the maximum support of the best PLAN warships. Alternatively, energy sources from Chinese offshore oil fields can be considered to be part of the green water SLOC defense problem.

In a fight to protect the SLOC, older diesel submarines could be used, but newer Songs and Yuans would be more effective. Shallow waters and complex acoustics (e.g., those of the littoral region close to the Malacca Strait) would be quite amenable to the effectiveness of these platforms, particularly if used to attack passing warships in choke points. New, high-speed nuclear submarines that China is developing (e.g., the Type 093 Shang-class SSN) would be better employed in other blue water operations either in the central Pacific or in the Indian Ocean.

Submarines have a role to play in protecting SLOC, but more important is the antiair warfare and escort capability provided by modern surface combatants.[1] Indeed, this new mission area can be used to help explain the accelerating pace of the PLAN's modernization of its surface combatant forces over the last five years.

New Momentum in the Surface Fleet

The first new generation PLAN warship designs acquired were two 5,000-ton Luhu DDGs. These ships, built between 1991 and 1993, feature French DUBV-23 and -43 hulls and variable depth sonars, American LM-2500 gas turbine power plants, two helicopters, and TAVITAC combat display system. The Five-Year Plan from 1996 to 2000 saw the PLAN add one 6,600-ton Luhai DDG to its order of battle. This vessel is equipped with French short-range Crotale surface-to-air missiles (SAM), Italian IPN-11 CDS, two Z9 helicopters, and the DUBV-23 bow sonar, 100 mm fast reload guns, and shows evidence of low radar cross section design considerations. The Luhai is powered by combined diesel/gas turbines. The Z-9 shipboard helicopters were later replaced with Russian Ka-28 antisubmarine warfare (ASW) helicopters.

In 1999 and 2000 (and later in 2005 and 2006) China imported from Russia a total of four 7,900-ton Sovremennyy DDGs, each armed with eight dreaded Mach 3 over the horizon SS-N-22 "carrier killer" surface to surface missiles (SSMs), 3D radar, SA-N-6 SAMs, and sophisticated medium frequency MG-552 sonar. Sovremennyys are powered by steam propulsion plants. Also at the end of the 1990s, eight first generation Jiangwei guided missile frigates (FFGs) were converted into Jiangwei II versions by replacing the existing short-range indigenous HQ-61 SAM launcher with French Crotale systems, and by adding the TAVITAC CDS and DUBV-23 sonar. The prioritization of underway replenishment capability was demonstrated with the launching of the 37,000-ton Nanyun auxiliary oiler replenishment (AOR) ship, which also features a helicopter deck. This ship is based in the South Sea Fleet. Added in 1991 were Houjian-class missile patrol boats, which first gave the PLAN a combat direction system (CDS). Later, Jianghu III, Jiangwei and Jiangkai frigates; and Luhai, Luda II, and Luda III DDGs all received CDS. Indigenous C-802 antiship cruise missiles (ASCMs) entered service in 1994 and are now found on many of the new Chinese-built warships.

As significant as those new PLAN warships and combat systems were, 2001–6 produced even more impressive additions. Two 7,000-ton Luyang I DDGs were constructed in 2004; they feature a Russian SA-N-12 SAM launcher, Type 630 close-in weapon system (CIWS), improved ZJK 5 cth ernet CDS, and a Bandstand ASCM supporting datalink. The following year a pair of Luyang II DDGs of similar displacement created a stir when they appeared with an AEGIS-like phased array radar and eight six-cell vertical launch system (VLS) modules. The real surprise was that neither was a copy of the Russian or American systems but were instead unique Chinese designs. Yet another pair of new Luzhou DDGs followed in 2006, armed with a long-ranged Russian area air defense system, the SA-N-6. Luzhous carry six eight-cell VLS modules coupled to a navalized 30N6E1 S-300 TOR air defense radar similar to those that protect major cities like Shanghai and Beijing. Surprisingly, however, Luzhous lack the stealth design and combined diesel/gas turbine propulsion of all other new DDGs, relying on a steam power plant instead. The bow sonar, CIWS, two helo hangers, and combat systems are similar to the other four new DDG classes.

A new class of two stealthy Jiangkai 054 frigates appeared in 2003, which were quickly followed in 2006 by the Jiangkai II class. The latter class is upgraded with a rectangular module VLS (which looks similar to the U.S. Navy's MK 41 missile launching system), four Headlight fire control SAM directors, and the Bandstand SSM link to eight new YJ-83 SSMs. Two new 23,000-ton, 10,000-mile range Fuchi AOR underway replenishment ships also joined the fleet in 2003. Complementing these larger ships are the serially produced (with over twenty already built) Houbei-class high-speed,

low-observable missile catamarans. While the Houbei's sea-keeping quali-
ties and endurance remain to be determined, its invulnerability to torpedoes
because of shallow draft and high speed, not to mention the considerable
punch of its eight indigenous ASCMs, means that the new patrol boat could
offer formidable capabilities for green water SLOC operations.

China has also made impressive progress in developing indigenous
ASCMs, as demonstrated by the successful strike by Hezbollah fighters
wielding a Chinese-made 120-km-range C-802 against Israeli naval vessel
INS *Hanit* on 14 July 2006. The follow-on 160-km-range C-803 may have
a supersonic terminal attack phase and is already being deployed on PLAN
surface combatants.

Despite ample progress of late, the PLAN surface forces still have glaring deficiencies that would present major problems for SLOC protection.
Remaining limitations include the PLAN's retaining of more than one hundred obsolete pre-1990 patrol craft, warships, and associated equipment and
continued reliance on Russian and Western sources for hulls, systems, and
maintenance. ASW weakness may pose the biggest challenge for Chinese surface combatants. Only three PLAN warships, Luda DDG 166 and two Luhu
DDGs, are equipped with variable depth sonars; none carries powerful low-
frequency sonars optimized to find submarines, and the PLAN does not yet
have a significant inventory of ASW helicopters. To date, there are no Chinese warships confirmed to carry the CY-1 long-range antisubmarine rocket–
type ASW weapons, but the Jiangkai II frigate VLS is a possible candidate.[2]

Before discussing the operational context for potential PLAN SLOC
operations, an important caveat is in order. This particular chapter focuses
on the Chinese navy's surface force, but this is in no way to suggest that sub-
surface and air forces are irrelevant to the SLOC protection mission. Quite
the contrary—naval air and submarine reconnaissance and attack capabilities would be absolutely crucial for any PLAN effort to undertake blue or
green water SLOC protection and support.

Green Water SLOC Defense

The challenges of coastal-water convoy protection constitute a vital strategic question for Beijing because of China's lengthy 14,500-km coastline.
Moreover, most of China's critical energy supplies lie in the direction of its
southwestern flank. A considerable amount of the country's heavy industry, not to mention many of the country's largest ports, including Dalian,
Qingdao, Shanghai, and Tianjin, are located in the northeast—a fact that

underscores the importance of China's coastal SLOC. Indeed, one plausible explanation for current Chinese naval development strategy is that it seeks to achieve the strategic depth necessary to drive an adversary sufficiently far into the Pacific so that this critical coastal sea lane and the eastern seaboard are more generally beyond the range of easy attack from naval and air strikes.

China has already deployed surface combatants to illustrate its determination to defend territorial waters and exclusive economic zones. Indeed, the PRC has employed some of the PLAN's most powerful warships to make a strong political statement of Beijing's resolution on such matters. Japan and China are both exploring for gas from the large Shirakaba/Chunxiao field in the East China Sea. There exist overlapping national exclusive economic zone claims, and China has increasingly intruded into the waters claimed by Japan since the 1980s.[3] China's maritime presence in these waters has escalated from trawlers or coast guard cutters, to intelligence and research ships, and, most recently, to warships. Frigates were the first PLAN warships to enter the fray, but in January 2005, a Sovremennyy destroyer entered the disputed area. The situation escalated significantly in August 2005 with a five ship surface action group (SAG) foray consisting of a Sovremennyy DDG 137, two Jianghu I frigates (hulls 515 and 517), a Fuqing-class 886 replenishment ship, and the Dondiao (hull 851) intelligence ship. Deployment of this SAG reflects the strongest statement yet of the PRC to Japan regarding rights to the energy deposits in the East China Sea. There are several future SLOC roles for SAGs such as this, including sanitizing a path a suitable distance ahead of tankers and clearing or nullifying opposition forces in critical contested zones.

At present, the PLAN lacks assets for ASW hunter/killer groups or convoy escorts, warfighting innovations that proved so effective for Allied forces during the World Wars. Until the mid-1980s, most PLAN frigates carried ineffective high-frequency hull-mounted Russian sonars. In 1983, however Hudong shipyard revised the bow rake and anchor locations and added an improved SJD-5A bow sonar to some Jianghu frigates. All new frigates since 1991, including Jiangwei and new Jiangkai I and II frigates are equipped with improved DUBV-23 French bow sonars. These ships can also carry helicopters with lightweight ASW torpedoes, and thus provide some ASW capability. The ships themselves, however, are limited to over-the-side lightweight torpedoes and do not have towed arrays or variable-depth sonars.[4]

Considering antiair warfare, the majority of PLAN frigates have only gun defense, but the dual-purpose, fully automatic French mounts found on the Jianghu, Jiangwei, and Jiangkai frigates and on all DDGs, are capable against both aircraft and surface ships, albeit at short ranges and against less capable threats. Although some newer Jiangwei and Jiangkai I frigates have SAMs, they are French HHQ-7 models with only 13-km range. Beijing is addressing this weakness, however. As previously mentioned, the four or five Jiangkai-II frigates under construction in early 2007 will have VLS SAMs, as do both pairs of the Luzhou- and Luyang II–class destroyers. Anticruise missile defense remains a challenge, with only the frigates and destroyers built after 2001 generally having such capabilities. Many navies adjoining China's littoral SLOC have minimal ASCM capability. Therefore, the PLAN's numerous gun and missile patrol boats could probably adequately provide SLOC security in these lower-threat areas. Many of the PLAN's missile patrol craft are copies of over-forty-year-old Soviet Osa and Komar (designated Hola and Hoku) designs, but the ASCMs carried by these vessels are still potent. Land-based aircraft, radars, and long-range SAMs provide helpful cover also. Despite their reported limitations, China's four Beidou satellites might be able to support at least some green water satellite communication and navigation needs.

Blue Water SLOC Defense

The forces conducting SLOC defense during World Wars I and II had to conduct antisubmarine, antisurface, and antiaircraft warfare. Antisurface warfare was a tremendous concern before the *Graf Spee*, *Bismark*, and other German surface raiders were destroyed. Q-ships, too, were a major problem in both world wars. One need only consider the enormous numbers of platforms that the Allies had to deploy to suppress the German submarine threat in both wars, and alternatively Japan's catastrophic failure to protect its sea lanes, in order to appreciate both the priority and complexity of SLOC defense missions. Although ASW and antiair warfare will likely retain high priority among sea lane protection missions, a fundamentally new dimension (overlapping to some extent, of course, with these other missions) is the difficult challenge of countering incoming ASCMs. In the near term, Chinese intelligence, surveillance, and reconnaissance (ISR) capabilities will remain relatively limited, so detecting and engaging adversary launch platforms will continue to be a problem, thus placing a larger onus on the capability to destroy incoming missiles as a vital mission for escort vessels.

The current distribution of PLAN ships has most vessels in the East Sea Fleet due to the Taiwan issue's priority, with the North Sea and South Sea fleets receiving equally the remainder of forces. Although most escort missions would depart from North and East Fleet ports, the South Sea Fleet would be the point of departure and arrival for distant blue water convoys. However, the PLAN has recently moved Luyang 052C DDG 170 and modernized frigates to naval bases on Hainan Island. If, as appears likely, the PLAN at Hainan is augmented with additional submarine forces, perhaps to include new nuclear submarines, then a new strategic orientation toward the critical energy SLOC on China's southwestern flank could be suggested. Regardless, a paucity of major U.S. bases in Southeast Asia will make this buildup difficult to counter.

Given that there would be multiple distant blue water sea lanes requiring PLAN warships to protect valuable tankers, which PLAN ships could meet the new mission requirements? Reviewing the bloody and costly campaigns during the twentieth century, it is clear that destroyers, destroyer escorts, and frigates are the all-around workhorses that defend critical sea lanes. Frigates, especially those possessing strong antisubmarine credentials (of which the PLAN has none), are likely to be in especially high demand. A similar situation exists with respect to ships with area air defense capabilities. With seventy-three Aegis warships, the U.S. Navy can hardly imagine how difficult it is for the PLAN at present to allocate its limited numbers of area air defense ships. Indeed, the PLAN seems to be in a rather preliminary experimental phase for its emerging surface force, wherein a wide variety of different advanced platforms are produced and tested. A crucial issue and indicator for future mission trajectory for Chinese naval development concerns if and when Beijing settles on warship designs that suit its needs and then proceeds with serial production—as has only recently occurred in the case of the Song-class diesel submarine and the Houbei-class missile catamaran. This may have already occurred in the case of the Jiangkai-II frigate, of which at least four, in 2007, are being built at two separate shipyards.

A major dilemma confronts China with respect to SLOC defense in the area of deck aviation.[5] Chinese naval analysts readily admit that air cover remains a major constraint for PLAN operations—in part motivating the evident Chinese priority on submarines over the last decade. While China's largest warship to date, a 10,000-ton landing ship dock helicopter, was launched in December 2006, its actual significance for deck aviation is not great, and the PLAN is still a very long way from being able to wield significant tactical air power over distant blue waters. Naturally, the potential introduction of PLAN aircraft carriers in the next decade would draw on the same surface forces discussed above for escort duties within an aircraft carrier battle group, thereby diverting these assets from convoy protection.

But on the other hand, such a battle group could form a vital component of SLOC defense, especially in the vast and vital expanse of the Indian Ocean, which is and will remain predominantly beyond the reach of land-based aviation even if China's air forces make substantial progress in aerial refueling.

Whether or not China acquires aircraft carriers, PLAN SAGs may still provide options for SLOC defense. Currently the Luyang-II and Luzhou vessels are likely flagships of a SLOC group, equipped with 100-km-range indigenous HHQ-9 vertical launch SAM and Russian 150-km-range Rif-M SAM respectively.[6] Both of these classes also carry long-range C-802 or C-803 ASCMs. The PLAN's four Sovremennyys, with their 160-km mach-2.5 long-range ASCMs, would also provide SAGs with a potent offensive punch.

For the near term, despite their age, China's fourteen Jiangwei FFGs, thirty-one Jianghu FFGs, and eighteen Luda DDGs will remain the backbone of China's surface combatant force. These ships, which all have approximately the same armaments, have significant limitations, including a lack of ASW capability, no ASCM defenses to speak of, and a lack of the modern communications equipment necessary to conduct real-time data sharing and coordinated operations, as would be necessary to engage in network centric warfare. The eighteen aged Luda-class destroyers, for example, need modern, long-range communications and especially satellite capability if they are to contribute meaningfully to a coordinated effort in a modern battlefield. This may be more difficult than expected. A certain Luda III was upgraded with a three-dimensional radar antenna. This antenna was later replaced with a satellite communications antenna. This hints that available topside space for command, control, and communications upgrades may be scarce and new platforms would be required.[7] Chinese satellites provide minimal support far from the mainland, but global positioning system and Russian GLONASS receivers have been used extensively by the PLAN. It is worth noting that China's frigates, in addition to their green water role, meet blue water missions when grouped with DDG consorts.

Naval mines could form a potent threat to Chinese SLOC defense forces, especially in narrow straits and points of departure or arrival. The bulk of Chinese minesweepers are crude mechanical sweepers in small units attached to military districts. These would be somewhat useful in the limited case of primitive mines deployed in Chinese coastal waters. The PLAN once had a fleet of about forty copies of Russian T-43 minesweepers but now has only about a dozen units. The only modern mine units in the PLAN inventory are the 1988-vintage 3,100-ton Wolei, four smaller Wosao coastal minesweepers, and one 2004 Wozang-class minesweeping vessel. The PLAN's fifty copies of German Troika remote-control sweepers are augmented with recent new unmanned mine hunting prototypes.[8]

High-speed boats using swarm tactics could also threaten PLAN surface ships conducting SLOC protection missions, suggesting a need for CIWS for defense. An interesting question for PLAN planners concerns whether the Chinese navy might receive assistance in its SLOC missions (e.g., from Burma, Pakistan, or Iran). Oil-exporting nations such as Iran might have a very direct strategic interest in keeping the energy flowing to China. While these states do not currently bring many SLOC defense assets to the table, this could change in the future, especially if Beijing takes an interest in the matter. It is worth considering, for example, whether—and if so, how— Chinese basing, either of patrol aircraft or of missile catamarans, to any of these states might alter the strategic balance in the Indian Ocean.[9] Supporting elements from other states or Chinese assets in theater could plausibly take some of the burden off Chinese surface combatants as convoy escorts.

Other than escorting warships, the most critical maritime element for SLOC defense operations is the replenishment at sea (RAS) vessels. The distance from PRC waters to the Persian Gulf is over 8,000 km, and to Latin American oil sources is approximately 15,000 km. These distances exceed PLAN surface warships' endurance, thus mandating underway replenishment capabilities.

It is not widely understood that the PLAN has been undertaking some form of RAS operations for decades. Indeed, the 1979-vintage 23,000-ton Fuqing AORs distant cruise replenishments actually date from the Chinese ICBM tests in 1980 when the PLAN dispatched eighteen ships to the South Pacific, and also played a conspicuous role in a five-month Antarctic expedition in 1985. The ideal replenishment ship for the SLOC protection mission is a large vessel that carries a full variety of fuel, food, and ammunition in one hull with multihighline RAS stations on each side. China has only three such vessels, the Nanyun, and two of the Fuching class. Sending to sea more than three simultaneous blue water SLOC task forces, therefore, would require additional replenishment ships. There are many single-purpose oil transporting ships available to the PLAN, some armed and attached to Maritime Border Defense Forces, that could support green water escort requirements, including the nineteen Fulin-class auxiliary oiler tankers. All of the PLAN destroyers and frigates have RAS handling equipment.

Contrary to conventional wisdom, the PLAN in 2007, by way of impressive incremental improvements over the last two decades, actually has already achieved a position whereby it could in a limited way contest for the main SLOC linking China to its main Middle East energy suppliers. By committing its large numbers of surface warships, and backed up by its much improved submarine force and its newly energized air forces, not to mention the heretofore-unmentioned support that might be provided by homing ballistic missiles of the Second Artillery, an incredibly difficult SLOC defense mission enters the realm of possibility.[10] However, the feasibility of defending the crucial route across the Indian Ocean to the Middle East depends on a number of key assumptions. First, the Indian navy would have to stay neutral. Second, it would depend on substantial air and naval base access and other support from regional allies, such as Pakistan and Burma. Third, if the U.S. Navy were the adversary, it would depend on combat action elsewhere (e.g., Taiwan, Guam), perhaps of an asymmetric nature (e.g., mine warfare), to tie down U.S. Navy forces in other theaters. It would also require suppression (preemptive) attacks against the main U.S. base in the Indian Ocean at Diego Garcia, and possibly attacks against U.S. space-based ISR—a capability suggested by the PLA's successful 11 January 2007 antisatellite test. A final (and possibly most tenuous) assumption is that professionalism is becoming truly pervasive in the PLAN—an unknown that assumes crucial importance when it is realized that the PLAN is lacking in major SLOC defense operational experience and, most concretely, has little actual experience in the Indian Ocean or other deep water areas to date.

Of course, some of these assumptions may strike the reader as far-fetched. Would New Delhi, for example, simply stand aside and watch as the Chinese navy conducted convoy escort operations in its backyard? Perhaps yes or perhaps no, but what is essential to realize is that five years ago the PLAN could not hope to even contest for this sea lane. That situation is beginning to change. If the PLAN continues to rapidly modernize at the current pace, the Indian Ocean will not necessarily remain beyond its growing reach, especially over the long term.

Improvements Will Move PLA Navy beyond Access Denial

Seriously preparing for a SLOC protection mission would force the PLAN to make many readily apparent force structure changes. This would include significantly increasing its current limited inventory of three underway replenishment vessels. Although there is no sign that such construction has started, China's booming shipyards could certainly design and build such vessels quickly.

Likewise all surface ships, not only the most modern, would have to be prepared to reliably defend against cruise missile attack. This would require the addition of modern defensive systems to the existing platform, but as this chapter has indicated, space and weight issues on older classes of ships appear to preclude this possibility. Similarly, the PLAN would also have to upgrade its many older ships with modern command and control systems, but again, limited evidence suggests that these vessels cannot readily support such modifications. These factors suggest, therefore, that for China to perform SLOC-protection missions, it would have to replace its entire inventory of Jiangwei, Jianghu, Luda and other obsolete classes. This would necessitate the construction of over sixty major surface combatants, assuming that overall force levels remained nearly constant.

In order to safeguard against underwater attacks, the PLAN would also have to devote much of its budget and training to learning the difficult and expensive art of blue water undersea warfare. This would involve acquiring and perfecting the use of modern (low-frequency) bow-mounted and deployable sonars, ASW helicopters, maritime patrol aircraft, and effective ASW weapons such as long-range ASW rockets. Effective ASW also requires the effective and coordinated use of modern SSNs. China has yet to demonstrate such an ability. Correcting this critical vulnerability would require many years of visible effort.

Modern naval warfare conducted at great distances also requires extensive space assets for reconnaissance, navigation, and communications. China is a relative newcomer to this field, but is making impressive strides. Even if the PLAN acquired all the assets required to conduct long-range, sea-lane defense missions, it would still require extensive experience in operating groups of warships at long distances from China for extended periods of time. Basing rights in deployment regions would greatly facilitate such a capability, but such experience and bases remain critical requirements that as yet have not materialized.

Despite these lingering deficiencies, it is nevertheless clear that China's effort to modernize its surface combatants has moved into high gear. For now, it must be admitted that China appears to remain focused on improving its ability to conduct access-denial operations, such as those appropriate to Taiwan scenarios. Jiankai-II frigates; Luzhou, Luyang-I, and Luyang-II destroyers; and even the Houbei missile corvettes—all less than five years old, and all equipped with advanced weapons and associated systems—could play roles in a Taiwan scenario. But these ships and weapons have the flexibility necessary to be useful in other mission areas as well, including SLOC protection.

China's ability to quickly build large classes of ships should not be underestimated, and recent production rates suggest that China could, if necessary, have within a decade all the modern surface fleet it needed for all missions, including the defense of critical sea lanes and Taiwan reunification.

Notes

1. During the first half of the Cold War, the submarine-centric Soviet navy experimented with this concept without much success, for example at the time of the Cuban Missile Crisis.

2. For more on this system, see the website of *China Defense Today* at http://www.sinodefence.com/navy/navalmissile/cy1.asp.

3. On the legal aspects of this dispute, see the chapter by Peter Dutton in this volume.

4. Jiangkai II frigates have bell mouths on their sterns from which towed arrays could be deployed.

5. On this subject, see for example Andrew Erickson and Andrew Wilson, "China's Aircraft Carrier Dilemma," *Naval War College Review* 59, no. 4 (2006): 13–46.

6. SA-N-6/20 "Grumble" (S-300 Fort/Rif) and "HQ-9/-15, HHQ-9A, RF-9," *Jane's Strategic Weapon Systems*, 29 December 2006, www.janes.com. That report credits the HHQ9 with a range of 150 km, but a second and more recent Jane's report says the HHQ-9 has a range of 100 km. See "Luyang II (Type 052C) class (DDGHM)" in *Jane's Fighting Ships*, 29 January 2007, www.janes.com.

7. When contemplating possible upgrades of the Luda, it should be recognized that it is a 1950s-era design, built in the 1970s. It is arguably obsolete, and part of the cost of being obsolete is that it cannot be readily upgraded. Some might maintain that this is really a moot point anyway because these ships are destined for the scrap yard as they have reached or exceeded their effective lives (thirty years). Their block obsolescence is probably one of the major reasons for the construction of the Jiangwei IIs, much as the Ming and Romeos diesel submarines being decommissioned probably at least partially explains the Kilo and Song acquisitions. Nevertheless, if China were willing to risk significant casualties and able to arm the *Ludas* sufficiently, they might be capable of diverting some of an adversary's attention and resources.

8. A picture of this new vessel was posted on the Internet in spring 2006 at http://www.anyboard.net/gov/mil/anyboard/uploads/minesweeper060515220200__1_p111.jpg.

9. For an extended discussion of China's prospects in the Indian Ocean, see the chapter by James Holmes and Toshi Yoshihara in this volume.

10. On the potential threat posed by China's Second Artillery conventionally armed ballistic missiles, see Eric McVadon, "China's Maturing Navy," *Naval War College Review* 59, no. 2 (2006): 90–107.

Bruce Elleman

A Comparative Historical Approach to Blockade Strategies

Implications for China

NAVAL BLOCKADES CAN BE an important military means to achieve national goals. With regard to East Asia, there have been seven naval blockades during the past century that are worth examining for relevant historical lessons: (a) the first Sino-Japanese War (1894–95), in which Japan used a short, rapid blockade of Weihaiwei Harbor, in Shandong province, in combination with land forces to defeat China's most modern naval forces; (b) the second Sino-Japanese War (1937–45), in which Japan used a long, tightening blockade of virtually all of China's coastline and major rivers but ended up creating an even larger hostile coalition; (c) World War II in the Pacific (1941–45), in which the U.S. Navy and Army Air Force utilized a medium-length, tightening blockade of Japan but which ultimately had little direct effect on Japanese decision to surrender, which came mainly due to the two atomic bombs and the massive Soviet invasion of the Japanese empire;[1] (d) the Korean War (1950–53), in which UN forces used a medium-length, rapid blockade that eventually forced North Korea and its supporters to recognize South Korea; (e) the Vietnam War (1965–73), in which a medium-length, tightening blockade did allow for the withdrawal of U.S. forces only to witness North Vietnam's victory a few years later; (f) the ROC-PRC (Republic of China [Taiwan] and People's Republic of China) blockade (1949–58), a long, loosening Nationalist blockade of the PRC that may have prevented a communist invasion but otherwise was a draw; and (g) PRC missile blockade (1995–96), which was a short, intermittent Chinese blockade of Taiwan using only missiles that backfired when the United States sent two carrier battle groups to intervene, resulting in a draw.[2]

To make relevant comparisons with the situation currently facing China, these seven blockades will be addressed in three sets: the two Japanese blockades of China; U.S.-led blockades of Japan, Korea, and Vietnam; and then the ROC blockade of the PRC and the PRC missile blockade of Taiwan.

Additional blockades, in particular during the Falklands War, in which a continental country attempted to invade and assert sovereignty over a nearby island, will also be considered for their possible relevance to China. Finally, this chapter will consider possible counterblockade scenarios by the United States or other powers, in particular with regard to the Malacca Strait. This historical examination suggests that, should China decide to adopt a naval blockade strategy against Taiwan, it would probably be rapidly enacted, of short to medium duration, and most likely lead to a negotiated settlement. If the blockade operation were to become protracted, then the likelihood of a counterblockade by Taiwan's allies would also become more likely.

The Time Factor in Successful Asian Blockades

The speed of implementation of a naval blockade can influence effectiveness, with implementation being rapid, intermittent, tightening, or loosening. Meanwhile, the duration can be short, medium, or long. As a good example of this difference, the Japanese rapidly blockaded China during the first Sino-Japanese War but for a short period, whereas during the second Sino-Japanese War, the blockade gradually tightened over a much longer period of time.

Table 1 shows how these factors played out in the seven Asian case studies.[3] The first Sino-Japanese War and the Korean War involved winning strategies that included rapidly implemented blockades involving sea powers cutting off land powers. The rapid blockade during the first was short, forcing a favorable negotiated settlement, while negotiations took two years in Korea. Rapid blockades can help to compel the blockaded country to accept a negotiated settlement, thus suggesting a possible relationship between speed and effectiveness. In the Korean War, where strategic success was not rapid, North Korea bordered powerful allies including the Union of Soviet Socialist Republics (U.S.S.R.) and China, which enabled Pyongyang to withstand the blockade.

Table 1. Time

Name	Implementation	Duration	Strategic Effectiveness	Win-Lose-Draw
SJW I	rapid	short	yes, forces war termination	win
SJW II	tightening	long	no, creates hostile coalition	lose
WW II	tightening	medium	yes, but A-bomb ends war	win
Korea	rapid	medium	yes, undermines morale, cuts supplies and ammunition	win
Vietnam	tightening	medium	no, temporarily delays war termination	lose
ROC-PRC	loosening	long	no/yes, prevents PRC invasion	draw
PRC missile	intermittent	short	yes/no, creates hostile coalition	draw

In the second Sino-Japanese and Vietnam Wars, tightening blockades did not lead to victory. The large size of the theaters perhaps explains why these blockades could not be conducted rapidly. The gradually tightening U.S. blockade of the Japanese home islands was more successful, as mines (dropped by heavy bombers), submarines, and attacks by tactical aircraft reversed Tokyo's military gains and reduced the resources available to fuel its military machine. While allied war planners were convinced that an invasion of Japan would be necessary to end the war, such an invasion became a moot point after the use of the atom bomb. When tightening blockades were imposed against a land power, the blockaded country usually had sufficient time to create alternative trade routes, like the Burma Road for Nationalist China during the late 1930s and early 1940s and the Ho Chi Minh Trail for the insurgents in South Vietnam during the 1960s. By contrast, island nations, such as Japan during World War II, can experience great difficulty in keeping sea lanes open.

The Nationalist blockade of the PRC was a loosening blockade, while the PRC missile blockade against Taiwan was an intermittent blockade. Arguably, neither was successful because neither led to strategic victory. Nevertheless, they may have had strategic effects in what they prevented from happening: China did not invade Taiwan in the 1950s, and Taiwan did not declare independence in 1996.

The second Sino-Japanese War and the ROC blockade were both long—each averaging ten years or more—and both attempted to interdict the blockaded country's logistics. The second Sino-Japanese War blockade tightened while the ROC blockade loosened over time. Neither blockade was particularly successful. Short- and medium-length blockades, by comparison, were usually carried out in combination with either a real land invasion, or at least the threat of one. The blockader generally focused on undermining the enemy's military forces. In the first Sino-Japanese War, for example, the Chinese navy was trapped in the port of Weihaiwei and was destroyed as a result of the blockade; in Korea, however, the focus of the blockade was the shipment of ammunition and supplies to North Korean troops. Should the PRC elect to blockade Taiwan, the rapid defeat of the Taiwanese navy would probably be considered a prerequisite for success.

The Space Factor in Successful Asian Blockades

Characteristics of the theater of operations can include close versus distant blockades, which is the distance of the blockade perimeter from the blockaded country; near versus far blockades, which is the distance of the theater from the blockading country; partial versus total blockades, measured by the blockade's porosity; and different levels of coercion, including paper, pacific, and belligerent blockades. Sea powers usually impose blockades on land powers while land powers have great difficulty in blockading sea powers; however, as the recent missile blockade of Taiwan suggests, the use of long-range aircraft and ballistic and cruise missiles may have the potential to alleviate this historic problem.

In Asia most blockades have been enacted near the border of the blockaded country while only in the U.S. blockade of Japan, the Korean War blockade, and the Vietnam War blockade were the blockaded areas far from the countries enforcing the blockades. Blockades can be executed unilaterally or in combination with a coalition, and can be broken by blockade runners or by creating alternate new land lines of communication or air routes.

As shown in table 2, six of the seven blockades—all but the PRC missile blockade—were close blockades, and these mainly involved sea powers opposing a land power. Meanwhile, of the six close blockades, three were near, including the first Sino-Japanese War, second Sino-Japanese War, and the ROC-PRC blockade. Arguably, in all of these cases the blockaded country was too weak to retaliate effectively against the blockading country; because armed retaliation was always a possibility, the enemy's navy usually became a prime target.

Table 2. Space

Name	Blockader	Blockaded	Neighbors	Type	Type
S-JW I	sea power	land power	no other powers intervene	close	near
S-JW II	sea power	land power	U.S.S.R. intervenes	close	near
WW II	sea power	sea power	U.S.S.R. enters war	distant	far
Korea	great power coalition	peninsula	U.S.S.R., PRC intervene	close	far
Vietnam	sea power	land power	U.S.S.R., PRC intervene	close	far
ROC-PRC	island sea power	land power	U.S., U.S.S.R. intervene	close	near
PRC missile	land power	island nation	U.S. intervenes	distant	near

As demonstrated by the second Sino-Japanese War, the Korean War, the Vietnam War, and the ROC-PRC blockade, land powers are extremely capable of rendering ineffective a sea power's blockades when their central geographic location provides alternate land lines of communication. In particular, if the blockaded country can form land lines with allies, then the costs of the blockade will increase and its effectiveness will decline. In the first Sino-Japanese War, in which a blockade succeeded anyway, the war ended quickly due to a negotiated settlement, before new land lines had been formed.

Any blockader of a country bordering on Russia should be prepared for Russian intervention. Historically, Russia has chosen sides in such conflicts to open up or close down alternate supply routes and sources of supplies. In six of the seven Asian blockades, Russian actions helped tip the balance in the blockade effort, including (a) opposition to Japan in the second Sino-Japanese War, (b) support for the United States against Japan, (c) opposition to the UN blockade of Korea, (d) opposition to the U.S. blockade of North Vietnam, (e) opposition to the Nationalist blockade of China during the 1950s, and finally, (f) continued weapons sales to the PRC during the 1995–96 missile crisis against Taiwan.[4]

While land powers can often compensate with alternate land lines of communication, sea powers and island nations require strong navies to overcome a blockade. Conversely, while strong naval powers can successfully conduct quick decisive blockades against land powers, land powers can rarely conduct quick operations against sea powers or island nations. This suggests that until the PRC has a sufficiently powerful navy, it will probably experience great difficulty should it choose to blockade Taiwan, except perhaps to produce a deterrent effect.

The Force Factor in Successful Asian Blockades

Bombs, missiles, torpedoes, or mines delivered from the air, surface assets, or submarines can be used to enforce a naval blockade. Surface patrols and mines were used in six of the seven blockades—the first Sino-Japanese War, the second Sino-Japanese War, World War II in the Pacific, the Korean War, the Vietnam War, and the ROC-PRC blockade. After the development of aerial bombing, it too was used extensively, including in the second Sino-Japanese War, World War II in the Pacific, the ROC-PRC blockade, the Korean War, and the Vietnam War. Finally, land-based missiles were the primary means of enforcement in only one of the blockades—that of the PRC versus Taiwan—but their potential for use in future blockades is great. Blockades like the Taiwan missile blockade, which attempt to cut off strategic points, have been referred to as "choke point" blockades and can be carried out by a wide range of means, including mines or other obstructions, such as sunken ships.[5]

According to table 3, land operations supported five of the seven blockades on the home territory of the target country. One exception was World War II in the Pacific, where use of the atom bomb precluded a land invasion of the major Japanese home islands. The other exception was the PRC Missile Blockade of Taiwan, a highly unusual blockade.

Table 3. Force

Name	Mines	Patrols	Subs	Bombing	Conquest	Invade	Land Ops.	Air Ops.
S-JW I	X	X				X	X	
S-JW II	X	X		X	X	X	X	X
WW II	X	X	X	X				X
Korea	X	X		X	X	X	X	X
Vietnam	X	X		X			X	X
ROC-PRC	X	X		X	X		X	X
PRC missile					X			X

In four of the blockades, the blockading power was intent on conquest or reconquest of territory, including Japan in the second Sino-Japanese War, the Nationalist blockade of China, UN efforts to defend South Korea, and the PRC missile blockade. However, in three cases there were land invasions that were not intended to be permanent conquests, including that by Japan in the first Sino-Japanese War, the U.S. postwar occupation of Japan, and the U.S. military presence in Vietnam.

Blockades without any land operations were rare, and many naval blockades entailed joint and combined operations that coordinated sea, land, and air operations. The first Sino-Japanese War, the second Sino-Japanese War, and the Korean War stand out in this regard. The single exception to this pattern was the PRC missile blockade, in which operations on land played little if any role in the blockade. Blockades are rarely conducted by surface ships alone. Submarines have played an important role in many European blockades, but less so in Asia, with the notable exception of the U.S. blockade of Japan. As airpower became more available and dependable, it too was used. Joint operations also played an increasingly important role, with joint sea–air operations increasingly substituting for joint land–sea operations in the modern period.

Finally, while wars of conquest usually included invasions (with the two notable exceptions being Chinese—the Nationalist blockade of the PRC and the PRC missile blockade of Taiwan, in which a full-blown invasion would have been an enormous undertaking) land invasions were not necessarily intended for permanent conquest. Rather, they were often for exerting pressure for a negotiated, as opposed to an unconditional, settlement. This happened in the first Sino-Japanese War, the Korean War, and during the Vietnam War. If the PRC were to conduct a full-blown naval blockade of Taiwan, it would likely involve attempts to invade territory under Taiwanese control, perhaps including a number of offshore islands, which would be useful during negotiations to end the war.

Operational and Strategic Goals during Naval Blockades

Blockades support diverse operational and strategic goals. Operational goals pursued with Asian blockades have included the destruction of enemy naval or land forces, the interruption of trade, and the occupation of territory. Strategic goals can include economic embargo, military degradation, and deterrence. Blockades can be total or partial, with total blockades completely halting prohibited traffic, while partial blockades, by intent or by default, allow either a percentage or certain categories of trade and population movement to continue. Blockades that are effective at cutting sea routes but fail to cut alternate land routes are still partial, even though they may make critical contributions to victory. Finally, the blockader's goals can be unlimited, meaning the overthrow of the enemy government, or limited, usually defined in terms of strategic objectives not in the quantity of resources devoted to the blockade. Arguably, only one blockading country—the PRC—was a continental power at the time it adopted a blockade strategy.

As shown in table 4, in the ROC-PRC blockade, during World War II, and PRC missile blockade the original objectives were unlimited, and in the second Sino-Japanese War and the Korean War the original, limited goals later became unlimited for at least a time. Only two blockades that began as limited conflicts remained so throughout, including the first Sino-Japanese War and the Vietnam War. In limited wars, blockades were usually partial, but of the two total blockades in Asia, only the blockade during the first Sino-Japanese War occurred during a limited war and focused on defeating the enemy's military forces, especially the Chinese navy whereas another, the U.S. blockade of Japan during World War II, supported an unlimited war that escalated to include the use of atomic weapons.

Table 4. Goals

Blockade	Operational Goal	Strategic Goal	Focus	Part/Tot	L/U	C
S-JW I	take key port for pincer on Beijing	wipe out Chinese navy	navy	total	L	
S-JW II	support ground ops punish China	China recognized Manchukuo	trade	partial	L-U	
WW II	cut Japan's foreign trade	full surrender	trade	total	U	
Korea	cut coastal + internal (S)LOCs	defeat North Korea	army	partial	L-U-L	
Vietnam	cut insurgent and weapons flow	protect South Vietnam	army	partial	L	
ROC-PRC	cut PRC trade, get forward bases	reunite China under KMT	trade	partial	U	
PRC missile	cut commerce, transport	prevent inde pendence	trade	partial	U	C

U = Unlimited; L = Limited; C = Continental power doing the blockading

In the majority of limited blockades the blockading countries instituted a close blockade of their enemy. This meant that their ships operated in close proximity to the enemy's shores, usually in order to isolate and destroy the enemy's navy as much or more than to halt trade. By contrast, a larger number of the distant blockades were part of unlimited wars. In these conflicts, blockades were usually intended to disrupt enemy trade as one point of leverage rather than to eliminate a specific military target or to take a set piece of territory. Unlimited wars by their very nature include a full array of military forces, often in a variety of theaters, so that blockade is just one instrument among many.

Naval blockades used alone have achieved limited objectives. This particularly applies to limited naval objectives, such as the first Sino-Japanese War's success at blockading an enemy navy in port, or during the Korean War and the Vietnam War, when the United States and its allies tried to block the transfer of weapons and supplies to the enemy. Naval blockades alone cannot easily or quickly achieve unlimited goals, which is perhaps best exemplified by President Truman's decision to use the atomic bomb against Japan. In addition, the strategic impact of limited blockades on trade can be difficult to measure, unless there are particular bottleneck items that the adversary can acquire only through trade and that are essential to continuing the war and that can be discriminately blockaded.

The number of cases in which land powers in Asia tried to use solely blockades to achieve their overall strategic goals includes only the PRC in 1995–96. It was a distant albeit near blockade, with the enemy close at hand, but because it relied only on missiles, it lacked the necessary capabilities to qualify as a total blockade. The PRC failed in part because of third-party intervention—the U.S. government elected to send two carrier battle groups to waters around Taiwan—but there may still have been an important deterrent effect because the Taiwanese government has yet to declare official independence from the PRC.

In the second Sino-Japanese War and the Korean War limited blockades escalated fully or for a time into unlimited blockades focusing on the adversary's military, and in particular against logistical lines. The geography of China and Korea made it difficult for naval forces, even in conjunction with air power and an active military presence, to cut the enemy's land lines of communication with contiguous powers. Interestingly, in both of these cases the shift from limited to unlimited proved to be a mistake, and in the Korean War the UN forces quickly returned to a limited conflict. In any PRC blockade of Taiwan, limited objectives would likely be easier to achieve than unlimited ones.

The Importance of Enemy Adaptation in Undermining Blockades

Enemies can adapt to changing circumstances and threats. If executed properly, the blockaded country's counterstrategies can make sustaining the blockade extraordinarily expensive in terms of money, manpower, and prestige so that costs ultimately outweigh benefits—in other words, a nightmare scenario. Meanwhile, if the blockaded country does not adapt well, naval blockades can deliver a quick decisive victory, usually including a negotiated settlement, thereby providing a dream scenario for the blockading country.

The first Sino-Japanese War was a good example of a dream scenario because China was unwilling to commit its naval forces to destroy Japan's sea lines of communication. In this case, the blockade ended as a result of negotiations, and no fighting took place on Japanese territory. In a dream scenario, the blockaded country also largely follows the script anticipated by the blockader; in this case, the Chinese obliged Japan by anchoring the northern fleet in port where the Japanese navy and army could find, surround, and destroy it. If China had been less of a cooperative adversary, its fleets should have been more than capable of denying Japan sea control.

Table 5 identifies the one nightmare scenario—the second Sino-Japanese War and the overlapping World War II in the Pacific. In this case, Japan's blockade of China helped forge powerful new enemy coalitions with even more unlimited goals than the blockader, ultimately destroying Imperial Japan, in part through a highly effective blockade, but mainly through the use of the atomic bomb and the entry of the U.S.S.R. into the Pacific theater.

Table 5. Enemy Adaptation

Name	Counterblockade	Third Party Action	Countermeasures	N/D
S-JW I				D
S-JW II	China embargoes J	U.S., U.K. help China	alternate LOCs, U.S.S.R.	N
WW II		U.K., U.S.S.R. help U.S.		
Korea			alternate LOCs, U.S.S.R.-PRC	
Vietnam			alternate LOCs, U.S.S.R.-PRC	
ROC-PRC	PRC attacks islands		alternate LOCs, U.S.S.R.	
PRC missile		U.S. deploys carriers		

D = Dream cooperative adversary; N = Nightmare triggers major adverse alliance shift

Most East Asian blockades involved neither dream nor nightmare scenarios. In most cases, both the blockader and blockaded power adapted to each other's strategies. Not all adaptations were effective. For example, one of the Nationalists' counterstrategies to oppose Japan's invasion was to enact trade barriers. These additional trade restrictions merely served to make the Japanese blockade tighter, although not enough to make a crucial difference to the outcome of the war. Other adaptations worked better. Extensive smug-

gling by land and sea undermined the effectiveness of many naval blockades. Creating alternate land lines of communication seriously degraded the
strategic effectiveness of many blockades and usually led to a certain degree
of protraction, including in the second Sino-Japanese War, the ROC-PRC
blockade, the Korean War, and the Vietnam War.

In one set of cases, that of Japan against China, the blockading power
used the same basic strategy twice, with much greater success the first time.
Better adaptation during the second blockade probably occurred because the
blockaded country knew what to expect and so made greater efforts to form
outside coalitions and to find alternate supply lines—the Nationalists, for
example, quickly moved their capital from Nanjing to Chongqing, in China's
interior, and so were able to create new land lines to evade Japan's blockade.
This suggests that countries must lower their expectations when employing
a blockade strategy for a second time.[6] Previous success cannot be construed
as an indicator of future victory; the opponent also has a learning curve.

When evaluating the efficacy of conducting a blockade strategy, it is
important to consider all possible enemy responses. The intervention of third
parties, such as the United States and United Kingdom in the second Sino-
Japanese War, the intervention of the PRC in the Korean War, or the U.S.
government's decision to send two carrier battle groups to Taiwan during
the PRC missile blockade, can effectively break a blockade. The likelihood
of strategic success plummeted for blockades that triggered major additions
to the blockaded country's coalition. Any future PRC decision to blockade
Taiwan would not only have to take American intervention into account but
would have to factor in possible Japanese intervention as well.[7]

Naval Blockades' Effectiveness in Obtaining Victory

The majority of Asian blockades have obtained some degree of strategic
and operational effectiveness due mainly to the fact that naval blockades can
exercise nonlethal economic and military pressure on an enemy as opposed
to an outright attack. Factors influencing effectiveness include the size of the
area under blockade, the extent of blockade running and smuggling, and the
availability of substitute markets or substitute products to overcome possible
bottlenecks.

Table 6 shows two blockades in which the blockading power obtained its
strategic objectives. One blockade was tight—the first Sino-Japanese War—
and was focused on quickly defeating the enemy's navy, while Korea was a
peninsula and so was porous. In porous blockades that resulted in draws—

that of the ROC-PRC and the PRC missile blockade—blockade runners, smuggling, and alternative trade routes undermined their effectiveness.

Table 6. Effectiveness

Name	Alternate Route	Geographical Coverage	Bottleneck	W/L	Effect
S-JW I		Weihaiwei	navy stuck in port	W	tight
S-JW II	Vietnam, Burma	huge	war matériel	L	porous
WW II		huge	oil, natural resources	W*	tight
Korea	U.S.S.R., PRC	limited coastline		W	porous
Vietnam	PRC, Laos, Cambodia	long coastline		L	porous
ROC-PRC	blockade running	huge		D	porous
PRC missile	blockade running	island nation		D	porous

W = blockader wins, L = blockader loses, D = draw

*Although the U.S. submarine blockade of Japan during World War II was very effective and had a devastating impact on the Japanese economy, it paled in comparison with the use of the atomic bomb and Russia's decision to enter the war. As a result, during Japanese discussions of whether to surrender, the blockade was not considered a major factor.

Of those blockades that were part of generally successful wars, surprisingly only one was a far blockade conducted by naval powers—the Korean War—and in this war success meant that the United Nations managed to save South Korea from destruction.[8] Success rates usually increased for sea powers conducting near blockades, but Japan failed at a near blockade in the second Sino-Japanese War primarily because its 1941 attack on Pearl Harbor brought it into conflict with other sea powers (primarily the United States).

When the goal is to deter and so a clear victory is difficult to ascertain, reasons for failure are often connected to the nature of the theater. In two cases—the second Sino-Japanese War and ROC-PRC blockade—the area under blockade was enormous and precluded effective enforcement. In the case of the Vietnam War, long porous land borders provided multiple alternate land lines of communication. The ultimate outcome of the one deterrent blockade—the PRC missile blockade—remains unresolved to this day.

Historical Blockades and China's Strategic Dilemmas

For more recent lessons on blockade, it seems likely that China has examined most closely the 1982 Falklands War,[9] which Admiral Elmo Zumwalt called the "classic example of modern limited blockade."[10] The geographic and maritime parallels with Taiwan are evident because the Falklands are 300 miles off Argentina's southeast coast, its 4,700-square-mile territory is claimed by Argentina as its sovereign territory, and the major sea power that might come to the Falklands' aid—the United Kingdom—is 8,000 miles away and, in theory at least, could be denied access to the region by the Argentine navy.

On 28 March 1982 Argentina secretly launched the operation to recover the Falkland/Malvinas Islands when naval task forces departed Puerto Belgrano, the Argentine navy's main base, and headed northeast to participate in exercises with the Uruguayan navy. On 2 April 1982, marines were landed and seized Port Stanley after a three-hour fight with minimal casualties; twelve thousand troops and their officers were deployed throughout the islands. Meanwhile, a six-thousand-mobile-reserve was stationed close to Port Stanley and Stanley's four-thousand-foot airfield was commandeered by the Argentine air force. On 3 April, South Georgia Island was seized far to the east to provide regional sea denial.

To make sure that British forces could not interfere, the Argentine navy tried to block sea access from the north should British forces come directly from Ascension Island, some 4,000 miles away from the Falklands, or from the southwest via Chile, after transiting through the Straits of Magellan. The Argentine navy stationed a carrier and escorts 450 miles to the north of the Falklands while a cruiser and escorts were stationed to the south. Argentina initially proclaimed a 200-mile exclusion zone around the Falklands and later extended this zone to include the entire South Atlantic area.

One of the most dangerous areas for the approaching British ships was after they left Ascension Island and continued south to the Falklands, traveling parallel to the 900-mile length of Argentina's coastline. The logistics ships made particularly good targets. But, surprisingly, Argentine surface raids were never executed against these logistics ships primarily because on

2 May 1982 a British nuclear-powered attack submarine *Conqueror* located and sank the Argentine cruiser *General Belgrano*. Argentina subsequently recalled all of its ships to home waters, which opened the sea lanes from Britain to the Falklands.

The Argentine navy withdrew to retain a "fleet in being" and attempted to protect its troops on the Falklands with its Étendards and A-4s. The British fleet sent to retake the Falklands included two light vertical or short runway takeoff and landing carriers *Hermes* and *Invincible*, in addition to eleven other warships and four supply ships; later, almost ninety British ships were involved in the operation. Because the carriers were the heart of the operation, Argentine jets tried to sink them. On 4 May 1982, two Argentine Super Étendard aircraft based out of Rio Grande launched a low-flying Exocet air-to-surface missile at the British Task Force. With only three or four seconds warning, the British destroyer *Sheffield* was badly damaged and twenty British were dead and another twenty-four injured. *Sheffield* was eventually scuttled on 10 May. Admiral Sandy Woodward later admitted that any "major damage to *Hermes* or to *Invincible* (our vital 'second deck'), would probably cause us to abandon the entire Falkland Islands operation."[11] Therefore, had the Argentine attack succeeded in hitting even one of the aircraft carriers, the outcome of the conflict might have been very different.

The British quickly declared a counterblockade and enforced a two-hundred-mile exclusion zone. Their goal was to use ships and planes to halt further reinforcement, and they later adopted an air quarantine. This cut virtually all logistics to the Argentine troops garrisoned on the islands. On 30 April, a total exclusion zone (TEZ) was adopted and any ship farther than twelve miles from Argentina was in a General Warning Area. By 7 May, the Admiralty extended the TEZ to within twelve miles, warning that any Argentine warship outside of the TEZ could be attacked.

At one stroke, both the northern and the southwestern approaches to the Falkland Islands had been cut off. Meanwhile Britain stationed two nuclear-powered attack submarines two hundred miles northwest of the Falklands, midway between the islands and Argentina.[12] Destroyers, which could detect incoming enemy aircraft, backed them up. At the same time, the British carriers and the amphibious group were located one hundred miles to the east of the Falklands to keep them safe from Argentine attack aircraft.

To retake the islands, British marines landed at Port San Carlos, west of Port Stanley. Beginning on 20–21 May, these forces moved east and took Port Stanley on 15 June. Within a month, all remaining Argentine forces had been captured. Following this decisive victory, the British blockade was lifted on

22 July. However, a 150-mile Falkland Islands Protection Zone temporarily replaced it.

By the end of the limited conflict "Argentine losses included cruiser *General Belgrano,* conventional (diesel-powered) submarine *Santa Fe*; dispatch boats *Alferez Sobral* and *Comodoro Somallera*; Coast Guard vessels *Rio Iguazu, Islas Malvinas*; merchant runners (in TEZ) *Rio Carcarana, Islas de los Estados*; and intelligence collector (fishing boat) *Narwal*."[13] Over one hundred Argentine planes were destroyed during the conflict. According to one estimate, 50–60 percent of the Argentine pilots were shot down.[14]

The British counterblockade in the Falklands War was a porous, far, distant, intermittent, air and naval blockade of the Argentine coast, even while it was a tight, far, close, continuous, and "total"—including air, naval, and commercial—blockade of the Falkland Islands. While naval blockades are sometimes the first step in challenging another country's naval forces, the Argentine navy decided to remain in port. This military decision virtually guaranteed that the war in general, and the naval conflict in particular, would remain limited. The landing of British troops and the seizure of the islands themselves led to the complete defeat of Argentine forces.

One lesson that China has probably learned from studying the Falklands War is the vulnerability of carriers to missile attack; China has reportedly invested in a new generation of "carrier-killing" surface-to-surface missiles to keep U.S. carriers away.[15] A second lesson is the importance of sea denial plus air denial; because China's navy and air force are insufficiently robust to exert unchallenged sea control, the use of missiles to create exclusion zones is highly likely. A third lesson is that invading Taiwan with amphibious marines could just as well lead to their being cut off and taken prisoner, especially if the land invasion is not firmly supported by air and sea. China's ability to sustain an invasion with strong logistical lines would be very important because otherwise its invading forces might be trapped on Taiwan.[16]

Finally, it is surely of great interest and concern to China to observe Britain's willingness to send a naval fleet to counterblockade Argentina's navy and to see that Britain was victorious from eight thousand miles away. By contrast with the United Kingdom, the close proximity of American bases in Japan, Okinawa, and Guam to the East Asian littoral gives the U.S. Navy much stronger regional basing than Britain enjoyed during the Falklands conflict. This makes China even more concerned that it could be vulnerable to a U.S. counterblockade.

How Vulnerable Is China to Counterblockade?

As we have seen, land powers have failed to produce victory when applying blockades to sea powers or to island nations. The Falklands War and the PRC missile blockade are good examples. Meanwhile, sea powers blockading land powers must take into account the probability that new land lines of communication with contiguous allies can be created to avoid the greatest effects of the blockade; the "nightmare" scenario discussed under enemy adaptation was of this type. Interestingly, it was Russia/U.S.S.R. that most often played this role of developing new land lines by utilizing its central geographic position. The PRC currently buys a substantial percentage of its new weapons from Russia.[17] China also buys a growing percentage of its oil from Russia and Central Asia. Russia and Central Asia could provide 10 percent of China's foreign energy needs, including natural gas, by 2020.[18] If the United States or another sea power were to adopt a counterblockade strategy against China, foreign oil supplies would be one bottleneck item that it might try to halt.

The United States has conducted three naval blockades in Asia, including close blockades against Japan, Korea, and Vietnam. Should the PRC decide to blockade Taiwan, it should expect that the U.S. Navy might attempt a counterblockade. However, given China's access denial capabilities, a close blockade may not be possible, thus making a distant blockade more likely. The December 2004–February 2005 Operation Unified Assistance in northern Sumatra showed China that U.S. naval forces could, without any prior warning, travel—granted during peacetime and unopposed—to the western entrance to the Malacca Strait in less than a week and begin operations there.[19]

Even though their mission was a humanitarian relief operation, jet fighters flew off the USS *Abraham Lincoln* on training flights because under U.S. Navy rules, carrier-based pilots who do not train for two weeks straight must undergo an extensive retraining program. Because the Indonesian government was unwilling to allow the ship's fighter pilots to use Indonesian airspace, the aircraft carrier had to use international waters. The *Abraham Lincoln's* daily training routine thus included flight operations off the western mouth of the Malacca Strait, which in a modest way simulated a naval blockade of the Strait, right where U.S. naval forces might choose to blockade oil supplies to China if there were ever a serious Sino–American conflict.

Prior to the 26 December 2004 tsunami, the viability of the continued U.S. presence throughout Southeast Asia had been questioned, especially by the spectacular rise of China's "soft power."[20] Beginning in 2007 China is expected to import natural gas from Indonesia's Tangguh field, which could increase Beijing's influence over Indonesia even more.[21] However, the U.S. decision to send "hard power" assets to Indonesia, like the *Abraham Lincoln* battle group, produced substantial "soft power" benefits. For example, the U.S. government immediately resumed the U.S. International Military Education and Training program for Indonesian officers, and military-to-military relations improved dramatically. Dr. Greg Fealy, an Australian National University lecturer, gives credit for this change to Operation Unified Assistance, since the "tsunami spurred unprecedented cooperation with Indonesia's military."[22]

Following Operation Unified Assistance, assessments of China's "soft power" throughout the region subtly changed, with some scholars arguing that "while China's soft power is increasing, Beijing faces serious constraints in translating these resources into desired foreign-policy outcomes."[23] China's inability to support large numbers of humanitarian forces overseas undoubtedly reemphasized to the Southeast Asian governments the importance of retaining the U.S. military as the primary security provider. As Jeffrey Bader, a National Security Council Asian expert during the Clinton administration, noted, "This gives us an opportunity to remind the countries in the region that there are things that we can do that no one else can do—and, in particular, China can't do."[24] As one journalist recently noted: "China was humiliated after the 2004 tsunami in the Indian Ocean drew swift responses from the United States, Japan, and other nations with air and naval assets, while China could do little to help."[25]

The U.S. naval operation in Aceh province, Indonesia, sent a potent military warning to China because less than a week after the tsunami, U.S. ships arrived off of the western mouth of the Malacca Strait. The training missions from *Abraham Lincoln* sent a clear message to China of how quickly U.S. forces could reach the area and begin operations. In case of a PRC blockade of Taiwan, a U.S.-led counterblockade would be capable of interdicting the bulk of China's oil trade from Africa and the Persian Gulf, nearly all of which passes through the Malacca Strait on its way to China.

Conclusion

An examination of historical blockades suggests that rapidly enacted, short- to medium-duration blockades have been most successful in producing a negotiated settlement. Sea powers have had greater success with blockades over land powers while close blockades are more common than distant ones. Instead of one skill set making all the difference, a full range of military capabilities are needed to conduct a successful blockade, and the PRC's new submarine and missiles forces alone might not be sufficient to effectively blockade Taiwan; a more robust surface fleet and tactical air cover would probably need to be utilized as well. Blockades in support of limited goals that focus on the enemy's naval forces and their military logistics tend to be resolved most quickly.

The most obvious category of successful naval blockades involved sea powers blockading islands or isolated peninsulas such as Shandong Peninsula during the first Sino-Japanese War, where blockade had the dual effect of halting trade and putting military pressure on the enemy. However, blockades of large peninsulas or coastal states that have adequate land transportation and powerful allies—for example, during the Korean War and the Vietnam War—were not nearly as rapid or effective.

Blockading powers that attempted to repeat a successful blockade have found themselves stymied the second time by enemy adaptation. While very successful during the 1890s, Imperial Japan failed to subdue China in the 1930s and 1940s. This suggests that blockaded countries learn the lessons of history as well, if not better, than the blockaders. This has implications for any future PRC attempt to blockade Taiwan. Since 1996 Taiwan has endeavored to augment its naval forces and has worked hard to add potential coalition members—in particular Japan—to its side.

As technology changes, so do naval blockades. Over time, blockading countries have moved away from primary reliance on surface patrols and underwater mines and toward more extensive use of air power, air-dropped mines, and missiles. As a result, invasion of territory has become less common while the threat of aerial attack has become more so. In "choke point" blockades, such as the PRC missile blockade of Taiwan, the target was not a particular navy unit or section of coastline but rather disruption of trade routes by the creation of exclusion zones; an important underlying goal of such a blockade may have been to disrupt stock markets or raise insurance rates, thus making the cost of doing business with Taiwan prohibitive.

A particularly important imperative for the blockading country is to keep third parties from intervening and adopting a counterblockade, in which case one of the counterblockade's primary goals would include cutting alternate land or sea lines of communication. History has shown that, thanks in part to China's geographical position, alternate supply routes can be formed through continental neighbors via secure land routes, such as Russia. Russia, of course, would become especially important since it provides spare parts for China's naval and military equipment. Therefore, in any counterblockade of China, it would be difficult to enforce an effective tight blockade without taking these land routes into consideration.

One useful alternate to a tight blockade would be to blockade bottleneck items, like foreign oil. In the case of a PRC blockade of Taiwan, Beijing must be concerned about a counterblockade by Taiwan's supporters, most likely led by the United States. One possible location of such a counterblockade would be west of the Malacca Strait, which is sufficiently distant from the PRC to make any strong retaliation on its part difficult, if not impossible.

However, China has also repeatedly been involved in naval blockades, beginning with the first Sino-Japanese War, usually as the blockaded country rather than the blockader. These historical experiences will likely play a role in China's strategic planning prior to adopting any blockade strategy. Specifically, the Chinese will probably plan a wide range of contingencies well in advance to counter any possible counterblockade.

Notes

1. A number of books—one of the most well known by Gar Alperovitz, *The Decision to Use the Atomic Bomb* (New York: Vintage Press, 1996)—have tried to argue that the atomic bombs were unnecessary because Japan was almost ready to surrender. However, General MacArthur's staff did not think surrender was imminent and estimated that a U.S. invasion of the Japanese home islands would result in hundreds of thousands of American casualties. State Department estimates of when the war might end cited 1947 as the most likely date. Gerhard Weinberg has argued that "the key point was that the atomic bombs were falling," and that Japan's decision to surrender was due mainly to the A-bomb, and secondarily on the entry of the U.S.S.R. into the Pacific theater; earlier, the one essential contribution of the U.S. blockade Weinberg noted was Japan's inability to "bring into effective use the new weapons" developed by Germany, and only very late in the war transferred with great difficulty through the blockade to Japan. Gerhard L. Weinberg, *A World at Arms: A Global History of World War II* (New York: Cambridge University Press, 1994), 402–3, 888–90. Due to the use of atomic weapons, the effectiveness of the U.S. blockade in forcing Japan's surrender is extremely difficult to determine. The economic toll on Japan is easier to document. One recent book concluded that the U.S. blockade against Japan was so effective that "if it had not been for the atom bomb, [the blockade] might have, and practically did, cripple the Japanese economy." Lance E. Davis and Stanley L. Engerman, *Naval Blockades in Peace and War: An Economic History Since 1750* (New York: Cambridge University Press, 2006), 381.

2. There is disagreement over whether the PRC missile "tests" should be considered a blockade. Indeed, the author acknowledges the methodological difficulty of comparing the firing of ten DF-15 short-range ballistic missiles with other cases that witnessed intense combat over the course of years. An alternative interpreta-

tion would describe this action as an exercise to be compared with other coercive exercises. For information concerning the number of Chinese missiles fired, see Andrew Scobell, "Show of Force. The PLA and the 1995–1996 Taiwan Strait Crisis," working paper, Walter H. Shorenstein Asia-Pacific Research Center, Stanford University, 1999, p. 5, http://iis-db.stanford.edu/pubs/10091/Scobell.pdf. However, China's two designated missile splash zones during the April 1996 crisis did interfere with maritime trade flowing to and from the Taiwanese ports of Keelung in the north and Kaohsiung in the south, which corresponds to the goals of more traditional blockades. For more on the PRC missile tests as a new form of blockade, see Chris Rahman, "Ballistic Missiles in China's Anti-Taiwan Blockade Strategy," in *Naval Blockades and Seapower: Strategies and Counter-strategies, 1805–2005,* ed. Bruce A. Elleman and S. C. M. Paine, 214–23 (London: Routledge Press, 2006).

3. The tables in this essay have been adapted from those presented in Bruce A. Elleman and S. C. M. Paine, "Conclusions: Naval Blockades and the Future of Seapower," in *Naval Blockades and Seapower,* ed. Elleman and Paine, 250–66.

4. In the first Sino-Japanese War, Russia intervened to help China as part of the so-called Triple Intervention, but this took place after the blockade had already ended. See S. C. M. Paine, *The Sino-Japanese War of 1894–1895: Perceptions, Power, and Primacy* (London: Cambridge University Press, 2003), 247–94. During 1995–96, the Russian Ministry of Defense sold China upper-stage rocket engines in violation of the Missile Technology Control Regime; there were unconfirmed reports that China was allowed to hire a Russian cruise missile research and development team, and by early 1997 Russia had sold China copies of its most advanced SS-N-22 Sunburn antiship missiles. See Stephen J. Blank, "The Dynamics of Russian Weapons Sales to China," *Strategic Studies Institute (SSI) Monograph,* 4 March 1997.

5. Kohei Hashimoto, *Japanese Energy Security and Changing Global Energy Markets: An Analysis of Northeast Asian Energy Cooperation and Japan's Evolving Leadership Role in the Region* (Houston, Texas: James A. Baker III Institute for Public Policy, Rice University, May 2000), 11.

6. Of course, blockaded countries do not always learn these lessons, or learn them as well as they perhaps should have, as best shown by Germany's initially effective, but ultimately unsuccessful, submarine blockade of Britain during World War II.

7. During a 2005 interview with the Taiwanese press, retired Rear Admiral Sumihiko Kawamura stated, "I believe that in an emergency [over Taiwan], the Japanese government would help the U.S." See "China's Navy Not Yet a Threat to Japan and US," *Taipei Times,* 31 October 2005.

8. Again, the U.S. blockade of Japan during World War II was cut short.

9. See, for example, 丁一平 [Ding Yiping (VADM-PLA Navy)] 世界海军史 [*The History of World Navies from the Chinese Perspective*] (Beijing: 海潮出版社 [Sea Tide Press], 2000), 761–80.

10. Elmo R. Zumwalt Jr., "Blockade and Geopolitics," *Comparative Strategy* 4, no. 2 (1983): 169–84; cited in Charles W. Koburger Jr., "SLOCs and Sidewinders: The 1982 Falklands War," in *Naval Blockades and Seapower,* ed. Elleman and Paine, 189–200.

11. Sandy Woodward, *One Hundred Days: The Memoirs of the Falklands Battle Group Commander* (Annapolis, Md.: Naval Institute Press, 1997), 5; cited in Charles W. Koburger, *Sea Power in the Falklands* (New York: Praeger Publishers, 1983).

12. A third nuclear submarine was stationed south of the Falklands to track the cruiser *General Belgrano*. "Falklands/Malvinas War," Global Security.org, http://www.global security.org/military/world/war/malvinas.htm.

13. Koburger, *Sea Power in the Falklands,* 196.

14. Bryan Perrett, *Weapons of the Falklands Conflict* (Dorset: Blandford Press, 1982), 95; Koburger, *Sea Power in the Falklands,* 95.

15. Roger Cliff et al., *Entering the Dragon's Lair: Chinese Antiaccess Strategies and Their Implications for the United States* (Washington, D.C.: RAND, 2007), 71–76.

16. James R. Holmes and Toshi Yoshihara, "Taiwan: Melos or Pylos?" *Naval War College Review* 58, no. 3 (2005): 43–63.

17. "Russia to Sell Arms Worth $6 Bln in 2006—Putin," *Novosti,* 7 December 2006, http://www.globalsecurity.org/wmd/library/news/russia/2006/russia-061207-rianovostio2.htm.

18. John C. K. Daly, "The Dragon's Drive for Caspian Oil," *China Brief* 4, no. 10 (2004), http://www.jamestown.org/images/pdf/cb_004_010.pdf.

19. For more extensive analysis, see Bruce A. Elleman, *Waves of Hope: The U.S. Navy's Response to the Tsunami in Northern Indonesia,* Naval War College Newport Paper No. 28, 2007.

20. Eric Teo Chu Cheow, "Paying Tribute to Beijing: An Ancient Model for China's New Power," *International Herald Tribune,* 21 January 2004.

21. Robert Collier, "China on Global Search to Quench Its Thirst for Oil," *San Francisco Chronicle,* 26 June 2005. See also "Indonesia Expects Bank of China's Loan for Gas Field Project," *People's Daily,* 4 March 2004, http://english.people.com.cn/200403/04/eng20040304_136457.shtml.

22. "Indonesia's Stature Rises with New Security Pact," *Christian Science Monitor,* 17 January 2006.

23. Bates Gill and Yanzhong Huang, "Sources and Limits of Chinese 'Soft Power,'" *Survival* 48, no. 2 (2006): 17–36.

24. Tom Raum, "U.S. May Boost Image if Efforts Seem Nonpolitical," *Philadelphia Inquirer,* 5 January 2005.

25. Richard Halloran, "China Intent on Aircraft Carrier Goal," *Washington Times,* 28 May 2007.

Gabriel B. Collins and William S. Murray

No Oil for the Lamps of China?

THE UBIQUITOUS "MADE IN CHINA" stickers and labels on consumer products remind us daily of China's incredible economic rise. The world seems accustomed to this powerful phenomenon; analysts expect that China's economy will grow at 10 percent annually for at least another decade. Such remarkable economic progress has lifted millions of Chinese out of poverty and also substantially benefited the global economy. It is also arguably the keystone of the Chinese Communist Party's legitimacy.

Western and Asian hunger for inexpensive Chinese goods fuels much of this growth, but China's economic engine cannot run without imports of raw materials such as bauxite, iron ore, timber, and, perhaps most significantly, crude oil. Once a significant exporter of crude, China became a net importer in 1993 and now struggles to deal with this dependency.

Chinese security analysts fear that oil import dependency is a potential pressure point that could be exploited by future People's Rebublic of China (PRC) adversaries.[1] Approximately 80 percent of China's 3.3 million barrels per day (bpd) in crude oil imports passes through the Strait of Malacca. Such funneling could facilitate interdiction of China's oil lifeline in times of crisis.[2] The United States, India, and Japan are all seen as potential blockaders, but Chinese observers appear to believe that only the United States has both the capability and the will to blockade oil shipments to China.[3] One recent

Chinese article postulated that the most likely triggers of an oil blockade of China include a conflict over Taiwan and a situation in which China's rise becomes hostile and directly threatening to other major powers.[4]

Some Chinese analysts argue that the need to protect shipments of oil and other vital raw materials is a key driver behind the PRC's intensive aerial and naval modernization programs.[5] Yet despite impressive improvements, the People's Liberation Army Navy (PLAN) lacks the ability to defend the sea lines of communication (SLOC) over which Chinese oil supplies flow. Among other limitations, the PLAN lacks guaranteed access to ports for refueling and replenishing as well as adequate numbers of at-sea replenishment vessels necessary to support long-range missions. More fundamentally, the PLAN rarely undertakes long-distance operations that would provide vital training experience for SLOC protection missions.

In contrast, some of Beijing's potential adversaries have decades of blue water experience, world-class logistical capacity, global access to replenishment ports, and doctrine and equipment oriented toward warfare on the high seas. Beijing's strategists recognize this disparity and are presumably devising plans to counter any possible future efforts to cut China's petroleum umbilical cord.

This chapter will examine potential Chinese responses to possible forms of energy blockade.[6] The first two sections discuss how a distant blockade might be conducted, and will survey possible Chinese responses to such an action. The third section hypothesizes a close blockade and then analyzes potential courses of action in response. The fourth section examines the possibility of a "blockade by convoy," and the final section considers an energy denial strategy that would target China's ability to transport and process crude oil.

The authors conclude that an energy blockade of China would send destructive shockwaves through the global economic and political landscape. It is hoped that frankly discussing energy sea-lane security will promote trust and lay a foundation for fostering deeper energy security cooperation between China and other major oil consumers.

Assumptions

The imperatives of continued economic growth and global interdependence among states make major wars unlikely. Nonetheless, this chapter assumes that a state of war exists between the PRC and the blockading state. Even an "embargo" implemented as a measure short of war would still likely trigger open hostilities because it would threaten China's continued economic growth and would be interpreted by Beijing as an intolerable and unjustifiable breach of sovereignty. We assume, therefore, that Beijing would interpret a blockade under any name as an act of war and would respond accordingly.

This chapter also assumes that, if faced with an energy blockade, China would restrict or prohibit the use of private automobiles and other nonessential transportation and would ration the sale of any liquid fuels to diesel generator owners and other nongovernmental oil users. These and similar measures would reduce PRC oil needs, perhaps even to levels that could be sustained with domestic production and Kazakh and Russian pipeline and rail imports. China's nonmaritime oil sources currently total more than 3.5 million bpd and by 2010 could reach 4 million bpd. For comparison purposes, in fiscal year 2004, the U.S. military, fighting wars in Iraq and Afghanistan and sustaining other normal operations, used approximately 395,000 bpd of oil.[7] While U.S. military fuel consumption levels cannot be directly correlated with the consumption of the Chinese military in a hypothetical context, these figures strongly suggest that even in a high-intensity conflict the PRC would have access to sufficient fuel levels to run its military machine, as well as most portions of its current economy, assuming that the export channels and the import of critical non-energy imports continued unabated.

We acknowledge that a blockade that prohibits fuel imports while permitting the continued shipment of other raw materials to China, as well as the export of finished products, is an artificial and unlikely circumstance. A comprehensive ban on maritime shipping in and out of Chinese ports would have a far more powerful effect than an energy blockade alone. However, much of the Chinese internal discussion on blockades deals directly with the possibility of a maritime energy blockade. For this reason, this analysis focuses exclusively on potential energy blockade mechanisms and possible PRC responses.

The Distant Blockade

An energy blockade of China could be initiated at choke points such as the Malacca and Hormuz straits, both of which lie far from the Chinese coast. Chinese analysts worry, perhaps with good reason, that a relatively small number of warships could effectively sever China's oil lifeline. After all, a distant maritime energy blockade might be very attractive to any civilian policymakers and military planners tasked with preparing for conflict with China. If successful such a course of action could offer the possibility of achieving political objectives with very low levels of violence.[8] Additionally, at least in the near term, there would seem to be little that China's conventional military forces could do to directly challenge such a blockade.

One of the greatest obstacles facing the PRC in such a scenario would be the distance of the energy choke points from PLAN naval bases. China's naval vessels rarely operate very far from their home waters, or for very long. With a few exceptions, their crews probably lack the experience necessary to undertake extended, distant missions during wartime. Compounding this weakness, Beijing's limited number of replenishment vessels is inadequate for and inexperienced in sustaining distant operations.[9] In the near term, therefore, any PLAN counterblockade task force would operate at or beyond the outer limits of its professional ability and combat range. Blockading forces, on the other hand, would probably not suffer from either limitation. Another feature of the long distances involved is that PLAN ships would also likely be detected well before they came within weapons range of enemy ships, if not immediately after departing their home ports. During its entire transit, therefore, a PRC surface action group would be vulnerable to a range of subsea, surface, and aerial threats, at locations of the blockading force's choosing.

Another symmetrical option available to the People's Liberation Army (PLA) would be to conduct air-launched antiship cruise missile (ASCM) attacks against blockading vessels. Yet the distances involved, the likely early detection of incoming aircraft, and the lack of an adequate in-flight refueling ability would work against any air strike force. Furthermore, PRC bombers and strike aircraft operating far from mainland China would be highly vulnerable to an opponent's surface-to-air missiles, land-based air superiority fighters, and any carrier-based aircraft. China possesses approximately ninety highly capable SU-30 fighter bombers that could conceivably reach the Strait of Malacca, conduct strikes against enemy surface warships there, and return to base. Conducting such an operation would, however, require a level of proficiency in aerial refueling and long-range strike operations that the PLA has yet to demonstrate. As such, successful PRC aerial attacks against blockading forces are presently unlikely although the situation could change if the PLA develops the doctrine, infrastructure, and experience necessary to conduct such actions.

Alternatively, China could threaten distant blockading ships with its submarine force. However, PLAN submarines would be at a disadvantage. Any submarine attempting to transit from its mainland base to the Strait of Malacca would have to penetrate the antisubmarine efforts of the blockading powers, some of which could be extremely sophisticated.[10] Beijing's diesel-powered submarines would be forced to snorkel frequently when making such a transit, greatly increasing the probability of detection and destruction. The PLAN's limited number of notoriously noisy nuclear attack submarines could deploy from their North Sea Fleet base but would be vulnerable while en route. PLAN submarines also rarely undertake long patrols, so it is very likely that there is little institutional knowledge in the PLAN submarine force of how to conduct such an operation.

PLAN submarines, furthermore, would have little utility if the blockade were conducted in the Strait of Malacca. Many portions of the strait are too shallow to allow the submerged passage or sustained submerged operation of any submarine. If the blockade were conducted on the western approaches to the strait, PLAN submarines would have to either pass through the strait on the surface and be readily detected and attacked or transit submerged around the Indonesian archipelago, making the journey that much more challenging. For a variety of reasons, shallow waters greatly inhibit the use of torpedoes, thereby depriving PLAN submarines of their most lethal weapons, at least in many areas of the strait. PLAN ASCMs would also be of limited use in the strait, since their difficulty in discriminating between targets would make their successful attack on a warship in the crowded strait statistically unlikely, especially from longer ranges.[11] The same arguments apply to the Strait of Hormuz. PLAN submarines, consequently, are not a counterblockade panacea, though the threat they represent cannot be completely dismissed. It must also be said that if the Shang (Type 093) or any follow-on classes of Chinese nuclear attack submarines (or even, to a somewhat more limited extent, air-independent propulsion diesel submarines) are sufficiently quiet and capably operated, then the threat they would pose to surface warships would be significantly increased.

Because Beijing has limited ability to directly oppose forces conducting a distant energy blockade, it might seriously consider taking retaliatory actions elsewhere.[12] One option available includes using submarines to mine the entrances to a blockader's commercial ports and naval bases. Other options include using short- and medium-range ballistic missiles to pummel regional targets and attacking a blockader's replenishment ships with submarines.[13] There is strong evidence that China has developed a land attack cruise missile similar to the Tomahawk.[14] In the near future this weapon, particularly long-range bomber or submarine-launched variants, could be employed against a wide range of critical regional targets thus giving China a powerful asymmetric response option. China could also mine the approaches to an opponent's harbors with submarines or converted merchant ships. Defending against these threats would tax the blockading navy by forcing individual ships to be on the tactical defensive throughout the region and would strain the theater's military forces overall as they struggled to protect vulnerable infrastructure. A host of other escalatory steps could be taken in response to an energy blockade, perhaps even including the use of nuclear weapons, not-withstanding China's No First Use pledge.

Although the distant blockade seems relatively attractive from a block-ading state's point of view, its implementation includes several critical chal-lenges. Captured ships, cargoes, and crews would have to be escorted to a central marshaling area. If the original crews proved unwilling to continue to operate the vessel, the blockader would have to provide a prize crew of mariners to undertake the journey in addition to escorting the seized ves-sels with a warship. This would be a complex undertaking, especially if mul-tiple vessels were seized in a short period of time. It is unlikely that many military sailors have the necessary knowledge to operate oil tankers, and it is certain that most naval ship-manning requirements are not set with an eye on providing prize crews. Selecting the marshalling area would also likely be problematic because Southeast Asian states might balk at openly abetting the blockading state. Furthermore, many if not most harbors are too shallow to allow the entry of deep-draft supertankers.

Aside from finding a location to anchor seized tankers, blockading forces would still face the perplexing issue of what to do with the seized crews and cargoes. Tanker crews are often multinational and the owners of any seized ships and cargoes would presumably vigorously protest to their govern-ments, whose pressure on the blockading state to release the ships might lead to the not-infrequent blockade phenomenon of having to seize the same ship multiple times.[15]

The oil trade's flexibility would make a distant blockade difficult to suc-cessfully execute. Fifty-two tankers pass through the Strait of Malacca daily carrying approximately 11.7 million barrels per day of crude oil.[16] A block-ading naval force would have to determine which of these tankers carried the roughly 3.3 million of these daily barrels that were bound for China.[17] Presumably, tankers sailing under PRC flags or having known PRC owner-ship would also be relatively easy to distinguish and stop. Yet only about 10 percent of China's energy imports are presently carried on domestic hulls, which would force a blockader to accurately identify and intercept the other 90 percent.[18] A 250,000-deadweight-ton very large crude carrier (VLCC) serving the Arabian Gulf–Far East route typically carries just under 2 million barrels of crude oil per trip. This suggests that as few as two VLCCs per day can carry China's daily crude oil imports, which might bode well for a navy contemplating how to conduct a distant maritime energy blockade against the PRC. Yet the number of tankers carrying oil to China on any given day could assume a wide range of configurations that would depend on commercial concerns, which will be discussed shortly. The volume could range from two vessels to ten or more. This larger prospective volume suggests that identifying in advance which tanker was destined for the PRC would be problematic. Each tanker passing through the strait, therefore, would have to be boarded, and have its shipping documents examined. Any tanker with a legitimate bill of lading that stated the oil was destined for Japan, Korea, the Philippines, or elsewhere would be allowed to proceed on its journey.[19] Those stating a PRC destination would be seized.

A distant blockade would be easy to defeat using conventional commercial means. For instance, it is not unusual for cargoes to be sold between ports of embarkation and destination, with some oil cargoes being resold on the spot market up to thirty times while a tanker is at sea.[20] This suggests that a tanker with a legitimate bill of lading for Korea could have its cargo sold to PRC interests after it had been inspected and allowed to pass through the blockade. This feature of the modern oil trade would greatly complicate any state's ability to determine a tanker's final destination by examining only the bill of lading. In addition, oil cargoes are frequently "parceled out" with one tanker carrying oil bound for several consumers.[21] For example, a VLCC might carry a 2-million-barrel crude oil cargo with 500,000 barrels headed to Singapore, 500,000 to South Korea, and 1 million to the PRC. If an embargo against oil shipments to China seemed imminent, parceling would likely quickly rise as Chinese oil importers sought to avoid being singled out. Even if a shipper honestly declared that one-quarter of his cargo was headed to China, a blockader might create very serious diplomatic and economic repercussions if it detained a vessel which was also carrying crude to South Korean and Singaporean buyers. This would be particularly true in the case of a conflict over Taiwan, as regional nations might resist taking sides in a confrontation between the PRC and an outside power.

Shipping documents can also be forged. Forgery could be quite sophisticated, especially if it were (as it no doubt would be) abetted by the PRC government. In a blockade scenario therefore, the blockading force would probably not find any tankers with bills of lading that declared China as their destination. The PRC government and its state-owned energy companies could almost certainly offer private shippers and oil producers sufficient compensation to ensure their complicity in such a scheme.

Another issue that might arise while enforcing a blockade is stopping a ship that simply refused to stop and be boarded. Sinking an uncooperative supertanker seems implausible in conditions short of total war, given the value of the cargo, the environmental havoc created by the resulting oil spill, and the threat to the civilian crew. With high enough stakes, a blockader might use minimal levels of violence to ensure compliance, but serious diplomatic repercussions could follow the use of disabling fire against a foreign vessel (e.g., a Greek or Norwegian supertanker). A blockader could probably stop uncooperative ships without using gunfire or other lethal force, but those means could be overtaxed if faced with significant numbers of ships that resisted being boarded. Beijing could orchestrate coordinated disobedience such that ten vessels in one day would refuse to stop.

The issue of maritime insurance and its effect on maritime oil transport during war is also worth consideration. Under normal operating conditions, hull insurance for a tanker runs between 2.5 percent and 3.75 percent of ship value on an annualized basis.[22] Thus, a tanker owner operating a $130 million VLCC can expect to pay $8,900–13,300 per day in insurance costs. Lloyd's of London and other insurers, however, would automatically revoke ships' hull insurance upon any outbreak of war between China and the United Kingdom, France, the United States, and Russia, suggesting that all shipping to and from China would automatically stop during hostilities.[23] In practice, however, cargo owners and shippers can obtain compensating coverage known as Hull War Risks and Strikes Policies if they operate in a declared War Risk Exclusion Zone.[24] In such declared waters, rates can climb to 7.5 percent to 10 percent of ship value on a per trip basis, meaning that the same VLCC operator would have to pay between $8,900,000 and $13,300,000 per trip to insure his ship while it was in the danger zone.[25] Beijing would have to subsidize such costs either directly or indirectly if it wanted continued delivery of oil on privately owned vessels.

PRC state-owned tankers could conceivably be self-insured and forego paying such premiums in order to maintain continued oil delivery service to the home country. This may explain recent efforts by Chinese nationally owned oil corporations to build and operate a larger fleet of oil tankers, as described in the chapter by Collins and Erickson in this volume. In addition, it is possible that the PRC could entice shippers and ship owners with direct payments or some type of laundering mechanism. A high enough return can induce some shippers to sail into war zones without insurance. Crews willing to sail can also be found for the right price.[26] Consequently, the challenges of overcoming insurance barriers during potential blockades would likely be overcome.

Yet another method of sidestepping the blockade would involve avoiding the Malacca Strait altogether by sailing tankers through the Lombok and Sunda straits, or even circumnavigating Australia and approaching East Asia from the open Pacific.[27] This would render a distant blockade even more unlikely to achieve its goal and would require additional blockading forces. If each strait required four surface warships, a protecting submarine, and a replenishment ship, then guarding these passages would require twelve additional surface warships, three submarines, and three replenishment ships.[28] Tanker rerouting would result in four to sixteen days of disrupted oil shipments to East Asian consumers depending on whether shippers re-routed through the Lombok Strait or were forced to go all the way around Australia. This, in turn, would drive up shipping rates and final oil prices for all oil consumers. Map 1 shows the increased tanker demand and delivery disruption times that would result from tankers being rerouted around the Malacca Strait.

Map 1. PRC Tanker Re-routing Options

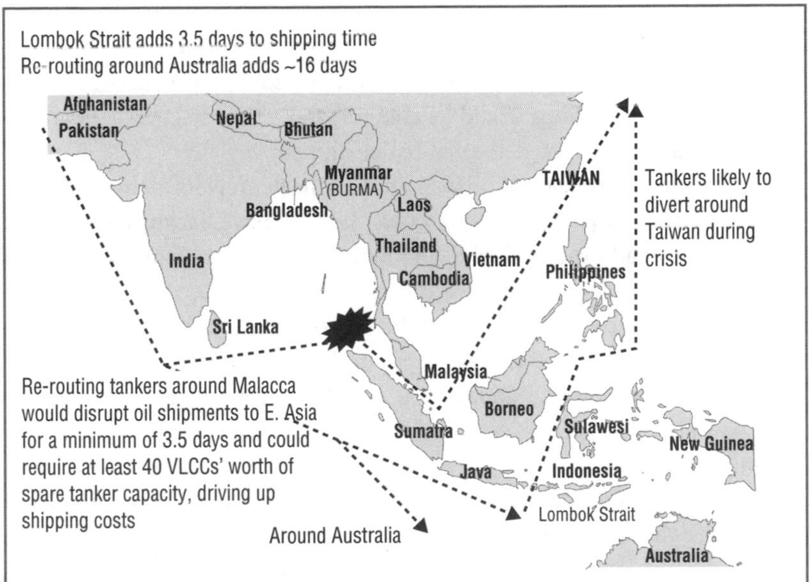

A distant blockade would also be unable to interdict oil transshipped from neighboring nations to China. The blockading state could exert pressure on East Asian nations to prohibit such transshipments, but the economic incentive to violate any such prohibitions would doubtless be considerable. Furthermore, preventing transshipment would mean intercepting—in close proximity to the mainland—large numbers of smaller ships carrying oil cargo into China, a problem that will be discussed shortly.

Estimating Required Forces

The practical problems associated with conducting a distant blockade as discussed above suggest a robust force structure. This would have a high opportunity cost because it reduces the number of ships available to deal with the conflict that prompted the blockade in the first place. The number of surface warships necessary to conduct a distant blockade can be roughly estimated. The driving factor is the need to ascertain which tankers passing through the Strait of Malacca contain oil bound for China. If each tanker must be boarded to make this determination, then perhaps a single warship could send boarding teams to four tankers in a twenty-four-hour period. This produces a need for thirteen surface warships, based on fifty-two tankers passing through the strait every day. If the number of tankers requiring boarding could be winnowed somehow, perhaps if bills of lading could somehow be verified electronically, then the number could be reduced. Perhaps then, six surface warships would be able to conduct the necessary boarding and inspections, with one dedicated replenishment vessel.[29]

Such a limited force would also require in-theater replacements for maintenance or combat casualties, and would have to have backups available if any of the blockading ships had to conduct escorting or pursuit functions. It appears then that upwards of ten surface warships and at least two replenishment vessels would be required to establish an effective and protected distant blockade in the Strait of Malacca. This number would increase proportionally if the Lombok Strait, Sunda Strait, and route around Australia also had to be patrolled. The authors estimate that three surface warships and accompanying replenishment vessels per additional strait would be necessary to provide reasonable assurances that all passing tankers could be boarded and inspected, and if necessary, escorted to a quarantine anchorage. This leads to a minimum total of sixteen surface warships and a minimum of four replenishment vessels, not counting supporting forces that would be necessary to interdict and defeat any attacking PRC counterblockade forces, and not counting the forces necessary to relieve the initial forces. Clearly, only large navies would be capable of contemplating such a blockade.

Further Limitations and PRC Options

In addition to the problems discussed earlier, a distant maritime energy blockade would also be unable to prevent the overland transport of oil into China. As with the transshipment to smaller ships, significant economic incentives would drive substantial oil delivery to China via pipeline, train, truck, or other means. Russia currently ships over 300,000 bpd of oil to China by rail and anticipates being able to pipeline up to 280,000 bpd of crude to northern China by year-end 2008. Severing these overland oil flows would require attacking critical infrastructure deep within Chinese territory, with all the escalatory risks such strikes would entail. It is worth noting that no blockade of China in history has succeeded without Russian acquiescence.

China has diplomatic options if subjected to a blockade. Unless China committed an act of such magnitude that it united the international community against itself, a blockading power would likely face Beijing alone. While a blockader might be militarily superior, China's vital role in the global economy means that a blockader would face extreme international pressure to conclude operations quickly. Such pressure would rise steadily as economic damage mounted with the net effect being that the blockader would alienate allies and could even become an international pariah. Resulting international diplomatic pressure would severely hamper a blockade, which even if conducted flawlessly would probably take months or even years to register its full effect. Undoubtedly, Beijing would also use its substantial diplomatic ability to align other states with its energy and economic interests, thus further raising the diplomatic, economic, and even military costs to the blockader.

Among other diplomatic options the PRC might decide to (or threaten to) proliferate previously denied arms to states unfriendly to those conducting the blockade, or might renege on previous agreements that benefited the blockading state. Beijing could also reflag its tankers to a third nation and thereby greatly complicate the legalities involved in boarding such vessels. Under the Statement of Interdiction Principles of the Proliferation Security Initiative, participating states have agreed "to seriously consider providing consent under the appropriate circumstances to the boarding and searching of its own flag vessels by other states, and to the seizure of such WMD-related cargoes in such vessels that may be identified by such states."[30] It is likely that in a roughly parallel manner Chinese planners believe an energy blockader could also convince or compel some states to acquiesce to allowing boarding, searching, and interdiction. Thus, China might try to reflag its vessels to states that a blockader would be reluctant to confront. Such ships could sail imperviously through a distant blockade, unless the blockading state was prepared to risk significantly broadening the conflict.

China might also attempt to disrupt the energy systems of its opponents. In the case of the United States, for example, Hurricane Katrina demonstrated the fragility of Gulf Coast oil production, refining, and distribution systems. Other nations dependent on hydrocarbon imports doubtless have similarly vulnerable concentrations of energy infrastructure. China could conduct physical or electronic attacks against these and other critical nodes that would limit the amount of oil blockading nations could import. Similar attacks against financial, electrical, and even food distribution networks are also conceivable and could have very profound effects.

In short, although China would not be able to effectively counter a distant oil blockade via traditional military might, it would likely be able to greatly reduce a blockade's effectiveness through commercial, diplomatic, and unconventional military means. Even if Beijing could not maintain its peacetime levels of oil imports through these mechanisms, restricted domestic consumption and domestically produced oil and overland imports would allow it to hold out for a length of time limited only by the ability of PRC leadership to convince its population that the costs were worth the value of the objective that led to the blockade's imposition. Simultaneously, global business and diplomatic interests would surely clamor for a resumption of trade with China. Such a scenario would seem to be to Beijing's, and not a blockader's, advantage.

"Supply-Side" Blockade

A state that contemplates an energy blockade against China might consider a "supply-side" blockade in which major oil exporters such as Iran, Oman, Angola, and Saudi Arabia would be forbidden to export oil to China. Such an approach could be enforced by either inducing the countries to reduce exports by an amount equal to their average exports to China, or by monitoring outbound tankers and taking punitive actions if they carried their cargoes to China. A supply-side blockade, however, would likely require the use of force to compel cooperation from recalcitrant oil exporters such as Iran or Venezuela, thereby substantially widening the conflict. By reducing the total amount of oil available to the world market, a supply-side embargo would also trigger frantic bidding by China and other major consumers, causing increased costs to all oil consumers, including those in the blockading state. Furthermore, as the 1973 Arab oil embargo eventually demonstrated, even the embargoed country eventually receives oil from the embargoing states, albeit at increased costs and through third parties. A supply-side blockade, consequently, would be neither effective nor feasible.

The Close Blockade

If a distant blockade cut off delivery of oil to China via large tankers, it is likely that delivery via smaller vessels would increase in response to this new demand signal. To defeat this delivery mechanism, a blockading state would be forced to consider employing a close blockade.

A close blockade would entail placing surface warships in close proximity to China's three major oil-handling port concentrations of Guangzhou/ Hong Kong, Shanghai/Ningbo, and Tianjin/Dalian. Each of these concentrations would likely require perhaps six surface combatants to board, inspect, and, if necessary, seize ships that attempt to run the blockade. Blockading forces would also have to be prepared to stop, or at least greatly reduce, the traffic of smaller ships that could transit in close proximity to the coastline between Chinese and other Asian countries. All of these methods would require placing dozens of surface warships near the Chinese coast. The risks to warships operating in such a wartime environment would be substantial, and the blockading state would probably quickly find itself in a naval and aerial war of attrition. To achieve the upper hand in such a scenario, a blockading state would be tempted to strike at PLAN-supporting infrastructure (e.g., command and control nodes, fleet headquarters, and naval vessel fueling depots). Such actions could prove dangerously escalatory and would define a critical difference between the distant and close blockades.

A Blockade by Convoy

Another option available to the blockading state would be to implement a system of convoys. These would not be formed for defensive purposes but would instead ensure compliance with an energy embargo against China. Each convoy would consist of tankers bound for neutral and friendly Asian states and would be escorted by a surface warship. No other tankers would be permitted to sail in Eastern Pacific waters. Assuming that five VLCCs per day would be needed to supply non-Chinese Asian oil demand, the logistics of implementing such a convoy system would overwhelm most or even all navies. We estimate that each group of five VLCCs would require a round-trip sailing time of upwards of twenty days from Singapore to Busan, plus a two-day turnaround. Each of the twenty-two daily convoys would need at least one escorting surface warship and corresponding replenishment ship. Additional ships would be required to ensure that maintenance and repair could be performed on the escorting ships, and to establish patrols to ensure that no cheaters entered China from the east or from other routes. This would require an enormous force structure and could only be conducted by the largest of navies, and only with the active cooperation of neighboring states.

Energy Denial

Given the shortcomings of the maritime blockade options discussed earlier, a blockading state might seek an alternative way to deny China energy imports. One possible method of achieving at least a partial energy blockade would involve preventing China from processing and distributing oil, regardless of how it entered the country. China, like all other major oil consumers, is vulnerable to precision attacks on key energy infrastructure such as refineries and pumping stations. The destruction of such critical infrastructure components could almost completely deny China the ability to process crude oil or efficiently transport refined products. This could conceivably be achieved with minimal destruction and violence while also minimizing risk to attacking forces.

A sufficiently capable adversary could conceivably destroy such a target set in a very short time. Conversely, an attacker might consider a calibrated approach as a method of demonstrating resolve and increasing incentives for negotiated settlement. In such a scheme oil off-loading wharves and adjacent strategic petroleum reserve facilities could be attacked first, followed perhaps by pumping stations on the Chinese portion of pipelines carrying oil from Kazakhstan and Russia and finally, if necessary, by strikes on oil refineries. With key refining units thus disabled, China would lose the ability to produce liquid fuels from petroleum for six or more months.[31] Yet unlike a naval blockade, which can be quickly reversed, destroying refinery components that take a half year or more to replace would have serious long-term repercussions for China's economy and would effectively constitute an irreversible act likely to trigger conflict escalation. Compounding these escalatory dangers, Russia and Kazakhstan could react strongly to the loss of significant portions of their energy exports and the prospect of political, social, and economic upheaval on the other side of their Chinese borders.

Possible Chinese Responses to Calibrated Energy Access Denial

PRC military planners undoubtedly realize that the destruction of energy infrastructure could appeal to an adversary. The PRC's heavy investment in advanced air defense systems such as the Russian SA-10 and S-300 and indigenous variants like the HQ-9 suggests that countermeasures to precision weaponry upon which such a scheme depends are being acquired.[32] China could also defend against such a campaign by stockpiling parts necessary for quickly rebuilding critical energy nodes. Fear of precision conventional attacks on energy infrastructure and other critical potential targets could also explain why China's naval modernization seems designed to be able to push opposing forces beyond the "first island chain" and, hence, eventually out of manned tactical aircraft and cruise missile range.[33]

If China were subjected to a precision energy infrastructure destruction campaign, it could employ the same retaliatory options described earlier. Yet, Beijing's symmetrical military response options would be less likely to be effective because naval forces supporting the precision campaign would operate at distances from China sufficient to provide some measure of safety. This difficulty in responding in a parallel manner would only increase the extant escalatory pressures that accompanied the crisis leading to the blockade's imposition.

An even more critical failing of an energy denial campaign is that it immediately involves strikes conducted against the PRC mainland. This is antithetical to the purpose of naval blockades, which could be considered a desirable use for military power because they rely on a limited use of force that can be modulated and, if necessary, withdrawn quickly, with little permanent damage done. Yet any actions, such as those involved in a precision energy denial campaign that significantly endanger Chinese economic growth, also threaten the survival of Chinese leaders as well as their regime's legitimacy, thereby producing extreme escalatory pressures. Beijing has long maintained a nuclear deterrent, which is being made extensively more survivable through the addition of a long-range SLBM on new SSBNs and road-mobile ICBM systems. Occasional mutterings and dark allusions from senior PLA officers who suggest a willingness to trade nuclear blows raise real questions concerning what constitutes Beijing's set of nuclear redlines.

One would hope that such scenarios would be avoided in all but the most fundamental and unconstrained struggles for national survival.

Conclusion

A distant naval energy blockade, though it could be conducted with low to moderate tactical risk with some navies' force structures, could probably not prevent the delivery of oil to China from alternative sea routes; from the falsification of bills of lading; or from the transshipment of oil via third parties. Such a blockade will become even less feasible as China extends the reach and lethality of its naval and aerial forces. A close blockade, on the other hand, would require large numbers of ships to operate in close proximity to the PRC's impressive and increasingly lethal anti-access weaponry where they would be subject to attrition, with attendant escalatory risk. A blockade by convoy would also require a very large force structure, and a supply-side blockade of oil shipments to the PRC would only drive up prices for all global oil consumers.

None of these blockade schemes could prevent the flow of oil into China via pipeline, rail, or truck, and none could prevent China from extracting oil from its interior oil fields. In 2005, domestic sources accounted for over 60 percent of the oil that China consumed. That same year imported oil comprised only about 10 percent of China's overall energy consumption. These numbers strongly suggest that China could withstand a complete denial of seaborne oil imports. Furthermore, effective blockades typically take years to achieve their goals and even then only succeed when they are a part of a comprehensive military action, which usually includes invasion or massive aerial bombardment of the country being blockaded.[34] It is difficult to imagine a limited-war scenario that would justify such actions by any blockading nation.

The fundamental conclusion of this chapter's examination of blockade scenarios is that, contrary to what appears to pass for conventional wisdom among PRC naval analysts and observers, China is not fundamentally vulnerable to a maritime energy blockade in circumstances other than global war.[35] This has far-reaching implications. Foremost, this suggests that China does not need to build up naval capacity for the purpose of defending energy SLOC against potentially hostile naval forces. Such a realization might recalibrate internal Chinese discussions in ways that increase transparency and engender increased trust between China and concerned regional powers. This in turn potentially opens the door for much more meaningful naval and SLOC security cooperation between the PLAN and other navies.

The twin trends of China's skyrocketing resource demands and regional countries' general move to modernize their navies create a dire need for frank discussions on core energy and maritime security issues. Including tough subjects such as blockades puts the discussion in concrete terms and may help participants move beyond the "talking" stage and into the policy "implementation" stage.

Seeking deeper understanding between China and other regional and global powers would help reduce tensions and foster more effective multilateral solutions to energy transport security. This might be accomplished by such measures as encouraging the International Energy Agency to accept China as a full member, increasing military–military contacts, and offering to share strategic petroleum reserve management expertise. Parties on either side of a potential conflict who play on China's sense of vulnerability to an energy blockade, whether by accident or by intent, destabilize and ultimately erode security for all sides.

Notes

1. See, for example, Gabe Collins, Andrew Erickson, and Lyle Goldstein, "Chinese Naval Analysts Consider the Energy Question," in *Maritime Implications of China's Energy Strategy*, Interim Report, Chinese Maritime Studies Institute, U.S. Naval War College, December 2006.

2. See P. Parameswaran, "U.S., China, India Flex Muscle over Energy-Critical Sea Lanes," Agence France-Presse, 4 October 2006, http://www.defensenews.com/story.php?F=2151823&C=asiapac.

3. 凌云 [Ling Yun], ["The Dragon's Arteries"], "龙脉" "现代舰船" *Modern Ships* (October 2006): 8–19.

4. Ling, "The Dragon's Arteries," 15.

5. Lei Wu and Shen Qinyu, "Will China Go to War over Oil?" *Far Eastern Economic Review* 169, no. 3 (2006): 38.

6. Throughout this chapter the word blockade will be used to describe efforts that seek to deny the transport and delivery of products—in this case petroleum-based energy—to a given nation. The authors recognize that the legal requirements and definitions of a blockade can differ from the hypothetical conditions put forth in this chapter but assert that such differences would not prove insurmountable to a nation intent on denying another's access to energy during war. The authors also recognize the many compelling reasons to believe that a war between China and the United States is highly unlikely and undesirable.

7. Sohbet Karbuz, "The U.S. Military Oil Consumption," 25 February 2006, http://www.energybulletin.net/13199.html.

8. The method of blockade assumed in this chapter is the boarding and searching of suspect ships. Those with contraband would be either seized or forced to proceed to holding ports while those with authorized cargoes and destinations would be allowed to proceed. This chapter does not envision the selective or indiscriminate sinking of suspect vessels in conditions other than unrestricted warfare.

9. Deployments by PLAN vessels such as those by the Luhu-class destroyer *Qingdao* and a replenishment vessel to the west coasts of Canada and the United States in the late summer of 2006 are infrequent exceptions to this rule.

10. The distance from the PLAN's submarine base on the south coast of Hainan Island to the Strait of Malacca is approximately 1,200 nautical miles. PLAN diesel submarines can travel submerged quietly at a maximum speed of approximately 4 knots without rapidly depleting their batteries. Assuming, then, that they could travel nearly 100 nautical miles a day, they would require twelve days to travel from their base to the Strait of Malacca. After arriving, PLAN submarines would have to operate in and around the very crowded and shallow waters of the Malacca Strait against the combined, formidable, and concentrated antisubmarine efforts of the blockading force. Success for a PLAN submarine in such an environment is far from assured.

11. Autonomous weapons such as ASCMs do not generally discriminate well between potential targets and instead attack whatever radar return first satisfies their arming and attack criteria. Hence, one Chinese manufactured C-802 ASCM fired by Hezbollah against the Israeli *Hanit* Sa'ar 5 corvette on 14 July 2006 missed its target and instead is alleged to have struck and destroyed an Egyptian merchant vessel. Another, of course, hit its target. See Yitzhak Shichor, "Silent Partner: China and the Lebanon Crisis," *China Brief* 6, no. 17 (2006), http://www.jamestown.org/publi cations_details.php?volume_id=415&issue_id=3837&article_id=2371390.

12. Bruce Blair, Chen Yali, and Eric Hagt noted a doctrine of PLAN escalation in naval warfare, quoting former PLAN commander Liu Huaqing as having written in his memoirs, "When enemies attack our coastlines, we will attack our enemies' home base." Bruce Blair, Chen Yali, and Eric Hagt, "The Oil Weapon: Myth of China's Vulnerability," *China Security*, no. 3 (Summer 2006): 43.

13. Although operations of this type could ultimately prove unsuccessful due to PLAN inexperience, any blockading force would have to honor the threat and deploy assets accordingly.

14. "Land Attack Cruise Missiles (LACM)," GlobalSecurity.org, http://www.globalse curity.org/wmd/world/china/lacm.htm.

15. For example, a Norwegian ship-owning company specializing in the maritime transport of petrochemical gases, liquid propane gas, crude oil, and liquid natural gas recruits officers and crews for its ships in St. Petersburg, Russia, and Wuhan, China. These ships are then chartered to major international companies. See "The I. M. Skaugen Group" at http://www.skaugen.com. Using modern communications, a ship about to be seized would surely tell its owners of this fact, who could inform the cargo owners, who could sell the cargo on the spot market. A very large crude carrier (VLCC) carrying a 300,000-ton shipment of crude (about 2.2 million bar-

rels) has a cargo value (at $60 a barrel) of over $130,000,000. Such enormous financial stakes would doubtless result in sophisticated maneuverings that would greatly complicate the challenge of determining cargo ownership. It is also conceivable that the PRC government and its oil companies could set up shell companies that would permit any tanker threatened with boarding to almost instantaneously sell its cargo to what appeared to be a non-PRC buyer. James Goldrick, "Maritime Sanctions Enforcement against Iraq, 1990–2003," in *Naval Blockades and Seapower, Strategies and Counter-Strategies, 1805–2005*, ed. Bruce Elleman and S. C. M. Paine (London: Routledge, 2006), 210.

16. The fifty-two tankers per day estimate is derived from information reported to the Malaysian Vessel Traffic Service at Klang, which is available from Malaysian Vessel Traffic Service statistics at the Malaysian Marine Department website at http://www.marine.gov.my/misc/index.html. See "World Oil Transit Chokepoints, Strait of Malacca," November 2005, http://www.eia.doe.gov/cabs/World_Oil_Transit_Chokepoints/Malacca.html.

17. In 2005 China imported approximately 27 percent of the oil that passed through the Strait of Malacca that was bound for either China (3.1 million bpd imported), Japan (5.2 million bpd), South Korea (2.2 million bpd), and Taiwan (1 million bpd). See "Top World Net Oil Importers, 2004," at http://www.eia.doe.gov/emeu/cabs/topworldtables3_4.html; 3.1 million barrels of oil can be carried on as few as two VLCCs or on any number of smaller ships.

18. "China Needs More Supertankers to Ensure Oil Supply Security: Report," Xinhua News Agency, 11 August 2006, http://english.people.com.cn/200608/11/eng20060811_292246.html.

19. A bill of lading is a document issued by a shipper acknowledging that specific items have been received on board as cargo to be shipped to a designated destination for delivery to a consignee who is usually stipulated.

20. *The International Crude Oil Market Handbook 2004*, 5th ed. (New York: Energy Intelligence Group, 2004), A12.

21. This observation was made during an interview with a former VLCC officer. It is also mentioned in John S. Burnett, *Dangerous Waters: Modern Piracy and Terror on the High Seas* (New York: Penguin Group, 2002), 43.

22. See, for example, P. Manoj, "War Risk Insurance for Indian Flag Ships Liberalized," *The Hindu Business Line*, 28 December 2004, http://www.thehindubusinessline.com/2004/12/29/stories/2004122902350100.htm.

23. Michael D. Tusiani, *The Petroleum Shipping Industry*, Volume II, *Operations and Practices* (Tulsa, Okla.: PennWell Publishing Company, 1996), 216–17.

24. Ibid.

25. See, for example, Perrine Faye, "Iraq Attacks Drive Up Oil Tanker Insurance, Middle East On Line," 28 April 2004, http://www.middle-east-online.com/english/?id=9821. Interviews with some industry specialists suggest that in some cases the charges cited in the text can be incurred daily.

26. During the Iran–Iraq Tanker War some crews agreed to sail in the Persian Gulf in return for triple pay. Tusiani, *Petroleum Shipping Industry*, 217. Willing crews would be even easier to find during a blockade marked by seizures rather than sinkings.

27. An excellent summary of the limitations and delays involved in rerouting oil tankers through alternative passages if the Strait of Malacca were closed can be found at Mokhzani Zubir, "The Strategic Value of the Strait of Malacca," Centre for Maritime Security and Diplomacy, Maritime Institute of Malaysia, 2, http://www.mima.gov.my/mima/htmls/papers/pdf/mokhzani/strategic-value.pdf.

28. Adding these forces to those required to patrol the Strait of Malacca produces the need for a fleet of approximately twenty-two surface warships, five submarines, an aircraft carrier, and at least five replenishment vessels. Maintenance, rest, and other reasons would probably increase the numbers required by 50 percent or more, creating an estimated need for fifty or more ships to conduct a distant blockade that has a reasonable chance of denying China access to seaborne oil imports. If the blockade were designed to stop other imports or exports, the number of warships required would be much larger.

29. This half dozen combatants would require protective forces because distance and shallow water alone would be insufficient to vouchsafe their safety. If the blockading navy possessed one or more aircraft carriers, then those vessels' air wings could provide welcome self-defense and surveillance and reconnaissance functions, all of which would benefit the blockade. Any such carrier, however, would require additional surface ships and submarines for self-defense, as well as a dedicated replenishment vessel.

30. See "The Proliferation Security Initiative," U.S. Department of State, June 2004, http://usinfo.state.gov/products/pubs/proliferation/. Readers should note a bedrock respect for sovereignty in the wording of those principles.

31. This estimate is based on author's conversations with experienced refining specialists.

32. China's SAM order of battle is partially described in "Surface-to-Air Missiles," *Chinese Defence Today*, http://www.sinodefence.com/army/surfacetoairmissile/default.asp, accessed 6 February 2008. China's advanced SAM acquisitions are also described in the 2005 "DoD Report to Congress on the Military Power of the People's Republic of China," at http://www.defenselink.mil/news/Jul2005/d20050719china.pdf., 12, 23, 32

33. For discussion of the imperative to extend the operational capabilities of China's navy in this fashion by a PLAN senior captain, see Xu Qi, "Maritime Geostrategy and the Development of the Chinese Navy in the Early Twenty-first Century," trans. Andrew S. Erickson and Lyle J. Goldstein, *Naval War College Review* 59, no. 4 (2006): 62.

34. The allied blockade of World War I, the Union blockade of the Confederacy, Britain's blockade of Napoleonic France, and the U.S. blockade of Japan in World War II are cases in point.

35. Other recent research supports this assertion. Using two calculation methods, a 2006 analysis concluded that a total stoppage of seaborne oil into China would reduce Beijing's gross domestic product (GDP) by only 5.4 to 10.0 percent. The study noted that this reduction in GDP would either halve (best case) or nearly eliminate (worst case) China's continued annual 10 percent GDP growth. This would certainly be painful for China but by itself would unlikely provide sufficient incentive for PRC leadership to enter negotiations to end whatever conflict precipitated the blockade. See Blair, Chen, and Hagt, "The Oil Weapon," 43.

PART IV

China's Energy Security and U.S.–China Relations

Ronald O'Rourke

China's Naval Modernization Effort: Potential Implications for Required U.S. Navy Capabilities

THIS CHAPTER DISCUSSES THREE ISSUES: the goals or significance of China's naval modernization effort; the implications of China's naval modernization effort for required U.S. Navy capabilities; and the possible tension between China-related contingencies and what the administration refers to as the global war on terror (GWOT) as U.S. Navy planning priorities.

Goals or Significance of China's Naval Modernization Effort

A perceived near-term goal of China's naval modernization effort is to prepare for a short-duration conflict involving Taiwan. Observers believe this goal includes the development of anti-access forces capable of deterring, stopping, or delaying the arrival of U.S. military forces (principally naval and air forces) that might seek to intervene in such a conflict.

Perceived broader or longer-term goals of China's naval modernization effort include asserting China's regional military leadership, defending China's maritime territorial claims, and protecting China's sea lines of communication. The maritime territorial claims and the sea lines of communication can be linked in part to China's energy interests—the former because they include potential sites for oil exploration, the latter because they are used to import oil.

Given its perceived broader or longer-term goals, China will likely continue its naval modernization effort even if the situation with Taiwan is resolved (peacefully or otherwise). If the broader or longer-term goals become more prominent in China's naval modernization effort, the composition of that effort might shift to include a stronger emphasis on one or more of the following:

- Larger surface combatants (i.e., serial production of one or more destroyer designs)
- Nuclear-powered attack submarines (SSNs)
- Aircraft carriers and sea-based aircraft
- Underway replenishment
- Overseas bases and support facilities

Potential Implications for Required U.S. Navy Capabilities

Responding to capabilities that China acquires in support of its broader or longer-term goals may require the U.S. Navy in coming years to have capabilities for the following:

- Maintaining presence and influence in the western Pacific
- Defeating Chinese general-purpose naval forces in potential non-Taiwan combat scenarios
- Tracking and countering Chinese nuclear-powered ballistic missile submarines (SSBNs)

Maintaining presence and influence in the western Pacific would require forces to be forward deployed into the region or capable of arriving there rapidly in response to contingencies. This in turn would require a navy with sufficient force structure, suitable basing arrangements, and suitable deployment and readiness practices. Suitable basing arrangements could include the homeporting of additional ships at forward locations such as Hawaii and Guam. Suitable deployment and readiness practices could include measures such as long-duration deployments with crew rotation, multiple crewing, and the Fleet Response Plan (FRP). Maintaining presence and influence in the western Pacific would also entail conducting port calls, exercises, military-to-military exchanges, as well as technical measures to promote interoperability of U.S. and allied or friendly forces.

Defeating Chinese general-purpose naval forces in potential non-Taiwan combat scenarios would involve investing in a variety of what might be called higher-end naval capabilities, including the following:

- Ballistic missile defense (BMD), including defense against potential ballistic missiles equipped with maneuvering reentry vehicles capable of hitting moving ships at sea
- Air-to-air warfare
- Antiair warfare against antiship cruise missiles
- Antisurface warfare
- Antisubmarine warfare and torpedo defense
- Mine warfare—offensive as well as defensive
- Resistance to information warfare/information operations
- Resistance to electromagnetic pulse and other nuclear-weapon effects

BMD capability is a relatively new area for the U.S. Navy; most of the other capabilities listed here can be viewed as more classic capabilities although they would be executed in the future with new technologies and operational concepts.

Tracking and countering Chinese SSBNs could require a certain number of U.S. SSNs, as well as modern analogs to the sound surveillance system, tactical auxiliary general ocean surveillance–type ocean surveillance ships, and P-3 maritime patrol aircraft that the Navy used during the Cold War to track and counter Soviet submarines, including SSBNs.

China and GWOT as U.S. Navy Planning Priorities

To what extent is the U.S. Navy divided between two contrasting futures—a GWOT future and a peer competitor (China contingency) future? What are the tradeoffs and choices?

Navy capabilities required for conducting GWOT-related operations overlap with, but are not identical to, capabilities required for conducting China-related operations, and capabilities for conducting a third category of operations—larger-scale land-oriented operations such as might take place under certain Southwest Asian or Korean Peninsula scenarios.

Table 1 shows selected Navy investment areas and which of these three types of operations they appear more strongly oriented toward. The purpose of the table is simply to suggest the idea of capability sets that overlap but are not identical. The table does not attempt to be exhaustive or systematic in the items listed—some of the items listed are platforms while others are groups of platforms, capability areas, or types of operations. Observers might score the listed items differently, or choose to list different items. Some items not listed in the table—such as aircraft carriers; SSNs; precision strike systems; special operations forces; and intelligence, surveillance and reconnaissance—appear to apply more evenly across all three types of operations. The potential planning tension for such assets appears to focus more on how their use is allocated among the three types of operations.

Table 1. U.S. Navy Investment Areas

Selected Navy investment areas, and the kinds of operations they appear more strongly oriented toward	GWOT-related operations	Larger-scale land-oriented operations	China-related operations
Maritime domain awareness and maritime interception operation	X		
Riverine force	X		
Global Fleet Stations	X		
Civil affairs/CBs/medical/disaster relief	X		
Antiterrorism/force protection measures	X		
Littoral combat ships	X	X	
Amphibious fleet	X	X	
Maritime prepositioning ships	X	X	
Naval surface fire support		X	
Ballistic missile defense		X	X
Air-to-air		X	X
Antiair warfare		X	X
Antisurface warfare		X	X
Antisubmarine warfare and torpedo defense		X	X
Mine warfare		X	X

Insofar as Navy resources in future years will be finite and likely insufficient to fully fund all desired capabilities for all three types of operations, it appears likely that there will be a tension in future years among these three types of operations as Navy planning priorities. Just how much tension will be a function in part of how limited Navy resources will be.

The cost of some of the GWOT-related investments shown in the table may be relatively modest. Other things held equal, this could mitigate the tension between GWOT-related priorities and other planning priorities.

A potentially larger source of tension relates to how much time the Navy spends emphasizing each of these planning priorities in its discussions with policymakers. Navy public statements in recent months have featured a strong emphasis on GWOT-related operations and almost no emphasis on preparing for a future maritime military challenge from China.

The Navy's current public emphasis on the GWOT appears intended in part to prevent or minimize a potential shift of budget resources from the Navy to the Army and Marine Corps. It may have some success in this regard. But over the longer run, the Navy's public emphasis on the GWOT can work against the Navy's goal to fund various desired programs by reinforcing in the minds of policymakers a GWOT-centered defense planning paradigm that inherently focuses thinking more on the needs of the Army and Marine Corps than on the needs of the Navy (or Air Force).

A GWOT-centered defense planning paradigm does little to justify higher-end Navy capabilities that may be needed for China-related operations. A few examples of planned or desired investments that could be put at risk under this paradigm due to inadequate justification are

- the procurement of a second SSN each year, even though SSNs have operational value in the GWOT;

- procurement of more than one CG(X) cruiser per year, and the eventual total number of CG(X)(s) procured;

- the Navy-desired initiation of a full replacement program for the canceled Navy Area Defense BMD program (also known as the sea-based terminal or Navy lower-tier program);

- the total number of F-35 Joint Strike Fighters (JSFs) procured for the Navy, and thus the percentage of JSFs in the Navy's strike-fighter force; and

- various antiair and antisubmarine warfare weapon and system acquisition efforts.

In short, this could be a situation of being careful of what you ask for. If the Navy continues to strongly emphasize its value in the GWOT while rarely mentioning the need for preparing for a potential future maritime military challenge from China, then the Navy one day might wind up with a fleet that is more oriented toward the former than the latter. Such a fleet might look a bit like a large version of the Coast Guard, with a lot of littoral combat ships and some extra logistics capabilities for disaster-relief operations but without some of the higher-end capabilities that might be needed for China-related operations.

Promoting a defense-planning paradigm that more evenly balances investing for GWOT-related operations with investing for China-related operations would require three things. The first is an ability to acknowledge more than one actual or potential major security challenge at a time, even when one of those challenges (China) is not immediately acute.

The second is an ability to understand and speak about China as a big country that is many things at the same time, some of them contradictory. China is a dynamic economy, a big trading partner, and an actual or potential partner on certain international issues. But it is also a potential major security challenge.

The third is an ability to speak clearly and openly about all aspects of China, including its potential for posing a major security challenge, without self-censorship (or exaggeration). It is legitimate to take into account China's perspectives and potential reactions on issues, but doing so should not become a barrier in U.S. discussions to openly identifying China as a potential regional peer competitor of major interest in U.S. defense planning, or to openly and fully discussing the defense-planning implications of China's military modernization effort.

Compared to the U.S. Navy, China's navy currently is not ten feet tall, or even six feet tall. But when measured against the missions that China appears to have in mind for its navy, it is on a path toward becoming six feet tall. Given the apparent goals of China's naval modernization effort, it seems unlikely that refraining from openly identifying China as a potential regional peer competitor of major interest in U.S. defense planning would induce China to stop this effort. Whether U.S. self-censorship would help slow China's naval modernization is not clear; conceivably, one might argue the contrary—that self-censorship could reinforce the effort by suggesting to Chinese leaders that it is helping to intimidate U.S. policymakers. Self-censorship on this matter could, however, distort U.S. defense planning by reducing policymaking attention devoted to, and the justification for investments that might be needed to respond to, China's naval modernization effort.

One potential place to start talking more openly and consistently about China as a major Navy planning issue would be the new Maritime Strategy that the Navy is writing. Since the end of the Cold War the Navy has issued a number of strategy-type documents. Most have had little lasting impact, at least with non-Navy audiences, because although they said useful and interesting things about a variety of issues, they did not say anything that readers could recognize as significantly new, different, and important. The reaction these documents garnered with non-Navy audiences reminds me of what Winston Churchill reportedly once said at a dinner when he was presented with a dessert he was not too impressed with: "Take this pudding away—it has no theme!" Today, these theme-deficient Navy strategy documents are largely forgotten.

An exception to this pattern was . . . *From the Sea*, first issued in late 1992. This document had some real impact because its central theme formalized and catalyzed a significant shift in Navy planning focus away from the Cold War–scenario of mid-ocean operations against Soviet/Russian naval forces and toward the post–Cold War scenario of operations in littoral waters against the land- and sea-based forces of potential adversaries other than Russia.

Does the Navy want its new strategy document to have a real impact? If so, it needs to include something significantly new, different, and important. China's naval modernization effort and its implications for U.S. Navy planning is arguably that issue.

In its new strategy document the Navy can certainly continue to talk about the Navy's role in the GWOT, the 1,000-ship Navy, Global Fleet Stations, humanitarian operations, and similar issues. But if talk is all there is, it may not have much impact. Incorporating a significant discussion of the need to prepare for a potential future maritime military challenge from China could give the document a more lasting impact. The discussion should present the issue calmly, respectfully, and without exaggeration but also plainly, clearly, and without self-censorship.

Like 1992's . . . *From the Sea*, the new strategy document could formalize a significant shift in Navy planning focus. In this case the shift would preserve a concern for GWOT-related operations and larger-scale land-oriented combat scenarios while elevating preparations for countering a potential maritime military challenge from China to openly equal status.

Dan Blumenthal

Concerns with Respect to China's Energy Policy

THE TREMENDOUS INCREASE IN China's appetite for energy, and the response to this by regional powers, is changing the dynamics of international politics. Over the past two decades, the growth in China's demand for natural resources has been dramatic. Twenty years ago China was East Asia's largest oil exporter; now it is the world's second largest oil importer. According to various estimates, in the last two years the increase in China's energy demand has made up anywhere from 20–40 percent of worldwide growth. China's expanding portion of the worldwide demand for energy and other natural resources helps to explain China's booming presence on the international stage. China's share of worldwide aluminum, nickel, and iron ore consumption, which are now each approximately 20 percent, doubled from 1990 to 2000 and will probably double again by the decade's end.[1]

As China scours the globe for energy resources, it has become a new player in some important regions. It receives between 40 and 45 percent of its energy imports from the Middle East, 11 percent from Iran alone. More than 30 percent of its oil now comes from Africa. President Hu Jintao and Premier Wen Jiabao have worked hard to secure and protect China's far-flung investments. Through high-level diplomacy, economic aid, and military relations,

Chinese leaders have increased Beijing's influence in oil-producing states. As a latecomer to the world energy consumption game, Beijing has entered markets forbidden to Americans. Some of these relationships have strengthened the hand of dangerous regimes looking for an alternative to the United States: for example, China's presence in Latin American resource markets has allowed Hugo Chavez to boast that no longer will the United States be the dominant consumer of Venezuelan oil; now, "[Venezuela is] free and place[s] this oil at the disposal of the great Chinese fatherland."[2]

Washington is concerned that China is underwriting dangerous and repressive dictatorships from Khartoum to Tehran. Its response, within the framework of a diplomacy that encourages China to become a "responsible stakeholder" in international affairs, is to persuade China to embrace the international energy market rather than "lock-up" upstream resources. The United States is also trying to convince China that supporting dictators in oil-producing states is not conducive to the long-term stability of the international system and does not even enhance Beijing's own oil supply security.

As Chinese energy investments expand around the globe, Chinese strategists and officials are debating options for securing China's oil supply. This debate is unfolding in the context of Beijing's larger debate regarding China's strategic direction. To be sure, the Chinese energy debate has produced some policies consistent with evolving international norms. For example, Beijing is constructing a Strategic Petroleum Reserve, participating in the spot oil market, and making efforts to increase energy efficiency at home and therefore decrease demand. Still, some major elements of China's energy security policy remain attempts to "lock-up" energy supplies at the source, develop strategic relationships with oil producers, and develop the military capability to deter hostile supply disruptions.[3] The policy is informed by suspicion of the United States and regionally powerful nations including Japan and India, as well as by the economic nationalist impulse that China should have as much control as possible over its own strategic resources.

Beijing perceives the United States to be opposed to key Chinese strategic objectives. China sees Washington as standing in the way of unification with Taiwan and suspects that the United States has a longer-term objective of containing China's rise. This perception reinforces a widespread Chinese belief that the United States "controls" the oil market and will manipulate it to China's detriment. Moreover, many in Beijing believe that the United States will use its dominance at sea to interrupt fuel supplies should China behave in a manner that displeases Washington. These views about American policy help to explain why China has not moved more toward the "liberal" end of the economic policy spectrum.[4]

Washington's response, as articulated by former deputy secretary of state Robert Zoellick, has been to convince China of the mutual benefits of sustaining the international energy system. Responding to Beijing's announcement of a peaceful rise (now called "peaceful development") strategy, Zoellick laid out what Washington believes a peaceful rise would look like. China, he said, benefits from the international system that America created and guarantees.[5] The system is characterized by an expansion of free and open trade, the promotion of human rights and democracy, efforts to counter proliferation, a well-functioning energy market, transparency in military affairs, and attempts to resolve disputes peacefully. China joined and benefited from the international system and is now being asked to help strengthen it. Today the system is under threat from jihadi terrorists, state sponsors of terrorism seeking to acquire nuclear weapons, and genocidal dictators. China is being asked to help thwart those threats and define its national interests more broadly.

A China that rejects the main characteristics of the international system and attempts to rewrite the rules will be viewed as a noncooperative rising power, one that challenges the guarantors of the system. Those guarantors will in turn more aggressively contain that rise. A China that helps sustain the system, instead of challenging it, will be accepted as a great power.

China's foreign policy is largely driven by its energy policy. Increasingly, Beijing's approach undermines the international system Zoellick described. China's oil diplomacy has provided cover to Iran as the United States and European Union work to thwart Tehran's nuclear ambitions. China's energy policy has protected Sudan and Burma from tough international sanctions, and China is providing African dictators with a shield against international pressure to reform.

In addition, current Chinese energy moves fuel tension with Washington's key Asian ally, Japan, and are causing consternation within India. China's actions have also reinforced economic nationalist impulses in both Japan and India, sucking them into an energy competition in countries such as Burma.[6]

Looming over the horizon is China's debate over military options to secure its energy supply. China has become more open about the People Liberation Army's (PLA) role in "safeguarding China's economic development." Indeed, China's 2006 defense white paper notes that "China's national defense provides the guarantee for maintaining China's security and unity, and realizing the goal of building a moderately prosperous society in an all-round way. To build a powerful and fortified national defense is a strategic task of China's modernization drive."[7] Chinese military officers talk about developing a blue water navy.[8] The ambition is real, but the future characteristics and capabilities of China's military are unknown. A China developing greater power projection capabilities would significantly alter the geopolitical landscape for an America used to dominating the sea.

If the Chinese perception of energy security as a zero-sum game persists alongside suspicion of U.S. strategic intentions, Sino–U.S. relations will become more competitive. If China continues to grow richer and stronger, Beijing will develop capabilities to defend its oil supply, just as other rising powers have done. While such a development need not inevitably lead to conflict with the United States, barring changes in China's national aspirations, Washington is likely to view greater Chinese power projection capability as threatening.

The United States is engaging China in countless attempts to cooperate on energy security in such areas as clean coal and the U.S.–China Oil and Gas Industry Forum. But these initiatives seem to be having a limited impact on China's strategic perceptions. Such efforts should continue, but Washington should be humble about its ability to change China's policy. As long as China vies for preeminence in Asia, it will view Washington as a threat standing in the way of that ambition. Beijing's strategies will be conceived with an "America threat" in mind. Because energy policy is closely tied to foreign policy, China will only change its approach to energy security if it accepts the current system of international politics.

Beijing's Perceptions

China's concern over energy security has become significantly more palpable since it became a net oil importer in 1993. But fears of containment accelerated since the United States launched the war on terror. For many Chinese strategists, the United States is boxing China in along its periphery, with a presence in Central Asia; partnerships with India, Pakistan, Japan, Korea, and Australia; and increased engagement with Vietnam and the Philippines. America's objective is said by some to be to prevent "China's influence from rising in the region."[9]

Washington's deployments and increased presence in Central and South Asia and in the Middle East have fueled the Chinese perception of a containment strategy that includes impeding Chinese access to oil. Although Beijing had initially supported U.S. operations in the region, China became increasingly suspicious of the American presence once the United States began to encourage Central Asian states to undertake political reform and the color revolutions unfolded.[10] The turbulence that China assumes will accompany political reform in Central Asia is perceived in Beijing to place its resource suppliers at risk and threaten Chinese Communist Party regime stability.

An overwhelming reliance on Middle Eastern suppliers has compounded Chinese anxiety over energy security. In particular, American naval control of regional sea lines of communication, through which most of Beijing's crude passes, is seen as a troubling vulnerability.[11] The fact that over 80 percent of the People's Republic of China's (PRC) oil imports pass through the Strait of Malacca in particular has caused some alarm in the Chinese media, who refer to it as the "Malacca dilemma."[12] Zhao Nianyu of the state council-run Shanghai Institute for International Studies pointed to the Regional Military Security Initiative (RMSI)—a collective security exercise to protect the sea lanes that was proposed in 2004—as a first step by the U.S. military to "garrison the Strait" under the "guise of counterterrorist measures."[13] It should be noted that the RMSI was mischaracterized by the media and soon scrapped as sovereignty-sensitive Indonesia and Malaysia quickly stepped up antipiracy measures such as patrols and aerial surveillance.

Chinese responses to an increased sense of vulnerability, as James Holmes and Toshi Yoshihara have documented, have included an important debate about the necessity of sea control for a nation reliant upon foreign commerce. Officers writing in Chinese military journals speak in Mahanian terms: "[he] who controls the seas controls the world;"[14] "the command of communications on the sea . . . is vital for the future and destiny of the nation;"[15] "it is extremely risky for a major power such as China to become overly dependent on foreign import without adequate protection."[16] Some Chinese scholars, such as Zhang Wenmu of the Center for Strategic Studies at Beijing University of Aeronautics & Astronautics, also advocate naval expansion. Zhang has bluntly stated that "[China] must build up our navy as quickly as possible" to prepare for "sea battle"—the way in which many seafaring nations have previously resolved economic disputes.[17]

In some quarters of the PLA, even Taiwan is viewed in geostrategic terms because its acquisition would ease China's breakout to the open ocean. For General Wen Zongren of the PLA Academy of Sciences, regaining control of Taiwan would be "of far reaching significance to breaking international forces' blockade against China's maritime security. . . . Only when we break this blockade shall we be able to talk about China's rise. . . . China must pass through oceans and go out of the oceans in its future development."[18]

The Chinese view of Washington as an obstacle to its rise reinforces mercantilist inclinations. Why would America *not* use its dominance to starve China of its economic lifeline if Washington objected to China's behavior? America controls the sea lane and the shipping chokepoints. From Beijing's perspective, the oil weapon is a potent one in America's arsenal.

America's oil weapon would be especially threatening if China thought its actions would provoke a response, for example in a Taiwan, South China Sea, or Japan contingency. A China that believes Washington is intent on containment will inevitably view its energy supply lines as insecure. Given the salience of these perceptions of geopolitics, China's energy policy is troubling but not altogether surprising.

China's Energy Policy and the Rogues

To circumvent America's perceived "control" of the energy market, Beijing is pursuing relationships with oil producers isolated by Washington. China views oil diplomacy, particularly the formation of special relationships with oil producers, as an important element of its energy security strategy. Sudan, Iran, and Burma are cases in point.

Sudan

China has been Sudan's biggest investor in its growing energy sector, giving Khartoum the means to expand its military. Sudan is the largest source of oil production by Chinese national oil companies and is Beijing's seventh largest supplier of crude imports at 133,000 barrels per day (bpd).[19] China is Sudan's largest trading partner, purchasing roughly two-thirds of Sudan's exports and providing some 20 percent of its imports. Over the past decade, Beijing has also been the chief supplier of weapons, military supplies, and weapons technology to the Khartoum regime, despite the 2005 UN arms embargo on the government.[20]

China has consistently protected Khartoum from serious diplomatic sanctions, even going so far as to threaten vetoes when UN efforts seem to squeeze Khartoum too tightly.[21] Beijing succeeded in watering down Security Council Resolution 1556, which imposed an arms embargo on nongovernmental combatants in Darfur and required Khartoum to allow humanitarian assistance into Darfur and disarm the Janjaweed militia.[22] In 2006, during debate on UNSCR 1672, China impeded efforts to sanction Sudanese government officials charged with war crimes, reducing from seventeen to four the list of individuals subject to Security Council travel bans and financial sanctions.

Although China has eased its obstructionism slightly in response to international pressure, it is unwilling to risk its oil investments by imposing serious costs on Khartoum. While Hu Jintao made a well publicized trip to Khartoum in February 2007 to urge its compliance with international demands, he also announced new economic agreements, including $104 million to write off Sudanese debt and $17 million to provide an interest-free loan for infrastructure projects, including a new presidential palace.[23]

Iran

Iran is China's third-largest supplier of crude oil at 287,000 bpd in 2005, and China became Iran's largest oil export market in 2004. Since 2002 Iran has supplied China with more than 15 percent of its annual oil imports (a narrow second to Saudi Arabia).[24] Bilateral trade totaled $10.09 billion in 2005, more than four times the amount of trade five years earlier ($2.49 billion in 2000).[25]

During the past few years, as the United States and European Union were trying to isolate Tehran in an effort to gain compliance with nonproliferation commitments, China signed several major energy deals. In February 2006 China signed a $33 million three-year contract with Iran to repair and maintain the Alborz semisubmersible drilling rig in the Caspian Sea.[26] In October 2004 Sinopec signed a $100 billion deal to import 250–270 million tons of liquefied natural gas from Iran's South Pars oil field over twenty-five years. The deal also provides China with 150,000 barrels of crude oil per day for the twenty-five-year period from the Yadavaran oil field and a 50 percent stake in Yadavaran's estimated 17 billion barrel reserve.[27]

In March 2004 Zhuhai Zhenrong Corporation, a state-owned Chinese oil trading company, signed a $20 billion, twenty-five-year deal to import 110 million tons of liquefied natural gas from Iran. At the same time, Beijing signed a seven-year deal worth $121 million when the Chinese state-owned oil company Sinopec purchased the Iranian subsidiary of Sheer Energy, a Canadian firm, and received a 49 percent stake in the Masjed-I-Suleiman oil field.[28] To consummate these deals, Chinese foreign minister Li Zhaoxing made several trips to Tehran, promising diplomatic support in Iran's showdown with the West.

Moreover, along with Russia, China has been key in promoting Iranian participation in the Shanghai Cooperation Organization (SCO). President

Mahmoud Ahmadinejad was given great moral support when he addressed the SCO in Shanghai, where he called upon the SCO to "prevent threats and interventions by bullying powers,"[29] and the Chinese publicly rebuked the United States for calling Iran a terror-sponsoring nation. While China plays a careful game—it will not jeopardize stable relations with the United States, which explains its UN Security Council vote to sanction Iran in 2006—it still allows Iran to believe that it has a powerful protector. After voting to sanction Iran, China quickly made clear that the vote would not jeopardize good bilateral relations.

Failure to bring collective will to bear against Iran strengthens Tehran's defiance of the international community, and leads to greater instability. While Washington is trying to convince Beijing that both have an interest in pressuring Iran to abandon its nuclear weapons program, China will not risk its energy investments.

Burma

China pursues a similar "energy security for protection" trade-off with Burma. China sees Burma as its outlet to the Indian Ocean and has invested in highways and oil and gas pipelines that would link it southwest to Burma's coast. China's relationship with Burma has three main military components: provision of military technology to the State Law and Order Restoration Council (SLORC), the building of various military facilities, and the construction of intelligence collection installations.[30] Weapons provided to the junta, such as communication gear, armored personnel carriers, and rocket-propelled grenades, helped the SLORC turn the tide against antijunta insurgents. Conventional Chinese weaponry is reportedly deployed along the Indian and Thai border for possible use by the Chinese in various contingencies, thereby pushing China's strategic perimeter out into Southeast Asia and closer to the Indian Ocean.[31]

Many observers, in India especially, believe that the grand prize in China's relationship with Burma has been the construction of ports and bases along the Indian Ocean coast, including a major base at Haingyi Island. The fact that this base can port ships larger than anything in the Burmese fleet has not gone unnoticed in India.[32] Chinese intelligence facilities on the Great Coco Island near the Nicobar and Andaman islands provide Beijing with the ability to monitor naval and air movements across a large expanse of the Indian Ocean. While the extent of Chinese influence over port construction and intelligence facilities has been disputed, there is little doubt that China seeks to maximize its access to maritime facilities along the Indian Ocean.[33]

Burma is an important component of China's pipeline strategy as well. In 2005 China provided Burma with nearly $300 million in financial assistance and trade deals, certainly key to securing Burma's support for a five-hundred-mile pipeline linked to Yunnan to transport offshore natural gas that PetroChina will extract from Burma. Beijing hopes this gas pipeline will pave the way for an oil pipeline with a terminal on the Arakan coast that would lead back along the same route to Yunnan.[34] A number of Chinese and Western observers believe these pipelines would help China bypass the Strait of Malacca and its security risks (e.g., blockades, piracy, terrorism).

To be sure, it can be argued that the proposed pipelines would do little to enhance Chinese oil security. The planned Burma line can only carry 200,000 bpd of crude while China's annual oil import demand grows by more than 200,000 bpd each year, meaning that the pipeline's already small relative contribution to import security would quickly be erased by demand growth. Moreover, the per barrel cost of pumping oil through Burma to Yunnan and then refining it and transporting it to market will likely be several times the cost of carrying it through Malacca on a supertanker to Eastern China's large demand centers. These costs would be even higher for a pipeline from Gwadar, Pakistan, to Xinjiang province in Western China.

Nevertheless, it is clear that China views Burma as a strategic asset of some significance. In return for some degree of economic, resource, and perhaps even security cooperation, China has protected Burma from UN sanctions and U.S. pressure. It has also created a "race to the bottom" dynamic with Japan and India. In the case of Japan, Tokyo announced an aid cutoff after the Burmese junta massacred dissidents in May 2003. However, by October 2003, Japan had resumed aid to nongovernmental organizations and many other development projects. According to some reports, Japan's decision to resume aid was influenced by China's deal to assist the Burmese government with the development of the Irrawaddy River. Japanese government officials "are in favor of providing more aid to the military regime in order to offset China's increasing influence."[35] The Japanese government's posture toward Burma was "due in part to apparent concern about China replacing Japan as a likely source of economic assistance to, and political influence on, Burma."[36] Then in 2006, despite strong pressure from the West, Japan defied international expectations and voted against a 2006 UN Security Council (UNSC) resolution condemning human rights abuses in Burma, leading some commentators to ponder whether Tokyo's action was motivated by

Beijing's growing influence.[37] These concerns are well founded, given Tokyo's expressed desire to place human rights and democracy at the forefront of its foreign policy.

Observers of the India–Burma relationship have also noted an Indian response to a perceived increase in Chinese influence in Burma. Despite India's rhetorical commitment to democracy promotion, it sent a $40 million aid package and consummated a large natural gas deal in 2006 just as the UNSC was addressing the issue of Burma, leaving one analyst to conclude, "India has also recently moved to offer substantial international, political and economic support for Myanmar in what is quite clearly a concerted policy by India to counter Chinese commercial and military influence in Myanmar."[38] Indian security officials believe that India is "10 years behind" China in a competition for influence in Burma, and must catch up.[39]

All three countries view Burma as being geopolitically important. Tokyo and Delhi have undermined their own stated desires to incorporate human rights into their foreign policy in response to Beijing's increased activity in the country after the 2003 massacre.[40]

India and Japan must be held accountable for these irresponsible actions. However, from a U.S. perspective, one of the most promising developments in Asia has been Tokyo's and Delhi's attempts to reshape their foreign policies toward the provision of collective rather than simply national goods. China's actions have reinforced less altruistic elements of Japanese and Indian foreign policy.

Increased Presence in Central Asia

Beijing's perception that it is vulnerable to naval blockade has made land-based energy supply routes more attractive. After first deciding that an oil pipeline from Kazakhstan was uneconomical, China changed course in 2003 and signed the deal for $3–3.5 billion. In July 2006, the pipeline began to transport oil, some 200,000 barrels daily, from Atasu in northern Kazakhstan to Xinjiang Uyghur Autonomous Region.[41] Beijing has not surprisingly taken a strong interest in Central Asian politics and has tried to strengthen the SCO. Chinese analysts talk of using the SCO to turn the old Central Asian Silk Road into an "energy road."[42] China and Russia together secured an SCO statement calling for a timeline for the American military departure from Central Asia in 2005.

Beijing similarly took advantage of Uzbekistan's souring on its relationship with the United States after the Andijon massacre of 2005 to provide moral support to Uzbek president Islam Karimov, receiving him in Beijing with a twenty-one-gun salute not two weeks after the crackdown.[43]

China's interest in piping energy from Central Asia and its concomitant need to increase its influence in that region pose challenges to American policy. First, as in the Middle East and Africa, Western goals of democratization are frustrated by a new China card in the hands of regional dictators. Projecting into the future, it is very likely that China will want to protect its land-based energy investments. China is already forming two powerful armor-heavy mechanized corps modeled after the 1980s Soviet Operational Maneuver Groups for land-based threats.[44] In the future China will have more ability to contest, and perhaps even to restrict, American freedom of action in Central Asia, a development that will conflict with U.S. goals in the war on terror.

The View from Tokyo and Delhi

Already suspicious of China's long-term intentions, India views China as a competitor for global energy resources. Prime Minister Manmohan Singh articulated India's angst in a speech in New Delhi in 2005: "China is ahead of us in planning for its energy security—India can no longer be so complacent."[45] Both countries are scouring the globe for oil and gas deals and have invested heavily in Iran. Indian Oil and Gas minister Shankar Aiyar has advocated more collaboration, and some have talked about extending the proposed Iran–Pakistan–India pipeline to China. But many Indian strategists view this proposal with skepticism, especially in light of an Indian view that China is a competitor for regional influence.

China's energy policy in Burma and along the Indian Ocean exacerbates Indian concerns. India views Chinese construction of roads and waterways, ports and intelligence posts along the Indian Ocean as an attempt to eventually contest the Indian Ocean.[46] Indian naval planners in particular worry about Chinese forays into the Indian Ocean and expect that as China's energy insecurities grow, the Chinese navy will accelerate attempts to project power.[47] Indian Army Officers see China as a land power, increasingly able to project power across the Eurasian landmass after investing heavily in road and rail networks.[48] The need to secure pipelines would undoubtedly accelerate this trend.

Indians remain suspicious of China's intentions regarding the Spratly and Paracel islands as well. Indian security officials similarly warn that they will not "cede" Iran—a country that Delhi believes is of vital strategic importance—to China.[49] Delhi is trying to foster cooperation with China on energy matters while keeping options open for more intensified competition. India's concern over a future in which China increases its influence in Central Asia explains its observership in the SCO, but it is concerned that a diluted American presence in that region will result in another portion of its backyard dominated by China.[50]

Tokyo, which used to be the dominant Asian player in energy markets, has been shocked by China's growing oil needs. Japan's view of Chinese energy policies is shaped by its perception that a stronger China is asserting itself regionally and globally to Tokyo's detriment. In particular, Japan views the dispute over territorial demarcation and oil and gas resources in the East China Sea as part of a more aggressive Chinese posture. Japan has responded assertively as well, chasing away a Chinese nuclear submarine that intruded into Japanese waters in 2004. In 2005 relations deteriorated when China and Japan accused one another of beginning to extract resources in contested regions of the East China Sea.[51] China sent a small fleet led by Sovremennyy-class destroyers in a show of force around the gas field, and a Chinese ship reportedly trained its guns on a Japanese P-3C patrol craft.[52] Japan declared for the first time in its 2004 defense white paper that Chinese naval power should be a cause of concern for all of Asia. The prospect of two Asian powers using military force to emphasize or settle competing claims for oil and gas is unsettling. The United States has significant treaty obligations to Japan, meaning that risk of conflict with Japan is a risk of conflict with the United States.

Japan is alarmed by the rate of China's energy consumption growth and a perceived mercantilist tilt in China's energy policy.[53] This Japanese perception has prompted Japanese national security policymakers to take a tougher line with China and upgrade the alliance with the United States. Japanese energy policy is likewise responding: following a two-decade period of liberalization, Japan's latest energy strategy has a more nationalist cast, with calls for government intervention to compete on an equal footing with China for international resources.[54] To be sure, Japan is also taking measures to reduce demand and proposing multilateral cooperation, but a view insisting that energy is a strategic resource, and that Japan will need to compete for it with China, has grown prominent of late in Tokyo. Tokyo's and Beijing's recent competition for Russian energy supplies from East Siberia and Sakhalin is a case in point.

An energy policy that fuels great power competition threatens the security of Asia. Given Japanese and Indian angst over Beijing's energy strategy, it is incumbent upon the United States to maintain its predominance in Asia through robust economic and military presence. The appearance of American withdrawal or inattention would create a vacuum to be filled by intensified security competition among the three major powers, two of whom have nuclear weapons.

Unfortunately as Beijing works to secure its energy supply it has also developed anti-access/area denial capabilities that have the potential to restrict American freedom of access to the Asian rim lands and the continent, and therefore call into question Washington's staying power as the regional hegemon. This, in turn, further fuels Japanese and Indian worries that they may have to face a dominant China alone, prompting less than optimal energy policies.

Speculating about China's Future Energy Security Strategy

The speculation game is a perilous one, but given China's importance it is necessary to engage in it. China is a dynamic country with a highly skilled population. As its economy continues to grow, so too does its defense industrial and technological base, as well as the capabilities of its military personnel. The PRC has developed its military in ways not predicted by analysts less than a decade ago. No longer can China watchers say that "the PRC's armed forces are not very good and not getting better fast."[55] Most national security analysts now believe that China can pose serious challenges to an American military trying to come to the defense of Taiwan or other allies in the region. In the past decade a very small arsenal of ballistic missiles has grown into an arsenal of some nine hundred more accurate and lethal ballistic and cruise missiles. A decade ago China had just a few modern Kilo-class diesel submarines; today China has Kilos, Songs, and Yuans as well as two nuclear submarine programs. A decade ago, China's fleet of fourth-generation aircraft was minimal, today it is significant: an increasing percentage incorporate fourth-generation technology.[56] China has made additional strides in mine warfare and information warfare, and is contesting the United States in space. China has also grown bolder in using its military capabilities as evidenced by its activity in and around the East China Sea. A decade ago few if any analysts predicted that China would provoke Japan in this way.

There is no reason to believe that China will stop improving its military capabilities. Its defense industrial base is improving, it has money to spend on military projects, and it has the ambitions of a country anxious to retake its place in the sun. The ongoing energy debate will obviously influence the PLA's course. If China continues to tend toward the energy-mercantilist side of the energy policy spectrum, as compared to relying solely on the open market, then the PLA will increase in importance to Beijing's energy strategy.

A continued Chinese perception that the United States remains committed to preventing it from taking Taiwan by force, controlling the energy market, and preventing its rise as a great power, will reinforce impulses to control energy supply lines. Moreover, as China increases its overseas investment in energy, it will feel more exposed to a spectrum of threats and will want to provide security for those investments. Finally, the "Mahanian" impulse is strong in rising powers. The idea that a great power must be able to protect its own seaborne trade is the norm—practiced in the past by a rising Great Britain, a rising America, a rising Germany, and by a rising Japan.

There are some positive indicators that China's energy security strategy may not be the cause of a more conflictual relationship with its neighbors or with the United States. Washington is deeply engaged in a cooperative energy policy with China, including over twenty ongoing official cooperative energy initiates, which may push the Chinese energy debate to the more economically liberal side of the energy spectrum.[57] In addition to bilateral cooperative programs, Washington is promoting China's entry into multilateral energy forums and greater engagement with the IEA. The purpose of this engagement policy is to encourage China to embrace the energy market and the international mechanisms of energy security.[58] China's own energy insecurities may be a motivation to seek more independence by investing in renewable energy sources and becoming more energy efficient. These developments would be welcome.

But there are reasons to be skeptical of optimistic scenarios. Unless China radically changes its national objectives, it will continue to anticipate an American response to actions Washington deems threatening. One response, in Beijing's view, is a disruption of energy supply. So long as Washington has the means to "control" Beijing's energy supply, China will seek ways to access and secure energy for itself.

Even more discouragingly, great powers often decide that to be considered truly great they must be capable of securing their own trade. In the early part of the twentieth century—an earlier example of economic globalization—Norman Angell suggested that Imperial Germany should rely on the collective good provided by the Royal Navy and continue to prosper from it. The Kaiser did not accept his advice, challenged the Royal Navy, and the rest is unfortunate history.

We can and should offer up more opportunities for cooperation with China on energy security. But we should also be humble. A real embrace of the current energy system will only materialize if China undergoes a profound strategic reorientation. China's current energy insecurity is a product of its fears over possible American reactions to a range of future Chinese actions. Washington thus infers that China holds out the possibility of taking actions that may provoke an American response. In turn, China's energy security policy seeks ways to circumvent American responses to Sino–American conflict. A change in Beijing's energy security policy—a true embrace of the market, an acceptance of the international system of energy security, a reneging of its support for dangerous regimes, a decision to forego blue water capabilities—may be a key indicator of China's peaceful intentions.

Notes

1. For statistics on demand growth see, for example, David Zweig and Bi Jianhui, "China's Global Hunt for Energy," *Foreign Affairs* 84, no. 5 (2005): 25–38.

2. Ibid.

3. Recently, some Chinese analysts have begun to question this logic, noting that the foreign equity oil obtained by China's national oil companies (almost exclusively by China National Petroleum Corporation) accounts for a small percentage (roughly 15 percent) of Beijing's oil imports. The very fact, however, that Beijing has so aggressively pursued upstream equity speaks to the still prevailing belief in many Chinese circles that equity oil constitutes a more secure supply than does the world market. Erica S. Downs, "China's Role in the World: Is China a Responsible Stakeholder?" testimony before the U.S.-China Economic and Security Review Commission, 4 August 2006, http://www.uscc.gov/hearings/2006hearings/hr06_08_03_04.php.

4. Erica Strecker Downs, "China's Energy Security" (PhD diss., Princeton University, January 2004).

5. "Deputy Secretary Zoellick Statement on Conclusion of the Second U.S.-China Senior Dialogue," U.S. Department of State, 8 December 2006, http://www.state.gov/r/pa/prs/ps/2005/57822.htm.

6. Jill McGivering, "India Signs Burma Gas Agreement," *BBC News*, 9 March 2006, http://news.bbc.co.uk/1/hi/world/south_asia/4791078.stm.

7. "China's National Defense in 2006," Information Office of the State Council, People's Republic of China, 29 December 2006, http://www.fas.org/nuke/guide/china/doctrine/wp2006.html.

8. Author's conversations with PLA officers in Beijing, April 2007.

9. Zhai Kun, "What Underlies the U.S.-Philippine Joint Military Exercise?," *Beijing Review*, 14 March 2002, 9. Quoted in Mohan Malik, *Dragon on Terrorism: Assess-*

ing China's Tactical Gains and Strategic Losses Post September 11 (Carlisle, Pa.: Strategic Studies Institute, 2002), 30.

10. Go Lido, "Will the United States Withdraw from Central and South Asla?" Beijing Review, 17 January 2001, 8–9.

11. Downs, "China's Role in the World," testimony.

12. Hu Jintao allegedly urged a closed-door government session in 2003 to find ways around the "Malacca dilemma"—the fact that much of China's seaborne trade, including oil, goes through the Malacca Strait. "Certain major powers," he is reported to have said, were trying to dominate the strait. Shi Hongtao, "Nengyuan anquan zaoyu 'Maliujia kunju' Zhong-Ri-Han nengfou xie shou" ["Energy Security Runs Up Against the 'Malacca Dilemma'; Will China, Japan and Korea Cooperate?"], Zhongguo qingnian bao [China Youth Daily], 15 June 2004, business.sohu.com/2004/06/15/49/article220534904.shtml.

13. Dan Blumenthal and Joseph Lin, "Oil Obsession," Armed Forces Journal (June 2006), http://www.armedforcesjournal.com/2006/06/1813592. Although Malaysia, Indonesia, and Singapore have taken the lead on patrols, the perception remains in some Chinese circles that "American control" of the strait is a strategic vulnerability. Indonesia and Singapore have declined the U.S. Navy offer to help patrol the strait and have instead embarked on a fairly successful multilateral effort themselves. Thus, China's fears of the United States controlling the Strait of Malacca are not well based.

14. Xie Zhijun, "Asian Seas in the 21st Century: With So Many Rival Navies, How Will China Manage?" Junshi Wenzhai (1 February 2001): 20–22, FBIS-CPP10010305000214. Quoted in Toshi Yoshihara and James Holmes, "The Influence of Mahan upon China's Maritime Strategy," Comparative Strategy 24, no. 1 (2005): 23–51.

15. Jiang Shiliang, "The Command of Communications," Zhongguo Junshi Kexue (2 October 2002): 106–14, FBIS-CPP20030107000189. Cited in James Holmes and Toshi Yoshihara, "China and the Commons: Angell or Mahan?," World Affairs 168, no. 4 (2006): 172–91.

16. Shi Hongtao, "China's 'Malacca Straits,'" Qingnian Bao, 15 June 2004, OSC# CPP 20040615000042.

17. Zhang Wenmu, "China's Energy Security and Policy Choices," Shijie Jingji Yu Zhengzhi 5, (14 May 2003): 11–16. Cited in James Holmes and Toshi Yoshihara "China and the Commons," 181–82.

18. "Annual Report: The Military Power of the People's Republic of China," Office of the Secretary of Defense (Washington, D.C.: Government Printing Office, 2005), 12.

19. Downs, "China's Role in the World," testimony; Amy Jaffe, "China's Role in the World: Is China a Responsible Stakeholder?" testimony, U.S.-China Economic and Security Review Commission, 4 August 2006, http://www.uscc.gov/hearings/2006hearings/hr06_08_03_04.php.

20. Eric Reeves, "Darfur and the Olympics: A Call for International Action," testimony before the House Committee on Oversight and Government Reform, Subcommittee on National Security and Foreign Affairs, 110th Cong., 1st sess., 7 June 2007.

21. Peter S. Goodman, "China Invests Heavily in Sudan's Oil Industry," *Washington Post*, 23 December 2004.

22. Yitzhak Shichor, "China's Voting Behavior in the UN Security Council," The Jamestown Foundation, 6 September 2006, http://www.jamestown.org.

23. House Committee on Foreign Affairs, "The Escalating Crisis in Darfur," introduction by Representative Tom Lantos, 110th Cong., 1st sess., 8 February 2007.

24. Ilan Berman, "The Impact of the Sino-Iranian Strategic Partnership," testimony before the U.S.-China Economic and Security Review Commission, 14 September 2006, http://www.uscc.gov/hearings/2006hearings/written_testimonies/06_09_14 wrts/06_09_14_berman_statement.pdf.

25. Global Investment cites International Monetary Fund Direction of Trade Statistics, March 2007, www.imf.org.

26. Ehsan Ahrari, "China's Proliferation to North Korea and Iran, and Its Role in Addressing the Nuclear and Missile Situations in Both Nations," testimony before the U.S.-China Economic and Security Review Commission, 14 September 2006, http://www.uscc.gov/hearings/2006hearings/written_testimonies/06_09_14wrts/ 06_09_14_ahrari_statement.php.

27. Jephraim Gundzik, "The Ties That Bind China, Russia and Iran," *Asia Times*, 4 June 2005.

28. Borzou Daragahi, "China Goes Beyond Oil in Forging Ties to Persian Gulf," *The New York Times*, 13 January 2005.

29. John Douglas, Matthew Nelson, and Kevin Schwartz, "Fueling the Dragon's Flame: How China's Energy Demands Affect Its Relationships in the Middle East," report prepared for the U.S.-China Economic and Security Review Commission, 14 September 2006.

30. Ross Munro, "China's Strategy Towards Countries on Its Land Borders," final report of study commissioned by the Director of Net Assessment of the Office of the Secretary of Defense (McLean, Va.: Booz Allen Hamilton, August 2006), 58.

31. Malik J. Mohan, "Myanmar's Role in Regional Security: Pawn or Pivot," *Contemporary Southeast Asia* 19 (June 1997): 52–73.

32. Rahul Bedi, "Rural India Trying to Build Military Ties with Burma," *The Asian Age*, 6 July 2000; Donald L. Berlin, "The Great Base Race in the Indian Ocean Littoral: Conflict Prevention or Stimulation," *Contemporary South Asia* 13, no. 3 (2004): 239–55. Quoted in Munro, "China's Strategy Towards Countries on Its Land Borders," 65.

33. Andrew Selth of the Griffith Asia Institute urges caution in claiming that Burmese ports or intelligence facilities are Chinese owned or controlled. See Andrew Selth, "Chinese Military Bases in Burma: The Explosion of a Myth," *Griffith Asia Institute: Regional Outlook* 10 (2007). Such analysts as Ross Munro and Juli MacDonald,

however, have found evidence of Chinese investment, influence, and some control over significant ports and intelligence facilities. Professors Toshi Yoshihara and James Holmes of the Naval War College likewise argue that China views the ports and facilities along the Indian Ocean as key elements of a Chinese energy security policy. See Dr. Yoshihara's U.S.-China Economic and Security Commission testimony, 14 June 2007.

34. Munro, "China's Strategy Towards Countries on Its Land Borders," 108–9.

35. "Did Japanese ODA to Burma Really Stop After the Massacre on May 30th, 2003?" *Mekong Watch*, 27 May 2004, http://www.mekongwatch.org/english/policy/oda. html.

36. "Is Japan Really Getting Tough on Burma? Not Likely," *Burma Information Network*, 28 June 2003, http://burmainfo.org/oda/analyseGOJpolicy20030628.pdf.

37. Michael Green, "Japan Fails Test on Democracy and Burma," *Washington Post*, 8 June 2006; "Japan's Lackluster Policy on Burma," editorial, *The Nation* (Thailand), 3 June 2006.

38. Helen James, "Myanmar's International Relations Strategy: The Search for Security," *Contemporary Southeast Asia* 26, no. 3 (2004): 530; Michael Jonathan Green, "U.S.-Burma Relations," testimony before the Senate Committee on Foreign Relations, Washington, 29 March 2006.

39. Bethany Danyluk, Amy Donahue, and Juli MacDonald, *Perspectives on China: A View from India*, (Washington, D.C.: Booz Allen Hamilton, 2005): 17.

40. On 30 May 2003, forces associated with Burma's ruling junta attacked a convoy carrying National League for Democracy leader Aung San Suu Kyi and her supporters. Several League members were killed or injured in the attack and many others including Suu Kyi were arrested. She remains under house arrest. See USAID, http://www.usaid.gov/policy/budget/cbj2006/ane/mm.html.

41. "China Country Analysis Brief," Energy Information Administration, August 2006, http://www.eia.doe.gov/emeu/cabs/China/Background.html.

42. John Douglas, Matthew Nelson, and Kevin Schwartz, "Fueling the Dragon's Flame: How China's Energy Demands Affect Its Relationships in the Middle East," report prepared for the U.S.-China Economic and Security Review Commission, 14 September 2006, 12.

43. Chris Buckley, "China 'Honors' Uzbekistan Crackdown," *The International Herald Tribune*, 27 May 2005.

44. Martin Andrew, "PLA Doctrine on Securing Energy Sources in Central Asia," *China Brief* 6, no. 11 (2006): 6.

45. Manmohan Singh, "Speech to Petrotech 2005," New Delhi, India, 17–18 January 2005, Prime Minister of India website, http://pmindia.nic.in/speech/content. asp?id=69.

46. Danyluk, Donahue, and MacDonald, "Perspectives on China," 17.

47. Ibid., 6.

48. Ibid., 7.

49. Ibid., 18.

50. Russia has maintained close ties to India, including energy and weapons sales, and it is not inconceivable that Moscow and Delhi might cooperate to balance against increased Chinese influence in Central Asia and elsewhere.

51. "Japan's Provocation in East China Sea Very Dangerous," *People's Daily Online*, Opinion, 21 July 2005, http://english.people.com.cn/200507/21/eng20050721_197493.html.

52. James Holmes and Toshi Yoshihara, "Japanese Maritime Thought: If Not Mahan, Who?" *Naval War College Review* 59, no. 3 (2006): 14.

53. Peter C. Evans, "Japan," *Brookings Energy Security Series* (December 2006): 2.

54. Ibid.

55. Bates Gill and Michael O'Hanlon, "China's Hollow Military," *The National Interest*, no. 56 (Summer 1999, 55–62).

56. "Annual Report: The Military Power of the People's Republic of China," Office of the Secretary of Defense (Washington, D.C.: Government Printing Office, 2007).

57. Some cooperative programs include the Energy Policy Dialogue, the United States–China Oil and Gas Industry, the Protocol for Cooperation in the field of Fossil Energy Technology Development and Utilization, the Peaceful Uses of Nuclear Technologies Agreement, and the United States–China Strategic Economic Dialogue (SED). "China's Energy Consumption and Opportunities for U.S.-China Cooperation to Address the Effects of China's Energy Use," testimony of Assistant Secretary Karen Harbert, U.S.-China Economic and Security Commission, Office of Policy and International Affairs of the Department of Energy, 14 June 2007.

58. "U.S.-China Relationship: Economics and Security in Perspective," testimony by Deputy Assistant Secretary David Pumphrey, U.S.-China Economic and Security Commission, Office of Policy and International Affairs of the Department of Energy, 1 February 2007.

Jonathan D. Pollack

Energy Insecurity with Chinese and American Characteristics: Realities and Possibilities

THE WORLD IS AWASH IN ENERGY ANXIETY, both real and imagined. These fears are driven by perception, domestic politics, corporate and governmental interests, psychology, and (not infrequently) media hyperventilation. Amid this cacophony of voices, the policy agendas of oil producers and consumers and the concerns of some defense strategists threaten to overwhelm the need for reasoned analysis.[1] This chapter therefore focuses on some basic issues in energy strategy debate in the United States and China. It presents data on Chinese and (to a lesser extent) U.S. energy requirements, briefly reviews policy debate in both countries over energy futures, and then weighs some potential implications for Sino–American relations in the longer term. By focusing on Chinese and American views of energy strategy and their consequences for national-level decision making, we can identify areas of overlapping interest, clarify misperceptions, and highlight the potential implications should the United States and China prove unable to achieve a collaborative energy future.

There are profound differences among analysts about how to define energy security, and its treatment as a defense planning issue, in particular its implications for maritime security. Many of these differences are highlighted in other contributions to this volume. However, the underlying assumptions and larger context of energy strategy are often insufficiently examined. A comprehensive assessment of energy alternatives requires careful attention to aggregate supply and demand factors, the political and bureaucratic context of energy decision making in both systems, science and technology for resource exploitation, conservation options, and the operation of global energy markets.[2]

China and the United States have undeniable shared interests in energy strategy, though these shared interests are often obscured or overlooked. These include the need to ensure the predictable availability of energy at reasonable cost, protect against any potential disruption in the shipment of energy resources, diversify the sources of supply, encourage energy exploration, and prevent further environmental degradation, primarily by reducing reliance on hydrocarbons. Despite the convergent interests of the two countries (which together presently consume close to 35 percent of global oil production), their respective perceptions of each other's energy strategies are often highly divergent. These differences bear in particular on Chinese purchases of equity shares in various overseas energy markets, especially in the Persian Gulf, Africa, and Central Asia, which are characterized by some analysts as part of a larger Chinese effort to lock up energy resources or to control sources of supply.[3] They extend as well to worrisome characterizations of China's longer-term maritime interests and naval modernization priorities.

Amid a range of competing interests and policy agendas, one conclusion seems inescapable: the United States and China are largely in the same global energy boat. There is a self-evident need for Washington and Beijing to approach energy issues without excessive preconception, forego where possible a measure of national autonomy for the sake of collective interests, and undertake potentially wrenching domestic changes to advance larger policy goals. These are all tall orders, and none will be achievable without major efforts by both governments to undertake serious, sustained exchanges on the energy issue. There is a parallel need for heightened awareness among policymakers of the maritime security futures of both the United States and China, and of how these respective futures could interact either in positive or negative fashions.

Moreover, energy security is a misnomer. Nearly all analysis dwells on energy *insecurity*. Governments, producers, and consumers seek predictability and assurance about energy availability and pricing precisely because there is very little of either. The plethora of imagined disasters seems boundless, though many of these concerns reflect the competition and instability inherent in the operation of energy markets. Prudence and self-interest often result in bureaucratic or company-specific solutions, and energy strategy is increasingly being viewed as a military planning issue.[4] National- and firm-level decisions can have a powerful lock-in effect on subsequent policy options. Energy availability and cost considerations also impinge on consumer behavior and on environmental well-being. Well-informed scientists, analysts, and policy planners in the United States and China are addressing longer-term options in energy strategy, but it is far from certain whether national decision makers will pay full heed to these judgments, or whether extant policy mechanisms allow for comprehensive policy solutions.[5] Although the efficacy of long-range planning remains to be proven, it is not too much to hope for a measure of common sense and enlightened self-interest.

Some caution on projections of energy supply, demand, and cost is also warranted. In March 1999, for example, *The Economist* declared that the world was "drowning in oil" and that this glut would persist indefinitely, likely resulting in oil prices of well under $10 a barrel.[6] Careful, well-informed observers can therefore get things very wrong, primarily because of the volatility of energy prices. Aggregate analysis tends to minimize the more contingent factors in energy forecasts. Projections of heightened oil production in post-Saddam Iraq, for example, provide an additional example of unwarranted optimism. Specific events or policy developments (in particular instability in the Persian Gulf) can therefore affect markets and national psychology, helping to explain sharp price fluctuations as well as hedging strategies that often depart from rational economic calculations. When presenting characteristically optimistic long-term projections in his renowned briefings, Herman Kahn would often conclude with a dual caution: "my estimates should hold, barring bad luck and bad management." There will likely be no shortage of either in the years to come.

The Big Picture

Longer-term oil projections have generated major anxieties in recent years, triggered in significant measure by China's rapidly increasing demand for imported oil, as distinct from its use of other energy resources. The International Energy Agency (IEA) projects that China's oil import requirements will increase from the current level of approximately 3.5 million barrels per day (bpd), or roughly 50 percent of daily oil requirements, to approximately 14 million bpd by 2030, which would comprise approximately 75 percent of China's oil requirements. The preponderance of these imports will derive from the Persian Gulf.[7] This growing supply and demand disparity is explained by numerous factors: a structural shift in the Chinese economy toward energy-intensive basic industries, exponential increases in automobile ownership, dwindling domestic oil reserves, highly inefficient energy use within China, and the leadership's decision to keep the domestic price of oil artificially low, lest rising energy product prices trigger social unrest. As a consequence, China has accounted for approximately 40 percent of the increases in worldwide oil demand over the past five years.[8] China only became a net oil importer in 1993, but it has quickly emerged as a major player in global energy markets, with other rapid developers in Asia (most notably India) also contributing to this process.

The United States and China are the world's first and second largest consumers of oil, respectively. Saudi Arabia, Russia, and the United States constitute the top tier of the world's oil producers, with Iran, Mexico, and China in the second-ranking tier. China is now the third largest oil importer, behind the United States and Japan, and it will not likely be third for much longer.[9] China is largely following in America's footsteps (albeit beginning from a vastly lower level of economic development): both countries are consuming far more oil than they produce.[10] According to a British Petroleum estimate, the United States in 2005 possessed 2.5 percent of the world's proven oil reserves but consumed 24.9 percent of global oil production; by contrast, China held 1.4 percent of proven world reserves, and consumed 8.2 percent of global production.[11] This latter percentage seems certain to increase markedly in coming years.

The primary asymmetry in the Sino–American import equation concerns the locations from which the two countries acquire oil, though these usage patterns reflect geography more than any other factor. The United States meets slightly more than 50 percent of its import requirements from the Western Hemisphere (i.e., Mexico, Canada, and South and Central America). Slightly less than 20 percent comes from West and North Africa, approximately 18 percent comes from the Middle East, and the remainder (less than 10 percent each) comes from the North Sea and from Russia.[12] By contrast, China's imports are primarily from Africa (25 percent), Saudi Arabia (17 percent), Iran (14 percent), and Russia (8 percent), with projections that Central Asia could ultimately meet up to 15 percent of China's projected needs.[13] Thus China's increasing oil inroads into the Persian Gulf, Africa, and Central Asia (and the presumed political influence that would follow from this involvement) are triggering growing anxieties among those wary of China's longer-term goals and policies.

However, this picture is deceiving. There may be keen competition for oil resources, but it is not a Hobbesian war of all against all. Though the global imbalance between supply and demand is exceedingly small, energy resources are inherently fungible.[14] As Daniel Yergin observes, "There is only one global oil market, and the United States is part of it. Moreover, energy markets, like the rest of trade and finance, are ever more internationally entwined. Energy security does not reside in a realm of its own, but is part of the larger pattern of relations among nations."[15] Indeed, the slim margins between supply and demand highlight the disproportionate effects of any potential disruption of energy supply. Some analysts see these circumstances triggering future crises, especially given global dependence on oil exports from the Persian Gulf and the Gulf of Guinea, both among the world's most volatile locales.[16]

Viewed in a more long-run perspective, the world (according to 2005 consumption rates) has approximately forty-one years of proven oil reserves. This does not mean that the world will abruptly run out of oil in 2047; more reserves may yet be discovered, and existing reserves previously not economical to extract may be exploited as technology improves and oil prices rise. Indeed, forty-one years represents a significant *increase* over the slightly more than thirty-year estimate that was operative until the early 1980s, notwithstanding major consumption increases over the past decade or more.[17] As Chen Fengying concludes, "insufficient production and demand driven [factors], not resource depletion are responsible for supply shortages and galloping price [increases] in recent years. In other words, the sources of risks are to be sought on the ground instead of under ground. So we should not confuse tension in market supplies with energy security in a strategic sense. Otherwise unnecessary hysteria would follow hot on the heels."[18]

Assessing China's Hopes and Fears

There is widespread debate among Chinese analysts about China's increased dependence on foreign sources of energy, the potential vulnerabilities this might create, and how China can most effectively ensure its vital interests under these altered circumstances. As Xuecheng Liu of the China Institute of International Studies observes, "from China's perspective, domestic energy strategy is rooted in the vulnerability of its access to external energy resources and defensiveness against the United States curtailing its energy supplies. Considering the [potential] vulnerability of the four-fifths of all Chinese imports that pass through the Strait of Malacca, China sees its maritime shipping security as a pressing priority."[19]

Potential pipeline vulnerabilities in locales facing internal instability and ethnic tensions add to this pessimistic picture. However, Zha Daojiong of People's University argues:

> Disruption of supply is an energy security issue when the movement of foreign energy resources into China becomes problematic. Yet . . . there has not been a single known major incident of deliberate interruption since the early 1990s, making such issues primarily psychological. . . . Although there is no physical evidence to support these fears, they have a deep impact on thinking about China's future fate in the global energy markets. This fear is exacerbated by the discussion among the major world powers of a "China threat" to their respective energy supplies. . . . [But] awareness about China's geographic vulnerability should be turned into a powerful strategic motivation for cooperation with the powers that have the capacity to adversely affect China's oil supply security.[20]

Zha's observations reflect larger deliberations within Chinese research circles about the implications of globalization for China's future economic development. Some Chinese strategists have opted for a much more cautionary, "hedged" vision of China's energy future. For example, Zhang Wenmu of the University of Aeronautics & Astronautics has argued that

> China's dependence on international energy imports is rapidly changing from a relationship of relative dependence to one of absolute dependence. . . . China is almost helpless to protect its overseas oil import routes. This is an Achilles heel to contemporary China, as it has forced China to entrust its fate (stable markets and access to resources) to others. Therefore, it is imperative that China, as a nation, pay attention to its maritime security and the means to defend its interests, through sea power, a critical capability in which China currently lags behind. . . . Once a nation-state takes part in globalization, it has the right to protect those national interests that have been integrated into the world. . . . The most crucial conduit connecting China with the region and the rest of the world is the sea lanes, and therefore China must have a powerful navy.[21]

Though Zhang believes that China can partially protect its maritime rights through multilateral consultations and full adherence to China's interpretation of the UN Convention on the Law of the Sea, he argues that the country must possess the military means for "maintaining what China has already accomplished regionally . . . [through] a policy of outward active defense."[22]

China's maritime rights and interests and the implications of these for future naval development are also receiving increased attention. In 2004, for example, Senior Captain Xu Qi of the Navy Research Institute published a particularly detailed assessment in *China Military Science*, among China's most authoritative journals on military and strategic affairs.[23] Xu advocated heightened development of maritime capabilities to ensure the long-term power and prosperity of the state, replete with obligatory references to Alfred Thayer Mahan. In the context of China's larger economic and energy transition, his arguments are hardly surprising.

Xu's assessment and other recently published views suggest ongoing internal debate about China's maritime future.[24] This debate seems more interest-driven than contingency-driven, though the augmentation of China's maritime capabilities would enable China to bring its power much more fully to bear in the event of a future crisis.[25] However, these arguments do not presuppose an "either/or" choice in Chinese external strategies, particularly in Chinese attitudes toward energy interdependence, including prospective policy collaboration with the United States. There is an increasing awareness and sophistication among Chinese analysts of the major choices in the country's modernization strategies, in particular how China's ever-larger envelopment in global commerce and energy transactions affects Chinese interests. These issues will increasingly shape Chinese deliberations over national strategy and influence policy decisions that the United States, China, and other maritime powers will face in coming years.

However, some recent Chinese actions have triggered ample agitation in the United States. Over the past half decade, China's three national oil companies have established a foothold in global energy production through purchases of equity shares, financing of exploratory drilling, and the building of refineries and pipelines in the Middle East, Africa, and Central Asia. Flynt Leverett and Jeffrey Bader date this "going out" (走出去) policy to 2002, with the explicit sanction of Hu Jintao, then newly established in the top leadership post.[26] However, this agitation reached a crescendo when Chinese actions (in the eyes of various U.S. politicians) literally hit close to home, with the $18.5 billion cash offer by the China National Offshore Oil Corporation (CNOOC) to purchase Unocal. CNOOC's ultimate decision to withdraw its bid reflected fierce political opposition to this transaction in the United States even as free trade advocates saw the bid as an opportunity to establish an important precedent by enabling a major Chinese firm to undertake an increased stake in the global economy.[27]

CNOOC's chairman, Fu Chengyu, was sobered by this experience, which he attributed less to the bid itself, and more as a portent of things to come. As Fu subsequently observed, "shock [in the United States] . . . was not just because of the size of the deal. In the U.S. and in the world capital markets, that kind of money is a common thing, it's not a big surprise. But there was shock because such a volume [of funds] came from a Chinese company. Nobody thought a Chinese company could do this at that time."[28] With Chinese companies an ever-larger force in global commerce, this will not be the last time that a major Chinese firm (perhaps CNOOC itself) makes a bid for a U.S. energy company. Lenovo's purchase of IBM's personal computer business is another such indication. But to various U.S. politicians, these purchases still remain disquieting, and perhaps even alarming.

Assessing America's Hopes and Fears

There is a highly skewed debate in the United States over its energy future, and an equally skewed discussion about the potential effects of China's foothold in various oil and natural gas markets on U.S. energy availability. In the United States, there are also renewed calls for "energy independence" that make neither economic nor empirical sense.[29] As Daniel Yergin notes, the United States remains 70 percent self-sufficient in the total energy mix. U.S. dependence disproportionately concerns oil imports. When President Nixon first enunciated the goal of energy independence in November 1973, the United States imported one-third of its oil, but this dependence has since increased to 60 percent, and will increase even more in the future. Imports of liquefied natural gas will also be a growing factor, from 3 percent of current demand to more than 25 percent by 2020.[30] Thus, the United States is the preeminent beneficiary and advocate of an open, globalized oil and natural gas market, and there is no reason to believe that this will change anytime soon.

However, some analysts (notably, Dan Blumenthal and Joseph Lin) draw highly worrisome implications from China's purchases of energy resources. Blumenthal and Lin perceive a growing risk that "China and the United States will clash over sources of fossil fuels in the Middle East and other oil-patch states that are not models of stability or representative governance." They characterize energy importation as a "zero-sum game" and describe China's energy purchases as reflecting "the paranoia that drives Chinese thinking on energy security." In a longer-run sense, Blumenthal and Lin foresee China's "perceived military necessity and an intense sense of national pride [that] may already be leading China to its own variant of sea control.

. . . American offers of cooperation [with China] . . . may well be overpowered by the nationalist instinct to control one's own trade . . . [leading China] to compete with America for sea control." Yet Blumenthal and Lin also criticize Chinese efforts to diversify sources of supply, failing to acknowledge that China's energy acquisitions (by increasing global oil availability, albeit in relatively modest amounts) reduce potential energy shortfalls for the United States and other oil consumers.[31]

Blumenthal elaborates on these arguments in his contribution to this volume. He contends that "China's foreign policy is largely driven by its energy policy," with Beijing's mounting energy anxieties purportedly determining China's larger strategic priorities and its perceptions of malign American intentions. In Blumenthal's view, both are rooted in abiding Chinese suspicions of American power and a supposed Chinese unwillingness to accept "a true embrace of the market [and] an acceptance of the international system of energy security." Such characterizations are indeed evident among some Chinese analysts. But Chinese actions as a whole seem more "all of the above" rather than zero-sum. Though Chinese planners have articulated a "supply side" dominant energy strategy, there is very little evidence of coherence or unanimity in Chinese energy planning. Competition *within* the Chinese energy system is at least as marked as any depictions of adversarial energy strategies between China and the United States. Much of the internal debate therefore reflects advocacy and bureaucratic rivalry within China, not a set of decisions orchestrated and coordinated from atop the Chinese system.

The larger issue concerns shared and ever-increasing American and Chinese needs for the unhampered movement of energy resources. In the characterization of the student authors of a recent Naval War College study, China and the United States confront a situation of "mutual assured dependence" in their respective energy needs.[32] Both have inherently complementary interests in underwriting additional energy exploration, enhancing energy efficiency, encouraging resource conservation, and reducing the horrendous environmental consequences of fossil fuel consumption. But such goals cannot be realized without greatly heightened Sino–American collaboration. If Washington and Beijing retreat into narrower, self-protective approaches to energy strategy, with neither prepared to accept their shared responsibility for the global energy future, both countries (and the world as a whole) will get the results that they deserve.

Some of these implications are evident in former deputy secretary of state Robert Zoellick's calls for China to emerge as a "responsible stakeholder" in

the international system. Zoellick argues that China's ever-growing participation in the global trading system (including the energy sector) has enabled
it to steadily augment its national power over the past three decades. He contends that (as a major beneficiary of the system) China "has a responsibility to
strengthen the international system that has enabled its success." By contributing more fully to extant norms and relationships, Zoellick asserts, China
would enhance its influence in international politics and reduce the possibilities for heightened rivalry with the United States. He further acknowledges
that the United States and China have a "shared interest in sustaining political, economic, and security systems that provide common benefits." But he
asserts that China's insufficient regard for intellectual property rights, its
maintenance of an undervalued currency, and engagement in a mercantilist energy policy all attest to China's falling short of American expectations.[33]
Irrespective of the tenor of Zoellick's remarks, his larger characterization of
long-term trends in the international system attests to the interlocking character of U.S. and Chinese interests, in which energy futures are assuming an
ever-more pivotal role.

The Case for Collaboration

As China's economic, political, and military power grows, U.S. policymakers face the obvious need to determine how Chinese strategic directions
and policy priorities comport with long-term American interests. However,
the United States has a capacity to shape and facilitate preferred outcomes
in Sino–American relations, including in the energy sector. China is pursuing its strategic interests as its leaders define them, and it increasingly has
the means to pursue them. A central animating concept in Chinese strategy is the expectation that there will be multiple seats at the great power
table. The future world order will therefore not be a simple extension of the
great power rule book of earlier decades, with the United States as its near-
exclusive author. The global order in the twenty-first century presupposes
additional major power entrants, and the United States has ample incentives
to facilitate China's full inclusion in this process. The pathways to a future
order need to be developed now, and Sino–American energy collaboration
affords clear opportunities to advance this process.

At present, both countries suffer from the lack of a coherent energy strategy. In the Chinese case, Kenneth Lieberthal and Mikkal Herberg observe:

China's outward energy thrust [does not represent] an organized strategic challenge to U.S. energy and security interests . . . but a more malleable, loosely connected set of policies that are not directly aimed at the United States but have collateral impacts on a number of key U.S. interests. . . . Rather than a coherent strategy, Beijing's energy policies are more a collection of ad hoc initiatives—some coordinated, some not, and some state driven, others market and commercially driven. . . . There is no central policy institution that effectively oversees this strategy. Rather, the Chinese leadership and supporting institutions seem to adhere to a more broad "mentality" in which the government, NOCs [national oil companies], and China's diplomatic corps all work to some extent in the same direction.[34]

These liabilities reflect the dysfunctional history of energy decision making within China, a process that has (if anything) become more problematic as China's energy requirements have increased. As Leland Miller argues, "for decades . . . the organizational structure of China's energy industry has undergone one facelift after another. Yet these changes have been mostly cosmetic. Hobbled by serious understaffing, overlapping areas of authority, feuding fiefdoms, and bureaucratic inertia, China's energy-regulation system has fibrillated between fragmentation and centralization, with no one held responsible for the system's continuous failures. This muddle has made a mockery of what Beijing now considers its most important national-security issue of the 21st century."[35]

However, the surge in world oil demand in recent years is leading experts and government officials in the United States and China to weigh more seriously long-term energy strategy.[36] For example, China in 2003 formulated plans for a comprehensive "Twenty-First-Century Oil Strategy," followed in 2004 by preparation of a National Energy Strategy and Report undertaken by the Development Research Center of the State Council.[37] But these efforts remain stymied by the lack of authoritative policy mechanisms for overseeing energy strategy. Establishment of a State Energy Office in April 2005 under the National Development and Reform Commission seemed to point in the right direction, but only weeks later this effort was seemingly trumped by creation of an executive task force under Premier Wen Jiabao and Vice Premiers Huang Ju and Zeng Peiyuan. Formal reestablishment of a Ministry of Energy continues to be deferred, which suggests that China will continue to labor under divided bureaucratic responsibilities when clear lines of authority are ever-more imperative. Indeed, even as there is widespread recognition with China of the need for an authoritative supraministerial authority, as distinct from a reestablished energy ministry that "would likely become another layer of bureaucracy captured by vested interests."[38]

The underlying premises and goals of strategic planning for energy policy in the United States and China also need to be carefully scrutinized. Though the goal of energy independence may seem laudable, it is hugely unrealistic for both countries.[39] There is, however, a compelling need for both governments to fully understand the longer-term implications of dependence on imported oil and to weigh potential policy options for mitigating the potential risks. But these cannot be stand-alone strategies for either the United States or China. The two countries need to interact and communicate fully on energy strategy. As the world's leading consumers of imported oil, *both* must demonstrate that they are "responsible stakeholders" with respect to their energy futures. Moreover, a larger set of initiatives and programs for energy collaboration could well exert a forcing function on the activities and responsibilities of the energy bureaucracies and corporations in both systems.

What might a U.S.–China agenda on energy strategy look like? Three major possibilities are already evident, at least in embryonic form: (a) a sustained high-level policy dialogue between the American and Chinese leaderships, (b) collaborative research and development on energy policy, especially conservation options, and (c) and assessment of the implications of potential energy vulnerabilities for U.S. and Chinese defense planning, especially as it affects both navies. All three issues require elaboration.

The United States and China initiated an annual energy policy dialogue in June 2005 and energy officials from both countries subsequently met in September 2006. Such a mechanism could prove an important venue for airing long-term issues. There is a compelling need for regular exchanges between policymakers and energy specialists from both countries, and the list of agenda items has begun to diversify. Annual dialogues should be one component of an ongoing process to which both governments would be fully obligated. Such discussions should encompass a full spectrum of issues, including comparing assessments of future energy requirements; reviewing options for strategic petroleum reserves (including measures to enhance transparency); and encouraging increased energy efficiency in China and changes to the energy mix, including heightened use of renewable energy. The September 2006 meetings, which participating U.S. officials characterized as wide-ranging and candid, encompassed exchanges on all these issues.[40] Subsequent progress on a framework agreement between the IEA and the National Development and Reform Commission on China's development of a strategic petroleum reserve (SPR) is also a positive development. According to the IEA, this includes an increased commitment from the Chinese side to enhance transparency and disclosure of its plans, which suggests how the U.S.–China policy dialogue can reinforce larger collaborative goals involving relevant international organizations.[41]

The second area for collaboration concerns future research and development on energy technology, including measures to enhance environmental security. This should encompass a full spectrum of conservation strategies to reduce dependence on fossil fuels. Transfer to clean coal technology also represents a promising avenue to diminish greenhouse gas emissions. China faces the added liability of horrific environmental damage associated with rapid modernization. The United States has ample experience and know-how that could benefit Chinese policymakers and energy firms in this regard. Such collaboration, moreover, offers promising possibilities for involving universities, research organizations, and the private sector, some of which are already undergoing active exploration.

The third area for potential Sino–American exchanges concerns the implications of energy supply for the national security strategies of both countries. This area necessarily entails major sensitivities for both the United States and China, yet there are obvious possibilities that warrant fuller examination and mutual discussion. As China has become an ever-larger factor in global commerce, Chinese strategists are increasingly posing issues related to the security of the sea lines of communication because these affect Chinese energy supply. This should surprise no one. Chinese planners can conceptualize two broad categories of future scenarios. The first set of scenarios posits the United States seeking to impede or prevent outright China's access to oil in a major crisis with the focus disproportionately on a Taiwan crisis. The second set of scenarios posits collaborative arrangements to ensure sea lane security with China as a prospective member of a multilateral coalition guarding against potential threats to all maritime nations.

These alternative possibilities touch upon the fundamental assumptions underlying long-term U.S. and Chinese defense planning. For example, the U.S. Navy is preparing a new maritime strategy that will balance the Navy's traditional focus on war fighting with a broader set of responsibilities. Some of the contours of this strategy are contained in *The National Strategy for Maritime Security*, which proposes enhanced international collaboration to ensure collective security interests in the maritime domain.[42] The Navy leadership is seeking to maintain decisive combat power for major contingencies while also pursuing a division of labor with regional collaborators.

In a speech delivered at the Naval War College in September 2005, the Chief of Naval Operations, Admiral Michael Mullen, described how new international circumstances have redefined the Navy's roles and missions:

> [Today] the joint application of sea power . . . is a critical part of [the] global community. . . . Without mastery of the sea—without sea power—we cannot protect trade, we cannot help those in peril, we cannot provide relief from natural disasters, and we cannot intercede when whole societies are torn asunder by slavery, weapons of mass destruction, drugs, and piracy. . . . We need a new [and] very different image of sea power.
>
> We've got a . . . fleet . . . that is particularly good at leveraging the joint application of sea power to fight and win during major combat operations. But we also need a fleet that can operate at the other end of the spectrum. . . . I'm after that proverbial 1,000 ship Navy—a fleet in being, if you will—composed of all freedom-loving nations, standing watch over the seas, standing watch over each other. . . . We have proven the awesome capability of the sea when used for war. But we have yet to realize the full potential of the sea when leveraged for peace, prosperity, increased understanding, transparency, and pervasive security. . . . The real potential of sea power . . . is the power of the sea to share and unite, to deter and defeat, to protect and endure.[43]

Admiral Mullen's allusion to a "1,000 ship Navy" (also known as the Global Maritime Partnership) has gained increasing currency in U.S. Navy circles. It is less a programmatic goal or operational concept than an imagined maritime future. As argued by Vice Admiral John Morgan Jr. and Rear Admiral Charles Martoglio, it presumes a collective capability against a diverse range of maritime threats that no single maritime force—including the U.S. Navy—can undertake on its own:

> Promoting and maintaining the security of the global maritime commons is a key element because freedom of the seas is critical to any nation's long-term economic well being. . . . Likewise, the exploitation of the maritime commons by nations, groups, or individuals who seek to disrupt, destroy, or otherwise degrade security in the maritime domain must be considered a global challenge. . . . Policing the maritime commons will require substantially more capability than the United States or any individual nation can deliver. . . . The 1,000 ship Navy is about the voluntary development of a network that vastly increases . . . [the means] available to monitor security in the maritime domain while increasing the number of responders capable of ensuring maritime security.[44]

Though neither of these assessments alludes directly to China, the underlying argument tacitly poses the issue of whether China is "in" or "out" of such a notional maritime coalition. On initial examination, the concept does not appear to preclude China's inclusion. Indeed, during the visit of People's Liberation Army Navy commander Wu Shengli to the United States in May 2007, Admiral Mullen signaled an interest in exploring such possibilities, and Admiral Wu indicated a readiness to consider this prospect as well. Admiral Timothy Keating, Commander of U.S. Pacific Forces, reinforced this message during a visit during the same month to China.

The question of China's incorporation in such a collaborative concept is not likely to receive a direct answer from ranking American or Chinese officials, all the more so because it represents a prospective vision of maritime security collaboration, not a fully realized set of concepts and practices. States will undertake what they deem necessary to protect their vital interests, but this does not rule out cooperation in areas where these interests overlap or intersect. The development of collaborative arrangements between the U.S. and Chinese coast guards has been one such quiet success story that does not involve the sensitivities inherent in the involvement of navies charged with war-fighting responsibilities. Their collaboration includes protection of coastal infrastructure, ensuring the security of shipping, and antipiracy and counterterrorism measures in the South China Sea. There may also be opportunities for both countries to facilitate the training of Southeast Asian maritime forces and other comparable capacity building measures that would also enhance energy security goals.[45]

However, in the absence of U.S. readiness to explore collaborative possibilities with China and without equivalent reciprocity from the Chinese side, contingency planning and autonomous capabilities will emerge as the ultimate and dominant default options for the maritime forces of both countries. An unwillingness to broach the possibilities for collaboration would foreordain the ultimate outcome. The United States and China have both voiced support for mutually validating their respective roles as major powers in the Asia-Pacific region. But does this mutual validation extend to the full range of both countries' security responsibilities and military capabilities? The implications could hardly be greater for the United States and China, and not just for their respective energy futures.

Notes

A different version of this chapter will appear in the *Journal of Contemporary China* 17, no. 54 (May 2008).

1. For a valuable corrective, see Daniel Yergin, "What Does 'Energy Security' Really Mean?" *Wall Street Journal*, 11 July 2006.

2. For full consideration of these issues, consult John Deutch and James R. Schlesinger, chairs, *National Security Consequences of U.S. Oil Dependency*, Independent Task Force Report No. 58 (New York: Council on Foreign Relations, 2006); *Energy Policy Act 2005, Section 1837: National Security Review of International Energy Requirements* (Washington, D.C.: The U.S. Department of Energy, February 2006); Erica Downs, *China*, Energy Security Series (Washington, D.C.: The Brookings Foreign Policy Studies, December 2006); Eugene Gholz and Daryl G. Press, *Energy Alarmism: The Myths That Make Americans Worry About Oil*, Report No. 589 (Washington, D.C.: Cato Institute, 5 April 2007); and Daniel H. Rosen and Trevor Houser, *China Energy: A Guide for the Perplexed* (Washington, D.C.: China Balance Sheet Project, May 2007).

3. See, for example, Josh Kurlantzick, "Crude Awakening," *The New Republic*, 25 September 2006.

4. James A. Russell and Trisha Bury, "Conference Report: The Militarization of Energy Security," *Strategic Insights* 6, no. 2, (2007), http://www.ccc.nps.navy.mil/si/2007/Mar/energyMar07.pdf.

5. See *Ending the Energy Stalemate: A Bipartisan Strategy to Meet America's Energy Challenges* (Washington, D.C.: The National Committee on Energy Policy, December 2004); for an assessment focused on U.S. defense requirements, consult *Reducing DoD Fossil-Fuel Dependence* (McLean, Va.: JASON, The MITRE Corporation, JSR-06-135, September 2006). On Chinese energy strategy, consult Chen Fengying, "World Energy Security in Flux," *Contemporary International Relations* 16, no. 7 (2006): 1–12; various essays in *China Security* (Washington, D.C.: World Security Institute China Program, Summer 2006); Xuecheng Liu, *China's Energy Security and Grand Strategy* (Muscatine, Iowa: The Stanley Foundation, Policy Analysis Brief, September 2006); and *11th Five-Year Program for Energy Development* (Beijing: National Development and Reform Commission of the State Council in Chinese, 10 April 2007).

6. "Drowning in Oil," *The Economist*, 6 March 1999.

7. Jeffrey Logan, "Energy Outlook for China: Focus on Oil and Gas," testimony before the U.S. Senate Committee on Energy and Natural Resources, 3 February 2005, as cited in *China's Global Activism: Strategy, Drivers, and Tools*, ed. Phillip C. Saunders, Occasional Paper 4 (Washington, D.C.: National Defense University Press, Institute for National Strategic Studies, October 2006), 6.

8. Flynt Leverett and Jeffrey Bader, "Managing China-U.S. Energy Competition in the Middle East," *Washington Quarterly* 29, no. 1 (2005–6): 189.

9. Despite the rapid growth in energy consumption in China and India, per capita energy use in both countries remains a pittance, compared to Canada and the United States. (Canada's per capita energy consumption amply exceeds that of the United States.) In 2004 China's per capita energy consumption was between one-seventh and one-eighth of that of the United States; India's per capita consumption was only about one-third of China's. "Leaders of the Pack," *The Atlantic*, January/February 2007, p. 125.

10. As Xuecheng Liu notes, however, China still relies disproportionately on domestic sources of energy supply. In 2005, 94 percent of China's energy requirements derived from domestic sources, although the preponderant role of coal in this mix (approximately two-thirds of this total) has deeply worrisome environmental consequences. Liu further notes that China projects that the domestic sources of total energy needs will drop to approximately 80 percent by 2020. Liu, *China's Energy Security and Grand Strategy*, 3, 5.

11. BP, *Statistical Review of World Energy*, June 2006, as cited in Chen, "World Energy in Flux," 6.

12. BP, *Statistical Review of World Energy*, June 2006, as tabulated in *Reducing DoD Fossil-Fuel Dependence*, vi.

13. Liu, *China's Energy Security and Grand Strategy*, 10–11.

14. Data from IEA website, 30 June 2006, as cited in Liu, *China's Energy Security and Grand Strategy*, 8.

15. Yergin, "What Does 'Energy Security' Really Mean?"

16. Chip Cummins, "As Threats to Oil Supply Grow, a General Says U.S. Isn't Ready," *Wall Street Journal*, 19 December 2006.

17. *Reducing DoD Fossil-Fuel Dependence*, 4–5.

18. Chen, "World Energy Security in Flux," 4.

19. Liu, *China's Energy Security and Its Grand Strategy*, 12.

20. Zha Daojiong, "Energy Interdependence," *China Security* (Summer 2006): 7, 9.

21. Zhang Wenmu, "Sea Power and China's Strategic Choices," *China Security* (Summer 2006): 19–22.

22. Ibid., 27.

23. Xu Qi, "Military Geostrategy and the Development of the Chinese Navy in the Early Twenty-first Century," trans. Andrew Erickson and Lyle Goldstein, *Naval War College Review* 59, no. 4 (2006): 47–67.

24. For the views of one leading Chinese strategist, see Yang Yi, "Occupy the Moral High Ground of a Rich Country with a Powerful Army," *Huanqiu Shibao* [*Global Times*], 27 April 2006. Rear Admiral Yang is director of the Institute of Strategic Studies at the China National Defense University.

25. For an additional review of these writings, consult James R. Holmes and Toshi Yoshihara, "China and the Commons: Angell or Mahan?" *World Affairs*, 22 March 2006.

26. Leverett and Bader, "Managing China-U.S. Energy Competition in the Middle East," 193. For additional perspective, consult Kenneth Lieberthal and Mikkal Herberg, "China's Search for Energy Security: Implications for U.S. Policy," *NBR Analysis* 17, no. 1 (April 2006): 11–16. Lieberthal and Herberg appear to date the "going out" policy somewhat earlier than Leverett and Bader.

27. See, for example, "China's Energy Thirst," *Wall Street Journal,* Editorial, 24 June 2005.

28. Fu made these comments in an interview with Shai Oster of the *Wall Street Journal.* Oster, "China's Offshore Oilman," *Wall Street Journal*, 31 July 2006.

29. For a pithy demolition of these arguments, see Charles Wolf Jr., "Energy Fables," *The International Economy* 19 (Fall 2005): 38–39, 54. For a valuable overview of these issues, consult Deutch and Schlesinger, *National Security Consequences of U.S. Oil Dependency.*

30. Daniel Yergin, "Energy Independence," *Wall Street Journal*, 23 January 2007.

31. Dan Blumenthal and Joseph Lin, "Oil Obsession," *Armed Forces Journal* (June 2006), www.armedforcesjournal.com/2006/06/1813592, 49–50. See also Blumenthal's essay in this volume, "Concerns with Respect to China's Energy Policy," as discussed below.

32. Matthew J. Bonnot et al., "Responding to China's Global Pursuit of Energy: U.S. Challenges and Strategic Options," paper submitted to the faculty of the Naval War College in partial satisfaction of the requirements of the China Energy Advanced Research Project, 1 June 2007.

33. Robert B. Zoellick, "Whither China: From Membership to Responsibility?" Remarks to the National Committee on U.S.-China Relations, New York, 21 September 2005. This paragraph draws on a useful analysis of the speech and implications for U.S. strategy by James J. Przystup and Phillip C. Saunders, *Visions of Order: Japan and China in U.S. Strategy,* Institute for National Strategic Studies *Strategic Forum* no. 220 (Washington, D.C.: National Defense University, June 2006).

34. Lieberthal and Herberg, "China's Search for Energy Security," 17. For a detailed and insightful rendering of the liabilities of the existing energy policymaking system, consult Downs, *China*, especially 16–24.

35. Leland R. Miller, "In Search of China's Energy Authority," *Far Eastern Economic Review* 169, no. 1 (2006): 39.

36. On U.S. policy debate, consult Deutch and Schlesinger, *National Security Consequences of U.S. Oil Dependency.* On potential initiatives involving China, consult Lieberthal and Herberg, "China's Search for Energy Security," 30–37.

37. Miller, "In Search of China's Energy Authority," 39.

38. Downs, *China*, 17, 19, 20.

39. For a cogent critique of energy independence as an explicit U.S. policy goal, consult Deutch and Schlesinger, *National Security Consequences of U.S. Oil Dependency.*

40. Karen Harbert, "U.S.-China Energy Policy Dialogue," Washington Foreign Press Center, 19 September 2006, fpc.state.gov/fpc/72880.htm.

41. Shai Oster and David Winning, "China, IEA Near Pact on Strategic Oil Reserve," *Wall Street Journal*, 18 January 2007.

42. *The National Strategy for Maritime Security* (Washington, D.C.: The White House, September 2005); see also "Maritime Security in the East Asia and Pacific Region," (Washington, D.C.: U.S. Department of State, Bureau of Public Affairs, 21 April 2006).

43. Adm. Michael Mullen, "Remarks as Delivered for the 17th international Seapower Symposium," Naval War College, Newport, RI, 21 September 2005. Available at http://www.navy.mil/palib/cno/speeches/mullen050921.txt.

44. John Morgan Jr. and Charles Martoglio, "The Thousand Ship Navy—A Global Maritime Network," *U.S. Naval Institute Proceedings*, November 2005, http://www.usni.org/magazines/proceedings/archive/story.asp?STORY_ID=247.

45. Lyle Goldstein, "Conceptualizing China as Maritime Stakeholder: USCG Opens Door to Cooperative Relationship," *U.S. Naval Institute Proceedings* (August 2007): http://www.usni.org/magazines/proceedings/archive/story.asp?STORY_ID=749.

Abbreviations and Acronyms

AAW	antiair warfare
AFRICOM	United States Africa Command
AIP	air-independent propulsion
AOR	auxiliary oiler replenishment
ASCM	antiship cruise missile
ASEAN	Association of Southeast Asian Nations
ASW	antisubmarine warfare
bcm	billion cubic meters
bpd	barrels of oil per day
BP/TNK	British Petroleum/Russian Oil Company
CAR	Central African Republic
CCP	Chinese Communist Party
CDS	combat direction system
CICIR	China Institute of Contemporary International Relations
CIWS	close-in weapon system
CMSI	China Maritime Studies Institute
CNOOC	China National Offshore Oil Corporation
CNPC	China National Petroleum Corporation
CODOG	combined diesel/gas turbine
CPECC	China Petroleum Engineering and Construction Corporation
CSIC	China Shipbuilding Industry Corporation

dwt	deadweight tons
E&P	exploration and production
EEZ	exclusive economic zone
FBM	fleet ballistic missile
FIPZ	Falkland Islands Protection Zone
FRP	Fleet Response Plan
GDP	gross domestic product
GNP	gross national product
GPS	global positioning system
GWDC	Great Wall Drilling Company
GWOT	global war on terror
IAEA	International Atomic Energy Agency
IEA	International Energy Agency
IPOs	initial public offerings
IRI	Islamic Republic of Iran
ISR	intelligence, surveillance, and reconnaissance
LNG	liquefied natural gas
mmt/y	million metric tonnes per year
MOU	memorandum of understanding
NDRC	National Development and Reform Commission
nm	nautical miles
NOCs	national oil companies
OECD	Organization for Economic Cooperation and Development
OPEC	Organization of Petroleum Exporting Countries
PLA	People's Liberation Army
PLAAF	People's Liberation Army Air Force
PLAN	People's Liberation Army Navy
PRC	People's Republic of China
PSA	production-sharing agreement
RAS	replenishment-at-sea
RMB	renminbi
ROC	Republic of China (Taiwan)
SABIC	Saudi Arabian Basic Industries Corporation
SAG	surface action group
SAM	surface-to-air missile

SCO	Shanghai Cooperation Organization
SCS	South China Sea
Sinopec	China Petrochemical Corporation
SLOC	sea lines of communication
SOSUS	sound surveillance system
SPR	strategic petroleum reserve
SSBN	nuclear-powered ballistic missile submarine
SSM	surface-to-surface missile
SSN	nuclear-powered attack submarine
TEZ	total exclusion zone
tpy	tons per year
UAE	United Arab Emirates
UNCLOS	United Nations Convention on the Law of the Sea
UNSC	United Nations Security Council
USN	U.S. Navy
VDS	variable depth sonar
VLCC	very large crude carrier
VSTOL	vertical or short runway takeoff and landing
WTO	World Trade Organization

About the Contributors

MR. DAN BLUMENTHAL is vice chairman of the U.S.-China Economic and Security Review Commission and a resident fellow in Asian studies at the American Enterprise Institute for Public Policy Research. He is a member of the Academic Advisory Group of the Congressional U.S.-China Work Group. Previously Mr. Blumenthal was senior director for China, Taiwan, and Mongolia in the Office of the Under Secretary of Defense for International Security Affairs from March to November 2004 during the first George W. Bush administration. He developed and implemented defense policy toward China, Taiwan, Hong Kong, and Mongolia, for which he received the Office of Secretary of Defense Medal for Exceptional Public Service. From January 2002 to March 2004 he was country director for China, Taiwan, and Hong Kong in the Office of the Secretary of Defense, International Security Affairs. Before his service at the Department of Defense, Mr. Blumenthal was an associate attorney, Corporate and Asia Practice Groups at Kelley Drye & Warren LLP. Earlier he was an editorial and research assistant at the Washington Institute for Near East Policy. Mr. Blumenthal received an MA in international relations and international economics from the Johns Hopkins University School of Advanced International Studies, and a JD from the Duke University School of Law in 2000. Mr. Blumenthal has written extensively on national security issues. He resides in Washington, D.C., with his wife and two children.

MR. JAMES BUSSERT has been Surface Warship ASW safety deputy at Naval Surface Warfare Center (NSWC) Dahlgren, Virginia, for ten years. He previously worked on system testability after retirement in 1979 as a contractor and a civil servant at Naval Ocean Systems Center. He has a BA from National University and was IEEE chair for San Diego and Richmond IEEE Sections. He has worked in ASW for fifty-two years since he enlisted in 1954 and served twenty-five years active duty on destroyers as a Master Chief Sonarman. His hobby is freelance writing about foreign technology. After winning the U.S. Naval Institute Enlisted Essay Contest in 1972 and 1973, Mr. Bussert has published nearly two hundred military/technical articles in various professional journals. His writing focus shifted from the U.S.S.R. to mainland China in 1990. A series of articles on the People's Liberation Army Navy combat systems technology are the genesis for a book manuscript on the subject, with co-author Prof. Bruce Elleman.

PROF. BERNARD D. COLE, USN (RET.), is professor of international history at the National War College in Washington, D.C., where he concentrates on the Chinese military and Asian energy issues. He previously served thirty years as a surface warfare officer in the Navy, all in the Pacific. He commanded USS *Rathburne* (FF 1057) and Destroyer Squadron 35, served as a naval gunfire liaison officer with the Third Marine Division in Vietnam, plans officer for Commander-in-Chief Pacific Fleet, and special assistant to the Chief of Naval Operations for Expeditionary Warfare. Dr. Cole has written numerous articles and has had four books published: *Gunboats and Marines: The United States Navy in China, 1925–1928* (University of Delaware Press, 1982); *The Great Wall at Sea: China's Navy Enters the 21st Century* (Naval Institute Press, 2001); *Oil for the Lamps of China: Beijing's 21st Century Search for Energy* (National Defense University Press, 2003); and *Taiwan's Security: History and Prospects* (Routledge, 2006). He is currently writing a book on the maritime aspects of energy security in East Asia. Dr. Cole earned an AB in history from the University of North Carolina, an MPA (National Security Affairs) from the University of Washington, and a PhD in history from Auburn University.

PROF. PETER DUTTON, JAGC, USN (RET.), is the Howard S. Levie Chair of Operational Law in the Joint Military Operations Department at the Naval War College where he is responsible for all international and operational law instruction in the joint military operations curriculum. Professor Dutton also teaches law of the sea and national security law at Roger Williams University in Bristol, Rhode Island. He began his Navy service as a naval flight officer in 1985, flying various electronic warfare aircraft until 1990 when he was selected for transition from aviation into the Judge Advocate General's Corps. As a Navy JAG, Professor Dutton served in various positions with the operating forces, including as the legal advisor to commander, Carrier Group Six (John F. Kennedy Battle Group). Professor Dutton received his JD degree from the College of William and Mary in 1993. He received an MA in national security and strategic studies, with honors, from the Naval War College in 1999, and his BA, cum laude, from Boston University in 1982.

PROF. BRUCE ELLEMAN received his BA from UC Berkeley in 1982, MA and Harriman Institute Certificate at Columbia University in 1984, followed by a MPhil in 1987, East Asian Certificate in 1988, and PhD in 1993. In addition, he completed the MSc in international history at the London School of Economics in 1985, and the MA in national security and strategic studies (with distinction) at the U.S. Naval War College in 2004. He is a research professor in the Maritime History Department, Center for Naval Warfare Studies, U.S. Naval War College, and author of *Japanese-American Civilian Prisoner Exchanges and Detention Camps, 1941–45* (Routledge, 2006); co-editor with S. C. M. Paine of *Naval Blockades and Seapower: Strategies and Counter-strategies, 1805–2005* (Routledge, 2006); co-editor with Christopher Bell of *Naval Mutinies of the Twentieth Century: An International Perspective* (Frank Cass, 2003); *Wilson and China: A Revised History of the Shandong Question* (M. E. Sharpe, 2002); *Modern Chinese Warfare, 1795–1989* (Routledge, 2001); co-editor with Stephen Kotkin of *Mongolia in the Twentieth Century: Landlocked Cosmopolitan* (M. E. Sharpe, 1999); and *Diplomacy and Deception: The Secret History of Sino-Soviet Diplomatic Relations, 1917–1927* (M. E. Sharpe, 1997). Several of Dr. Elleman's books have been translated into foreign languages, including a Chinese translation of *Modern Chinese Warfare, Jindai Zhongguo de junshi yu zhanzheng* (Taipei: Elite Press, 2002), and a Czech translation of the naval mutiny book, *Námoøní vzpoury ve dvacátém století : mezinárodní souvislosti* (Prague: BBart, 2004).

AMBASSADOR CHAS W. FREEMAN JR. is chairman of Projects International, Inc., a three-decade-old business development firm with activities and clients on six continents; president of the Middle East Policy Council; a co-chair of the United States China Policy Foundation; vice chair of the Atlantic Council; a trustee of the Institute for Defense Analyses; a director of the American Academy of Diplomacy; and a member of several other boards. As ambassador to Saudi Arabia during the 1990–91 Gulf War, he managed the largest diplomatic mission in history under crisis conditions while doubling

U.S. nonmilitary exports to the kingdom. As assistant secretary of defense, responsible for defense relations with all countries other than the successor states of the former Soviet Union 1993–94, he conceived successful plans for NATO enlargement, restored military contacts with the Chinese People's Liberation Army, and laid the basis for renewed inter-American defense dialogue. During thirty years of public service, Chas Freeman negotiated on behalf of the United States with over one hundred foreign governments in Africa, East and South Asia, Europe, the Middle East, and Latin America. He served as the principal American interpreter during President Nixon's 1972 visit to China and was the recipient of numerous high honors and awards for international negotiation and policy innovation. Educated at the Universidad Nacional Autónoma de México, Yale University, Harvard Law School, and the Foreign Service Institute, he is the author of *The Diplomat's Dictionary* (NDU Press, 1995) and *Arts of Power: Statecraft and Diplomacy* (U.S. Institute of Peace Press, 1997) as well as of numerous speeches and articles on current policy issues and events.

PROF. JOHN GAROFANO is Jerome Levy Chair of Economic Geography and professor of national security affairs, National Security Decision Making Department at the U.S. Naval War College, where he teaches U.S. policymaking and Asian security. Dr. Garofano's research interests include military intervention, Asian alliances and security problems, and the making of U.S. foreign policy. His writings have appeared in *International Security, Contemporary Southeast Asia, Asian Survey,* and *Naval War College Review,* among others. Prior to joining the Naval War College Dr. Garofano was senior fellow at the Kennedy School of Government, Harvard University, and has taught at the U.S. Army War College, the Five Colleges of western Massachusetts, and the University of Southern California. Dr. Garofano received a PhD from Cornell University and an MA from Johns Hopkins School of Advanced International Studies.

PROF. AHMED HASHIM is professor of strategic studies in the Center for Naval Warfare Studies at the Naval War College. He recently completed his fourth tour in Iraq as advisor to Multinational Forces-Iraq on security sector reform of the Iraqi armed forces. Dr. Hashim specializes in Middle Eastern and South Asian strategic issues, with a particular emphasis on Iraqi and Iranian affairs. He explores functional security issues such as the revolution in military affairs, asymmetric warfare, and terrorism. Previously he worked for four years at the Center for Naval Analyses on issues such as the revolution in military affairs and asymmetric warfare. Between 1994 and 1996 Dr. Hashim was senior fellow at the Center for International and Strategic Studies in Washington, D.C., where he worked on Middle East security issues. He was a research associate at the International Institute for Strategic Studies in London between 1993 and 1994, where he wrote a monograph titled *The Crisis of the Iranian State*. Dr. Hashim received his PhD and MS from the Massachusetts Institute of Technology and his BS from Warwick University in Coventry, Great Britain. His latest publications include "The World According to Usama Bin Laden," *Naval War College Review*, Autumn 2001; "Saddam Husayn and Civil-Military Relations in Iraq: The Quest for Legitimacy and Power," *Middle East Journal*, Winter 2003; "Iraq's Chaos," *Boston Review*, October 2004; "Iraq: From Insurgency to Civil War," *Current History*, January 2005; and *Insurgency and Counterinsurgency in Iraq* (Ithaca: Cornell University Press, 2006). Dr. Hashim is currently writing on the politics of energy in the Middle East and North Africa, with emphasis on the terrorist threat to oil and gas infrastructure.

MR. MIKKAL HERBERG is research director of the energy security program at the National Bureau (NBR) of Asian Research in Seattle, Washington. NBR is a nonpartisan, independent research institution devoted to advanced research on U.S. policy in Asia. He is also a senior consultant with PFC Energy, an international energy consulting firm located in Washington, D.C., and a visiting faculty member at the graduate school of International Relations and Pacific Studies at the University of California, San Diego. Previously he spent twenty years in the oil industry in Strategic Planning roles for ARCO, where from 1997–2000 he was director for global energy and economics, responsible for worldwide energy, economic, and political analysis. He also headed country risk analysis responsible for advising the executive management on risk conditions and investment strategies in countries and regions where ARCO had major investments. His previous positions with ARCO included director of portfolio risk management and director for emerging markets. Mr. Herberg writes and speaks extensively on Asian energy issues to the energy industry and governments in the Asia-Pacific region, including the United States, China, and Japan. He is cited frequently in the media, including the *Wall Street Journal*, *Washington Post*, National Public Radio, *Asahi Shimbun*, Reuters, *NIKKEI News*, and *Caijing*. His recent writings include "China's Search for Energy Security: Implications for U.S. Policy" (2006), a special study by NBR co-authored with Kenneth Lieberthal; "China's Search for Energy Security: Implications for

Southeast Asia," in *China, the United States, and Southeast Asia: Contending Perspectives on Economics, Politics, and Security* (Routledge, forthcoming); and "The China, India and United States Strategic Energy Triangle: U.S. Perspectives" (Emirates Center for Strategic Studies and Research, Abu Dhabi, forthcoming).

PROF. JAMES R. HOLMES is a Phi Beta Kappa graduate of Vanderbilt University and earned graduate degrees at Salve Regina University, Providence College, and the Fletcher School of Law and Diplomacy at Tufts University, where he was awarded a PhD in 2003. He graduated from the Naval War College with highest distinction in 1994 and, as the top graduate in his class, received the Naval War College Foundation Award. Before joining the Naval War College faculty in the spring of 2007, he was a senior research associate at the University of Georgia Center for International Trade and Security, Athens, Georgia; a research associate at the Institute for Foreign Policy Analysis, Cambridge, Massachusetts; and a U.S. Navy surface warfare officer, serving in the engineering and weapons departments on board the battleship *Wisconsin*, directing an engineering course at the Surface Warfare Officers School Command, and teaching strategy and policy at the Naval War College, College of Distance Education. He is the author of *Theodore Roosevelt and World Order: Police Power in International Relations* (Potomac Books, 2005), co-author of *Chinese Naval Strategy in the 21st Century: The Turn to Mahan* (Routledge, 2007), and co-editor of *Asia Looks Seaward: Power and Maritime Strategy* (Praeger, 2008).

MR. TREVOR HOUSER is a director at China Strategic Advisory (CSA), a specialized practice helping decision makers in the public and private sectors analyze and understand commercial, economic, and policy trends in Greater China. Mr. Houser leads CSA's energy sector activities and divides his time between New York and China where he meets regularly with government officials, business leaders, academics, and NGOs about developments in the energy space. He is additionally responsible for seminars and presentations on overall China macroeconomic development and regularly advises policymakers in the United States regarding China's economic growth. Mr. Houser is also a visiting fellow at the Colin Powell Center for Policy Studies at the City College of New York where his research focuses on analyzing trends in China's energy sector and the effects on international markets, the global environment, and relations with the United States. His recent publications include "China Energy: A Guide for the Perplexed" (CSIS/IIE China

Balance Sheet Project, May 2007), "Chávez-China Oil Deal May Produce Unsuspected Winners" (*YaleGlobal*, September 2006), "The China Energy Specter: Perceptions and Prospects" (Pudong Institute for the U.S. Economy, May 2006), and "Alternative Measures of Chinese Economic Development" (Aspenia, February 2006). Mr. Houser and Daniel H. Rosen of the Peterson Institute for International Economics are currently writing a guidebook for policymakers that addresses the energy and environmental impacts of China's rise. Houser lives in New York City with his wife, Jennifer, and can be reached at tghouser@chinaadvise.com.

PROF. VITALY KOZYREV is Karl Loewenstein Visiting Professor of Political Science at Amherst College and associate professor at the Institute of Asian and African Studies of Moscow State University (Russia). He is an expert on conflicts in Eurasia, Chinese foreign policy, Russo–Chinese relations, energy cooperation in East Asia, and China's war history. He served as advisor to the Moscow city government (1999–2003) and as China analyst of the influential Russian News Agency (2002–3). Since 2005 he has been a member of the Russian think tank at the Shanghai Cooperation Organization Analytic Center at the Institute of International Relations of the Russian Foreign Ministry (MGIMO). As a negotiator and consultant of a number of Russo–Chinese projects he worked closely with a wide range of institutions and organizations in Kazakhstan, Kyrgyzstan, and Uzbekistan. Dr. Kozyrev has intensively published in Russia, the United States, and China/Taiwan, including his contribution to *Normalization of U.S.-China Relations: An International History* (edited by W. C. Kirby and R. S. Ross, Harvard University Press, 2006); *IISS Survival* (co-authored with Lyle Goldstein) (Spring 2006), *Chinese Society at War, 1937–45* (Moscow, forthcoming in 2007), and *The Revolution and Reforms in Contemporary China: The Search for Developmental Paradigm* (Moscow University Press, 2004). Since 1999 he has taught in a number of international universities, including Amherst College, University of Delaware, Fengchia University (Taiwan), Yunnan University (China), and Yale University.

DR. JAMES MULVENON is director of advanced studies and analysis at DGI's Center for Intelligence Research and Analysis. Previously Dr. Mulvenon was a political scientist at the RAND Corporation in Washington, D.C., and deputy director of RAND's Center for Asia-Pacific Policy. A specialist on the Chinese military, his current research focuses on Chinese C4ISR, defense research/development/acquisition organizations and policy, strategic weapons doctrines (computer network attack and nuclear warfare), patriotic hackers, and the military and civilian implications of the information revolution in China. His book *Soldiers of Fortune* (M. E. Sharpe, 2001) examines the Chinese military's multibillion dollar business empire. Dr. Mulvenon received his PhD in political science from the University of California, Los Angeles.

MR. RONALD O'ROURKE is a Phi Beta Kappa graduate of the Johns Hopkins University, where he received his BA in international studies, and a valedictorian graduate of the University's Paul Nitze School of Advanced International Studies where he received his MA in the same field. Since 1984 Mr. O'Rourke has worked as a naval analyst for the Congressional Research Service of the Library of Congress. Mr. O'Rourke has written numerous reports for Congress on various issues relating to the Navy. He regularly briefs members of Congress and congressional staffers and has testified before congressional committees on several occasions. In 1996 Mr. O'Rourke received a Distinguished Service Award from the Library of Congress for his service to Congress on naval issues. Mr. O'Rourke is the author of several journal articles on naval issues, and is a past winner of the U.S. Naval Institute's Arleigh Burke essay contest. Mr. O'Rourke has given presentations on Navy-related issues to a variety of audiences in government, industry, and academia.

DR. DAVID PIETZ is an associate professor of modern Chinese history and the director of the Asia Program at Washington State University. His research focuses on the economic and state-building consequences of natural resource policy in twentieth-century China. He is currently conducting research on the state's management of water on the North China Plain after 1949. In addition to holding a Mellon Fellowship at the Needham Center for the History of Chinese Science, Technology, and Medicine in Cambridge, England, in 2003, Dr. Pietz has received grants from the National Science Foundation, the National Endowments for the Humanities, the American Philosophical Society, and the American Council of Learned Societies. Prior to his current position at Washington State University Dr. Pietz was an Asian oil and gas market analyst for Energy Security Analysis Inc. (ESAI) in Boston. In 2001 he authored "Fueling China: Oil and Gas Demand to 2010," a multi-client study for ESAI.

PROF. JONATHAN D. POLLACK is professor of Asian and Pacific studies and chairman of the Asia-Pacific Studies Group at the Naval War College.

Between 2000 and 2004 he also served as chairman of the College's Strategic Research Department. Prior to joining the War College he served in a wide variety of research and management capacities at the RAND Corporation. Dr. Pollack's major research interests include U.S.–China relations, East Asian international politics, Chinese national security strategy, U.S. strategy in the Asia-Pacific region, Korean politics and foreign policy, and East Asian technological and military development. He has recently completed a three-part series of major conference symposia focused on Asia's strategic transition and its implications for American policy. The publications include *Asia Eyes America: Regional Perspectives on the U.S. Power* (2007), *Korea: The East Asian Pivot* (2006), and *Strategic Surprise? U.S.-China Relations in the Early 21st Century* (2004). In addition to numerous reports, research monographs, and edited volumes, Dr. Pollack contributes regularly to leading professional journals in the United States, Asia, and Europe, and has written chapters for numerous edited volumes, with particular attention to China's international strategies, East Asian international politics, regional security, and U.S. foreign policy. He is also a regular media contributor in the United States and abroad, including numerous op-eds and strategic commentaries.

MR. SAAD RAHIM is a manager in PFC Energy's Country Strategies Group. His primary focus is managing PFC Energy's National Oil Companies Service (NOCS), which analyses the strategies, goals, and outlook for national oil companies worldwide. He is also responsible for regional political analysis, concentrated specifically on the Middle East, South Asia, and East Asia regions. Mr. Rahim's additional area of focus is global and regional economic analysis, and he is responsible for coordinating PFC Energy's economic outlook and growth forecasts. Mr. Rahim graduated from Stanford University with degrees in economics and political science. He is a frequent guest analyst with CNBC, Bloomberg, Reuters, *Wall Street Journal, Financial Times,* and NPR, and has had his work published in the *Petroleum Economist, Middle East Report* and other major publications. His areas of expertise include national oil companies, political economy of the Middle East and Asia, and petroleum sector risk and market analysis.

MR. DANIEL H. ROSEN is an economic advisor specializing in China's commercial development. He writes and speaks extensively on U.S.–China economic relations. He is the principal of China Strategic Advisory, a specialized practice helping decision makers in the public and private sectors analyze and understand commercial, economic, and policy trends in Greater

China. Mr. Rosen is an adjunct associate professor at Columbia University and a visiting fellow with the Institute for International Economics (IIE) in Washington, D.C. His fourth book, on changes in China's agrobusinesses sector, was published by IIE in July 2004; his fifth, on U.S.–Taiwan trade dynamics, was published in December 2004. He was a resident fellow at IIE until 1999. In 2001 and 2002 Mr. Rosen directed research for an investment venture in Beijing and Shanghai focused on the value chain partners of American multinationals. From 2000–2001 he was senior advisor for international economic policy at the White House National Economic Council (NEC) where he played a managing role in completing China's accession to the World Trade Organization, accompanied President Bill Clinton to Asia for summit meetings, and participated in cabinet-level meetings and meetings with foreign heads of state. Mr. Rosen was a research fellow at IIE until 1999 when his book *Behind the Open Door: Foreign Enterprises in the Chinese Marketplace* was co-published by the IIE and the Council on Foreign Relations. He has worked at IBM Governmental Relations, the U.S. International Trade Administration, and the Woodrow Wilson Center for Scholars. He was educated at the Graduate School of Foreign Service at Georgetown University and at the department of Asian Studies at the University of Texas, Austin. He is a member of the Council on Foreign Relations and the National Committee for U.S.-China Relations, and he resides in New York City with his wife, Anna.

MR. CLIFFORD SHELTON has substantial professional and research expertise on Chinese economic interests in the developing world. He has advised the U.S. Navy's European command on West Africa strategies and has lived in both China and Egypt where he worked with the state of Utah Beijing Trade Representative Office, Chinese Yeaoco Investment Company, and Arab radio and television. He was also a research fellow with the Corporate Council on Africa. Mr. Shelton is a recent graduate of the Fletcher School of Law and Diplomacy specializing in international business and development economics. He has also taken courses in advanced finance at Harvard Business School. Mr. Shelton reads and speaks both Arabic and Mandarin and has had his research published by *The Africa Journal* and the Corporate Council on Africa.

PROF. TOSHI YOSHIHARA is an assistant professor in the Strategy and Policy Department at the Naval War College, Newport, Rhode Island. Previously he was a visiting professor in the strategy department at the Air War College,

Montgomery, Alabama. Dr. Yoshihara has also served as a senior research fellow at the Institute for Foreign Policy Analysis in Cambridge, Massachusetts. His research interests include U.S. alliances in the Asia-Pacific region, China's military modernization, security dynamics on the Korean peninsula, Japan's defense policy, and China–Taiwan relations. Dr. Yoshihara's current research agenda focuses on the influence of geopolitics in Asia, China's naval strategy, and Japan's maritime strategy. Over the past two years, he co-authored journal articles on Chinese maritime strategy that appeared in *Comparative Strategy, Naval War College Review, Issues and Studies,* and *Orbis.* Dr. Yoshihara holds a PhD in international relations from the Fletcher School of Law and Diplomacy, Tufts University, an MA in international relations from the School of Advanced International Studies, Johns Hopkins University, and a BS in international relations from the School of Foreign Service, Georgetown University.

The Editors

MR. GABRIEL B. COLLINS is a research fellow in the U.S. Naval War College's China Maritime Studies Institute. He is an honors graduate of Princeton University (2005, AB politics) and is proficient in Mandarin Chinese and Russian. His primary research areas are Chinese and Russian energy policy, maritime energy security, Chinese shipbuilding, and Chinese naval modernization. Mr. Collins's energy-related work has been published in *Oil & Gas Journal, Geopolitics of Energy, The National Interest, Hart's Oil & Gas Investor, LNG Observer, Pacific Focus,* and *Orbis.*

PROF. ANDREW S. ERICKSON is assistant professor in the Strategic Research Department at the U.S. Naval War College and a founding member of the department's China Maritime Studies Institute (CMSI). He recently completed his PhD dissertation at Princeton University on Chinese aerospace development. Dr. Erickson previously worked for Science Applications International Corporation (SAIC) as a Chinese translator and technical analyst. He has also worked at the U.S. Embassy in Beijing, the U.S. Consulate in Hong Kong, the U.S. Senate, and the White House. Proficient in Mandarin Chinese and Japanese, he has traveled extensively in Asia. Dr. Erickson graduated magna cum laude from Amherst College with a BA in history and political science, and received an MA from Princeton in international relations and comparative politics. Hvvis research, which focuses on East Asian defense, foreign policy, and technology issues, has been published in *Journal of Strategic Studies, Comparative Strategy, Undersea Warfare, Space Policy, Naval War College Review, Geopolitics of Energy, Pacific Focus, Orbis,* and *Technology in Society* (forthcoming).

PROF. LYLE J. GOLDSTEIN is an associate professor in the strategic research department of the Naval War College in Newport, Rhode Island, and is also director of NWC's new China Maritime Studies Institute (CMSI), which was established in October 2006. Proficient in Chinese and Russian, Professor Goldstein has conducted extensive field research in both China and Russia. His research on Chinese defense policies, especially concerning naval development, has been published in *China Quarterly, International Security, Jane's Intelligence Review, Journal of Strategic Studies,* and *U.S. Naval Institute Proceedings.* Professor Goldstein's first book, which compared proliferation crises and focused particularly on Chinese nuclear strategy, was published by Stanford University Press in 2005. He earned a PhD from Princeton University in 2001 and has an MA from Johns Hopkins School of Advanced International Studies. Dr. Goldstein has also worked in the Office of the Secretary of Defense.

PROF. WILLIAM S. MURRAY is an associate research professor in the research and analysis division of the United States Naval War College's War Game Department. He joined the Navy in 1983 immediately after graduating cum laude from the State University of New York at Buffalo with a BS in electrical engineering. Professor Murray served as a junior officer and plank owner on the USS *Pittsburgh* (SSN 720) and as the navigator on the USS *Houston* (SSN 713). He conducted overseas deployments in those vessels in both the Atlantic and Pacific oceans. He is a 1990 recipient of the David Lloyd Award for excellence and is qualified to command nuclear-powered submarines. In 1994 he received an MA from the U.S. Naval War College. Professor Murray has served as a fire control instructor at the United States Submarine School, on the operations staff at the United States Strategic Command, and as a member of the faculty of the Naval War College's Strategic Research Department. He retired from the Navy with the rank of lieutenant commander in 2003. He has published articles in *International Security, Parameters, Comparative Strategy,* U.S. Naval Institute *Proceedings, Jane's Intelligence Review,* and *Undersea Warfare.*

Index

THE NAVAL INSTITUTE PRESS is the book-publishing arm of the U.S. Naval Institute, a private, nonprofit, membership society for sea service professionals and others who share an interest in naval and maritime affairs. Established in 1873 at the U.S. Naval Academy in Annapolis, Maryland, where its offices remain today, the Naval Institute has members worldwide.

Members of the Naval Institute support the education programs of the society and receive the influential monthly magazine *Proceedings* or the colorful bimonthly magazine *Naval History* and discounts on fine nautical prints and on ship and aircraft photos. They also have access to the transcripts of the Institute's Oral History Program and get discounted admission to any of the Institute-sponsored seminars offered around the country.

The Naval Institute's book-publishing program, begun in 1898 with basic guides to naval practices, has broadened its scope to include books of more general interest. Now the Naval Institute Press publishes about seventy titles each year, ranging from how-to books on boating and navigation to battle histories, biographies, ship and aircraft guides, and novels. Institute members receive significant discounts on the Press's more than eight hundred books in print.

Full-time students are eligible for special half-price membership rates. Life memberships are also available.

For a free catalog describing Naval Institute Press books currently available, and for further information about joining the U.S. Naval Institute, please write to:

Member Services
U.S. NAVAL INSTITUTE
291 Wood Road
Annapolis, MD 21402-5034
Telephone: (800) 233-8764
Fax: (410) 571-1703
Web address: www.usni.org